# BARRON'S

# PSAT/ NMSQT*

## 17TH EDITION

**Sharon Weiner Green, M.A.**
Former Instructor in English
Merritt College
Oakland, California

**Ira K. Wolf, Ph.D.**
President, PowerPrep, Inc.
Former High School Teacher, College Professor,
and University Director of Teacher Preparation

BARRON'S

## ABOUT THE AUTHORS

*Sharon Green* started helping prepare students for the PSAT and SAT as a 13-year-old assistant at her father's college entrance tutoring course; she has never stopped since. A National Merit Scholar, she holds degrees from Harvard College, New York University School of Education, and the University of California at Berkeley. Her test preparation books, all published by Barron's, run the gamut from the California High School Proficiency Examination to the GRE. Whenever she can dig her way out from under multiple dictionaries, Sharon enjoys folk dancing, reading Jane Austen and science fiction, and watching Little League baseball.

*Dr. Ira Wolf*, who earned his bachelor's, master's, and doctoral degrees at Tufts, Yale, and Rutgers, respectively, has had a long career in math education. In addition to teaching math at the high school level for several years, he was a professor of mathematics at Brooklyn College and the Director of the Mathematics Teacher Preparation program at SUNY Stony Brook.

Dr. Wolf has been helping students prepare for college entrance exams, including the PSAT, SAT, ACT, and SAT Subject Tests, for more than 35 years. He is the founder and president of PowerPrep, Inc., a test preparation company on Long Island that currently works with more than 1,000 high school students each year.

© Copyright 2014, 2012, 2010, 2008 by Barron's Educational Series, Inc.

Previous editions © copyright 2006, 2004, 2003, 1999, 1997, 1993, 1989, 1986, 1982, 1976, 1973, 1971, 1966, 1965 by Barron's Educational Series, Inc., under the title *How to Prepare for the PSAT/NMSQT.*

*All inquiries should be addressed to:*
Barron's Educational Series, Inc.
250 Wireless Boulevard
Hauppauge, NY 11788
**www.barronseduc.com**

**International Standard Serial No.: 1941-7055 (print with CD-ROM)**

ISBN: 978-1-4380-0354-2 (book)
ISBN: 978-1-4380-7440-5 (book/CD-ROM package)

PRINTED IN THE UNITED STATES OF AMERICA
9 8 7 6 5 4 3 2 1

# Contents

# Preface

---

**W**elcome to the seventeenth edition of *Barron's PSAT/NMSQT*. If you are preparing for the PSAT, this is the book you need.

This edition updates America's leading book focused on the PSAT. Along with the best of the time-tested features of earlier editions, today's seventeenth edition provides much, much more.

- It features four full-length sample tests modeled on the PSAT in length and difficulty, four crucial "dress rehearsals" for the day you walk into the examination room. If you purchased this book with a CD-ROM, you have two additional tests for practice.
- It clears up misconceptions you may have about the PSAT and gives you a brief rundown of the entire test.
- It prepares you for the Writing Skills section, teaching you how to spot errors and polish rough drafts so that you can shine on the PSAT and eventually on the SAT. **Note:** Although there's a Writing Skills section on the PSAT, you *don't* have to write an essay! The section contains only multiple-choice questions that test the mechanics of writing.
- It briefs you on vocabulary-in-context and reading comprehension questions, giving you key tips on how to tackle these important verbal question types.
- It takes you step by step through the double reading passages, showing you how to work your way through a pair of reading passages without wasting effort or time.
- It introduces you to the "grid-in" non-multiple-choice questions in the Mathematics section, teaching you shortcuts to solving problems and entering your own answers on a sample grid.
- It offers you advice on how (and when) to use a calculator in dealing with both multiple-choice and "grid-in" questions.
- It contains a separate chapter that reviews every math topic you need to know.
- It gives you the 300-word PSAT High-Frequency Word List, 300 vital words that have been shown by computer analysis to occur and reoccur on actual published PSATs, plus Barron's PSAT Basic Word List, more than 1,300 words that you'll want to master as you work to build a college-level vocabulary. (For quick review, you can consult the list of Basic Word Parts.)

Most important, it teaches you the special tactics and strategies essential for scoring high on the PSAT.

No other book tells you as much about the test. No other book offers you as many questions modeled on the PSAT.

The PSAT is your chance to get yourself set for the all-important SAT. It's also your chance to qualify for some of the nation's most prestigious college scholarships. Go for your personal best; take the time to learn how to prepare for the PSAT.

This edition of *Barron's PSAT/NMSQT* is evidence of Barron's ongoing commitment to make this publication America's outstanding PSAT study guide.

# PSAT/NMSQT Test Format

**Section 1**                    25 minutes          24 questions
Critical Reading
    8 sentence completions
    4 short-paragraph reading comprehension
  12 long-passage reading comprehension

#### 1-MINUTE BREAK

**Section 2**                    25 minutes          20 questions
Mathematics
    20 multiple-choice

#### 1-MINUTE BREAK

**Section 3**                    25 minutes          24 questions
Critical Reading
    5 sentence completions
    4 short-paragraph reading comprehension
  15 long-passage reading comprehension

#### 5-MINUTE BREAK

**Section 4**                    25 minutes          18 questions
Mathematics
    8 multiple-choice
    10 student-produced response (grid-in)

#### 1-MINUTE BREAK

**Section 5**                    30 minutes          39 questions
Writing Skills
    20 improving sentences
    14 identifying sentence errors
    5 improving paragraphs

# Acknowledgments

The authors gratefully acknowledge all those sources who granted permission to use materials from their publications:

Pages 14–15, 126–127: From *Summer of '49* by David Halberstam, © 1989 by David Halberstam. (HarperCollins Publishers Inc.)

Pages 15, 127: From *Take Time for Paradise,* © 1989 by the Estate of A. Bartlett Giamatti.

Page 35: From *Life Nature Library: The Forest* by Peter Farb and the editors of Time-Life Books, © Time-Life Books Inc., pp. 75–76.

Pages 36–37: From "Introduction" from *Bury My Heart at Wounded Knee: An Indian History of the American West* by Dee Brown, Copyright © 1970 by Dee Brown. (Henry Holt & Co., LLC.)

Page 44: From *Modern Dancer's Primer for Action,* by Martha Graham, © 1941 by PUP. Reprinted by permission of Princeton University Press.

Pages 44–45: From *Chez Panisse Menu Cookbook* by Alice Waters, copyright © 1982 by Alice L. Waters. Used by permission of Random House, Inc.

Pages 104, 106, 108, 112, 114, 116, 118: From "The Odds Are You're Innumerate" by John Allen Paulos in *The New York Times Book Review,* © by the New York Times Co., January 1, 1989, pp. 16–17. Reprinted by permission.

Page 395: Excerpt from "Yonder Peasant, Who Is He?" in *Memories of a Catholic Girlhood,* copyright 1948 and renewed 1975 by Mary McCarthy, p. 57. Reprinted with permission by Houghton Mifflin Harcourt Publishing Company.

Page 403: Excerpts from *Renaissance to Modern Tapestries in The Metropolitan Museum of Art* (pp. 4–6) by Edith Appleton Standen. Copyright © 1987, the Metropolitan Museum of Art. Reprinted by permission.

Page 405: From *King Solomon's Ring* by Konrad Z. Lorenz, © 1952, Harper & Row, pp. 128–129.

Pages 405–406: From "Social Behavior of the Jackdaw, *Corvus monedula,* in Relation to its Niche" by A. Röell, in *Behavior* vol. 64, no. 1/2 (1978), pp. 1–124.

Pages 436–437: From "Huge Conservation Effort Aims to Save Vanishing Architect of the Savannah" by William K. Stevens, from *The New York Times* © 2/28/1989 The New York Times. All rights reserved. Used by permission and protected by the Copyright Laws of the United States. The printing, copying, redistribution, or retransmission of this Content without express written permission is prohibited.

Page 444: From "Let's Say You Wrote Badly This Morning" by David Huddle in *The Writing Habit,* University Press of New England, Lebanon, NH. Reprinted with permission.

## ON THE CD

# PART ONE

# INTRODUCTION

**Note the following icons, used throughout this book:**

 Time saver

 Educated guess

 Did you notice?

 Look it up; math reference fact

 Prefixes, roots, and suffixes

 Positive or negative?

 Helpful Hint

 Caution!

 A calculator might be useful.

# The PSAT/National Merit Scholarship Qualifying Test

Your plan to take the PSAT/NMSQT is perhaps your first concrete step toward planning a college career. The PSAT/NMSQT and the SAT—what do they mean to you? When do you take them? What sort of hurdles do you face? How do these tests differ from the tests you ordinarily face in school? In this section we answer these basic questions so that you will be able to move on to the following chapters and concentrate on preparing yourself for this test.

## Some Basic Questions Answered

### What Is the PSAT/NMSQT?

The PSAT/NMSQT is the first step in getting ready for the SAT. It is given only in mid-October. Schools generally administer the exam on a Saturday or a Wednesday. You will take the PSAT on the day it is offered in your school.

The test consists of five sections: two test critical reading skills, two test mathematical reasoning skills, and one tests writing skills. The time allowed for each of the reading and math sections is twenty-five minutes; the time allowed for the writing skills section is thirty minutes.

### Why Is the Test Called the PSAT/NMSQT?

The "P" in PSAT stands for "preliminary." So first and foremost the PSAT is the Preliminary SAT. As such, its job is to familiarize students with the types of questions that are on the SAT and to help students assess their strengths and weaknesses.

The PSAT also serves as the National Merit Scholarship Qualifying Test (NMSQT). Approximately 50,000 students nationally gain recognition in the NMSQT competition by earning high scores on the PSAT.

### Who Takes the PSAT/NMSQT?

Essentially, all high school students who plan to take the SAT take the PSAT in October of their junior year. In addition, about 50 percent of freshman and sophomores take the PSAT for practice. **Note:** You can only qualify for recognition in the National Merit Scholarship competition as a junior. Even if you had perfect scores on the PSAT as a freshman or sophomore, you would have to take it again as a junior to receive a National Merit letter of commendation or to qualify as a semifinalist.

## What Are Merit Scholarships?

Merit Scholarships are prestigious national awards that carry with them a chance for solid financial aid. Conducted by NMSC, an independent, nonprofit organization with offices at 1560 Sherman Avenue, Suite 200, Evanston, Illinois 60201-4897, the Merit Program today is supported by grants from more than 500 corporations, private foundations, colleges and universities, and other organizations. The top-scoring PSAT/NMSQT participants in every state are named Semifinalists. Those who advance to Finalist standing compete for one-time National Merit $2500 Scholarships and renewable, four-year Merit Scholarships, which may be worth as much as $10,000 a year for four years.

Check out Merit Scholarships at *www.nationalmerit.org.*

## What Is the National Achievement Scholarship Program for Outstanding Black Students?

This program is aimed at honoring and assisting promising African-American high school students throughout the country. It is also administered by NMSC. Students who enter the Merit Program by taking the PSAT/NMSQT and who are also eligible to participate in the Achievement program mark a space on their test answer sheets asking to enter this competition as well. Top-scoring African-American students in each of the regions established for the competition compete for nonrenewable National Achievement $2500 Scholarships and for four-year Achievement Scholarships supported by many colleges and corporate organizations.

**Note:** To be considered for this program, you *must* mark the appropriate space on your answer sheet.

Check out the National Achievement Scholarship Program at *www.nationalmerit.org.*

## How Can the PSAT/NMSQT Help Me?

If you are a high school junior, it will help you gauge your potential scores on the SAT that you will take in the spring. It will give you some idea of which colleges you should apply to in your senior year. It will give you access to scholarship competitions. It will definitely give you practice in answering multiple-choice questions, where timing is an important factor.

In addition, you may choose to take advantage of the College Board's Student Search Service. This service is free for students who fill out the biographical section of the PSAT/NMSQT. If you fill out this section, you will receive mail from colleges and search programs.

## How Do I Apply for This Test?

You apply through your school. Fees, when required, are collected by your school. Fee waivers are available for students whose families cannot afford the test fee; if this applies to you, talk to your counselor.

The test is given in October. In December the results are sent to your school and to the scholarship program that you indicated on your answer sheet in the examination room. Your school will send you your score report.

## What if I Am a Home-Schooled Student?

If you are a home-schooler, you must make arrangements with the principal or counselor of a nearby high school (public or independent) to take the test. Do not wait until the school year starts to make your arrangements. If you want to take the test in October, start the process the previous June.

Because you are a home-schooler, your score report is supposed to be sent to your home address. When you fill out your answer sheet, you must enter the state's home school code in the school code section of the answer sheet. This will ensure that you will receive your score report. You should be able to get this number from the exam proctor or supervisor.

## What Makes the PSAT Different from Other Tests?

The PSAT is trying to measure your ability to reason using facts that are part of your general knowledge or facts that are included in your test booklet. You are not required to recall any history or literature or science. You are not even required to recall most math formulas—they are printed right in the test booklet.

Your score depends upon how many questions you answer correctly. You can't go too slowly, but, accuracy is more important than speed. You have to pace yourself so that you don't sacrifice speed to gain accuracy (or sacrifice accuracy to gain speed).

The biggest mistake most students make is trying to answer too many questions. It is better to answer fewer questions correctly, even if you have to leave some out at the end of a section. See page 11 for a full discussion of how to pace yourself.

## How Is the PSAT Different from the SAT?

The PSAT is a mini-version of the SAT. For most students, it serves as a practice test. The PSAT takes two hours and ten minutes; the SAT takes almost twice as long. You have to answer fewer reading, math, and writing skills questions on the PSAT than you do on the SAT; however, the questions are similar in level of difficulty.

Unlike the SAT, the PSAT has *no* essay-writing section. *You do not have to write an essay*. Your school may recommend that you participate in the College Board's practice essay-writing program, *Score Write*. However, your participation in *Score Write* will *not* affect your PSAT score.

## How Is the PSAT Scored?

The PSAT has three parts: critical reading, math, and writing skills. On each part you will receive a score between 20 and 80, and a combined Selection Index, which is the sum of your three scores. For example, if your score report listed scores of 53 in critical reading, 61 in math, and 48 in writing skills, your Selection Index would be 53 + 61 + 48 = 162.

| Score Report (Example) | | | |
| --- | --- | --- | --- |
| Critical Reading | Math | Writing Skills | Selection Index |
| 53 | 61 | 48 | 162 |

For each individual score, as well as the Selection Index, you will receive a percentile ranking that shows how your scores compare with those of the other students who took the PSAT the same day you did.

Because SAT scores range from 200 to 800, many students multiply their PSAT scores by 10 to make them look like SAT scores. So, if you earned the scores given in the previous paragraph, you might say that your PSAT score was a 1620.

## How Are the Results of Your PSAT/NMSQT Reported?

About six to eight weeks after the test, you will receive, from your school, the following:

1. an official score report that includes:
   a) the answer you gave for each question
   b) the correct answer for each question
   c) the difficulty level of each question
   d) a Selection Index, which is used to determine eligibility for NMSC programs
2. a copy of the original test booklet that you used in the examination room

## Can I Do Anything if I Miss the Test but Still Want to Participate in Scholarship Competitions?

If you fail to take the PSAT/NMSQT because you were ill or involved in an emergency, you still may be able to qualify for a National Merit or National Achievement Scholarship. You need to contact the NMSC to find out about alternative testing arrangements that would enable you to take part in the National Merit competitions.

If you are of Hispanic descent, you need to contact the National Hispanic Scholar Recognition Program run by the College Board. You can arrange to be considered for this program by communicating with The College Board, Suite 600, 1233 20th Street NW, Washington, DC 20036.

# How to Approach the PSAT/NMSQT

## TEST-TAKING TACTICS

## What Tactics Can Help Me When I Take the PSAT?

1. **Memorize the directions given in this book for each type of question.** These are only slightly different from the exact words you'll find on the PSAT you'll take. During the test, you won't have to waste even a few seconds reading any directions or sample questions.

2. **Know the format of the test.** The number and kinds of questions will break down roughly as follows:

   *48 Critical Reading Questions (2 sections, 25 minutes each)*

   *38 Math Questions (2 sections, 25 minutes each)*

   *39 Writing Skills Questions (1 section, 30 minutes)*

   See the chart on page vi for the breakdown within each section.

**3.** **Expect easier questions at the beginning of many sets of the same question type.** Within these sets (except for the reading comprehension and improving paragraph questions), the questions progress from easy to difficult. In other words, the first few sentence completion questions in a set will be easier than the last few sentence completion questions in that set. Similarly, the first two grid-in questions will be easier than the fifth and sixth ones and much easier than the last two grid-in questions.

**4.** **Take advantage of the easy questions to boost your score.** Each question is worth the same number of points. Whether it is easy or difficult, whether it takes you ten seconds or two minutes to answer, you get the same number of points for each question you answer correctly. Your job is to answer as many questions as you possibly can without rushing ahead so fast that you make careless errors and lose points for failing to give some questions enough thought. So take enough time to get those easy questions right!

**5.** ***First* answer all the easy questions; *then* tackle the hard ones if you have time.** The questions in each segment of the test get harder as you go along (except for the reading comprehension and improving paragraph questions). But there's no rule that says you have to answer the questions in order. You're allowed to skip. So skip the hard sentence completion questions and move on to the short reading passages right away. If you finish all the reading and still have time, you can go back to the hard sentence completion questions you skipped. Test-wise students know when it's time to move on. Test-wise students also know how to keep track of what they have skipped. Be sure to mark skipped questions in your test booklet. Be sure to skip that number on your answer sheet. Always be aware of where you are on the answer sheet.

**6.** **Eliminate as many wrong answers as you can and then make an educated guess.** Deciding between two choices is easier than deciding among five. The more choices you eliminate, the better your chance of guessing correctly.

**7.** **Change answers *only* if you have a reason for doing so.** Don't give in to last-minute panic. It's usually better not to change your answers on a sudden hunch or whim.

**8.** **Calculators are permitted in the test room, so bring along a calculator that you are comfortable using.** No question on the test will *require* the use of a calculator, but a calculator will be helpful for some questions. **Note:** You may *not* use the calculator on your cell phone. (You may not even have a phone on your desk, so do not bring your phone into the testing area.) Make sure that whatever calculator you bring is on the College Board's approved list. For a complete list of authorized and unauthorized calculators, go to *http://www.collegeboard.org/student/ testing/psat/about/calculator.html.*

**9.** **Remember that you are allowed to write anything you want in your test booklet. Make good use of it.** Circle questions you skip, and put big question marks next to questions you answer but are unsure about. In sentence completion questions, circle or underline key words such as *although, therefore, not,* and so on. In reading passages, circle key words and underline or put a mark in the margin next to any major point. On math questions, mark up diagrams, adding lines when necessary. And, of course, use all the space provided to solve the problem. In short, write anything that will help you, using whatever symbols you like. But remember, the only thing that counts is what you enter on your answer sheet. No one will ever see anything that you write in your test booklet.

10. **Be careful not to make any stray marks on your answer sheet.** This test is graded by a machine, and a machine cannot tell the difference between an accidental mark and a filled-in answer. When the machine sees two marks instead of one, the answer is marked wrong.

11. **Check frequently to make sure you are answering the questions in the right spots.** No machine is going to notice that you made a mistake early in the test, that you answered question 4 in the space for question 5, and that all your following answers are in the wrong place. One way to avoid this problem is to mark your answers in your test booklet and transfer them to your answer sheet by blocks.

12. **Line up your test book with your answer sheet to avoid making careless errors.** Whether you choose to fill in the answers question by question or in blocks, you will do so most efficiently if you keep your test booklet and your answer sheet aligned.

13. **Be particularly careful in marking the student-produced responses on the math grid.** Before you fill in the appropriate blanks in the grid, write your answer at the top of the columns. Then go down each column and make sure you fill in the right spaces. Be sure to answer every grid-in question.

14. **Don't get bogged down on any one question.** By the time you get to the actual PSAT, you should have a fair idea of how much time to spend on each question. If a question is taking too long, leave it and go on to the next question. This is no time to try to show the world that you can stick to a job no matter how long it takes. All the machine that grades the test will notice is that after a certain point you didn't have any correct answers.

## REDUCING ANXIETY

## How Can I Prevent PSAT Anxiety from Setting In?

1. Use this book to prepare conscientiously. The better prepared you are, the less anxiety you will have.

2. Get a good night's sleep before the test so that you are well rested and alert, and be sure to eat a good breakfast. You have a full morning ahead of you; you should have a full stomach as well.

3. Allow plenty of time for getting to the test site. Taking a test is pressure enough. You don't need the extra tension that comes from worrying about whether you will get there on time.

4. Be aware of the amount of time the test is going to take. There are five sections. They will take two hours and ten minutes total. Add to that a five-minute break after the third section, one-minute breaks between the others, plus thirty minutes for paper pushing. If the test starts at 8:00 A.M., don't make a dentist appointment for 11:00 A.M. You can't possibly get there on time, and you'll just spend the last half hour of the test worrying about it.

5. The College Board tells you to bring two sharpened No. 2 pencils to the test. Bring four. They don't weigh much, and this might be the one day in the decade when two pencil points decide to break. Bring full-size pencils, not little stubs. They are easier to write with, and you might as well be comfortable.

6. Speaking of being comfortable, wear comfortable clothes. This is a test, not a fashion show. Aim for the layered look. Wear something light, but bring a sweater. The test room may be hot, or it may be cold. You can't change the room, but you can put on the sweater.

**7.** Bring a watch or small travel clock, which you may keep on your desk. You need one. The room in which you take the test may not have a clock, and some proctors are not very good about posting the time on the blackboard. Don't depend on them. Each time you begin a test section, write down in your booklet the time according to your watch. That way you will always know how much time you have left. **Note:** The College Board does not permit you to bring any timer or watch with an audible alarm into the testing room. No beeps! And no cell phones!

**8.** Bring along some quick energy in your pocket—trail mix, raisins, a candy bar. Even if the proctors don't let you eat in the test room, you can still grab a bite en route to the restrooms during the five-minute break. Taking the test can leave you feeling drained and in need of a quick pickup—bring along your favorite comfort food.

**9.** There will be a break after the third section. Use this period to clear your thoughts. Take a few deep breaths. Stretch. Close your eyes and imagine yourself floating or sunbathing. In addition to being under mental pressure, you're under physical pressure from sitting so long in an uncomfortable seat with a No. 2 pencil clutched in your hand. Anything you can do to loosen up and get the kinks out will ease your body and help the oxygen get to your brain.

**10.** Most important of all, remember: very little, if anything, is riding on the result of this test. If you do poorly, no one will know; your PSAT scores are not reported to the colleges to which you plan to apply. So relax!

## GUESSING

If you try answering a question on the PSAT, but are unsure of the correct answer, should you guess?

The answer to the above question is very simple: in general, if you are an intelligent guesser, *it pays to guess*. To understand why this is so and why so many people are confused about it, you must understand how the PSAT is scored.

Two types of scores are associated with the PSAT: raw scores and scaled scores. First, three raw scores are calculated—one for each part of the test. Each raw score is then converted to a scaled score between 20 and 80. If you multiply a PSAT scaled score by 10, it becomes equivalent to an SAT scaled score. So, for example, a PSAT score of 56 is equivalent to an SAT score of 560.

On the PSAT, every question is worth exactly the same amount: 1 raw score point. A correct answer to a critical reading question for which you may have to read a whole paragraph is worth no more than a correct response to a sentence completion question that you can answer in a few seconds. You get no more credit for a correct answer to the hardest math question than you do for the easiest. For each question that you answer correctly, you receive 1 raw score point. For each multiple-choice question that you answer incorrectly, you lose ¼ point. Questions that you leave out have no effect on your score. So on each of the PSAT's three parts—critical reading, math, and writing skills—the raw score is calculated as follows:

$$(\text{\# of correct answers}) - \left( \frac{\text{\# of incorrect multiple-choice answers}}{4} \right) = \text{Raw Score}$$

There are 48 critical reading questions on the PSAT, 24 in each section. Let's assume that on each of the two sections you leave out the last 5 questions because you run out of time, and of the first 19 questions, you answer 15 correctly and 4 incorrectly. What would your raw score be? For the 30 correct answers you would earn 30 points and for the 8 incorrect answers you would lose $\frac{8}{4} = 2$ points. So your raw score on the critical reading part would be $30 - 2 = 28$, which would be converted to a scaled score of about 56.

In this scenario, what would happen to your score if during your last few seconds, you quickly bubbled in an answer for each of the 10 questions that you didn't have time to answer? Since there are five choices for each question, on average you would answer one-fifth of them correctly and four-fifths of them incorrectly. That is, you would probably get about 2 right and 8 wrong. How would that affect your score? Well, for 2 right answers you would gain 2 raw score points, and for 8 wrong answers you would lose $\frac{8}{4} = 2$ raw score points. So your raw score, and hence your scaled score, would be the same. If you were lucky and answered 3 questions correctly or a bit unlucky and answered only 1 question correctly, your raw score, and hence your scaled score, would go up or down slightly, but most likely it would remain the same. This leaves us with the following important conclusion:

*On average, on the PSAT, wild guessing does not affect your score.*

Although, as we have just seen, on average wild guessing doesn't affect your score, *educated guessing* can have an enormous effect on your score—it can increase it dramatically! To see what we mean by educated guessing and how it can increase your score on the PSAT, let's look at two examples. The first is a sentence completion question.

1. In Victorian times, countless Egyptian mummies were ground up to produce dried mummy powder, hailed by quacks as a near-magical ----, able to cure a wide variety of ailments.
   (A) toxin   (B) diagnosis   (C) symptom
   (D) panacea   (E) placebo

Clearly, what is needed is a word such as *medicine*—something capable of curing ailments. Let's assume that you know that *toxin* means poison; so you immediately eliminate A. You also know that although *diagnosis* and *symptom* are medical terms, neither means a medicine or a cure; so you eliminate B and C. You now know that the correct answer must be D or E, but unfortunately you have no idea what *panacea* or *placebo* means. You *could* guess, but you don't want to be wrong; after all, there's that ¼-point penalty for incorrect answers. So, should you leave it out? Absolutely not. *You must guess!* We'll explain why and how in a moment, but first let's look at the other example, this time a math one.

2. From 2000 to 2010 the number of students participating in a school's community service program increased by 25 percent. If the number of participants in 2010 was *P*, how many students participated in 2000?
   (A)  $0.75P$
   (B)  $0.80P$
   (C)  $1.20P$
   (D)  $1.25P$
   (E)  $1.50P$

Even if you are not very good at percent problems (especially when they involve letters!), you should realize that since participation in the program increased, the number of students who participated in 2000 must be *less than P*. So you know the answer must be A or B. What do you do? Do you guess and risk losing points for a wrong answer, or do you leave it out because you have no idea which answer is correct? *You must guess!*

Suppose that on the entire PSAT there are 16 questions on which you can eliminate three of the five answer choices, as we did on the two examples above, but you have no idea whatsoever about which of the two remaining choices is correct. What would be the result of guessing on those questions? You would probably get about 8 right answers and 8 wrong answers. Would that be good or bad? *It would be great!* For the 8 right answers you would earn 8 raw score points, but for the 8 wrong answers you would lose only $\frac{8}{4} = 2$ raw score points. Those 16 guesses gained you 6 raw score points, which would raise your scaled score by about 5 points (50 SAT points). You can't give up 50 points because you're afraid to guess.

When you take the PSAT, what if you find questions on which you can eliminate only one or two of the answer choices? You still have to guess. Remember—if you can't eliminate anything and you take wild guesses, you will break even. Whenever you can eliminate any choices at all, you must guess.

As you read this book, you will learn strategies that will enable you to narrow down the choices on every question you attempt. So the only questions you should leave out are the ones you didn't attempt, because you ran out of time.

*If you read a question but are unsure of the answer, use one of the strategies in this book to narrow down the choices and guess!*

## PACING

The biggest mistake that most students make when they take the PSAT is that they try to answer too many questions. Therefore, an important strategy is to slow down and answer fewer questions. Let's see why this is true.

Section 2 of a PSAT is always a math section with 20 multiple-choice questions. The questions in this section are presented in order of difficulty. Although this varies slightly from test to test, typically questions 1–6 are considered easy, questions 7–14 are considered medium, and questions 15–20 are considered hard. Even within the groups, the questions increase in difficulty: questions 7 and 14, for example, may both be ranked medium, but question 14 will definitely be harder than question 7. Of course, this depends slightly on each student's math skills. Some students might find question 8 or 9 or even 10 to be easier than question 7, but everyone will find questions 11 and 12 to be harder than questions 1 and 2, and questions 19 and 20 to be harder than questions 13 and 14.

However, all questions have the same value. You earn 1 point for a correct answer to question 1, which might take you only fifteen seconds to solve, and 1 point for a correct answer to question 20, which might take two or three minutes to solve. Knowing that it will probably take at least ten minutes to answer the last 5 questions, many students try to race through the first 15 questions in fifteen minutes or less and, as a result, miss many questions that they could have answered correctly, had they slowed down.

Suppose Michael rushed through questions 1–15 and got 9 right answers and 6 wrong ones and then worked on the 5 hardest questions and got 2 right and 3 wrong. His raw score would be $8\frac{3}{4}$: 11 for the 11 correct answers minus $2\frac{1}{4}$ points for the 9 wrong answers. Had he gone slowly and carefully, and not made any careless errors on the easy and medium questions, he might have run out of time and not answered any of the 5 hard questions at the end. But if spending all twenty-five minutes on the first 15 questions meant that he answered 13 correctly, 2 incorrectly, and omitted 5, his raw score would have been $12\frac{1}{2}$. If Michael had a similar improvement on Section 4, the other math section, his scaled score would have been about 7 points (70 SAT points) higher.

The only questions on the PSAT that do not proceed from easy to difficult are the reading comprehension questions; but the sentence completion questions at the beginning of each reading section do. So when a section begins with 8 sentence completions, for example, a winning strategy is to answer the 5 easy and medium ones, intentionally skip the 3 hardest ones, and go directly to the reading questions. It would be a shame to have to leave out a few reading questions that might be easy or medium because you wasted too much time trying to answer some very hard sentence completions, which you might very well miss, anyway. It is not only OK to intentionally leave out questions on the PSAT, for almost all students, even very good ones, it is advisable to do so. So it is worth repeating:

*The biggest mistake that most students make when they take the PSAT is that they try to answer too many questions.*

# Sample PSAT Questions

The purpose of this section is to familiarize you with the kinds of questions that appear on the PSAT by presenting questions like those on recent PSATs. Knowing what to expect when you take the examination is an important step in preparing for the test and succeeding in it.

If you wish, you can head straight for the diagnostic test that follows to learn about your strengths and weaknesses as a test taker and to get a sense of how well you might do on the PSAT. However, before you tackle the diagnostic test, we recommend that you take a few minutes to acquaint yourself with the kinds of questions you're going to encounter.

The directions that precede the various types of questions are similar to those on the PSAT. For all except the student-produced response questions, you are to choose the best answer and fill in the corresponding blank on the answer sheet.

## CRITICAL READING

There are two types of questions on the Critical Reading portion of the PSAT:

- sentence completion questions
- reading comprehension questions

The critical reading questions on the PSAT are in Section 1 (questions 1–24) and Section 3 (questions 25–48). You are allowed twenty-five minutes to complete each section.

| | Sentence Completion | Short Passages | Long Passages |
|---|---|---|---|
| Section 1 | 1–8 | 9–12 [2 passages] | 13–24 [2 passages] |
| Section 3 | 25–29 | 30–33 [2 passages] | 34–48 [2 passages] |
| | 13 questions total | 8 questions total | 27 questions total |

## Sentence Completion

Sentence completion questions are straightforward fill-in-the-blank questions. Each group of sentence completion questions starts with easy questions and gets harder as it goes along.

## Sentence Completion Directions

Each of the following sentences contains one or two blanks; these blanks indicate that a word or set of words has been left out. Below the sentence are five words or phrases, lettered A through E. Select the word or set of words that best completes the sentence.

**EXAMPLE:**

Fame is ----; today's rising star is all too soon tomorrow's washed-up has-been.

(A) rewarding   (B) gradual   (C) essential
(D) spontaneous   (E) transitory

1. Folk dancing is ---- senior citizens, and it is also economical; they need neither great physical agility nor special equipment to enjoy participating in the dance.

   (A) bewildering to   (B) thrilling for
   (C) foreign to   (D) appropriate for
   (E) impracticable for

2. Holding her infant son, the new mother felt an ---- greater than any other joy she had known.

   (A) affluence   (B) incentive   (C) assurance
   (D) incredulity   (E) elation

3. The author maintained that his insights were not ---- but had been made independently of others.

   (A) derivative   (B) esoteric   (C) fallacious
   (D) hypothetical   (E) concise

4. Suspicious of the ---- actions of others, the critic Edmund Wilson was in many ways a ---- man, unused to trusting anyone.

   (A) altruistic . . cynical
   (B) questionable . . contrite
   (C) generous . . candid
   (D) hypocritical . . cordial
   (E) benevolent . . dauntless

5. Although Roman original contributions to government, jurisprudence, and engineering are commonly acknowledged, the artistic legacy of the Roman world continues to be judged widely as ---- the magnificent Greek traditions that preceded it.

   (A) an improvement on   (B) an echo of
   (C) a resolution of   (D) a precursor of
   (E) a consummation of

6. ---- though she appeared, her journals reveal that her outward maidenly reserve concealed a passionate nature unsuspected by her family and friends.

   (A) Effusive   (B) Suspicious   (C) Tempestuous
   (D) Domineering   (E) Reticent

7. Crabeater seal, the common name of *Lobodon carcinophagus*, is ----, since the animal's staple diet is not crabs, but krill.

   (A) a pseudonym   (B) a misnomer
   (C) an allusion   (D) a digression
   (E) a compromise

## Answer Explanations

### Sentence Completion Questions

1. **(D)** *Because* senior citizens don't need great physical agility to enjoy folk dancing, it is an *appropriate* activity for them. It is not by definition *thrilling* for them.

2. **(E)** If the missing word is an emotion greater than *any other joy*, then it too must be a form of joy. *Elation* is a feeling of great joy.

3. **(A)** If the author got his insights independently, then he did not get or derive them from the insights of other people. In other words, his insights were not *derivative*.

4. **(A)** Someone given to distrusting the motives and actions of others is by definition *cynical*. Such a person would question even the *altruistic*, unselfish deeds of others, suspecting there to be ulterior motives for these charitable acts.

5. **(B)** The view of Rome's contributions to government, law, and engineering is wholly positive: these original additions to human knowledge are generally acknowledged or recognized. *In contrast*, Rome's original contributions to art are *not* recognized; they are seen as just an *echo* or imitation of the art of ancient Greece.

   Note that *Although* sets up the contrast here.

6. **(E)** Her outward appearance was one of "maidenly reserve" (self-restraint; avoidance of intimacy). Thus, she seemed to be *reticent* (reserved; disinclined to speak or act freely), even though she actually felt things passionately.

7. **(B)** Because these seals eat far more krill than crabs, it *misnames* them to call them crabeater seals. The term is thus a *misnomer*, a name that's wrongly applied to someone or something.

   Beware of eye-catchers. Choice A is incorrect. A *pseudonym* isn't a mistaken name; it's a false name that an author adopts.

# Critical Reading

Your ability to read and understand the kind of material found in college texts and the more serious magazines is tested in the critical reading section of the PSAT/NMSQT. There are two types of passages on the test, short passages and long passages. Short passages are approximately 100 words in length; long passages generally range from 400–850 words. Some passages are paired: you will be asked to answer two or three questions that compare the viewpoints of two passages on the same subject.

---

## Critical Reading Directions

The passages below are followed by questions on their content; questions following a pair of related passages may also be based on the relationship between the paired passages. Answer the questions on the basis of what is stated or implied in the passages and in any introductory material that may be provided.

---

**Questions 8 and 9 are based on the following passage.**

"Ladybug, ladybug, fly away home. Your house is on fire; your children do roam." Few farmers would seek to chase away ladybugs, or ladybird
Line beetles, with this familiar children's rhyme, for
5 ladybugs are known as the farmer's friend. Clusters of ladybugs are often gathered and sold to farmers, who employ them to control the spread of insect pests. In 1888, for example, when California's orange orchards were threatened by an out-
10 break of cottony-cushion scale, farmers imported the Australian ladybird beetle to devour the scale. In less than two years, the ladybugs had saved the orchards.

**8.** The quotation in the opening lines of the passage primarily serves to
(A) alert the ladybugs to an actual danger
(B) introduce the passage's subject informally
(C) demonstrate a common misapprehension
(D) provide a critical literary allusion
(E) diminish the importance of ladybird beetles

**9.** As used in line 12, the word "scale" most likely refers to
(A) a form of cotton
(B) a variety of insect
(C) a type of orange
(D) a plant nutrient
(E) a measure of weight

**Questions 10–16 are based on the following passages.**

*The following passages are excerpted from books on America's national pastime, baseball.*

**Passage 1**

DiMaggio had size, power, and speed. McCarthy, his longtime manager, liked to say that DiMaggio might have stolen 60 bases a season if
Line he had given him the green light. Stengel, his
5 new manager, was equally impressed, and when DiMaggio was on base he would point to him as an example of the perfect base runner. "Look at him," Stengel would say as DiMaggio ran out a base hit, "he's always watching the ball. He isn't watching
10 second base. He isn't watching third base. He knows they haven't been moved. He isn't watching the ground, because he knows they haven't built a canal or a swimming pool since he was last there. He's watching the ball and the outfielder, which is
15 the one thing that is different on every play."

DiMaggio complemented his natural athletic ability with astonishing physical grace. He played the outfield, he ran the bases, and he batted not just effectively but with rare style. He would glide
20 rather than run, it seemed, always smooth, always ending up where he wanted to be just when he wanted to be there. If he appeared to play effort-lessly, his teammates knew otherwise. In his first season as a Yankee, Gene Woodling, who played
25 left field, was struck by the sound of DiMaggio chasing a fly ball. He sounded like a giant truck horse on the loose, Woodling thought, his feet thudding down hard on the grass. The great, clear noises in the open space enabled Woodling to
30 measure the distances between them without looking.

He was the perfect Hemingway hero, for Hem-ingway in his novels romanticized the man who exhibited grace under pressure, who withheld
35 any emotion lest it soil the purer statement of his deeds. DiMaggio was that kind of hero; his grace and skill were always on display, his emotions always concealed. This stoic grace was not achieved without a terrible price: DiMaggio was a man

40  wound tight. He suffered from insomnia and
    ulcers. When he sat and watched the game he
    chain-smoked and drank endless cups of coffee. He
    was ever conscious of his obligation to play well.
    Late in his career, when his legs were bothering
45  him and the Yankees had a comfortable lead in a
    pennant race, columnist Jimmy Cannon asked him
    why he played so hard—the games, after all, no
    longer meant so much. "Because there might be
    somebody out there who's never seen me play
50  before," he answered.

**Passage 2**

    Athletes and actors—let actors stand for the
    set of performing artists—share much. They share
    the need to make gestures as fluid and economical
    as possible, to make out of a welter of choices the
55  single, precisely right one. They share the need for
    thousands of hours of practice in order to train the
    body to become the perfect, instinctive instrument
    to express. Both athlete and actor, out of that
    abundance of emotion, choice, strategy, knowl-
60  edge of the terrain, mood of spectators, condition
    of others in the ensemble, secret awareness of
    injury or weakness, and as nearly an absolute *con-
    centration* as possible so that all externalities are
    integrated, all distraction absorbed to the self,
65  must be able to change the self so successfully that
    it changes us.
    When either athlete or actor can bring all
    these skills to bear and focus them, then he or she
    will achieve that state of complete intensity and
70  complete relaxation—complete coherence or
    integrity between what the performer wants to do
    and what the performer has to do. Then, the per-
    former is free; for then, all that has been learned,
    by thousands of hours of practice and discipline
75  and by repetition of pattern, becomes natural.
    Then, intellect is upgraded to the level of an
    instinct. The body follows commands that precede
    thinking.
    When athlete and artist achieve such self-
80  knowledge that they transform the self so that we
    are re-created, it is finally an exercise in power.
    The individual's power to dominate, on stage or
    field, invests the whole arena around the locus of
    performance with his or her power. We draw from
85  the performer's energy, just as we scrutinize the
    performer's vulnerabilities, and we criticize as if
    we were equals (we are not) what is displayed. This
    is why all performers dislike or resent the audience
    as much as they need and enjoy it. Power
90  flows in a mysterious circuit from performer to

spectator (I assume a "live" performance) and
back, and while cheers or applause are the hoped-
for outcome of performing, silence or gasps are the
most desired, for then the moment has
95  occurred—then domination is complete, and as
the performer triumphs, a unity rare and inspiring
results.

**10.** In Passage 1, Stengel is most impressed by DiMaggio's
   (A) indifference to potential dangers
   (B) tendency to overlook the bases in his haste
   (C) ability to focus on the variables
   (D) proficiency at fielding fly balls
   (E) overall swiftness and stamina

**11.** It can be inferred from the content and tone of
Stengel's comment (lines 7–15) that he would
regard a base runner who kept his eye on second
base with
   (A) trepidation   (B) approbation
   (C) resignation   (D) exasperation
   (E) tolerance

**12.** The phrase "a man wound tight" (lines 39–40)
means a man
   (A) wrapped in confining bandages
   (B) living in constricted quarters
   (C) under intense emotional pressure
   (D) who drank alcohol to excess
   (E) who could throw with great force

**13.** Which best describes what the author is doing in
the parenthetical comment "let actors stand for the
set of performing artists" (lines 51–52)?
   (A) indicating that actors should rise out of
       respect for the arts
   (B) defining the way in which he is using a partic-
       ular term
   (C) encouraging actors to show tolerance for their
       fellow artists
   (D) emphasizing that actors are superior to other
       performing artists
   (E) correcting a misinterpretation of the role of
       actors

**14.** To the author of Passage 2, freedom for performers
depends on
   (A) their subjection of the audience
   (B) their willingness to depart from tradition
   (C) the internalization of all they have learned
   (D) their ability to interpret material
       independently
   (E) the absence of injuries or other weaknesses

**15.** The author's attitude toward the concept of the equality of spectators and performers (lines 83–87) is one of

(A) relative indifference
(B) mild skepticism
(C) explicit rejection
(D) strong embarrassment
(E) marked perplexity

**16.** The author of Passage 2 would most likely react to the characterization of DiMaggio presented in lines 43–50 by pointing out that DiMaggio probably

(A) felt some resentment of the spectator whose good opinion he supposedly sought
(B) never achieved the degree of self-knowledge that would have transformed him
(C) was unaware that his audience was surveying his weak points
(D) was a purely instinctive natural athlete
(E) was seldom criticized by his peers

## Answer Explanations

### Critical Reading Questions

8. **(B)** Rather than launch immediately into a formal discussion of the beneficial qualities of ladybugs or ladybird beetles, the author chooses to *introduce the subject informally* by quoting a familiar nursery rhyme.

9. **(B)** Cottony-cushion scale is just one of the insect pests combatted by ladybird beetles. The correct answer is Choice B, *a variety of insect*.

10. **(C)** Stengel's concluding sentence indicates that DiMaggio watches "the one thing that is different on every play." In other words, DiMaggio *focuses on the variables*, the factors that change from play to play.

11. **(D)** The sarcastic tone of Stengel's comment suggests that he would be *exasperated* or irritated by a base runner who had his eye on second base when he should have been watching the ball and the outfielder.

12. **(C)** Look at the sentences following this phrase. They indicate that DiMaggio was a man *under intense emotional pressure*, one who felt so much stress that he developed ulcers and had problems getting to sleep.

13. **(B)** The author is taking a moment away from his argument to make sure the reader knows exactly who the subjects of his comparison are. He is not simply comparing athletes and actors. He is comparing athletes and *all* performing artists, "the set of performing artists," to use his words. Thus, in his side comment, he is *defining* how he intends to use the word *actors* throughout the discussion.

14. **(C)** Performers are free when all they have learned becomes so natural, so internalized, that it seems instinctive. In other words, freedom depends on *the internalization* of what they have learned.

15. **(C)** The author bluntly states that we spectators are not the performers' equals. Thus, his attitude toward the concept is one of *explicit rejection*.

16. **(A)** Passage 1 indicates DiMaggio always played hard to live up to his reputation and to perform well for anyone in the stands who had never seem him play before. Clearly, he wanted the spectators to have a good opinion of him. Passage 2, however, presents a more complex picture of the relationship between the performer and his audience. On the one hand, the performer needs the audience, needs its good opinion and its applause. On the other hand, the performer also resents the audience, resents the way spectators freely point out his weaknesses and criticize his art. Thus, the author of Passage 2 might well point out that DiMaggio *felt some resentment* of the audience, whom he hoped to impress with his skill.

# MATHEMATICS

There are two types of questions on the Mathematics portion of the PSAT:

**1.** multiple-choice questions

**2.** grid-in questions

The math questions are in Sections 2 and 4 of the PSAT. You have twenty-five minutes to work on each section.

- Section 2 has 20 multiple-choice questions (Questions 1–20)
- Section 4 has 8 multiple-choice questions (Questions 21–28) followed by 10 grid-in questions (Questions 29–38).

Within each group, the questions are presented approximately in order of increasing difficulty. In fact, on the score report, which you will receive about seven or eight weeks after taking the PSAT, each question will be rated E (Easy), M (Medium), or H (Hard), depending on how many students answered that question correctly. A typical ranking of the math questions would be as follows:

|  | Easy | Medium | Hard |
| --- | --- | --- | --- |
| Section 2: Multiple-choice | 1–6 | 7–14 | 15–20 |
| Section 4: Multiple-choice | 21–22 | 23–25 | 26–28 |
| Section 4: Grid-in | 29–31 | 32–35 | 36–38 |

As a result, the amount of time you spend on any one question should vary greatly.

## Multiple-Choice Questions

Twenty-eight of the 38 mathematics questions on the PSAT are multiple-choice questions. Although you have certainly taken multiple-choice tests before, the PSAT uses a few different types of questions in these sections, and you must become familiar with all of them. By far, the most common type of question is one in which you are asked to solve a problem. The straightforward way to answer such a question is to do the necessary work, get the solution, then look at the five choices and choose the one that corresponds to your answer. In Chapter 6 we will discuss other techniques for answering these questions, but for now let's look at a couple of examples.

## EXAMPLE 1

What is the average (arithmetic mean) of –2, –1, 0, 1, 2, 3, and 4?

(A) 0

(B) $\frac{3}{7}$

(C) 1

(D) $\frac{7}{6}$

(E) $\frac{7}{2}$

To solve this problem requires only that you know how to find the average of a set of numbers. Ignore the fact that this is a multiple-choice question. *Don't even look at the choices.*

- Calculate the average by adding the 7 numbers and dividing by 7.

- $\dfrac{-2 + -1 + 0 + 1 + 2 + 3 + 4}{7} = \dfrac{7}{7} = 1.$

- Now look at the five choices. Find 1, listed as Choice C, and blacken in C on your answer sheet.

## EXAMPLE 2

Emily was born on Wednesday, April 16, 2008. Her sister Erin was born exactly 1200 days later. On what day of the week was Erin born?

   (A) Tuesday
   (B) Thursday
   (C) Friday
   (D) Saturday
   (E) Sunday

Again, you are not helped by the fact that this question is a multiple-choice question. You need to determine the day of the week on which Erin was born and then select the choice that matches your answer.

- The 7 days keep repeating in exactly the same order: 1 day after Emily was born was a Thursday, 2 days after Emily was born was a Friday, and so on. Make a table.

|  | Thurs. | Fri. | Sat. | Sun. | Mon. | Tues. | Wed. |
|---|---|---|---|---|---|---|---|
| Days after Emily | 1 | 2 | 3 | 4 | 5 | 6 | 7 |
| was born | 8 | 9 | 10 | 11 | 12 | 13 | 14 |
|  | and so on. | | | | | | |

- Note that whenever the number of days is a multiple of 7 (7, 14, 21, . . . , 70, . . .) a whole number of weeks has gone by, and it is again a Wednesday.
- If 1200 were a multiple of 7, the 1200th day would be a Wednesday.
- Is it? To find out, use your calculator: $1200 \div 7 = 171.4285 \ldots$
- 1200 days is <u>not</u> a whole number of weeks; it is a little more than 171 weeks.
- Since $171 \times 7 = 1197$, the 1197th day completes the 171st week and hence is a Wednesday.
- The 1198th day starts the next week. It is a Thursday; the 1199th day is a Friday; and the 1200th day is a Saturday.
- The answer is D.

   **Note:** Did you notice that the solution didn't use the fact that Emily was born on April 16, 2008? This is unusual. Occasionally, but not often, a PSAT problem contains extraneous information.

   In contrast to Examples 1 and 2, some questions *require* you to look at all five choices in order to find the answers. Consider Example 3.

## EXAMPLE 3

For any numbers $a$ and $b$: let the operation ☺ be defined by $a ☺ b = a^2 + b^2$. Which of the following is *not* equal to $6 ☺ 8$?

(A) $-10 ☺ 0$
(B) $-8 ☺ -6$
(C) $9 ☺ \sqrt{19}$
(D) $(6 ☺ 9) - (4 ☺ 1)$
(E) $2(3 ☺ 4)$

The words *which of the following* alert you to the fact that you are going to have to examine each of the five choices and determine which of them satisfies the stated condition—in this case, that it is *not* equal to $6 ☺ 8$.

Do not be concerned that you have never seen the symbol "☺" used this way before. No one has. On the PSAT there is almost always at least one question that uses a symbol that the test makers have made up. All you have to do is read the question very carefully and follow the directions exactly. In this case we have: $6 ☺ 8 = 6^2 + 8^2 = 36 + 64 = 100$.

Now check each of the five choices, and find the one that is *not* equal to 100.

(A) $-10 ☺ 0 = (-10)^2 + 0^2 = 100 + 0 = 100$
(B) $-8 ☺ -6 = (-8)^2 + (-6)^2 = 64 + 36 = 100$
(C) $9 ☺ \sqrt{19} = 9^2 + (\sqrt{19})^2 = 81 + 19 = 100$
(D) $(6 ☺ 9) - (4 ☺ 1) = (6^2 + 9^2) - (4^2 + 1^2) = (36 + 81) - (16 + 1) =$
    $117 - 17 = 100$
(E) $2(3 ☺ 4) = 2(3^2 + 4^2) = 2(9 + 16) = 2(25) = 50$, which is *not* equal to 100.

So, the correct answer is E.

Another kind of multiple-choice question that appears on the PSAT is the Roman numeral-type question. These questions consist of three statements labeled I, II, and III. The five answer choices give various possibilities for which of the statements are true. So, really, a Roman numeral question consists of three separate true–false questions. Here is a typical example.

## EXAMPLE 4

In $\triangle ABC$, $AB = 3$ and $BC = 4$. Which of the following could be the perimeter of $\triangle ABC$?

   I. 8
  II. 12
 III. 16

(A) I only
(B) II only
(C) I and II only
(D) II and III only
(E) I, II, and III

● Note that "I. 8" is simply an abbreviation of the statement, "The perimeter of $\triangle ABC$ could be 8." The same is true for "II. 12" and "III. 16." To solve this problem, examine each of the three statements independently.

   I. Could the perimeter be 8? If it were, then the third side would be 1. But in any triangle, the smallest side must be greater than the difference of the other two sides. So, the third side must be *greater* than $4 - 3 = 1$. It cannot equal 1. I is false.

II.   Could the perimeter be 12? That is, could the third side be 5? Yes. The three sides could be 3, 4, and 5. In fact, the most common right triangle to appear on the PSAT is a 3-4-5 right triangle. II is true.

III.   Could the perimeter be 16? If it were, then the third side would be 9. But in any triangle, the largest side must be less than the sum of the other two sides. So, the third side must be less than $4 + 3 = 7$. It cannot equal 9. III is false.

- Only statement II is true. The answer is B.

## Grid-In Questions

Ten of the 38 mathematics questions on the PSAT are what the College Board calls student-produced response questions. These are the only questions on the PSAT that are not multiple-choice. Since the answers to these questions are entered on a special grid, they are usually referred to as *grid-in* questions. Except for the method of entering your answer, this type of question is probably the one with which you are most familiar. In your math class, most homework problems and test questions require you to determine an answer and write it down, and this is what you will do on the grid-in problems. The only difference is that on the PSAT, you must record your answer on a special grid, such as the one shown, so that it can be read by a computer.

**There is no deduction for wrong answers to grid-in questions, so if you can't solve a problem, you should always guess.**

Here is a typical grid-in question.

## EXAMPLE 5

John has a rectangular garden. He decides to enlarge it by increasing its length by 20% and its width by 30%. If the area of the new garden is *a* times the area of the original garden, what is the value of *a*?

**Solution.** From the wording of the question, it is clear that the answer does not depend on the actual original dimensions. Therefore, pick an easy value. For example, assume that the original garden is a square whose sides are 10. Since 20% of 10 is 2 and 30% of 10 is 3, then the new garden is a 12 by 13 rectangle. Therefore, the area of the original garden is $10 \times 10 = 100$, and the area of the new garden is $12 \times 13 = 156$. So $156 = a(100)$, and $a = 1.56$.

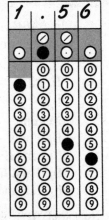

To enter this answer, you write 1.56 in the four spaces at the top of the grid and blacken in the appropriate circle under each space. In the first column, under the 1, blacken the oval marked 1; in the second column, under the decimal point, blacken the oval with the decimal point; in the third column, under the 5, blacken the oval marked 5; and finally, in the fourth column, under the 6, blacken the oval marked 6.

Note that the only symbols that appear in the grid are the digits from 0 to 9, a decimal point, and a fraction bar ( / ). The grid does not have a minus sign, so *answers to grid-in problems can never be negative*. In Chapter 5, you will read suggestions for the best way to fill in grids. You will also learn the special rules concerning the proper way to grid-in fractions, mixed numbers, and decimals that won't fit in the grid's four columns. When you take the diagnostic test, just enter your answers exactly as was done in Example 5.

# WRITING SKILLS

The Writing Skills section consists of 39 questions to be answered in thirty minutes. A typical test has 20 improving sentences questions, 14 identifying sentence errors questions, and 5 improving paragraphs questions.

## Improving Sentences Questions

The improving sentences questions test your ability to select the wording that makes the strongest sentence—the clearest, the smoothest, the most compact.

---

### Improving Sentences Directions

Some or all parts of the following sentences are underlined. The first answer choice, (A), simply repeats the underlined part of the sentence. The other four choices present four alternative ways to phrase the underlined part. Select the answer that produces the most effective sentence, one that is clear and exact, and blacken the appropriate space on your answer sheet. In selecting your choice, be sure that it is standard written English and that it expresses the meaning of the original sentence.

**EXAMPLE:**

The first biography of author Eudora Welty came out in 1998, <u>and she was eighty-nine years old at the time.</u>

(A) and she was eighty-nine years old at the time
(B) at the time when she was eighty-nine
(C) upon becoming an eighty-nine year old
(D) when she was eighty-nine
(E) at the age of eighty-nine years old

---

1. <u>More than any animal,</u> the wolverine exemplifies the unbridled ferocity of "nature red in tooth and claw."

   (A) More than any animal
   (B) More than any other animal
   (C) More than another animal
   (D) Unlike any animal
   (E) Compared to other animals

2. The reviewer knew that Barbara Cartland had written several Gothic <u>novels, she didn't remember any of their titles.</u>

   (A) novels, she didn't remember any of their titles
   (B) novels, however she didn't remember any of their titles
   (C) novels, their titles, however, she didn't remember
   (D) novels without remembering any of their titles
   (E) novels, but she remembered none of their titles

3. I think the United States will veto the resolution imposing sanctions against Israel <u>regardless of the desires of the Arab nations</u> for strong action.

   (A) regardless of the desires of the Arab nations
   (B) irregardless of the Arab nations' desires
   (C) regardless of the Arab nations desires
   (D) irregardless of the Arab nation's desires
   (E) mindful of the desires of the Arab nations

## Answer Explanations

1. **(B)** Choice B includes the necessary word *other*, which makes the comparison correct. Choice D changes the meaning of the sentence by its implication that the wolverine is *not* an animal.

2. **(E)** Choices A, B, and C are run-on sentences. Choice D changes the meaning of the sentence by implying that it was Barbara Cartland who could not remember the titles.

3. **(A)** *Irregardless* in Choices B and D is incorrect. Also, in Choices C and D, the case of *nations* is incorrect. The correct form of the plural possessive case of *nation* is *nations'*. Choice E changes the meaning of the sentence; in fact, it reverses it.

# Identifying Sentence Errors

The identifying sentence errors questions test your ability to spot faults in usage and sentence structure.

---

## Identifying Sentence Errors Directions

The sentences in this section may contain errors in grammar, usage, choice of words, or idioms. There is either just one error per sentence, or the sentence is correct. Some words or phrases are underlined and lettered; everything else in the sentence is correct.

If an underlined word or phrase is incorrect, choose that letter; if the sentence is correct, select <u>No error</u>. Then blacken the appropriate space on your answer sheet.

**EXAMPLE:**

The region has a climate <u>so severe that</u> plants
                          A

<u>growing there</u> rarely <u>had been</u> more than twelve
   B                       C

inches <u>high</u>. <u>No error</u>        ⒶⒷ●ⒹⒺ
        D        E

---

4. <u>Despite the fact that</u> <u>some states</u> have resisted,
       A                        B

   Congress <u>have passed</u> legislation <u>permitting</u>
              C                             D

   highway speed limits to 65 miles per hour on rural

   interstates. <u>No error</u>
                   E

5. J. M. Barrie's *Peter Pan*, <u>which</u> <u>originated as</u>
                                 A         B

   a play for children, later <u>was reworked</u> as a
                                   C

   novel, a popular animated film, and

   <u>it was turned into a hit musical comedy</u>.
                        D

   <u>No error</u>
     E

6. Joe DiMaggio, <u>whose</u> style was one of
                   A

   <u>quiet excellence</u>, was consistently the New York
        B

   Yankees' <u>outstanding player</u> <u>during</u> his thirteen
                  C                    D

   years on the team. <u>No error</u>
                          E

7. When Ms. Rivera <u>was</u> <u>truly</u> happy, she does
                     A      B

   not <u>constantly</u> complain <u>that</u> she has no purpose
          C                        D

   in life. <u>No error</u>
               E

## Answer Explanations

4. **(C)** Error in subject-verb agreement. The antecedent, *Congress*, is singular. Change *have passed* to *has passed*.

5. **(D)** Error in parallelism. All sentence parts listed in a series should have the same form. Change *it was turned into a hit musical comedy* to *a hit musical comedy*.

6. **(E)** Sentence is correct.

7. **(A)** Error in sequence of tenses. The sentence should read: *When Ms. Rivera is truly happy, she does not constantly complain.*

# Improving Paragraphs Questions

The improving paragraphs questions test your ability to polish an essay by combining sentences or manipulating sentence parts. You may need to arrange sentences to improve the essay's logical organization or to pick evidence to strengthen the writer's argument.

---

**Improving Paragraphs Directions**

The passage below is the unedited draft of a student's essay. Some of the essay needs to be rewritten to make the meaning clearer and more precise. Read the essay carefully.

The essay is followed by questions about changes that might improve all or part of its organization, development, sentence structure, use of language, appropriateness to the audience, or use of standard written English. Choose the answer that most clearly and effectively expresses the student's intended meaning. Indicate your choice by filling in the corresponding space on the answer sheet.

---

**[1]** As people grow older, quite obviously, the earth does too. **[2]** And with the process of the earth aging, we must learn to recycle. **[3]** The idea of using things over and over again to conserve our supply of natural resources is a beautiful one. **[4]** Those who don't see how easy it is to recycle should be criticized greatly.

**[5]** As we become more aware of the earth's problems, we all say "Oh, I'd like to help." **[6]** However, so few really do get involved. **[7]** Recycling is a simple, yet effective place to start. **[8]** Taking aluminum cans to the supermarket to be recycled is an ingenious idea. **[9]** It attracts those who want the money (5 cents a can), and it is also a convenient place to go to. **[10]** In addition, in almost every town, there is a Recycling Center. **[11]** I know that there are separate bins for paper, bottles, cans, etc. **[12]** This is a convenient service to those who recycle. **[13]** It is so easy to drive a few blocks to a center to drop off what needs to be recycled. **[14]** This is just another simple example of how easy it really is to recycle and to get involved. **[15]** Those who don't see its simplicity should be criticized for not doing their part to help make the world a better place.

**[16]** When I go to other people's houses and see aluminum cans in the garbage, I can honestly say I get enraged. **[17]** Often I say, "Why don't you just recycle those cans instead of throwing them out?" **[18]** What makes me even more angry is when they say "We have no time to recycle them." **[19]** Those people, I feel, should be criticized for not recycling in the past and should be taught a lesson about our earth and how recycling can conserve it.

8. Which of the following most effectively expresses the underlined portion of sentence 2 below?

   *And <u>with the process of the earth aging</u>, we must learn to recycle.*

   (A) with the aging process of the earth
   (B) the process of the earth's aging
   (C) as the earth ages
   (D) with the aging earth's process
   (E) as the process of the earth's aging continues

9. Considering the essay as a whole, which of the following best explains the main purpose of the second paragraph?

   (A) to explain the historical background of the topic
   (B) to provide a smooth transition between the first and third paragraphs
   (C) to define terms introduced in the first paragraph
   (D) to give an example of an idea presented in the first paragraph
   (E) to present a different point of view on the issue being discussed

10. Which of the sentences below most effectively combines sentences 10, 11, and 12?

   (A) Recycling centers offer recyclers convenience by providing separate bins for paper, bottles, and cans and by being located in almost every town.
   (B) Recycling centers, located in almost every town, serve recyclers by providing convenient bins to separate paper, bottles, and cans.
   (C) Almost every town has a recycling center with separate bins for paper, bottles, and cans, and this is a convenient service for people who want to recycle.
   (D) People who want to recycle will find recycling centers in almost every town, providing a convenient separation of paper, bottles, and cans into bins.
   (E) For the convenience of recyclers, separate bins for paper, bottles, and cans are provided by almost every town's recycling center.

## Answer Explanations

8. **(C)** This question asks you to find an alternative to a rather awkward group of words, composed of two phrases, *with the process* and *of the earth aging*. The second is graceless and ungrammatical. It should have read *of the earth's aging*, because in standard usage, nouns and pronouns modifying gerunds are usually written as possessives. Knowing what it should have been, however, is not much help in answering the question. You still must select from the five alternatives the one best way to express the essay writer's idea. In the context of the whole sentence, two of the choices, B and D, make no sense at all. A also borders on incomprehensibility. Left with C and E, the better choice is C because it is more concise and it expresses exactly what the writer intended.

9. **(D)** To answer this question, you need to have read the whole essay. You also need to know the way individual paragraphs function in an essay—any essay. Here, all five choices describe legitimate uses of a paragraph, but they don't all apply to this particular essay. Choices A, C, and E can be quickly discarded. Choice B is a possibility because in a unified essay every paragraph (except the first and last) in some sense serves as a bridge between paragraphs. Because the second paragraph is the longest in the essay, however, its main function is probably more than transitional. In fact, it develops by example an idea originating in the first paragraph—how easy it is to recycle. Therefore, D is the best choice.

10. **(B)** In a series of short sentences, every idea carries equal weight. By combining short sentences, writers may emphasize the important ideas and subordinate the others. To answer this question, then, you have to decide which idea expressed by the three sentences ought to be emphasized. Since two of the sentences (11 and 12) refer to the convenient arrangement of recycling centers, that's the point to stress. In the context of the whole essay, the other sentence (10), which pertains to the location of recycling centers, contains less vital information. Usually, the main point of a sentence is contained in the main, or independent, clause, and secondary ideas are found in subordinate, or dependent, clauses.

With that principle in mind, read each of the choices. A and C give equal weight to the location and convenience of recycling centers. D stresses the location rather than the convenience. E subordinates properly but changes the meaning. Therefore, B is the correct answer. In B, information about the location of recycling centers is contained in a subordinate clause included parenthetically inside the main clause.

## TACTICAL WRAP-UP

 1. Memorize the directions given in this book for each type of question. That way, during the test you won't have to waste precious time reading the directions and sample questions.

2. Know the format of the test.

3. Expect easy questions at the beginning of many sets of the same question type.

4. Take advantage of the easy questions to boost your score.

 5. First answer all the easy questions; then tackle the hard ones if you have time.

 6. Eliminate as many wrong answers as you can and then make an educated guess.

7. Change answers *only* if you have a reason for doing so.

8. Calculators are permitted on the math portion of the test, so bring along a calculator that you are comfortable using.

9. Remember that you are allowed to write anything you want in your test booklet. Make good use of it.

10. Be careful not to make any stray marks on your answer sheet.

11. Check frequently to make sure you are answering the questions in the right spots.

12. Line up your test book with your answer sheet to avoid making careless errors.

 13. Be particularly careful in marking the student-produced responses on the math grids.

14. Don't get bogged down on any one question. If a question has you dithering or bogged down, circle it in the test booklet and return to it only after you have answered all the questions you are sure of.

# PART TWO

# A DIAGNOSTIC TEST

- IDENTIFY YOUR WEAKNESSES
- KNOW YOUR STRENGTHS

# A Diagnostic Test

On the following pages you will find a sample PSAT test. Take this test, following the directions below; then score your answers and go over the results using the self-rating guides provided. This should give you a fairly good sense of what your score would be if you didn't do any special preparation for the test.

Once you've done this, you'll be in good shape to come with up with a review plan that meets your needs. You'll know which types of questions you have to practice, which topics in math you must review, which reading skills you have to concentrate on, and which writing skills you need to improve.

## HERE'S WHAT YOU NEED TO KNOW:

- Each correct answer is worth 1 point (raw score).
- Except for 10 grid-in math questions in Section 4, every question on the PSAT is multiple-choice.
- The multiple-choice questions have a ¼-point penalty for wrong answers.
- There is *no* penalty for wrong answers on the 10 grid-in math questions.
- If you don't answer a question, your raw score is not affected.

## SIMULATE TEST CONDITIONS (TAKE THIS DIAGNOSTIC PSAT AS IF IT WERE THE REAL THING)

Total Time: 2 hours, 10 minutes*
- Find a quiet place to work.
- Keep an accurate record of your time.
- If you finish a section early, do not start the next section. Use the remaining minutes to check your work.
- Read the questions closely.
- Work carefully, even if it means you don't get to all the questions.
- Do not spend too much time on questions that seem hard for you.
- If time permits, go back to any questions you left out.
- Do not guess wildly, but whenever you can eliminate one or more answer choices, make an educated guess.

*This does not count the short breaks between the sections (see page vi).

# Answer Sheet–Diagnostic Test

Each mark should completely fill the appropriate space, and should be as dark as all other marks. Make all erasures complete. Traces of an erasure may be read as an answer.

## Section 1 – Critical Reading
### 25 minutes

1 Ⓐ Ⓑ Ⓒ Ⓓ Ⓔ
2 Ⓐ Ⓑ Ⓒ Ⓓ Ⓔ
3 Ⓐ Ⓑ Ⓒ Ⓓ Ⓔ
4 Ⓐ Ⓑ Ⓒ Ⓓ Ⓔ
5 Ⓐ Ⓑ Ⓒ Ⓓ Ⓔ
6 Ⓐ Ⓑ Ⓒ Ⓓ Ⓔ
7 Ⓐ Ⓑ Ⓒ Ⓓ Ⓔ
8 Ⓐ Ⓑ Ⓒ Ⓓ Ⓔ
9 Ⓐ Ⓑ Ⓒ Ⓓ Ⓔ
10 Ⓐ Ⓑ Ⓒ Ⓓ Ⓔ
11 Ⓐ Ⓑ Ⓒ Ⓓ Ⓔ
12 Ⓐ Ⓑ Ⓒ Ⓓ Ⓔ
13 Ⓐ Ⓑ Ⓒ Ⓓ Ⓔ
14 Ⓐ Ⓑ Ⓒ Ⓓ Ⓔ
15 Ⓐ Ⓑ Ⓒ Ⓓ Ⓔ
16 Ⓐ Ⓑ Ⓒ Ⓓ Ⓔ
17 Ⓐ Ⓑ Ⓒ Ⓓ Ⓔ
18 Ⓐ Ⓑ Ⓒ Ⓓ Ⓔ
19 Ⓐ Ⓑ Ⓒ Ⓓ Ⓔ
20 Ⓐ Ⓑ Ⓒ Ⓓ Ⓔ
21 Ⓐ Ⓑ Ⓒ Ⓓ Ⓔ
22 Ⓐ Ⓑ Ⓒ Ⓓ Ⓔ
23 Ⓐ Ⓑ Ⓒ Ⓓ Ⓔ
24 Ⓐ Ⓑ Ⓒ Ⓓ Ⓔ

## Section 2 – Math
### 25 minutes

1 Ⓐ Ⓑ Ⓒ Ⓓ Ⓔ
2 Ⓐ Ⓑ Ⓒ Ⓓ Ⓔ
3 Ⓐ Ⓑ Ⓒ Ⓓ Ⓔ
4 Ⓐ Ⓑ Ⓒ Ⓓ Ⓔ
5 Ⓐ Ⓑ Ⓒ Ⓓ Ⓔ
6 Ⓐ Ⓑ Ⓒ Ⓓ Ⓔ
7 Ⓐ Ⓑ Ⓒ Ⓓ Ⓔ
8 Ⓐ Ⓑ Ⓒ Ⓓ Ⓔ
9 Ⓐ Ⓑ Ⓒ Ⓓ Ⓔ
10 Ⓐ Ⓑ Ⓒ Ⓓ Ⓔ
11 Ⓐ Ⓑ Ⓒ Ⓓ Ⓔ
12 Ⓐ Ⓑ Ⓒ Ⓓ Ⓔ
13 Ⓐ Ⓑ Ⓒ Ⓓ Ⓔ
14 Ⓐ Ⓑ Ⓒ Ⓓ Ⓔ
15 Ⓐ Ⓑ Ⓒ Ⓓ Ⓔ
16 Ⓐ Ⓑ Ⓒ Ⓓ Ⓔ
17 Ⓐ Ⓑ Ⓒ Ⓓ Ⓔ
18 Ⓐ Ⓑ Ⓒ Ⓓ Ⓔ
19 Ⓐ Ⓑ Ⓒ Ⓓ Ⓔ
20 Ⓐ Ⓑ Ⓒ Ⓓ Ⓔ

## Section 3 – Critical Reading
### 25 minutes

25 Ⓐ Ⓑ Ⓒ Ⓓ Ⓔ
26 Ⓐ Ⓑ Ⓒ Ⓓ Ⓔ
27 Ⓐ Ⓑ Ⓒ Ⓓ Ⓔ
28 Ⓐ Ⓑ Ⓒ Ⓓ Ⓔ
29 Ⓐ Ⓑ Ⓒ Ⓓ Ⓔ
30 Ⓐ Ⓑ Ⓒ Ⓓ Ⓔ
31 Ⓐ Ⓑ Ⓒ Ⓓ Ⓔ
32 Ⓐ Ⓑ Ⓒ Ⓓ Ⓔ
33 Ⓐ Ⓑ Ⓒ Ⓓ Ⓔ
34 Ⓐ Ⓑ Ⓒ Ⓓ Ⓔ
35 Ⓐ Ⓑ Ⓒ Ⓓ Ⓔ
36 Ⓐ Ⓑ Ⓒ Ⓓ Ⓔ
37 Ⓐ Ⓑ Ⓒ Ⓓ Ⓔ
38 Ⓐ Ⓑ Ⓒ Ⓓ Ⓔ
39 Ⓐ Ⓑ Ⓒ Ⓓ Ⓔ
40 Ⓐ Ⓑ Ⓒ Ⓓ Ⓔ
41 Ⓐ Ⓑ Ⓒ Ⓓ Ⓔ
42 Ⓐ Ⓑ Ⓒ Ⓓ Ⓔ
43 Ⓐ Ⓑ Ⓒ Ⓓ Ⓔ
44 Ⓐ Ⓑ Ⓒ Ⓓ Ⓔ
45 Ⓐ Ⓑ Ⓒ Ⓓ Ⓔ
46 Ⓐ Ⓑ Ⓒ Ⓓ Ⓔ
47 Ⓐ Ⓑ Ⓒ Ⓓ Ⓔ
48 Ⓐ Ⓑ Ⓒ Ⓓ Ⓔ

## Section 4 – Math
### 25 minutes

21 Ⓐ Ⓑ Ⓒ Ⓓ Ⓔ
22 Ⓐ Ⓑ Ⓒ Ⓓ Ⓔ
23 Ⓐ Ⓑ Ⓒ Ⓓ Ⓔ
24 Ⓐ Ⓑ Ⓒ Ⓓ Ⓔ
25 Ⓐ Ⓑ Ⓒ Ⓓ Ⓔ
26 Ⓐ Ⓑ Ⓒ Ⓓ Ⓔ
27 Ⓐ Ⓑ Ⓒ Ⓓ Ⓔ
28 Ⓐ Ⓑ Ⓒ Ⓓ Ⓔ

29 [grid-in answer field]
30 [grid-in answer field]
31 [grid-in answer field]
32 [grid-in answer field]
33 [grid-in answer field]
34 [grid-in answer field]
35 [grid-in answer field]
36 [grid-in answer field]
37 [grid-in answer field]
38 [grid-in answer field]

## Section 5 – Writing Skills
### 30 minutes

1 Ⓐ Ⓑ Ⓒ Ⓓ Ⓔ
2 Ⓐ Ⓑ Ⓒ Ⓓ Ⓔ
3 Ⓐ Ⓑ Ⓒ Ⓓ Ⓔ
4 Ⓐ Ⓑ Ⓒ Ⓓ Ⓔ
5 Ⓐ Ⓑ Ⓒ Ⓓ Ⓔ
6 Ⓐ Ⓑ Ⓒ Ⓓ Ⓔ
7 Ⓐ Ⓑ Ⓒ Ⓓ Ⓔ
8 Ⓐ Ⓑ Ⓒ Ⓓ Ⓔ
9 Ⓐ Ⓑ Ⓒ Ⓓ Ⓔ
10 Ⓐ Ⓑ Ⓒ Ⓓ Ⓔ
11 Ⓐ Ⓑ Ⓒ Ⓓ Ⓔ
12 Ⓐ Ⓑ Ⓒ Ⓓ Ⓔ
13 Ⓐ Ⓑ Ⓒ Ⓓ Ⓔ
14 Ⓐ Ⓑ Ⓒ Ⓓ Ⓔ
15 Ⓐ Ⓑ Ⓒ Ⓓ Ⓔ
16 Ⓐ Ⓑ Ⓒ Ⓓ Ⓔ
17 Ⓐ Ⓑ Ⓒ Ⓓ Ⓔ
18 Ⓐ Ⓑ Ⓒ Ⓓ Ⓔ
19 Ⓐ Ⓑ Ⓒ Ⓓ Ⓔ
20 Ⓐ Ⓑ Ⓒ Ⓓ Ⓔ
21 Ⓐ Ⓑ Ⓒ Ⓓ Ⓔ
22 Ⓐ Ⓑ Ⓒ Ⓓ Ⓔ
23 Ⓐ Ⓑ Ⓒ Ⓓ Ⓔ
24 Ⓐ Ⓑ Ⓒ Ⓓ Ⓔ
25 Ⓐ Ⓑ Ⓒ Ⓓ Ⓔ
26 Ⓐ Ⓑ Ⓒ Ⓓ Ⓔ
27 Ⓐ Ⓑ Ⓒ Ⓓ Ⓔ
28 Ⓐ Ⓑ Ⓒ Ⓓ Ⓔ
29 Ⓐ Ⓑ Ⓒ Ⓓ Ⓔ
30 Ⓐ Ⓑ Ⓒ Ⓓ Ⓔ
31 Ⓐ Ⓑ Ⓒ Ⓓ Ⓔ
32 Ⓐ Ⓑ Ⓒ Ⓓ Ⓔ
33 Ⓐ Ⓑ Ⓒ Ⓓ Ⓔ
34 Ⓐ Ⓑ Ⓒ Ⓓ Ⓔ
35 Ⓐ Ⓑ Ⓒ Ⓓ Ⓔ
36 Ⓐ Ⓑ Ⓒ Ⓓ Ⓔ
37 Ⓐ Ⓑ Ⓒ Ⓓ Ⓔ
38 Ⓐ Ⓑ Ⓒ Ⓓ Ⓔ
39 Ⓐ Ⓑ Ⓒ Ⓓ Ⓔ

# SECTION 1/CRITICAL READING

TIME: 25 MINUTES
24 QUESTIONS (1–24)

**Directions:** For each question in this section, select the best answer from among the choices given and fill in the corresponding circle on the answer sheet.

---

Each sentence below has one or two blanks, each blank indicating that something has been omitted. Beneath the sentence are five words or sets of words labeled A through E. Choose the word or set of words that, when inserted in the sentence, best fits the meaning of the sentence as a whole.

**EXAMPLE:**

Medieval kingdoms did not become constitutional republics overnight; on the contrary, the change was ----.

(A) unpopular  (B) unexpected
(C) advantageous  (D) sufficient  (E) gradual

Ⓐ Ⓑ Ⓒ Ⓓ ●

---

1. For Miró, art became a ---- ritual: paper and pencils were holy objects to him, and he worked as though he were performing a religious rite.

(A) superficial  (B) sacred  (C) banal
(D) cryptic  (E) futile

2. Many Wright scholars, striving for accurate reconstructions of the architect's life, have been ---- by the palpable ---- and smoke screens of Wright's autobiography.

(A) delighted..truths  (B) amazed..facts
(C) vexed..errors  (D) confused..precision
(E) entertained..omissions

3. A certain ---- in Singer's prose always keeps one at arm's length from his protagonist's emotions.

(A) detachment  (B) lyricism  (C) fluency
(D) brevity  (E) rhythm

4. The books' topics are no less varied than their bindings, for their prolific author has ---- specialization as energetically as some of his colleagues have ---- it.

(A) resisted..pursued
(B) admired..supported
(C) endorsed..accepted
(D) defended..attacked
(E) repudiated..deliberated

5. The mayfly is an ---- creature: its adult life lasts little more than a day.

(A) elegant  (B) ephemeral  (C) idiosyncratic
(D) impulsive  (E) omnivorous

**GO ON TO NEXT PAGE** ▶

**Directions:** The passages below are followed by questions on their content; questions following a pair of related passages may also be based on the relationship between the paired passages. Answer the questions on the basis of what is stated or implied in the passages and in any introductory material that may be provided.

**Questions 6–9 are based on the following passage.**

**Passage 1**

      Knighthoods are not what they used to be. Members of the press have had a field day with the recent knighting of Mick Jagger, rock and roll's
Line perennial bad boy. Though Sir Mick, as he is now
5 to be called, is not the first rock and roller to be dubbed a knight—Sir Elton John was knighted in 1997, Sir Paul McCartney in 1996—he is the most notorious. One reporter even quipped that Jagger's trip to Buckingham Palace was not his
10 first experience with royal hospitality: in 1967 he had spent a night in Her Majesty's Prison, Brixton, convicted of drug possession.

**Passage 2**

      What factors led to the decline of the armored knight? Although some scholars have hypothe-
15 sized that developing technology, in particular the invention of firearms, rendered knights in armor obsolete, this suggestion seems unlikely. On the contrary, throughout the Middle Ages and well into the fifteenth century, technological develop-
20 ments contributed to the effectiveness of the chivalry, enabling them to consolidate their positions both politically and economically. Rather than technological obsolescence spelling the doom of these mounted warriors, it seems more
25 likely that changes in basic army structure—the development of the modern professional army, based on the Swiss model—and the high costs of outfitting themselves with steeds and armor led many knights to abandon their careers as profes-
30 sional fighting men.

6. The reaction of the press to the news of Jagger's knighting (lines 2–4) can best be characterized as one of
   (A) indifference
   (B) disappointment
   (C) outrage
   (D) envy
   (E) glee

7. The phrase "royal hospitality" (line 10) is being used
   (A) literally
   (B) ironically
   (C) colloquially
   (D) descriptively
   (E) objectively

8. Both passages make the point that the institution of knighthood
   (A) glorifies professional fighting men
   (B) has undergone changes over time
   (C) reached its high point in the fifteenth century
   (D) depends on technological progress
   (E) requires a mounted order of chivalry

9. Which best expresses the relationship between Passage 2 and Passage 1?
   (A) Passage 2 provides a technical explanation for the examples cited in Passage 1.
   (B) Passage 2 advocates particular changes as a result of the situation described in Passage 1.
   (C) Passage 2 expresses reservations about the value of a tradition whose vitality is acclaimed in Passage 1.
   (D) Passage 2 offers historical perspective on an institution whose current guise is mocked in Passage 1.
   (E) Passage 2 questions an assumption underlying the ideas expressed in Passage 1.

**GO ON TO NEXT PAGE** ▶

**Directions:** Each passage below is followed by questions based on its content. Answer the questions following each passage on the basis of what is stated or implied in that passage and in any introductory material that may be provided.

**Questions 10–15 are based on the following passage.**

*The world's tropical rain forests contain varieties of plant and animal life found nowhere else on earth. The following passage presents background information on the epiphytes and their relatives the strangler trees, fascinating specimens of rain forest plant life.*

The great trees furnish support for much of
the other plant life of the forest. Climbers are
abundant, much more so than elsewhere. Greedy
Line for light, they have various adaptations for hoist-
(5) ing themselves to the upper canopy—some are
twiners, others are equipped with tendrils, hooks
or suckers. An entire group of plants is unfitted to
start low and climb high to reach the light. These
are epiphytes, plants that grow on trees without
(10) parasitizing them or deriving any advantage
except a platform near the sun. They are extraordinarily common. However, in order to grow close
to the sunlight, they have had to pay a price—
they have lost their root connection with the for-
(15) est floor and its abundant moisture. For soil, they
must often make do with the small amounts of
debris that lodge in crannies in the trees, with
dust from the atmosphere and organic matter and
seeds deposited by ants that often nest in the roots
(20) of epiphytes—a small but vital source of humus
and minerals. So well have these plants managed
to create their own environment that the spoonfuls of soil in which they grow do not differ significantly from normal soil in microbiological
(25) processes.
Some of the epiphytes have developed
remarkable adaptations for conserving water.
Many are encased in a waxy layer that retards
evaporation. The roots of some orchids have a
(30) spongy tissue that not only soaks up water but
also carries on photosynthesis. The staghorn fern
accumulates water-holding humus in a sort of
bucket structure at the base of its leaves. The
large group of tropical plants known as bromeli-
(35) ads are living cisterns—their long branching
leaves spring from the same place around the
stem, and overlap so tightly at their bases that
they can hold water, as much as four-and-a-half
quarts in a large plant. These bromeliad tanks
(40) become a center of life, holding breeding frogs,
snails and aquatic insects, all of which add to the
supply of nutrients in the water. Hairs at the base

of the leaves line the tank and perform the job of
absorbing water and nutrients, making the
(45) bromeliad independent of a root connection with
the soil.
The problems of living in the dark rain forest,
and the unusual efforts made to rise into the sun,
are best symbolized by the strangler trees. They
(50) achieve their place in the sun by stealth. The
strangler begins life as an epiphyte, its seed ger-
minating high up in the fork of a large tree. The
seedling puts out two kinds of roots: one seizes
the branch and serves as a grapple to hold the
(55) plant in place, and the other dangles like a cable,
growing steadily closer to the soil. Until it makes
contact with the ground, the strangler grows like
any other epiphyte, obtaining small quantities of
water and nutrients from the debris in the tree
(60) crevice. But once the descending root reaches the
soil its source of supply is increased enormously
and the plant's growth quickens. It sprouts more
leaves high in the canopy and grows upward
toward a sunlit window between the leaves; a
(65) maze of additional feeding cables descends to the
soil and eventually the supporting tree is encased
in a network of them. It was once thought that
the strangler kills the forest giant by the simple
process of enwrapping it and preventing its trunk
(70) from expanding, but it is now known that it actually squeezes its host to death. As the hold tight-
ens, the strangler's roots thicken to a marked
degree, preparing for the time when it will need
props to stand by itself in the sunlight it has cap-
(75) tured. The host finally expires, thoroughly
encased inside the "trunk" (actually the fused
roots) of the strangler tree which now stands on
its own pedestal as a member of the high forest
canopy.

**10.** According to the passage, some epiphytes are par-
ticularly adapted to
(A) the floor of the tropical rain forest
(B) a sunless environment
(C) the dissipation of rainwater
(D) drawing sustenance from a host
(E) the retention of liquid

**GO ON TO NEXT PAGE ▶**

**11.** It can be inferred from the passage that one of the following is true of epiphytes.

    (A) They lack root systems.
    (B) They do not require large amounts of soil for growth.
    (C) They are incapable of photosynthesis.
    (D) They are hard to perceive in the dense rain forest canopy.
    (E) They need different nutrients than other plants do.

**12.** The passage can best be described as

    (A) enthusiastic exhortation
    (B) sophisticated analysis
    (C) straightforward description
    (D) indirect exposition
    (E) forceful argument

**13.** The author states all of the following about the strangler tree EXCEPT

    (A) It eventually becomes self-supporting.
    (B) Its feeding cables ascend toward the forest canopy.
    (C) Its roots extend far from its point of germination.
    (D) It undergoes a rapid growth spurt.
    (E) Its roots become conspicuously larger.

**14.** In line 72, "marked" most nearly means

    (A) noticeable
    (B) branded
    (C) graded
    (D) doomed
    (E) unique

**15.** Which of the following does the passage suggest about the strangler tree?

    (A) It needs only a small supply of nutrients for full growth.
    (B) All its roots seek the forest floor.
    (C) It outgrows its need for its host.
    (D) It is killed by the forest giant that supports it.
    (E) It eventually sheds its feeder cables.

**Questions 16–24 are based on the following passage.**

*The passage below is excerpted from the introduction to* Bury My Heart at Wounded Knee, *written in 1970 by the Native American historian Dee Brown.*

Since the exploratory journey of Lewis and Clark to the Pacific Coast early in the nineteenth century, the number of published accounts
Line describing the "opening" of the American West
5 has risen into the thousands. The greatest concentration of recorded experience and observation came out of the thirty-year span between 1860 and 1890—the period covered by this book. It was an incredible era of violence, greed, audacity, sen-
10 timentality, undirected exuberance, and an almost reverential attitude toward the ideal of personal freedom for those who already had it.

During that time the culture and civilization of the American Indian was destroyed, and out of
15 that time came virtually all the great myths of the American West—tales of fur traders, mountain men, steamboat pilots, goldseekers, gamblers, gunmen, cavalrymen, cowboys, harlots, missionaries, schoolmarms, and homesteaders. Only occa-
20 sionally was the voice of the Indian heard, and then more often than not it was recorded by the pen of a white man. The Indian was the dark menace of the myths, and even if he had known how to write in English, where would he have found a
25 printer or a publisher?

Yet they are not all lost, those Indian voices of the past. A few authentic accounts of American western history were recorded by Indians either in pictographs or in translated English, and some
30 managed to get published in obscure journals, pamphlets, or books of small circulation. In the late nineteenth century, when the white man's curiosity about Indian survivors of the wars reached a high point, enterprising newspaper
35 reporters frequently interviewed warriors and chiefs and gave them an opportunity to express their opinions on what was happening in the West. The quality of these interviews varied greatly, depending upon the abilities of the inter-
40 preters, or upon the inclination of the Indians to speak freely. Some feared reprisals for telling the truth, while others delighted in hoaxing reporters with tall tales and shaggy-dog stories.

**GO ON TO NEXT PAGE ▶**

Contemporary newspaper statements by Indians
45 must therefore be read with skepticism, although
some of them are masterpieces of irony and others burn with outbursts of poetic fury.

Among the richest sources of first-person
statements by Indians are the records of treaty
50 councils and other formal meetings with civilian
and military representatives of the United States
government. Isaac Pitman's new stenographic
system was coming into vogue in the second half
of the nineteenth century, and when Indians
55 spoke in council a recording clerk sat beside the
official interpreter.

Even when the meetings were in remote parts
of the West, someone usually was available to
write down the speeches, and because of the slow-
60 ness of the translation process, much of what was
said could be recorded in longhand. Interpreters
quite often were half-bloods who knew spoken
languages but seldom could read or write. Like
most oral peoples they and the Indians depended
65 upon imagery to express their thoughts, so that
the English translations were filled with graphic
similes and metaphors of the natural world. If an
eloquent Indian had a poor interpreter, his words
might be transformed to flat prose, but a good
70 interpreter could make a poor speaker sound
poetic.

Most Indian leaders spoke freely and candidly
in councils with white officials, and as they
became more sophisticated in such matters dur-
75 ing the 1870's and 1880's, they demanded the
right to choose their own interpreters and
recorders. In this latter period, all members of the
tribes were free to speak, and some of the older
men chose such opportunities to recount events
80 they had witnessed in the past, or sum up the histories of their peoples. Although the Indians who
lived through this doom period of their civilization have vanished from the earth, millions of
their words are preserved in official records. Many
85 of the more important council proceedings were
published in government documents and reports.

Out of all these sources of almost forgotten
oral history, I have tried to fashion a narrative of
the conquest of the American West as the victims
90 experienced it, using their own words whenever
possible. Americans who have always looked west-
ward when reading about this period should read
this book facing eastward.

This is not a cheerful book, but history has a
95 way of intruding upon the present, and perhaps
those who read it will have a clearer understanding of what the American Indian is, by knowing
what he was. They may learn something about
their own relationship to the earth from a people
100 who were true conservationists. The Indians knew
that life was equated with the earth and its
resources, that America was a paradise, and they
could not comprehend why the intruders from the
East were determined to destroy all that was
105 Indian as well as America itself.

**16.** A main concern of the author in this passage is to

(A) denounce the white man for his untrustwor-
thiness and savagery
(B) evaluate the effectiveness of the military
treaty councils
(C) argue for the improved treatment of Indians
today
(D) suggest that Indian narratives of the conquest
of the West are similar to white accounts
(E) introduce the background of the original
source materials for his text

**17.** In line 4, the quotation marks around the word
"opening" serve to

(A) emphasize the author's belief that the
conquest of the West took place much
earlier
(B) demonstrate the uniqueness of the author's
choice of words
(C) indicate the author's disagreement with a
term in common use
(D) emphasize the need for the word to be
stressed when it is spoken aloud
(E) criticize the rapid growth in number of
these published accounts

**18.** In lines 5–6, "concentration" most nearly means

(A) memory
(B) attention
(C) diligence
(D) imprisonment
(E) cluster

**GO ON TO NEXT PAGE ▶**

**19.** According to the passage, nineteenth-century newspaper accounts of interviews with Indians are variable in quality for which of the following reasons?

   I. Lack of skill on the part of the translators
   II. The tendency of the reporters to overstate what they were told by the Indians
   III. The Indians' misgivings about possible retaliations

(A) I only
(B) III only
(C) I and II only
(D) I and III only
(E) I, II, and III

**20.** The author's tone in describing the Indian survivors can best be described as

(A) skeptical    (B) detached    (C) elegiac
(D) obsequious    (E) impatient

**21.** The author is most impressed by which aspect of the English translations of Indian speeches?

(A) Their vividness of imagery
(B) Their lack of frankness
(C) The inefficiency of the process
(D) Their absence of sophistication
(E) Their brevity of expression

**22.** In line 69, "flat" most nearly means

(A) smooth    (B) level    (C) pedestrian
(D) horizontal    (E) unequivocal

**23.** The author most likely suggests that Americans should read this book facing eastward

(A) in an inappropriate attempt at levity
(B) out of respect for Western superstitions
(C) in order to read by natural light
(D) because the Indians came from the East
(E) to identify with the Indians' viewpoint

**24.** In line 101, "equated with" most nearly means

(A) reduced to an average with
(B) necessarily tied to
(C) numerically equal to
(D) fulfilled by
(E) differentiated by

IF YOU FINISH IN LESS THAN 25 MINUTES, YOU MAY CHECK YOUR WORK ON THIS SECTION ONLY. DO NOT TURN TO ANY OTHER SECTION IN THE TEST.

**STOP**

# SECTION 2 /MATHEMATICS

TIME: 25 MINUTES

20 QUESTIONS (1–20)

## Directions:

For each question in this section, determine which of the five choices is correct, and blacken that choice on your answer sheet. You may use any blank space on the page for your work.

NOTES:

• You may use a calculator whenever you believe it will be helpful.

• Use the diagrams provided to help you solve the problems. Unless you see the phrase <u>Note: Figure not drawn to scale</u> under a diagram, it has been drawn as accurately as possible. Unless it is stated that a figure is three dimensional, you may assume that it lies in a plane.

## Reference

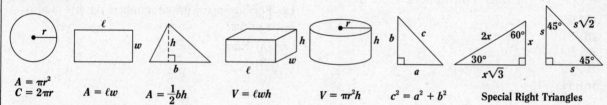

$A = \pi r^2$
$C = 2\pi r$

$A = \ell w$

$A = \frac{1}{2}bh$

$V = \ell wh$

$V = \pi r^2 h$

$c^2 = a^2 + b^2$

**Special Right Triangles**

Number of degrees in a circle: 360

Sum of the measures, in degrees, of the three angles of a triangle: 180

---

**1.** If $4x = 12$, then $12x =$

(A) 4
(B) 6
(C) 24
(D) 36
(E) 48

**2.** Which of the following numbers has the same digit in the hundreds and hundredths places?

(A) 3300.0033
(B) 3335.3553
(C) 3353.5353
(D) 3357.3573
(E) 3357.7533

**3.** In the figure above, what is the value of $x$?

(A) 50
(B) 60
(C) 70
(D) 110
(E) It cannot be determined from the information given.

**4.** For how many integers $n$ is it true that $n^2 - 10$ is negative?

(A) 5
(B) 6
(C) 7
(D) 10
(E) More than 10

**GO ON TO NEXT PAGE ▶**

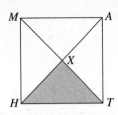

**5.** In the figure above, *MATH* is a square. If *MX* = 3, what is the area of the shaded triangle?

(A) $\frac{9}{4}$

(B) $\frac{9\sqrt{3}}{4}$

(C) 4.5

(D) 9

(E) 18

**6.** If $7x + 5 = 74$, what is the value of $\sqrt{7x - 5}$?

(A) 7

(B) 8

(C) 9

(D) 10

(E) 11

**7.** How many primes less than 100 are divisible by 3?

(A) none

(B) 1

(C) more than 1 but less than 33

(D) 33

(E) more than 33

**8.** If $f(x) = x^2 - 2^x$, what is the value of $f(3)$?

(A) −17

(B) −1

(C) 0

(D) 1

(E) 17

**9.** If Michael can paint $\frac{2}{5}$ of a room in an hour at this rate, how many rooms can he paint in *h* hours?

(A) $\frac{2h}{5}$

(B) $\frac{5h}{2}$

(C) $h - \frac{2}{5}$

(D) $\frac{2}{5h}$

(E) $\frac{5}{2h}$

**10.** If $x^2 + 1 = 50$, which of the following could be the value of $x + 1$?

(A) −8

(B) −6

(C) $\sqrt{50}$

(D) 6

(E) 7

**11.** Evelyn's average (arithmetic mean) on her six math tests this marking period is 80. Fortunately for Evelyn, her teacher drops each student's lowest grade; doing so raises Evelyn's average to 90. What was her lowest grade?

(A) 20

(B) 25

(C) 30

(D) 40

(E) 50

**12.** For how many prime numbers *p* is $p + 1$ also a prime?

(A) None

(B) 1

(C) 2

(D) 3

(E) More than 3

**Questions 13 and 14 refer to the following definition.**

$\boxed{W \quad X \quad Y \quad Z}$ is a *number bar* if $W + Z = X + Y$ and $2W = 3X$.

**13.** If $\boxed{3 \quad X \quad Y \quad 7}$ is a *number bar*, what is the value of *Y*?

(A) 0

(B) 2

(C) 4

(D) 6

(E) 8

**14.** If $\boxed{W \quad X \quad Y \quad W}$ is a *number bar*, $Y =$

(A) $\frac{3}{4}W$

(B) $W$

(C) $\frac{4}{3}W$

(D) $3W$

(E) $4W$

**GO ON TO NEXT PAGE** ▶

**15.** If $m$ is an integer, which of the following could be true?

  I.  $\frac{16}{m}$ is an odd integer

  II. $\frac{m}{16}$ is an odd integer

  III. $16m$ is an odd integer

  (A) I only

  (B) II only

  (C) III only

  (D) I and II only

  (E) I, II, and III

**16.** What is the volume, in cubic inches, of a cube whose surface area is 60 square inches?

  (A) $10\sqrt{10}$
  (B) $15\sqrt{15}$
  (C) $60\sqrt{60}$
  (D) 1000
  (E) 3375

**17.** In rectangle *PQRS*, diagonal *PR* makes a 60° angle with side *PS*. If $PR = 10$, what is the area of the rectangle?

  (A) $25\sqrt{2}$
  (B) $25\sqrt{3}$
  (C) 48
  (D) 50
  (E) 100

**18.** If $25 - 2\sqrt{x} = 7$, then $x =$

  (A) $-81$
  (B) 9
  (C) 36
  (D) 49
  (E) 81

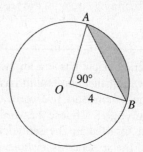

**19.** In the figure above, the radius of circle *O* is 4, and m∠*AOB* = 90°. What is the perimeter of the shaded region?

  (A) $4 + 2\pi$
  (B) $4\sqrt{2} + \pi$
  (C) $4\sqrt{2} + 2\pi$
  (D) $4\sqrt{3} + \pi$
  (E) $4\sqrt{3} + 2\pi$

**20.** Because her test turned out to be more difficult than she intended it to be, a teacher decided to adjust the grades by deducting only half the number of points a student missed. For example, if a student missed 20 points, she received a 90 instead of an 80. Before the grades were adjusted Mary's grade was *G*. What was her grade after the adjustment?

  (A) $50 + \frac{G}{2}$
  (B) $\frac{1}{2}(100 - G)$
  (C) $100 - \frac{G}{2}$
  (D) $\frac{100 - G}{2}$
  (E) $G + 25$

IF YOU FINISH IN LESS THAN 25 MINUTES, YOU MAY CHECK YOUR WORK ON
THIS SECTION ONLY. DO NOT TURN TO ANY OTHER SECTION IN THE TEST.

**STOP**

# SECTION 3 /CRITICAL READING

TIME: 25 MINUTES
24 QUESTIONS (25–48)

**Directions:** For each question in this section, select the best answer from among the choices given and fill in the corresponding circle on the answer sheet.

Each sentence below has one or two blanks, each blank indicating that something has been omitted. Beneath the sentence are five words or sets of words labeled A through E. Choose the word or set of words that, when inserted in the sentence, best fits the meaning of the sentence as a whole.

**EXAMPLE:**

Medieval kingdoms did not become constitutional republics overnight; on the contrary, the change was ----.

(A) unpopular    (B) unexpected
(C) advantageous    (D) sufficient    (E) gradual

25. Feeling ---- about her latest victories, the tennis champion looked smugly at the row of trophies on her mantelpiece.

    (A) downcast    (B) agitated    (C) indifferent
    (D) complacent    (E) philosophical

26. Normally an individual thunderstorm lasts about 45 minutes, but under certain conditions the storm may ----, becoming ever more severe, for as long as four hours.

    (A) wane    (B) moderate    (C) persist
    (D) vacillate    (E) disperse

27. The newest fiber-optic cables that carry telephone calls cross-country are made of glass so ---- that a piece 100 miles thick is clearer than a standard windowpane.

    (A) fragile    (B) immaculate    (C) tangible
    (D) transparent    (E) iridescent

28. Her employers could not complain about her work because she was ---- in the ---- of her duties.

    (A) derelict..performance
    (B) importunate..observance
    (C) meticulous..postponement
    (D) assiduous..execution
    (E) hidebound..conception

29. Decorated in ---- style, his home contained bits and pieces of furnishings from widely divergent periods, strikingly juxtaposed to create a unique decor.

    (A) an aesthetic    (B) a lyrical    (C) a traditional
    (D) an eclectic    (E) a perfunctory

30. Equipped with mechanisms that deliberately delay sprouting, woodland seeds often seem sadly ---- to germinate.

    (A) prone    (B) reluctant    (C) qualified
    (D) prolific    (E) modified

31. Soap operas and situation comedies, though given to distortion, are so derivative of contemporary culture that they are inestimable ---- the attitudes and values of our society in any particular decade.

    (A) contradictions of    (B) antidotes to
    (C) indices of    (D) prerequisites for
    (E) determinants of

32. Although eighteenth-century English society as a whole did not encourage learning for its own sake in women, nonetheless it illogically ---- women's sad lack of education.

    (A) palliated    (B) postulated
    (C) decried    (D) brooked
    (E) vaunted

**GO ON TO NEXT PAGE** ▶

**Directions:** Each of the passages below precedes two questions based on its content. Answer the questions following each passage on the basis of what is stated or implied in that passage.

**Questions 33 and 34 are based on the following passage.**

One of the world's most celebrated crusaders for social justice and peace is South Africa's Archbishop Desmond Tutu. Despite his prominence, however, Archbishop Tutu has always
Line
5   made time for his people. On the day in 1984 that he was named winner of the Nobel Peace Prize, reporters and photographers mobbed the seminary where he was staying. A press conference was hastily set up. Just as it was to begin, the arch-
10  bishop's student assistant entered the courtyard, returning from a family funeral. Leaving the microphones and cameras behind, the archbishop went to comfort her. The world press could wait; her grief could not.

**33.** The anecdote about Archbishop Tutu serves primarily to demonstrate his
(A) fame   (B) anguish   (C) distraction
(D) compassion   (E) peacefulness

**34.** In lines 3–4, "prominence" most nearly means
(A) projection   (B) high altitude
(C) land elevation   (D) emphasis   (E) renown

**Questions 35 and 36 are based on the following passage.**

Although most of the world's active volcanoes are located along the edges of the great shifting plates that make up Earth's surface, there are
Line
5   more than 100 isolated areas of volcanic activity far from the nearest plate boundary. Geologists call these volcanic areas hot spots. Lying deep in the interior of a plate, hot spots or intra-plate volcanoes are sources of magma, the red-hot, molten material within the earth's crust. These intra-
10  plate volcanoes often form volcanic chains, trails of extinct volcanoes. Such volcanic chains serve as landmarks signaling the slow but relentless passage of the plates.

**35.** The term "hot spot" is being used in the passage
(A) rhetorically   (B) colloquially
(C) technically   (D) ambiguously
(E) ironically

**36.** Hot spots differ from other areas of volcanic activity in their
(A) temperature   (B) location   (C) composition
(D) volatility   (E) relevance

**GO ON TO NEXT PAGE ▶**

**Directions:** The passages below are followed by questions on their content; questions following a pair of related passages may also be based on the relationship between the paired passages. Answer the questions on the basis of what is stated or implied in the passages and in any introductory material that may be provided.

**Questions 37–48 are based on the following passages.**

*In Passage 1, the author, the dancer-choreographer Martha Graham, draws on her experience as a dancer to generalize about her art. In Passage 2, the author, California chef Alice Waters, presents her approach to cooking, as practiced at her restaurant, Chez Panisse.*

**Passage 1**

I am a dancer. My experience has been with dance as an art.

Each art has an instrument and a medium.
Line The instrument of the dance is the human body;
5   the medium is movement. The body has always
been to me a thrilling wonder, a dynamo of
energy, exciting, courageous, powerful; a deli-
cately balanced logic and proportion. It has not
been my aim to evolve or discover a new method
10  of dance training, but rather to dance significantly. To dance significantly means "through the
medium of discipline and by means of a sensitive,
strong instrument, to bring into focus unhackneyed movement: a human being."
15      I did not want to be a tree, a flower, or a
wave. In a dancer's body, we as audience must see
*ourselves*, not the imitated behavior of everyday
actions, not the phenomena of nature, not exotic
creatures from another planet, but something of
20  the miracle that is a human being, motivated, disciplined, concentrated.
Technique and training have never been a
substitute for that condition of awareness which is
talent, for that complete miracle of balance which
25  is genius, but it can give plasticity and tension,
freedom and discipline, balancing one against the
other. It can awaken memory of the race through
muscular memory of the body. Training and technique are means to strength, to freedom, to
30  spontaneity.
Contrary to popular belief, spontaneity as one
sees it in dance or in theater, is not wholly dependent on emotion at that instant. It is the condition of emotion objectified. It plays that part in
35  theater that light plays in life. It illumines. It
excites. Spontaneity is essentially dependent on
energy, upon the strength necessary to perfect
timing. It is the result of perfect timing to the
Now. It is not essentially intellectual or emo-
40  tional, but is nerve reaction.

To me, the acquirement of nervous, physical,
and emotional concentration is the one element
possessed to the highest degree by the truly great
dancers of the world. Its acquirement is the result
45  of discipline, of energy in the deep sense. That is
why there are so few great dancers.
A great dancer is not made by technique
alone any more than a great statesman is made by
knowledge alone. Both possess true spontaneity.
50  Spontaneity in behavior, in life, is due largely to
complete health; on the stage to a technical use—
often so ingrained by proper training as to seem
instinctive—of nervous energy. Perhaps what we
have always called intuition is merely a nervous
55  system organized by training to perceive.

**Passage 2**

Flexibility is an essential component of good
cooking. You should never feel locked in to a
recipe or a menu unless it involves a basic principle regarding procedure or technique such as
60  those involved in breadmaking and pastry. I don't
ever want to write anything in this book that is so
precise that the reader must invoke great powers
of concentration on every last detail in order to
ensure the success of a recipe or a dinner; ingre-
65  dients are simply too variable. I want to *suggest*
the expected taste; I want to *suggest* the appearance of the complete dish; I want to *suggest* the
combination of ingredients; and I want to *suggest*
the overall harmony and balance of the meal.
70  Then it will be up to you to determine the correct
balance and composition. Perhaps the garlic is
sharp and strong and you will use it sparingly in a
particular presentation, or you may find the garlic
to be sweet and fresh and you will want to use
75  twice as much!

**GO ON TO NEXT PAGE ▶**

Learn to trust your own instincts. A good cook needs only to have positive feelings about food in general, and about the pleasures of eating and cooking. I have known some cooks who did
80 not seem to discover pleasure and gratification in things culinary. At the restaurant, I look for employees who are interested in working in the kitchen for reasons above and beyond those of simply needing a job, any job. This applies equally
85 to the home cook: a cook who dislikes food is a bad cook. Period. Even an ambivalent cook is a bad cook. Yet a person who responds to the cooking processes and the mound of fresh ingredients with a genuine glow of delight is likely to be, or
90 become, a very good cook indeed. Technical skills can be acquired and perfected along the way, but dislike or ambivalence toward food cannot always be overcome.

In the early stages of my culinary pursuits,
95 I cooked as I had seen cooking done in France. I copied some of the more traditional cooks, and I stayed within the bounds they had laid out so carefully because I didn't trust my own instincts yet. Having imitated their styles, I found that with
100 time and experience, their fundamental principles had become a part of my nature and I began to understand why they had done certain things in a particular way. Then I could begin to develop a different and more personal style based on the
105 ingredients available to me here in California.

**37.** Graham rejects movement in dance that is

(A) jerky  (B) spontaneous  (C) brief
(D) trite  (E) natural

**38.** In saying that she "did not want to be a tree, a flower, or a wave" (lines 15–16), Graham

(A) emphasizes that dancers must express their humanity
(B) reveals an innate discomfort with natural phenomena
(C) suggests a budding desire to imitate other phenomena
(D) conveys a sense of unsatisfied longings
(E) indicates impatience with how long such transformations take

**39.** In line 25, "plasticity" most nearly means

(A) nervous energy
(B) strength and endurance
(C) mobility and pliancy
(D) organic coherence
(E) muscular memory

**40.** According to Graham, most people believe that spontaneous theatrical moments

(A) are the product of disciplined rehearsal and training
(B) happen only because the actor is gripped by a sudden emotion
(C) are dependent on the audience's willingness to suspend their disbelief
(D) depends upon the quickness of the actor's reaction time
(E) are more objective than subjective

**41.** Graham attempts to clarify the function of spontaneity in dance or theater (lines 34–36) by means of

(A) a digression
(B) an analogy
(C) a hypothesis
(D) an anecdote
(E) a quotation

**42.** In Passage 2, Waters is discussing cooking from the point of view of

(A) a chef on the verge of opening her own restaurant
(B) someone uninformed about traditional methods of French cuisine
(C) an accomplished practitioner of the culinary arts
(D) a gifted home cook and collector of recipes
(E) a professional determined to outstrip her competitors

**43.** Waters uses the example of the garlic (lines 71–75) to show

(A) the variability of ingredients
(B) the importance of every last detail
(C) her insistence on fresh ingredients
(D) the need to be a flexible shopper
(E) her preference for strong flavors

**GO ON TO NEXT PAGE ▶**

44. In writing her cookbook, Waters is trying to

    (A) anticipate any pitfalls those using her recipes might run into
    (B) provide precise measurements for her readers to follow
    (C) limit herself to basic principles and procedures
    (D) dictate the spices going into each meal
    (E) allow scope for the reader's own culinary initiative

45. To Waters, to produce superior results, the cook must possess

    (A) an excellent sense of smell
    (B) first-rate technical skills
    (C) the finest kitchen equipment
    (D) detailed recipes to follow
    (E) a love of her medium

46. In lines 81–84 Waters indicates she seeks restaurant employees who share her

    (A) level of expertise
    (B) classical French training
    (C) enjoyment of culinary processes
    (D) willingness to work long hours
    (E) respect for tradition

47. In these passages, both Graham and Waters are

    (A) examining their consciences
    (B) presenting their artistic creeds
    (C) criticizing their opponents
    (D) analyzing their impact on their fields
    (E) reassessing their chosen professions

48. Waters and Graham seem alike in that they both

    (A) have an abundant supply of nervous energy
    (B) benefited from extensive classical training
    (C) occasionally distrust their own instincts
    (D) are passionately involved with their art
    (E) believe in maintaining a positive attitude

IF YOU FINISH IN LESS THAN 25 MINUTES, YOU MAY CHECK YOUR WORK ON THIS SECTION ONLY. DO NOT TURN TO ANY OTHER SECTION IN THE TEST.

**STOP**

# SECTION 4/MATHEMATICS

TIME: 25 MINUTES

18 QUESTIONS (21–38)

---

**Directions:**

For questions 21–28, determine which of the five choices is correct, and blacken that choice on your answer sheet. You may use any blank space on the page for your work.

NOTES:
- You may use a calculator whenever you believe it will be helpful.
- Use the diagrams provided to help you solve the problems. Unless you see the phrase
  <u>Note: Figure not drawn to scale</u>
  under a diagram, it has been drawn as accurately as possible. Unless it is stated that a figure is three dimensional, you may assume that it lies in a plane.

**Reference**

     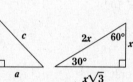 

$A = \pi r^2$
$C = 2\pi r$     $A = \ell w$     $A = \frac{1}{2}bh$     $V = \ell wh$     $V = \pi r^2 h$     $c^2 = a^2 + b^2$     **Special Right Triangles**

Number of degrees in a circle: 360
Sum of the measures, in degrees, of the three angles of a triangle: 180

---

**21.** If $7d + 5 = 5d + 7$, what is the value of $d$?

(A) $-1$
(B) 0
(C) 1
(D) 5
(E) 7

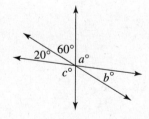

**22.** In the figure above, what is the value of $a + b + c$?

(A) 210
(B) 220
(C) 240
(D) 270
(E) 280

**23.** If $5\sqrt{x} + 1 = 46$, what is the value of $x$?

(A) 1
(B) 3
(C) 9
(D) 81
(E) 729

**24.** If $x^2 = y^2$, which of the following must be true?

(A) $x = y$
(B) $x = -y$
(C) $y = |x|$
(D) $x = |y|$
(E) $|x| = |y|$

**GO ON TO NEXT PAGE ▶**

**Diagnostic Test**

Questions 25 and 26 refer to the following definition.

For all integers *a* and *b, let the operation* ✛ *be defined by*:

$$a ✛ b = a, \text{ if } a + b \text{ is even;}$$
$$a ✛ b = b, \text{ if } a + b \text{ is odd.}$$

**25.** What is the value of $-5 ✛ 5$?

(A) 10
(B) 5
(C) 0
(D) −5
(E) −10

**26.** If $a \neq b$ and $a ✛ b = 10$, which of the following could be true?

   I. $a + b$ is even
  II. $a + b$ is odd
 III. $b ✛ a = 10$

(A) I only
(B) II only
(C) III only
(D) I and II only
(E) I, II, and III

**27.** A bag contains 4 red, 5 white, and 6 blue marbles. Sarah begins removing marbles from the bag at random, one at a time. What is the least number of marbles she must remove to be sure that she has at least one of each color?

(A) 3
(B) 6
(C) 9
(D) 12
(E) 15

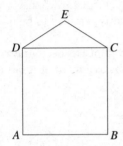

Note: Figure not drawn to scale

**28.** In the figure above, $ED = EC$, the area of square *ABCD* is 100, and the area of $\triangle DEC$ is 10. Find the distance from *A* to *E*.

(A) 11
(B) 12
(C) $\sqrt{146}$
(D) 13
(E) $\sqrt{44}$

**GO ON TO NEXT PAGE ▶**

## Student-Produced Response Directions

In questions 29–38, first solve the problem, and then enter your answer on the grid provided on the answer sheet. The instructions for entering your answers follow.

- First, write your answer in the boxes at the top of the grid.
- Second, grid your answer in the columns below the boxes.
- Use the fraction bar in the first row or the decimal point in the second row to enter fractions and decimals.

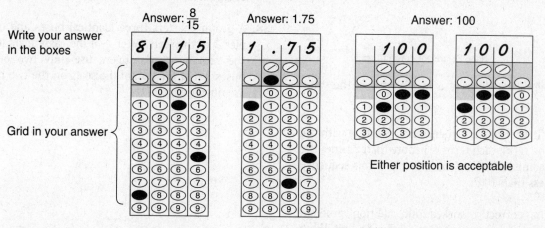

- Grid only one space in each column.
- Entering the answer in the boxes is recommended as an aid in gridding but is not required.
- The machine scoring your exam can read only what you grid, so you **must grid-in your answers correctly to get credit.**
- If a question has more than one correct answer, grid-in only one of them.
- The grid does not have a minus sign; so no answer can be negative.
- A mixed number *must* be converted to an improper fraction or a decimal before it is gridded. Enter $1\frac{1}{4}$ as $\frac{5}{4}$ or 1.25; the machine will interpret 11/4 as $\frac{11}{4}$ and mark it wrong.

- **All decimals must be entered as accurately as possible.** Here are three acceptable ways of gridding

$$\frac{3}{11} = 0.272727\ldots$$

- Note that rounding to .273 is acceptable because you are using the full grid, but you would receive **no credit** for .3 or .27, because they are less accurate.

---

**29.** If $5 - w = 4.99$, then what is the value of $w$?

**31.** If $xy = 30$ and $x = -6$, what is the value of $x^2 - y^2$?

**32.** If 25% of $x$ equals 35% of $x$, what is 45% of $x$?

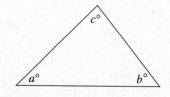

**30.** If, in the figure above, $a:b:c = 5:7:12$, what is the value of $c$?

**GO ON TO NEXT PAGE** ▶

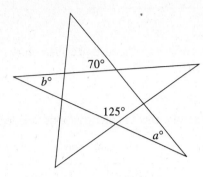

Note: Figure not drawn to scale

**33.** In the figure above, if $a = 30$, what is the value of $b$?

**34.** The first term of a sequence is 2. Starting with the second term, each term is 1 more than 2 times the preceding term. How many terms of this sequence are less than 100?

**35.** In the correctly worked out addition problem below, each letter represents a different digit. What is the number *ABC*?

$$2B$$
$$4B$$
$$+\ 6B$$
$$\overline{ABC}$$

**36.** If circle $O$ has its center at $(1, 1)$, and line $l$ is tangent to circle $O$ at $P\ (4, -4)$, then what is the slope of $l$?

**37.** What is the height, in feet, of a rectangular box whose width and length are 5 feet and 7 feet, respectively, and whose total surface area is 298 square feet?

**38.** A group charters three identical buses and occupies $\frac{4}{5}$ of the seats. After $\frac{1}{4}$ of the passengers leave, the remaining passengers use only two of the buses. What fraction of the seats on the two buses are now occupied?

IF YOU FINISH IN LESS THAN 25 MINUTES, YOU MAY CHECK YOUR WORK ON THIS SECTION ONLY. DO NOT TURN TO ANY OTHER SECTION IN THE TEST.

**STOP**

# SECTION 5/WRITING SKILLS

TIME: 30 MINUTES

39 QUESTIONS (1–39)

**Directions:** For each question in this section, select the best answer from among the choices given and fill in the corresponding circle on the answer sheet.

---

Some or all parts of the following sentences are underlined. The first answer choice, (A), simply repeats the underlined part of the sentence. The other four choices present four alternative ways to phrase the underlined part. Select the answer that produces the most effective sentence, one that is clear and exact, and blacken the appropriate space on your answer sheet. In selecting your choice, be sure that it is standard written English and that it expresses the meaning of the original sentence.

**EXAMPLE:**

The first biography of author Eudora Welty came out in 1998, <u>and she was eighty-nine years old at the time.</u>

(A) and she was eighty-nine years old at the time
(B) at the time when she was eighty-nine
(C) upon becoming an eighty-nine year old
(D) when she was eighty-nine
(E) at the age of eighty-nine years old

---

1. If <u>he was to decide to go to college</u>, I, for one, would recommend that he plan to go to Yale.

    (A) If he was to decide to go to college
    (B) If he were to decide to go to college
    (C) Had he decided to go to college
    (D) In the event that he decides to go to college
    (E) Supposing he was to decide to go to college

2. <u>Except for you and I, everyone brought</u> a present to the party.

    (A) Except for you and I, everyone brought
    (B) With the exception of you and I, everyone brought
    (C) Except for you and I, everyone had brought
    (D) Except for you and me, everyone brought
    (E) Except for you and me, everyone had brought

3. <u>Had I realized how close</u> I was to failing, I would not have gone to the party.

    (A) Had I realized how close
    (B) If I would have realized how close
    (C) Had I had realized how close
    (D) When I realized how close
    (E) If I realized how close

4. <u>Being a realist,</u> I could not accept his statement that supernatural beings had caused the disturbance.

    (A) Being a realist
    (B) Due to the fact that I am a realist
    (C) Being that I am a realist
    (D) Being as I am a realist
    (E) Realist that I am

5. Having finished the marathon in record-breaking time, <u>the city awarded him its Citizen's Outstanding Performance Medal.</u>

    (A) the city awarded him its Citizen's Outstanding Performance Medal
    (B) the city awarded the Citizen's Outstanding Performance Medal to him
    (C) he was awarded the Citizen's Outstanding Performance Medal by the city
    (D) the Citizen's Outstanding Performance Medal was awarded to him
    (E) he was awarded by the city the Citizen's Outstanding Performance Medal

**GO ON TO NEXT PAGE ▶**

6. The football team's winning its first game of the season excited the student body.

    (A) The football team's winning its first game of the season
    (B) The football team having won its first game of the season
    (C) Having won its first game of the season, the football team
    (D) Winning its first game of the season, the football team
    (E) The football team winning its first game of the season

7. Anyone interested in the use of computers can learn much if you have access to a copy of *PC Magazine* or of *MacUser*.

    (A) if you have access to
    (B) if he or she has access to
    (C) if access is available to
    (D) by access to
    (E) from access to

8. I have to make dinner, wash the dishes, do my homework, and then relaxing.

    (A) to make dinner, wash the dishes, do my homework, and then relaxing
    (B) to make dinner, washing the dishes, my homework, and then relaxing
    (C) to make dinner, wash the dishes, doing my homework, and then relax
    (D) to prepare dinner, wash the dishes, do my homework, and then relaxing
    (E) to make dinner, wash the dishes, do my homework, and then relax

9. The climax occurs when he asks who's in the closet.

    (A) occurs when he asks who's
    (B) is when he asks who's
    (C) occurs when he is asking who's
    (D) is when he is asking who's
    (E) occurs when he asked who's

10. Setting up correct bookkeeping procedures is important to any new business, it helps to obtain the services of a good accountant.

    (A) is important to any new business, it helps
    (B) are important to any new business, it
    (C) is important to any new business, therefore, try
    (D) is important to any new business; it helps
    (E) are important to any new business, so try

11. The grocer hadn't hardly any of those kind of canned goods.

    (A) hadn't hardly any of those kind
    (B) hadn't hardly any of those kinds
    (C) had hardly any of those kind
    (D) had hardly any of those kinds
    (E) had scarcely any of those kind

12. Having spent five years in the Appalachian Mountains collecting mountain ballads, an anthology entitled *English Folk Songs from the Southern Appalachians* was produced by Olive Dame Campbell

    (A) an anthology entitled *English Folk Songs from the Southern Appalachians* was produced by Olive Dame Campbell
    (B) Olive Dame Campbell produced an anthology entitled *English Folk Songs from the Southern Appalachians*
    (C) Olive Dame Campbell's anthology entitled *English Folk Songs from the Southern Appalachians* was produced
    (D) an anthology entitled *English Folk Songs from the Southern Appalachians* has been produced by Olive Dame Campbell
    (E) there is an anthology entitled *English Folk Songs from the Southern Appalachians* produced by Olive Dame Campbell

13. Juan broke his hip, he has not and possibly never will be able to run the mile again.

    (A) hip, he has not and possibly never will be able to run
    (B) hip; he has not been able to run and possibly never will be able to run
    (C) hip; he has not and possibly never will be able to run
    (D) hip, he has not been and possibly never would be able to run
    (E) hip; he has not and possibly will never be able to run

14. I came late to class today; the reason being that the bus broke down.

    (A) today; the reason being that
    (B) today, the reason being that
    (C) today because
    (D) today;
    (E) today; since

**GO ON TO NEXT PAGE ▶**

15. Young children's fevers are <u>erratic, furthermore they can spike unpredictably, and, just as unpredictably, can subside.</u>

   (A) erratic, furthermore they can spike unpredictably, and, just as unpredictably, can subside
   (B) erratic; nevertheless, they can spike unpredictably, and, just as unpredictably, they can subside
   (C) erratic, and can spike unpredictably, and, just as unpredictable, they can subside
   (D) erratic: they can spike unpredictably, and, just as unpredictably, can subside
   (E) erratic, they can spike just as unpredictably as they can subside

16. <u>Of all the characters in *A Christmas Carol*, sweet and saintly Tiny Tim is the more beloved.</u>

   (A) Of all the characters in *A Christmas Carol*, sweet and saintly Tiny Tim is the more beloved.
   (B) Of all the characters in *A Christmas Carol*, sweet and saintly Tiny Tim was the more beloved.
   (C) In *A Christmas Carol*, of all the characters, sweet and saintly Tiny Tim is the more beloved.
   (D) Of all the characters in *A Christmas Carol*, sweet and saintly Tiny Tim is the most beloved.
   (E) Sweet and saintly Tiny Tim is more beloved than all the characters in *A Christmas Carol*.

17. The history of the past quarter century illustrates how a president may increase his power to act aggressively in international <u>affairs, and he does not consider the wishes of Congress.</u>

   (A) affairs, and he does not consider the wishes of Congress
   (B) affairs, therefore he did not consider the wishes of Congress
   (C) affairs without considering the wishes of Congress
   (D) affairs, but he does not consider what Congress wishes
   (E) affairs, and he may not have considered the wishes of Congress

18. With the exception of a few publications like *The New York Times*, American newspapers tend to ignore world news <u>unless the event to be reported immediately affects American citizens.</u>

   (A) unless the event to be reported immediately affects American citizens
   (B) unless the event being reported immediately effects American citizens
   (C) except the event to be reported has immediately affected American citizens
   (D) unless the event immediately to be reported affecting American citizens
   (E) unless the immediate event they reported affects American citizens

19. When he was a war correspondent during the Spanish Civil War (1936–1939), the American novelist Ernest <u>Hemingway has written movingly about the struggle</u> of the Republican forces against General Francisco Franco's Nationalist troops.

   (A) Hemingway has written movingly about the struggle
   (B) Hemingway has written while moving about the struggle
   (C) Hemingway has written movingly from the struggle
   (D) Hemingway has been writing movingly about the struggle
   (E) Hemingway wrote movingly about the struggle

20. Fearful that Rome's hungry, restless throngs might grow unruly, Roman <u>emperors catered to the masses, providing the mob with bread</u> and circuses.

   (A) emperors catered to the masses, providing the mob with bread
   (B) emperors catered to the masses, provided that the mob with bread
   (C) emperors catered for the masses, providing the mob with bread
   (D) emperors catered to the masses, they provided the mob with bread
   (E) emperors catered for the masses by providing the mob with bread

**GO ON TO NEXT PAGE** ▶

The sentences in this section may contain errors in grammar, usage, choice of words, or idioms. There is either just one error per sentence, or the sentence is correct. Some words or phrases are underlined and lettered; everything else in the sentence is correct.

If an underlined word or phrase is incorrect, choose that letter; if the sentence is correct, select <u>No error</u>. Then blacken the appropriate space on your answer sheet.

**EXAMPLE:**

The region has a climate <u>so severe that</u> plants
                              A

<u>growing there</u> rarely <u>had been</u> more than twelve
   B                    C

inches <u>high</u>. <u>No error</u>
        D        E

21. <u>In order to</u> conserve valuable gasoline, motorists
        A

    <u>had ought to</u> check their speedometers <u>while</u>
        B                                        C

    driving along the highways <u>since it is</u> very easy to
                                   D

    exceed 55 miles per hour while driving on open

    roads.  <u>No error</u>
              E

22. The book <u>must</u> be old, <u>for</u> its cover <u>is torn</u> <u>bad</u>.
              A          B              C        D

    <u>No error</u>
      E

23. <u>Not one</u> of the children <u>has ever sang</u> <u>in public</u>
        A                            B               C

    before. <u>No error</u>
       D        E

24. Neither you nor <u>I</u> can realize the <u>affect</u> his behav-
                     A                        B

    ior <u>will have</u> on his chances <u>for promotion</u>.
           C                              D

    <u>No error</u>
      E

25. The <u>apparently</u> <u>obvious solution to</u> the problem
              A              B

    <u>was overlooked</u> by <u>many of</u> the contestants.
           C                  D

    <u>No error</u>
      E

26. After he <u>had drank</u> the warm milk, he began
        A        B

    <u>to feel sleepy</u> and <u>finally decided</u> to go to bed.
           C                    D

    <u>No error</u>
      E

27. <u>Without hardly</u> a moment's delay, the computer
        A

    began to <u>print out</u> the <u>answer to</u> the problem.
                 B              C         D

    <u>No error</u>
      E

28. <u>Of</u> the two candidates for this newly <u>formed</u>
      A                                          B

    government position, Ms. Rivera is the

    <u>most qualified</u> <u>because</u> of her experience in
           C               D

    the field. <u>No error</u>
                    E

29. Diligence and honesty <u>as well as</u> <u>being intelligent</u>
                              A               B

    are qualities that personnel directors look for
    C

    <u>when</u> they interview applicants. <u>No error</u>
      D                                        E

30. Neither the San Francisco earthquake <u>or</u> the
                                            A

    subsequent fire <u>was</u> able to destroy the <u>spirit</u> of the
        B            C                                D

    city dwellers. <u>No error</u>
                        E

**31.** The <u>impatient customer</u> had <u>scarcely enough</u>
         A                  B

money <u>to pay</u> the clerk <u>at</u> the checkout counter.
      C            D

<u>No error</u>
 E

**32.** The <u>principal</u> of equal justice <u>for all</u> is <u>one</u> of the
      A               B   C

cornerstones of the democratic <u>way of life</u>.
                          D

<u>No error</u>
 E

**33.** Although alchemy anticipated science in its belief

<u>that</u> physical reality was <u>determined by</u> an
 A                      B

<u>unvarying</u> set of natural laws, the alchemist's
 C

experimental method <u>was not hardly</u> scientific.
                    D

<u>No error</u>
 E

**34.** If anyone <u>calls</u> while the delegates are in
  A     B

conference, tell <u>them</u> the chairman will
            C

<u>return the call</u> after the meeting. <u>No error</u>
    D                    E

**GO ON TO NEXT PAGE** ▶

## Improving Paragraphs Directions

The passage below is the unedited draft of a student's essay. Some of the essay needs to be rewritten to make the meaning clearer and more precise. Read the essay carefully.

The essay is followed by questions about changes that might improve all or part of its organization, development, sentence structure, use of language, appropriateness to the audience, or use of standard written English. Choose the answer that most clearly and effectively expresses the student's intended meaning. Indicate your choice by filling in the corresponding space on the answer sheet.

[1] There are many reasons making it cruel to keep animals penned up in zoos for the sole purpose of letting families gawk at caged creatures. [2] There has to be a better reason to imprison animals than merely to allow visitors to drop a quarter into a food dispenser so that one can feed the monkeys or the elephant. [3] One might argue that it is educational. [4] If someone is so dumb that they don't know what a zebra looks like, they should pull out an encyclopedia and look it up. [5] Humans have no right to pull animals from their natural environment and to seal their fate forever behind a set of cold metal bars. [6] Animals need to run free and live, but by putting them in zoos we are disrupting and disturbing nature.

[7] Then there is the issue of sanitary conditions for animals at the zoo. [8] When the animals have been at the zoo for a while they adopt a particular lifestyle. [9] They lounge around all day, and they're fed at a particular time. [10] They get used to that. [11] That means that they would never again be able to be placed back in their natural environment. [12] They would never survive. [13] And if they reproduce while in captivity, the offspring are born into an artificial lifestyle. [14] After a few generations the animals become totally different from their wild and free ancestors, and visitors to the zoo see animals hardly resembling the ones living in their natural habitat.

[15] The vicious cycle should be stopped before it is too late. [16] The whole idea of a zoo is cruel. [17] If zoos are not cruel and if, as some people say, they serve a useful purpose, then why not put homo sapiens on display, too?

35. Which is the most effective revision of the underlined segment of sentence 1 below?

    *There are many reasons making it cruel to keep animals penned up in zoos* for the sole purpose of letting families gawk at caged creatures.

    (A) Many reasons exist for the cruelty of keeping animals penned up in zoos
    (B) It is a cruel practice to keep animals penned up in zoos
    (C) The reasons are numerous to object to the cruelty experienced by animals locked in cages
    (D) There are several reasons for it being cruel toward animals to lock them up in zoos
    (E) Locking up animals in zoos a cruel practice especially

36. Taking sentence 3 into account, which of the following is the most effective revision of sentence 4?

    (A) Reading about animals in the encyclopedia rather than studying them first hand.
    (B) In the encyclopedia you can gain more information about zebras and other animals.
    (C) Viewing the animal in a zoo is clearly more informative than looking at a picture in a book.
    (D) Doesn't everyone know what a zebra looks like, even little children?
    (E) But if someone is so dumb that they don't know what a zebra looks like, they should look it up in an encyclopedia.

**37.** Which of the following reasons most accurately describes the author's intention in the selection of words used in the underlined segment of sentence 5 below?

*Humans have no right to pull animals from their natural environment and to seal their fate forever behind a set of cold metal bars.*

(A) to inform the reader that animals in the zoo live in cages

(B) to propose a solution to the plight of animals in the zoo

(C) to arouse in the reader an emotional response to the problem

(D) to appeal to the reader to weigh both sides of the issue

(E) to convince the reader that animals don't enjoy being in the zoo

**38.** Which of the following revisions of sentence 7 is the best topic sentence for paragraph 2?

(A) Life in captivity causes animals to change.

(B) No one favors zoos that deliberately try to change the lifestyle of animals in captivity.

(C) Living conditions for animals in the zoo are ordinarily harsh and cruel.

(D) Living in the zoo, conditions for animals affect them permanently.

(E) Life in the zoo for animals is not a bowl of cherries.

**39.** Which revision most effectively combines sentences 10, 11, and 12?

(A) Because they would never be able to survive again back in their natural environment, they grow used to being fed.

(B) Having grown used to regular feedings, the animals would be unable to survive back in their native environment.

(C) Growing accustomed to that, placing them back in their native habitat and being unable to survive on their own.

(D) They, having gotten used to being fed regularly, in their natural environment would never survive.

(E) Being unable to survive back in their natural environment, the animals have grown accustomed to regular feedings.

IF YOU FINISH IN LESS THAN 30 MINUTES, YOU MAY CHECK YOUR WORK ON THIS SECTION ONLY. DO NOT TURN TO ANY OTHER SECTION IN THE TEST.

**STOP**

# Answer Key

## Section 1    Critical Reading

| | | | | | | | | | |
|---|---|---|---|---|---|---|---|---|---|
| 1. | B | 6. | E | 11. | B | 16. | E | 21. | A |
| 2. | C | 7. | B | 12. | C | 17. | C | 22. | C |
| 3. | A | 8. | B | 13. | B | 18. | E | 23. | E |
| 4. | A | 9. | D | 14. | A | 19. | D | 24. | B |
| 5. | B | 10. | E | 15. | C | 20. | C | | |

## Section 2    Mathematics

| | | | | | | | | | |
|---|---|---|---|---|---|---|---|---|---|
| 1. | D | 5. | C | 9. | A | 13. | E | 17. | B |
| 2. | C | 6. | B | 10. | B | 14. | C | 18. | E |
| 3. | C | 7. | B | 11. | C | 15. | D | 19. | C |
| 4. | C | 8. | D | 12. | B | 16. | A | 20. | A |

## Section 3    Critical Reading

| | | | | | | | | | |
|---|---|---|---|---|---|---|---|---|---|
| 25. | D | 30. | B | 35. | C | 40. | B | 45. | E |
| 26. | C | 31. | C | 36. | B | 41. | B | 46. | C |
| 27. | D | 32. | C | 37. | D | 42. | C | 47. | B |
| 28. | D | 33. | D | 38. | A | 43. | A | 48. | D |
| 29. | D | 34. | E | 39. | C | 44. | E | | |

## Section 4    Mathematics

| | | | | | | | | | |
|---|---|---|---|---|---|---|---|---|---|
| 21. | C | 23. | D | 25. | D | 27. | D | | |
| 22. | B | 24. | E | 26. | D | 28. | D | | |

29. .01

30. 90

31. 11

32. 0

33. **40**

34. **6**

35. **126**

36. **3/5**  or **.6**

37. **9.5**

38. **9/10**  or **.9**

# Section 5   Writing Skills

| | | | | | | | | | |
|---|---|---|---|---|---|---|---|---|---|
| 1. | B | 9. | A | 17. | C | 25. | E | 33. | D |
| 2. | D | 10. | D | 18. | A | 26. | B | 34. | C |
| 3. | A | 11. | D | 19. | E | 27. | A | 35. | B |
| 4. | A | 12. | B | 20. | A | 28. | C | 36. | C |
| 5. | C | 13. | B | 21. | B | 29. | B | 37. | C |
| 6. | A | 14. | C | 22. | D | 30. | A | 38. | A |
| 7. | B | 15. | D | 23. | B | 31. | E | 39. | B |
| 8. | E | 16. | D | 24. | B | 32. | A | | |

## Scoring Chart—Diagnostic Test

### Critical Reading Sections

**Section 1: 24 Questions (1–24)**

| | | |
|---|---|---|
| Number correct | _____ | (A) |
| Number omitted | _____ | (B) |
| Number incorrect | _____ | (C) |
| $\frac{1}{4}$ (C) | _____ | (D) |
| (A) − (D) | _____ | Raw Score I |

**Section 3: 24 Questions (25–48)**

| | | |
|---|---|---|
| Number correct | _____ | (A) |
| Number omitted | _____ | (B) |
| Number incorrect | _____ | (C) |
| $\frac{1}{4}$ (C) | _____ | (D) |
| (A) − (D) | _____ | Raw Score II |

**Total Critical Reading Raw Score**
Raw Scores I + II          _____

### Mathematics Sections

**Section 2: 20 Questions (1–20)**

| | | |
|---|---|---|
| Number correct | _____ | (A) |
| Number omitted | _____ | (B) |
| Number incorrect | _____ | (C) |
| $\frac{1}{4}$ (C) | _____ | (D) |
| (A) − (D) | _____ | Raw Score I |

**Section 4: First 8 Questions (21–28)**

| | | |
|---|---|---|
| Number correct | _____ | (A) |
| Number omitted | _____ | (B) |
| Number incorrect | _____ | (C) |
| $\frac{1}{4}$ (C) | _____ | (D) |
| (A) − (D) | _____ | Raw Score II |

**Section 4: Next 10 Questions (29–38)**
Number correct          _____ Raw Score III

**Total Mathematics Raw Score**
Raw Scores I + II + III          _____

**NOTE: In each section (A) + (B) + (C) should equal the number of questions in that section.**

### Writing Skills Section

**Section 5: 39 Questions (1–39)**

| | | |
|---|---|---|
| Number correct | _____ | (A) |
| Number omitted | _____ | (B) |
| Number incorrect | _____ | (C) |
| $\frac{1}{4}$ (C) | _____ | (D) |

**Writing Skills Raw Score**
(A) − (D)          _____

## Evaluation Chart

Study your score. Your raw score is an indication of your probable achievement on the PSAT/NMSQT. As a guide to the amount of work you need or want to do with this book, study the following.

| Raw Score | | | Self-Rating |
|---|---|---|---|
| *Critical Reading* | *Mathematics* | *Writing Skills* | |
| 42–48 | 35–38 | 33–39 | Superior |
| 37–41 | 30–34 | 28–32 | Very good |
| 32–36 | 25–29 | 23–27 | Good |
| 26–31 | 21–24 | 17–22 | Above average |
| 20–25 | 17–20 | 12–16 | Average |
| 12–19 | 10–16 | 7–11 | Below average |
| less than 12 | less than 10 | less than 7 | Inadequate |

# ANSWER EXPLANATIONS

## Section 1 Critical Reading

1. **(B)** For Miró, art was holy or *sacred*. Note how the second clause clarifies what kind of ritual art became for Miró.

    Choice A is incorrect. *Superficial* means shallow or not profound. If Miró worked as though he were performing a religious rite, he would not think of creating art as superficial. Choice C is incorrect. *Banal* means commonplace or trite. If Miró looked on paper and pencil as holy objects, he would not regard his art as banal. Choice D is incorrect. *Cryptic* means mysterious or obscure. The word has no necessary connection with holiness. Choice E is incorrect. *Futile* means useless or pointless. The word makes no sense in this context.

2. **(C)** The key term here is "smoke screen," something designed to obscure or mislead. How would accuracy-loving scholars react to an autobiography filled with misleading remarks? They would be *vexed* (annoyed) by the smoke screens and other misleading *errors*.

    Choice A is incorrect. How would Wright scholars react to the misleading, deceptive smoke screens in Wright's autobiography? They definitely would not have been *delighted* or pleased by them. Choice B is incorrect. While Wright scholars might have been *amazed* or surprised by misleading smoke screens in Wright's autobiography, their reaction is likely to have been far more negative. Choice D is incorrect. While Wright scholars might have been *confused* or puzzled by misleading smoke screens in Wright's autobiography, their reaction is likely to have been far more negative. Choice E is incorrect. Wright scholars are unlikely to have been *entertained* or amused by *omissions* (lapses) and misleading smoke screens in Wright's autobiography.

3. **(A)** To be kept "at arm's length" from someone's emotions is to feel an emotional distance between you and that person. Singer's own quality of uninvolvement or *detachment* makes the reader feel distant from his main character.

    Choice B is incorrect. *Lyricism* refers to emotional, poetic expression. It would be more likely to put the reader in touch with the character's emotions than to distance the reader from what the character feels. Choice C is incorrect. *Fluency* means ease in speech or writing. That would be unlikely to distance the reader from what the character feels. Choice D is incorrect. *Brevity* means conciseness or terseness, the ability to express

much in a few words. That would be unlikely to distance the reader from what the character feels. Choice E is incorrect. *Rhythm* is the recurrence of a pattern (in writing) or a beat (in music). Again, that would be unlikely to distance the reader from what the character feels.

4. **(A)** Break down the sentence. The prolific (highly productive) author has written many different books, bound in many different bindings. The fact that the books' topics vary as much as their bindings indicates the author has not specialized in any one topic. Instead, he has *resisted* or fought specialization as strongly as some other writers have *pursued* it.

    Choice B is incorrect. The author has not specialized in one topic; he has not *admired* or looked positively on specialization. Choice C is incorrect. The author has not specialized in one topic; he has not *endorsed* or formally approved specialization. Choice D is incorrect. The author has not specialized in one topic; he has not *defended* or supported specialization. Choice E is incorrect. The author has not gone so far as to *repudiate* or disown specialization. In addition, it makes little sense to say that his colleagues have energetically *deliberated* or thought about specialization.

5. **(B)** If the mayfly's adult life lasts for such a short time, it clearly is an *ephemeral* (short-lived, fleeting) creature. Note how the second clause clarifies what the author means by *ephemeral*.

    Choice A is incorrect. *Elegant* means tastefully refined or graceful. You are looking for a word that means short-lived. Choice C is incorrect. *Idiosyncratic* means quirky or peculiar to an individual. You are looking for a word that means short-lived. Choice D is incorrect. *Impulsive* means rash or impetuous. You are looking for a word that means short-lived. Choice E is incorrect. *Omnivorous* means eating both animal and plant food. You are looking for a word that means short-lived.

6. **(E)** Reporters "have had a field day" commenting on the controversial knighting. In other words, they have had an occasion for unrestrained ridicule and hilarity, to which their response has been one of pure *glee* (high-spirited delight, often prompted by a malicious joy in someone else's discomfiture).

7. **(B)** Consider that the original instance of royal hospitality to which the reporter refers is a night in a prison cell. Does that sound hospitable to you? Clearly, the reporter is using the phrase *ironically*, in an amusingly surprising way.

8. **(B)** The opening sentence of Passage 1 is "Knighthoods are not what they used to be." The opening sentence of Passage 2 is "What factors led to the decline of the armored knight?" Although the passages greatly differ in focus and tone, both make the point that the institution of knighthood has *undergone changes over time*.

9. **(D)** Passage 2 discusses the institution of knighthood from the Middle Ages through the fifteenth century: it *offers historical perspective* on the institution. Passage 1 discusses the current *guise* or form the institution takes today, with rock-and-roll knights whose not-so-shining reputations the author cheerfully *mocks* (makes fun of). The correct answer is Choice D: *Passage 2 offers historical perspective on an institution whose current guise is mocked in Passage 1.*

10. **(E)** The second paragraph discusses the various methods epiphytes adopt in order to retain or conserve moisture.

    Choice A is incorrect. Epiphytes have lost their root connection with the forest floor. Choice B is incorrect. Epiphytes seek the sun; they are not adapted to a sunless environment. Choice C is incorrect. Epiphytes have developed ways to conserve rainwater, not to dissipate or squander it. Choice D is incorrect. Epiphytes are not parasites; they do not derive nourishment ("sustenance") from the tree trunks to which they attach themselves.

11. **(B)** The first paragraph states that epiphytes grow in "spoonfuls" of soil. We can infer from this that they do not need particularly large amounts of soil for growth.

    Choice A is incorrect. Although epiphytes have lost their root connection with the forest floor, they do possess root systems. Choice C is incorrect. The passage states that the roots of some orchids carry on photosynthesis; epiphytes clearly are not incapable of photosynthesis. Choice D is incorrect. Nothing in the passage suggests epiphytes are hard to spot. Choice E is incorrect. Epiphytes have "managed to create their own environment" so well that the soil in which they grow does not differ significantly from normal soil in microbiological processes. This fact does not suggest that their need for nutrients differs from that of plants that grow in normal soil.

12. **(C)** Epiphytes are described in a straightforward, direct manner.

    Choice A is incorrect. The author is not exhorting or urging anyone to do anything. Choice B is incorrect. The author is not analyzing epiphytes, that is, thoroughly studying each of the individual features that comprise these plants in order to

understand their structure. He is simply saying what they are like. Choice D is incorrect. The author is being direct rather than indirect in presenting what he knows about epiphytes. Choice E is incorrect. The author is not being particularly forceful in his presentation; neither is he presenting an argument.

13. **(B)** The strangler tree's feeding cables do not ascend toward the canopy; they descend to the forest floor. You can double-check your answer by using the process of elimination.

    The strangler tree eventually stands on its own pedestal or supports itself. You can eliminate Choice A. One set of the strangler tree's roots (the "feeding cable") extends all the way from high up in the fork of the host tree down to the forest floor. You can eliminate Choice C. When the feeder cable reaches the soil, the plant's growth quickens. You can eliminate Choice D. The strangler's roots "thicken to a marked degree," becoming *conspicuously larger*. You can eliminate Choice E. Only Choice B is left. It is the correct answer.

14. **(A)** The roots thicken to a marked or *noticeable* degree, eventually growing thick enough to support the strangler tree.

15. **(C)** The concluding sentence states that the host expires and the strangler tree stands on its own pedestal of thickened roots (its original feeding cables, now fused together). Thus, the strangler tree has *outgrown its need for its host*.

16. **(E)** Throughout the passage the author presents and comments on the nature of the original documents that form the basis for his historical narrative. Thus, it is clear that a major concern of his is to *introduce* these "sources of almost forgotten oral history" to his readers.

    Choice A is incorrect. The author clearly regrets the fate of the Indians. However, he does not take this occasion to denounce or condemn the white man. Choice B is incorrect. While the author discusses the various treaty councils, he does not evaluate or judge how effective they were. Choice C is incorrect. The author never touches on the current treatment of Indians. Choice D is incorrect. The author indicates no such thing.

17. **(C)** Because Brown looks on the conquest of the West from a Native American perspective, he views it as the tragic destruction of Indian civilization rather than as the heroic opening of new, uncivilized territory by European civilization. Thus, by putting quotation marks around the word "opening," Brown indicates his *disagreement with* the notion of "the opening of the West," *a term in common use* in typical narratives of the period.

18. **(E)** Of all the thousands of published descriptions of the opening of the West, the greatest concentration or *cluster* of accounts date from the period of 1860 to 1890.

19. **(D)** You can arrive at the correct choice by the process of elimination.

    Statement I is true. The passage states that the quality of the interviews depended on the interpreters' abilities. Inaccuracies could creep in because of the translators' lack of skill. Therefore, you can eliminate Choice B.

    Statement II is untrue. The passage indicates that the Indians sometimes exaggerated, telling the reporters tall tales. It does not indicate that the reporters in turn overstated what they had been told. Therefore, you can eliminate Choices C and E.

    Statement III is true. The passage indicates that the Indians sometimes were disinclined to speak the whole truth because they feared reprisals (retaliation) if they did. Therefore, you can eliminate Choice A.

    Only Choice D is left. It is the correct answer.

20. **(C)** Brown speaks of the Indians who lived through the "doom period of their civilization," the victims of the conquest of the American West. In doing so, his tone can best be described as *elegiac*, expressing sadness about their fate and lamenting their vanished civilization.

21. **(A)** In the fifth paragraph Brown comments upon the "graphic similes and metaphors of the natural world" found in the English translations of Indian speeches. Thus, he is impressed by their *vividness of imagery*.

22. **(C)** Commenting about inadequate interpreters who turned eloquent Indian speeches into "flat" prose, Brown is criticizing the translations for their *pedestrian*, unimaginative quality.

23. **(E)** Brown has tried to create a narrative of the winning of the West from the victims' perspective. In asking his readers to read the book facing eastward (the way the Indians would have been looking when they first saw the whites headed west), he is asking them metaphorically to look at things from the Indians' point of view.

24. **(B)** In the sentence immediate preceding the one in which this phrase appears, Brown calls the Indians "true conservationists." Such conservationists know that life is *necessarily tied to* the earth and to its resources and that by destroying these resources by imbalancing the equation, so to speak, you destroy life itself.

## Section 2  Mathematics

For many problems, the explanation provides a reference to one or more **KEY FACTS** from Chapter 7. These are the mathematical facts that you need to solve that problem. If a solution refers to **KEY FACT J2**, for example, the solution depends on the second **KEY FACT** discussed in Section J of Chapter 7.

For some problems, an alternative solution, indicated by two asterisks (**), follows the first solution. When this occurs, usually one of the solutions is the direct mathematical one and the other is based on one of the tactics discussed in Chapters 6 and 7.

See page 244 for an explanation of the symbol $\Rightarrow$, which is used in several answer explanations.

1. **(D)** $4x = 12 \Rightarrow x = 3 \Rightarrow 12x = 36$.

2. **(C)** Just look at each number carefully. The hundreds place is the third from the left of the decimal point and the hundredths place is the second to the right of the decimal point: 3353.5353.

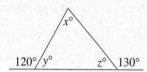

3. **(C)** In the figure above, by **KEY FACT J1**, $x + y + z = 180$, and by **KEY FACT I2**, $y = 60$ and $z = 50$. Therefore,
   $$x = 180 - (50 + 60) = 180 - 110 = 70.$$

4. **(C)** The expression $n^2 - 10$ is negative whenever $n^2 < 10$. This is true for all integers between $-3$ and 3 inclusive: $-3, -2, -1, 0, 1, 2, 3$—7 in all.

5. **(C)** The diagonals of a square bisect each other and bisect the right angles. So the measure of $\angle XHT$ and $\angle XTH$ are each $45°$, and $\triangle HXT$ is a 45-45-90 right triangle. Therefore,
   $$MX = 3 \Rightarrow XT = 3 \Rightarrow XH = 3,\ \text{and}$$
   $$\text{area of } \triangle HXT = \tfrac{1}{2}(3)(3) = 4.5.$$
   **$MX = 3 \Rightarrow MT = 6$. By **KEY FACT K6**, the area of a square equals $\frac{d^2}{2}$, where $d$ is the length of a diagonal. So the area of square *MATH* is $\frac{1}{2}(6)^2 = 18$, and the area of the shaded triangle is $18 \div 4 = 4.5$.

6. **(B)** $7x + 5 = 74 \Rightarrow 7x = 69 \Rightarrow 7x - 5 = 64$. So $\sqrt{7x - 5} = \sqrt{64} = 8$. (Note that, since the given equation and what you want both involve $7x$, you should *not* solve for $x$.)

7. **(B)** 3 is the only prime divisible by 3.

8. **(D)** $f(3) = 3^2 - 2^3 = 9 - 8 = 1$.

**Diagnostic Test**

9. **(A)** Just multiply: $\frac{2}{5}(h) = \frac{2h}{5}$.

   \*\*Use **TACTIC 6-2** and pick an easy-to-use number for $h$: 2, for example. Michael can paint $\frac{2}{5}$ of a room in the first hour and another $\frac{2}{5}$ of a room in the second hour, for a total of $\frac{4}{5}$ of a room. Check the choices. Only $\frac{2h}{5}$ equals $\frac{4}{5}$ when $h = 2$.

10. **(B)** $x^2 + 1 = 50 \Rightarrow x^2 = 49 \Rightarrow x = 7$ or $x = -7$. Therefore, $x + 1 = 8$ or $x + 1 = -6$. Since 8 is not one of the choices, the answer is $-6$.

11. **(C)** On her 6 tests combined, Evelyn earned a total of $6 \times 80 = 480$ points (see **KEY FACT E1**). The total of her 5 best grades is $5 \times 90 = 450$ points. So, her lowest grade was $480 - 450 = 30$.

12. **(B)** Of the two consecutive integers $p$ and $p + 1$, one is odd and one is even. Since 2 is the only even prime number, there is only one possibility:

    $p = 2$ and $p + 1 = 3$. ($p = 1$ and $p + 1 = 2$ does *not* work, because 1 is *not* a prime number.)

13. **(E)** Since $W = 3$ and $Z = 7$, then

    $$W + Z = 10 \Rightarrow X + Y = 10$$

    Since $3X = 2W = 2(3) = 6$, $X = 2$ and $Y = 8$.

14. **(C)** Here $Z = W$. So by definition of a number bar, $W + Z = X + Y \Rightarrow 2W = X + Y$; but the definition also states that $2W = 3X$, so $X = \frac{2}{3}W$. Therefore,

    $$2W = \frac{2}{3}W + Y \Rightarrow Y = \frac{4}{3}W.$$

15. **(D)** Check each statement.

    • Could $\frac{16}{m}$ be odd? Yes, if $m = 16$, then $\frac{16}{m} = 1$, an odd integer. (I is true.)

    • Could $\frac{m}{16}$ be an odd integer? Sure, it could be any odd integer; for example, if $m = 16$, $\frac{m}{16} = 1$, and if $m = 80$, $\frac{m}{16} = 5$. (II is true.)

    • Could $16m$ be odd? No, the product of 16 and any integer is even. (III is false.)

    • Only statements I and II are true.

16. **(A)** By **KEY FACT M2**, if $e$ is the edge of the cube, the surface area, $A$, is $6e^2$ and the volume, $V$, is $e^3$. Then

    $$A = 6e^2 = 60 \Rightarrow e^2 = 10 \Rightarrow e = \sqrt{10} \Rightarrow$$
    $$V = \left(\sqrt{10}\right)^3 = \left(\sqrt{10}\right)\left(\sqrt{10}\right)\left(\sqrt{10}\right) = 10\sqrt{10}.$$

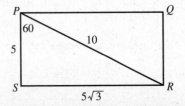

17. **(B)** *PR* is the hypotenuse of a 30-60-90 right triangle. By **KEY FACT J11**, *PS*, the leg opposite the 30° angle, is 5 (half the hypotenuse), and *SR* is $5\sqrt{3}$. So the area of the rectangle is $5 \times 5\sqrt{3} = 25\sqrt{3}$.

18. **(E)** $25 - 2\sqrt{x} = 7 \Rightarrow -2\sqrt{x} = -18 \Rightarrow \sqrt{x} = 9 \Rightarrow x = 9^2 = 81$.

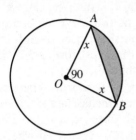

19. **(C)** Since each radius is 4, $OA = OB$ and $\triangle AOB$ is an isosceles right triangle. So by **KEY FACT J5**, $AB = 4\sqrt{2}$. The length of arc $AB$ is $\frac{90}{360} = \frac{1}{4}$ of the circumference, which by **KEY FACT L4** is $2\pi(4) = 8\pi$; so the length of arc $AB = 2\pi$. The perimeter of the region, then, is $4\sqrt{2} + 2\pi$.

20. **(A)** If Mary earned a grade of $G$ on the test, she missed $(100 - G)$ points. In adjusting the grades, the teacher decided to deduct only half that number: $\frac{100-G}{2}$. So Mary's new grade was

    $$100 - \left(\frac{100-G}{2}\right) = 100 - 50 + \frac{G}{2} = 50 + \frac{G}{2}.$$

    \*\*Pick a number for $G$. For example, if $G$ is 80, as explained in the question, Mary's adjusted grade would be 90. Only Choice A is equal to 90 when $G$ is 80.

## Section 3  Critical Reading

25. **(D)** The key word here is *smugly*. The tennis champion is smug or *complacent* about her victories.

    Choice A is incorrect. *Downcast* means sad. A smug, self-satisfied tennis champion would be unlikely to feel downcast about winning victories. Choice B is incorrect. *Agitated* means anxious or disturbed. A smug, self-satisfied tennis champion would be unlikely to feel agitated about winning victories. Choice C is incorrect. *Indifferent* means uncaring or neutral. A smug, self-satisfied tennis champion would be unlikely to be indifferent to having won victories. Choice E is incorrect. *Philosophical* means calm and stoical, governed by reason rather than emotion. The tennis champion, however, is not entirely philosophical; she looks on her trophies smugly, viewing them with satisfaction.

26. **(C)** *But* signals a contrast. Normally thunderstorms last for a short time. However, sometimes they last or *persist* for a long time. Note the effect of the phrase "becoming ever more severe." If the storm keeps on getting worse, it is not *waning* (declining), *moderating* (becoming less severe), *vacillating* (wavering), or *dispersing* (being scattered).

27. **(D)** Why is this 100-mile-thick piece of glass clearer than a standard windowpane? *Because* the glass is exceptionally *transparent*. The "so . . . that" structure signals cause and effect.

    Choice A is incorrect. *Fragile* means breakable. The sentence emphasizes the clearness of the glass, not its fragility. Choice B is incorrect. *Immaculate* means perfectly clean. The sentence emphasizes the clearness of the glass, not its cleanliness. Choice C is incorrect. *Tangible* means able to be touched. The sentence emphasizes the clearness of the glass, not its tangibility. Choice E is incorrect. *Iridescent* means lustrous and rainbowlike. The sentence emphasizes the clearness of the glass, not its iridescence.

28. **(D)** The *assiduous* or diligent *execution* (performance) of one's job would give one's employer no cause for complaint. Note the signal word *because* indicating the sentence's cause and effect structure.

    Choice A is incorrect. *Derelict* means neglectful in the performance of one's duties. Her employers would have had every right to complain if she had been derelict in the performance of her duties. Choice B is incorrect. *Importunate* means annoyingly demanding and overeager. It is related to the word *persistent*, but has negative connotations. The first missing word should be entirely positive. Choice C is incorrect. *Meticulous* means painstaking and careful. However, employers would not necessarily be happy to have an employee who was meticulous about postponing or putting off doing her work. Choice E is incorrect. *Hidebound* means narrow-minded and unwilling to change. Employers might easily have complaints about an employee who was hidebound in her notion of what her duties were.

29. **(D)** Something *eclectic* is by definition composed of items drawn from many different sources. In this case, the style of interior decoration is eclectic.

    Choice A is incorrect. *Aesthetic* means characterized by a love of beauty. The key phrase here is "bits and pieces . . . from widely divergent periods." The author is not emphasizing the beauty of the style of decoration; he is emphasizing its unusual variety. Choice B is incorrect. *Lyrical* means musi-

cal or songlike. The word is an unlikely choice to describe a style of decoration. Choice C is incorrect. *Traditional* means customary or established. A unique mix of furnishings from very different periods would be unlikely to be described as customary or traditional. Choice E is incorrect. *Perfunctory* means hasty and superficial; it also can mean uninterested. Neither meaning makes sense in the context.

30. **(B)** One expects seeds to germinate or sprout within a relatively short period of time. However, for woodland seeds, the process takes longer than normal; the seeds seem sadly *reluctant* to sprout.

    Choice A is incorrect. *Germinate* means to put forth shoots or sprout. If the mechanisms delay sprouting, then the woodland seeds would not be unfortunately *prone* or inclined to germinate. Choice C is incorrect. *Qualified* means fitted or competent to do something. It makes no sense in the context. Choice D is incorrect. *Prolific* means highly productive or fruitful. If the mechanisms delay the seeds' sprouting, then the seeds would not be sadly *prolific* or productive. Choice E is incorrect. *Modified* means changed. It makes no sense in the context.

31. **(C)** Because these shows are highly derivative of (stem from) our culture, they reflect what our culture is like. Thus, they are good *indices* (indicators or signs) of our culture's attitudes and values. *Indices* is the plural form of *index*.

    Choice A is incorrect. The soap operas are derivative of contemporary culture; they are based on or derived from it. They do not *contradict* or disagree with it. Choice B is incorrect. Because soap operas are derived from contemporary culture, they are unlikely to be *antidotes* or medicines that can serve to counteract its effects. Choice D is incorrect. Soap operas are derivative of contemporary culture; they are based on or derived from it. Thus, they cannot be *prerequisites* (preconditions or requirements that must be met *before* something can occur) for contemporary culture. Choice E is incorrect. According to the author, soap operas are derivative of contemporary culture; they are based on or derived from it. Thus, they are unlikely be *determinants* (determining agents) of the culture from which they derive.

32. **(C)** Given that English society didn't encourage women to get an education, you would expect it not to care that women were uneducated. However, English society was illogical: it *decried* or expressed its disapproval of women's lack of education.

Choice A is incorrect. *Palliated* means alleviated or relieved without curing. It makes no sense in the context. Choice B is incorrect. *Postulated* means assumed without proof, or claimed. It makes little sense here. Choice D is incorrect. *Brooked* means tolerated or endured. It makes little sense here. Choice E is incorrect. *Vaunted* means boasted or bragged about. It makes little sense here.

33. **(D)** The passage depicts Archbishop Tutu's *compassion*, his feeling for someone in need that leads him to ignore the importunate demands of the press. Choice B is incorrect: it is the distressed student assistant who feels grief or anguish, not the archbishop.

34. **(E)** The archbishop's prominence is his fame or *renown*.

35. **(C)** The author uses the term "hot spot" to indicate a geological phenomenon; she uses the term *technically*, as it is used by geologists.

    Choice B is incorrect. In its informal, or colloquial, sense, a hot spot is a nightclub.

36. **(B)** The opening sentence states that "most of the world's active volcanoes are located along the edges of the great shifting plates." However, there are "isolated areas of volcanic activity" that are located "far from the nearest plate boundary." These hot spots differ from other areas of volcanic activity in their *location*: they occur within the plates, not along the plates' edges.

37. **(D)** Graham's goal is "to bring into unhackneyed movement." Thus, she rejects movement in dance that is hackneyed or *trite*.

38. **(A)** Graham insists that, in the dancer's body, the audience must see themselves, "something of the miracle that is a human being." In rejecting the idea of their imitating natural phenomena (trees, flowers, waves), she emphasizes that dancers must embody or *express their humanity*.

39. **(C)** Graham is pairing opposite qualities that are held in balance by training and technique. Thus, technique and training give freedom and its opposite, discipline; tension and its opposite, plasticity (*mobility and pliancy*).

40. **(B)** What do most people believe? Most people believe that spontaneity in dance or in theater *is* wholly dependent on emotion at that moment. That is what Graham refers to as the "popular belief." It is the belief that spontaneous theatrical moments *happen only because the actor is gripped by a sudden emotion*.

41. **(B)** Graham draws an *analogy* or comparison between the function of spontaneity in dance or theater and that of light in life.

42. **(C)** Waters is an experienced cook and restaurateur, an *accomplished practitioner of the culinary arts*.

    You can determine the answer to this question by using the process of elimination. Waters is not a cook on the verge of opening a restaurant or simply a gifted home cook; she has run her own restaurant for years, long enough to have developed criteria for hiring employees (lines 81–84). Therefore, you can eliminate Choices A and D. She is not uninformed about traditional methods of French cooking; she served her culinary apprenticeship in France. You can eliminate Choice B. Though she is a professional, there is nothing in the passage to suggest that she is set on outstripping her competition. You can eliminate Choice E. Only Choice C is left; it is the correct answer.

43. **(A)** Sometimes sharp and strong, sometimes sweet and fresh, garlic varies in quality. Waters uses the example of the garlic to show the *variability of ingredients*.

44. **(E)** Waters stresses that she is only making suggestions and that it is up to the reader to "determine the correct balance and composition" of the meal. Thus, she is trying to *allow scope* (room) *for the reader's own culinary initiative*.

45. **(E)** Waters states firmly that "a person who responds to the cooking processes and the mound of fresh ingredients with a genuine glow of delight is likely to be, or become, a very good cook indeed." Thus, to be a good cook, one who will produce superior results, one must have *a love of one's medium* (material for artistic expression; in this case, food).

46. **(C)** Waters is looking for employees who will take great personal satisfaction in what they are doing, people who enjoy the *culinary processes*.

47. **(B)** Waters and Graham are expressing their belief as artists in spontaneity, in flexibility, in energy, in joy. They are *presenting their artistic creeds*.

48. **(D)** Graham and Waters resemble one another in their marked enthusiasm and love for their work. Both clearly *are passionately involved with their art*.

# Section 4 Mathematics

## MULTIPLE-CHOICE QUESTIONS

For many problems, the explanation provides a reference to one or more **KEY FACTS** from Chapter 7. These are the mathematical facts that you need to solve that problem. If a solution refers to **KEY FACT J2**, for example, the solution depends on the second **KEY FACT** discussed in Section J of Chapter 7.

For some problems, an alternative solution, indicated by two asterisks (**), follows the first solution. When this occurs, usually one of the solutions is the direct mathematical one and the other is based on one of the tactics discussed in Chapters 6 and 7.

See page 244 for an explanation of the symbol ⇒, which is used in several answer explanations.

21. **(C)** Solve the given equation using the six-step method discussed in Section 9-G.
$$7d + 5 = 5d + 7 \Rightarrow$$
$$2d + 5 = 7 \Rightarrow 2d = 2 \Rightarrow d = 1.$$
**Use **TACTIC 6-1**. Test the answer choices, starting with C, which happens to work.

22. **(B)** The unmarked angle opposite the 60° angle also measures 60° (**KEY FACT I4**), and the sum of the measures of all six angles in the diagram is 360° (**KEY FACT I3**). Then,
$$360 = a + b + c + 20 + 60 + 60 =$$
$$a + b + c + 140.$$

Subtracting 140 from each side, we get
$$a + b + c = 220.$$

23. **(D)** If $5\sqrt{x} + 1 = 46$, then $5\sqrt{x} = 45$, and so $\sqrt{x} = 9$ and $x = 81$.

24. **(E)** If $y = 1$, then $x$ could be 1 or $-1$; so neither Choice A nor Choice B is correct. If $x = 1$ and $y = -1$, Choice C is wrong, and if $y = 1$ and $x = -1$, Choice D is wrong. Only Choice E is correct.
$$**x^2 = y^2 \Rightarrow x^2 - y^2 = 0 \Rightarrow (x - y)(x + y) = 0$$
Therefore,
$$x - y = 0 \text{ or } x + y = 0 \Rightarrow$$
$$x = y \text{ or } x = -y \Rightarrow |x| = |y|.$$

25. **(D)** Since $-5 + 5 = 0$, and since 0 is an even integer, $-5 ⊹ 5 = -5$.

26. **(D)**
- Could $a + b$ be even? Yes, if $a = 10$ and $b = 2$, then $a + b$ is even and $a ⊹ b = 10$.
- Could $a + b$ be odd? Yes, if $a = 1$ and $b = 10$, then $a + b$ is odd and $a ⊹ b = 10$.

- Could $b ⊹ a = 10$? No. If $b ⊹ a$ were 10, then $b ⊹ a$ would be equal to $a ⊹ b$, which would imply that $a = b$, contrary to the given information.
- Statements I and II only are true.

27. **(D)** If Sarah were really unlucky, what could go wrong in her attempt to get one marble of each color? Well, her first 11 picks *might* yield 6 blue marbles and 5 white ones. But then the twelfth marble would be red, and she would have at least one of each color. The answer is 12.

28. **(D)** Since the area of square $ABCD$ is 100, each side is 10. In the diagram, draw in line segment $\overline{AE}$ and line segment $\overline{EXY}$ perpendicular to $\overline{AB}$ and $\overline{CD}$, and then label the diagram.

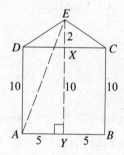

$XY = 10$ since it is the same length as a side of the square. $\overline{EX}$ is the height of $\triangle ECD$, whose base is 10 and whose area is 10. So $10 = \frac{1}{2}(10)(EX) \Rightarrow EX = 2$, and so $EY = 12$.
Since $\triangle ECD$ is isosceles, $DX = 5$; so $AY = 5$. Finally, recognize $\triangle AYE$ as a 5-12-13 right triangle, or use the Pythagorean theorem to find the hypotenuse, $AE$, of the triangle:
$$(AE)^2 = 5^2 + 12^2 = 25 + 144 = 169,$$
so $AE = 13$.

## GRID-IN QUESTIONS

29. **(.01)** First, add $w$ to each side of the given equation, and then subtract 4.99:
$$5 - w = 4.99 \Rightarrow 5 = 4.99 + w \Rightarrow w = .01.$$

30. **(90)** In a ratio problem write the letter $x$ after each number (**TACTIC D-1**). Then $a = 5x$, $b = 7x$, and $c = 12x$; and since, by **KEY FACT J1**, the sum of the measures of the angles of a triangle is 180°:
$$5x + 7x + 12x = 180 \Rightarrow 24x = 180 \Rightarrow x = 7.5.$$
So $c = 12x = 12(7.5) = 90$.

31. **(11)** Since $xy = 30$ and $x = -6$, we have $y = -5$. So $x^2 - y^2 = (-6)^2 + (-5)^2 = 36 - 25 = 11$.

32. **(0)** For any numbers $a$ and $b$, if $a \neq b$ and $ax = bx$, then $x$ must be 0. Therefore,
$$25\% \text{ of } x = 35\% \text{ of } x \Rightarrow x = 0 \Rightarrow 45\% \text{ of } x = 0.$$

33. **(40)** Consider the diagram below in which several additional angles have been labeled and repeatedly use **KEY FACTS I2**, **I4**, and **J1**.

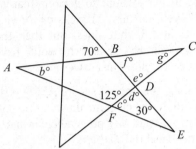

Since $125 + c = 180$, then $c = 55$; so in $\triangle DEF$, $55 + 30 + d = 180 \Rightarrow d = 95$. Also, since vertical angles are equal, $e = 95$ and $f = 70$. Then in $\triangle BCD$,
$$95 + 70 + g = 180 \Rightarrow g = 15.$$
Finally, in $\triangle CAF$,
$$15 + 125 + b = 180 \Rightarrow b = 40.$$

34. **(6)** Write out the first few terms being careful to follow the directions. The first term is 2. The second term is 1 more than 2 times the first term: $2(2) + 1 = 5$. The third term is 1 more than 2 times the second term: $2(5) + 1 = 11$. Continuing in this way, you find that the terms less than 100 are: 2, 5, 11, 23, 47, 95. There are 6 of them.

35. **(126)** In the tens column, $2 + 4 + 6 = 12$; so if nothing was carried from the units column, $A = 1$ and $B = 2$. In fact, this works, because if $B = 2$, the units column adds up to 6, and $ABC = 126$.

36. $\left(\frac{3}{5} \text{ or } .6\right)$ A quick sketch can eliminate a few choices and guard against carelessness.

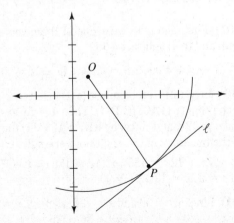

From the diagram, we see that the slope of $l$ is positive (**KEY FACT N5**), and so we can eliminate

choices A and B. By **KEY FACT N4**, the slope of $\overline{OP}$ is $\frac{-4-1}{4-1} = \frac{-5}{3}$. Since by **KEY FACT N6**, $\overline{OP} \perp l$, the slope of $l$ is the negative reciprocal of $-\frac{5}{3}$, namely $\frac{3}{5}$.

37. **(9.5)** By **KEY FACT M2**, the surface area of a rectangular box is given by $A = 2(\ell w + wh + \ell h)$. Replacing $w$ by 5, $\ell$ by 7, and $A$ by 298, we get
$$298 = 2(35 + 5h + 7h) = 70 + 24h.$$
Therefore, $24h = 228$ and $h = 9.5$.

38. $\left(\frac{9}{10} \text{ or } .9\right)$ If there are $x$ seats on each bus, then the group is using $\frac{4}{5}(3x) = \frac{12}{5}x$ seats. After $\frac{1}{4}$ of the passengers get off, $\frac{3}{4}$ of them, or $\frac{3}{1}\frac{4}{5}\left(\frac{12^3}{5}x\right) = \frac{9}{5}x$ remain. The fraction of the $2x$ seats now being used on the two buses is
$$\frac{\frac{9}{5}x}{2x} = \frac{\frac{9}{5}}{2} = \frac{9}{10}.$$

\*\*To avoid working with $x$, assume there are 20 seats on each bus. At the beginning, the group is using $\frac{4}{5}$ of the 60 seats on the three buses: $\frac{4}{5}(60) = 48$. When $\frac{1}{4}$ of the 48 people left, 12 left and the 36 remaining people used $\frac{36}{40} = \frac{9}{10}$ of the 40 seats on the two buses.

## Section 5  Writing Skills

1. **(B)** Choice B corrects the misuse of the subjunctive.

2. **(D)** Choice D corrects the error in the case of the pronoun. Choice E corrects the error in case but introduces an error in tense.

3. **(A)** The clause is correct.

4. **(A)** Sentence is correct.

5. **(C)** Error in modification and word order. Choice C corrects the dangling participle.

6. **(A)** Sentence is correct.

7. **(B)** This corrects the unnecessary switch in the pronouns, *anyone–you*.

8. **(E)** Error in parallelism. *Relax* matches *make*, *wash*, and *do*.

9. **(A)** Sentence is correct.

10. **(D)** Comma splice. The run-on sentence is corrected by the use of a semicolon.

11. **(D)** Error in following conventions. Choice D corrects the double negative *hadn't hardly* and the misuse of *those* with *kind*.

12. **(B)** Error in modification and word order. Choice B corrects the dangling participle.

13. **(B)** Comma splice. In Choice B, the run-on sentence is corrected by the use of a semicolon, and the omission of the past participle *been* is also corrected.

14. **(C)** Errors in following conventions. Choice C expresses the author's meaning directly and concisely. All other choices are either indirect or ungrammatical.

15. **(D)** Incorrect conjunction. The conjunction *furthermore* fails to link the two clauses logically. Choice D corrects the error by eliminating the incorrect conjunction and substituting a colon to separate the two main clauses. (A colon may separate two main clauses when the second explains the first. In Choice D, the second clause ["they . . . subside"] explains in what way young children's fevers are erratic.)

16. **(D)** Error in degree of comparison. Because there are many characters in *A Christmas Carol,* you must describe Tiny Tim as the *most* beloved of them all.

17. **(C)** Wordiness. Choice C eliminates the unnecessary words.

18. **(A)** Sentence is correct.

19. **(E)** Error in sequence of tenses. Because Hemingway worked as a correspondent at a definite time in the past (during the Spanish Civil War), the verb should be in the past tense ("wrote"), not the present perfect tense ("has written").

20. **(A)** Sentence is correct.

21. **(B)** Error in diction. Change *had ought* to *ought*.

22. **(D)** Adjective and adverb confusion. Change *bad* to *badly*.

23. **(B)** Error in tense. Change *has sang* to *has sung*.

24. **(B)** Error in diction. Change *affect* to *effect*.

25. **(E)** Sentence is correct.

26. **(B)** Error in verb. Change *had drank* to *had drunk*.

27. **(A)** Error in diction. Since *without hardly* is a double negative, change *without hardly* to either *without* or *with hardly*.

28. **(C)** Error in comparison of modifiers. Incorrect use of the superlative. Change *most* to *more*.

29. **(B)** Error in parallelism. Change *being intelligent* to *intelligence*.

30. **(A)** Error in diction. Change *or* to *nor*.

31. **(E)** Sentence is correct.

32. **(A)** Error in diction. Change *principal* to *principle*.

33. **(D)** Double negative. Do not combine *hardly* with *not*. Either say the alchemist's method was not scientific, or say that it was hardly scientific.

34. **(C)** Error in agreement. Change *them* to *him* or *her*.

35. **(B)** Choice A is awkwardly constructed. The phrase *for the cruelty of keeping animals* is cumbersome. Moreover, the sentence suggests that cruelty to animals can be justified—the opposite of what the writer intended to say.

    Choice B states the idea clearly and economically. It is the best answer.

    Choice C is wordy and awkwardly expressed.

    Choice D is wordy and awkwardly expressed.

    Choice E, which lacks a main verb, is a sentence fragment.

36. **(C)** Choice A is a sentence fragment. It lacks a main verb.

    Choice B contradicts the idea that zoos can be educational.

    Choice C accurately develops the idea introduced in sentence 3 that zoos can be educational. It is the best answer.

    Choice D is irrelevant to the idea in sentence 3.

    Choice E is written with a hostile and inappropriate tone.

37. **(C)** Choice A is not the best answer because most readers probably know that zoos house animals in cages. Moreover, highly charged language is not ordinarily used merely to pass along information.

    Choice B is unrelated to the words in question.

    Choice C is the best answer. The choice of words is meant to shock and disturb the reader.

    Choice D suggests that the author is trying to be objective, but the words in question are hardly objective.

    Choice E describes the purpose of the entire essay but not the particular words in question.

38. **(A)** Choice A introduces the main idea of the paragraph. It is the best answer.

    Choice B raises an issue not mentioned in the remainder of the paragraph. Therefore, it is not a good topic sentence of the paragraph.

Choice C contains an idea not discussed in the paragraph. The paragraph focuses on how animals behave in captivity, not on living conditions at the zoo.

Choice D contains a dangling modifier. The phrase *Living in the zoo*s should modify *animals* instead of *conditions*.

Choice E contains a frivolous cliché that is not consistent with the tone of the essay.

39. **(B)** Choice A is grammatically correct, but it reverses the cause-effect relationship stated by the original sentences.

Choice B accurately and economically conveys the ideas of the original sentences. It is the best answer.

Choice C is a sentence fragment. It lacks a main verb. The *-ing* forms of verbs (e.g., *growing, placing, being*) may not be used as the main verb without a helping verb, as in *was growing, is placing*, and so on.

Choice D is grammatically correct but stylistically awkward mainly because the subject *They* is too far removed from the verb *would . . . survive*.

Choice E is virtually meaningless because the cause-effect relationship has been reversed.

# PART THREE

# CRITICAL READING

# The Sentence Completion Question

## CHAPTER 1

> *The sentence completion questions ask you to choose the best way to complete a sentence from which one or two words have been omitted. You must be able to recognize the logic, style, and tone of the sentence so that you can choose the answer that makes sense in this context. You must also be able to recognize the way words are normally used.*
>
> *The sentences cover a wide variety of topics of the sort you have probably encountered in your general reading. However, this is not a test of your general knowledge. You may feel more comfortable if you are familiar with the topic the sentence is discussing, but you should be able to handle any of the sentences using your understanding of the English language.*

## TIPS FOR HANDLING SENTENCE COMPLETION QUESTIONS

### Tip 1

**Before you look at the answer choices, read the sentence, substituting the word "blank" for the missing word.** Think of words you know that might make sense in the context. You may not come up with the exact word, but you may come up with a synonym. You will definitely have a feel for what word belongs in the frame.

### EXAMPLE 1

See how the first tip works in dealing with the following sentence:

> The psychologist set up the experiment to test the rat's _____: he wished to see how well the rat adjusted to the changing conditions it had to face.

Even before you look at the answer choices, you can figure out what the answer *should* be.

Look at the sentence. The psychologist is trying to test the rat's "blank." In other words, the psychologist is trying to test some particular quality or characteristic of the rat. What quality? How do you get the answer?

Look at the second part of the sentence, the part following the colon (the second clause, in technical terms). This clause defines or clarifies what the psychologist is trying to test. He is trying to see how well the rat adjusts. What words does this suggest to you? *Flexibility*, possibly, or *adjustment* comes to mind. Either of these words could logically complete the sentence's thought.

Here are the five answer choices given:

(A) reflexes    (B) communicability    (C) stamina
(D) sociability    (E) adaptability

Which one is the best synonym for *flexibility* or *adjustment*? Clearly, the closest synonym is *adaptability*, Choice E.

To make sure you are correct, reread the sentence, substituting the word *adaptability* in the blank.

> The psychologist set up the experiment to test the rat's adaptability: he wished to see how well the rat adjusted to the changing conditions it had to face.

The correct answer is Choice E.

## Power Practice

Practice Tip 1 as you work through the following questions, step by step.

1. It is foolish to boast about your wealth or accomplishments; no one likes a

   _____ .

   What word makes sense in the context?
   Write down your word: _____

Now look at the answer choices:

(A) miser    (B) turncoat    (C) braggart
· (D) charlatan    (E) mentor

Reread the sentence, substituting your answer choice in the blank.

2. Usually several skunks live together; however, adult male striped skunks are

   _____ during the summer.

   What word makes sense in the context?
   Write down your word: _____

Now look at the answer choices:

    (A) nocturnal    (B) solitary    (C) predatory
      (D) cooperative    (E) dormant

Reread the sentence, substituting your answer choice in the blank.

3. Justice Brandeis was noted for his legal _____ : his biographers often comment about the keenness of his insights into the workings of the law.

    What word makes sense in the context?
    Write down your word: _____

Now look at the answer choices:

    (A) ethics    (B) malpractice    (C) defense
      (D) acumen    (E) representation

Reread the sentence, substituting your answer choice in the blank.

## Check Your Answers:

1. **(C)** A *braggart* is a boaster.
2. **(B)** *Solitary* means alone, without companions.
3. **(D)** *Acumen* means shrewdness, keenness of judgment.

---

 **DID YOU NOTICE?**
Each of the sentences in the preceding questions is actually two statements linked by a semicolon (;) or a colon (:). The punctuation mark is your clue that the two statements support each other.
    A semicolon signals you that the second statement develops the idea expressed in the first statement.
Statement 1: It is foolish to boast about your wealth or accomplishments.
Why?
Statement 2: No one likes a braggart.
A colon signals you that the second statement serves to explain or clarify the first. It gives examples, or it defines terms.
    Statement 1: Justice Brandeis was noted for his legal acumen.
    What is legal acumen?
    Statement 2: His biographers often comment about *the keenness of his insights into the workings of the law*.
    Legal acumen is keenness of insight into the workings of the law.

**Look for words or phrases that indicate a contrast between one idea and another—words like *although*, *however*, *despite*, or *but*.** In such cases, an antonym or near-antonym for another word in the sentence may be the correct answer.

## EXAMPLE 2

See how the second tip works in dealing with the following sentence:

> We expected the winner of the race to be jubilant about his victory, but he was _____ instead.

How do you expect someone to feel who has won a victory? Even if you do not know the word *jubilant*, you can guess that it means overjoyed and triumphant.

*But* signals a contrast. The winner is *not* jubilant. Instead, he is the opposite of jubilant: he is sad.

Here are the five answer choices given:

(A) triumphant    (B) mature    (C) morose
(D) talkative    (E) culpable

You are looking for an antonym of *jubilant*. *Triumphant* is a synonym of *jubilant*, not an antonym; its antonym is *sad* or *disappointed*. You can cross out Choice A. *Mature* means grown-up; its antonym is *immature*. You can cross out Choice B. The next choice, *morose*, may be an unfamiliar word to you. For the moment, skip Choice C. The antonym of *talkative* is *silent* or *uncommunicative*. You can cross out Choice D. *Culpable* means guilty; its antonym is *innocent*. You can cross out Choice E. Only Choice C is left. *Morose* means gloomy and ill-humored; it is the opposite of *jubilant*.

## Power Practice

Practice Tip 2 as you work through the following questions, step by step.

1. Although it appeared quite _____ , the vase was actually very sturdy; even a fall from the top shelf left it undamaged.

*Although* signals a contrast. The vase is actually *sturdy* (tough). Even a fall does not shatter or damage it. However, the vase appears to be the opposite of sturdy. You are looking for the antonym of *sturdy*. What word makes sense in the context?

Write down your word: _____

Now look at the answer choices:

(A) expensive    (B) floral    (C) capacious
(D) ornate    (E) fragile

Reread the sentence, substituting your answer choice in the blank.

2. Despite his seemingly hopeless position, Bond felt _____ that he would escape from the trap.

*Despite* signals a contrast. Bond's position seems hopeless. He is caught in a trap. However, Bond feels the opposite of hopeless. You are looking for the antonym of *hopeless*. What word makes sense in the context?

Write down your word: _____

Now look at the answers:

(A) problematic    (B) dubious    (C) optimistic
(D) unwarranted    (E) tolerant

Reread the sentence, substituting your answer choice in the blank.

3. Most birds of prey hunt by day; owls, however, are _____ hunters.

*However* signals a contrast. Owls do the opposite of what most birds of prey do. You are looking for the antonym of *by day*. What word makes sense in the context?

Write down your word: _____

Now look at the answer choices:

(A) migratory    (B) nocturnal    (C) persistent
(D) clandestine    (E) fierce

**HOW'S YOUR WORD POWER?**
Did you know all the words in the answer choices? Look up any unfamiliar words in our Word List, in a dictionary, or online at sites like *www.onelook.com* or *www.dictionary.com*.

## Check Your Answers:

1. **(E)** The opposite of sturdy or durable is *fragile*.
2. **(C)** The opposite of hopeless is *optimistic* or hopeful.
3. **(B)** Unlike most birds of prey, owls do not hunt by day. They hunt by night. They are *nocturnal* hunters.

## Tip 3

**Look for words or phrases that indicate support for a concept—words such as *likewise, similarly, in the same way, and, in addition, additionally,* and *also.*** What follows logically develops the writer's idea. In such cases, a synonym or near-synonym for another word in the sentence may provide the correct answer.

## EXAMPLE 3

See how the third tip works in dealing with the following sentence:

> The simplest animals are those whose bodies are least complex in structure, and that do the same things done by all animals, such as eating, breathing, moving, and feeling, in the most _____ way.

The transition word *and* signals you that the writer intends to develop the idea of simplicity introduced in the sentence. Which of the answer choices is closest in meaning to *simplest* and to *least complex*?

Here are the five answer choices given:

(A) haphazard    (B) bizarre    (C) advantageous
(D) primitive    (E) unique

You are looking for a word that develops the idea of simplicity, possibly a synonym for the word *simplest*. In biology class, you most likely learned that primitive life forms were simple in structure, and that the more complex forms of life evolved later. Clearly, Choice D, *primitive*, is best. It is the only answer choice that develops the idea of simplicity.

## Power Practice

Practice Tip 3 as you work through the following questions, step by step.

1. Studies have shown that women are faster than men at certain precision manual tasks; moreover, they also _____ men in arithmetic calculation and in recalling landmarks from a route.

*Moreover* signals support. You are looking for a word that supports and develops the idea of women being *faster than* men at certain tasks. What word makes sense in the context?

Write down your word: _____

Now look at the answer choices:

(A) outnumber     (B) conspire against     (C) acknowledge
(D) outperform     (E) lag behind

Reread the sentence, substituting your answer choice in the blank.

2. After the El Salvadoran rebels ousted President Hernandez Martinez, the revolution spread to Guatemala, whose authoritarian president was similarly _____ .

*Similarly* signals support. You are looking for a word that supports and develops the idea of being *ousted* (forced out). What word makes sense in the context?

Write down your word: _____

Now look at the answer choices:

(A) overthrown     (B) nominated     (C) elected
(D) derided     (E) astounded

Reread the sentence, substituting your answer choice in the blank.

3. During World War II, Finland was conspicuous for its refusal to take sides with either warring power, while Sweden likewise refused to do anything that might damage its traditional_____ .

*Likewise* signals support. Finland and Sweden both acted in a similar way. You are looking for a word or phrase that develops the idea of Finland's *refusal to take sides*. What word makes sense in the context?

Write down your word: _____

Now look at the answer choices:

(A) monarchy     (B) neutrality     (C) economy
(D) belligerence     (E) dignity

Reread the sentence, substituting your answer choice in the blank.

## Check Your Answers:

1. **(D)** According to the studies, women *outperform* (do better than) men at certain tasks.
2. **(A)** The president was *overthrown* (removed from power; thrown out of office).
3. **(B)** Sweden did not want to damage its traditional *neutrality*. Like Finland, it refused to take sides.

**Tip 4**

Look for words or phrases that indicate that one thing causes another—words like *because*, *since*, *therefore*, or *thus*.

## EXAMPLE 4

See how the fourth tip works in dealing with the following sentence:

Because her delivery was _____ , the effect of her speech on the voters was nonexistent.

*Because* signals a relationship of cause and effect. One thing causes another. Which of the answer choices expresses such a logical relationship?

Here are the five answer choices given:

  (A) halting    (B) plausible    (C) moving
     (D) respectable    (E) audible

What sort of delivery would cause a speech to have no effect? Obviously you would not expect a *moving* (eloquent) delivery to have such a poor result. A *halting* or stumbling speech, however, might logically have little or no effect on its audience. Thus, Choice A is best.

## Power Practice

Practice Tip 4 as you work through the following questions, step by step.

  1. We ran out of food toward the middle of the day, so by the time we returned to camp that evening we were _____ .

*So* signals cause and effect. You are looking for a word that expresses the effect of running out of food on a group of campers. What word makes sense in the context?

Write down your word: _____

Now look at the answer choices:

  (A) footsore    (B) reckless    (C) envious
     (D) ravenous    (E) tasteless

Reread the sentence, substituting your answer choice in the blank.

2. He valued his colleagues for the soundness of their opinions and therefore _____ with them often.

*Therefore* signals cause and effect. You are looking for a word that expresses the result of a person's valuing his colleagues' sound (sensible) opinions. What word makes sense in the context?

Write down your word: _____

Now look at the answer choices:

    (A) differed    (B) consulted    (C) embarked
      (D) celebrated    (E) struggled

Reread the sentence, substituting your answer choice in the blank.

3. Since the polar bear uses Arctic sea ice as a platform from which to hunt and feed upon seals, to seek mates and breed, and to travel long distances, any threat to the existence of sea ice would have _____ effect on all stages of the animal's life cycle.

*Since* signals cause and effect. You are looking for a word that expresses the effect on the polar bear of a threat to its habitat. What word makes sense in the context?

Write down your word: _____

Now look at the answer choices:

    (A) an innocuous    (B) a characteristic    (C) a detrimental
      (D) a peripheral    (E) a positive

Reread the sentence, substituting your answer choice in the blank.

## Check Your Answers:

1. **(D)** A day of hiking on an empty stomach would result in people being *ravenous* (very hungry).
2. **(B)** *Because* he valued his colleagues' sensible opinions, he *consulted* or discussed matters with them.
3. **(C)** Something that threatened the polar bear's habitat by definition would have *a detrimental* (harmful) effect on its life cycle.

### Tip 5

**Look for signals that indicate a word is being defined—phrases such as *in other words*, *that is*, or *which means*, and special punctuation clues.** Commas, hyphens, and parentheses all are used to set off definitions.

## EXAMPLE 5

See how the fifth tip works in dealing with the following sentence:

> As a child, Menuhin was considered a _____ , gifted with extraordinary musical ability.

This sentence is a straightforward definition. The missing word is defined in the section set off by the comma. Ask yourself what word in the dictionary is defined as a person *gifted with extraordinary musical ability*?

Here are the five answer choices given:

(A) heretic   (B) prodigy   (C) mendicant
(D) renegade   (E) precursor

Menuhin was a child *prodigy*. The correct answer is Choice B.

## Power Practice

Practice Tip 5 as you work through the following questions, step by step.

1. In her old age, Miss Emily became _____; in other words, she grew to shun society, preferring to live alone in her decaying house.

The phrase *in other words* signals a definition. Whatever word you choose has something to do with avoiding society. What word makes sense in the context?

Write down your word: _____

Now look at the answer choices:

(A) forgetful   (B) reclusive   (C) obdurate
(D) ironic   (E) avaricious

Reread the sentence, substituting your answer choice in the blank.

2. Gladiators were trained in the use of the net and the _____ (three-pronged spear).

The phrase in the parentheses defines the missing word. What word makes sense in the context?

Write down your word: _____

Now look at the answer choices:

   (A) rapier     (B) implement     (C) crescent
   (D) triage     (E) trident

Reread the sentence, substituting your answer choice in the blank.

3. I am a habitual _____, that is, a person who puts off doing things until another day.

The phrase *that is* signals a definition. Whatever word you choose should mean someone who delays doing what he or she ought to do. What word makes sense in the context?

Write down your word: _____

Now look at the answer choices:

   (A) miser     (B) ingrate     (C) proponent
   (D) procrastinator     (E) debunker

Reread the sentence, substituting your answer choice in the blank.

## Check Your Answers:

1. **(B)** By definition, someone who shuns or avoids society is *reclusive*. Miss Emily acts like a recluse or hermit.
2. **(E)** A gladiator's three-pronged weapon is a *trident*.
3. **(D)** A person who habitually puts off doing things is a *procrastinator*.

**If you're having vocabulary trouble, look for familiar word parts—prefixes, suffixes, and roots—in unfamiliar words.**

## EXAMPLE 6

See how the sixth tip works in dealing with the following sentence:

> After a tragedy, many people claim to have had a _____ of disaster.

Some of the following answer choices are unfamiliar words that you can figure out if you know the meaning of the prefixes, suffixes, and roots involved.

Here are the five answer choices given:

(A) deviation    (B) proclamation    (C) presentiment
(D) brink    (E) verdict

Go through the answer choices, trying to figure out the meaning of any unfamiliar words by breaking them down into parts.

*Deviation*    The prefix *de-* means down or away.
The root *via* means way or road.
A *deviation* is a departure from the way, that is, a divergence or difference.

Does this word work in the context? If it does not, you can eliminate Choice A.

*Proclamation*    The prefix *pro-* means forward or in favor of.
The root *clam* means cry out.
A *proclamation* is a public statement or announcement, something cried out to the people.

Does this word work in the context? If it does not, you can eliminate Choice B.

*Presentiment*    The prefix *pre-* means before.
The root *sens* means feel. A *sentiment* is a feeling.
A *presentiment* is something you feel before it happens, a premonition or foreboding.

*Presentiment* works in the context. Your best answer is Choice C.

# Power Practice

Practice Tip 6 as you work through the following questions, step by step.

1. Breaking with established artistic traditions, Dalí was a genius whose _____ works infuriated the traditionalists of his day.

The opening phrase is your key to the meaning of the missing word. What word makes sense in the context?

Write down your word: _____

Now look at the answer choices:

    (A) derivative    (B) magnanimous    (C) insignificant
    (D) uncontroversial    (E) heterodox

Break down any unfamiliar words into parts. Reread the sentence, substituting your answer choice in the blank.

2. The Declaration of Independence proclaimed the _____ of the American colonies and an end to English rule.

The phrase *an end to English rule* is a strong clue to the meaning of the missing word. What word makes sense in the context?

Write down your word: _____

Now look at the answer choices:

    (A) manipulation    (B) consecration    (C) abasement
    (D) autonomy    (E) heresy

Break down any unfamiliar words into parts. Reread the sentence, substituting your answer choice in the blank.

3. After many years of working together as a comedy duo, Dean Martin and Jerry Lewis ended their _____ on a sour note.

The opening phrase is your key to the meaning of the missing word. What word makes sense in the context?

Write down your word: _____

Now look at the answer choices:

(A)  resolution      (B) tenacity      (C) collaboration
(D) duplicity      (E) commemoration

Break down any unfamiliar words into parts. Reread the sentence, substituting your answer choice in the blank.

## Check Your Answers:

1.  **(E)**  The prefix *hetero-* means other. The root *dox-* means opinion. In breaking with established artistic traditions, Dalí created works that were *heterodox* (unorthodox; not in accordance with established opinions).
2.  **(D)**  The prefix *auto-* means self. The root *nom-* means law or custom. The Declaration proclaimed the colonies' *autonomy* or right of self-government.
3.  **(C)**  The prefix *col-* means with or together. The root *labor* of course means work. The comedians ended their *collaboration*.

| Tip 7 |
| --- |

**Work out whether the missing word is positive (+) or negative (–). Then test the answer choices for their positive or negative sense, eliminating those that don't work.**

## EXAMPLE 7

See how the seventh tip works in the following sentence.

> No matter how hard Ichabod tried to appear smooth and debonair, he still struck those who met him as a particularly _____ young man.

The sentence contrasts Ichabod's desired image—smooth and debonair (both positive terms)—with the actual negative impression he makes. You are looking for a negative term. Ask yourself what negative words would describe a young man who is *not* smooth and debonair (suave; sophisticated; elegant).

Here are the five answer choices given:

(A)  heroic      (B) promising      (C) mendacious
(D) ungainly      (E) precocious

**TIME FOR AN EDUCATED GUESS**
At this point, even if you do not know the meaning of the words *mendacious* and *ungainly*, you *must* guess.

*Heroic* (gallant; brave), *promising* (likely to turn out well), and *precocious* (unusually advanced, especially mentally) are all positive terms. Since you are looking for a negative term, you can eliminate Choices A, B, and E.

The Sentence Completion Question  **87**

Both *mendacious* and *ungainly* are negative terms. *Mendacious* means untruthful. Ichabod isn't being untruthful; he's just unsuccessful at looking cool and suave. No matter how hard he tries, he still looks *ungainly*: ungraceful and clumsy, the opposite of smooth. The correct answer is Choice D.

## Power Practice

Practice Tip 7 as you work through the following questions, step by step.

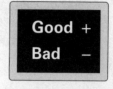

1. When the students were told that the popular class trip to Washington, D.C. had been cancelled for lack of funds, they predictably were greatly _____ .

Analyze the sentence to see whether the missing word is positive or negative. The opening clause is your key to the meaning of the missing word. What word makes sense in the context?

Write down your word: _____

Now look at the answer choices:

    (A) relieved      (B) accommodated      (C) disgruntled
       (D) emancipated      (E) disseminated

Reread the sentence, substituting your answer choice in the blank.

2. Eugene Lang was a public _____ , creating scholarships that enabled hundreds of poor children to attend college.

Analyze the sentence to see whether the missing word is positive or negative. The long descriptive phrase is your key to the meaning of the missing word. What word makes sense in the context?

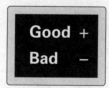

Write down your word: _____

Now look at the answer choices:

    (A) partisan      (B) benefactor      (C) misanthrope
       (D) official      (E) nuisance

Reread the sentence, substituting your answer choice in the blank.

3. Although General Benedict Arnold originally distinguished himself by his brave service in the Continental Army, his later betrayal of the American cause so_____ his name that few people today recognize his contribution to America's independence.

Analyze the sentence to see whether the missing word is positive or negative. The phrase "his later betrayal of the American cause" is your key to the meaning of the missing word. What word makes sense in the context?

Write down your word: _____

Now look at the answer choices:

    (A) exalted    (B) blackened    (C) misconstrued
       (D) proclaimed    (E) cleared

Reread the sentence, substituting your answer choice in the blank.

### Check Your Answers:

1. **(C)** The students' reaction to losing their trip clearly is negative. They are *disgruntled* (displeased and sulky).
2. **(B)** Someone who creates scholarships enabling poor children to attend college is a public *benefactor* (one who does good works).
3. **(B)** What effect would betraying a cause have on someone's good name? Clearly, it would have a negative effect. Arnold's betrayal *blackened* his name.

### Tip 8

**In a sentence completion question with two blanks, eliminate answer choices by testing one blank at a time.** First read through the entire sentence and decide which blank you want to work on. Then insert the appropriate word of each answer pair in that blank. Ask yourself whether this particular word makes sense in this blank. If a word makes *no* sense in the sentence, you can eliminate that answer pair.

### EXAMPLE 8

See how the eighth tip works in the following sentence.

    The author portrays research psychologists not as disruptive _____ in the field of psychotherapy, but as effective _____ working ultimately toward the same ends as the psychotherapists.

Two additional tips can help you answer this question. **Tip 2:** Look for words that signal a contrast. The *not as…but as* structure signals a contrast; the missing words may be antonyms or near-antonyms. **Tip 7:** Test the answer choices for their positive or negative sense, eliminating those that don't work.

Here are the five answer choices given:

(A) proponents..opponents
(B) antagonists..pundits
(C) interlocutors..surrogates
(D) meddlers..usurpers
(E) intruders..collaborators

Turn to the second part of the sentence. The research psychologists are portrayed as effective "blanks" working ultimately toward the same ends as the psychotherapists. The key phrase here is "working ultimately toward the same ends." Thus, the research psychologists are in effect working together with the psychotherapists to achieve a common goal. This immediately suggests that the correct answer is *collaborators*, Choice E. Test the first word of that answer pair in the first blank. The adjective "disruptive" suggests that the first missing word is negative in tone. *Intruders* (people who rudely or inappropriately barge in) definitely have negative connotations. Choice E continues to look good.

Reread the sentence with both words in place, making sure both words make sense. "The author portrays research psychologists not as disruptive intruders in the field of psychotherapy, but as effective collaborators working ultimately toward the same ends as the psychotherapists." Both words make perfect sense. The correct answer is Choice E.

## Power Practice

Practice Tip 8 as you work through the following questions, step by step.

1. Barbara's new classmates were neither _____ nor _____: they were not unfriendly, but they were not precisely welcoming either.

Quickly decide which blank you are going to test. The second clause (the part following the colon) is your key to the meaning of both missing words. What word makes sense in the blank you have chosen?

Write down your word: _____

Now look at the answer choices:

(A) curious..intelligent
(B) aloof..scholarly
(C) standoffish..cordial
(D) magnanimous..pragmatic
(E) diligent..affable

Eliminate any answer pair that did not work in the blank you tested. Then work on the other blank. Reread the sentence, substituting *both words* of your answer pair in the blanks.

2. Although his personal appearance is _____, the homework that he hands in is always neat, well-organized, and _____ executed.

Quickly decide which blank you are going to test. The contrast signal *Although* is your key to the meaning of both missing words. What word makes sense in the blank you have chosen?

Write down your word: _____

Now look at the answer choices:

    (A) immaculate..flawlessly
    (B) disheveled.. poorly
    (C) stylish..indifferently
    (D) curious..hastily
    (E) unkempt..meticulously

Eliminate any answer pair that did not work in the blank you tested. Then work on the other blank. Reread the sentence, substituting *both words* of your answer pair in the blanks.

3. Scrooge's hatred of _____ grew so strong that he came to regard people who spent any money at all on Christmas presents and holiday entertainments as _____.

Quickly decide which blank you are going to test. The cause-and-effect signal "so..that" is your key to the meaning of both missing words. What word makes sense in the blank you have chosen?

Write down your word: _____

Now look at the answer choices:

    (A) parsimony..ingrates
    (B) philanthropy..misers
    (C) extravagance..wastrels
    (D) frugality..traitors
    (E) seclusion..prodigals

Eliminate any answer pair that did not work in the blank you tested. Then work on the other blank. Reread the sentence, substituting *both words* of your answer pair in the blanks.

## Check Your Answers:

1. **(C)** Barbara's classmates were not unfriendly and *standoffish* (cold and aloof). However, they were also not welcoming and *cordial* (warm and friendly).
2. **(E)** Although the student's appearance is *unkempt* (untidy; uncared for), his homework is *meticulously* (carefully and properly) executed.
3. **(C)** Scrooge hates *extravagance* (excessive or unnecessary spending). Because of this, he looks on people who spend money on things he regards unnecessary as *wastrels* (spendthrifts).

# Practice Exercises

The following exercises are set up to give even National Merit Scholars a challenge. If you don't get every answer right, it's No Big Deal. Just do your best, and check the answer explanations for tips on how to do even better next time round.

## EXERCISE A

1. Although the play was not praised by the critics, it did not _____ thanks to favorable word-of-mouth comments.

   (A) succeed    (B) translate
   (C) function    (D) close
   (E) continue

2. Because the hawk is _____ bird, farmers try to keep it away from their chickens.

   (A) a migratory    (B) an ugly
   (C) a predatory    (D) a reclusive
   (E) a huge

3. If you are trying to make a strong impression on your audience, you cannot do so by being understated, tentative, or _____.

   (A) hyperbolic    (B) restrained
   (C) argumentative    (D) authoritative
   (E) expressive

4. Despite the mixture's _____ nature, we found that by lowering its temperature in the laboratory we could dramatically reduce its tendency to vaporize.

   (A) resilient    (B) homogeneous
   (C) insipid    (D) volatile
   (E) acerbic

5. Milton's poem *Lycidas* is renowned as an example of _____ verse, for it laments the death of the young clergyman Edward King.

   (A) satiric    (B) moribund
   (C) elegiac    (D) free
   (E) didactic

6. Despite his _____ appearance, he was chosen by his employer for a job that required neatness and polish.

   (A) disheveled    (B) impressive
   (C) prepossessing    (D) aloof
   (E) tardy

7. The earthquake caused some damage, but the tidal wave that followed was more _____ because it _____ many villages.

   (A) culpable..bypassed
   (B) surreptitious..absorbed
   (C) deleterious..renovated
   (D) beneficial..congested
   (E) devastating..inundated

8. Several manufacturers now make biodegradable forms of plastic: some plastic six-pack rings, for example, gradually _____ when exposed to sunlight.

   (A) harden    (B) stagnate
   (C) inflate    (D) propagate
   (E) decompose

9. Although Barbara Tuchman never earned a graduate degree, she nevertheless _____ a scholarly career as a historian noted for her vivid style and _____ erudition.

   (A) interrupted..flawed
   (B) relinquished..immense
   (C) abandoned..capricious
   (D) pursued..prodigious
   (E) followed..scanty

10. Since the chief executive officer had promised to give us a definite answer to our proposal, we were _____ by his _____ reply.

   (A) pleased..equivocal
   (B) vexed..negative
   (C) annoyed..noncommittal
   (D) delighted..perfunctory
   (E) baffled..decisive

## EXERCISE B

1. The insurance company rejected his application for accident insurance, because his _____ occupation made him a poor risk.

   (A) desultory      (B) haphazard
   (C) esoteric      (D) hazardous
   (E) sedentary

2. No other artist rewards the viewer with more sheer pleasure than Miró: he is one of those blessed artists who combine profundity and

   _____.

   (A) education      (B) wisdom
   (C) faith      (D) depth
   (E) fun

3. The tapeworm is an example of _____ organism, one that lives within or on another creature, deriving some or all of its nutriment from its host.

   (A) a hospitable      (B) an exemplary
   (C) a parasitic      (D) an autonomous
   (E) a protozoan

4. The young woman was quickly promoted when her employers saw how _____ she was.

   (A) indigent      (B) indifferent
   (C) assiduous      (D) irresolute
   (E) cursory

5. Though she was theoretically a friend of labor, her voting record in Congress _____ that impression.

   (A) implied      (B) created
   (C) confirmed      (D) belied
   (E) maintained

6. The reasoning in this editorial is so _____ that I cannot see how anyone can be _____ by it.

   (A) coherent..convinced
   (B) astute..persuaded
   (C) cogent..moved
   (D) specious..deceived
   (E) dispassionate..incriminated

7. To _____ the problem of contaminated chicken, the panel recommends shifting inspections from cursory visual checks to a more scientifically _____ random sampling for bacterial and chemical contamination.

   (A) alleviate..rigorous
   (B) eliminate..perfunctory
   (C) analyze..symbolic
   (D) document..unreliable
   (E) obviate..dubious

8. Unable to hide his _____ for the police commissioner, the inspector imprudently made _____ remarks about his superior officer.

   (A) disdain..detached
   (B) respect..ambiguous
   (C) liking..unfathomable
   (D) contempt..interminable
   (E) scorn..scathing

9. We were amazed that a woman who had been up to now the most _____ of public speakers could, in a single speech, electrify an audience and bring them cheering to their feet.

   (A) enthralling     (B) accomplished
   (C) pedestrian     (D) auspicious
   (E) masterful

10. Shy and hypochondriacal, Madison was _____ at public gatherings; his character made him a most _____ lawmaker and practicing politician.

    (A) ambivalent..conscientious
    (B) uncomfortable..unlikely
    (C) inaudible..fervent
    (D) aloof..gregarious
    (E) awkward..effective

## EXERCISE C

1. In place of the more general debate about abstract principles of government that many delegates expected, the Constitutional Convention put _____ proposals on the table.

   (A) theoretical     (B) vague
   (C) concrete     (D) tentative
   (E) redundant

2. He was so _____ in meeting the payments on his car that the finance company threatened to seize the automobile.

   (A) dilatory     (B) mercenary
   (C) solvent     (D) diligent
   (E) compulsive

3. The child was so spoiled by her indulgent parents that she pouted and became _____ when she did not receive all of their attention.

   (A) discreet     (B) suspicious
   (C) elated     (D) sullen
   (E) tranquil

4. Modern architecture has abandoned the use of _____ trimming on buildings and has concentrated on an almost Greek simplicity of line.

   (A) flamboyant     (B) austere
   (C) inconspicuous     (D) hypothetical
   (E) derivative

5. We lost confidence in him because he never _____ the grandiose promises he had made.

   (A) forgot about
   (B) reneged on
   (C) tired of
   (D) delivered on
   (E) retreated from

6. Perhaps because something in us instinctively distrusts such displays of natural fluency, some readers approach John Updike's fiction with _____.

   (A) indifference     (B) suspicion
   (C) veneration     (D) enthusiasm
   (E) eloquence

7. Because she had a reputation for _____ , we were surprised and pleased when she greeted us so _____ .

   (A) insolence..informally
   (B) insouciance..cordially
   (C) graciousness..amiably
   (D) arrogance..disdainfully
   (E) aloofness..affably

8. Just as disloyalty is the mark of the traitor, _____ is the mark of the _____.

   (A) timorousness..hero
   (B) temerity..renegade
   (C) avarice..philanthropist
   (D) cowardice..craven
   (E) vanity..flatterer

9. We now know that what constitutes practically all of matter is empty space: relatively enormous _____ in which revolve infinitesimal particles so _____ that they have never been seen or photographed.

   (A) crescendos..minute
   (B) enigmas..static
   (C) conglomerates..vague
   (D) abstractions..colorful
   (E) voids..small

10. Brilliant yet disturbing, James Baldwin's *The Fire Next Time* is both so eloquent in its passion and so _____ in its candor that it is bound to _____ any reader.

    (A) bitter..soothe
    (B) romantic..appall
    (C) searing..unsettle
    (D) indifferent..disappoint
    (E) frank..bore

## EXERCISE D

1. The scientist maintains that any hypothesis must explain what has already been discovered and must be constantly _____ by future findings.

   (A) confirmed    (B) invalidated
   (C) disregarded    (D) equaled
   (E) reversed

2. Traffic speed limits are set at a level that achieves some balance between the danger of _____ speed and the desire of most people to travel as quickly as possible.

   (A) minimal    (B) normal
   (C) prudent    (D) inadvertent
   (E) excessive

3. Written in an engaging style, the book provides a comprehensive overview of European wines that should prove inviting to everyone from the virtual _____ to the experienced connoisseur.

   (A) prodigal    (B) novice
   (C) zealot    (D) miser
   (E) glutton

4. In view of the interrelationships among the African-American leaders treated in this anthology, a certain amount of _____ among some of the essays presented is inevitable.

   (A) overlapping    (B) inaccuracy
   (C) pomposity    (D) exaggeration
   (E) objectivity

5. Most Antarctic animals _____ depend on the tiny shrimplike krill, either feeding on them directly, like the humpback whale, or consuming species that feed on them.

   (A) seldom    (B) ultimately
   (C) needlessly    (D) immediately
   (E) marginally

6. Andy Warhol was an inspired _____ of his own art: he had a true gift for publicity.

   (A) assessor    (B) promoter
   (C) curator    (D) benefactor
   (E) luminary

7. Japan's industrial success is _____ in part to its tradition of group effort and _____ , as opposed to the tradition of individual personal achievement common in many other industrial nations.

   (A) responsive..independence
   (B) related..misdirection
   (C) equivalent..solidarity
   (D) subordinate..individuality
   (E) attributable..cooperation

8. Aimed at _____ European attempts to seize territory in the Americas, the Monroe Doctrine was a strong warning to _____ foreign powers.

   (A) abetting..impertinent
   (B) eliminating..credulous
   (C) assisting..remote
   (D) preventing..overt
   (E) curbing..predatory

9. Because he was cynical, he was reluctant to _____ the _____ of any kind act until he had ruled out all possible hidden uncharitable motives.

   (A) question..benevolence
   (B) acknowledge..wisdom
   (C) credit..unselfishness
   (D) endure..loss
   (E) witness..outcome

10. The concept of individual freedom grew from political and moral convictions that _____ the closed and _____ world of feudalism into a more open and dynamic society.

    (A) galvanized..vibrant
    (B) converted..irreverent
    (C) transformed..hierarchical
    (D) recast..vital
    (E) merged..unregulated

## EXERCISE E

1. Some students are _____ in choosing their classes; that is, they want to take only the courses for which they see immediate value.

   (A) theoretical   (B) impartial
   (C) pragmatic   (D) idealistic
   (E) opinionated

2. Chaotic in conception but not in _____, Kelly's canvases are as neat as the proverbial pin.

   (A) conceit   (B) theory
   (C) execution   (D) origin
   (E) intent

3. Although Josephine Tey was arguably as good a mystery writer as Agatha Christie, she was clearly far less _____ than Christie, having written only six books in comparison to Christie's sixty.

   (A) coherent   (B) prolific
   (C) equivocal   (D) pretentious
   (E) gripping

4. In the North American tribes, men were the representational artists, creating drawings of hunters and animals; women, on the other hand, traditionally _____ abstract, geometrical compositions.

   (A) devised   (B) shunned
   (C) decried   (D) impersonated
   (E) prefigured

5. The counselor viewed divorce not as a single circumscribed event but as _____ of changing family relationships—as a process that begins during the failing marriage and extends over many years.

   (A) a continuum     (B) an episode
   (C) a parody     (D) a denial
   (E) an elimination

6. The systems analyst hesitated to talk to strangers about her highly specialized work, because she feared it was too _____ for people uninitiated in the field to understand.

   (A) intriguing     (B) derivative
   (C) frivolous     (D) esoteric
   (E) rudimentary

7. Lavish in visual beauty, the film *Lawrence of Arabia* nevertheless boasts _____ of style: it knows how much can be shown in a single shot, how much can be said in a few words.

   (A) nonchalance     (B) economy
   (C) autonomy     (D) frivolity
   (E) arrogance

8. The verbose and _____ style of the late Victorian novel is totally unlike the _____ of a minimalist like Hemingway.

   (A) chatty..prolixity
   (B) awkward..consistency
   (C) redundant..terseness
   (D) eloquent..logistics
   (E) concise..floridity

9. Both the popular shows *China Beach* and *Tour of Duty* reflect the way dissent has become _____ in America; what were radical antiwar attitudes in the 1960s are now _____ TV attitudes.

   (A) domesticated..mainstream
   (B) obsolete..militant
   (C) meaningful..unfashionable
   (D) sensationalized..trite
   (E) troublesome..conventional

10. He was a _____ employee, but the _____ and exhaustive research that he performed made it worthwhile for his employers to put up with his difficult moods.

    (A) domineering..biased
    (B) congenial..exemplary
    (C) popular..pretentious
    (D) fastidious..garbled
    (E) cantankerous..meticulous

# Answer Key

## EXERCISE A

1. **D**   3. **B**   5. **C**   7. **E**   9. **D**
2. **C**   4. **D**   6. **A**   8. **E**   10. **C**

## EXERCISE B

1. **D**   3. **C**   5. **D**   7. **A**   9. **C**
2. **E**   4. **C**   6. **D**   8. **E**   10. **B**

## EXERCISE C

1. **C**   3. **D**   5. **D**   7. **E**   9. **E**
2. **A**   4. **A**   6. **B**   8. **D**   10. **C**

## EXERCISE D

1. **A**   3. **B**   5. **B**   7. **E**   9. **C**
2. **E**   4. **A**   6. **B**   8. **E**   10. **C**

## EXERCISE E

1. **C**   3. **B**   5. **A**   7. **B**   9. **A**
2. **C**   4. **A**   6. **D**   8. **C**   10. **E**

# Answer Explanations

## EXERCISE A

1. **(D)** Because the word-of-mouth comments were good, the play did not *close*. Watch out for the word *not*. It's a small but important word, one easy to overlook.
2. **(C)** The hawk is a *predatory* bird; it preys on chickens and other small creatures.
3. **(B)** You will not make a strong impression on your audience if you are *restrained* (reserved; reticent).
4. **(D)** By definition, a *volatile* (unstable) mixture tends to vaporize or evaporate.
5. **(C)** By definition, *elegiac* (like an elegy; sorrowful) verse is melancholy; often, such verse laments a death.
6. **(A)** *Despite* is a contrast clue. Despite his *disheveled* (untidy) appearance, he got a job that required him to be neat.
7. **(E)** The tidal wave was *devastating* (extremely destructive) because it *inundated* (flooded) many villages.
8. **(E)** By definition, biodegradable products *decompose* (disintegrate; break down).
9. **(D)** Barbara Tuchman *pursued* (followed) a scholarly career. She was famous for her vivid style and her *prodigious* (exceptional; extraordinary) erudition. Note that the second missing word must be positive. If you tested the second blank first, you could have eliminated Choices A, C, and E.
10. **(C)** A person who had been promised a definite answer would most likely be *annoyed* by a *noncommittal* (evasive; vague; indefinite) reply.

## EXERCISE B

1. **(D)** A *hazardous* (dangerous) occupation would make someone a poor insurance risk.
2. **(E)** The artist combines profundity and *fun*. The sentence's first clause is your key to the meaning of the missing word.
3. **(C)** An organism that derives some or all of its nourishment from a host is by definition *parasitic*.
4. **(C)** Employers would most likely promote an *assiduous* (diligent; hard-working) worker.

5. **(D)** The Congresswoman voted against bills that would have benefited labor. Her voting record *belied* (contradicted) the impression that she was a friend of labor.
6. **(D)** *Specious* (faulty) reasoning would be unlikely to *deceive* (fool) anyone.
7. **(A)** The panel wishes to *alleviate* (ease; lessen) the problem by switching to a more *rigorous* (exact) method of the inspection.
8. **(E)** The inspector could not hide his *scorn* for his superior officer. Instead, he imprudently (unwisely) made *scathing* (scornful; cutting) remarks about his boss.
9. **(C)** People would most likely be surprised to have a dull, *pedestrian* speaker make an electrifying, dynamic speech.
10. **(B)** Because he was shy, Madison was *uncomfortable* at public gatherings. His shyness and his hypochondria (excessive worrying about his health) made him an *unlikely* person to be involved in politics.

## EXERCISE C

1. **(C)** Instead of discussing abstract principles, the Convention dealt with *concrete* (specific; actual) proposals.
2. **(A)** He was *dilatory* (tardy; slow) in making his car payments.
3. **(D)** The child pouted (showed her displeasure) and became *sullen* (angry; sulky) when her parents ignored her. Note that you are looking for a negative word.
4. **(A)** The sentence contrasts the simple lines of modern architecture with the *flamboyant* (showy; flashy) trimming on older buildings.
5. **(D)** Someone who never *delivered on* (lived up to) the promises he made would soon cause people to distrust him.
6. **(B)** Some readers approach Updike's fluent prose with *suspicion* (doubt; mistrust). They distrust his fluency.
7. **(E)** Because she had a reputation for *aloofness* (coldness; standoffishness), they were pleasantly surprised when she greeted them *affably* (warmly; cordially). Note the cause and effect signal here.
8. **(D)** *Cowardice* is the mark of the *craven* (coward).

9. **(E)** Matter consists of *voids* (empty spaces) in which extremely *small* particles revolve. The opening clause contains your key to the first missing word.

10. **(C)** Baldwin's book is so *searing* (severely critical; scorching) in its frankness or candor that it is bound to *unsettle* (disturb) any reader. The opening phrase "Brilliant yet disturbing" is your key to the missing words.

## EXERCISE D

1. **(A)** A hypothesis must be *confirmed* (corroborated; backed up) by future discoveries. Otherwise, it will be proven worthless.

2. **(E)** *Excessive* (extreme) speed is dangerous.

3. **(B)** The book should interest a wide range of readers: everyone from the *novice* (beginner) wine-taster to the experienced connoisseur.

4. **(A)** The African-American leaders discussed in the essays were involved with one another in various ways. (There were *interrelationships* among them.) Therefore, it makes sense for there to be some *overlapping* (elements in common) among the essays.

5. **(B)** Most of these animals *ultimately* (in the end) get their nourishment from krill, either directly, by eating krill themselves, or indirectly, by feeding on other species that eat krill.

6. **(B)** Someone who has a gift for publicity clearly would be a good *promoter* (publicity organizer; advocate) of his own art.

7. **(E)** Japan's success is *attributable* (can be ascribed or credited) to Japan's tradition of group effort and *cooperation* (working together). The contrast signal "as opposed to" provides a key to the meaning of the second missing word.

8. **(E)** The Monroe Doctrine was aimed at *curbing* (restraining) attempts to seize land by *predatory* (plundering; exploiting) foreign powers. Note that the second missing word must be negative.

Good + Bad –

9. **(C)** Someone cynical (disbelieving) would be reluctant to *credit* (believe) the *unselfishness* of any kind act without checking further.

10. **(C)** Altered political and moral convictions *transformed* (changed) the *hierarchical* (organized by rank; ruled by a closed elite) world of feudalism into a more dynamic society.

## EXERCISE E

1. **(C)** *Pragmatic* (practical) students choose classes that have immediate value.

2. **(C)** The sentence contrasts the conception of Kelly's paintings with their *execution* (implementation; the way the idea is carried out).

3. **(B)** Tey was less *prolific* (productive) than Christie: she wrote fewer books.

4. **(A)** Women *devised* (created; planned) abstract designs.

5. **(A)** The counselor saw divorce as a *continuum* (a continuous whole that can be divided only arbitrarily) or ongoing process.

6. **(D)** Something highly specialized that is hard to discuss with people uninitiated in the field is by definition *esoteric* (obscure; arcane; only for initiates).

7. **(B)** By accomplishing a great deal with just a few words or a single shot, the film demonstrates *economy* (efficient use of resources) of style. The contrast clue *nevertheless* sets up the contrast between the film's lavishness or extravagance of visual beauty and its economy of style.

8. **(C)** The late Victorian novel tends to be wordy and *redundant* (repetitive). The novels of Hemingway tend to be *terse* (concise and to the point). Note the contrast signal *unlike*.

9. **(A)** Dissent has become *domesticated* (tame); radical attitudes are now *mainstream* (conventional).

10. **(E)** A *cantankerous* (bad-tempered) person by definition has difficult moods. Employers would not put up with such a difficult employee unless he did exceptionally good work, in this case, *meticulous* (extremely careful) and exhaustive research.

## SENTENCE COMPLETION WRAP-UP

1. Before you look at the answer choices, read the sentence, substituting the word "blank" for the missing word.

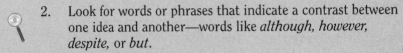

2. Look for words or phrases that indicate a contrast between one idea and another—words like *although, however, despite,* or *but*.

3. Look for words or phrases that indicate support for a concept—words such as *likewise, similarly, in the same way, and, in addition, additionally,* and *also*.

4. Look for words or phrases that indicate that one thing causes another—words like *because, since, therefore,* or *thus*.

5. Look for signals that indicate a word is being defined—phrases such as *in other words, that is,* or *which means,* and special punctuation clues, such as commas, hyphens, and parentheses.

6. If you're having vocabulary trouble, look for familiar word parts—prefixes, suffixes, and roots—in unfamiliar words.

7. Work out whether the missing word is positive (+) or negative (−). Then test the answer choices for their positive or negative sense, eliminating those that don't work.

8. In a sentence completion question with two blanks, eliminate answer choices by testing one blank at a time.

## CHAPTER 2

# Improving Critical Reading Comprehension

*Now more than ever, doing well on the critical reading questions can make the difference between success and failure on the PSAT. The most numerous questions in each verbal section, they are also the most time-consuming and the ones most likely to bog you down. However, you* can *handle them, and this chapter will show you how.*

## FREQUENTLY ASKED QUESTIONS

1. **How can I become a better reader?**
   **Read, Read, Read!**
   Just do it.

   There is no substitute for extensive reading to prepare you for the PSAT and for college work. The only way to build up your proficiency in reading is by reading books of all kinds. As you read, you will develop speed, stamina, and the ability to comprehend the printed page. But if you want to turn yourself into the kind of reader the colleges are looking for, you must develop the habit of reading—closely and critically—every day.

2. **What sort of material should I read?**
   Challenge yourself. Don't limit your reading to light fiction, graphic novels, and Xbox reviews. Branch out a bit. Try to develop an interest in as many fields as you can.

   Check out some of these magazines:

   - *The New Yorker*
   - *Smithsonian*
   - *The New York Review of Books*
   - *National Geographic*
   - *Natural History*
   - *Harper's Magazine*

   Explore popular encyclopedias on the Web. You'll find articles on literature, music, science, philosophy, history, the arts—the whole range of fields touched on by the PSAT. If you take time to sample these fields, you won't find the subject matter of the reading passages on the PSAT strange.

**3.** **On the PSAT, is it better to read the passage first or the questions first?**
The answer is, it depends on the passage, and *it depends on you*. If you are a super fast reader faced with one of the 100-word short reading passages, you may want to head for the questions first. It all depends on how good your visual memory is and on how good at scanning you are. If you're not a speed demon at reading, your best move may be to skim the whole passage before you read the questions. Only you can decide which method suits you best.

**THE QUESTIONS-FIRST APPROACH**
• As you read each question, be on the lookout for key words, either in the question itself or among the answer choices.
• Run your eye down the passage, looking for those key words or their synonyms. (That's called *scanning*.)
• When you spot a key word in a sentence, read that sentence and a couple of sentences around it.
• Decide whether you can confidently answer the question on the basis of just that part of the passage.
• Check to see whether your answer is correct.

## GENERAL TIPS: WORKING YOUR WAY THROUGH THE READING SECTIONS

**1.** **Tackle the short passages before the long ones.** Use them as a warm-up for the longer passages that follow.

**2.** **Tackle passages with familiar subjects before passages with unfamiliar ones.** It's hard to concentrate when you read about something wholly unfamiliar to you. Give yourself a break. In each section, first tackle the reading passage that interests you or deals with the topic about which you have a clue. Then move on to the other passage. You'll do better that way.

**3.** **If you are stumped by a tough reading question, move on, but do *not* skip the other questions on that passage.** Remember, the critical reading questions following each passage are not arranged in order of difficulty. They tend to be arranged sequentially: questions on paragraph 1 come before questions on paragraph 2. So try *all* the questions on the passage. That tough question may be just one question away from one that's easy for you.

**4.** **Do not zip back and forth between passages.** Stick with one passage until you feel sure you've answered all the questions you can on that passage. (If you don't, you'll probably have to waste time rereading the passage when you come back to it.) Before moving on to the next passage, be sure to go back over any questions you marked to come back to. In answering other questions on the passage, you may have acquired some information that will help you answer the questions you skipped.

5. **Read as fast as you can with understanding, but don't force yourself to rush.** Do not worry about the time. If you worry about not finishing the test, you will start taking shortcuts and miss the correct answer in your rush.

6. **Try to anticipate what the passage will be about.** As you read the italicized introductory material and tackle the passage's opening sentences, ask yourself who or what the author is talking about.

7. **Read with a purpose.** Try to spot what kind of writing this is, what techniques are used, who its intended audience is, and how the author feels about the subject. Be on the lookout for names, dates, and places. In particular, try to remember where in the passage the author makes major points. Then, when you start looking for the phrase or sentence that will justify your answer choice, you may be able to save time by zipping back to that section of the passage without having to reread the whole thing.

8. **Read the footnotes.** Duh!

9. **When you tackle the questions, go back to the passage to check each answer choice.** Do not rely on your memory, and above all, do not ignore the passage and just answer questions based on other things you've read. Remember, the questions are asking you about what this author has to say about the subject, not about what some other author you once read said about it in another book.

10. **Use the line references in the questions to get quickly to the correct spot in the passage.** It takes less time to locate a line number than to spot a word or phrase. Use the line numbers to orient yourself in the text.

11. **When dealing with the double passages, tackle them one at a time.** The questions are organized sequentially: questions about Passage 1 come before questions about Passage 2. So, do things in order. First read Passage 1; then jump straight to the questions and answer all the questions on Passage 1. Next read Passage 2; then answer all the questions on Passage 2. Finally, tackle the two or three questions that refer to both passages. Go back to both passages as needed.

    Occasionally a couple of questions referring to both passages will come before the questions on Passage 1. Do not let this throw you. Use your common sense. You've just read the first passage. Skip the one or two questions on both passages, and head straight for the questions about Passage 1. Answer them. Then read Passage 2. Answer the questions on Passage 2. Finally, go back to the questions you skipped and answer them (plus any other questions at the end of the set that refer to both passages). This is not rocket science. One thing, though: whenever you skip from question to question or from passage to passage, *be sure you are filling in the right spaces on your answer sheet.*

12. **Watch out for words or phrases in the questions that can clue you in to the kind of question being asked.** If you can recognize just what a given question is asking for, you'll be better able to tell which particular reading tactic to apply.

Now that you have a general idea about how to work your way through the reading sections, it's time to think about how to handle the different reading question types.

- **Vocabulary**—quick questions (you have to figure out the meaning of an individual word)
- **Main Idea**—big picture questions (you have to figure out the central point the author is trying to make)
- **Specific Detail**—narrow focus questions (you have to zoom in on specific facts)
- **Inference**—logic questions (you have to figure out what the author is suggesting or stating indirectly)
- **Attitude/Tone**—emotion questions (you have to figure out how the author feels about something or someone)
- **Literary Technique**—technical questions (you have to know the meaning of literary terms)
- **Logic/Application**—advanced logic questions (you have to judge the strength or weakness of the author's argument and figure out how it might apply in other situations)

On the following pages you will get to work through several questions of each type, learning to handle them as you go. All these questions are based on a long reading passage from *The New York Times*. You may find the passage challenging, but you can take as much time as you need to figure it out.

---

*The following passage is taken from an article on mathematical and scientific illiteracy published in* The New York Times *in January 1989, as Ronald and Nancy Reagan left the White House.*

The abstractness of mathematics is a great obstacle for many intelligent people. Such people may readily understand narrative particulars, but strongly resist impersonal generalities. Since numbers, science, and such generalities are
*Line* intimately related, this resistance can lead to an almost willful mathematical and
(5) scientific illiteracy. Numbers have appeal for many only if they're associated with them personally—hence part of the attraction of astrology, biorhythms, Tarot cards and the I Ching, all individually customized "sciences."
Mathematical illiteracy and the attitudes underlying it provide in fact a fertile soil for the growth of pseudoscience. In *Pseudoscience and Society in Nine-*
(10) *teenth-Century America,* Arthur Wrobel remarks that belief in phrenology, homeopathy, and hydropathy was not confined to the poor and the ignorant, but pervaded much of nineteenth-century literature. Such credulity is not as extensive in contemporary literature, but astrology is one pseudoscience that does seem to engage a big segment of the reading public. Literary allusions to it
(15) abound, appearing in everything from Shakespeare to Dom DeLillo's *Libra*. A 1986 Gallup poll showed that 52 percent of American teenagers subscribe to it, as does at least 50 percent of the nation's departing First Couple.
Given these figures, it may not be entirely inappropriate to note here that no mechanism through which the alleged zodiacal influences exert themselves has
(20) ever been specified by astrologers. Gravity certainly cannot account for these natal influences, since even the gravitational pull of the attending obstetrician is orders of magnitude greater than that of the relevant planet or planets. Nor is there any empirical evidence; top astrologers (as determined by their peers) have failed repeatedly to associate personality profiles with astrological data at a rate
(25) higher than that of chance. Neither of these fatal objections to astrology, of course, is likely to carry much weight with literate but innumerate people who don't estimate magnitudes or probabilities, or who are over-impressed by vague coincidences yet unmoved by overwhelming statistical evidence.

# VOCABULARY QUESTIONS

Vocabulary-in-context questions are easy to spot. They look like this:

> In line 13, "frabbledrab" most nearly means
>
> (A) snipsnop
> (B) kangasplat
> (C) replix
> (D) oggitty
> (E) thrumble

**Tip 1**

**Tackle vocabulary-in-context questions the same way you do sentence completion questions.** First, read the sentence, substituting "blank" for the word in quotes. Think of words you know that might make sense in the context. Then test each answer choice, substituting it in the sentence for the word in quotes. Ask yourself whether this particular answer choice makes sense in the specific context.

## Vocabulary Power Practice

1. In line 11, "confined" most nearly means

   (A) enclosed
   (B) jailed
   (C) isolated
   (D) restricted
   (E) preached

**WORDS HAVE MULTIPLE MEANINGS**

A *run* in baseball is *not* the same thing as a *run* in your stocking.

2. In line 14, "engage" most nearly means

   (A) hire
   (B) reserve
   (C) attract
   (D) confront
   (E) interlock

 Vocabulary-in-context questions take hardly any time to answer. If you're running out of time, answer them first.

3. In line 16, "subscribe to" most nearly means

   (A) sign up for
   (B) agree with
   (C) write about
   (D) suffer from
   (E) pay for

## Check Your Answers

1. **(D)** The original sentence states that "belief...was not _____ to the poor and the ignorant, but pervaded much of nineteenth-century literature." Non-scientific belief was widespread in the nineteenth century; it pervaded or filled the literature of the period. Therefore, it was not *restricted* or confined to poor, ignorant people, but had spread to the well-to-do, literate classes.

Note that *many* of the answer choices could be substitutes for "confined" *in other contexts*. For example, if the sentence were "The dogcatcher *confined* dozens of stray animals in the pound," Choice A, *enclosed*, would be the best word to substitute. Your job is to spot which meaning of the word works this time.

2. **(C)** Again, look at the sentence, substituting "blank" for the key word. "Astrology...does seem to *blank* a big segment of the reading public." What word would make sense in the context? Summarize what's going on. The author is reacting to the strong hold that astrology has on the reading public. Despite its being a pseudoscience, astrology has managed to *attract* or involve many members of the reading public. The correct answer is Choice C.

3. **(B)** "52 percent of American teenagers *blank* it, as does at least 50 percent of the nation's departing First Couple." The author has been talking about how many people have been attracted or drawn to astrology. Many of these people have been more or less won over by it: they accept it as a valid belief. Thus, the teenagers (and the Reagans) who *subscribe to* astrology *agree with* it, going along with its doctrines. Once again, you've found a word that makes sense in context.

*The following passage is taken from an article on mathematical and scientific illiteracy published in* The New York Times *in January 1989, as Ronald and Nancy Reagan left the White House.*

The abstractness of mathematics is a great obstacle for many intelligent people. Such people may readily understand narrative particulars, but strongly resist impersonal generalities. Since numbers, science, and such generalities are

*Line*
*(5)* intimately related, this resistance can lead to an almost willful mathematical and scientific illiteracy. Numbers have appeal for many only if they're associated with them personally—hence part of the attraction of astrology, biorhythms, Tarot cards and the I Ching, all individually customized "sciences."

Mathematical illiteracy and the attitudes underlying it provide in fact a fertile soil for the growth of pseudoscience. In *Pseudoscience and Society in Nine-*
*(10)* *teenth-Century America,* Arthur Wrobel remarks that belief in phrenology, homeopathy, and hydropathy was not confined to the poor and the ignorant, but pervaded much of nineteenth-century literature. Such credulity is not as extensive in contemporary literature, but astrology is one pseudoscience that does seem to engage a big segment of the reading public. Literary allusions to it
*(15)* abound, appearing in everything from Shakespeare to Dom DeLillo's *Libra*. A 1986 Gallup poll showed that 52 percent of American teenagers subscribe to it, as does at least 50 percent of the nation's departing First Couple.

Given these figures, it may not be entirely inappropriate to note here that no mechanism through which the alleged zodiacal influences exert themselves has
*(20)* ever been specified by astrologers. Gravity certainly cannot account for these natal influences, since even the gravitational pull of the attending obstetrician is orders of magnitude greater than that of the relevant planet or planets. Nor is there any empirical evidence; top astrologers (as determined by their peers) have failed repeatedly to associate personality profiles with astrological data at a rate
*(25)* higher than that of chance. Neither of these fatal objections to astrology, of course, is likely to carry much weight with literate but innumerate people who don't estimate magnitudes or probabilities, or who are over-impressed by vague coincidences yet unmoved by overwhelming statistical evidence.

# MAIN IDEA QUESTIONS

Main idea questions look like this:

> Which of the following best states the central thought of the passage?
> The primary purpose of the passage is to…
> In the second paragraph of the passage, the author primarily stresses that…

## Tip 2

**When asked to find a passage's main idea, be sure to check the opening and summary sentences of each paragraph.** Authors often orient readers with a sentence that expresses a paragraph's main idea concisely. Although such *topic sentences* may appear anywhere in the paragraph, you can usually find them in the opening or closing sentences.

In PSAT reading passages, topic sentences are sometimes implied rather than stated directly. If you cannot find a topic sentence, ask yourself these questions:

- Who or what is this passage about?
- What feature of this subject is the author talking about?
- What is the author trying to get across about this feature of the subject?

You'll be on your way to locating the passage's main idea.

## Main Idea Power Practice

1. In the final paragraph of the passage, the author stresses that

   (A) astrologers are working to discover the mechanisms through which the zodiac affects human lives
   (B) the planets are able to influence people in mysterious, imperceptible ways
   (C) top astrologers strive to maintain accurate personality profiles of their clientele
   (D) astrologers have been unable to corroborate their theories scientifically
   (E) astrologers are more mechanically minded than mathematically literate

2. The author's primary purpose throughout the passage is to

   (A) contrast astrology and other contemporary pseudosciences with phrenology, homeopathy, and hydropathy
   (B) trace the development of the current belief in astrology to its nineteenth-century roots
   (C) apologize for the rise of mathematical and scientific illiteracy in the present day
   (D) disprove the difficulty of achieving universal mathematical and scientific literacy
   (E) relate mathematical illiteracy to the prevalence of invalid pseudoscientific beliefs today

### Check Your Answers

1. **(D)** The author spends the final paragraph debunking (discrediting; exposing) the claims of astrologers. To their claim that the planets in the heavens at the time of one's birth influence one's destiny, he retorts that the attending physician exerts more gravitational pull on the infant than the distant planets do. To their claim that astrological data can be used to predict personality types, he retorts that no valid correlation exists between astrological predictions and the results of scientifically legit-

imate personality profiles. Throughout the paragraph, he stresses that *astrologers have been unable to corroborate* (confirm or back up) *their theories scientifically*.

2. **(E)** Go back to the passage and look at the opening sentences of the three paragraphs and the final sentence of the third paragraph. (The shaded bits.) What are these sentences talking about? Mathematical illiteracy. What aspect of mathematical illiteracy are they talking about? They're talking about how it *relates to the prevalence* (widespread acceptance) of astrology and other *invalid pseudoscientific beliefs today*.

Choice A is incorrect. Although the author mentions phrenology and the other pseudosciences, he never contrasts them with astrology. Choice B is incorrect; although the author discusses astrology at length, his chief purpose is to use astrology as an example of a contemporary pseudoscientific belief, not to trace its nineteenth-century connections. Choice C is incorrect; the author is irritated by the state of mathematical and scientific illiteracy today, not apologetic about it. Choice D is incorrect; nothing in the passage supports it.

---

*The following passage is taken from an article on mathematical and scientific illiteracy published in* The New York Times *in January 1989, as Ronald and Nancy Reagan left the White House.*

The abstractness of mathematics is a great obstacle for many intelligent people. Such people may readily understand narrative particulars, but strongly resist impersonal generalities. Since numbers, science, and such generalities are

*Line* intimately related, this resistance can lead to an almost willful mathematical and
*(5)* scientific illiteracy. Numbers have appeal for many only if they're associated with them personally—hence part of the attraction of astrology, biorhythms, Tarot cards and the I Ching, all individually customized "sciences."

Mathematical illiteracy and the attitudes underlying it provide in fact a fertile soil for the growth of pseudoscience. In *Pseudoscience and Society in Nine-*
*(10)* *teenth-Century America,* Arthur Wrobel remarks that belief in phrenology, homeopathy, and hydropathy was not confined to the poor and the ignorant, but pervaded much of nineteenth-century literature. Such credulity is not as extensive in contemporary literature, but astrology is one pseudoscience that does seem to engage a big segment of the reading public. Literary allusions to it
*(15)* abound, appearing in everything from Shakespeare to Dom DeLillo's *Libra.* A 1986 Gallup poll showed that 52 percent of American teenagers subscribe to it, as does at least 50 percent of the nation's departing First Couple.

Given these figures, it may not be entirely inappropriate to note here that no mechanism through which the alleged zodiacal influences exert themselves has
*(20)* ever been specified by astrologers. Gravity certainly cannot account for these natal influences, since even the gravitational pull of the attending obstetrician is orders of magnitude greater than that of the relevant planet or planets. Nor is there any empirical evidence; top astrologers (as determined by their peers) have failed repeatedly to associate personality profiles with astrological data at a rate
*(25)* higher than that of chance. Neither of these fatal objections to astrology, of course, is likely to carry much weight with literate but innumerate people who don't estimate magnitudes or probabilities, or who are over-impressed by vague coincidences yet unmoved by overwhelming statistical evidence.

# SPECIFIC DETAIL QUESTIONS

Specific detail questions often begin like this:

> According to the author, what is the reason for…
> The "fatal objections" to astrology referred to in line 25 are…
> To the author, a belief in astrology is…

## Tip 3

**When you answer specific detail questions, point to the precise words in the passage that support your answer choice.** You must be *sure* that the answer you select is in the passage. That means you must find a word or sentence or group of sentences that justifies your choice. Do *not* pick an answer just because it agrees with your personal opinions or with information on the subject that you've gotten from other sources.

---

**FACT VS. OPINION**

**Fact:** In 1986, a Gallup poll sampled American teenagers' views on astrology.
(You can verify this by checking old newspaper reports and Gallup poll publications.)

**Opinion:** Patsy believes that people born under the sign of Scorpio are passionate.
(Well, that's what *she* believes…)

---

## Specific Detail Power Practice

1. Which of the following best summarizes the reason given in lines 1–5 for the extent of mathematical and scientific illiteracy today?

   (A) Many intelligent people dislike the intimacy of the connection between numbers and science.
   (B) Many otherwise intelligent people have difficulty dealing with impersonal, abstract concepts.
   (C) Intelligent people prefer speaking in generalities to narrating particular incidents.
   (D) Few people are able to appreciate the benefits of an individually customized science.
   (E) People today no longer cherish their personal associations with numbers.

2. According to the author, "phrenology, homeopathy, and hydropathy" (lines 10–11) are all

   (A) scholarly allusions
   (B) pseudosciences
   (C) branches of astrology
   (D) forms of society
   (E) mechanisms

3. The "figures" referred to in line 18 are the

   (A) pseudosciences
   (B) literary references
   (C) prominent political leaders
   (D) numbers involved in calculating horoscopes
   (E) statistics concerning believers in astrology

4. The term "innumerate" (line 26) is best interpreted to mean

   (A) various in kind
   (B) too numerous to count
   (C) scientifically sophisticated
   (D) unable to use mathematics
   (E) indifferent to astrology

## Check Your Answers

1. **(B)** In the opening lines, the author states that the abstractness of mathematics is a problem for many intelligent people. People resist dealing with abstractions ("impersonal generalities"). However, to work in science or math, you must deal with abstractions: numbers, science, and abstractions are "intimately connected." *Because* many otherwise intelligent people have difficulty dealing with impersonal, abstract concepts, these people wind up mathematically and scientifically illiterate. That, according to the author, is the reason for much of the mathematical and scientific illiteracy we see today. The correct answer is Choice B.

2. **(B)** Phrenology, homeopathy, and hydropathy are three beliefs mentioned in the book titled *Pseudoscience and Society in Nineteenth-Century America*. Throughout the passage, the author is critical of various beliefs he categorizes as unscientific. He groups such beliefs together as *pseudosciences*, false sciences in which many otherwise intelligent individuals believe. Phrenology is the belief that the shape of your skull indicates your character traits and mental abilities. Homeopathy is the belief that you can cure disease by giving someone who is ill extremely small doses of a substance that would produce in someone healthy symptoms similar to those of the disease. Hydropathy is the belief that you can cure disease by giving someone ill huge amounts of water (both internally and externally). To the author, all three beliefs are *pseudosciences*.

   Note the phrase "to the author." The question is not asking you what *you* think about phrenology, homeopathy, and hydropathy. It is asking you what *the author* thinks of these beliefs.

3. **(E)** The paragraph immediately preceding line 18 gives the percentage of American teenagers who go along with astrology. It also refers to the well-known fact that Nancy Reagan (half of "the nation's departing First Couple") believed in astrology (she followed the advice of astrologers in setting up her husband's engagements during his presidency) and that her husband might possibly have believed in it as well. Thus, the figures referred to are *statistics concerning believers in astrology*.

4. **(D)** The author contrasts the word "innumerate" with the word "literate." Since *illiterate* means unable to read, *innumerate* must mean unable to use mathematics.

   You can use your knowledge of word parts to answer this question. *In-* means not; *numer-* means number. *Innumerate* means not having numbers, unable to use numbers. Watch out, however, for eye-catchers. *Innumerable* means uncountable, too many or too numerous for anyone to count.

*The following passage is taken from an article on mathematical and scientific illiteracy published in* The New York Times *in January 1989, as Ronald and Nancy Reagan left the White House.*

The abstractness of mathematics is a great obstacle for many intelligent people. Such people may readily understand narrative particulars, but strongly resist impersonal generalities. Since numbers, science, and such generalities are
Line intimately related, this resistance can lead to an almost willful mathematical and
(5) scientific illiteracy. Numbers have appeal for many only if they're associated with them personally—hence part of the attraction of astrology, biorhythms, Tarot cards and the I Ching, all individually customized "sciences."

Mathematical illiteracy and the attitudes underlying it provide in fact a fertile soil for the growth of pseudoscience. In *Pseudoscience and Society in Nine-*
(10) *teenth-Century America,* Arthur Wrobel remarks that belief in phrenology, homeopathy, and hydropathy was not confined to the poor and the ignorant, but pervaded much of nineteenth-century literature. Such credulity is not as extensive in contemporary literature, but astrology is one pseudoscience that does seem to engage a big segment of the reading public. Literary allusions to it
(15) abound, appearing in everything from Shakespeare to Dom DeLillo's *Libra*. A 1986 Gallup poll showed that 52 percent of American teenagers subscribe to it, as does at least 50 percent of the nation's departing First Couple.

Given these figures, it may not be entirely inappropriate to note here that no mechanism through which the alleged zodiacal influences exert themselves has
(20) ever been specified by astrologers. Gravity certainly cannot account for these natal influences, since even the gravitational pull of the attending obstetrician is orders of magnitude greater than that of the relevant planet or planets. Nor is there any empirical evidence; top astrologers (as determined by their peers) have failed repeatedly to associate personality profiles with astrological data at a rate
(25) higher than that of chance. Neither of these fatal objections to astrology, of course, is likely to carry much weight with literate but innumerate people who don't estimate magnitudes or probabilities, or who are over-impressed by vague coincidences yet unmoved by overwhelming statistical evidence.

# INFERENCE QUESTIONS

Inference questions often begin like this:

> The author implies that...
> The passage suggests that...
> It can be inferred from the passage that...
> The author would most likely...
> The author probably considers...

**Tip 4**

**When you answer inference questions, look for what the passage logically suggests, but does *not* directly state.** Inference questions require you to use your judgment. You are drawing a conclusion based on what you have read in the text. Think about what the passage suggests. You must not take anything directly stated in the passage as an inference. Instead, you must look for clues in the passage that you can use in coming up with your own conclusion. Then you should choose as your answer a statement that logically follows from the information the author has given you.

## Inference Power Practice

1. Lines 5–7 ("Numbers . . . 'sciences'") suggest that the author thinks the individually customized sciences that he mentions are

   (A) impersonal
   (B) rewarding
   (C) personally appealing
   (D) fundamentally sound
   (E) unscientific

**DID YOU NOTICE?**
There are quotation marks around the word "sciences." Quotation marks often indicate that the word in quotes is being used in a special sense.

2. The author most likely regards the lack of empirical evidence for astrology as

   (A) an oversight on the part of the astrologers
   (B) a key argument against its validity
   (C) a flaw that will be corrected in time
   (D) the unfortunate result of too small a sampling
   (E) a major reason to keep searching for fresh data

## Check Your Answers

1. **(E)** Note the quotation marks around the word *sciences*. They are your clue that the author does not regard astrology, biorhythms, Tarot cards, and the I Ching as real sciences. Instead, he considers them *unscientific*.

2. **(B)** The final sentence of the paragraph characterizes these absences of empirical evidence as "fatal objections to astrology." In general, the author sees astrology as invalid, a pseudoscience, not a real science. If he were handed empirical experimental data that supported astrological theory, he probably would have a harder time rejecting it so sharply. Thus, he most likely regards the lack of empirical, observable evidence for astrology as *a key argument against its validity*.

*The following passage is taken from an article on mathematical and scientific illiteracy published in* The New York Times *in January 1989, as Ronald and Nancy Reagan left the White House.*

The abstractness of mathematics is a great obstacle for many intelligent people. Such people may readily understand narrative particulars, but strongly resist impersonal generalities. Since numbers, science, and such generalities are
*Line* intimately related, this resistance can lead to an almost willful mathematical and
(5) scientific illiteracy. Numbers have appeal for many only if they're associated with them personally—hence part of the attraction of astrology, biorhythms, Tarot cards and the I Ching, all individually customized "sciences."

Mathematical illiteracy and the attitudes underlying it provide in fact a fertile soil for the growth of pseudoscience. In *Pseudoscience and Society in Nine-*
(10) *teenth-Century America,* Arthur Wrobel remarks that belief in phrenology, homeopathy, and hydropathy was not confined to the poor and the ignorant, but pervaded much of nineteenth-century literature. Such credulity is not as exten-sive in contemporary literature, but astrology is one pseudoscience that does seem to engage a big segment of the reading public. Literary allusions to it
(15) abound, appearing in everything from Shakespeare to Dom DeLillo's *Libra.* A 1986 Gallup poll showed that 52 percent of American teenagers subscribe to it, as does at least 50 percent of the nation's departing First Couple.

Given these figures, it may not be entirely inappropriate to note here that no mechanism through which the alleged zodiacal influences exert themselves has
(20) ever been specified by astrologers. Gravity certainly cannot account for these natal influences, since even the gravitational pull of the attending obstetrician is orders of magnitude greater than that of the relevant planet or planets. Nor is there any empirical evidence; top astrologers (as determined by their peers) have failed repeatedly to associate personality profiles with astrological data at a rate
(25) higher than that of chance. Neither of these fatal objections to astrology, of course, is likely to carry much weight with literate but innumerate people who don't estimate magnitudes or probabilities, or who are over-impressed by vague coincidences yet unmoved by overwhelming statistical evidence.

# ATTITUDE/TONE QUESTIONS

Attitude/tone questions often look like this:

> The author's attitude toward...is...
> The author regards the idea that...with...
> The author's tone in the passage...

**Tip 5**

**When asked to figure out an author's attitude or tone, look for words that convey emotion, express values, or paint pictures.** These images and descriptive phrases get the author's feelings across.

## Attitude/Tone Power Practice

1. The author's attitude toward believers in astrology can best be described as one of

   (A) grudging respect
   (B) amused tolerance
   (C) open disdain
   (D) disguised hostility
   (E) puzzled fascination

2. The author's tone in referring to the nation's departing First Couple can best be described as

   (A) respectful
   (B) nostalgic
   (C) negative
   (D) mocking
   (E) effusive

---

**KNOW YOUR ATTITUDES**
(If you don't know any of these words, look them up.)

| | | |
|---|---|---|
| 😞 | SAD | *somber, melancholy, pessimistic, regretful* |
| 🙂 | HAPPY | *optimistic, sanguine, amused* |
| 😈 | EVIL GRIN | *mocking, sardonic, sarcastic, ironic, cynical, disdainful* |
| 😠 | ANGRY | *irate, outraged, incensed* |
| 😕 | FOOLISH | *baffled, puzzled, bemused, bewildered* |
| 😲 | SURPRISED | *astonished, astounded, awestruck* |
| 😬 | EMBARRASSED | *discomfited, mortified* |
| 😐 | WHATEVER | *indifferent, ambivalent, equivocal* |

---

## Check Your Answers

1. **(C)** The author states that people who believe in astrology are the sort who are "over-impressed by vague coincidences." Clearly, he feels that people should not be impressed by such vague coincidences. In his opinion, astrology as a science is fatally flawed. He looks down on the innumerate souls who continue to believe in it despite all the evidence against it. Thus, his attitude toward those who believe in astrology is one of *open disdain* or contempt.

2. **(D)** In saying that at least 50 percent of the Reagans subscribes to a belief in astrology, the author is making a little joke. He is referring to Nancy Reagan's dependence on astrologers and, at the same time, implying that 100 percent of the Reagans, that is, the first lady *and* the president, may believe in a subject he considers nonsensical. Even the term *First Couple*, all dressed up in capital letters, has a mocking ring. The correct answer is *mocking*, Choice D.

---

*The following passage is taken from an article on mathematical and scientific illiteracy published in* The New York Times *in January 1989, as Ronald and Nancy Reagan left the White House.*

The abstractness of mathematics is a great obstacle for many intelligent people. Such people may readily understand narrative particulars, but strongly resist impersonal generalities. Since numbers, science, and such generalities are
*Line* intimately related, this resistance can lead to an almost willful mathematical and
*(5)* scientific illiteracy. Numbers have appeal for many only if they're associated with them personally—hence part of the attraction of astrology, biorhythms, Tarot cards and the I Ching, all individually customized "sciences."

Mathematical illiteracy and the attitudes underlying it provide in fact a fertile soil for the growth of pseudoscience. In *Pseudoscience and Society in Nine-*
*(10)* *teenth-Century America,* Arthur Wrobel remarks that belief in phrenology, homeopathy, and hydropathy was not confined to the poor and the ignorant, but pervaded much of nineteenth-century literature. Such credulity is not as extensive in contemporary literature, but astrology is one pseudoscience that does seem to engage a big segment of the reading public. Literary allusions to it
*(15)* abound, appearing in everything from Shakespeare to Dom DeLillo's *Libra*. A 1986 Gallup poll showed that 52 percent of American teenagers subscribe to it, as does at least 50 percent of the nation's departing First Couple.

Given these figures, it may not be entirely inappropriate to note here that no mechanism through which the alleged zodiacal influences exert themselves has
*(20)* ever been specified by astrologers. Gravity certainly cannot account for these natal influences, since even the gravitational pull of the attending obstetrician is orders of magnitude greater than that of the relevant planet or planets. Nor is there any empirical evidence; top astrologers (as determined by their peers) have failed repeatedly to associate personality profiles with astrological data at a rate
*(25)* higher than that of chance. Neither of these fatal objections to astrology, of course, is likely to carry much weight with literate but innumerate people who don't estimate magnitudes or probabilities, or who are over-impressed by vague coincidences yet unmoved by overwhelming statistical evidence.

# LITERARY TECHNIQUE QUESTIONS

Literary technique questions often look like this:

> Which of the following best describes the development of this passage?
> In presenting the argument, the author does all of the following EXCEPT...
> The statement in lines 8–9 is an example of...
> In the passage, the author makes the central point primarily by...

### Tip 6

**Familiarize yourself with the common terms used to describe an author's technique.** Even if you don't learn them all, once you've mastered a few, you'll be in a good position to eliminate incorrect answer choices and make an educated guess among the rest.

| COMMON LITERARY TERMS | |
|---|---|
| **allusion** | reference to something |
| **analogy** | comparison; similarity of functions or properties; likeness |
| **anecdote** | short account of an incident (often autobiographical) |
| **antithesis** | direct opposite |
| **argumentative** | presenting a logical argument |
| **assertion** | positive statement; declaration |
| **cite** | to refer to; to quote as an authority |
| **euphemism** | mild or indirect expression substituted for one felt offensive or harsh (Example: "Downsizing employees" is a euphemism for firing them.) |
| **expository** | concerned with explaining ideas, facts, etc. |
| **generalization** | simplification; general idea or principle |
| **metaphor** | an expression used to suggest a similarity between two things that are not literally equivalent (Example: "He's a tiger!") |
| **narrative (adj.)** | relating to telling a story |
| **paradox** | statement that contradicts itself (Example: "I always lie.") |
| **rhetorical** | relating to the effective use of language |
| **thesis** | the central idea in a piece of writing; a point to be defended |

## Literary Technique Power Practice

1. The opening sentence of the second paragraph contains an example of

   (A) an apology
   (B) a metaphor
   (C) a paradox
   (D) a euphemism
   (E) an understatement

2. The author's point about the popularity of astrology is made through both

(A) personal testimony and generalizations
(B) assertions and case histories
(C) comparisons and anecdotes
(D) literary and statistics references
(E) observation and analogy

## Check Your Answers

1. **(B)** The phrase "a fertile soil for...growth" is an example of *a metaphor*. People's attitudes aren't really dirt.
2. **(D)** The author offers as evidence of astrology's popularity both *literary references* (allusions to Dom DeLillo's *Libra* and to Shakespeare) and *statistics* based on Gallup poll figures.

---

*The following passage is taken from an article on mathematical and scientific illiteracy published in* The New York Times *in January 1989, as Ronald and Nancy Reagan left the White House.*

The abstractness of mathematics is a great obstacle for many intelligent people. Such people may readily understand narrative particulars, but strongly resist impersonal generalities. Since numbers, science, and such generalities are
*Line* intimately related, this resistance can lead to an almost willful mathematical and
(5) scientific illiteracy. Numbers have appeal for many only if they're associated with them personally—hence part of the attraction of astrology, biorhythms, Tarot cards and the I Ching, all individually customized "sciences."

Mathematical illiteracy and the attitudes underlying it provide in fact a fertile soil for the growth of pseudoscience. In *Pseudoscience and Society in Nine-*
(10) *teenth-Century America,* Arthur Wrobel remarks that belief in phrenology, homeopathy, and hydropathy was not confined to the poor and the ignorant, but pervaded much of nineteenth-century literature. Such credulity is not as extensive in contemporary literature, but astrology is one pseudoscience that does seem to engage a big segment of the reading public. Literary allusions to it
(15) abound, appearing in everything from Shakespeare to Dom DeLillo's *Libra*. A 1986 Gallup poll showed that 52 percent of American teenagers subscribe to it, as does at least 50 percent of the nation's departing First Couple.

Given these figures, it may not be entirely inappropriate to note here that no mechanism through which the alleged zodiacal influences exert themselves has
(20) ever been specified by astrologers. Gravity certainly cannot account for these natal influences, since even the gravitational pull of the attending obstetrician is orders of magnitude greater than that of the relevant planet or planets. Nor is there any empirical evidence; top astrologers (as determined by their peers) have failed repeatedly to associate personality profiles with astrological data at a rate
(25) higher than that of chance. Neither of these fatal objections to astrology, of course, is likely to carry much weight with literate but innumerate people who don't estimate magnitudes or probabilities, or who are over-impressed by vague coincidences yet unmoved by overwhelming statistical evidence.

# LOGIC/APPLICATION QUESTIONS

Logic/application questions look like this:

> With which of the following statements would the author be most in agreement?
>
> The author's argument would be most weakened by the discovery of which of the following?
>
> The author's contention would be most clearly strengthened if which of the following were found to be true?

## Tip 7

**Think about how the ideas in the passage are logically organized.** Break down the author's argument. The author is making a point. Ask yourself which statements support that point. How could you attack that point? What other statements could you make to support it?

 Logic/application questions take lots of time to think through. If you're running out of time, you may want to skip that logic question and try a detail or vocabulary one.

Why get bogged down answering one time-consuming question when in the same amount of time you can answer two less demanding ones?

## Logic/Application Power Practice

1. Which of the following would most weaken the author's assumption that mathematical and scientific literacy would make people less likely to believe in a pseudoscience such as astrology?

   (A) Assertions by professional astrologers that astrology has a firm scientific basis in astronomy.

   (B) Anecdotal reports that an individual astrologer has been known to use a calculator in computing horoscopes.

   (C) Poll results showing that the percentage of American teenagers believing in astrology has radically decreased since 1989.

   (D) Evidence that the majority of practicing astrologers have also taught mathematics or a scientific discipline.

   (E) A statement by ex-president Reagan denying that he had ever believed in astrology.

2. With which of the following statements would the author be most likely to disagree?

   (A) Phrenology may be of some interest to sociologists and cultural historians, but it has no real value as a scientific discipline.

   (B) A rigorous training in mathematics would benefit young people by equipping them to estimate magnitudes and probabilities.

   (C) People were somewhat less apt to be taken in by pseudoscientific claims in the nineteenth century than they are today.

   (D) Despite the weight of the evidence against astrology, scientifically illiterate individuals will continue to believe in it.

   (E) Determining biorhythms and computing astrological horoscopes may require people to perform some mathematical calculations.

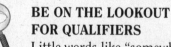 **BE ON THE LOOKOUT FOR QUALIFIERS**

Little words like "somewhat," "often," and "almost" limit the meaning of other words. Little words, but they can have a big impact. Which would you rather have the Terminator say, "No problem," or "Almost no problem"?

## Check Your Answers

1. **(D)** If we assume that people who have professionally taught math or science are therefore not mathematically and scientifically illiterate, and if we also assume that practicing astrologers believe in astrology, then *evidence that the majority of practicing astrologers have also taught mathematics or a scientific discipline* would clearly weaken the author's assumption that mathematical and scientific literacy would make people less likely to believe in astrology.

2. **(C)** You can answer this question by using the process of elimination.

   The key word here is "disagree." Examine each statement in turn, asking yourself whether it does or does not reflect the author's point of view. Eliminate every answer choice with which the author would agree.

   First check Choice A. Phrenology is one of the pseudosciences mentioned in the second paragraph; clearly, the author would agree *it has no real value as a scientific discipline* or field of study. You can eliminate Choice A.

   Next check Choice B. In the concluding sentence of the passage, the author mentions the failure to estimate magnitudes and probabilities as a characteristic of innumerate, mathematically illiterate people. The author wishes people to be mathematically *literate*; therefore, he would agree that *a rigorous training in mathematics* that enabled them to estimate magnitudes and probabilities *would benefit young people*. You can eliminate Choice B.

   In the second paragraph, the author states that belief in various pseudosciences "pervaded much of nineteenth-century literature"; it was widespread in earlier days. He then asserts that "such credulity is not as extensive in contemporary literature." In other words, the author argues that *people are somewhat less apt to be taken in by pseudoscientific claims today than they were a century ago*. This directly contradicts what is stated in Choice C. Therefore, Choice C is most likely the correct answer.

   Double-check yourself. Test the other two answer choices.

   In lines 25–28, the author states directly that the "fatal objections to astrology" he has just pointed out are unlikely to convince the innumerate scientifically illiterate believers in astrology that the powers of the zodiac are nonexistent. Clearly, the author would agree that *scientifically illiterate individuals will continue to believe* in astrology despite the evidence. You can eliminate Choice D.

   The author asserts that the only numbers that appeal to some people are ones with which they have personal associations—numbers connected to individual biorhythms or astrological horoscopes, for example. Given this personal connection with numbers, even non-mathematically inclined individuals might wind up having *to perform mathematical computations*, though the author would most likely look down on such computations as unscientific. You can eliminate Choice E.

   Only Choice C is left. As you suspected, it is the correct answer.

# Practice Exercises

## SHORT PASSAGES

### Passage 1

Too many parents force their children into group activities. They are concerned about the child who loves to do things alone, who
*Line* prefers a solitary walk with a camera to a
(5) game of ball. They want their sons to be "team players" and their daughters "good mixers." In such foolish fears lie the beginnings of the blighting of individuality, the thwarting of personality, the stealing of the
(10) wealth of one's capital for living joyously and well in a confused world. What America needs is a new army of defense, manned by young men and women who, through guidance and confidence, encouragement and wisdom, have
(15) built up values for themselves and away from crowds and companies.

1. According to the passage, too many parents push their children to be

   (A) unnecessarily gregarious
   (B) foolishly timorous
   (C) pointlessly extravagant
   (D) acutely individualistic
   (E) financially dependent

2. The primary point the author wishes to make is that

   (A) young people need time to themselves
   (B) group activities are harmful to children
   (C) parents knowingly thwart their children's personalities
   (D) independent thinking is of questionable value
   (E) America needs universal military training

3. The author puts quotation marks around the words *team players* and *good mixers* to indicate that he

   (A) is using vocabulary that is unfamiliar to the reader
   (B) intends to define these terms later in the course of the passage
   (C) can readily distinguish these terms from one another
   (D) prefers not to differentiate roles by secondary factors such as gender
   (E) refuses to accept the assumption that these are entirely positive values

4. By "the wealth of one's capital for living joyously and well in a confused world" (lines 9–11), the author most likely means the

   (A) financial security that one attains from one's individual professional achievements
   (B) riches that parents thrust upon children who would far prefer to be left alone to follow their own inclinations
   (C) hours spent in solitary pursuits that enable one to develop into an independent, confident adult
   (D) happy memories of childhood days spent in the company of good friends
   (E) profitable financial and personal contacts young people make when they engage in group activities

**Passage 2**
"Sticks and stones can break my bones,
But names will never harm me."

No doubt you are familiar with this child-
*Line* hood rhyme; perhaps, when you were
(5) younger, you frequently invoked whatever
protection it could offer against unpleasant
epithets. But like many popular slogans and
verses, this one will not bear too close
scrutiny. For names will hurt you. Sometimes
(10) you may be the victim, and find yourself an
object of scorn, humiliation, and hatred just
because other people have called you certain
names. At other times you may not be the
victim, but clever speakers and writers may,
(15) through name-calling, blind your judgment
so that you will follow them in a course of
action wholly opposed to your own interests
or principles. Name-calling can make you
gullible to propaganda which you might
(20) otherwise readily see through and reject.

5. The author's primary purpose in quoting the
rhyme in lines 1 and 2 is to

   (A) remind readers of their childhood vulnera-
   bilities
   (B) emphasize the importance of maintaining
   one's good name
   (C) demonstrate his conviction that only physical attacks can harm us
   (D) affirm his faith in the rhyme's ability to
   shield one from unpleasant epithets
   (E) introduce the topic of speaking abusively
   about others

6. By "this one will not bear too close scrutiny"
(lines 8–9), the author means that

   (A) the statement will no longer seem valid if
   you examine it closely
   (B) the literary quality of the verse does not
   improve on closer inspection
   (C) people who indulge in name-calling are
   embarrassed when they are in the spotlight
   (D) the author cannot stand having his comments looked at critically
   (E) a narrow line exists between analyzing a
   slogan and overanalyzing it

7. According to the passage, name-calling may
make you more susceptible to

   (A) poetic language
   (B) biased arguments
   (C) physical abuse
   (D) risky confrontations
   (E) offensive epithets

8. The author evidently believes that slogans and
verses frequently

   (A) appeal to our better nature
   (B) are disregarded by children
   (C) are scorned by unprincipled speakers
   (D) represent the popular mood
   (E) oversimplify the situation

**Passage 3**
*The following passage was written by
Phillips Brooks, a nineteenth-century
Anglican bishop.*

To keep clear of concealment, to keep clear of
the need of concealment, to do nothing
which you might not do out on the middle of
*Line* Boston Common at noonday—I cannot say
(5) how more and more it seems to me the glory
of a young person's life. It is an awful hour
when the first necessity of hiding anything
comes. The whole life is different thenceforth.
When there are questions to be feared and
(10) eyes to be avoided and subjects which must
not be touched, then the bloom of life is
gone. Put off that day as long as possible. Put
it off forever if you can.

9. The author regards the occasion when one first
must conceal something as

   (A) anticlimactic
   (B) insignificant
   (C) fleeting
   (D) momentous
   (E) enviable

10. The author's tone throughout the passage can best be described as

    (A) hostile
    (B) condescending
    (C) playful
    (D) earnest
    (E) impersonal

11. The passage as a whole can best be described as

    (A) an apology
    (B) a rebuttal
    (C) an exhortation
    (D) an understatement
    (E) a paradox

## Passage 4
*The following passage was written by a twentieth-century naturalist.*

We were about a quarter mile away when quiet swept over the colony. A thousand or more heads periscoped. Two thousand eyes
*Line* glared. Save for our wading, the world's busi-
(5) ness had stopped. A thousand avian personalities were concentrated on us, and the psychological force of this was terrific. Contingents of home-coming feeders, suddenly aware of four strange specks moving across
(10) the lake, would bank violently and speed away. Then the chain reaction began. Every throat in that rookery let go with a concatenation of wild, raspy, terrorized trumpet bursts. With all wings now fully spread and
(15) churning, and quadrupling the color mass, the birds began to move as one, and the sky was filled with the sound of Judgment Day.

12. The author's primary purpose in this passage is to

    (A) explain a natural catastrophe
    (B) issue a challenge
    (C) criticize an expedition
    (D) evoke an experience
    (E) document an experiment

13. The "four strange specks" (line 9) are

    (A) wild birds
    (B) animal predators
    (C) intruding humans
    (D) unusual clouds
    (E) members of the colony

14. In line 10, "bank" most nearly means

    (A) cover
    (B) heap up
    (C) count on
    (D) tilt laterally
    (E) reserve carefully

15. The visitors' response to the episode described in this passage was most likely one of

    (A) impatience
    (B) trepidation
    (C) outrage
    (D) grief
    (E) awe

## Passage 5
How is a newborn star formed? For the answer to this question, we must look to the familiar physical concept of gravitational
*Line* instability. It is a simple concept, long-known
(5) to scientists, having been first recognized by Isaac Newton in the late 1600's.

   Let us envision a cloud of interstellar atoms and molecules, slightly admixed with dust. This cloud of interstellar gas is static
(10) and uniform. Suddenly, something occurs to disturb the gas, causing one small area within it to condense. As this small area increases in density, becoming slightly denser than the gas around it, its gravitational field likewise
(15) increases somewhat in strength. More matter now is attracted to the area, and its gravity becomes even stronger; as a result, it starts to contract, in process increasing in density even more. This in turn further increases its
(20) gravity, so that it accumulates still more matter and contracts further still. And so the process continues, until finally the small area of gas gives birth to a gravitationally bound object, a newborn star.

16. The primary purpose of the passage is to

    (A) demonstrate the evolution of the meaning of a term
    (B) support a theory considered outmoded
    (C) depict the successive stages of a phenomenon
    (D) establish the pervasiveness of a process
    (E) describe a static condition

17. In line 11, "disturb" most nearly means

    (A) hinder
    (B) perplex
    (C) unsettle
    (D) pester
    (E) inconvenience

18. It can be inferred from the passage that the author views the information contained within it as

    (A) controversial but irrefutable
    (B) commonly accepted and factual
    (C) speculative and unprofitable
    (D) original but obscure
    (E) sadly lacking in elaboration

19. The author provides information that answers which of the following questions?

    I. How does the small region's increasing density affect its gravitational field?
    II. What causes the disturbance that changes the cloud from its original static state?
    III. What is the end result of the gradually increasing concentration of the small region of gas?

    (A) I only
    (B) II only
    (C) I and II only
    (D) I and III only
    (E) I, II, and III

20. Throughout the passage, the author's manner of presentation is

    (A) argumentative
    (B) convoluted
    (C) anecdotal
    (D) expository
    (E) hyperbolic

## LONG PASSAGES

**Passage 1**

Although patience is the most important quality a treasure hunter can have, the trade demands a certain amount of courage, too. I
*Line* have my share of guts, but make no boast
(5) about ignoring the hazards of diving. As all good divers know, the business of plunging into an alien world with an artificial air supply as your only link to the world above can be as dangerous as stepping into a den of
(10) lions. Most of the danger rests within the diver himself.

The devil-may-care diver who shows great bravado underwater is the worst risk of all. He may lose his bearings in the glimmering
(15) dim light that penetrates the sea and become separated from his diving companions. He may dive too deep, too long and suffer painful, sometimes fatal, bends.

He may surface too quickly and force his
(20) lungs to squeeze their supply of high pressure air into his bloodstream, causing an embolism—a bubble of air in the blood—which often kills. He may become trapped in a submarine rockslide, get lost in an underwa-
(25) ter cave, or be chopped to bits by a marauding shark. These are not occasional dangers such as crossing a street in busy traffic. They are always with you underwater. At one time or another, I have faced all of them except bends
(30) and embolism, which can be avoided by common sense and understanding of human physical limits beneath the surface.

Once, while salvaging brass from the sunken hulk of an old steel ship, I brushed
(35) lightly against a huge engine cylinder, which looked as if it were as solid as it was on the day the ship was launched. Although the pressure of my touch was hardly enough to topple a toy soldier, the heavy mass of cast
(40) iron collapsed, causing a chain reaction in which the rest of the old engine crumbled. Tons of iron dropped all around me. Sheer luck saved me from being crushed. I have been wary of swimming around steel ship-
(45) wrecks ever since.

1. The author's attitude toward divers who show "great bravado underwater" (lines 12–13) is primarily one of

   (A) admiration for their courage
   (B) resentment of their success
   (C) distaste for their methods
   (D) disapproval of their rashness
   (E) dismay over their laziness

2. The passage most probably appeared in

   (A) a short story
   (B) an autobiographical article
   (C) a diver's logbook
   (D) an article in an encyclopedia
   (E) a manual of skin diving instructions

3. Which of the following does the author not do?

   (A) define a term
   (B) give an example
   (C) make a comparison
   (D) pose a question
   (E) list a possibility

4. According to the passage, the solidity of the steel engine cylinder was

   (A) flawless
   (B) massive
   (C) flexible
   (D) illusory
   (E) fortunate

5. In line 42, "sheer" most nearly means

   (A) steep
   (B) pure
   (C) sharp
   (D) filmy
   (E) abrupt

**Passage 2**
*The following passage is taken from a basic geology text.*

Rocks which have solidified directly from molten materials are called igneous rocks.
Igneous rocks are commonly referred to as
*Line* primary rocks because they are the original
*(5)* source of material found in sedimentaries and
metamorphics. Igneous rocks compose the greater part of the earth's crust, but they are generally covered at the surface by a relatively thin layer of sedimentary or metamorphic
*(10)* rocks. Igneous rocks are distinguished by the following characteristics: (1) they contain no fossils; (2) they have no regular arrangement of layers; and (3) they are nearly always made up of crystals.
*(15)*    Sedimentary rocks are composed largely of minute fragments derived from the disintegration of existing rocks and in some instances from the remains of animals. As sediments are transported, individual frag-
*(20)* ments are sorted according to size. Distinct layers of such sediments as gravel, sand, and clay build up, as they are deposited by water and occasionally wind. These sediments vary in size with the material and the power of the
*(25)* eroding agent. Sedimentary materials are laid down in layers called strata.
   When sediments harden into sedimentary rocks, the names applied to them change to indicate the change in physical state. Thus,
*(30)* small stones and gravel cemented together are known as conglomerates; cemented sand becomes sandstone; and hardened clay becomes shale. In addition to these, other sedimentary rocks such as limestone fre-
*(35)* quently result from the deposition of dis- solved material. The ingredient parts are normally precipitated by organic substances, such as the shells of clams or hard skeletons of other marine life.
*(40)*    Both igneous and sedimentary rocks may be changed by pressure, heat, solution, or cementing action. When individual grains from existing rocks tend to deform and inter- lock, they are called metamorphic rocks. For
*(45)* example, granite, an igneous rock, may be metamorphosed into a gneiss or a schist. Limestone, a sedimentary rock, when sub- jected to heat and pressure may become marble, a metamorphic rock. Shale under
*(50)* pressure becomes slate.

6. The primary purpose of the passage is to

   (A) explain the factors that may cause rocks to change in form
   (B) show how the scientific names of rocks reflect the rocks' composition
   (C) present a new hypothesis about the nature of rock formation
   (D) define and describe several diverse kinds of rocks
   (E) explain why rocks are basic parts of the earth's structure

7. In line 29, "state" most nearly means

   (A) mood
   (B) pomp
   (C) territory
   (D) predicament
   (E) condition

8. According to the passage, igneous rocks are characterized by

   (A) their inability to be changed by heat or pressure
   (B) the wealth of fossils they incorporate
   (C) the lack of crystals in their makeup
   (D) their relative rarity
   (E) the absence of a regular grouping of layers

9. The passage contains information that would answer which of the following questions?

   I. Which elements form igneous rocks?
   II. What produces sufficient pressure to alter a rock?
   III. Why is marble called a metamorphic rock?

   (A) I only
   (B) III only
   (C) I and II only
   (D) II and III only
   (E) I, II, and III

10. The author does all of the following EXCEPT
    (A) provide an example
    (B) define a term
    (C) describe a process
    (D) cite an authority
    (E) enumerate specific attributes

## DOUBLE PASSAGES

*The following set of paired passages is the same set that appeared at the beginning of the book. The questions following the paired passages, however, will be new to you. The passages are excerpted from books on America's national pastime, baseball.*

### Passage 1

DiMaggio had size, power, and speed. McCarthy, his longtime manager, liked to say that DiMaggio might have stolen 60 bases a
*Line* season if he had given him the green light.
(5) Stengel, his new manager, was equally impressed, and when DiMaggio was on base he would point to him as an example of the perfect base runner. "Look at him," Stengel would say as DiMaggio ran out a base hit,
(10) "he's always watching the ball. He isn't watching second base. He isn't watching third base. He knows they haven't been moved. He isn't watching the ground, because he knows they haven't built a canal or a swimming pool
(15) since he was last there. He's watching the ball and the outfielder, which is the one thing that is different on every play."

DiMaggio complemented his natural athletic ability with astonishing physical grace.
(20) He played the outfield, he ran the bases, and he batted not just effectively but with rare style. He would glide rather than run, it seemed, always smooth, always ending up where he wanted to be just when he wanted
(25) to be there. If he appeared to play effortlessly, his teammates knew otherwise. In his first season as a Yankee, Gene Woodling, who played left field, was struck by the sound of DiMaggio chasing a fly ball. He sounded like a
(30) giant truck horse on the loose, Woodling thought, his feet thudding down hard on the grass. The great, clear noises in the open space enabled Woodling to measure the distances between them without looking.

(35) He was the perfect Hemingway hero, for Hemingway in his novels romanticized the man who exhibited grace under pressure, who withheld any emotion lest it soil the purer statement of his deeds. DiMaggio was
(40) that kind of hero; his grace and skill were always on display, his emotions always con-

cealed. This stoic grace was not achieved
without a terrible price: DiMaggio was a man
wound tight. He suffered from insomnia and
*(45)* ulcers. When he sat and watched the game he
chain smoked and drank endless cups of
coffee. He was ever conscious of his obliga-
tion to play well. Late in his career, when his
legs were bothering him and the Yankees had
*(50)* a comfortable lead in a pennant race, columnist Jimmy Cannon asked him why he played
so hard—the games, after all, no longer
meant so much. "Because there might be
somebody out there who's never seen me play
*(55)* before," he answered.

**Passage 2**
Athletes and actors—let actors stand for the
set of performing artists—share much. They
share the need to make gestures as fluid and
economical as possible, to make out of a welter
*(60)* of choices the single, precisely right one. They
share the need for thousands of hours of practice in order to train the body to become the
perfect, instinctive instrument to express. Both
athlete and actor, out of that abundance of
*(65)* emotion, choice, strategy, knowledge of the
terrain, mood of spectators, condition of
others in the ensemble, secret awareness of
injury or weakness, and as merely an absolute
concentration as possible so that all externali-
*(70)* ties are integrated, all distraction absorbed to
the self, must be able to change the self so successfully that it changes us.
    When either athlete or actor can bring all
these skills to bear and focus them, then he
*(75)* or she will achieve that state of complete
intensity and complete relaxation—complete
coherence or integrity between what the performer wants to do and what the performer
has to do. Then, the performer is free; for
*(80)* then, all that has been learned, by thousands
of hours of practice and discipline and by repetition of pattern, becomes natural. Then,
intellect is upgraded to the level of an
instinct. The body follows commands that
*(85)* precede thinking.

    When athlete and artist achieve such self-
knowledge that they transform the self so that
we are recreated, it is finally an exercise in
power. The individual's power to dominate, on
*(90)* stage or field, invests the whole arena around
the locus of performance with his or her
power. We draw from the performer's energy,
just as we scrutinize the performer's vulnera-
bilities, and we criticize as if we were equals
*(95)* (we are not) what is displayed. This is why all
performers dislike or resent the audience as
much as they need and enjoy it. Power flows
in a mysterious circuit from performer to
spectator (I assume a "live" performance) and
*(100)* back, and while cheers or applause are the
hoped-for outcome of performing, silence or
gasps are the most desired, for then the
moment has occurred—then domination is
complete, and as the performer triumphs, a
*(105)* unity rare and inspiring results.

11. Stengel's comments in lines 8–17 serve
    chiefly to

    (A) point out the stupidity of the sort of error
        he condemns
    (B) suggest the inevitability of mistakes in
        running bases
    (C) show it is easier to spot problems than to
        come up with answers
    (D) answer the criticisms of DiMaggio's
        baserunning
    (E) modify his earlier position on DiMaggio's
        ability

12. In line 28, "struck" most nearly means

    (A) halted
    (B) slapped
    (C) afflicted
    (D) enamored
    (E) impressed

13. By quoting Woodling's comment on DiMaggio's running (lines 29–32), the author most likely intends to emphasize

    (A) his teammates' envy of DiMaggio's natural gifts
    (B) how much exertion went into DiMaggio's moves
    (C) how important speed is to a baseball player
    (D) Woodling's awareness of his own slowness
    (E) how easily DiMaggio was able to cover territory

14. In the last paragraph of Passage 1, the author acknowledges which negative aspect of DiMaggio's heroic image?

    (A) His overemphasis on physical grace
    (B) His emotional romanticism
    (C) The uniformity of his performance
    (D) The obligation to answer the questions of reporters
    (E) The burden of living up to his reputation

15. The author makes his point about DiMaggio's prowess through all the following except

    (A) literary allusion
    (B) quotations
    (C) personal anecdotes
    (D) generalization
    (E) understatement

16. In line 56, "stand for" most nearly means

    (A) tolerate
    (B) represent
    (C) advocate
    (D) withstand
    (E) surpass

17. In lines 73–74, "bring all these skills to bear" most nearly means

    (A) come to endure
    (B) carry toward
    (C) apply directly
    (D) cause to behave
    (E) induce birth

18. Why, in line 99, does the author of Passage 2 assume a "live" performance?

    (A) His argument assumes a mutual involvement between performer and spectator that can occur only when both are physically present.
    (B) He believes that televised and filmed images give a false impression of the performer's ability to the spectators.
    (C) He fears the use of "instant replay" and other broadcasting techniques will cause performers to resent spectators even more strongly.
    (D) His argument dismisses the possibility of combining live performances with filmed segments.
    (E) He prefers audiences not to have time to reflect about the performance they have just seen.

19. Which of the following characteristics of the ideal athlete mentioned in Passage 2 is NOT illustrated by the anecdotes about DiMaggio in Passage 1?

    (A) Knowledge of the terrain
    (B) Secret awareness of injury or weakness
    (C) Consciousness of the condition of other teammates
    (D) Ability to make gestures fluid and economical
    (E) Absolute powers of concentration

20. Which of the following statements is best supported by a comparison of the two passages?

    (A) Both passages focus on the development of a specific professional athlete.
    (B) The purpose of both passages is to compare athletes with performing artists.
    (C) The development of ideas in both passages is similar.
    (D) Both passages examine the nature of superior athletic performance.
    (E) Both passages discuss athletic performance primarily in abstract terms.

## Answer Key

### SHORT PASSAGES

|     |   |     |   |     |   |     |   |
|-----|---|-----|---|-----|---|-----|---|
| 1.  | A | 6.  | A | 11. | C | 16. | C |
| 2.  | A | 7.  | B | 12. | D | 17. | C |
| 3.  | E | 8.  | E | 13. | C | 18. | B |
| 4.  | C | 9.  | D | 14. | D | 19. | D |
| 5.  | E | 10. | D | 15. | E | 20. | D |

### LONG PASSAGES

|     |   |     |   |     |   |     |   |     |   |
|-----|---|-----|---|-----|---|-----|---|-----|---|
| 1.  | D | 3.  | D | 5.  | B | 7.  | E | 9.  | B |
| 2.  | B | 4.  | D | 6.  | D | 8.  | E | 10. | D |

### DOUBLE PASSAGES

|     |   |     |   |     |   |     |   |     |   |
|-----|---|-----|---|-----|---|-----|---|-----|---|
| 11. | A | 13. | B | 15. | E | 17. | C | 19. | C |
| 12. | E | 14. | E | 16. | B | 18. | A | 20. | D |

## Answer Explanations

### SHORT PASSAGES

1. **(A)** The passage criticizes parents who force their children into group activities and push them to be *unnecessarily gregarious* (social; outgoing).

   Word Parts Clue: The root *greg-* means crowd. Gregarious people like crowds.

2. **(A)** The author is in favor of doing things on one's own and pursuing individual interests. Therefore, he feels that *young people need time to themselves.*

3. **(E)** Quotation marks often indicate that words are being used in a special sense.
   Here, the author puts quotes around *team players* and *good mixers* to show that he does not believe being a team player or a social mixer is an entirely good thing. In other words, he *refuses to accept the assumption that these are entirely positive values.*

4. **(C)** The author believes that by developing one's individual personality, one stores up the confidence and strong sense of self one needs to do well in adult life. Thus, "the wealth of one's capital" consists of the *hours spent in solitary*

*pursuits that enable one to develop into an independent, confident adult.*

5. **(E)** Authors frequently use a quotation—a proverb, an epigram, a bit of verse—to introduce a topic. Here the author quotes the rhyme to *introduce the topic of speaking abusively about others,* that is, name-calling.

6. **(A)** The rhyme says names will never harm you; the author says the opposite: names *will* hurt you. The author's point is that, if you think closely about what the rhyme is saying, you'll realize it isn't true. In other words, *the statement will no longer seem valid if you examine it closely.*

7. **(B)** The passage's concluding sentence states that "Name-calling can make you gullible to propaganda which you might otherwise readily see through and reject."
   In other words, name-calling can make you susceptible (vulnerable) to the *biased arguments* and half-truths of the propagandists.

8. **(E)** Go back to the sentence where the author mentions slogans and verses. What does it say? "(L)ike many popular slogans and verses, this one will not bear too close scrutiny." The author evidently believes that such popular slogans and

bits of verse frequently do not hold up under close examination. They don't tell the whole story. Instead, they *oversimplify the situation.*

9. **(D)** The author calls the occasion on which one first must hide something "an awful hour" and says one's "whole life is different" afterwards. Clearly, he regards the occasion as *momentous* (crucial; highly significant).

10. **(D)** The author is dead serious about his subject; his tone throughout the passage is *earnest* (intensely serious and sincere).

11. **(C)** Throughout the passage Bishop Brooks is urging young people to live virtuously and honorably, so that they never have any dark secrets they feel they must hide. Thus, the passage can best be described as *an exhortation* (a speech or address communicating urgent advice or recommendations).

    Did you already know the word *exhortation*? If not, you still had a good chance of answering this question correctly. Remember the process of elimination? If you go through the answer choices crossing out the ones you know are wrong, you'll be in a great position to make an educated guess.

12. **(D)** The author is *evoking* (imaginatively creating; producing a vivid impression of) *an experience* that a group of naturalists had visiting a rookery (colony or breeding ground of wild birds).

13. **(C)** The "four strange specks" of whom the birds become aware are the naturalists, the *intruding humans* who have invaded the birds' territory.

14. **(D)** Think of how birds fly. They swoop, they wheel, they bank, that is, *tilt laterally*, tipping as they go into a turn.

15. **(E)** The author describes the scene in vivid terms: trumpet bursts, churning wings, a sky "filled with the sound of judgment day." Clearly, the most likely response on the part of the visiting naturalists would have been *awe* (mixed reverence, fear, and wonder).

    Note how the words that painted pictures helped you identify the emotion the visitors most likely felt.

16. **(C)** The entire second paragraph serves to describe or *depict the successive stages of* the formation of a gravitationally bound object. (*Successive stages* are steps that follow in order,

one after another.) Key words that let you know that the passage is depicting the successive stages of a phenomenon are: *now, even more, further, further still,* and *finally.*

17. **(C)** The process of gravitational instability begins when something occurs to *unsettle* or disturb the static cloud of gas so that one small region becomes a little denser than the gas around it.

18. **(B)** To the author, the concept is both *commonly accepted* (it has been known since Newton's day) *and factual* (it is a simple, realistic concept, based on fact).

19. **(D)** You can answer this question by using the process of elimination.

    Question I is answerable on the basis of the passage. As the area's density increases, its gravitational field increases in strength. Therefore, you can eliminate Choice B.

    Question II is *not* answerable on the basis of the passage. The passage nowhere states what disturbs the gas. Therefore, you can eliminate Choices C and E.

    Question III is answerable on the basis of the passage. The end result of the process is the formation of a gravitationally bound object, a newborn star. Therefore, you can eliminate Choice A.

    Only Choice D is left. It is the correct answer.

20. **(D)** The author's manner of presentation is *expository*: he is explaining a physical concept.

## LONG PASSAGES

1. **(D)** The author clearly criticizes divers who fail to treat the underwater perils they face with proper caution. Condemning their devil-may-care bravado (swaggering pretense of courage; bluster), he shows his *disapproval of their rashness.*

    Choice C is incorrect. To feel distaste for something is to have no particular liking for it. You might have a personal distaste for drinking coffee, for example, but have no problem with other people's drinking some. The author here is strongly critical of the devil-may-care divers whose lack of caution exposes them to mortal danger.

2. **(B)** The personal, chatty tone and the use of the first person pronoun ("I have my share of guts," "I have been wary") suggest that this passage most likely appeared in *an autobiographical article.*

3. **(D)** You can answer this question by using the process of elimination.

Does the author *define a term*? Yes. He defines the word *embolism*. You can eliminate Choice A.

Does the author *give an example*? Yes. He gives examples of different underwater perils. You can eliminate Choice B.

Does the author *make a comparison*? Yes. He compares the danger of deep-sea diving to the danger of "stepping into a den of lions." You can eliminate Choice C.

Does the author *pose a question*? Scan the passage looking for a question mark. If you don't see one, the author most likely did *not* ask any questions. Therefore, Choice D is probably the correct answer. To be sure you are right, check Choice E.

Does the author *list a possibility*? Yes. He lists all the possible dangers that a devil-may-care, careless diver may face. You can eliminate Choice E.

Only Choice D is left. It is the correct answer.

4. **(D)** The engine cylinder *looked* solid but fell apart at a touch. Its solidity was *illusory* (deceptive; like an illusion).

5. **(B)** The author was saved by *pure* luck.

6. **(D)** Throughout the passage, the author attempts to *define and describe several diverse kinds of rocks*.

When you look for a passage's *primary* purpose, you are trying to discover its chief intent *as a whole*. Do not be misled into selecting an answer that is true as far as it goes but does not hold true for the passage as a whole. For example, one purpose of the passage is to *explain the factors that may cause rocks to change in form*. However, this is not the passage's primary purpose.

7. **(E)** Sandstone's new name reflects the change in sand's physical state or *condition*.

8. **(E)** According to the passage, igneous rocks "have no regular arrangement of layers." Thus, they are characterized by "the absence of a regular grouping (or arrangement) of layers."

9. **(B)** You can answer this question by using the process of elimination.

Question I is *not* answerable on the basis of the passage. The passage nowhere states which elements go into forming igneous rocks. Therefore, you can eliminate Choices A, C, and E.

Question II is *not* answerable on the basis of the passage. The passage nowhere states what force produces enough pressure to make a rock change from one physical state to another. Therefore, you can eliminate Choice D. Only Choice B is left, and it is the correct answer. Question III is answerable on the basis of the passage. Marble is called a metaphoric rock because it comes into existence when limestone, a sedimentary rock, is subjected to heat and pressure and undergoes a metamorphosis or change.

10. **(D)** You can use the process of elimination to answer this question.

Does the author *provide an example*? Yes. He gives the example of limestone as a type of sedimentary rock. You can eliminate Choice A.

Does the author *define a term*? Yes. He defines *igneous rocks, sedimentary rocks, metamorphic rocks*. You can eliminate Choice B.

Does the author *describe a process*? Yes. In paragraph 2 he describes how sedimentary rocks are formed. You can eliminate Choice C.

Does the author *cite* or refer to *an authority* (expert)? Scan the passage looking for people's names and for titles of books (Clue: they'll begin with capital letters). If you don't see one, the author most likely did *not* cite an authority. Therefore, Choice D is probably the correct answer. To be sure you are right, check Choice E.

Does the author *enumerate* (list) *specific attributes* or characteristics? Yes. He lists three characteristics that distinguish igneous rocks. You can eliminate Choice E.

Only Choice D is left. It is the correct answer.

## DOUBLE PASSAGES

11. **(A)** Manager Stengel's sarcastic comments about the mistakes DiMaggio *doesn't* make indicate just how dumb the manager thinks it is to look down at the ground when you should have your attention on the outfielder and the ball. Clearly, if one of his players made such an error, Stengel's response would be to say, "What's the matter, stupid? Are you afraid you're going to fall in a ditch down there?"

12. **(E)** Woodling was struck, or *impressed*, by the sound of DiMaggio's running; he found the impact of DiMaggio's feet hitting the ground

impressive.

13. **(B)** Note the context of the reference to Woodling. In the sentence immediately before it, the author says that, if DiMaggio "appeared to play effortlessly, his teammates knew otherwise." The author then introduces a comment by Woodling, one of DiMaggio's teammates. Woodling knew a great deal of effort went into DiMaggio's playing: he describes how DiMaggio's feet pounded as he ran. Clearly, the force of DiMaggio's running is mentioned to illustrate *how much exertion went into DiMaggio's moves*.

14. **(E)** In the final paragraph, the author describes DiMaggio pushing himself to play hard, despite his injuries. DiMaggio does this because he is trying to live up to the image his public has of him. He feels *the burden of living up to his reputation*.

15. **(E)** You can answer this technique question by using the process of elimination.

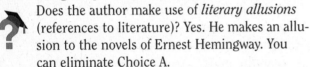

Does the author make use of *literary allusions* (references to literature)? Yes. He makes an allusion to the novels of Ernest Hemingway. You can eliminate Choice A.

Does the author make use of *quotations*? Yes. He quotes the comments of Casey Stengel and of DiMaggio himself. You can eliminate Choice B.

Does the author make use of *personal anecdotes*? Yes. He tells an anecdote or story about Gene Woodling's first impression of DiMaggio. You can eliminate Choice C.

Does the author make use of *generalizations* (general statements)? Yes. He makes several generalizations about DiMaggio ("He was the perfect Hemingway hero..."). You can eliminate Choice D.

Does the author make use of *understatements*? (Understatements are a form of irony in which you purposely describe something as if it is weaker or less than it really is. To say "Joe DiMaggio was a pretty good hitter" is an understatement.) No. The author always expresses himself emphatically, using strong, extremely positive words to describe his subject. He never uses any understatements. Therefore, the correct answer is Choice E.

16. **(B)** At this point, the questions on Passage 2 begin. In this brief aside or side comment, the author is defining how he intends to use a word. He wishes to use the word *actors* to stand for, or *represent*, all other performers. This way every time he makes his comparison between athletes and performers he won't have to list all the various sorts of performing artists (actors, dancers, singers, acrobats, clowns) who resemble athletes in their need for physical grace, extensive rehearsal, and total concentration.

17. **(C)** The author has been describing the wide range of skills a performer uses in crafting an artistic or athletic performance. It is by taking these skills and *applying them directly* and with concentration to the task at hand that the performer achieves his or her goal.

18. **(A)** Although a spectator may feel powerfully involved with the filmed or televised image of a performer, the filmed image is unaffected by the spectator's feelings. Thus, for power to "flow in a mysterious circuit" from performer to spectator *and back*, the assumption is that *both performer and spectator must be physically present*.

19. **(C)** Although DiMaggio's teammates clearly were aware of his condition (as the Woodling anecdote illustrates), none of the anecdotes in Passage 1 indicate or even suggest that DiMaggio was specifically *conscious of his teammates' condition*.

You can answer this question by using the process of elimination.

Do the anecdotes about DiMaggio show that he had *knowledge of the terrain*? Yes. In running bases, DiMaggio never lets himself be distracted by looking at the bases or down at the ground; as Stengel says, he knows where they are. Clearly he knows the terrain. You can eliminate Choice A.

Do the anecdotes about DiMaggio show that he had a *secret awareness of injury or weakness*? Yes. When DiMaggio's legs are failing him late in his career, he still pushes himself to perform well for the fan in the stands who hasn't seen him play before. In doing so, he takes into account his secret awareness of his legs' weakness. You can eliminate Choice B.

Do the anecdotes about DiMaggio show that he had an *ability to make gestures fluid and economical*? Yes. Gliding rather than running, always smooth, never wasting a glance on inessentials, DiMaggio clearly shows that he can move fluidly and economically. You can eliminate Choice D.

Do the anecdotes about DiMaggio show that he had *absolute powers of concentration*? Yes. Running bases, DiMaggio *always* keeps his eye on the ball and the outfielder; he concentrates absolutely on them. You can eliminate Choice E. Only Choice C is left. It is the correct answer.

20. **(D)** Although one passage presents an abstract discussion of the nature of the ideal athlete and the other describes the achievements and character of a specific superior athlete, *both passages examine the nature of superior athletic performance*.

## READING WRAP-UP

1. Tackle the short passages before the long ones.

2. Tackle passages with familiar subjects before passages with unfamiliar ones.

 3. If you are stumped by a tough reading question, move on, but do *not* skip the other questions on that passage without giving them a shot.

4. Whenever you skip a question, *be sure you are filling in the right spaces on your answer sheet*.

 5. Do not zip back and forth between passages.

6. Read as fast as you can with understanding, but don't force yourself to rush.

7. Try to anticipate what the passage will be about.

8. Read with a purpose.

9. Read the footnotes.

10. When you tackle the questions, go back to the passage to check each answer choice.

 11. Use the line references in the questions to get quickly to the correct spot in the passage.

12. When dealing with the double passages, tackle them one at a time.

13. Be on the lookout for words or phrases in the questions that can clue you in to the kind of question being asked.

14. Tackle vocabulary-in-context questions the same way you do sentence completion questions, substituting "blank" for the word in quotes.

15. When asked to find a passage's main idea, be sure to check the opening and summary sentences of each paragraph.

16. When you answer specific detail questions, point to the precise words in the passage that support your answer choice.

17. When you answer inference questions, look for what the passage logically suggests, but does *not* directly state.

18. When asked to figure out an author's attitude or tone, look for words that convey emotion, express values, or paint pictures.

19. Familiarize yourself with the common terms used to describe an author's technique.

20. Think about how the ideas in the passage are logically organized.

# Building Your Vocabulary

## CHAPTER 3

*Recognizing the meaning of words is essential to comprehending what you read. The more you stumble over unfamiliar words in a text, the more you have to take time out to look up words in your dictionary, the more likely you are to wind up losing track of what the author has to say.*

*To succeed in college, you must develop a college-level vocabulary. You must familiarize yourself with technical words in a wide variety of fields, mastering each field's special vocabulary. You must learn to use these words, and reuse them until they become second nature to you. The time you put in now learning vocabulary-building techniques for the PSAT will pay off later on and not just on the PSAT.*

## LONG-RANGE STRATEGY

There is only one effective long-range strategy for vocabulary building: READ.

Read—widely and well. Sample different fields—physics, art history, political science, geology—and different styles. Extensive reading is the one sure way to make your vocabulary grow.

As you read, however, take some time to acquaint yourself specifically with the kinds of words you must know to do well on the PSAT. No matter how little time you have before the test, you still can familiarize yourself with the sort of vocabulary you will be facing on the PSAT. First, look over the 300 words you will find on our PSAT high-frequency word list (pages 136–137): each of these 300 words, ranging from everyday words such as *ample* and *meek* to less commonly known ones such as *esoteric* and *pervasive* has appeared (as answer choices or as question words) at least four times in PSATs in the past two decades.

Next, proceed to master these high-frequency words. First check off the words you think you know. Then *look up all 300 words and their definitions in our abridged basic word list* (pages 138–187). Pay particular attention to the words you thought you knew. See whether any of them are defined in an unexpected way. If they are, make a special note of them. As you know from the preceding chapters, the PSAT often stumps students with questions based on unfamiliar meanings of familiar-looking words.

For extra practice with these high-frequency words, turn to page 188. There, at the end of the Basic Word List, you will find vocabulary practice exercises for 100 words on the PSAT High-Frequency Word List. The more times you work with these high-frequency words, the sooner you will master them.

Not only will looking over the high-frequency word list and doing the practice exercises reassure you that you do know some PSAT-type words, but also familiarizing yourself with these words may well help you on the actual day of the test. These words have turned up on recent tests; some of them may appear on the test you take.

## A PLAN FOR USING THE WORD LIST

For those of you who wish to work your way through the word list and feel the need for a plan, we recommend that you follow the procedure described below in order to use the lists most profitably:

1. Set aside a definite time each day for the study of a list.
2. Devote at least one hour to each list.
3. First, go through the list looking at the short, simple-looking words (six letters at most). Mark those you don't know. In studying, pay particular attention to them.
4. Go through the list again looking at the longer words. Pay particular attention to words with more than one meaning and familiar-looking words that have unusual definitions that come as a surprise to you. Many tests make use of these secondary definitions.
5. List unusual words on index cards so that you can shuffle and review them from time to time. (Study no more than five cards at a time.)
6. Use the illustrative sentences in the list as models and make up new sentences of your own.

For each word, the following is provided:

- The word (printed in heavy type)
- Its part of speech (abbreviated)
- A brief definition
- A sentence illustrating the word's use

Whenever appropriate, related words are provided, together with their parts of speech. The forty-eight word lists are arranged in alphabetical order.

# PSAT High-Frequency Word List

| | | | | |
|---|---|---|---|---|
| absolve | ambivalence | banal | collaborate | convoluted |
| abstract | amenable | beneficial | compliance | corrosion |
| accessible | ample | benign | component | curtail |
| acclaim | antagonism | betray | composure | dawdle |
| accommodate | apathy | brittle | compromise | dearth |
| acknowledge | apprehension | buoyant | condone | debilitate |
| acrimony | apprenticeship | candor | confirm | decorous |
| adversary | appropriate | captivate | conformity | decry |
| adverse | aristocracy | caricature | confront | defamation |
| aesthetic | aspire | censor | congenial | deference |
| affable | assert | chronicle | conscientious | defiance |
| affinity | assumption | circumspect | consistency | degenerate |
| alleviate | authentic | cite | consolidation | demean |
| altruistic | autonomous | cliché | contentious | denounce |
| ambiguous | aversion | coalesce | convention | depict |

deplete
deplore
derision
derivative
detached
deterrent
didactic
diffident
digression
discernible
disclaimer
disclose
discord
discrepancy
disgruntled
disinterested
dismiss
disparage
disparate
dispatch
dispel
disperse
dissent
dissipate
distinction
divulge
docile
doctrine
dogmatic
eclectic
eclipse
elated
elicit
elusive
embellish
endorse
enhance
enigma
entice
enumerate
ephemeral
erode
erratic
erroneous
esoteric

espouse
esteem
excerpt
exemplary
exonerate
expedite
exploit
facilitate
fallacious
farce
fastidious
fawning
feasible
fervor
flippant
forthright
frail
frivolous
garrulous
generate
genre
gluttonous
gratify
gregarious
hackneyed
hamper
hindrance
hostility
hypocritical
hypothetical
iconoclastic
immutable
impede
imperceptible
implacable
implement
implication
impromptu
incarcerate
incongruity
inconsequential
inconsistency
incorporate
indict
indifferent

induce
industrious
inept
infallible
ingenious
ingenuous
ingrate
inherent
initiate
innate
innocuous
inscrutable
insightful
intangible
integrity
intricacy
introspective
irony
judicious
languid
larceny
lethargic
loathe
malice
meek
meticulous
misconception
misrepresent
mock
monarchy
monotony
mutability
naïveté
nocturnal
nonchalance
nostalgia
notorious
nurture
obnoxious
obscure
opaque
optimist
orator
ostentatious
outmoded

pacifist
pacify
paradox
patronize
pedantic
perjury
perpetual
pervasive
pessimism
petulant
phenomena
philanthropist
plagiarize
potency
pragmatic
precedent
predator
premise
premonition
presumptuous
prevail
prey
profound
proliferation
prolific
prologue
prominent
promote
prophetic
prosperity
provocative
prudent
ramble
random
recluse
refute
rejuvenate
relinquish
renown
reprehensible
repudiate
reserved
resignation
resolution
resolve

restraint
retain
reticent
reverent
ruthless
satirize
scrutinize
seclusion
serenity
sever
severity
singular
skeptical
steadfast
stoic
stratagem
subdued
subversive
superficial
superfluous
suppress
surpass
susceptible
suspend
sustain
symmetry
synthesis
taciturn
tedious
temper
temperament
termination
thwart
toxic
transcendent
transparent
trepidation
turbulence
urbane
utopia
vacillate
versatile
volatile
voracious
wary

# Basic Word List

The abridged Basic Word List follows. *Do not let this list overwhelm you.* You do not need to memorize every word. An entry preceded by a bullet (•) is a High-Frequency Word.

## Word List 1     abase–accommodate

**abase** V. lower; humiliate. Defeated, Queen Zenobia was forced to *abase* herself before the conquering Romans, who forced her to march before the emperor Aurelian in the procession celebrating his triumph.

**abate** V. subside; decrease; lessen. Rather than leaving immediately, they waited for the storm to *abate*. abatement, N.

**abdicate** V. renounce; give up. When Edward VIII *abdicated* the British throne to marry the woman he loved, he surprised the entire world. When the painter Gauguin *abdicated* his family responsibilities to run off to Samoa, he surprised no one at all.

**aberration** N. deviation from the expected or the normal; mental irregularity or disorder. Survivors of a major catastrophe are likely to exhibit *aberrations* of behavior because of the trauma they have experienced. aberrant, ADJ. and N.

**abet** V. encourage; aid. She was accused of aiding and *abetting* the drug dealer by engaging in a money-laundering scheme to help him disguise his illegal income. abettor, N.

**abeyance** N. suspended action. The deal was held in *abeyance* until her arrival.

**abject** ADJ. hopeless and crushed; servile and spiritless; wretched. On the streets of New York, the homeless live in *abject* poverty, lying huddled in doorways to find shelter from the wind.

**abrade** V. wear away by friction; scrape; erode. The sharp rocks *abraded* the skin on her legs; so she put iodine on her *abrasions*.

**abscond** V. depart secretly to avoid capture. The teller who *absconded* with the bonds was not captured until someone recognized him from his photograph on *America's Most Wanted*.

**absolute** ADJ. complete; totally unlimited; certain. Although the king of Siam was an *absolute* monarch, he did not want to behead his unfaithful wife without *absolute* evidence of her infidelity.

• **absolve** V. pardon (an offense); free from blame. The father confessor *absolved* him of his sins. absolution, N.

**abstain** V. refrain; hold oneself back voluntarily from an action or practice (especially one regarded as improper or unhealthy). After considering the effect of alcohol on his athletic performance, he decided to *abstain* from drinking while he trained for the race. abstinence, N.; abstinent or abstemious, ADJ.

• **abstract** ADJ. theoretical; not concrete; nonrepresentational. To him, hunger was an *abstract* concept; he had never missed a meal.

**abstruse** ADJ. obscure; profound; difficult to understand. She carries around *abstruse* works of philosophy, not because she understands them but because she wants her friends to think she does.

**accelerate** V. move faster. In our science class, we learn how falling bodies *accelerate*.

• **accessible** ADJ. easy to approach; obtainable. We asked our guide whether the ruins were *accessible* on foot.

**accessory** N. additional object; useful but not essential thing. The *accessories* she bought cost more than the dress. also ADJ.

• **acclaim** V. applaud; announce with great approval. The NBC sportscasters *acclaimed* every American victory in the Olympics and lamented every American defeat. acclamation, acclaim, N.

**accolade** N. award of merit. In the world of public relations, a Clio is the highest *accolade* an advertising campaign can receive.

• **accommodate** V. provide lodgings. Mary asked the room clerk whether the hotel would be able to *accommodate* the tour group on such short notice. accommodations, N.

• **accommodate** V. oblige or help someone; adjust or bring into harmony; adapt. Mitch always did everything possible to *accommodate* his elderly relatives, from driving them to medical appointments to helping them with paperwork. accommodating, ADJ. (secondary meaning)

## Word List 2     accomplice–alacrity

**accomplice** N. partner in crime. Because he had provided the criminal with the lethal weapon, he was arrested as an *accomplice* in the murder.

• **acknowledge** V. recognize; admit. Although Ira *acknowledged* that the Beatles' tunes sounded pretty dated nowadays, he still preferred them to the punk rock songs his nephews played.

**acquittal** N. declaration of innocence; deliverance from a charge. His *acquittal* by the jury surprised those who had thought him guilty. acquit, V.

- **acrimony** N. bitterness of words or manner. The candidate attacked his opponent with great *acrimony*. acrimonious, ADJ.

**acumen** N. mental keenness. His business *acumen* helped him to succeed where others had failed.

**adamant** ADJ. hard; inflexible. Bronson played the part of a revenge-driven man, *adamant* in his determination to punish the criminals who had destroyed his family. adamancy, N.

**adapt** V. alter; modify. Some species of animals have become extinct because they could not *adapt* to a changing environment.

**addiction** N. compulsive, habitual need. His *addiction* to drugs caused his friends much grief.

**adhere** V. stick fast to. I will *adhere* to this opinion until someone comes up with solid proof that I am wrong. adhesive, ADJ.

**adjacent** ADJ. adjoining; neighboring; close by. Philip's best friend Jason lived only four houses away, close but not immediately *adjacent*.

**adjudicate** V. pass legal judgment on; sit in judgment. Do you trust Judge Judy to *adjudicate* disputes impartially?

**admonish** V. warn; scold. The preacher *admonished* his listeners to change their wicked ways. admonition, N.

**adroit** ADJ. skillful; nimble. The juggler's admirers particularly enjoyed his *adroit* handling of difficult balancing tricks.

**adulation** N. flattery; admiration. The rock star relished the *adulation* she received from her groupies and yes-men.

**adulterate** V. make impure by adding inferior or tainted substances. It is a crime to *adulterate* foods without informing the buyer; when consumers learned that the manufacturer had *adulterated* its apple juice by mixing it with water, they protested vigorously.

- **adversary** N. opponent. "Aha!" cried Holmes. "Watson, I suspect this delay is the work of my old *adversary* Professor Moriarty." adversarial, ADJ.

- **adverse** ADJ. unfavorable; hostile. The recession had a highly *adverse* effect on Father's investment portfolio: he lost so much money that he could no longer afford the butler and the upstairs maid. adversity, N.

**adversity** N. poverty; misfortune. We must learn to meet *adversity* gracefully.

**advocate** V. urge; plead for. Noted abolitionists such as Frederick Douglass and Sojourner Truth *advocated* the eradication of the Southern institution of slavery. also N.

- **aesthetic** ADJ. artistic; dealing with or capable of appreciation of the beautiful. The beauty of Tiffany's stained glass appealed to Alice's *aesthetic* sense. aesthete, N.

- **affable** ADJ. easily approachable; warmly friendly. Accustomed to cold, aloof supervisors, Nicholas was amazed by how *affable* his new employer was.

**affected** ADJ. artificial; pretended; assumed in order to impress. His *affected* mannerisms—his "Harvard" accent, his air of boredom, his flaunting of obscure foreign words—irritated many of us who had known him before he had gone away to school. affectation, N.

- **affinity** N. kinship; attraction to. She felt an *affinity* with all who suffered; their pains were her pains. Her brother, in contrast, had an *affinity* for political wheeling and dealing; he manipulated people shamelessly, not caring who got hurt.

**affirmation** N. positive assertion; confirmation; solemn pledge by one who refuses to take an oath. Despite Tom's *affirmations* of innocence, Aunt Polly still suspected he had eaten the pie. affirm, V.

**affix** V. add on; fasten; attach. First the registrar had to *affix* her signature to the license; then she had to *affix* her official seal.

**affluence** N. wealth; prosperity; abundance. Galvanized by his sudden, unexpected *affluence*, the lottery winner dashed out to buy himself a brand new Ferrari. affluent, ADJ.

**affront** V. insult; offend. Accustomed to being treated with respect, Miss Challoner was *affronted* by Vidal's offensive behavior.

**aggregate** V. gather; accumulate. Before the Wall Street scandals, dealers in so-called junk bonds managed to *aggregate* great wealth in short periods of time. aggregation, N.

**agility** N. nimbleness. The acrobat's *agility* amazed and thrilled the audience. agile, ADJ.

**agitate** V. stir up; disturb. Her fiery remarks further *agitated* the already angry mob.

**alacrity** N. cheerful promptness. Phil and Dave were raring to get off to the mountains; they packed up their ski gear and climbed into the van with *alacrity*.

## Word List 3   alias–ancillary

**alias** N. an assumed name. John Smith's *alias* was Bob Jones. also ADV.

**alienate** V. make hostile; separate. Her attempts to *alienate* the two friends failed because they had complete faith in each other.

- **alleviate** V. relieve; lessen. This should *alleviate* the pain; if it does not, we will use stronger drugs.

**alloy** V. mix; make less pure; lessen or moderate. Our delight at the victory was *alloyed* by our concern for the pitcher, who injured his pitching arm in the game.

**allude** V. refer indirectly. Try not to mention divorce in John's presence because he will think you are *alluding* to his marital problems with Jill.

**allure** V. entice; attract. *Allured* by the song of the sirens, the helmsman steered the ship toward the reef. also N.

**allusion** N. indirect reference. When Amanda said to the ticket scalper, "One hundred bucks? What do you want, a pound of flesh?," she was making an *allusion* to Shakespeare's *Merchant of Venice*.

**aloft** ADV. upward. The sailor climbed *aloft* into the rigging. To get into a loft bed, you have to climb *aloft*.

**aloof** ADJ. apart; reserved; standoffish. People thought James was a snob because he remained *aloof* while all the rest of the group conversed.

**altercation** N. noisy quarrel; heated dispute. In that hot-tempered household, no meal ever came to a peaceful conclusion; the inevitable *altercation* occasionally even ended in blows.

• **altruistic** ADJ. unselfishly generous; concerned for others. The star received no fee for appearing at the benefit; it was a purely *altruistic* act. altruism, N.

**amalgam** N. mixture of different elements; alloy. In character, King Gustav was a strange *amalgam* of hard-headed practicality and religious zeal. amalgamate, V.

• **ambiguous** ADJ. unclear or doubtful in meaning. The proctor's *ambiguous* instructions thoroughly confused us; we didn't know which columns we should mark and which we should leave blank. ambiguity, N.

• **ambivalence** N. having contradictory or conflicting emotional attitudes. Torn between loving her parents one minute and hating them the next, she was confused by the *ambivalence* of her feelings. ambivalent, ADJ.

**ambulatory** ADJ. able to walk; not bedridden. Jonathan was a highly *ambulatory* patient; not only did he refuse to be confined to bed, but also he insisted on riding his skateboard up and down the halls.

**ameliorate** V. improve; make more satisfactory. Carl became a union organizer because he wanted to join the fight to *ameliorate* working conditions in the factory.

• **amenable** ADJ. readily managed; willing to give in; agreeable; submissive. A born snob, Wilbur was *amenable* to any suggestions from those he looked up to, but he resented advice from his supposed inferiors. Unfortunately, his incorrigible snobbery was not *amenable* to improvement.

**amiable** ADJ. agreeable; lovable; warmly friendly. In *Little Women*, Beth is the *amiable* daughter whose loving disposition endears her to all who have dealings with her.

**amorous** ADJ. moved by sexual love; loving. "Love them and leave them" was the motto of the *amorous* Don Juan.

**amorphous** ADJ. formless; lacking shape or definition. As soon as we have decided on our itinerary, we shall send you a copy; right now, our plans are still *amorphous*.

• **ample** ADJ. abundant. Bond had *ample* opportunity to escape. Why did he let us catch him?

**amplify** V. broaden or clarify by expanding; intensify; make stronger. Charlie Brown tried to *amplify* his remarks, but he was drowned out by jeers from the audience. Lucy, however, used a loudspeaker to *amplify* her voice and drowned out all the hecklers.

**anachronism** N. something regarded as outmoded; something or someone misplaced in time. In today's world of personal copiers and fax machines, the old-fashioned mimeograph machine is clearly an *anachronism*; even the electric typewriter seems *anachronistic* next to a laptop PC.

**analogy** N. similarity; parallelism. A well-known *analogy* compares the body's immune system with an army whose defending troops are the lymphocytes or white blood cells. *Analogies* are useful, but you can't take them too far: cells, after all, are not soldiers; there is no boot camp for lymphocytes.

**anarchist** N. person who seeks to overturn the established government; advocate of abolishing authority. Denying she was an *anarchist*, Katya maintained she wished only to make changes in our government, not to destroy it entirely.

**anarchy** N. absence of governing body; state of disorder. For weeks China was in a state of *anarchy*, with soldiers shooting down civilians in the streets and rumors claiming that Premier Deng was dead. Foreigners fleeing the country reported conditions were so *anarchic* that it was a miracle they escaped.

**ancillary** ADJ. serving as an aid or accessory; auxiliary. In an *ancillary* capacity Doctor Watson was helpful; however, Holmes could not trust the good doctor to solve a perplexing case on his own. also N.

# Word List 4    animated–aristocracy

**animated** ADJ. lively; spirited. Jim Carrey's facial expressions are highly *animated*: when he played Ace Ventura, he looked practically rubber-faced.

**animosity** N. active enmity. Mr. Fang incurred the *animosity* of the party's rulers because he advocated limitations of their power.

**anomaly** N. irregularity; something out of place or abnormal. A bird that cannot fly is an *anomaly*. A classical harpist in the middle of a heavy metal band is *anomalous;* she is also inaudible.

• **antagonism** N. hostility; active resistance. Barry showed his *antagonism* toward his new stepmother by ignoring her whenever she tried talking to him. antagonistic, ADJ.

**antecedents** N. preceding events or circumstances that influence what comes later; ancestors or early background. Susi Bechhofer's ignorance of her Jewish background had its *antecedents* in the chaos of World War II. Smuggled out of Germany and adopted by a Christian family, she knew nothing of her birth and *antecedents* until she was reunited with her family in 1989.

**anticlimax** N. letdown in thought or emotion. After the fine performance in the first act, the rest of the play was an *anticlimax*. anticlimactic, ADJ.

**antipathy** N. aversion; dislike. Tom's extreme *antipathy* for disputes keeps him from getting into arguments with his temperamental wife. Noise in any form is *antipathetic* to him. Among his particular *antipathies* are honking cars, boom boxes, and heavy metal rock.

**antiquated** ADJ. obsolete; outdated. Accustomed to editing his papers on word processors, Philip thought typewriters were too *antiquated* for him to use.

**antiseptic** N. substance that prevents infection. It is advisable to apply an *antiseptic* to any wound, no matter how slight or insignificant. also ADJ.

**antithesis** N. contrast; direct opposite of or to. This tyranny was the *antithesis* of all that he had hoped for, and he fought it with all his strength.

• **apathy** N. lack of caring; indifference. A firm believer in democratic government, she could not understand the *apathy* of people who never bothered to vote. She wondered whether they had ever cared or whether they had always been *apathetic*.

**aplomb** N. poise; assurance. Gwen's *aplomb* in handling potentially embarrassing moments was legendary around the office; when one of her clients broke a piece of her best crystal, she coolly picked up her own goblet and hurled it into the fireplace.

**apocryphal** ADJ. untrue; made up. To impress his friends, Tom invented *apocryphal* tales of his adventures in the big city.

**apostate** N. one who abandons his religious faith or political beliefs. Because he switched from one party to another, his former friends shunned him as an *apostate*.

**append** V. attach. I shall *append* this chart to my report. When you *append* a bibliography to a text, you have just created an *appendix*.

• **apprehension** N. fear; discernment; capture. The tourist refused to drive his rental car through downtown Miami because he felt some *apprehension* that he might be carjacked.

• **apprenticeship** N. time spent as a novice learning a trade from a skilled worker. As a child, Pip had thought it would be wonderful to work as Joe's *apprentice;* now he hated his *apprenticeship* and scorned the blacksmith's trade.

• **appropriate** ADJ. fitting or suitable; pertinent. Madonna spent hours looking for a suit that would be *appropriate* to wear at a summer wedding.

• **appropriate** V. acquire; take possession of for one's own use; set aside for a special purpose. The ranchers *appropriated* lands that had originally been intended for Indian use. In response, Congress *appropriated* additional funds for the Bureau of Indian Affairs.

**arable** ADJ. fit for growing crops. The first settlers wrote home glowing reports of the New World, praising its vast acres of *arable* land ready for the plow.

**arbiter** N. a person with power to decide a dispute; judge. As an *arbiter* in labor disputes, she is skillful: she balances the demands of both sides and hands down rulings with which everyone agrees. As an *arbiter* of style, however, she is worthless: she wears such unflattering outfits that no woman in her right mind would imitate her.

**arbitrary** ADJ. unreasonable or capricious; randomly selected without any reason; based solely on one's unrestricted will or judgment. The coach claimed the team lost because the umpire made some *arbitrary* calls.

**archipelago** N. group of closely located islands. When Gauguin looked at the map and saw the *archipelagoes* in the South Seas, he longed to visit them.

**arduous** ADJ. hard; strenuous. Bob's *arduous* efforts had sapped his energy. Even using a chain saw, he found chopping down trees an *arduous*, time-consuming task.

**aria** N. operatic solo. At her Metropolitan Opera audition, Marian Anderson sang an *aria* from the opera *Norma*.

**arid** ADJ. dry; barren. The cactus has adapted to survive in an *arid* environment.

• **aristocracy** N. hereditary nobility; privileged class. Americans have mixed feelings about hereditary *aristocracy:* we say all men are created equal, but we describe people who bear themselves with grace and graciousness as natural *aristocrats*.

# Word List 5   arrogance–authoritative

**arrogance** N. pride; haughtiness. Convinced that Emma thought she was better than anyone else in the class, Ed rebuked her for her *arrogance*.

**articulate** ADJ. effective; distinct. Her *articulate* presentation of the advertising campaign impressed her employers. also V.

**ascendancy** N. controlling influence. President Marcos failed to maintain his *ascendancy* over the Philippines. He was overthrown by the forces of Corazon Aquino when she *ascended* to power.

**ascetic** ADJ. practicing self-denial; austere. The wealthy, self-indulgent young man felt oddly drawn to the strict, *ascetic* life led by members of some monastic orders. also N.

• **aspire** V. seek to attain; long for. Because he *aspired* to a career in professional sports, Philip enrolled in a graduate program in sports management. aspiration, N.

**assail** V. assault. He was *assailed* with questions after his lecture.

• **assert** V. state strongly or positively; insist on or demand recognition of (rights, claims, etc). When Jill *asserted* that nobody else in the junior class had such an early curfew, her parents *asserted* themselves, telling her that if she didn't get home by nine o'clock, she would be grounded for the week. assertion, N.

**assiduous** ADJ. diligent. It took Rembrandt weeks of *assiduous* labor before he was satisfied with his self-portrait. assiduity, N.

**assuage** V. ease or lessen (pain); Jilted by Jane, Dick tried to *assuage* his heartache by indulging in ice cream.

• **assumption** N. something taken for granted; taking over or taking possession of. The young princess made the foolish *assumption* that the regent would not object to her *assumption* of power. assume, V.

**assurance** N. promise or pledge; certainty; self-confidence. When Guthrie gave Guinness his *assurance* rehearsals were going well, he spoke with such *assurance* that Guinness felt relieved. assure, V.; assured, ADJ.

**astute** ADJ. wise; shrewd; keen. As tutor, she made *astute* observations about how to take multiple-choice tests. She was an *astute* observer: she noticed every tiny detail and knew exactly how important each one was.

**asylum** N. place of refuge; safety. Fleeing persecution, the political refugee sought *asylum* in the United States.

**atrophy** V. waste away. After three months in a cast, Stan's biceps had *atrophied* somewhat; however, he was sure that if he pumped iron for a while he would soon build it up.

**attain** V. reach or accomplish; gain. It took Bolingbroke years to *attain* his goal of gaining the throne.

**attentive** ADJ. watching carefully; considerate; thoughtful. Spellbound, the *attentive* audience watched the final game of the match, never taking their eyes from the ball. Stan's *attentive* daughter slipped a sweater over his shoulders without distracting his attention from the game.

**attire** N. clothing (especially, splendid clothes). At the Academy Awards ceremony, the television host commented on the highly fashionable *attire* worn by the nominees. also N.

**attribute** N. essential quality. His outstanding *attribute* was his kindness.

**attribute** V. ascribe or credit (to a cause); regard as characteristic of a person or thing. I *attribute* Andrea's success in science to the encouragement she received from her parents.

**attrition** N. gradual decrease in numbers; reduction in the work force without firing employees; wearing away of opposition by means of harassment. In the 1960s urban churches suffered from *attrition* as members moved from the cities to the suburbs. Rather than fire staff members, church leaders followed a policy of *attrition*, allowing elderly workers to retire without replacing them.

**audacity** N. boldness. Luke could not believe his own *audacity* in addressing the princess. Where did he get the nerve?

**augment** V. increase. Armies *augment* their forces by calling up reinforcements; teachers *augment* their salaries by taking odd jobs. Lexy *augments* her salary by working in a record store. Her *augmentation* of wealth has not been great; however, she has *augmented* her record collection considerably.

**aura** N. distinctive atmosphere; luminous glow. Radiant with happiness, the bride seemed surrounded by an *aura* of brightness.

**auspicious** ADJ. favoring success; fortunate. With favorable weather conditions, it was an *auspicious* moment to set sail. Prospects for trade were good: under such promising *auspices* we were bound to thrive. Thomas, however, had doubts: a paranoid, he became suspicious whenever conditions seemed *auspicious*.

**austere** ADJ. forbiddingly stern; severely simple and unornamented. The headmaster's *austere* demeanor tended to scare off the more timid students, who never visited his study willingly. The room reflected the man, for it was *austere* and bare, like a monk's cell, with no touches of luxury to moderate its *austerity*.

- **authentic** ADJ. genuine. The art expert was able to distinguish the *authentic* van Gogh painting from the forged copy. authenticate, V.
- **authoritative** ADJ. having the weight of authority; overbearing and dictatorial. Impressed by the young researcher's well-documented presentation, we accepted her analysis of the experiment as *authoritative*.

# Word List 6    autonomous–blasphemy

- **autonomous** ADJ. self-governing. This island is a colony; however, in most matters, it is *autonomous* and receives no orders from the mother country. The islanders are an independent lot and would fight to preserve their *autonomy*.
- **autopsy** N. examination of a dead body; postmortem. The medical examiner ordered an *autopsy* to determine the cause of death. also V.
- **avarice** N. greediness for wealth. King Midas is a perfect example of *avarice*, for he was so greedy that he wished everything he touched would turn to gold.
- **averse** ADJ. reluctant. The reporter was *averse* to revealing the sources of his information.
- **aversion** N. firm dislike. Bert had an *aversion* to yuppies; Alex had an *aversion* to punks. Their mutual *aversion* was so great that they refused to speak to one another.
- **avert** V. prevent; turn aside. "Watch out!" she cried, hoping to *avert* an accident. She *averted* her eyes from the dead cat on the highway.
- **avid** ADJ. greedy; eager for. Abner was *avid* for pleasure and partied with great *avidity*.
- **awe** N. solemn wonder. The tourists gazed with *awe* at the tremendous expanse of the Grand Canyon.
- **babble** V. chatter idly. The little girl *babbled* about her dolls and pets.
- **badger** V. pester; annoy; harass. Madge was forced to change her telephone number because she was *badgered* by obscene phone calls.
- **baffle** V. frustrate; perplex. The new code *baffled* the enemy agents.
- **balk** V. foil or thwart; stop short; refuse to go on. When the warden learned that several inmates were planning to escape, he took steps to *balk* their attempt. However, he *balked* at punishing them by shackling them to the walls of their cells.
- **banal** ADJ. hackneyed; commonplace; trite; lacking originality. The hack writer's worn-out clichés made his comic sketch seem *banal*. He even resorted to the *banality* of having someone slip on a banana peel!

- **bane** N. cause of ruin; curse. Lucy's little brother was the *bane* of her existence: his attempts to make her life miserable worked so well that she could have fed him some ratsbane for having such a *baneful* effect.
- **bastion** N. stronghold; something seen as a source of protection. The villagers fortified the town hall, hoping this improvised *bastion* could protect them from the guerrilla raids.
- **begrudge** V. resent. I *begrudge* every minute I have to spend attending meetings; they're a complete waste of time.
- **beguile** V. mislead or delude; cheat; pass time. With flattery and big talk of easy money, the con men *beguiled* Kyle into betting his allowance on the shell game. Broke, Kyle *beguiled* himself during the long hours by playing solitaire.
- **belie** V. contradict; give a false impression of. His coarse, hard-bitten exterior *belied* his underlying sensitivity.
- **benefactor** N. gift giver; patron. In later years Scrooge became Tiny Tim's *benefactor* and gave him many gifts.
- **beneficial** ADJ. helpful; advantageous; useful. Tiny Tim's cheerful good nature had a *beneficial* influence on Scrooge's disposition.
- **beneficiary** N. person entitled to benefits or proceeds of an insurance policy or will. In Scrooge's will, he made Tiny Tim his *beneficiary*. Everything he left would go to the benefit of young Tim.
- **benevolent** ADJ. generous; charitable. Mr. Fezziwig was a *benevolent* employer, who wished to make Christmas merrier for young Scrooge and his other employees.
- **benign** ADJ. kindly; favorable; not malignant. Though her *benign* smile and gentle bearing made Miss Marple seem a sweet little old lady, in reality she was a tough-minded, shrewd observer of human nature. benignity, N.
- **bestial** ADJ. beastlike; brutal. According to legend, the werewolf was able to abandon its human shape to take on a *bestial* form.
- **bestow** V. confer. The president wished to *bestow* great honors upon the hero.
- **betray** V. be unfaithful; reveal (unconsciously or unwillingly). The spy *betrayed* his country by selling military secrets to the enemy. When he was taken in for questioning, the tightness of his lips *betrayed* his fear of being caught.
- **biased** ADJ. slanted; prejudiced. Because the judge played golf regularly with the district attorney's father, we feared he might be *biased* in the prosecution's favor. bias, N.
- **bizarre** ADJ. fantastic; violently contrasting. The plot of the novel was too *bizarre* to be believed.

**bland** ADJ. soothing; mild; dull. Unless you want your stomach lining to be eaten away, stick to a *bland* diet. blandness, N.

**blandishment** N. flattery. Despite the salesperson's *blandishments,* the customer did not buy the outfit.

**blare** N. loud, harsh roar; screech. I don't know which is worse: the steady *blare* of a teenager's boom box deafening your ears or a sudden blaze of flashbulbs dazzling your eyes.

**blasphemy** N. irreverence; sacrilege; cursing. In my father's house, the Dodgers were the holiest of holies; to cheer for another team was to utter words of *blasphemy.* blasphemous, ADJ.

## Word List 7    blatant–cant

**blatant** ADJ. flagrant; conspicuously obvious; loudly offensive. To the unemployed youth from Dublin, the "No Irish Need Apply" placard in the shop window was a *blatant* mark of prejudice.

**blithe** ADJ. gay; joyous; carefree. Without a care in the world, Beth went her *blithe,* light-hearted way.

**bloat** V. expand or swell (with water or air); puff up with conceit. Constant flattery from his hangers-on *bloated* the heavyweight champion's already sizable ego.

**boisterous** ADJ. rough and noisy; rowdy; stormy. The unruly crowd of demonstrators became even more *boisterous* when the mayor tried to quiet them.

**bolster** V. support; reinforce. The debaters amassed file boxes full of evidence to *bolster* their arguments.

**boon** N. blessing; benefit. The recent rains that filled our empty reservoirs were a *boon* to the whole community.

**boundless** ADJ. unlimited; vast. Mike's energy was *boundless:* the greater the challenge, the more vigorously he tackled the job.

**bountiful** ADJ. abundant; graciously generous. Thanks to the good harvest, we had a *bountiful* supply of food, and we could be as *bountiful* as we liked in distributing food to the needy.

**bourgeois** ADJ. middle class; selfishly materialistic; dully conventional. Technically, anyone who belongs to the middle class is *bourgeois,* but, given the word's connotations, most people resent it if you call them that.

**boycott** V. refrain from buying or using. In an effort to stop grape growers from using pesticides that harmed the farm workers' health, Cesar Chavez called for consumers to *boycott* grapes.

**brackish** ADJ. somewhat salty. Following the stream, we noticed its fresh, springlike water grew increasingly *brackish* as we drew nearer to the bay.

**brandish** V. wave around; flourish. Alarmed, Doctor Watson wildly *brandished* his gun until Holmes told him to put the thing away before he shot himself.

**breach** N. breaking of contract or duty; fissure; gap. Jill sued Jack for *breach* of promise, claiming he had broken his promise to marry her. They found a *breach* in the enemy's fortifications and penetrated their lines. also V.

**brevity** N. conciseness. Since you are charged for every transmitted word, *brevity* is essential when you send a telegram or cablegram.

**brine** N. salt water; seawater (as opposed to fresh). If you pack a peck of peppers in *brine,* what do you get? A peck of pickled peppers! briny, ADJ.

• **brittle** ADJ. easily broken; difficult. My employer's self-control was as *brittle* as an eggshell. Her *brittle* personality made it difficult for me to get along with her.

**brochure** N. pamphlet. This free *brochure* on farming was issued by the Department of Agriculture.

**brusque** ADJ. blunt; abrupt. Jill was offended by Jack's *brusque* reply; he had no right to be so impatient with her.

**bungle** V. mismanage; blunder. Don't botch this assignment, Bumstead; if you *bungle* the job, you're fired!

• **buoyant** ADJ. able to float; cheerful and optimistic. When the boat capsized, her *buoyant* life jacket kept Jody afloat. Scrambling back on board, she was still in a *buoyant* mood, certain that despite the delay she'd win the race. buoyancy, N.

**burgeon** V. bloom; develop rapidly; flourish. From its start as a small Seattle coffeehouse, Starbucks seemed to *burgeon* almost overnight into a major national chain.

**bustle** V. move about energetically; teem. David and the children *bustled* about the house getting in each other's way as they tried to pack for the camping trip.

**buttress** V. support or prop up. The government is considering price supports to *buttress* the declining economy. The huge cathedral walls were supported by flying *buttresses.* also N.

**cajole** V. coax; wheedle. Jill tried to *cajole* Jack into buying her a fur coat, but no matter how much she coaxed him, he wouldn't give in to her *cajolery.*

**calamity** N. disaster; misery. As news of the *calamity* spread, offers of relief poured in to the stricken community. calamitous, ADJ.

**calligraphy** N. beautiful writing; excellent penmanship. In the Middle Ages, before a novice scribe was allowed to copy an important document, he had to spend years practicing *calligraphy.*

**callous** ADJ. hardened; unfeeling. Carl had worked in the hospital for so many years that he was *callous* to the suffering in the wards. It was as if he had a *callus* on his soul.

**camaraderie** N. good-fellowship. What Ginger loved best about her job was the sense of *camaraderie* she and her coworkers shared.

• **candor** N. frankness; open honesty. Jack can carry *candor* too far: when he told Jill his honest opinion of her, she nearly slapped his face. Instead of being so *candid,* try keeping your opinions to yourself.

**canine** ADJ. related to dogs; doglike. Some days the *canine* population of Berkeley seems almost to outnumber the human population.

**cant** N. insincere, hypocritical speech; "pious" talk; jargon of thieves. Shocked by news of the minister's extramarital love affairs, the worshippers dismissed his talk about the sacredness of marriage as mere *cant. Cant* is a form of hypocrisy: those who can, pray; those who can't, pretend.

# Word List 8  capricious–choreography

**capricious** ADJ. unpredictable; fickle. The storm was *capricious:* it changed course constantly. Jill was *capricious,* too: she changed boyfriends almost as often as she changed clothes.

**caption** N. title; chapter heading; text under illustration. The capricious *captions* that accompany "The Far Side" cartoons are almost as funny as the pictures. also V.

• **captivate** V. charm; fascinate. Although he was predisposed to dislike Elizabeth, Darcy found himself *captivated* by her charm and wit.

**cardiac** ADJ. pertaining to the heart. Since no one in his family had ever had *cardiac* problems, Bill was unconcerned about the possibility of a heart attack.

• **caricature** N. exaggerated picture or description; distortion. The cartoonist's *caricature* of Senator Foghorn grossly exaggerated the size of the senator's nose and ears. also V.

**carping** ADJ. finding fault. A *carping* critic is a nit-picker, someone who loves to point out flaws. carp, V.

**caste** N. one of the hereditary classes in Hindu society; social stratification; prestige. She bore a mark on her forehead signifying she was a Brahmin, a member of the highest *caste.*

**castigation** V. punishment, severe criticism. Sensitive to even mild criticism, Virginia Woolf could not bear the *castigation* that she met in certain reviews. castigate, V.

**casualty** N. serious or fatal accident. The number of *casualties* on this holiday weekend was high.

**catacomb** N. subterranean cemetery; underground passageway. Londoners refer to their *catacomb*-like subway system as the Underground.

**catastrophe** N. calamity; disaster. The 1906 San Francisco earthquake was a *catastrophe* that destroyed most of the city.

**caustic** ADJ. burning; sarcastically biting. The critic's *caustic* review humiliated the actors, who resented his cutting remarks.

**cede** V. yield (title, territory) to; surrender formally. Eventually the descendants of England's Henry II were forced to *cede* their French territories to the King of France.

• **censor** N. inspector overseeing public morals; official who prevents publication of offensive material. Because certain passages in his novel *Ulysses* had been condemned by the *censor,* James Joyce was unable to publish the novel in England for many years.

**censure** V. blame; criticize. Though I don't blame Tony for leaving Tina, I do *censure* him for failing to pay child support.

**cerebral** ADJ. pertaining to the brain or intellect. The content of philosophical works is *cerebral* in nature and requires much thought.

**cessation** N. stopping. The airline workers threatened a *cessation* of all work if management failed to meet their demands. cease, V.

**chafe** V. warm by rubbing; make sore (by rubbing). Chilled, he *chafed* his hands before the fire. The collar of his school uniform *chafed* Tom's neck, but not as much the school's strict rules *chafed* his spirit. also N.

**chaff** N. husks and stems left over when grain has been threshed; worthless, leftover by-products. When you separate the wheat from the *chaff,* be sure you throw out the *chaff.*

**chagrin** N. vexation (caused by humiliation or injured pride); disappointment. Embarrassed by his parents' shabby, working-class appearance, Doug felt their visit to his school would bring him nothing but *chagrin.* Someone filled with *chagrin* doesn't grin: he's too mortified.

**chameleon** N. lizard that changes color in different situations. Like the *chameleon,* the candidate assumed the political thinking of every group he met.

**chaotic** ADJ. in utter disorder. He tried to bring order into the *chaotic* state of affairs. chaos, N.

**charlatan** N. quack; pretender to knowledge. When they realized that the Wizard didn't know how to get them back to Kansas, Dorothy and her friends were sure they'd been duped by a *charlatan.*

**chary** ADJ. cautious; sparing or restrained about giving. A prudent, thrifty, New Englander, DeWitt was as *chary* of investing money in junk bonds as he was *chary* of paying people unnecessary compliments.

**chasm** N. abyss. They could not see the bottom of the *chasm.*

**chastise** V. punish physically; scold verbally. "Spare the rod and spoil the child," Miss Watson said, grabbing her birch wand and proceeding to *chastise* poor Huck thoroughly.

**chauvinist** N. blindly devoted patriot. *Chauvinists* cannot recognize any faults in their country, no matter how flagrant they may be. Likewise, a male *chauvinist* cannot recognize how biased he is in favor of his own sex, no matter how flagrant that may be.

**chicanery** N. trickery; deception. Those sneaky lawyers misrepresented what occurred, made up all sorts of implausible alternative scenarios to confuse the jurors, and in general depended on *chicanery* to win the case.

**choreography** N. art of representing dances in written symbols; arrangement of dances. Merce Cunningham has begun to use a computer in designing *choreography:* a software program allows him to compose arrangements of possible moves and to view them immediately onscreen.

## Word List 9   chronic–compute

**chronic** ADJ. long established (as a disease). The doctors were finally able to attribute his *chronic* headaches and nausea to traces of formaldehyde gas in his apartment.

• **chronicle** V. report; record (in chronological order). The gossip columnist was paid to *chronicle* the latest escapades of the socially prominent celebrities. also N.

**circumscribe** V. limit; confine. Although I do not wish to *circumscribe* your activities, I must insist that you complete this assignment before you start anything else.

• **circumspect** ADJ. prudent; cautious. Investigating before acting, she tried always to be *circumspect.*

• **cite** V. quote; refer to; commend. Because Virginia could *cite* hundreds of biblical passages from memory, her pastor *cited* her for her studiousness. citation, N.

**clairvoyant** ADJ., N. having foresight; fortune-teller. Cassandra's *clairvoyant* warning was not heeded by the Trojans. clairvoyance, N.

**clandestine** ADJ. secret. After avoiding their chaperone, the lovers had a *clandestine* meeting.

**claustrophobia** N. fear of being shut in. If Santa Claus got stuck in a chimney and couldn't get out, would he wind up suffering from *claustrophobia?*

**clemency** N. disposition to be lenient; mildness, as of the weather. The lawyer was pleased when the case was sent to Judge Smith's chambers because Smith was noted for her *clemency* toward first offenders. We decided to eat dinner in the garden to enjoy the unexpected *clemency* of the weather.

• **cliché** N. phrase dulled in meaning by repetition. High school compositions are often marred by such *clichés* as "strong as an ox."

**climactic** ADJ. relating to the highest point. When Jack reached the *climactic* portions of the book, he could not stop reading. climax, N.

**clique** N. small exclusive group. Fitzgerald wished that he belonged to the *clique* of popular athletes and big men on campus who seemed to run Princeton's social life.

• **coalesce** V. combine; fuse. The brooks *coalesced* into one large river. When minor political parties *coalesce,* their *coalescence* may create a major coalition.

**coalition** N. association; union. Jesse Jackson's Rainbow *Coalition* brought together people of many different races and creeds.

**cogitate** V. think over. *Cogitate* on this problem; the solution will come.

**coincidence** N. two or more things occurring at the same time by chance. Was it just a *coincidence* that John and she had chanced to meet at the market for three days running, or was he deliberately trying to seek her out? coincident, ADJ.

• **collaborate** V. work together. Two writers *collaborated* in preparing this book.

**colossal** ADJ. huge. Radio City Music Hall has a *colossal* stage.

**collusion** N. conspiring in a fraudulent scheme. The swindlers were found guilty of *collusion.* collude, V.

**comely** ADJ. attractive; agreeable. I would rather have a poor but *comely* wife than a rich and homely one.

**commiserate** V. feel or express pity or sympathy for. Her friends *commiserated* with the widow.

**compact** ADJ. tightly packed; firm; brief. His short, *compact* body was better suited to wrestling than to basketball.

**compact** N. agreement; contract. The signers of the Mayflower *Compact* were establishing a form of government.

**comparable** ADJ. similar. People whose jobs are *comparable* in difficulty should receive *comparable* pay.

**compatible** ADJ. harmonious; in harmony with. They were *compatible* neighbors, never quarreling over unimportant matters. compatibility, N.

**compile** V. assemble; gather; accumulate. We planned to *compile* a list of the words most frequently used on SAT examinations. compilation, N.

**complacent** ADJ. self-satisfied; smug. Feeling *complacent* about his latest victories, he looked smugly at the row of trophies on his mantelpiece. complacency, N.

**complement** V. complete; make perfect. The waiter recommended a glass of port to *complement* the cheese. also N.

• **compliance** N. readiness to yield; conformity in fulfilling requirements. Bill was so bullheaded that we never expected his easy *compliance* to our requests. As an architect, however, Bill recognized that his design for the new school had to be in *compliance* with the local building code.

• **component** N. element; ingredient. I wish all the *components* of my stereo system were working at the same time.

• **composure** N. mental calmness. Even the latest work crisis failed to shake her *composure*.

**compress** V. close; squeeze; contract. She *compressed* the package under her arm.

• **compromise** V. adjust or settle by making mutual concessions; endanger the interests or reputation of. Sometimes the presence of a neutral third party can help adversaries *compromise* their differences. Unfortunately, your presence at the scene of the dispute *compromises* our claim to neutrality in this matter. also N.

**compute** V. reckon; calculate. He failed to *compute* the interest; so his bank balance was not accurate.

## Word List 10   concerted–contention

**concerted** ADJ. mutually agreed on; done together. All the Girl Scouts made a *concerted* effort to raise funds for their annual outing. When the movie star appeared, his fans let out a *concerted* sigh.

**concise** ADJ. brief but comprehensive. The instructions were *concise* and to the point: they included every necessary detail and not one word more. Precision indicates exactness; *concision* indicates compactness. To achieve *conciseness,* cut out unnecessary words.

**concoct** V. prepare by combining; make up in concert. How did the inventive chef ever *concoct* such a strange dish? concoction, N.

**concurrent** ADJ. happening at the same time. In America, the colonists were resisting the demands of the mother country; at the *concurrent* moment in France, the middle class was sowing the seeds of rebellion. The two revolutionary movements took place *concurrently.*

**condescend** V. act conscious of descending to a lower level; patronize. Though Jill was a star softball player in college, when she played a pickup game at the local park she never *condescended* to her teammates or acted as if she thought herself superior to them. condescension. N.

**condole** V. express sympathetic sorrow. Bill's friends gathered to *condole* with him over his loss. Those unable to attend the funeral sent letters of *condolence*.

• **condone** V. overlook voluntarily; forgive. Unlike the frail widow, who indulged her only son and *condoned* his mischievous behavior, the boy's stern uncle did nothing but scold.

**confine** V. shut in; restrict. The terrorists had *confined* their prisoner in a small room. However, they had not chained him to the wall or done anything else to *confine* his movements further. confinement, N.

• **confirm** V. corroborate; verify; support. I have several witnesses who will *confirm* my account of what happened.

**conflagration** N. great fire. In the *conflagration* that followed the 1906 earthquake, much of San Francisco burned to the ground.

• **conformity** N. agreement or compliance; actions in agreement with prevailing social customs. In *conformity* with the bylaws of the Country Dance and Song Society, I am submitting a petition nominating Susan Murrow as president of the society. Because Kate had always been a rebellious child, we were surprised by her *conformity* to the standards of behavior prevalent at her new school.

• **confront** V. face someone or something; encounter, often in a hostile way. Fearing his wife's hot temper, Stanley was reluctant to *confront* her about her skyrocketing credit card bills.

**congeal** V. freeze; coagulate. His blood *congealed* in his veins as he saw the dreaded monster rush toward him.

• **congenial** ADJ. pleasant; friendly. My father loved to go out for a meal with *congenial* companions.

**connotation** N. suggested or implied meaning of an expression. Foreigners frequently are unaware of the *connotations* of the words they use.

• **conscientious** ADJ. scrupulous, careful. A *conscientious* editor, she checked every definition for its accuracy.

**consensus** N. general agreement. Every time the garden club members had nearly reached a *consensus* about what to plant, Mistress Mary, quite contrary, disagreed.

**consequence** N. self-importance; pomposity. Convinced of his own importance, the actor strutted about the dressing room with such an air of *consequence* that it was hard for his valet to keep a straight face. consequential, ADJ.

• **consistency** N. harmony of parts; dependability; uniformity; degree of thickness. Holmes judged puddings and explanations on their *consistency*: he liked his puddings without lumps and his explanations without contradictions or improbabilities. consistent, ADJ.

**console** V. lessen sadness or disappointment; give comfort. When her father died, Marius did his best to *console* Cosette.

• **consolidation** N. unification; process of becoming firmer or stronger. The recent *consolidation* of several small airlines into one major company has left observers of the industry wondering whether room still exists for the "little guy" in aviation. consolidate, V.

**conspicuous** ADJ. easily seen; noticeable; striking. Janet was *conspicuous* both for her red hair and for her height.

**constituent** N. resident of a district represented by an elected official. The congressman received hundreds of letters from angry *constituents* after the Equal Rights Amendment failed to pass.

**constraint** N. compulsion; repression of feelings. There was a feeling of *constraint* in the room because no one dared to criticize the speaker. constrain, V.

**contagion** N. infection. Fearing *contagion,* the health authorities took great steps to prevent the spread of the disease.

**contempt** N. scorn; disdain. The heavyweight boxer looked on ordinary people with *contempt,* scorning them as weaklings who couldn't hurt a fly. We thought it was *contemptible* of him to be *contemptuous* of people for being weak.

**contention** N. claim; thesis. It is our *contention* that, if you follow our tactics, you will boost your score on the PSAT. contend, V.

## Word List 11  contentious–curtail

• **contentious** ADJ. quarrelsome. Disagreeing violently with the referees' ruling, the coach became so *contentious* that they threw him out of the game.

**context** N. writings preceding and following the passage quoted. Because these lines are taken out of *context,* they do not convey the message the author intended.

**contingent** ADJ. dependent on; conditional. Cher's father informed her that any increase in her allowance was *contingent* on the quality of her final grades. contingency, N.

**contingent** N. group that makes up part of a gathering. The New York *contingent* of delegates at the Democratic National Convention was a boisterous, sometimes rowdy lot.

**contortion** N. twisting; distortion. Watching the *contortions* of the gymnast as he twisted and heaved his body from one side to the other of the pommel horse, we were awed by his strength and flexibility.

**contrite** ADJ. penitent. Her *contrite* tears did not influence the judge when he imposed sentence.

• **convention** N. social or moral custom; established practice. Flying in the face of *convention,* George Sand shocked society by taking lovers and wearing men's clothes.

**converge** V. approach; tend to meet; come together. African-American men from all over the United States *converged* on Washington to take part in the historic Million Man march.

**convert** N. one who has adopted a different religion or opinion. On his trip to Japan, though the president spoke at length about the merits of American automobiles, he made few *converts* to his beliefs. also V.

**conviction** N. judgment that someone is guilty of a crime; strongly held belief. Even her *conviction* for murder did not shake Peter's *conviction* that Harriet was innocent of the crime.

• **convoluted** ADJ. complex and involved; intricate; winding; coiled. Talk about twisted! The new tax regulations are so *convoluted* that even my accountant can't unravel their mysteries.

**cordial** ADJ. gracious; heartfelt. Our hosts greeted us at the airport with a *cordial* welcome and a hearty hug.

**corroborate** V. confirm; support. Though Huck was quite willing to *corroborate* Tom's story, Aunt Polly knew better than to believe either of them.

• **corrosion** N. destruction by chemical action. The *corrosion* of the girders supporting the bridge took place so gradually that no one suspected any danger until the bridge suddenly collapsed. corrode, V.

**cosmic** ADJ. pertaining to the universe; vast. *Cosmic* rays derive their name from the fact that they bombard the earth's atmosphere from outer space. cosmos, N.

**cosmopolitan** ADJ. sophisticated. Her years in the capital had transformed her into a *cosmopolitan* young woman highly aware of international affairs.

**countenance** V. approve; tolerate. He refused to *countenance* such rude behavior on their part.

**covert** ADJ. secret; hidden; implied. Investigations of the Central Intelligence Agency and other secret service networks reveal that such *covert* operations can get out of control.

**covetous** ADJ. avaricious; eagerly desirous of. The child was *covetous* by nature and wanted to take the toys belonging to his classmates. covet, V.

**cower** V. shrink quivering, as from fear. The frightened child *cowered* in the corner of the room.

**crass** ADJ. very unrefined; grossly insensible. The film critic deplored the *crass* commercialism of moviemakers who abandon artistic standards in order to make a quick buck.

**credibility** N. believability. Because the candidate had made some pretty unbelievable promises, we began to question the *credibility* of everything she said.

**credulity** N. belief on slight evidence; gullibility; naïveté. Con artists take advantage of the *credulity* of inexperienced investors to swindle them out of their savings. credulous, ADJ.

**criterion** N. standard used in judging. What *criterion* did you use when you selected this essay as the prizewinner? criteria, Pl.

**cryptic** ADJ. mysterious; hidden; secret. Thoroughly baffled by Holmes's *cryptic* remarks, Watson wondered whether Holmes was intentionally concealing his thoughts about the crime.

**culinary** ADJ. relating to cooking. Many chefs attribute their *culinary* skill to the wise use of spices.

**cull** V. pick out; reject. Every month the farmer *culls* the nonlaying hens from his flock and sells them to the local butcher. also N.

**culmination** N. attainment of highest point. Her inauguration as president of the United States marked the *culmination* of her political career. culminate, V.

**culpable** ADJ. deserving blame. Corrupt politicians who condone the illegal activities of gamblers are equally *culpable*.

**cumbersome** ADJ. heavy; hard to manage. He was burdened down with *cumbersome* parcels.

**curb** V. restrain. The overly generous philanthropist had to *curb* his beneficent impulses before he gave away all his money and left himself with nothing.

**cursory** ADJ. casual; hastily done. Because a *cursory* examination of the ruins indicates the possibility of arson, we believe the insurance agency should undertake a more extensive investigation of the fire's cause.

• **curtail** V. shorten; reduce. When Elton asked Cher for a date, she said she was really sorry she couldn't go out with him, but her dad had ordered her to *curtail* her social life.

## Word List 12  cynical–demolish

**cynical** ADJ. skeptical or distrustful of human motives. *Cynical* from birth, Sidney was suspicious whenever anyone give him a gift "with no strings attached." cynic, N.

**dabble** V. work at in a nonserious fashion; splash around. The amateur painter *dabbled* at art, but seldom produced a finished piece. The children *dabbled* their hands in the bird bath, splashing one another gleefully.

**daunt** V. intimidate; frighten. "Boast all you like of your prowess. Mere words cannot *daunt* me," the *dauntless* hero answered the villain.

• **dawdle** V. loiter; waste time. At the mall, Mother grew impatient with Jo and Amy because they tended to *dawdle* as they went from store to store.

• **dearth** N. scarcity. The *dearth* of skilled labor compelled the employers to open trade schools.

**debase** V. reduce in quality or value; lower in esteem; degrade. In *The King and I*, Anna refuses to kneel down and prostrate herself before the king, for she feels that to do so would *debase* her position, and she will not submit to such *debasement*.

• **debilitate** V. weaken; enfeeble. Michael's severe bout of the flu *debilitated* him so much that he was too tired to go to work for a week.

**decadence** N. decay or decline, especially moral; self-indulgence. We named our best-selling ice cream flavor "chocolate *decadence*" because only truly self-indulgent people would treat themselves to something so calorific and cholesterol laden.

**decipher** V. decode. I could not *decipher* the doctor's handwriting.

• **decorous** ADJ. proper. Prudence's *decorous* behavior was praised by her teachers, who wished they had a classroom full of such polite and proper little girls. decorum, N.

**decoy** N. lure or bait. The wild ducks were not fooled by the *decoy*. also V.

• **decry** V. express strong disapproval of; disparage. The founder of the Children's Defense Fund, Marian Wright Edelman, strongly *decries* the lack of financial and moral support for children in America today.

**deducible** ADJ. derived by reasoning. If we accept your premise, your conclusions are easily *deducible*.

**deface** V. mar; disfigure. If you *deface* a library book, you will have to pay a hefty fine.

• **defamation** N. harming a person's reputation. *Defamation* of character may result in a slander suit. If rival candidates persist in *defaming* one another, the voters may conclude that all politicians are crooks.

**defeatist** ADJ. attitude of one who is ready to accept defeat as a natural outcome. If you maintain your *defeatist* attitude, you will never succeed. also N.

• **deference** N. courteous regard for another's wish. In *deference* to the minister's request, please do not take photographs during the wedding service.

• **defiance** N. opposition; willingness to resist. In learning to read and write in *defiance* of his master's orders, Frederick Douglass showed exceptional courage. defy, V.

**definitive** ADJ. final; complete. Carl Sandburg's *Abraham Lincoln* may be regarded as the *definitive* work on the life of the Great Emancipator.

**defrock** V. strip a priest or minister of church authority. We knew the minister had violated church regulations, but we had not realized his offense was serious enough for people to seek to *defrock* him.

**defunct** ADJ. dead; no longer in use or existence. The lawyers sought to examine the books of the *defunct* corporation.

• **degenerate** V. become worse; deteriorate. As the fight dragged on, the champion's style *degenerated* until he could barely keep on his feet.

**deign** V. condescend; stoop. The celebrated fashion designer would not *deign* to speak to a mere seamstress; his overburdened assistant had to convey the master's wishes to the lowly workers assembling his great designs.

**delete** V. erase; strike out. Less is more: if you *delete* this paragraph, the composition will have more appeal.

**deleterious** ADJ. harmful. If you believe that smoking is *deleterious* to your health (and the surgeon general certainly does), then quit!

**delineate** V. portray; depict; sketch. Using only a few descriptive phrases, Jane Austen *delineates* the character of Mr. Collins so well that we can predict his every move. delineation, N.

**delirium** N. mental disorder marked by confusion. In his *delirium,* the drunkard saw pink panthers and talking pigs. Perhaps he wasn't *delirious;* he might just have wandered into a movie.

**delusion** N. false belief; hallucination. Don suffers from *delusions* of grandeur: he thinks he's a world-famous author when he's published just one paperback book.

• **demean** V. degrade; humiliate. Standing on his dignity, he refused to *demean* himself by replying to the offensive letter. If you truly believed in the dignity of labor, you would not think it would *demean* you to work as a janitor.

**demeanor** N. behavior; bearing. His sober *demeanor* quieted the noisy revelers.

**demolish** V. destroy; tear down. Before building a new hotel along the waterfront, the construction company had to *demolish* several rundown warehouses on that site. demolition, N.

## Word List 13   demur–dichotomy

**demur** V. object (because of doubts, scruples); hesitate. When offered a post on the board of directors, David *demurred*: he had doubts about taking on the job because he was unsure he could handle it in addition to his other responsibilities.

**demure** ADJ. grave; serious; coy. She was *demure* and reserved, a nice modest girl whom any young man would be proud to take home to his mother.

• **denounce** V. condemn; criticize. The reform candidate *denounced* the corrupt city officials for having betrayed the public's trust. denunciation, N.

**deny** V. contradict; refuse. Do you *deny* his story, or do you support what he says? How could Pat *deny* the truth of the accusation that he'd been swiping the

Oreos when he'd been caught with his hand in the cookie jar? denial, N.

• **depict** V. portray. In this sensational exposé, the author *depicts* John Lennon as a drug-crazed neurotic. Do you question the accuracy of this *depiction* of Lennon?

• **deplete** V. reduce; exhaust. We must wait until we *deplete* our present inventory before we order replacements.

• **deplore** V. regret strongly; express grief over. Although Ann Landers *deplored* the disintegration of the modern family, she recognized that not every marriage could be saved.

**deprecate** V. express disapproval of; protest against. A firm believer in old-fashioned courtesy, Miss Post *deprecated* the unfortunate modern tendency to address new acquaintances by their first names. deprecatory, ADJ.

**depreciate** V. lessen in value. If you neglect this property, it will *depreciate.*

**deprivation** N. loss. In prison she faced the sudden *deprivation* of rights she had taken for granted: the right to stay up late reading a book, the right to privacy, the right to make a phone call to a friend.

**derelict** ADJ. abandoned; negligent. The *derelict* craft was a menace to navigation. Whoever abandoned it in mid harbor was *derelict* in living up to his or her responsibilities as a boat owner. dereliction, N.

• **derision** N. ridicule; mockery. Greeting his pretentious dialogue with *derision,* the critics refused to consider his play seriously. deride, V.

• **derivative** ADJ. unoriginal; derived from another source. Although her early poetry was clearly *derivative* in nature, the critics felt she had promise and eventually would find her own voice.

**desecrate** V. profane; violate the sanctity of. The soldiers *desecrated* the temple, shattering the altar and trampling the holy objects underfoot.

**designation** N. identifying name; appointment to a position or office. For years the president's home had no proper *designation*; eventually it was called the White House. Given Gary's background in accounting, his *designation* as treasurer came as no surprise to his fellow board members.

**despise** V. look on with scorn; regard as worthless or distasteful. Mr. Bond, I *despise* spies; I look down on them as mean, *despicable,* honorless men, whom I would cheerfully wipe from the face of the earth.

**despondent** ADJ. depressed; gloomy. To the dismay of his parents, William became so seriously *despondent* after he broke up with Jan that they despaired of finding a cure for his gloom. despondency, N.

**desultory** ADJ. aimless; haphazard; digressing at random. In prison Malcolm X set himself the task of reading straight through the dictionary; to him, reading was purposeful, not *desultory.*

• **detached** ADJ. emotionally removed; calm and objective; indifferent. A psychoanalyst must maintain a *detached* point of view and stay uninvolved with her patients' personal lives. detachment, N. (secondary meaning)

**determination** N. resolve; measurement or calculation; decision. Nothing could shake his *determination* that his children would get the best education that money could buy. Thanks to my pocket calculator, my *determination* of the answer to the problem took only seconds of my time.

• **deterrent** N. something that discourages; hindrance. Does the threat of capital punishment serve as a *deterrent* to potential killers? deter, V.

**detrimental** ADJ. harmful; damaging. The candidate's acceptance of major financial contributions from a well-known racist ultimately proved *detrimental* to his campaign, for he lost the backing of many of his early grassroots supporters. detriment, N.

**deviate** V. turn away from (a principle, norm); depart; diverge. Richard never *deviated* from his daily routine: every day he set off for work at eight o'clock, had his sack lunch (peanut butter on whole wheat) at 12:15, and headed home at the stroke of five.

**devious** ADJ. roundabout; erratic; not straightforward. The Joker's plan was so *devious* that it was only with great difficulty we could follow its shifts and dodges.

**dexterous** ADJ. skillful. The magician was so *dexterous* that we could not follow him as he performed his tricks.

**diagnosis** N. art of identifying a disease; analysis of a condition. In medical school Margaret developed her skill at *diagnosis,* learning how to read volumes from a rapid pulse or a hacking cough. diagnose, V.; diagnostic, ADJ.

**dichotomy** N. split; branching into two parts (especially contradictory ones). Willie didn't know how to resolve the *dichotomy* between his ambition to go to college and his childhood longing to run away to join the circus. Then he heard about Ringling Brothers Circus College, and he knew he'd found the perfect school.

# Word List 14   didactic–disparate

• **didactic** ADJ. teaching; instructional. Pope's lengthy poem *An Essay on Man* is too *didactic* for my taste: I dislike it when poets turn preachy and moralize.

**diehard** N. unyielding opponent (to a measure, position, etc.). Even the popular new president could not win support for his universal health care plan from the *diehards* in his party.

• **diffident** ADJ. shy; lacking confidence; reserved. Can a naturally *diffident* person become a fast-talking, successful used car salesman?

**diffuse** ADJ. wordy; rambling; spread out (like a gas). If you pay authors by the word, you tempt them to produce *diffuse* manuscripts rather then brief ones. diffusion, N.

• **digression** N. wandering away from the subject. Nobody minded when Professor Renoir's lectures wandered away from their official theme; his *digressions* were always more fascinating than the topic of the day. digress, V.

**dilemma** N. problem; choice of two unsatisfactory alternatives. In this *dilemma,* he knew no one to whom he could turn for advice.

**dilettante** N. aimless follower of the arts; amateur; dabbler. He was not serious in his painting; he was rather a *dilettante.*

**diligence** N. steadiness of effort; persistent hard work. Her employers were greatly impressed by her *diligence* and offered her a partnership in the firm. diligent, ADJ.

**dilute** V. make less concentrated; reduce in strength. She preferred her coffee *diluted* with milk.

**diminutive** ADJ. small in size. Looking at the tiny gymnast, we were amazed that anyone so *diminutive* could perform with such power.

**din** N. continued loud noise. The *din* of the jackhammers outside the classroom window drowned out the lecturer's voice. also V.

**dirge** N. lament with music. The funeral *dirge* stirred us to tears.

**disavowal** N. denial; disclaiming. His *disavowal* of his part in the conspiracy was not believed by the jury. disavow, V.

• **discernible** ADJ. distinguishable; perceivable. The ships in the harbor were not *discernible* in the fog.

**discerning** ADJ. mentally quick and observant; having insight. Though no genius, the star was sufficiently *discerning* to tell her true friends from the countless phonies who flattered her.

• **disclaimer** N. denial of a legal claim or right; disavowal. Though reporter Joe Klein issued a *disclaimer* stating that he was *not* Anonymous, the author of *Primary Colors,* eventually he admitted that he had written the controversial novel. disclaim, V.

• **disclose** V. reveal. Although competitors offered him bribes, he refused to *disclose* any information about his company's forthcoming product. disclosure, N.

**disconcert** V. confuse; upset; embarrass. The lawyer was *disconcerted* by the evidence produced by her adversary.

• **discord** N. lack of harmony; conflict; Watching Tweedledum battle Tweedledee, Alice wondered what had caused this pointless *discord.*

**discount** V. discredit; reduce in price. Be prepared to *discount* what he has to say about his ex-wife.

• **discrepancy** N. lack of consistency; contradiction; difference. "Observe, Watson, the significant *discrepancies* between Sir Percy's original description of the crime and his most recent testimony. What do these contradictions suggest?"

**discriminating** ADJ. able to see differences; prejudiced. A superb interpreter of Picasso, she was sufficiently *discriminating* to judge the most complex works of modern art. [secondary meaning] discrimination, N.

**discursive** ADJ. digressing; rambling. As the lecturer wandered from topic to topic, we wondered what if any point there was to his *discursive* remarks.

**disdain** V. view with scorn or contempt. In the film *Funny Face,* the bookish heroine *disdained* fashion models for their lack of intellectual interests. also N.

**disembark** V. go ashore; unload cargo from a ship. Before the passengers could *disembark,* they had to pick up their passports from the ship's purser.

• **disgruntled** ADJ. discontented; sulky and dissatisfied. The numerous delays left the passengers feeling *disgruntled.* disgruntle, V.

**disheveled** ADJ. untidy. Your *disheveled* appearance will hurt your chances in this interview.

• **disinterested** ADJ. unprejudiced. Given the judge's political ambitions and the lawyers' financial interest in the case, the only *disinterested* person in the courtroom may have been the court reporter.

**dismay** V. discourage; frighten. The huge amount of work she had left to do *dismayed* her. also N.

• **dismiss** V. put away from consideration; reject. Believing in John's love for her, she *dismissed* the notion that he might be unfaithful. [secondary meaning]

• **disparage** V. belittle. A doting mother, Emma was more likely to praise her son's crude attempts at art than to *disparage* them.

• **disparate** ADJ. basically different; unrelated. Unfortunately, Tony and Tina have *disparate* notions of marriage: Tony sees it as a carefree extended love affair, while Tina sees it as a solemn commitment to build a family and a home.

## Word List 15   disparity–duplicity

**disparity** N. difference; condition of inequality. Their *disparity* in rank made no difference at all to the prince and Cinderella.

**dispassionate** ADJ. calm; impartial. Known in the company for his cool judgment, Bill could impartially examine the causes of a problem, giving a *dispassionate* analysis of what had gone wrong, and go on to suggest how to correct the mess.

• **dispatch** N. speediness; prompt execution; message sent with all due speed. Young Napoleon defeated the enemy with all possible *dispatch*; he then sent a *dispatch* to headquarters, informing his commander of the great victory. also V.

• **dispel** V. scatter; cause to vanish. The bright sunlight eventually *dispelled* the morning mist.

• **disperse** V. scatter. The police fired tear gas into the crowd to *disperse* the protesters.

**disputatious** ADJ. argumentative; fond of arguing. Convinced he knew more than his lawyers, Tom was a *disputatious* client, ready to argue about the best way to conduct the case.

**dissemble** V. disguise; pretend. Even though John tried to *dissemble* his motive for taking modern dance, we all knew he was there not to dance but to meet girls.

**disseminate** V. distribute; spread; scatter (like seeds). By their use of the Internet, propagandists have been able to *disseminate* their pet doctrines to new audiences around the globe.

• **dissent** V. disagree. In the recent Supreme Court decision, Justice Kennedy *dissented* from the majority opinion. also N.

**dissertation** N. formal essay. In order to earn a graduate degree from many of our universities, a candidate is frequently required to prepare a *dissertation* on some scholarly subject.

**dissident** ADJ. dissenting; rebellious. In the purge that followed the student demonstrations at Tiananmen Square, the government hunted down the *dissident* students and their supporters. also N.

• **dissipate** V. squander; waste; scatter. He is a fine artist, but we fear he may *dissipate* his gifts if he keeps wasting his time doodling on napkins.

**dissuade** V. persuade not to do; discourage. Since Tom could not *dissuade* Huck from running away from home, he decided to run away with him. dissuasion, N.

• **distinction** N. honor; contrast; discrimination. A holder of the Medal of Honor, George served with great *distinction* in World War II. He made a *distinction,* however, between World War II and Vietnam, which he considered an immoral conflict.

**distort** V. twist out of shape. It is difficult to believe the newspaper accounts of the riots because of the way some reports *distort* and exaggerate the actual events. distortion, N.

**divergent** ADJ. differing; deviating. Since graduating from medical school, the two doctors have taken *divergent* paths, the one going on to become a nationally prominent surgeon, the other dedicating himself to a small family practice in his hometown. divergence, N.

**diverse** ADJ. differing in some characteristics; various. The professor suggested *diverse* ways of approaching the assignment and recommended that we choose one of them. diversity, N.

**diversion** N. act of turning aside; pastime. After studying for several hours, he needed a *diversion* from work. divert, V.

• **divulge** V. reveal. No lover of gossip, Charlotte would never *divulge* anything that a friend told her in confidence.

• **docile** ADJ. obedient; easily managed. As *docile* as he seems today, that old lion was once a ferocious, snarling beast.

• **doctrine** N. teachings, in general; particular principle (religious, legal, etc.) taught. He was so committed to the *doctrines* of his faith that he was unable to evaluate them impartially.

**document** V. provide written evidence. She kept all the receipts from her business trip in order to *document* her expenses for the firm. also N.

• **dogmatic** ADJ. opinionated; arbitrary; doctrinal. We tried to discourage Doug from being so *dogmatic* but never could convince him that his opinions might be wrong.

**dormant** ADJ. sleeping; lethargic; latent. At fifty her long-*dormant* ambition to write flared up once more; within a year she had completed the first of her great historical novels.

**doubtful** ADJ. uncertain; undecided. From the outset, the outcome of the battle was *doubtful*: we had no certainty that we were going to win.

**downcast** ADJ. disheartened; sad. Cheerful and optimistic by nature, Beth was never *downcast* despite the difficulties she faced.

**draconian** ADJ. extremely severe. When the principal canceled the senior prom because some seniors had been late to school that week, we thought the *draconian* punishment was far too harsh for such a minor violation of the rules.

**dregs** N. sediment; worthless residue. David poured the wine carefully to avoid stirring up the *dregs*.

**dross** N. waste matter; worthless impurities. Many methods have been devised to separate the valuable metal from the *dross*.

**ductile** ADJ. malleable; flexible; pliable. Copper is an extremely *ductile* material: you can stretch it into the thinnest of wires, bend it, even wind it into loops.

**duplicity** N. double-dealing; hypocrisy. When Tanya learned that Mark had been two-timing her, she was furious at his *duplicity*.

# Word List 16   duty–enhance

**duty** N. tax on imported or exported goods. Because he was too stingy to pay the *duty* on the watch he'd bought in Switzerland, Rex foolishly tried to smuggle it through Customs.

**dwindle** V. shrink; reduce. The food in the lifeboat gradually *dwindled* away to nothing.

**ebb** V. recede; lessen. Mrs. Dalloway sat on the beach and watched the tide *ebb*. also N.

**ebullient** ADJ. showing excitement; overflowing with enthusiasm. Her *ebullient* nature could not be repressed; she was always bubbling over with exuberance. ebullience, N.

**eccentric** ADJ. irregular; odd; whimsical; bizarre. The comet veered dangerously close to the earth in its *eccentric* orbit. eccentricity, N.

• **eclectic** ADJ. composed of elements drawn from disparate sources. His style of interior decoration was *eclectic*: bits and pieces of furnishings from widely divergent periods strikingly juxtaposed to create a unique decor. eclecticism, N.

• **eclipse** V. darken; extinguish; surpass. The new stock market high *eclipsed* the previous record set in 1995.

**ecstasy** N. rapture; joy; any overpowering emotion. When Allison received her long-hoped-for letter of acceptance from Harvard, she was in *ecstasy*. ecstatic, ADJ.

**effervescence** N. inner excitement or exuberance; bubbling from fermentation or carbonation. Nothing depressed Sue for long; her natural *effervescence* soon reasserted itself. Soda that loses its *effervescence* goes flat. effervescent, ADJ., effervesce, V.

**effrontery** N. insolent boldness. Lady Bracknell was shocked that Jack, a man of no rank or breeding, had possessed the *effrontery* to court the daughter of a noble family.

**egotistical** ADJ. excessively self-centered; self-important; conceited. Typical *egotistical* remark: "But enough of this chit-chat about you and your little problems. Let's talk about what's really important: *Me!*"

**egregious** ADJ. notorious; gross; shocking. She was an *egregious* liar; we all knew better than to believe a word she said.

• **elated** ADJ. overjoyed; in high spirits. Grinning from ear to ear, Carl Lewis was clearly *elated* by his ninth Olympic gold medal. elation, N.

• **elicit** V. draw out (by discussion); call forth. The camp counselor's humorous remarks finally *elicited* a smile from the shy new camper.

**eloquence** N. expressiveness; persuasive speech. The crowds were stirred by Martin Luther King's *eloquence*. eloquent, ADJ.

**elucidate** V. explain; enlighten. He was called upon to *elucidate* the disputed points in his article.

• **elusive** ADJ. evasive; baffling; hard to grasp. Trying to pin down exactly when the contractors would be done remodeling the house, Nancy was frustrated by their *elusive* replies. elude, V.

**emanate** V. issue forth. A strong odor of sulphur *emanated* from the spring.

**emancipate** V. set free. At first, the attempts of the abolitionists to *emancipate* the slaves were unpopular in New England as well as in the South.

• **embellish** V. adorn. We enjoyed my mother-in-law's stories about how she came here from Russia, in part because she *embellished* the bare facts of the journey with humorous anecdotes and vivid descriptive details.

**embrace** V. hug; adopt or espouse; accept readily; encircle; include. Clasping Maid Marian in his arms, Robin Hood *embraced* her lovingly. In joining the outlaws in Sherwood Forest, she had openly *embraced* their cause.

**empathy** N. ability to identify with another's feelings, ideas, etc. What made Ann such a fine counselor was her *empathy,* her ability to put herself in her client's place and feel his emotions as if they were her own. empathize, V.

**empirical** ADJ. based on experience. He distrusted hunches and intuitive flashes; he placed his reliance entirely on *empirical* data.

**emulate** V. imitate; rival. In a brief essay, describe a person you admire, someone whose virtues you would like to *emulate*.

**encumber** V. burden. Some people *encumber* themselves with too much luggage when they go for short trips.

• **endorse** V. approve; support. Everyone waited to see which one of the rival candidates for the city council the mayor would *endorse*. endorsement, N. (secondary meaning).

**enduring** ADJ. lasting; surviving. Keats believed in the *enduring* power of great art, which would outlast its creators' brief lives. endure, V.

**energize** V. invigorate; make forceful and active. Rather than exhausting Maggie, dancing *energized* her.

**engage** V. attract; hire; pledge oneself; confront. "Your case has *engaged* my interest, my lord," said Holmes. "You may *engage* my services."

**engaging** ADJ. charming; attractive. Everyone liked Nancy's pleasant manners and *engaging* personality.

**engender** V. cause; produce. To receive praise for real accomplishments *engenders* self-confidence in a child.

**engross** V. occupy fully. John was so *engrossed* in his studies that he did not hear his mother call.

• **enhance** V. increase; improve. You can *enhance* your chances of being admitted to the college of your choice by learning to write well; an excellent essay can *enhance* any application.

## Word List 17    enigma–explicate

• **enigma** N. puzzle; mystery. "What *do* women want?" asked Dr. Sigmund Freud. Their behavior was an *enigma* to him.

**enterprising** ADJ. ready to undertake ambitious projects. An *enterprising* young man, Matt saw business opportunities on every side and was always eager to capitalize on them.

• **entice** V. lure; attract; tempt. She always tried to *entice* her baby brother into mischief.

• **enumerate** V. list; mention one by one. Huck hung his head in shame as Miss Watson *enumerated* his many flaws.

**enunciate** V. speak distinctly. Stop mumbling! How will people understand you if you do not *enunciate*?

• **ephemeral** ADJ. short-lived; fleeting. The mayfly is an *ephemeral* creature: its adult life lasts little more than a day.

**epic** N. long heroic poem, novel, or similar work of art. Kurosawa's film *Seven Samurai* is an *epic* portraying the struggle of seven warriors to destroy a band of robbers. also ADJ.

**epilogue** N. short speech at conclusion of dramatic work. The audience was so disappointed in the play that many did not remain to hear the *epilogue*.

**equivocal** ADJ. ambiguous; intentionally misleading. Rejecting the candidate's *equivocal* comments on tax reform, the reporters pressed him to state clearly where he stood on the issue. equivocate, V.

• **erode** V. eat away. The limestone was *eroded* by the dripping water until only a thin shell remained. erosion, N.

• **erratic** ADJ. odd; unpredictable. Investors become anxious when the stock market appears *erratic*.

• **erroneous** ADJ. mistaken; wrong. I thought my answer was correct, but it was *erroneous*.

**eschew** V. avoid. Hoping to present himself to his girlfriend as a totally reformed character, he tried to *eschew* all the vices, especially chewing tobacco and drinking bathtub gin.

• **esoteric** ADJ. hard to understand; known only to the chosen few. *New Yorker* short stories often included *esoteric* allusions to obscure people and events; the implication was, if you were in the in-crowd, you'd get the reference; if you came from Cleveland, you would not.

- **espouse** V. adopt; support. She was always ready to *espouse* a worthy cause.

- **esteem** V. respect; value; Jill *esteemed* Jack's taste in music, but she deplored his taste in clothes.

**estranged** ADJ. separated; alienated. The *estranged* wife sought a divorce. estrangement, N.

**ethereal** ADJ. light; heavenly; unusually refined. In Shakespeare's *The Tempest,* the spirit Ariel is an *ethereal* creature, too airy and unearthly for our mortal world.

**euphemism** N. mild expression used in place of an unpleasant one. Until recently, many American southerners avoided the word *bull* in polite speech, replacing it by a *euphemism,* such as *he-cow* or *male beast.*

**euphonious** ADJ. pleasing in sound. *Euphonious* even when spoken, the Italian language is particularly pleasing to the ear when sung. euphony, N.

**evenhanded** ADJ. impartial; fair. Do men and women receive *evenhanded* treatment from their teachers, or, as recent studies suggest, do teachers pay more attention to male students than to females?

**eventuality** N. possible occurrence. The government instituted new security procedures to prepare for the *eventuality* of a terrorist attack.

**evocative** ADJ. tending to call up (emotions, memories). Scent can be remarkably *evocative:* the aroma of pipe tobacco *evokes* the memory of my father; a whiff of talcum powder calls up images of my daughter as a child.

**exacting** ADJ. extremely demanding. Cleaning the ceiling of the Sistine Chapel was an *exacting* task, one that demanded extremely meticulous care on the part of the restorers. exaction, N.

- **excerpt** N. selected passage (written or musical). The cinematic equivalent of an *excerpt* from a novel is a clip from a film.

**exculpate** V. clear from blame. Though Sid came up with excuse after excuse to *exculpate* himself, Samantha still blamed him for his conduct.

**execute** V. put into effect; carry out; put to death. The prima ballerina *executed* the pirouette so badly that the infuriated choreographer was ready to tear out his hair. execution, N.

- **exemplary** ADJ. serving as a model; outstanding. At commencement the dean praised Ellen for her *exemplary* behavior as class president.

- **exonerate** V. acquit; exculpate. The defense team feverishly sought fresh evidence that might *exonerate* its client.

**expansive** ADJ. outgoing and sociable; broad and extensive; able to increase in size. Mr. Fezziwig was in an *expansive* humor, cheerfully urging his guests to join in the Christmas feast. Looking down on his *expansive* paunch, he sighed: if his belly *expanded* any further, his pants would need an *expansive* waistline.

**expedient** ADJ. suitable to achieve a particular end; practical; politic. A pragmatic politician, he was guided by what was *expedient* rather than by what was ethical. expediency, N.

- **expedite** V. hasten. Because we are on a tight schedule, we hope you will be able to *expedite* the delivery of our order. expeditious, ADJ.

**explicate** V. explain; interpret; clarify. Harry Levin *explicated* James Joyce's often bewildering novels with such clarity that even *Finnegan's Wake* seemed comprehensible to his students.

## Word List 18 explicit–fleeting

**explicit** ADJ. totally clear; definite; outspoken. Don't just hint around that you're dissatisfied: be *explicit* about what's bugging you.

- **exploit** N. deed or action, particularly a brave deed. Raoul Wallenberg was noted for his *exploits* in rescuing Jews from Hitler's forces.

**exploit** V. make use of, sometimes unjustly. Cesar Chavez fought attempts to *exploit* migrant farmworkers in California. exploitation, N.

**expunge** V. wipe out; remove; destroy. If you hit the "Delete" key by mistake, you can accidentally *expunge* an entire block of text.

**expurgate** V. clean; remove offensive parts of a book. The editors felt that certain passages in the book had to be *expurgated* before it could be used in the classroom.

**extraneous** ADJ. not essential; superfluous. No wonder Ted can't think straight! His mind is so cluttered up with *extraneous* trivia, he can't concentrate on the essentials.

**extrapolate** V. infer; project from known data into the unknown; make a conjecture. On the basis of what they could *extrapolate* from the results of the primaries on Super Tuesday, the networks predicted that John McCain would be the Republican candidate for the presidency.

**extricate** V. free; disentangle. The fox could not *extricate* itself from the trap.

**exuberant** ADJ. joyfully enthusiastic; flamboyant; lavish; abundant. I was bowled over by Amy's *exuberant* welcome. What an enthusiastic greeting!

**fabricate** V. build; lie. If we *fabricate* the buildings in this project out of standardized sections, we can reduce construction cost considerably. Because of

Jack's tendency to *fabricate,* Jill had trouble believing a word he said.

**facile** ADJ. easily accomplished; ready or fluent; superficial. Words came easily to Jonathan: he was a *facile* speaker and prided himself on being ready to make a speech at a moment's notice.

• **facilitate** V. help bring about; make less difficult. Rest and proper nourishment should *facilitate* the patient's recovery.

• **fallacious** ADJ. false; misleading. Paradoxically, *fallacious* reasoning does not always yield erroneous results: even though your logic may be faulty, the answer you get may nevertheless be correct. fallacy, N.

**fallible** ADJ. liable to err. I know I am *fallible,* but I feel confident that I am right this time.

• **farce** N. broad comedy; mockery. Nothing went right; the entire interview degenerated into a *farce.* farcical, ADJ.

• **fastidious** ADJ. difficult to please; squeamish. Bobby was such a *fastidious* eater that he would eat a sandwich only if his mother first cut off every scrap of crust.

• **fawning** ADJ. seeking favor by cringing and flattering; obsequious. "Stop crawling around like a boot-licker, Uriah! I can't stand your flattery and *fawning* ways." fawn, V.

• **feasible** ADJ. practical. Was it *feasible* to build a new stadium for the Yankees on New York's West Side? Without additional funding, the project was clearly unrealistic.

**feint** N. trick; shift; sham blow. Fooled by his opponent's *feint,* the boxer unwisely dropped his guard. also V.

**ferment** N. agitation; commotion. With the breakup of the Soviet Union, much of Eastern Europe was in a state of *ferment.*

• **fervor** N. glowing ardor; intensity of feeling. At the protest rally, the students cheered the strikers and booed the dean with equal *fervor.* fervent, fervid, ADJ.

**fester** V. provoke keen irritation or resentment. Joe's insult *festered* in Anne's mind for days and made her too angry to speak to him.

**fetid** ADJ. having a foul, disgusting odor. Change the kitty litter in the cat box right now! No self-respecting cat would use a litter box with such a *fetid* smell.

**fetter** V. shackle. The prisoner was *fettered* to the wall.

**fiasco** N. total failure. Tanya's attempt to look sophisticated by smoking was a *fiasco*: she lit the wrong end of the cigarette, choked when she tried to inhale, and burned a hole in her boyfriend's couch.

**fiery** ADJ. easily provoked; passionate; burning. By reputation, redheads have *fiery* tempers; the least little thing can cause them to explode.

**finesse** N. delicate skill. The *finesse* and adroitness with which the surgeon wielded her scalpel impressed the observers in the operating theater.

**finite** ADJ. having an end; limited. Though Bill really wanted to win the pie-eating contest, the capacity of his stomach was *finite,* and he had to call it quits after eating only seven cherry pies.

**firebrand** N. hothead; troublemaker. The police tried to keep track of all the local *firebrands* when the president came to town.

**fissure** N. crevice. The mountain climbers secured footholds in tiny *fissures* in the rock.

**fitful** ADJ. spasmodic; intermittent. After several *fitful* attempts, he decided to postpone the start of the project until he felt more energetic.

**fleeting** ADJ. transitory; vanishing quickly. The glory of a New England autumn is *fleeting*: the first gust of wind strips the trees of their colorful leaves.

# Word List 19   flippant–garble

• **flippant** ADJ. lacking proper seriousness. When Mark told Mona he loved her, she dismissed his earnest declaration with a *flippant* "Oh, you say that to all the girls!" flippancy, N.

**flout** V. reject; mock. The headstrong youth *flouted* all authority; he refused to be curbed.

**fluctuate** V. waver; shift. The water pressure in our shower *fluctuates* wildly; you start rinsing yourself off with a trickle, and, two minutes later, a blast of water nearly knocks you down.

**fluency** N. smoothness of speech. He spoke French with *fluency* and ease.

**foible** N. weakness; slight fault. We can overlook the *foibles* of our friends; no one is perfect.

**foliage** N. masses of leaves. Every autumn before the leaves fell, he promised himself he would drive through New England to admire the colorful fall *foliage.*

**forbearance** N. patience. We must use *forbearance* in dealing with him because he is still weak from his illness.

**foreboding** N. premonition of evil. Suspecting no conspiracies against him, Caesar gently ridiculed his wife's *forebodings* about the ides of March.

**foreshadow** V. give an indication beforehand; portend; prefigure. In retrospect, political analysts realized that Yeltsin's defiance of the attempted coup *foreshadowed* his emergence as the dominant figure of the new Russian republic.

**foresight** N. ability to foresee future happenings; careful provision for the future. A shrewd investor, she had the *foresight* to buy land just before the current real estate boom.

**forestall** V. prevent by taking action in advance. By setting up a prenuptial agreement, the prospective bride and groom hoped to *forestall* any potential arguments about money in the event of a divorce.

**forfeit** V. lose; surrender. Convicted murderers *forfeit* the right to inherit anything from their victims; the law does not allow them to benefit financially from their crimes.

**forgo** V. give up; do without. Determined to lose weight over the summer, Michelle decided to *forgo* dessert until she could fit into a size eight again.

**formidable** ADJ. inspiring fear or apprehension; difficult; awe inspiring. In the film *Meet the Parents,* the hero is understandably nervous about meeting his fiancée's father, a *formidable* CIA agent.

• **forthright** ADJ. outspoken; frank. Never afraid to call a spade a spade, she was perhaps too *forthright* to be a successful party politician.

**fortuitous** ADJ. accidental; by chance. Though he pretended their encounter was *fortuitous,* he'd actually been hanging around her usual haunts for the past two weeks, hoping she'd turn up.

**foster** V. rear; encourage. According to the legend, Romulus and Remus were *fostered* by a she-wolf who raised the abandoned infants as her own. also ADJ.

• **frail** ADJ. weak. The delicate child seemed too *frail* to lift the heavy carton.

**franchise** N. right granted by authority; right to vote; business licensed to sell a product in a particular territory. The city issued a *franchise* to the company to operate surface transit lines on the streets for 99 years. For most of American history, women lacked the right to vote: not until the early twentieth century was the *franchise* granted to women. Stan owns a Carvel's ice cream *franchise* in Chinatown.

**frantic** ADJ. wild. At the time of the collision, many people became *frantic* with fear.

**fraudulent** ADJ. cheating; deceitful. The government seeks to prevent *fraudulent* and misleading advertising.

• **frivolous** ADJ. lacking in seriousness; self-indulgently carefree; relatively unimportant. Though Nancy enjoyed Bill's *frivolous,* lighthearted companionship, she sometimes wondered whether he could ever be serious. frivolity, N.

**fugitive** ADJ. fleeting or transient; elusive; fleeing. How can a painter capture on canvas the *fugitive* beauty of clouds moving across the sky? also N.

**fundamental** V. basic; primary; essential. The committee discussed all sorts of side issues without ever getting down to addressing the *fundamental* problem.

**furtive** ADJ. stealthy; sneaky. Noticing the *furtive* glance the customer gave the diamond bracelet on the counter, the jeweler wondered whether he had a potential shoplifter on his hands.

**fusion** N. union; coalition. The opponents of the political party in power organized a *fusion* of disgruntled groups and became an important element in the election.

**futile** ADJ. useless; hopeless; ineffectual. It is *futile* for me to try to get any work done around here while the telephone is ringing every thirty seconds. futility, N.

**gainful** ADJ. profitable. After having been out of work for six months, Brenda was excited by the prospect of *gainful* employment.

**gale** N. windstorm; gust of wind; emotional outburst (laughter, tears). The Weather Channel warned viewers about a rising *gale,* with winds of up to 60 miles per hour.

**galvanize** V. stimulate by shock; stir up; revitalize. News that the prince was almost at their door *galvanized* the ugly stepsisters into a frenzy of combing and primping.

**garble** V. mix up; jumble; distort. A favorite party game involves passing a whispered message from one person to another, till, by the time it reaches the last player, everyone has totally *garbled* the message.

## Word List 20 garish–hazardous

**garish** ADJ. overbright in color; gaudy. She wore a gaudy rhinestone necklace with an excessively *garish* gold lamé dress.

• **garrulous** ADJ. loquacious; wordy; talkative. My Uncle Henry can outtalk any three people I know. He is the most *garrulous* person in Cayuga County. garrulity, N.

**gastric** ADJ. pertaining to the stomach. Clutching his stomach and grimacing broadly, the acting student feigned *gastric* distress.

**gavel** N. hammerlike tool; mallet. "Sold!" cried the auctioneer, banging her *gavel* on the table to indicate she'd accepted the final bid.

**genealogy** N. record of descent; lineage. He was proud of his *genealogy* and constantly referred to the achievements of his ancestors.

• **generate** V. cause; produce; create. In his first days in office, President Obama managed to *generate* a new mood of optimism; we hoped he could *generate* a few new jobs.

**generic** ADJ. characteristic of an entire class or species. Sue knew so many computer programmers who spent their spare time playing fantasy games that she began to think that playing Dungeons & Dragons was a *generic* trait.

• **genre** N. particular variety of art or literature. Both a short story writer and a poet, Langston Hughes proved himself equally skilled in either *genre*.

**genteel** ADJ. well-bred; elegant. We are looking for a man with a *genteel* appearance who can inspire confidence by his cultivated manner.

**germane** ADJ. pertinent; bearing upon the case at hand. The lawyer objected that the witness's testimony was not *germane* to the case and should be ignored by the jury.

**gibberish** N. nonsense; babbling. "Did you hear that fool boy spouting *gibberish* about monsters from outer space? I never heard anything so nonsensical in all my . . ."

**giddy** ADJ. lighthearted; dizzy. The silly, *giddy* young girls rode ride after ride on the Tilt-a-Whirl until they were *giddy* and sick.

**gingerly** ADV. very carefully. To separate egg whites, first crack the egg *gingerly*, avoiding breaking the yolk.

**glimmer** V. shine erratically; twinkle. In the darkness of the cavern, the glowworms hanging from the cavern roof *glimmered* like distant stars.

**gloss over** V. explain away. No matter how hard he tried to talk around the issue, the president could not *gloss over* the fact that he had raised taxes after all.

**glower** V. scowl. The angry boy *glowered* at his father.

• **gluttonous** ADJ. greedy for food. The *gluttonous* boy ate all the cookies.

**gorge** N. small, steep-walled canyon. The white-water rafting guide warned us about the rapids farther downstream, where the river cut through a narrow *gorge*.

**gorge** V. stuff oneself. The gluttonous guest *gorged* himself, cramming food into his mouth as fast as he could.

**grandeur** N. impressiveness; stateliness; majesty. No matter how often he hiked through the mountains, David never failed to be struck by the *grandeur* of the Sierra Nevada range.

**grandiose** ADJ. pretentious; high-flown; ridiculously exaggerated; impressive. The aged matinee idol still had *grandiose* notions of his supposed importance in the theatrical world.

**graphic** ADJ. pertaining to the art of delineating; vividly described. I was particularly impressed by the *graphic* presentation of the storm.

• **gratify** V. please. Amy's success in her new job *gratified* her parents.

**gratuitous** ADJ. given freely; unwarranted; uncalled for. Quit making *gratuitous* comments about my driving; no one asked you for your opinion.

• **gregarious** ADJ. sociable. Typically, party-throwers are *gregarious;* hermits are not.

**guile** N. deceit; duplicity; wiliness; cunning. Iago uses considerate *guile* to trick Othello into believing that Desdemona has been unfaithful.

**gullible** ADJ. easily deceived. Overly *gullible* people have only themselves to blame if they fall for scams repeatedly. As the saying goes, "Fool me once, shame on you. Fool me twice, shame on me."

• **hackneyed** ADJ. commonplace; trite. When the reviewer criticized the movie for its *hackneyed* plot, we agreed; we had seen similar stories hundreds of times before.

• **halting** ADJ. hesitant; faltering. Novice extemporaneous speakers often talk in a *halting* fashion as they grope for the right words.

• **hamper** V. obstruct. The new mother didn't realize how much the effort of caring for an infant would *hamper* her ability to keep an immaculate house.

**harangue** N. noisy speech. In her lengthy *harangue,* the principal berated the offenders. also V.

**harass** V. to annoy by repeated attacks. When he could not pay his bills as quickly as he had promised, he was *harassed* by his creditors.

**harbor** V. provide a refuge for; hide. The church *harbored* illegal aliens who were political refugees.

**haughtiness** N. pride; arrogance. When she realized that Darcy believed himself too good to dance with his inferiors, Elizabeth took great offense at his *haughtiness*.

**hazardous** ADJ. dangerous. Your occupation is too *hazardous* for insurance companies to consider your application.

# Word List 21   headstrong–imbue

**headstrong** ADJ. stubborn; willful; unyielding. Because she refused to marry the man her parents had chosen for her, everyone scolded Minna and called her a foolish *headstrong* girl.

**heckle** V. harass; taunt; jeer at. The home team's fans mercilessly *heckled* the visiting pitcher, taunting him whenever he let anyone get on base.

**heed** V. pay attention to; consider. We hope you *heed* our advice and get a good night's sleep before the test. also N.

**herculean** ADJ. very strong; extremely difficult to perform; like the mythological hero Hercules.

Muscles rippling, the action hero was a *herculean* figure, lifting enormous weights with ease.

**heresy** N. opinion contrary to popular belief; opinion contrary to accepted religion. Galileo's assertion that the earth moved around the sun directly contradicted the religious teachings of his day; as a result, he was tried for *heresy*. heretic, N.

**hermetic** ADJ. sealed by fusion so as to be airtight. After you sterilize the bandages, place them in a container and seal it with a *hermetic* seal to protect them from contamination by airborne bacteria.

**hermit** N. someone who chooses to live in solitude; recluse. Abandoning society, Thoreau chose to go off and live in the woods like a *hermit*.

**hiatus** N. gap; pause. Except for a brief two-year *hiatus*, during which she enrolled in the Peace Corps, Ms. Clements has devoted herself to her medical career.

**hibernate** V. sleep throughout the winter. Bears are one of the many species of animals that *hibernate*. hibernation, N.

**hierarchy** N. arrangement by rank or standing; authoritarian body divided into ranks. To be low man on the totem pole is to have an inferior place in the *hierarchy*.

• **hindrance** N. block; obstacle. Stalled cars along the highway are a *hindrance* to traffic that tow trucks should remove without delay. hinder, V.

**homespun** ADJ. domestic; made at home. *Homespun* wit like *homespun* cloth was often coarse and plain.

• **hostility** N. unfriendliness; hatred. Children who have been the sole objects of their parents' attention often feel *hostility* toward a new baby in the family, resenting the newcomer who has taken their place.

**humane** ADJ. marked by kindness or consideration. It is ironic that the *Humane* Society sometimes must show its compassion toward mistreated animals by killing them to put them out of their misery.

**humble** ADJ. modest; not proud. He spoke with great feeling of how much he loved his *humble* home, which he would not trade for a palace. humility, N.

**husband** V. use sparingly; conserve; save. Marathon runners must *husband* their energy so that they can keep going for the entire distance.

**hyperbole** N. exaggeration; overstatement. As far as I'm concerned, Apple's claims about the new computer are pure *hyperbole:* no machine is that good!

• **hypocritical** ADJ. pretending to be virtuous; deceiving. It was *hypocritical* of Martha to say such nice things about my poetry to me and then make fun of my verses behind my back. hypocrisy, N.

• **hypothetical** ADJ. based on assumptions or hypotheses; supposed. Suppose you are accepted by Harvard, Stanford, and Brown. Which one would you choose to attend? Remember, this is only a *hypothetical* situation. hypothesis, N.

• **iconoclastic** ADJ. attacking cherished traditions. Deeply *iconoclastic,* Jean Genet deliberately set out to shock conventional theatergoers with his radical plays.

**ideology** N. system of ideas of a group. For people who had grown up believing in the communist *ideology,* it was hard to adjust to capitalism.

**idiom** N. expression whose meaning as a whole differs from the meanings of its individual words; distinctive style. The phrase "to lose one's marbles" is an *idiom:* if I say that Joe's lost his marbles, I'm not asking you to find some for him. I'm telling you *idiomatically* that he's crazy.

**idiosyncrasy** N. individual trait, usually odd in nature; eccentricity. One of Richard Nixon's little *idiosyncrasies* was his liking for ketchup on cottage cheese. One of Hannibal Lecter's little *idiosyncrasies* was his liking for human flesh.

**ignite** V. kindle; light. When Desi crooned "Baby, light my fire," literal-minded Lucy looked around for some paper to *ignite*.

**ignoble** ADJ. unworthy; base in nature; not noble. Sir Galahad was so pure in heart that he could never stoop to perform an *ignoble* deed.

**illuminate** V. brighten; clear up or make understandable; enlighten. Just as a lamp can *illuminate* a dark room, a perceptive comment can *illuminate* a knotty problem.

**illusory** ADJ. deceptive; not real. Unfortunately, the costs of running the lemonade stand were so high that Tom's profits proved *illusory*.

**imbalance** N. lack of balance or symmetry; disproportion. To correct racial *imbalance* in the schools, school boards have bussed black children into white neighborhoods and white children into black ones.

**imbibe** V. drink in. The dry soil *imbibed* the rain quickly.

**imbue** V. permeate completely; dye thoroughly; fill. The sight of her grandparents' names inscribed on the wall of Ellis Island *imbued* Sarah with a sense of her special heritage as the descendant of immigrants.

## Word List 22   immaterial–incarcerate

**immaterial** ADJ. unimportant; irrelevant; intangible. Though Kit said it was wholly *immaterial* whether she had a birthday party or not, we wanted to throw her a party.

**imminent** ADJ.; near at hand; impending. Rosa was such a last-minute worker that she could never start writing a paper till the deadline was *imminent*.

**immobilize** V. make unable to move. For a moment, Peter's fear of snakes *immobilized* him; then the use of his limbs returned to him and he bolted from the room.

**immune** ADJ. resistant to; free or exempt from. Fortunately, Florence had contracted chicken pox as a child and was *immune* to it when her baby broke out in spots.

• **immutable** ADJ. unchangeable. All things change over time; nothing is *immutable*.

**impair** V. injure; hurt. Drinking alcohol can *impair* your ability to drive safely; if you're going to drink, don't drive.

**impart** V. give or convey; communicate. A born dancer, she *imparted* her love of movement to her audience with every step she took.

**impartial** ADJ. not biased; fair. Knowing she could not be *impartial* about her own child, Jo refused to judge any match in which Billy was competing.

**impassable** ADJ. not able to be traveled or crossed. A giant redwood had fallen across the highway, blocking all four lanes: the road was *impassable*.

**impasse** N. predicament offering no escape; deadlock; dead end. The negotiators reported they had reached an *impasse* in their talks and had little hope of resolving the deadlock swiftly.

**impecunious** ADJ. without money. Though Scrooge claimed he was too *impecunious* to give alms, he easily could have afforded to be charitable.

• **impede** v. hinder; block; delay. A series of accidents *impeded* the launching of the space shuttle.

**impel** V. drive or force onward. A strong feeling of urgency *impelled* her; if she failed to finish the project right then, she knew that she would never get it done.

• **imperceptible** ADJ. unnoticeable; undetectable. Fortunately, the stain on the blouse was *imperceptible* after the blouse had gone through the wash.

**impermeable** ADJ. impervious; not permitting passage through its substance. Sue chose a raincoat made of Gore-Tex because the material was *impermeable* to liquids.

**impertinent** ADJ. insolent; rude. His neighbors' *impertinent* curiosity about his lack of dates angered Ted. It was downright rude of them to ask him such personal questions.

**imperturbable** ADJ. calm; placid; composed. In the midst of the battle, the Duke of Wellington remained *imperturbable* and in full command of the situation despite the hysteria and panic all around him. imperturbability, N.

**impetuous** ADJ. violent; hasty; rash. "Leap before you look" was the motto suggested by one particularly *impetuous* young man.

**impiety** N. irreverence; lack of respect for God. When members of the youth group draped the church in toilet paper one Halloween, the minister reprimanded them for their *impiety*. impious, ADJ.

• **implacable** ADJ. incapable of being pacified. Relentlessly seeking revenge, Madame Defarge was the *implacable* enemy of the Evremonde family.

• **implement** V. put into effect; supply with tools. The mayor was unwilling to *implement* the plan until she was sure it had the governor's backing. also N.

**implicate** V. incriminate; show to be involved. Here's the deal: If you agree to take the witness stand and *implicate* your partners in crime, the prosecution will recommend that the judge go easy in sentencing you.

• **implication** N. something hinted at or suggested. When Miss Watson said she hadn't seen her purse since the last time Jim was in the house, the *implication* was that she suspected Jim had taken it. imply, V.

**implicit** ADJ. understood but not stated. Jack never told Jill he adored her; he believed his love was *implicit* in his deeds.

**importune** V. beg persistently. Democratic and Republican phone solicitors *importuned* her for contributions so frequently that she decided to give nothing to either party.

**impotent** ADJ. weak; ineffective. Although he wished to break the nicotine habit, he found himself *impotent* to resist the craving for a cigarette.

• **impromptu** ADJ. without previous preparation; off the cuff; on the spur of the moment. The judges were amazed that she could make such a thorough, well-supported presentation in an *impromptu* speech.

**inadvertently** ADV. unintentionally; by oversight; carelessly. Judy's great fear was that she might *inadvertently* omit a question on the exam and mismark her whole answer sheet.

**inane** ADJ. silly; senseless. There's no point in what you're saying. Why are you bothering to make such *inane* remarks? inanity, N.

**inanimate** ADJ. lifeless. She was asked to identify the still and *inanimate* body.

**inarticulate** ADJ. speechless; producing indistinct speech. He became *inarticulate* with rage and uttered sounds without meaning.

**incapacitate** V. disable. During the winter, many people were *incapacitated* by respiratory ailments.

• **incarcerate** V. imprison. The civil rights workers were willing to be arrested and even *incarcerated* if by their imprisonment they could serve the cause.

## Word List 23 incentive–infallible

**incentive** N. spur; motive. Mike's strong desire to outshine his big sister was all the *incentive* he needed to do well in school.

**incessant** ADJ. uninterrupted; unceasing. In a famous TV commercial, the frogs' *incessant* croaking goes on and on until eventually it turns into a single word: "Bud-weis-er."

**incipient** ADJ. beginning; in an early stage. I will go to sleep early for I want to break an *incipient* cold.

**incite** V. arouse to action; goad; motivate; induce to exist. In a fiery speech, Mario *incited* his fellow students to go out on strike to protest the university's anti-affirmative-action stand.

**inclusive** ADJ. tending to include all. The comedian turned down the invitation to join the Players' Club, saying any club that would let him in was too *inclusive.*

• **incongruity** N. lack of harmony; absurdity. The *incongruity* of his wearing sneakers with formal attire amused the observers. incongruous, ADJ.

**incoherent** ADJ. unintelligible; muddled; illogical. The excited fan blushed and stammered, her words becoming almost *incoherent* in the thrill of meeting her favorite rock star face to face. incoherence, N.

• **inconsequential** ADJ. insignificant; unimportant. Brushing off Ali's apologies for having broken the wine glass, Tamara said, "Don't worry about it; it's *inconsequential.*"

• **inconsistency** N. state of being self-contradictory; lack of uniformity or steadiness. How are lawyers different from agricultural inspectors? While lawyers check *inconsistencies* in witnesses' statements, agricultural inspectors check *inconsistencies* in Grade A eggs. inconsistent, ADJ.

• **incorporate** V. introduce something into a larger whole; combine; unite. Breaking with precedent, President Truman ordered the military to *incorporate* blacks into every branch of the armed services. also ADJ.

**incorporeal** ADJ. lacking a material body; insubstantial. Although Casper the friendly ghost is an *incorporeal* being, he and his fellow ghosts make a decided impact on the physical world.

**incorrigible** ADJ. uncorrectable. Though Widow Douglass hoped to reform Huck, Miss Watson pronounced him *incorrigible* and said he would come to no good end.

**incredulous** ADJ. unwilling or unable to believe; skeptical. When Marco claimed he hadn't eaten the jelly doughnut, Joyce took one *incredulous* look at his smeared face and laughed.

**incrustation** N. hard coating or crust. In dry dock, we scraped off the *incrustation* of dirt and barnacles that covered the hull of the ship.

**incumbent** N. officeholder. The newly elected public official received valuable advice from the previous *incumbent.* also ADJ.

**indefatigable** ADJ. tireless. Although the effort of taking out the garbage tired Wayne out for the entire morning, when it came to partying, he was *indefatigable.*

**indelible** ADJ. not able to be erased. The *indelible* ink left a permanent mark on my shirt. Young Bill Clinton's meeting with President Kennedy made an *indelible* impression on the youth.

• **indict** V. charge. The district attorney didn't want to *indict* the suspect until she was sure she had a strong enough case to convince a jury. indictment, N.

• **indifferent** ADJ. unmoved or unconcerned by; mediocre. Because Consuela felt no desire to marry, she was *indifferent* to Edward's constant proposals. Not only was she *indifferent* to him personally, but she felt that, given his general silliness, he would make an *indifferent* husband.

**indigenous** ADJ. native. Cigarettes are made of tobacco, a plant *indigenous* to the New World.

**indisputable** ADJ. too certain to be disputed. In the face of these *indisputable* statements, I withdraw my complaint.

**indomitable** ADJ. unconquerable; unyielding. Focusing on her final vault despite her twisted ankle, gymnastics star Kerri Strug proved she had an *indomitable* will to win.

**indubitable** ADJ. unable to be doubted; unquestionable. Auditioning for the chorus line, Molly was an *indubitable* hit: the director fired the leading lady and hired Molly in her place!

• **induce** V. persuade; bring about. After the quarrel, Tina said nothing could *induce* her to talk to Tony again. inducement, N.

**indulgent** ADJ. humoring; yielding; lenient. Jay's mom was excessively *indulgent:* she bought him every Nintendo cartridge and video game on the market. She *indulged* Jay so much, she spoiled him rotten.

• **industrious** ADJ. diligent; hard-working. Look busy when the boss walks past your desk; it never hurts to appear *industrious.* industry, N.

**ineffable** ADJ. unutterable; unable to be expressed in speech. Looking down at her newborn daughter, Ruth felt such *ineffable* joy that, for the first time in her adult life, she had no words to convey what was in her heart.

• **inept** ADJ. lacking skill; unsuited; incompetent. The *inept* glove maker was all thumbs. ineptitude, ineptness, N.

**inevitable** ADJ. unavoidable. Though death and taxes are both supposedly *inevitable,* some people avoid paying taxes for years.

• **infallible** ADJ. unerring; faultless. Jane refused to believe the pope was *infallible,* reasoning: "All human beings are capable of error. The pope is a human being. Therefore, the pope is capable of error."

# Word List 24 infamous–insurgent

**infamous** ADJ. notoriously bad. Charles Manson and Jeffrey Dahmer are both *infamous* killers.

**infer** V. deduce; conclude. From the students' glazed looks, it was easy for me to *infer* that they were bored out of their minds. inference, N.

**infernal** ADJ. pertaining to hell; devilish. Batman was baffled: he could think of no way to hinder the Joker's *infernal* scheme to destroy the city.

**infinitesimal** ADJ. exceedingly small; so small as to be almost nonexistent. Making sure everyone was aware she was on an extremely strict diet, Melanie said she would have only an *infinitesimal* sliver of pie.

**infraction** N. violation (of a rule or regulation); breach. When Dennis Rodman butted heads with the referee, he committed a clear *infraction* of NBA rules.

• **ingenious** ADJ. clever; resourceful. Kit admired the *ingenious* way that her computer keyboard opened up to reveal the built-in CD-ROM below. ingenuity, N.

• **ingenuous** ADJ. naive and trusting; young; unsophisticated. The woodsman had not realized how *ingenuous* Little Red Riding Hood was until he heard that she had gone off for a walk in the woods with the Big Bad Wolf.

• **ingrate** N. ungrateful person. That *ingrate* Bob sneered at the tie I gave him.

**ingratiate** V. make an effort to become popular with others. In *All About Eve,* the heroine, an aspiring actress, wages a clever campaign to *ingratiate* herself with Margo Channing, an established star.

• **inherent** ADJ. firmly established by nature or habit. Katya's *inherent* love of justice caused her to champion anyone she considered treated unfairly by society.

**inhibit** V. restrain; retard or prevent. Only two things *inhibited* him from taking a punch at Mike Tyson: Tyson's left hook and Tyson's right jab. The protective undercoating on my car *inhibits* the formation of rust.

• **initiate** V. begin; originate; receive into a group. The college is about to *initiate* a program for reducing math anxiety among students.

**inkling** N. hint. This came as a complete surprise to me as I did not have the slightest *inkling* of your plans.

**inlet** N. small bay; narrow passage between islands; entrance. Seeking shelter from the gale, Drake sailed the *Golden Hind* into a protected *inlet,* where he hoped to wait out the storm.

• **innate** ADJ. inborn. Mozart's parents soon recognized young Wolfgang's *innate* talent for music.

• **innocuous** ADJ. harmless. An occasional glass of wine with dinner is relatively *innocuous* and should have no ill effect on you.

**innovation** N. change; introduction of something new. Although Richard liked to keep up with all the latest technological *innovations,* he didn't always abandon tried-and-true techniques in favor of something new. innovate, V.

**inopportune** ADJ. untimely; poorly chosen. A punk rock concert is an *inopportune* setting for a quiet conversation.

**inordinate** ADJ. unrestrained; excessive. She had an *inordinate* fondness for candy, eating two or three boxes in a single day.

**inquisitor** N. questioner (especially harsh); investigator. Fearing being grilled ruthlessly by the secret police, Masha faced her *inquisitors* with trepidation.

**insatiable** ADJ. not easily satisfied; greedy. Welty's thirst for knowledge was *insatiable;* she was in the library day and night.

• **inscrutable** ADJ. impenetrable; not readily understood; mysterious. Experienced poker players try to keep their expressions *inscrutable,* hiding their reactions to the cards behind a so-called poker face.

**insidious** ADJ. treacherous; stealthy; sly. The fifth column is *insidious* because it works secretly within our territory for our defeat.

• **insightful** ADJ. discerning; perceptive. Sol thought he was very *insightful* about human behavior, but he was actually clueless as to why people acted the way they did.

**insinuate** V. hint; imply; creep in. When you say I look robust, do you mean to *insinuate* that I'm getting fat?

**insipid** ADJ. lacking in flavor; dull. Flat prose and flat ginger ale are equally *insipid*: both lack sparkle.

**insolence** N. impudent disrespect; haughtiness. How dare you treat me so rudely! The manager will hear of your *insolence.* insolent, ADJ.

**insolvent** ADJ. bankrupt; lacking money to pay. When rumors that he was *insolvent* reached his creditors, they began to press him to pay the money he owed them. insolvency, N.

**insomnia** N. wakefulness; inability to sleep. He refused to join us in a midnight cup of coffee because he claimed it gave him *insomnia.*

**instigate** V. urge; start; provoke. Rumors of police corruption led the mayor to *instigate* an investigation into the department's activities.

**insubordination** N. disobedience; rebelliousness. At the slightest hint of *insubordination* from the sailors of the *Bounty,* Captain Bligh had them flogged; finally, they mutinied.

**insubstantial** ADJ. lacking substance; insignificant; frail. His hopes for a career in acting proved *insubstantial;* no one would cast him, even in an *insubstantial* role.

**insurgent** ADJ. rebellious. Because the *insurgent* forces had occupied the capital and had gained control of the railway lines, several of the war correspondents covering the uprising predicted a rebel victory.

## Word List 25   insurrection–jeopardize

**insurrection** N. rebellion; uprising. In retrospect, given how badly the British treated the American colonists, the eventual *insurrection* seems inevitable.

• **intangible** ADJ. not able to be perceived by touch; vague. Though the financial benefits of his Oxford post were meager, Lewis was drawn to it by its *intangible* rewards: prestige, intellectual freedom, the fellowship of his peers.

• **integrity** N. uprightness; wholeness. Lincoln, whose personal *integrity* has inspired millions, fought a civil war to maintain the *integrity* of the Republic, that these United States might remain undivided for all time.

**interminable** ADJ. endless. Although his speech lasted for only twenty minutes, it seemed *interminable* to his bored audience.

**intermittent** ADJ. periodic; on and off. The outdoor wedding reception had to be moved indoors to avoid the *intermittent* showers that fell all afternoon.

**interrogate** V. question closely; cross-examine. Knowing that the Nazis would *interrogate* him about his background, the secret agent invented a cover story that would help him meet their questions.

**intimidate** V. frighten. I'll learn karate and then those big bullies won't be able to *intimidate* me any more.

**intransigence** N. refusal of any compromise; stubbornness. When I predicted that the strike would be over in a week, I didn't expect to encounter such *intransigence* from both sides. intransigent, ADJ.

• **intricacy** N. complexity; knottiness. Philip spent many hours designing mazes of such great *intricacy* that none of his classmates could solve them. intricate, ADJ.

**intrigue** V. fascinate; interest. Holmes's air of reserve *intrigued* Irene Adler; she wanted to know just what made the great detective tick.

**intrinsic** ADJ. essential; inherent; built-in. Although my grandmother's china has little *intrinsic* value, I shall always cherish it for the memories it evokes.

• **introspective** ADJ. looking within oneself. Though young Francis of Assisi led a wild and worldly life, even he had *introspective* moments during which he examined his soul.

**intrude** V. trespass; enter as an uninvited person. She hesitated to *intrude* on their conversation.

**intuition** N. immediate insight; power of knowing without reasoning. Even though Tony denied that anything was wrong, Tina trusted her *intuition* that something was bothering him. intuitive, ADJ.

**inundate** V. overwhelm; flood; submerge. This semester I am *inundated* with work: you should see the piles of paperwork flooding my desk. Until the great dam was build, the waters of the Nile used to *inundate* the river valley every year.

**invalidate** V. discredit; nullify. The relatives who received little or nothing sought to *invalidate* the will by claiming that the deceased had not been in his right mind when he signed the document.

**invective** N. abuse. He had expected criticism but not the *invective* that greeted his proposal.

**inviolable** ADJ. secure from corruption, attack, or violation; unassailable. Batman considered his oath to keep the people of Gotham City safe *inviolable*: nothing on earth could make him break this promise.

**irascible** ADJ. irritable; easily angered. Pop had what people call a hair-trigger temper; he was a hot-tempered, *irascible* guy.

**irksome** ADJ. annoying; tedious. The petty rules and regulations Bill had to follow at work irritated him: he found them uniformly *irksome*.

• **irony** N. hidden sarcasm or satire; use of words that seem to mean the opposite of what they actually mean. Gradually his listeners began to realize that the excessive praise he was lavishing on his opponent was actually *irony;* he was in fact ridiculing the poor fool.

**irrational** ADJ. illogical; lacking reason; insane. Many people have such an *irrational* fear of snakes that they panic at the sight of a harmless garter snake.

**irrelevant** ADJ. not applicable; unrelated. No matter how *irrelevant* the patient's mumblings may seem, they give us some indications of what he has on his mind.

**isolate** V. keep apart; pinpoint; quarantine. The medical researchers *isolated* themselves in a remote village. Until they could *isolate* the cause of the plague and develop an effective vaccine, they had to avoid potential carriers of the disease. Anyone infected they *isolated* immediately.

**itinerant** ADJ. wandering; traveling. He was an *itinerant* peddler and traveled through Pennsylvania and Virginia selling his wares. also N.

**jabber** V. chatter rapidly or unintelligibly. Why does the fellow insist on *jabbering* away in French when I can't understand a word he says?

**jargon** N. language used by a special group; technical terminology; gibberish. The computer salesmen at the store used a *jargon* of their own that we simply couldn't follow; we had no idea what they were jabbering about.

**jaunty** ADJ. lighthearted; animated; easy and carefree. In *Singing in the Rain*, Gene Kelly sang and danced his way through the lighthearted title number in a properly *jaunty* style.

**jeopardize** V. endanger; imperil; put at risk. You can't give me a D in chemistry; you'll *jeopardize* my chances of getting into M.I.T. jeopardy, N.

# Word List 26  jocose–lurk

**jocose** ADJ. giving to joking. The salesman was so *jocose* that many of his customers suggested that he become a stand-up comic.

**jocular** ADJ. said or done in jest. Although Bill knew the boss hated jokes, he couldn't resist making one *jocular* remark. jocularity, N.

• **judicious** ADJ. sound in judgment; wise. At a key moment in his life, he made a *judicious* investment that was the foundation of his later wealth.

**justification** N. good or just reason; defense; excuse. The jury found him guilty of the more serious charge because they could see no possible *justification* for his actions.

**juxtapose** V. place side by side. You'll find it easier to compare the two paintings if you *juxtapose* them.

**kindle** V. start a fire; inspire. One of the first things Ben learned in the Boy Scouts was how to *kindle* a fire by rubbing two dry sticks together. Her teacher's praise for her poetry *kindled* a spark of hope inside Maya.

**knit** V. contract into wrinkles; grow together. Whenever David worries, his brow *knits* in a frown. When he broke his leg, he sat around the house all day waiting for the bones to *knit*.

**laborious** ADJ. demanding much work or care; tedious. In putting together his dictionary of the English language, Doctor Johnson undertook a *laborious* task.

**laconic** ADJ. brief and to the point. Many of the characters portrayed by Clint Eastwood are *laconic* types, rugged men of few words.

**laggard** ADJ. slow; sluggish. The sailor had been taught not to be *laggard* in carrying out orders. lag, N., V.

**lair** N. wild animal's living place; den; hideaway. Jack London called his remote dwelling place the *Lair* of the Wolf.

**lament** V. grieve; express sorrow. Even advocates of the war *lamented* the loss of so many lives in combat. lamentation, N.

**lampoon** V. ridicule. This hilarious article *lampoons* the pretensions of some movie moguls. also N.

• **languid** ADJ. weary; feeble; listless; apathetic. The chronic invalid's most recent siege of illness left her *languid* and drooping. languor, N. languish, V.

• **larceny** N. theft. Because of the prisoner's long record of thefts, the district attorney refused to reduce the charge from grand *larceny* to petty *larceny*.

**latent** ADJ. potential but undeveloped; dormant; hidden. Polaroid pictures are popular at parties, because you can see the *latent* photographic image gradually appear before your eyes.

**laud** V. praise. The NFL *lauded* Boomer Esiason's efforts to raise money to combat cystic fibrosis. laudable, laudatory, ADJ.

**leaven** V. cause to rise or grow lighter; mix in something that transforms, alleviates, or enlivens. As bread dough is *leavened*, it puffs up, expanding in volume. also N.

**lenience** N. mildness; permissiveness. Considering the gravity of the offense, we were surprised by the *lenience* of the sentence. also leniency; lenient, ADJ.

**lethal** ADJ. deadly. It is unwise to leave *lethal* weapons where children may find them.

• **lethargic** ADJ. drowsy; dull. The stuffy room made her *lethargic:* she felt as if she was about to nod off.

**levity** N. lack of seriousness; lightness. Stop giggling and wiggling around in your seats: such *levity* is improper in church.

**libel** N. defamatory statement; act of writing something that smears a person's character. If Batman wrote that the Joker was a dirty, rotten, mass-murdering criminal, could the Joker sue Batman for *libel*?

**lilliputian** ADJ. extremely small. Tiny and delicate, the model was built on a *lilliputian* scale. also N.

**linger** V. loiter or dawdle; continue or persist. Hoping to see Juliet pass by, Romeo *lingered* outside the Capulet house for hours. Though Mother made stuffed cabbage on Monday, the smell *lingered* around the house for days.

**loath** ADJ. reluctant; disinclined. Fearing for her son's safety, the overprotective mother was *loath* to let him go on the class trip.

• **loathe** V. detest. Booing and hissing, the audience showed how much they *loathed* the wicked villain.

**lofty** ADJ. very high. Though Barbara Jordan's fellow students used to tease her about her *lofty* ambitions, she rose to hold one of the highest positions in the land.

**longevity** N. long life. When he reached 90, the old man was proud of his *longevity*.

**loquacious** ADJ. talkative. She is very *loquacious* and can speak on the telephone for hours.

**lucid** ADJ. easily understood; clear; intelligible. Her explanation was *lucid* enough for a child to grasp.

**lucrative** ADJ. profitable. He turned his hobby into a *lucrative* profession.

**lugubrious** ADJ. mournful; funereal. Gloomy Gus walked around town with a *lugubrious* expression on his face.

**luminous** ADJ. shining; issuing light. The sun is a *luminous* body.

**lure** V. entice; attract. Baiting his hook with the latest fly he had put together, Grandpa Joe swore that this new fly was so attractive that it could *lure* the wariest trout out of hiding.

**lurk** V. stealthily lie in waiting; slink; exist unperceived. "Who knows what evils *lurk* in the hearts of men? The Shadow knows!"

## Word List 27 luxuriant–meticulous

**luxuriant** ADJ. abundant; rich and splendid; fertile. Lady Godiva was completely covered by her *luxuriant* hair.

**maelstrom** N. whirlpool. The canoe was tossed about in the *maelstrom*.

**magnanimous** ADJ. generous. Philanthropists by definition are *magnanimous;* misers, by definition, are not. magnanimity, N.

• **malice** N. hatred; spite. Jealous of Cinderella's beauty, her wicked stepsisters expressed their *malice* by forcing her to do menial tasks.

**malign** V. speak evil of; bad-mouth; defame. Her hatred of her ex-husband ran so deep that she *maligned* anyone who even casually dated him.

**malignant** ADJ. having an evil influence; virulent. This is a *malignant* disease; we may have to use drastic measures to stop its spread.

**malleable** ADJ. capable of being shaped by pounding; impressionable. Gold is a *malleable* metal, easily shaped into bracelets and rings. Fagin hoped Oliver was a *malleable* lad, easily shaped into a thief.

**manifest** ADJ. evident; visible; obvious. Digby's embarrassment when he met Madonna was *manifest:* his ears turned bright pink, he kept scuffing one shoe in the dirt, and he couldn't look her in the eye.

**marked** ADJ. noticeable; targeted for vengeance. He walked with a *marked* limp, a souvenir of an old I.R.A. attack. As British ambassador, he knew he was a *marked* man.

**marshal** V. put in order. At a debate tournament, extemporaneous speakers have only a minute or two to *marshal* their thoughts before they address their audience.

**martinet** N. strict disciplinarian. Captain Bligh was a *martinet* who observed each regulation to the letter.

**massive** ADJ. solid or heavy; large in scope; severe. The bust of Beethoven emphasizes his high forehead and *massive* brow. The composer suffered a *massive* hearing loss that left him unable to hear the music the orchestra played.

**materialism** N. preoccupation with physical comforts and things. By its nature, *materialism* is opposed to idealism, for where the *materialist* emphasizes the needs of the body, the idealist emphasizes the needs of the soul. materialistic, ADJ.

**maverick** N. rebel; nonconformist. To the masculine literary establishment, George Sand, with her insistence on wearing trousers and smoking cigars, was clearly a *maverick* who fought her proper womanly role.

**mawkish** ADJ. mushy and gushy; sentimental; maudlin. Whenever Gigi and her boyfriend would sigh and get all lovey-dovey, her little brother would shout, "Yuck!," protesting their *mawkish* behavior.

**maxim** N. proverb; a truth pithily stated. Aesop's fables illustrate moral *maxims*.

**meager** ADJ. scanty; inadequate. Still hungry after his *meager* serving of porridge, Oliver Twist asked for a second helping.

**mealymouthed** ADJ. indirect in speech; hypocritical; evasive. Rather than tell Jill directly what he disliked, Jack made a few *mealymouthed* comments and tried to change the subject.

**meander** V. wind or turn in its course. Needing to stay close to a source of water, he followed every twist and turn of the stream as it *meandered* through the countryside.

**mediate** V. settle a dispute through the services of an outsider. King Solomon was asked to *mediate* a dispute between two women, each of whom claimed to be the mother of the same child.

**mediocre** ADJ. ordinary; commonplace. We were disappointed because he gave a rather *mediocre* performance in this role.

**meditation** N. reflection; thought. She reached her decision only after much *meditation*.

• **meek** ADJ. quiet and obedient; spiritless. Can Lois Lane see through Superman's disguise and spot the superhero masquerading as the *meek*, timorous Clark Kent?

**melancholy** ADJ. gloomy; morose; blue. To Eugene, stuck in his small town, a train whistle was a *melancholy* sound, for it made him think of all the places he would never get to see.

**mellifluous** ADJ. sweetly or smoothly flowing; melodious. What a *mellifluous* language Italian is! Even the street vendors' cries sound like little songs.

**mentor** N. counselor; teacher. During this very trying period, she could not have had a better *mentor*, for her adviser was sympathetic and understanding.

**mercantile** ADJ. concerning trade. Selling candy bars to his classmates whose parents had packed their lunch boxes with apples and carrot sticks, George clearly was destined to be a *mercantile* success.

**mercenary** ADJ. interested in money or gain. Andy's every act was prompted by *mercenary* motives: his first question was always, "What's in it for me?"

**mercurial** ADJ. capricious; changing; fickle. Quick as quicksilver to change, he was *mercurial* in nature and therefore unreliable.

**mesmerize** V. hypnotize; fascinate. On a long stretch of road between Fresno and Los Angeles, the open highway began to *mesmerize* Richard; he pulled over to the side of the road and rested to free himself from highway hypnosis.

• **meticulous** ADJ. excessively careful; painstaking; scrupulous. Martha Stewart, a *meticulous* housekeeper, fusses about each and every detail that goes into making up her perfect home.

## Word List 28  migratory–nadir

**migratory** ADJ. wandering. The return of the *migratory* birds to the northern sections of this country is a harbinger of spring.

**ministration** N. act of giving care; attending to someone's needs. Red Cross founder Florence Nightingale was honored for her *ministrations* to wounded soldiers during the Crimean War.

**minute** ADJ. extremely small. The twins resembled one another closely; only *minute* differences set them apart.

**misanthrope** N. one who hates mankind. In *Gulliver's Travels,* Swift portrays human beings as vile, degraded beasts; for this reason, some critics consider him a *misanthrope.*

• **misconception** N. misunderstanding; misinterpretation. I'm afraid you are suffering from a *misconception,* Mr. Collins: I do not want to marry you at all.

**misconstrue** v. interpret incorrectly; misjudge. She took the passage seriously rather than humorously because she *misconstrued* the author's ironic tone.

**miserly** ADJ. stingy; mean. The *miserly* old man greedily counted the gold coins he had hoarded over the years.

**misnomer** N. wrong name; incorrect designation. His tyrannical conduct proved to us all that his nickname, King Eric the Just, was a *misnomer.*

• **misrepresent** V. give a false or incorrect impression, usually intentionally. The ad "Lovely Florida building site with water view" *misrepresented* the property, which was actually ten acres of bottomless swamp.

**mitigate** V. appease; moderate. Nothing Jason did could *mitigate* Medea's anger; she refused to forgive him for betraying her.

**mobile** ADJ. movable; not fixed. The *mobile* blood bank operated by the Red Cross visited our neighborhood today. mobility, N.

• **mock** V. ridicule; imitate, often in derision. It is unkind to *mock* anyone; it is stupid to *mock* anyone significantly bigger than you. mockery, N.

**mode** N. prevailing style; manner; way of doing something. The rock star had to have her hair done in the latest *mode:* frizzed, with occasional moussed spikes for variety. Henry plans to adopt a simpler *mode* of life: he is going to become a mushroom hunter and live off the land.

**mollify** V. soothe. The airline customer service representative tried to *mollify* the angry passenger by offering her a seat in first class.

**momentous** ADJ. very important. When Marie and Pierre Curie discovered radium, they had no idea of the *momentous* impact their discovery would have upon society.

• **monarchy** N. government under a single ruler. Though England today is a *monarchy,* there is some question whether it will be one in 20 years, given the present discontent at the prospect of Prince Charles as king.

**monochromatic** ADJ. having only one color. Most people who are color blind actually can distinguish several colors; some, however, have a truly *monochromatic* view of a world all in shades of gray.

• **monotony** N. sameness leading to boredom. What could be more deadly dull than the *monotony* of punching numbers into a computer hour after hour?

**monumental** ADJ. massive; immense. Writing a dictionary is a *monumental* task; so is reading one.

**moratorium** N. suspension of activity; authorized period of delay (of a payment, etc.). If we declare a *moratorium* and delay collecting all debts for six months, I am sure the farmers will be able to meet their bills.

**morose** ADJ. ill-humored; sullen; melancholy. Forced to take early retirement, Bill acted *morose* for months; then, all of a sudden, he shook off his sullen mood and was his usual cheerful self.

**morsel** N. small bit of food. "No, thank you, Aunt Polly," he said. "I'm so stuffed I can't eat another *morsel.*"

**mortify** V. humiliate; punish the flesh. She was so *mortified* by her blunder that she ran to her room in tears.

**muddle** V. confuse; mix up. His thoughts were *muddled* and chaotic. also N.

**mural** N. wall painting. The walls of the Chicano Community Center are covered with *murals* painted in the style of Diego Rivera, the great Mexican artist.

**murky** ADJ. dark and gloomy; thick with fog; vague. The *murky* depths of the swamp were so dark that you couldn't tell the vines and branches from the snakes.

**muse** V. ponder. For a moment he *mused* about the beauty of the scene, but his thoughts soon changed as he recalled his own personal problems. also N.

• **mutability** N. ability to change in form; fickleness. Going from rags to riches and then back to rags again, the bankrupt financier was a victim of the *mutability* of fortune.

**muted** ADJ. silent; muffled; toned down. Thanks to the thick, sound-absorbing walls of the cathedral, only *muted* traffic noise reached the worshippers within.

**mutinous** ADJ. unruly; rebellious. The captain had to use force to quiet his *mutinous* crew.

**myriad** N. very large number. *Myriads* of mosquitoes from the swamps invaded our village every evening at twilight. also ADJ.

**nadir** N. lowest point. Although few people realized it, the Dow-Jones averages had reached their *nadir* and would soon begin an upward surge.

## Word List 29   naïveté–obnoxious

• **naïveté** N. quality of being unsophisticated; simplicity; artlessness; gullibility. Touched by the *naïveté* of sweet, convent-trained Cosette, Marius pledges himself to protect her innocence. naive, ADJ.

**narrative** ADJ. related to telling a story. A born teller of tales, Olsen used her impressive *narrative* skills to advantage in her story, "I Stand Here Ironing."

**navigable** ADJ. wide and deep enough to allow ships to pass through; able to be steered. So much sand had built up at the bottom of the canal that the waterway was barely *navigable*.

**nebulous** ADJ. vague; hazy; cloudy. After 20 years, she had only a *nebulous* memory of her grandmother's face.

**negligence** N. neglect; failure to take reasonable care. Tommy failed to put back the cover on the well after he fetched his pail of water; because of his *negligence*, Kitty fell in.

**negligible** ADJ. so small, trifling, or unimportant that it may be easily disregarded. Because the damage to his car had been *negligible*, Michael decided he wouldn't bother to report the matter to his insurance company.

**neologism** N. new or newly coined word or phrase. As we invent new devices and professions, we must also invent *neologisms* such as "microcomputer" and "astronaut" to describe them.

**neophyte** N. recent convert; beginner. This mountain slope contains slides that will challenge experts as well as *neophytes*.

• **nocturnal** ADJ. relating to, occurring, or active in the night. Mr. Jones obtained a watchdog to prevent the *nocturnal* raids on his chicken coops.

• **nonchalance** N. indifference; lack of concern; composure. Cool, calm, and collected under fire, James Bond shows remarkable *nonchalance* in the face of danger.

**nondescript** ADJ. undistinctive; ordinary. The private detective was a *nondescript* fellow with no outstanding features, the sort of person one would never notice in a crowd.

**nonentity** N. person or thing of no importance; nonexistence. Don't dismiss John as a *nonentity*; in his quiet way, he's very important to the firm.

• **nostalgia** N. homesickness; longing for the past. My grandfather seldom spoke of life in the old country; he had little patience with *nostalgia*. nostalgic, ADJ.

**notable** ADJ. conspicuous; important; distinguished. Normally *notable* for his calm in the kitchen, today the head cook was shaking, for the *notable* chef Julia Child was coming to dinner.

• **notorious** ADJ. disreputable; widely known; scandalous. To the starlet, any publicity was good publicity: if she couldn't have a good reputation, she'd settle for being *notorious*. notoriety, N.

**novelty** N. something new; newness. The computer is no longer a *novelty* around the office; every office has one. novel, ADJ.

**novice** N. beginner. Even a *novice* at working with computers can install *Barron's Computer Study Program for the SAT* by following the easy steps outlined in the user's manual.

**nozzle** N. projecting spout; tapering tube. Did you leave the garden hose on? I see a trail of water leaking from its *nozzle*.

**nucleus** N. central point or core; component of protoplasm; central part of atom. Kathryn, Lexy, and Steven formed the *nucleus* of the debate team, which eventually grew to include most of the senior class.

**nullify** V. to make invalid; make null or void. Once the contract was *nullified*, it no longer had any legal force.

• **nurture** V. nourish; educate; foster. The Head Start program attempts to *nurture* pre-kindergarten children so that they will do well when they enter public school. also N.

**nutrient** N. nourishing substance. As a budding nutritionist, Kim has learned to design diets that contain foods rich in important basic *nutrients*.

**obdurate** ADJ. stubborn. The manager was *obdurate* in refusing to discuss the workers' grievances.

**obfuscate** V. confuse; muddle; make unclear. Occasionally in talking with patients, doctors seem to use medical terms to *obfuscate* rather than to inform them about the state of their health.

**objective** ADJ. not influenced by emotions; fair. Even though he was her son, she tried to be *objective* about his behavior.

**objective** N. goal; aim. A degree in medicine was her ultimate *objective*.

**obligatory** ADJ. required; legally or morally binding. It is *obligatory* that books borrowed from the library be returned within two weeks.

**oblique** ADJ. indirect; slanting (deviating from the perpendicular or from a straight line). Casting a quick, *oblique* glance at the reviewing stand, the sergeant ordered the company to march "*Oblique* Right."

**obliterate** V. destroy completely. In the film *Independence Day* the explosion *obliterated* the White House, vaporizing it completely.

**oblivion** N. obscurity; forgetfulness. After a brief period of popularity, Hurston's works fell into *oblivion;* no one bothered to reprint them or even to read them any more.

**oblivious** ADJ. inattentive or unmindful; wholly absorbed. Deep in her book, Nancy was *oblivious* of the noisy squabbles of her brother and his friends.

• **obnoxious** ADJ. offensive; objectionable. A sneak and a tattletale, Sid was an *obnoxious* little brat.

## Word List 30  obscure–painstaking

• **obscure** ADJ. dark; vague; unclear. Even after I read the poem a fourth time, its meaning was still *obscure*. obscurity, N.

• **obscure** V. darken; make unclear. At times he seemed purposely to *obscure* his meaning, preferring mystery to clarity.

**obsequious** ADJ. slavishly attentive; servile; fawning; sycophantic. Why are some waiters in fancy restaurants so *obsequious*? What makes them think diners want to have people fawning all over them?

**obsessive** ADJ. related to thinking about something constantly; preoccupying. Ballet, which had been a hobby, began to dominate her life; her love of dancing became *obsessive*.

**obsolescent** ADJ. going out of use. Given how quickly computer technology changes, I've had to reconcile myself to the fact that, no matter how up-to-date a system I buy, it's practically *obsolescent* as soon as I've gotten it out of its box.

**obsolete** ADJ. outmoded. "Hip" is an *obsolete* expression; it went out with love beads and tie-dye shirts.

**obtrude** V. push (oneself or one's ideas) forward or intrude; butt in; stick out or extrude. Because Fanny was reluctant to *obtrude* her opinions about child raising upon her daughter-in-law, she kept a close watch on her tongue. obtrusive, ADJ.

**offensive** ADJ. attacking; insulting; distasteful. Getting into street brawls is no minor matter for professional boxers, who are required by law to restrict their *offensive* impulses to the ring.

**officious** ADJ. meddlesome; excessively pushing in offering one's services. After her long flight, Jill just wanted to nap, but the *officious* bellboy was intent on showing her all the special features of the deluxe suite.

**olfactory** ADJ. concerning the sense of smell. A wine taster must have a discriminating palate and a keen *olfactory* sense, for a good wine appeals both to the taste buds and to the nose.

**ominous** ADJ. threatening. Those clouds are *ominous*; they suggest a severe storm is on the way.

**omnivorous** ADJ. eating both plant and animal food; devouring everything. Some animals, including man, are *omnivorous* and eat both meat and vegetables; others are either carnivorous or herbivorous.

• **opaque** ADJ. not transparent; impenetrable to light. The *opaque* window shade kept the sunlight out of the room. opacity, N.

**opportunist** N. individual who sacrifices principles for expediency by taking advantage of circumstances. Forget ethics! He's such an *opportunist* that he'll vote in favor of any deal that will give him a break.

**opprobrium** N. public disgrace or reproach; vilification. How did the Republicans manage to turn the once-honored name of "liberal" into a term of *opprobrium?*

**opt** V. decide in favor of; choose. Given the choice between the movie and the folk dance, Sharon *opted* to go to the dance.

• **optimist** N. person who looks on the good side. The pessimist says the glass is half empty; the *optimist* says it is half full.

**opulence** N. extreme wealth; luxuriousness; abundance. The glitter and *opulence* of the ballroom took Cinderella's breath away. opulent, ADJ.

• **orator** N. public speaker. The abolitionist Frederick Douglass was a brilliant *orator* whose speeches brought home to his audience the evils of slavery.

**ordeal** N. severe trial or affliction. June was so painfully shy that it was an *ordeal* for her to speak up when the teacher called on her in class.

**ornate** ADJ. excessively or elaborately decorated. The furnishings of homes that were shown on *Lifestyles of the Rich and Famous* tended to be highly *ornate*.

• **ostentatious** ADJ. showy; pretentious; trying to attract attention. Trump's latest casino in Atlantic City is the most *ostentatious* gambling palace in the East: it easily outglitters its competitors. ostentation, N.

**outlandish** ADJ. bizarre; peculiar; unconventional. The eccentric professor who engages in markedly *outlandish* behavior is a stock figure in novels with an academic setting.

• **outmoded** ADJ. no longer stylish; old-fashioned. Unconcerned about keeping in style, Lenore was perfectly happy to wear *outmoded* clothes as long as they were clean and unfrayed.

**outwit** V. outsmart; trick. By disguising himself as an old woman, Holmes was able to *outwit* his pursuers and escape capture.

**overbearing** ADJ. bossy; arrogant; decisively important. Certain of her own importance and of the unimportance of everyone else, Lady Bracknell was intolerably *overbearing* in her manner. "In choosing a husband," she said, "good birth is of *overbearing* importance; compared to that, neither wealth nor talent signifies."

**overt** ADJ. open to view. According to the United States Constitution, a person must commit an *overt* act before he or she may be tried for treason.

• **pacifist** N. one opposed to force; antimilitarist. Shooting his way through the jungle, Rambo was clearly not a *pacifist*.

• **pacify** V. soothe; make calm or quiet; subdue. Dentists criticize the practice of giving fussy children sweets to *pacify* them.

**painstaking** ADJ. expending or showing diligent care and great effort. The new high-frequency word list is the result of *painstaking* efforts on the part of our research staff.

# Word List 31   palatable–perjury

**palatable** ADJ. agreeable; pleasing to the taste. Neither Jack's underbaked opinions nor his overcooked casseroles were *palatable* to me.

**pallid** ADJ. pale; wan. Because his occupation required that he work at night and sleep during the day, he had an exceptionally *pallid* complexion.

**panacea** N. cure-all; remedy for all diseases. Some people claim that vitamin C is a *panacea* that can cure everything from cancer to the common cold.

**pandemonium** N. wild tumult. When the ships collided in the harbor, *pandemonium* broke out among the passengers.

**parable** N. short tale illustrating a moral principle. In the *parable* of the good shepherd, Jesus encourages his followers to seek those who have strayed from the flock.

• **paradox** N. something apparently contradictory in nature; statement that looks false but is actually correct. Richard presents a bit of a *paradox,* for he is a card-carrying member of both the National Rifle Association and the relatively pacifist American Civil Liberties Union.

**paragon** N. model of perfection. The class disliked him because the teacher was always pointing him out as a *paragon* of virtue.

**paramount** ADJ. foremost in importance; supreme. Proper nutrition and hygiene are of *paramount* importance in adolescent development and growth.

**parched** ADJ. extremely dry; very thirsty. The *parched* desert landscape seemed hostile to life.

**parody** N. humorous imitation; spoof; takeoff; travesty. The show *Forbidden Broadway* presents *parodies* spoofing the year's new productions playing on Broadway.

**partial** ADJ. incomplete; having a liking for something. In this issue we have published only a *partial* list of contributors because we lack space to acknowledge everyone. I am extremely *partial* to chocolate eclairs.

**partisan** ADJ. one-sided; prejudiced; committed to a party. On certain issues of principle, she refused to take a *partisan* stand but let her conscience be her guide. also N.

**partition** V. divide into parts. Before their second daughter was born, Jason and Lizzie decided each child needed a room of her own, and so they *partitioned* a large bedroom into two small but separate rooms. also N.

**passive** ADJ. not active; acted upon. Mahatma Gandhi urged his followers to pursue a program of *passive* resistance rather than resort to violence and acts of terrorism.

**passport** N. legal document identifying the bearer as a citizen of a country and allowing him or her to travel abroad. In arranging your first trip abroad, be sure to allow yourself enough time to apply for and receive your *passport*: you won't be allowed to travel without one.

**pastoral** ADJ. rural; simple and peaceful; idyllic; relating to shepherds. Tired of city living, David dreamed of moving to the country and enjoying the tranquillity of *pastoral* life.

• **patronize** V. support; act superior toward; be a customer of. Penniless artists hope to find some wealthy art lover who will *patronize* them. If a wine steward *patronized* me because he saw I knew nothing about fine wine, I'd refuse to *patronize* his restaurant.

**paucity** N. scarcity; lack. They closed the restaurant because the *paucity* of customers made it a losing proposition to operate.

• **pedantic** ADJ. showing off learning; bookish. Leavening his decisions with humorous, down-to-earth anecdotes, Judge Walker was not at all the *pedantic* legal scholar. pedant, N.

**pedestrian** ADJ. ordinary; unimaginative. Unintentionally boring, he wrote page after page of *pedestrian* prose. (secondary meaning)

**peerless** ADJ. having to equal; incomparable. To his admirers, the reigning operatic tenor of his generation, Luciano Pavarotti, was *peerless*; no one could compare with him.

**pendulum** N. suspended body that swings freely. Watching the swinging *pendulum* of the grandfather clock, Johnny swayed from side to side, echoing its movement.

**penitent** ADJ. feeling regret or sorrow for one's offenses; repentant. When he realized the enormity of his crime, he became remorseful and *penitent*. also N.

**perceptive** ADJ. insightful; aware; wise. Although Maud was a generally *perceptive* critic, she had her blind spots: she could never see flaws in the work of her friends.

**perdition** N. damnation; complete ruin. Praying for salvation, young Steven feared he was damned to eternal *perdition*.

**peremptory** ADJ. demanding and leaving no choice. From Jack's *peremptory* knock on the door, Jill could tell he would not give up until she let him in.

**perfidious** ADJ. treacherous; disloyal. When Caesar realized that Brutus had betrayed him, he reproached his *perfidious* friend. perfidy, N.

**perfunctory** ADJ. superficial; not thorough; lacking interest, care, or enthusiasm. Giving the tabletop only a *perfunctory* swipe with her dust cloth, Betty promised herself she'd clean it more thoroughly tomorrow.

• **perjury** N. false testimony while under oath. Rather than lie under oath and perhaps be indicted for *perjury*, the witness chose to take the Fifth Amendment, refusing to answer any questions on the grounds that he might incriminate himself.

## Word List 32   permutation–ponderous

**permutation** N. transformation; rearrangement of elements. I'm pretty sure Ted's phone number ends in 5236 or some *permutation* of those digits.

**pernicious** ADJ. very destructive. Crack cocaine has had a *pernicious* effect on urban society: it has destroyed families, turned children into drug dealers, and increased the spread of violent crimes.

**perpetrate** V. commit an offense. Only an insane person could *perpetrate* such a horrible crime.

• **perpetual** ADJ. everlasting. Ponce de León hoped to find the legendary fountain of *perpetual* youth. perpetuity, N.

**perpetuate** V. make something last; preserve from extinction. Some critics attack *The Adventures of Huckleberry Finn* because they believe Twain's book *perpetuates* a false image of blacks in this country.

**peruse** V. read with care. After the conflagration that burned down her house, Joan closely *perused* her home insurance policy to discover exactly what benefits her coverage provided her. perusal, N.

• **pervasive** ADJ. pervading; spread throughout every part. Despite airing them for several hours, she could not rid her clothes of the *pervasive* odor of mothballs that clung to them. pervade, V.

**perverse** ADJ. stubbornly wrongheaded; wicked and perverted. When Jack was in a *perverse* mood, he would do the opposite of whatever Jill asked him. When Hannibal Lecter was in a *perverse* mood, he ate the flesh of his victims.

• **pessimism** N. belief that life is basically bad or evil; gloominess. Considering how well you have done in the course so far, you have no real reason for such *pessimism* about your final grade.

• **petulant** ADJ. touchy; peevish. If you'd had hardly any sleep for three nights and people kept on phoning and waking you up, you'd sound pretty *petulant*, too.

• **phenomena** N. Pl. observable facts or events. We kept careful records of the *phenomena* we noted in the course of these experiments.

• **philanthropist** N. lover of mankind; doer of good. In his role as *philanthropist* and public benefactor, John D. Rockefeller Sr., donated millions to charity; as an individual, however, he was a tight-fisted old man.

**phlegmatic** ADJ. not easily excited to action or emotional displays; calm; sluggish. The nurse was a cheerful but *phlegmatic* person, untroubled by sudden emergencies.

**pious** ADJ. devout; religious. The challenge for church members today is how to be *pious* in the best sense, that is, to be devout without becoming hypocritical or sanctimonious. piety, N.

**pique** V. provoke or arouse; annoy. "I know something *you* don't know," said Lucy, trying to *pique* Ethel's interest.

**pique** N. irritation; resentment. She showed her *pique* at her loss by refusing to appear with the other contestants at the end of the competition.

**pivotal** ADJ. crucial; key; vital. The new "smart weapons" technology played a *pivotal* role in the quick resolution of the war with Iraq.

**placate** V. pacify; conciliate. The store manager, trying to *placate* the angry customer, offered to replace the damaged merchandise or to give back her money right away.

**placid** ADJ. calm; peaceful. Looking at the storm-tossed waters of the lake, Bob wondered why they ever called it Lake *Placid*.

• **plagiarize** V. steal another's ideas and pass them off as one's own. The teacher could tell that the student had *plagiarized* parts of his essay; she could recognize whole paragraphs straight from *Barron's Book Notes*.

**platitude** N. trite remark; commonplace statement. In giving advice to his son, old Polonius expressed himself only in *platitudes;* every word out of his mouth was commonplace.

**plausible** ADJ. having a show of truth but open to doubt; specious. Your mother made you stay home from school because she needed you to program the VCR? I'm sorry, you'll have to come up with a more *plausible* excuse than that.

**plethora** N. excess; overabundance. She offered a *plethora* of excuses for her shortcomings.

**pliable** ADJ. flexible; yielding; adaptable. In remodeling the bathroom, we have replaced all the old, rigid lead pipes with new, *pliable* copper tubing.

**plight** N. condition, state (especially a bad state or condition); predicament. Loggers, unmoved by the *plight* of the spotted owl, plan to keep on logging whether or not they ruin the owl's habitat.

**pluck** N. courage. Even the enemies of young Indiana Jones were impressed by the boy's *pluck* in trying to rescue the archaeological treasure they had stolen. plucky, ADJ.

**plunder** N. loot; takings from a raid. Rubbing his hands with glee, the robber gloated over his ill-gotten *plunder.* also V.

**podium** N. pedestal; raised platform. The audience applauded as the conductor made his way to the *podium*.

**polemical** ADJ. aggressive in verbal attack; disputatious. Lexy was a master of *polemical* rhetoric; she should have worn a T-shirt with the slogan "Born to Debate."

**ponderous** ADJ. weighty; unwieldy. His humor lacked the light touch; his jokes were always *ponderous*.

# Word List 33  pore–preside

**pore** V. study deeply; stare. In doing research on the SAT, we *pored* over back issues of *Scientific American* to locate articles from which reading passages had been excerpted.

**porous** ADJ. full of pores; like a sieve. Dancers like to wear *porous* clothing because it allows the ready passage of air.

**portend** V. foretell; presage. The king did not know what these omens might *portend* and asked his soothsayers to interpret them.

**portly** ADJ. stout; corpulent. The salesclerk diplomatically referred to the overweight customer as not fat but *portly*.

**posterity** N. descendants; future generations. We hope to leave a better world to *posterity*.

• **potency** N. power; effectiveness; influence. Looking at the expiration date on the cough syrup bottle, we wondered whether the medication still retained its *potency*. potent, ADJ.

**potentate** N. monarch; sovereign. The *potentate* spent more time at Monte Carlo than he did at home on his throne.

**practical** ADJ. based on experience; useful. Sharon gained *practical* experience in hospital work by acting as an emergency room volunteer.

• **pragmatic** ADJ. practical (as opposed to idealistic); concerned with the practical worth or impact of something. This coming trip to France should provide me with a *pragmatic* test of the value of my conversational French class.

**prairie** N. vast, level, or slightly rolling tract of grassland. The *prairie* is "big sky" country: your views are unobstructed by buildings or trees.

**prate** V. speak foolishly; boast idly. Despite Elizabeth's obvious disinclination for the topic, Mr. Collins *prated* on and on about his wonderful prospects as a husband, thanks to his noble patron, Lady Catherine de Burgh.

**prattle** V. babble. Baby John *prattled* on and on about the cats and his ball and the Cookie Monster.

**preamble** N. introductory statement. In the *preamble* to the Constitution, the purpose of the document is set forth.

**precarious** ADJ. uncertain; risky. Saying the stock would be a *precarious* investment, the broker advised her client against purchasing it.

• **precedent** N. something preceding in time that may be used as an authority or guide for future action. If I buy you a car for your sixteenth birthday, your brothers will want me to buy them cars when they turn sixteen, too; I can't afford to set such an expensive *precedent*.

**precipitate** ADJ. rash; premature; abrupt; hasty; sudden. Though I was angry enough to resign on the spot, I had enough sense to keep myself from quitting a job in such a *precipitate* fashion.

**precipitous** ADJ. steep; overhasty. This hill is difficult to climb because it is so *precipitous*; one slip, and our descent will be *precipitous* as well.

**preclude** V. make impossible; eliminate. Because the band was already booked to play in Hollywood on New Year's Eve, that booking *precluded* their accepting the New Year's Eve gig in London they were offered.

**precursor** N. forerunner. Though Gray and Burns share many traits with the Romantic poets who followed them, most critics consider them *precursors* of the Romantic movement, not true Romantics.

• **predator** N. creature that seizes and devours another animal; person who robs or exploits others. Not just cats, but a wide variety of *predators*—owls, hawks, weasels, foxes—catch mice for dinner. A carnivore is by definition *predatory,* for it *preys* on weaker creatures.

**predetermine** V. predestine; settle or decide beforehand; influence markedly. Romeo and Juliet believed that Fate had *predetermined* their meeting. Bea gathered estimates from caterers, florists, and stationers so that she could *predetermine* the costs of holding a catered buffet. Philip's love of athletics *predetermined* his choice of a career in sports marketing.

**predilection** N. partiality; preference. Although my mother wrote all sorts of poetry over the years, she had a definite *predilection* for occasional verse.

**preeminent** ADJ. outstanding; superior. The king traveled to Boston because he wanted the *preeminent* surgeon in the field to perform the operation.

**preempt** V. head off; forestall by acting first; appropriate for oneself; supplant. Hoping to *preempt* any attempts by the opposition to make educational reform a hot political issue, the candidate set out her own plan to revitalize the public schools. preemptive, ADJ.

**prelate** N. church dignitary. The archbishop of Moscow and other high-ranking *prelates* visited the Russian Orthodox seminary.

• **premise** N. assumption; postulate. Acting on the *premise* that there's no fool like an old fool, P. T. Barnum hired a 90-year-old clown for his circus.

• **premonition** N. forewarning. In horror movies, the hero often has a *premonition* of danger, yet he foolishly ignores it.

**preposterous** ADJ. absurd; ridiculous. When he tried to downplay his youthful experiments with marijuana by saying he hadn't inhaled, we all thought, "What a *preposterous* excuse!"

**prescience** N. ability to foretell the future. Given the current wave of Japan bashing, it does not take *prescience* for me to foresee problems in our future trade relations with Japan.

**preside** V. act as president or chairman; exercise control. When the club president cannot attend a meeting, the vice president will *preside* over that session.

## Word List 34 prestige–prophetic

**prestige** N. impression produced by achievements or reputation. Many students want to go to Harvard College not for the education offered but for the *prestige* of Harvard's name.

• **presumptuous** ADJ. taking liberties; overstepping bounds; nervy. I thought it was *presumptuous* of Mort to butt into Bishop Tutu's talk with Mrs. Clinton and ask them for their autographs; I wouldn't have had the nerve.

**pretentious** ADJ. ostentatious; pompous; making unjustified claims; overly ambitious. None of the other prizewinners are wearing their medals; isn't it a bit *pretentious* of you to wear yours?

• **prevail** V. triumph; predominate; prove superior in strength, power, or influence; be current. A radical committed to social change, Reed had no patience with the conservative views that *prevailed* in the America of his day. prevalent, ADJ.; prevailing, ADJ.

**prevaricate** V. lie. Some people believe that to *prevaricate* in a good cause is justifiable and regard their false statement as a "white lie."

• **prey** N. target of a hunt; victim. In *Stalking the Wild Asparagus,* Euell Gibbons has as his *prey* not wild beasts but wild plants. also V.

**privation** N. hardship; want. In his youth, he knew hunger and *privation.*

**procrastinate** V. postpone; delay or put off. Looking at four years of receipts and checks he still had to sort through, Bob was truly sorry he had *procrastinated* for so long and not finished filing his taxes long ago.

**prodigal** ADJ. wasteful; reckless with money. Don't be so *prodigal* spending my money; when you've earned some money, you can waste it as much as you want! also N.

**prodigious** ADJ. marvelous; enormous. Watching the champion weight lifter heave the weighty barbell to shoulder height and then boost it overhead, we marveled at his *prodigious* strength.

**prodigy** N. highly gifted child; extraordinary accomplishment or event. Menuhin was a *prodigy,* performing wonders on his violin when he was barely eight years old.

**profane** V. violate; desecrate; treat unworthily. The members of the mysterious Far Eastern cult sought to kill the British explorer because he had *profaned* the sanctity of their holy goblet by using it as an ashtray. also ADJ.

**profligate** N. dissipated; wasteful; wildly immoral. Although surrounded by wild and *profligate* companions, she nevertheless managed to retain some sense of decency.

• **profound** ADJ. deep; not superficial; complete. Freud's remarkable insights into human behavior caused his fellow scientists to honor him as a *profound* thinker. profundity, N.

**profusion** N. overabundance; lavish expenditure; excess. Freddy was so overwhelmed by the *profusion* of choices on the menu that he knocked over his wine glass and soaked his host. He made *profuse* apologies to his host, the waiter, the busboy, the people at the next table, and the man in the men's room giving out paper towels.

**progenitor** N. ancestor. The Roth family, whose *progenitors* emigrated from Germany early in the nineteenth century, settled in Peru, Illinois.

• **proliferation** N. rapid growth; spread; multiplication. Times of economic hardship inevitably encourage the *proliferation* of countless get-rich-quick schemes. proliferate, V.

• **prolific** ADJ. abundantly fruitful. My editors must assume I'm a *prolific* writer: they expect me to revise six books this year!

• **prologue** N. introduction (to a poem or play). In the *prologue* to *Romeo and Juliet*, Shakespeare introduces the audience to the feud between the Montagues and the Capulets.

**prolong** V. make longer; draw out; lengthen. In their determination to discover ways to *prolong* human life, doctors fail to take into account that longer lives are not always happier ones.

• **prominent** ADJ. conspicuous; notable; sticking out. Have you ever noticed that Prince Charles's *prominent* ears make him resemble the big-eared character in *Mad* comics?

**promontory** N. high point of land jutting out into a body of water; headland. They erected a lighthouse on the *promontory* to warn approaching ships of their nearness to the shore.

• **promote** V. help to flourish; advance in rank; publicize. Founder of the Children's Defense Fund, Marian Wright Edelman ceaselessly *promotes* the welfare of young people everywhere.

**promulgate** V. proclaim a doctrine or law; make known by official publication. When Moses came down from the mountaintop all set to *promulgate* God's commandments, he was shocked to discover his followers worshipping a golden calf.

**prone** ADJ. inclined to; prostrate. She was *prone* to sudden fits of anger during which she would lie *prone* on the floor, screaming and kicking her heels.

**propagate** V. multiply; spread. Since bacteria *propagate* more quickly in unsanitary environments, it is important to keep hospital rooms clean.

**propensity** N. natural inclination. Convinced of his own talent, Sol has an unfortunate *propensity* to belittle the talents of others.

**property** N. quality or aspect; belongings; land. In science class we learned that each element has certain physical and chemical *properties*.

• **prophetic** ADJ. foretelling the future. I have no magical *prophetic* powers; when I predict what will happen, I base my predictions on common sense. prophesy, V.

# Word List 35    proponent–qualified

**proponent** N. supporter; backer. In the Senate, *proponents* of the universal health care measure lobbied to gain additional support for the controversial legislation.

**propriety** N. fitness; correct conduct. Miss Manners counsels her readers so that they may behave with due *propriety* in any social situation and not embarrass themselves.

**prosaic** ADJ. dull and unimaginative; matter-of-fact; factual. Though the ad writers had come up with a wildly imaginative campaign to publicize the company's newest product, the head office rejected it for a more *prosaic,* down-to-earth approach.

• **prosperity** N. good fortune; financial success; physical well-being. Promising to stay together "for richer, for poorer," the newlyweds vowed to be true to one another in *prosperity* and hardship alike.

**protagonist** N. principal character; leading actor. Emma, the *protagonist* of Jane Austen's novel, is an overindulged young woman convinced of her ability as a matchmaker.

**prototype** N. original work used as a model by others. The National Air and Space Museum displays the Wright brothers' first plane, the *prototype* of all the American aircraft that came after.

**protract** V. prolong. Seeking to delay the union members' vote, the management team tried to *protract* the negotiations endlessly, but the union representatives saw through their strategy.

**protrude** V. stick out. His fingers *protruded* from the holes in his gloves. protrusion, N.

**protuberance** N. protrusion; bulge. A ganglionic cyst is a fluid-filled tumor that develops near a joint membrane or tendon sheath and that bulges beneath the skin, forming a *protuberance*.

**provident** ADJ. displaying foresight; thrifty; preparing for emergencies. In his usual *provident* manner, he had insured himself against this type of loss.

**provincial** ADJ. pertaining to a province; limited in outlook; unsophisticated. As *provincial* governor, Sir Henry administered the queen's law in his remote corner of Canada. Caught up in local problems, out of touch with London news, he became sadly *provincial*.

**provisional** ADJ. tentative. Kim's acceptance as an American Express cardholder was *provisional:* before issuing her a card, American Express wanted to check her employment record and credit history.

• **provocative** ADJ. arousing anger or interest; annoying. In a typically *provocative* act, the bully kicked sand into the weaker man's face.

**proximity** N. nearness. Blind people sometimes develop a compensatory ability to sense the *proximity* of objects around them.

• **prudent** ADJ. cautious; careful. A miser hoards money not because he is *prudent* but because he is greedy. prudence, N.

**prune** V. cut away; trim. With the help of her editor, she was able to *prune* her manuscript into publishable form.

**pseudonym** N. pen name. Samuel Clemens's *pseudonym* was Mark Twain.

**puerile** ADJ. childish; immature. Throwing tantrums? You should have outgrown such *puerile* behavior years ago.

**pugnacious** ADJ. combative; disposed to fight. "Put up your dukes!" he cried, making a fist to show how *pugnacious* he was.

**pulverize** V. crush or grind into dust. Before sprinkling the dried herbs into the stew, Michael first *pulverized* them into a fine powder.

**pummel** V. beat or pound with fists. Swinging wildly, Pammy *pummeled* her brother around the head and shoulders.

**punctilious** ADJ. laying stress on niceties of conduct or form; minutely attentive to fine points (perhaps too much so). Percy is *punctilious* about observing the rules of etiquette whenever Miss Manners invites him to stay. punctiliousness, N.

**pungent** ADJ. stinging; sharp in taste or smell; caustic. The *pungent* odor of ripe Limburger cheese appealed to Simone but made Stanley gag.

**puny** ADJ. insignificant; tiny; weak. Our *puny* efforts to stop the flood were futile.

**purge** V. remove or get rid of something unwanted; free from blame or guilt; cleanse or purify. The Communist government *purged* the party to get rid of members suspected of capitalist sympathies. also N.

**purveyor** N. furnisher of foodstuffs; caterer. As *purveyor* of rare wines and viands, he traveled through France and Italy every year in search of new products to sell.

**quack** N. charlatan; impostor. Don't let that *quack* fool you with his wild claims; he can't cure what ails you. quackery, N.

**quagmire** N. soft wet boggy land; complex or dangerous situation from which it is difficult to free oneself. Up to her knees in mud, Myra wondered how on earth she was going to extricate herself from this *quagmire*.

**qualified** ADJ. limited; restricted. Unable to give the candidate full support, the mayor gave him only a *qualified* endorsement. (secondary meaning)

## Word List 36   quandary–reconcile

**quandary** N. dilemma. When both Harvard and Stanford accepted Lori, she was in a *quandary* as to which school she should attend.

**quarry** N. victim; object of a hunt. The police closed in on their *quarry*.

**quarry** V. dig into. They *quarried* blocks of marble out of the hillside. also N.

**quell** V. extinguish; put down; quiet. Miss Minchin's demeanor was so stern and forbidding that she could *quell* any unrest among her students with one intimidating glance.

**quench** V. douse or extinguish; assuage or satisfy. What's the favorite song of the fire department? "Baby, *Quench* My Fire!"

**querulous** ADJ. fretful; whining. Even the most agreeable toddlers can begin to act *querulous* if they miss their nap.

**quibble** N. minor objection or complaint. Aside from a few hundred teensy-weensy *quibbles* about the set, the script, the actors, the director, the costumes, the lighting, and the props, the hypercritical critic loved the play. also V.

**quip** N. witty jest; wisecrack; taunt. Whenever the reporters asked him a tough question, he never gave them a straight answer but joked around, tossing off one-liners and humorous *quips*. also V.

**quiver** V. tremble; shake. The bird dog's nose twitched and his whiskers *quivered* as he strained eagerly against the leash. also N.

**quiver** N. case for arrows. Robin Hood reached back and plucked one last arrow from his *quiver*. (secondary meaning)

**quixotic** ADJ. idealistic but impractical. Simon's head is in the clouds; he constantly comes up with *quixotic*, unworkable schemes.

**rabid** ADJ. like a fanatic; furious. He was a *rabid* follower of the Dodgers and watched them play whenever he could go to the ball park.

**raconteur** N. storyteller. My father was a gifted *raconteur* with an unlimited supply of anecdotes.

**rally** V. call up or summon (forces, vital powers, etc.); revive or recuperate. Washington quickly *rallied* his troops to fight off the British attack. The patient had been sinking throughout the night, but at dawn she *rallied* and made a complete recovery.

• **ramble** V. wander aimlessly (physically or mentally). Listening to the teacher *ramble*, Shelby wondered whether he'd ever get to the point. also N.

**rampant** ADJ. growing in profusion; unrestrained. In the garden, the weeds were *rampant*: they killed all the flowers that had been planted in the spring. In the city, crime was *rampant*: the burglars and muggers were out of control.

**ramshackle** ADJ. rickety; falling apart. The boys propped up the *ramshackle* clubhouse with a couple of boards.

**rancid** ADJ. having the odor of stale fat. The *rancid* odor that filled the ship's galley nauseated the crew.

**rancor** N. bitterness; deep-seated hatred. Thirty years after the war, she could not let go of the past but still felt an implacable *rancor* against the foe.

• **random** ADJ. without definite purpose, plan, or aim; haphazard. Although the sponsor of the raffle claimed all winners were chosen at *random,* people had their suspicions when the grand prize went to the sponsor's brother-in-law.

**rant** V. rave; talk excitedly; scold; make a grandiloquent speech. When he heard that I'd totaled the family car, Dad began to *rant* at me like a complete madman.

**rarefied** ADJ. made less dense [of a gas]. The mountain climbers had difficulty breathing in the *rarefied* atmosphere. rarefy, V.

**raucous** ADJ. harsh and shrill; disorderly and boisterous. The *raucous* crowd of New Year's Eve revelers got progressively noisier as midnight drew near.

**raze** V. destroy completely. Spelling is important: to raise a building is to put it up; to *raze* a building is to tear it down.

**reactionary** ADJ. recoiling from progress; politically ultraconservative. Opposing the use of English in worship services, *reactionary* forces in the church fought to reinstate the mass in Latin.

**rebuff** V. snub; beat back. She *rebuffed* his invitation so smoothly that he did not realize he had been snubbed.

**recalcitrant** ADJ. obstinately stubborn. Which animal do you think is more *recalcitrant,* a pig-headed pig or a stubborn mule?

**recant** V. disclaim or disavow; retract a previous statement; openly confess error. Those who can, keep true to their faith; those who can't, *recant.*

**recapitulate** V. summarize. Let us *recapitulate* what has been said thus far before going ahead.

**recession** N. withdrawal; time of low economic activity. The slow *recession* of the floodwaters created problems for the crews working to restore power to the area.

**reciprocate** V. repay in kind. It was kind of Donna to have us over to dinner; I'd like us to *reciprocate* in some way, if we can.

• **recluse** N. hermit; loner. Disappointed in love, Miss Emily became a *recluse;* she shut herself away in her empty mansion and refused to see another living soul. reclusive, ADJ.

**reconcile** V. correct inconsistencies; become friendly after a quarrel. Every time we try to *reconcile* our checkbook with the bank statement, we quarrel.

However, despite these monthly lovers' quarrels, we always manage to *reconcile.*

## Word List 37   recount–renovate

**recount** V. narrate or tell; count over again. About to *recount* the latest adventure of Sherlock Holmes, Watson lost track of exactly how many cases Holmes had solved and refused to begin his tale until he'd *recounted* them one by one.

**rectify** V. set right; correct. You had better send a check to *rectify* your account before American Express cancels your credit card.

**rectitude** N. uprightness; moral virtue; correctness of judgment. The Eagle Scout was a model of *rectitude.*

**recumbent** ADJ. reclining; lying down completely or in part. The command "at ease" does not permit you to take a *recumbent* position.

**recuperate** V. recover. The doctors were worried because the patient did not *recuperate* as rapidly as they had expected.

**recurrent** ADJ. occurring again and again. Because Phil suffered from *recurrent* ear infections, the doctors were concerned that these periodic attacks might eventually affect his hearing.

**redundant** ADJ. superfluous; repetitious; excessively wordy. The bottle of wine I brought to Bob's was certainly *redundant*: how was I to know Bob owned a winery? In your essay, you repeat several points unnecessarily; try to be less *redundant* in the future. redundancy, N.

**refine** V. free from impurities; perfect. Just as you can *refine* sugar by removing bits of cane and other unwanted material, you can *refine* verse by removing awkward metaphors and polishing rough rhymes. refinement, N.

**reflect** V. consider or deliberate; show; mirror. Mr. Collins *reflected* on Elizabeth's rejection of his proposal. Did it *reflect* her true feelings, he wondered. Looking at his *reflection* in the mirror, he refused to believe that she could reject such a fine figure of a man.

**refraction** N. bending of a ray of light. Insert a stick in a glass of water and look at it carefully. It looks bent because of the *refraction* of the light by the water.

**refrain** V. abstain from; resist. Whenever he heard a song with a lively chorus, Sol could never *refrain* from joining in on the refrain.

**refrain** N. chorus. Whenever he heard a song with a lively chorus, Sol could never refrain from joining in on the *refrain.*

• **refute** V. disprove. At his trial, Socrates attempte *refute* the claims of those who accused him o rupting the youth of Athens through his teac

**regress** V. move backward to an earlier, generally more primitive state. Although Timmy outgrew his need for a pacifier well over a year ago, occasionally when he's tired or nervous, he *regresses* and starts sucking his thumb.

**reiterate** V. repeat. He *reiterated* the warning to make sure that everyone understood it.

**rejoinder** N. retort; comeback; reply. When someone has been rude to me, I find it particularly satisfying to come up with a quick *rejoinder*.

• **rejuvenate** V. make young again. The charlatan claimed that his elixir would *rejuvenate* the aged and weary.

**relegate** V. banish to an inferior position; delegate; assign. After Ralph dropped his second tray of drinks that week, the manager swiftly *relegated* him to a minor post cleaning up behind the bar.

**relevant** ADJ. pertinent; referring to the case in hand. How *relevant* Virginia Woolf's essays are to women writers today; it's as if Woolf in the 1930s foresaw our current literary struggles. relevancy, N.

**relic** N. surviving remnant; memento. Egypt's Department of Antiquities prohibits tourists from taking mummies and other ancient *relics* out of the country. Mike keeps his photos of his trip to Egypt in a box with other *relics* of his travels.

• **relinquish** V. give up something with reluctance; yield. Once you get used to fringe benefits like expense account meals and a company car, it's very hard to *relinquish* them.

**relish** V. savor; enjoy. Watching Peter enthusiastically chow down, I thought, "Now there's a man who *relishes* a good dinner!" also N.

**reminiscence** N. recollection. Her *reminiscences* of her experiences are so fascinating that she ought to write a book.

**remiss** ADJ. negligent. The prison guard was accused of being *remiss* in his duty when the prisoner escaped.

**remnant** N. remainder. I suggest that you wait until the store places the *remnants* of these goods on sale.

**remonstrance** N. protest; objection. The authorities were deaf to the pastor's *remonstrances* about the lack of police protection in the area. remonstrate, V.

**remorse** N. guilt; self-reproach. The murderer felt no *remorse* for his crime.

**remunerative** ADJ. lucrative; rewarding. Because work as an insurance agent was far more *remunerative* than work as a church organist, Ives eventually resigned from his church job. remuneration, N.

**renegade** N. deserter; traitor. Because he had abandoned his post and joined forces with the Indians, his fellow officers considered the hero of *Dances with Wolves* a *renegade*. also ADJ.

**renounce** V. abandon; disown; repudiate. Even though she knew she would be burned at the stake as a witch, Joan of Arc refused to *renounce* her belief that her voices came from God. renunciation, N.

**renovate** V. restore to good condition; renew. We *renovated* our kitchen, replacing the old cabinets and countertop and installing new appliances.

## Word List 38    renown–reticent

• **renown** N. fame. For many years an unheralded researcher, Barbara McClintock gained international *renown* when she won the Nobel Prize in physiology and medicine.

**rent** N. rip; split. Kit did an excellent job of mending the *rent* in the lining in her coat. rend, V.

**repatriate** V. return to one's own country. Although the Western powers hoped to *repatriate* the refugees swiftly, they were unable to do so because of the still dangerous conditions in the refugees' homeland.

**repeal** V. revoke; annul. What would the effect on our society be if we decriminalized drug use by *repealing* the laws against the possession and sale of narcotics?

**repel** V. drive away; disgust. At first, the Beast's ferocious appearance *repelled* Beauty, but she came to love the tender heart hidden behind that beastly exterior.

**repertoire** N. list of works of music, drama, etc., a performer is prepared to present. The opera company decided to include *Madame Butterfly* in its *repertoire* for the following season.

**replenish** V. fill up again. Before she could take another backpacking trip, Carla had to *replenish* her stock of freeze-dried foods.

• **reprehensible** ADJ. deserving blame. Shocked by the viciousness of the bombing, politicians of every party uniformly condemned the terrorists' *reprehensible* deed.

**repress** V. restrain; hold back; crush; suppress. Anne's parents tried to curb her impetuosity without *repressing* her boundless high spirits.

**reprieve** N. temporary stay. During the twenty-four-hour *reprieve*, the lawyers sought to make the stay of execution permanent. also V.

**reprimand** V. reprove severely; rebuke. Every time Ermengarde made a mistake in class, she was afraid that Miss Minchin would *reprimand* her and tell her father how badly she was doing in school. also N.

**reproachful** ADJ. expressing disapproval. He never could do anything wrong without imagining the *reproachful* look in his mother's eye.

**reprove** V. censure; rebuke. Though Aunt Bea at times would *reprove* Opie for inattention in church, she believed he was at heart a God-fearing lad.

• **repudiate** V. disown; disavow. On separating from Tony, Tina announced that she would *repudiate* all debts incurred by her soon-to-be ex-husband.

**repulsion** N. distaste; act of driving back. Hating blood-shed, she viewed war with *repulsion*. Even defensive battles distressed her, for the *repulsion* of enemy forces is never accomplished bloodlessly.

**reputable** ADJ. respectable. If you want to buy antiques, look for a *reputable* dealer; far too many dealers today pass off fakes as genuine antiques.

**rescind** V. cancel. Because of the public outcry against the new taxes, the senator proposed a bill to *rescind* the unpopular financial measure.

• **reserved** ADJ. self-controlled; careful in expressing oneself. They made an odd couple: she was outspoken and uninhibited; he was cautious and *reserved*. (secondary meaning)

• **resignation** N. patient submissiveness; statement that one is quitting a job. If Bob Cratchit had not accepted Scrooge's bullying with such *resignation*, he might have gotten up the nerve to hand in his *resignation*. resigned, ADJ.

**resilient** ADJ. elastic; having the power of springing back. Highly *resilient*, steel makes excellent bed-springs. resilience, N.

• **resolution** N. determination. Nothing could shake his *resolution* that his children would get the best education that money could buy. resolute, ADJ.

• **resolve** V. decide; settle; solve. "I have *resolved*, Watson, to travel to Bohemia to *resolve* the dispute between Irene Adler and the King. In my absence, do your best to *resolve* any mysteries that arise."

**resonant** ADJ. echoing; resounding; deep and full in sound. The deep, *resonant* voice of the actor James Earl Jones makes him particularly effective when he appears on stage.

**respiration** N. breathing. The doctor found that the patient's years of smoking had adversely affected both his lung capacity and his rate of *respiration*. respire, V.

**restive** ADJ. restlessly impatient; obstinately resisting control. Waiting impatiently in line to see Santa Claus, even the best-behaved children grow *restive* and start to fidget.

• **restraint** N. moderation or self-control; controlling force; restriction. Control yourself, young lady! Show some *restraint*!

**resumption** N. taking up again; recommencement. During summer break, Don had not realized how much he missed university life; at the *resumption* of classes, however, he felt marked excitement and pleasure. resume, V.

**resurge** V. rise again; flow to and fro. It was startling to see the spirit of nationalism *resurge* as the Soviet Union disintegrated into a loose federation of ethnic and national groups. resurgence, N.

• **retain** V. keep; employ. Fighting to *retain* his seat in Congress, Senator Foghorn *retained* a new manager to head his reelection campaign.

**retaliation** N. repayment in kind (usually for bad treatment). Because everyone knew the Princeton Band had stolen Brown's mascot, the whole Princeton student body expected some sort of *retaliation* from Brown. retaliate, V.

• **reticent** ADJ. reserved; uncommunicative; inclined to be silent. Fearing his competitors might get advance word about his plans from talkative staff members, Hughes preferred *reticent* employees to loquacious ones.

## Word List 39  retract–saturate

**retract** V. withdraw; take back. When I saw how Fred and his fraternity brothers had trashed the frat house, I decided to *retract* my offer to let them use our summer cottage for the weekend. retraction, N.

**retrieve** V. recover; find and bring in. The dog was intelligent and quickly learned to *retrieve* the game killed by the hunter.

**retroactive** ADJ. taking effect prior to its enactment (as a law) or imposition (as a tax). Because the new pension law was *retroactive* to the first of the year, even though Martha had retired in February, she was eligible for the pension.

**revelry** N. boisterous merrymaking. New Year's Eve is a night of *revelry*.

• **reverent** ADJ. respectful; worshipful. Though I bow my head in church and recite the prayers, sometimes I don't feel properly *reverent*. revere, V.

**revoke** V. cancel; retract. Repeat offenders who continue to drive under the influence of alcohol face having their driver's license permanently *revoked*.

**revulsion** N. sudden, violent change of feeling; distaste; repugnance. Normally Cecil had a good appetite, but when he felt seasick he viewed his shipboard supper with *revulsion*.

**rift** N. opening made by splitting; open space; break in friendly relations. After the recent earthquake, geologists observed several fresh *rifts* in the Hayward hills. Through a *rift* in the dense clouds the pilot glimpsed a beacon light far below. Unsure how he had offended Jo, Laurie tried to think of some way to mend the *rift* in their friendship.

**rigid** ADJ. stiff and unyielding; strict; hard and unbending. By living with a man to whom she was not married, George Eliot broke Victorian society's most *rigid* rule of respectable behavior.

**rigor** N. severity. Many settlers could not stand the *rigors* of the New England winters.

**rile** V. vex; irritate. Red had a hair-trigger temper: he was an easy man to *rile*.

**rivulet** N. small stream. As the rains continued, the small trickle of water running down the hillside grew into a *rivulet* that threatened to wash away a portion of the slope.

**rousing** ADJ. lively; stirring. "And now, let's have a *rousing* welcome for TV's own Roseanne Barr, who'll lead us in a *rousing* rendition of 'The Star Spangled Banner.'"

**ruddy** ADJ. reddish; healthy looking. Santa Claus's *ruddy* cheeks nicely complement Rudolph the Reindeer's bright red nose.

**rue** V. regret; lament; mourn. Tina *rued* the night she met Tony and wondered how she'd ever fallen for such a jerk. rueful, ADJ.

**rummage** V. ransack; thoroughly search. When we *rummaged* through the trunks in the attic, we found many souvenirs of our childhood days. also N.

**rupture** N. act of breaking; fracture; break in harmony or peaceful relations. The *rupture* of gas lines caused by the earthquake contributed greatly to the fire that ensued.

**ruse** N. trick; stratagem. Because they wanted to decorate the living room for their mother's surprise birthday party, the girls tried to think of some good *ruse* to lure her out of the house for a couple of hours.

• **ruthless** ADJ. pitiless; cruel. Captain Hook was a dangerous, *ruthless* villain who would stop at nothing to destroy Peter Pan.

**saboteur** N. one who commits sabotage; destroyer of property. Members of the Resistance acted as *saboteurs,* blowing up train lines to prevent supplies from reaching the Nazi army.

**saccharine** ADJ. cloyingly sweet. She tried to ingratiate herself, speaking sweetly and smiling a *saccharine* smile.

**sagacious** ADJ. keen; shrewd; having insight. Holmes is far too *sagacious* to be fooled by a simple trick like that. sagacity, N.

**salutary** ADJ. tending to improve; beneficial; wholesome. The punishment had a *salutary* effect on the boy, for he became a model student.

**sanction** V. approve; ratify. Nothing will convince me to *sanction* the engagement of my daughter to such a worthless young man.

**sap** V. diminish; undermine. The element kryptonite has an unhealthy effect on Superman: it *saps* his strength.

**sarcasm** N. scornful remarks; stinging rebuke. Though Ralph tried to ignore the mocking comments of his supposed friends, their *sarcasm* wounded him deeply.

**sate** V. satisfy to the full; cloy. Its hunger *sated,* the lion dozed.

**satiate** V. satisfy fully. Having stuffed themselves until they were *satiated,* the guests were so full they were ready for a nap.

• **satirize** V. mock. Cartoonist Gary Trudeau often *satirizes* contemporary politicians; through the comments of the *Doonesbury* characters, Trudeau ridicules political corruption and folly. satirical, ADJ.

**saturate** V. soak thoroughly. Thorough watering is the key to lawn care: you must *saturate* your new lawn well to encourage its growth.

## Word List 40   saunter–shyster

**saunter** V. stroll slowly. Too tired for his usual brisk walk, Stan *sauntered* through the park, taking time to enjoy the spring flowers.

**savant** N. learned scholar. Despite all her academic honors, Dr. Diamond refused to be classed as a *savant:* considering herself a simple researcher, she refused to describe herself in such grandiose terms.

**savory** ADJ. tasty; pleasing, attractive, or agreeable. Julia Child's recipes enable amateur chefs to create *savory* delicacies for their guests.

**scamper** V. run about playfully. Looking forward to the game of hide-and-seek, the children *scampered* off to find good spots in which to hide.

**scanty** ADJ. meager; insufficient. Thinking his helping of food was *scanty,* Oliver Twist asked for more.

**scapegoat** N. someone who bears the blame for others. After the *Challenger* disaster, NASA searched for *scapegoats* on whom they could cast the blame.

**scavenge** V. hunt through discarded materials for usable items; search, especially for food. If you need parts for an old car that the dealers no longer have in stock, try *scavenging* for odd bits and pieces at the auto wreckers' yards. scavenger, N.

**schism** N. division; split. Let us not widen the *schism* by further bickering.

**scintillate** V. sparkle; flash. I enjoy her dinner parties because the food is excellent and the conversation *scintillates*.

**scrupulous** ADJ. conscientious; extremely thorough. Though Alfred is *scrupulous* in fulfilling his duties at work, he is less conscientious about his obligations to his family and friends.

• **scrutinize** V. examine closely and critically. Searching for flaws, the sergeant *scrutinized* every detail of the private's uniform.

**scuffle** V. struggle confusedly; move off in a confused hurry. The twins briefly *scuffled,* wrestling to see which of them would get the toy. When their big brother yelled, "Let go of my Gameboy!" they *scuffled* off down the hall.

**seasoned** ADJ. experienced. Though pleased with her new batch of rookies, the basketball coach wished she had a few more *seasoned* players on the team. (secondary meaning)

• **seclusion** N. isolation; solitude. One moment she loved crowds; the next, she sought *seclusion*.

**sect** N. separate religious body; faction. As university chaplain, she sought to address universal religious issues and not limit herself to concerns of any one *sect*.

**secular** ADJ. worldly; not pertaining to church matters. The church leaders decided not to interfere in *secular* matters.

**sedate** ADJ. calm and composed; grave. To calm the agitated pony, we teamed him with a *sedate* mare that easily accepted the harness.

**sedition** N. resistance to authority; insubordination; rebellion. Her words, though not treasonous in themselves, were calculated to arouse thoughts of *sedition*. seditious, ADJ.

**seep** V. leak through; trickle. After all the times we'd tried to repair the leaky roof, we were discouraged to see the water *seep* through the ceiling once again.

**sensory** ADJ. pertaining to the physical senses. Blasted by sound waves, dazzled by flashing lights, jostled by crowds, a newcomer to rock concerts can suffer from *sensory* overload.

**sequester** V. isolate; retire from public life; segregate; seclude. Banished from his kingdom, the wizard Prospero *sequestered* himself on a desert island.

**serendipity** N. gift for finding valuable or desirable things by accident; accidental good fortune or luck. Many scientific discoveries are a matter of *serendipity*: Newton was not sitting there thinking about gravity when the apple dropped on his head.

• **serenity** N. calmness; placidity. The *serenity* of the sleepy town was shattered by a tremendous explosion.

**servile** ADJ. slavishly submissive; fawning; cringing. Constantly fawning over his employer, Uriah Heep was a *servile* creature.

**servitude** N. slavery; compulsory labor. Born a slave, Douglass resented his life of *servitude* and plotted to escape to the North.

• **sever** V. cut; separate. Dr. Guillotin invented a machine that could neatly *sever* an aristocratic head from its equally aristocratic body.

• **severity** N. harshness; intensity; austerity; rigidity. The *severity* of Jane's migraine attack was so great that she took to her bed for a week.

**shackle** V. chain; fetter. In a chain gang, convicts are *shackled* together to prevent their escape. also N.

**shambles** N. wreck; mess; slaughterhouse. After the hurricane, the Carolina coast was a *shambles*. After the New Year's Eve party, the apartment was a *shambles*.

**shimmer** V. glimmer intermittently. The moonlight *shimmered* on the water as the moon broke through the clouds for a moment. also N.

**shortcomings** N. failures; deficiencies. Aware of his own *shortcomings* as a public speaker, the candidate worked closely with debate coaches to prepare for the coming campaign.

**shrewd** ADJ. clever; astute. A *shrewd* investor, he took clever advantage of the fluctuations of the stock market.

**shun** V. keep away from. Cherishing his solitude, the recluse *shunned* the company of other human beings.

**shyster** N. lawyer using questionable methods. The respectable attorney was horrified to learn that his newly discovered half brother was nothing but a cheap *shyster*.

## Word List 41 simile–spoke

**simile** N. comparison of one thing with another, using the word *like* or *as*. "My love is like a red, red rose" is a *simile*.

**simplistic** ADJ. oversimplified. Though Jack's solution dealt adequately with one aspect of the problem, it was *simplistic* in failing to consider various complications that might arise.

**simulate** V. feign; pretend. The judge ruled that the accused racketeer had *simulated* insanity and was in fact sane enough to stand trial.

• **singular** ADJ. unique; extraordinary; odd. Though the young man tried to understand Father William's *singular* behavior, he still found it odd that the old man incessantly stood on his head. singularity, N.

**sinister** ADJ. evil; conveying a sense of ill omen. Aware of the Penguin's *sinister* purpose, Batman wondered how he could save Gotham City from the ravages of his evil enemy.

**sinuous** ADJ. winding; bending in and out; not morally honest. The snake moved in a *sinuous* manner.

• **skeptical** ADJ. doubting; suspending judgment until having examined the evidence supporting a point of view. I am *skeptical* about this project; I want some proof that it can work. skepticism, N.

**skulk** V. move furtively and secretly. He *skulked* through the less fashionable sections of the city in order to avoid meeting any of his former friends.

**slacken** V. slow up; loosen. As they passed the finish line, the runners *slackened* their pace.

**slag** N. residue from smelting metal; dross; waste matter. The blast furnace had a special opening at the bottom to allow the workers to remove the worthless *slag*.

**slapdash** ADJ. haphazard; careless; sloppy. From the number of typos and misspellings I found in it, it's clear that Mario proofread the report in a remarkably *slapdash* fashion.

**slather** V. spread abundantly. Johnny *slathered* jelly on his toast so generously that it oozed over the edge and dripped on the clean tablecloth below.

**slothful** ADJ. lazy. Lying idly on the sofa while others worked, Reggie denied he was *slothful:* "I just supervise better lying down."

**sluggish** ADJ. slow; lazy; lethargic. After two nights without sleep, she felt *sluggish* and incapable of exertion.

**smelt** V. melt or blend ores, changing their chemical composition. The furnaceman *smelts* tin with copper to create a special alloy used in making bells.

**smolder** V. burn without flame; be liable to break out at any moment. The rags *smoldered* for hours before they burst into flame.

**smuggler** N. one who illegally moves goods across national borders. Suspecting Randy might be a *smuggler,* the customs inspector made a thorough search of his luggage but found nothing illicit.

**sneer** V. smile or laugh contemptuously; make an insulting comment or face. "I could paint better than that with both hands tied behind my back," *sneered* Marvin.

**sobriety** N. moderation (especially regarding indulgence in alcohol); seriousness. Neither falling-down drunks nor stand-up comics are noted for *sobriety.* sober, ADJ.

**sodden** ADJ. soaked; dull, as if from drink. He set his *sodden* overcoat near the radiator to dry.

**solemnity** N. seriousness; gravity. The minister was concerned that nothing should disturb the *solemnity* of the marriage service.

**soliloquy** N. talking to oneself. Dramatists use the *soliloquy* as a device to reveal a character's innermost thoughts and emotions.

**somber** ADJ. gloomy; depressing; dark; drab. Dull brown and charcoal gray are pretty *somber* colors; can't you wear something bright?

**somnolent** ADJ. half asleep. The heavy meal and the overheated room made us all *somnolent* and indifferent to the speaker.

**soporific** ADJ. sleep-causing; marked by sleepiness. Professor Pringle's lectures were so *soporific* that even he fell asleep in class. also N.

**sordid** ADJ. vile; filthy; wretched; mean. Talk show hosts seem willing to discuss any topic, no matter how *sordid* and disgusting it may be.

**spartan** ADJ. avoiding luxury and comfort; sternly disciplined. Looking over the bare, unheated room with its hard cot, he wondered what he was doing in such *spartan* quarters. Only his *spartan* sense of duty kept him at his post.

**spat** N. squabble; minor dispute. What had started out as a mere *spat* escalated into a full-blown argument.

**specious** ADJ. seemingly reasonable but incorrect; misleading (often intentionally). To claim that, because houses and birds both have wings, both can fly, is extremely *specious* reasoning.

**speculate** V. theorize or ponder; assume a financial risk; gamble. Students of the stock market *speculate* that the seeds of the financier's downfall were planted when he *speculated* heavily in junk bonds.

**spendthrift** N. someone who wastes money. Easy access to credit encourages people to turn into *spendthrifts* who shop till they drop.

**splendor** N. magnificence; grandeur; brilliance. Awed by the glittering chandeliers and finely costumed courtiers, Cinderella was overwhelmed by the *splendor* of the ball.

**spoke** N. radiating bar supporting the rim of a wheel. The repair man at the bicycle shop took less than half an hour to fix the bent *spokes* on Bob's rear wheel.

# Word List 42    spontaneity–subsequent

**spontaneity** N. lack of premeditation; naturalness; freedom from constraint. When Betty and Jennifer met, Jen impulsively hugged her roommate-to-be, but Betty drew back, unprepared for such *spontaneity.* spontaneous, ADJ.

**sporadic** ADJ. occurring irregularly. Although you can still hear *sporadic* outbursts of laughter and singing outside, the big Halloween parade has passed; the party's over till next year.

**spurious** ADJ. false; counterfeit; forged; illogical. The hero of Jonathan Gash's mystery novels is an antique dealer who gives the reader advice on how to tell *spurious* antiques from the real thing.

**spurt** V. gush forth; squirt. Water suddenly *spurted* from the fountain and splashed Bert right in the face.

**squabble** N. minor quarrel; bickering. Children invariably get involved in petty *squabbles*; wise parents know when to interfere and when to let the children work things out on their own.

**squalor** N. filth; degradation; dirty, neglected state. With rusted, broken-down cars in its yard, trash piled up on the porch, and tar paper peeling from the roof, the shack was the picture of *squalor.*

**squander** V. waste. If you *squander* your allowance on candy and comic books, you won't have any money left to buy the new box of crayons you want.

**stagnant** ADJ. motionless; stale; dull. Mosquitoes commonly breed in ponds of *stagnant* water. Mike's career was *stagnant;* it wasn't going anywhere, and neither was he! stagnate, V.

**staid** ADJ. sober; sedate. The wild parties at the fraternity house appealed to the jocks and slackers, but appalled the more *staid* and serious students on campus.

**stalemate** N. deadlock. Negotiations between the union and the employers have reached a *stalemate*: neither side is willing to budge from its previously stated position.

**stalwart** ADJ. strong and vigorous; unwaveringly dependable. We thought the congressman was a *stalwart* Democrat until he voted against the president's health care plan.

**stamina** N. strength; staying power. I doubt that she has the *stamina* to run the full distance of the marathon race.

**stanza** N. division of a poem. We all know the first *stanza* of the "The Star Spangled Banner." Does anyone know the last?

**static** ADJ. unchanging; lacking development. Why watch chess on TV? I like watching a game with action, not something *static* where nothing seems to be going on. stasis, N.

**statute** N. law enacted by the legislature. The *statute* of limitations sets the limits on how long you have to take legal action in specific cases.

• **steadfast** ADJ. loyal; unswerving. Penelope was *steadfast* in her affections, faithfully waiting for Ulysses to return from his wanderings.

**stem** V. check the flow. The paramedic used a tourniquet to *stem* the bleeding from the slashed artery.

**stem from** V. arise from. Morton's problems in school *stemmed from* his poor study habits.

**stereotyped** ADJ. oversimplified; lacking individuality; seen as a type. My chief objection to the book is that the characters are *stereotyped;* they don't come across as real people with individual quirks, fears, and dreams. stereotype, N., V.

**stifle** V. suppress; extinguish; inhibit. Halfway through the boring lecture, Laura gave up trying to *stifle* her yawns.

**stodgy** ADJ. stuffy; boringly conservative. For a young person, Winston seems remarkably *stodgy:* you'd expect someone his age to show a little more life.

• **stoic** ADJ. impassive; unmoved by joy or grief. I wasn't particularly *stoic* when I had my flu shot; I squealed like a stuck pig. also N.

**stolid** ADJ. unruffled; impassive; dull. Marianne wanted a romantic, passionate suitor like Willoughby, not a *stolid*, unimaginative one like Colonel Brandon.

• **stratagem** N. deceptive scheme. Though Wellington's forces seemed to be in full retreat, in reality their withdrawal was a *stratagem* intended to lure the enemy away from its sheltered position.

**strident** ADJ. loud and harsh; insistent. Whenever Sue became angry, she tried not to raise her voice; she had no desire to appear *strident*.

**stringent** ADJ. binding; rigid; strict. Protesting that the school dress code was too *stringent*, Katya campaigned to have the rules relaxed.

**stupefy** V. make numb; stun; amaze. Disapproving of drugs in general, Laura refused to take sleeping pills or any other medicine that might *stupefy* her. stupefaction, N.

**stupor** N. state of apathy; daze; lack of awareness. The paramedics shook the unconscious man but could not rouse him from his drunken *stupor*.

• **subdued** ADJ. less intense; quieter. Bob liked the *subdued* lighting at the restaurant because he thought it was romantic. I just thought it was dimly lit.

**subjective** ADJ. existing in the mind, rather than in the object itself; opposite of objective; personal. Your analysis is highly *subjective*; you have permitted your emotions and your opinions to color your thinking.

**sublime** ADJ. exalted; noble and uplifting; utter. Lucy was in awe of Desi's *sublime* musicianship, while he was in awe of her *sublime* naïveté.

**subordinate** ADJ. occupying a lower rank; inferior; submissive. Bishop Proudie's wife expected all the *subordinate* clergy to behave with great deference to the wife of their superior.

**subsequent** ADJ. following; later. In *subsequent* lessons, we shall take up more difficult problems.

# Word List 43  subside–tarry

**subside** V. sink to a low(er) level; grow quiet, less active, or less violent. The doctor assured us that the fever would eventually *subside*.

**subsidiary** N. something secondary in importance or subordinate; auxiliary. The Turner Broadcasting System is a wholly owned *subsidiary* of AOL Time Warner. First deal with the critical issues, then with the *subsidiary* ones. also ADJ.

**substantial** ADJ. ample; solid; in essentials. The scholarship represented a *substantial* sum of money.

**substantiate** V. establish by evidence; verify; support. These endorsements from satisfied customers *substantiate* our claim that Barron's *PSAT/NMSQT* is the best PSAT-prep book on the market.

**subtlety** N. perceptiveness; ingenuity; delicacy. Never obvious, she expressed herself with such *subtlety* that her remarks went right over the heads of most of her audience. subtle, ADJ.

• **subversive** ADJ. tending to overthrow or destroy. At first glance, the notion that styrofoam cups may actually be more ecologically sound than paper cups strikes most environmentalists as *subversive*.

**succinct** ADJ. brief; terse; compact. Don't bore your audience with excess verbiage: be *succinct*.

**succulent** ADJ. juicy; full of richness. To some people, Florida citrus fruits are more *succulent* than those from California. also N.

**suffragist** N. advocate of voting rights (for women). In recognition of her efforts to win the vote for women, Congress authorized coining a silver dollar honoring the *suffragist* Susan B. Anthony.

• **superficial** ADJ. trivial; shallow. Since your report gave only a *superficial* analysis of the problem, I cannot give you more than a passing grade.

• **superfluous** ADJ. excessive; unnecessary. Please try not to include so many *superfluous* details in your report; just give me the bare facts. superfluity, N.

**supplant** V. replace; usurp. Did the other woman actually *supplant* Princess Diana in Prince Charles's affections, or did Charles never love Diana at all?

**supple** ADJ. flexible; pliant. Years of yoga exercises made Grace's body *supple*.

• **suppress** V. crush; subdue; inhibit. Too polite to laugh in anyone's face, Roy did his best to *suppress* his amusement at Ed's inane remark.

**surfeit** V. satiate; stuff; indulge to excess in anything. Every Thanksgiving we are *surfeited* with an overabundance of holiday treats. also N.

• **surpass** V. exceed. Her PSAT scores *surpassed* our expectations.

**surreptitious** ADJ. secret; furtive; sneaky. Hoping to discover where Mom had hidden the Christmas presents, Tommy took a *surreptitious* peek into the master bedroom closet.

• **susceptible** ADJ. impressionable; easily influenced; having little resistance, as to a disease; receptive to. Said the patent medicine man to the extremely *susceptible* customer, "Buy this new miracle drug, and you will no longer be *susceptible* to the common cold."

• **suspend** V. defer or postpone; expel or eject; halt or discontinue; hang from above. When the judge *suspended* his sentence, Bill breathed a sigh of relief. When the principal *suspended* her from school, Wanda tried to look as if she didn't care. When the trapeze artist broke her arm, she had to *suspend* her activities: she no longer could be *suspended* from her trapeze.

• **sustain** V. experience; support; nourish. Stuart *sustained* such a severe injury that the doctors feared he would be unable to work to *sustain* his growing family.

**swill** V. drink greedily. Singing "Yo, ho, ho, and a bottle of rum," Long John Silver and his fellow pirates *swilled* their grog.

**swindler** N. cheat. She was gullible and trusting, an easy victim for the first *swindler* who came along.

**sycophant** N. servile flatterer; bootlicker. Fed up with the toadies and flatterers who made up his entourage, the star cried, "Get out, all of you! I'm sick to death of *sycophants!*"

• **symmetry** N. arrangement of parts so that balance is obtained; congruity. Something lopsided by definition lacks *symmetry*.

• **synthesis** N. combining parts into a whole. Now that we have succeeded in isolating this drug, our next problem is to plan its *synthesis* in the laboratory. synthesize, V.

• **taciturn** ADJ. habitually silent; talking little. The stereotypical cowboy is a *taciturn* soul, answering lengthy questions with "Yep" or "Nope."

**tactile** ADJ. pertaining to the organs or sense of touch. His callused hands had lost their *tactile* sensitivity.

**taint** V. contaminate; cause to lose purity; modify with a trace of something bad. One speck of dirt on your utensils may contain enough germs to *taint* an entire batch of preserves.

**tangential** ADJ. peripheral; only slightly connected; digressing. Despite Clark's attempts to distract her with *tangential* remarks, Lois kept on coming back to her main question: why couldn't he come out to dinner with Superman and her?

**tantalize** V. tease; torture with disappointment. Tom *tantalized* his younger brother, holding the ball just too high for Jimmy to reach.

**tarry** V. delay; dawdle. We can't *tarry* if we want to get to the airport on time.

# Word List 44    tedious–transcendent

• **tedious** ADJ. boring; tiring. The repetitious nature of work on the assembly line made Martin's job very *tedious*. tedium, N.

• **temper** V. moderate; tone down or restrain; toughen (steel). Not even her supervisor's grumpiness could *temper* Nancy's enthusiasm for her new job.

• **temperament** N. characteristic frame of mind; disposition; emotional excess. Although the twins look alike, they differ markedly in *temperament*: Todd is calm, but Rod is excitable. Racket-throwing tennis star John McEnroe was famed for his displays of *temperament*.

**temperate** ADJ. restrained; self-controlled; moderate in respect to temperature. Try to be *temperate* in your eating this holiday season; if you control your appetite, you won't gain too much weight.

**tempestuous** ADJ. stormy; impassioned; violent. Racket-throwing tennis star John McEnroe was famed for his displays of *tempestuous* temperament.

**tenet** N. doctrine; dogma. The agnostic did not accept the *tenets* of their faith.

**tentative** ADJ. hesitant; not fully worked out or developed; experimental; not definite or positive. Unsure of his welcome at the Christmas party, Scrooge took a *tentative* step into his nephew's drawing room.

**tenuous** ADJ. thin; weak; unsubstantial. Napoleon's alliance with Russia quickly proved *tenuous*: it disintegrated altogether in 1812.

• **termination** N. end. Though the time for *termination* of the project was near, we still had a lot of work to finish before we shut up shop.

**terrestrial** ADJ. earthly (as opposed to celestial); pertaining to the land. In many science fiction films, alien invaders from outer space plan to destroy all *terrestrial* life.

**terse** ADJ. concise; abrupt; pithy. There is a fine line between speech that is *terse* and to the point and speech that is too abrupt.

**theocracy** N. government run by religious leaders. Though some Pilgrims aboard the *Mayflower* favored the establishment of a *theocracy* in New England, many of their fellow voyagers preferred a nonreligious form of government.

**theoretical** ADJ. not practical or applied; hypothetical. Bob was better at applied engineering and computer programming than he was at *theoretical* physics and math. While I can still think of some *theoretical* objections to your plan, you've convinced me of its basic soundness.

**therapeutic** ADJ. curative. Now better known for its racetrack, Saratoga Springs first gained attention for the *therapeutic* qualities of its famous "healing waters."

**thrifty** ADJ. careful about money; economical. A *thrifty* shopper compares prices before making major purchases.

**thrive** V. prosper; flourish. Despite the impact of the recession on the restaurant trade, Philip's cafe *thrived*.

• **thwart** V. baffle; frustrate. Batman searched for a way to *thwart* the Joker's evil plan to destroy Gotham City.

**tiff** ADJ. minor quarrel; fit of annoyance. Whenever the Kramdens had a *tiff*, Ralph would bluster, "That's it, Alice!" and storm out of the apartment.

**tiller** N. handle used to move a boat's rudder (to steer). Fearing the wind might shift suddenly and capsize the skiff, Tom kept one hand on the *tiller* at all times.

**timidity** N. lack of self-confidence or courage. If you are to succeed as a salesman, you must first lose your *timidity* and fear of failure.

**tirade** N. extended scolding; denunciation; harangue. Every time the boss holds a meeting, he goes into a lengthy *tirade*, scolding us for everything from tardiness to padding our expenses.

**titanic** ADJ. gigantic. *Titanic* waves beat against the majestic S.S. *Titanic*, driving it against the concealed iceberg.

**title** N. right or claim to possession; mark of rank; name (of a book, film, etc.). Though the penniless Duke of Ragwort no longer had *title* to the family estate, he still retained his *title* as head of one of England's oldest families. The *title* of his autobiography was *From Riches to Rags*.

**toady** N. servile flatterer; yes man. Never tell the boss anything he doesn't wish to hear: he doesn't want an independent adviser, he just wants a *toady*. also V.

**torpor** N. lethargy; sluggishness; dormancy. Throughout the winter, nothing aroused the bear from his *torpor*: he would not emerge from hibernation until spring. torpid, ADJ.

**torrent** N. rushing stream; flood. Day after day of heavy rain saturated the hillside until the water ran downhill in *torrents*. torrential, ADJ.

**totter** V. move unsteadily; sway, as if about to fall. On unsteady feet, the drunk *tottered* down the hill to the nearest bar.

• **toxic** ADJ. poisonous. Caution: poison! Manufacturers put the skull and crossbones on bottles of iodine to warn purchasers that iodine is *toxic* if taken internally. toxicity, N.

**tractable** ADJ. docile; easily managed. Although Susan seemed a *tractable* young woman, she had a stubborn streak of independence that occasionally led her to defy the powers-that-be when she felt they were in the wrong.

**traduce** V. slander; malign. His opponents tried to *traduce* the candidate's reputation by spreading rumors about his past.

• **transcendent** ADJ. surpassing; exceeding ordinary limits; superior. Standing on the hillside watching the sunset through the Golden Gate was a *transcendent* experience for Lise: it was so beautiful it surpassed her wildest dreams.

# Word List 45   transcribe–unfeasible

**transcribe** V. copy. It took hours for the secretary to *transcribe* his shorthand notes of the conference into a form others could read.

**transgression** N. violation of a law; sin. Forgive us our *transgressions;* we know not what we do. transgress, V.

**transient** ADJ. momentary; temporary; staying for a short time. Lexy's joy at finding the perfect Christmas gift for Phil was *transient;* she still had to find presents for Roger, Laura, Allison, and Uncle Bob. Located near the airport, this hotel caters to a largely *transient* trade.

**transition** N. going from one state of action to another. During the period of *transition* from oil heat to gas heat, the furnace will have to be shut off.

**transitory** ADJ. impermanent; fleeting. Fame is *transitory*: today's rising star is all too soon tomorrow's washed-up has-been. transitoriness, N.

**translucent** ADJ. partly transparent. We could not recognize the people in the next room because of the *translucent* curtains that separated us.

• **transparent** ADJ. easily detected; permitting light to pass through freely. Bobby managed to put an innocent look on his face; to his mother, however, his guilt was *transparent*.

**travail** N. painful physical or mental labor; drudgery; torment. Like every other high school student she knew, Sherry detested the yearlong *travail* of cramming for the SAT.

**trek** N. travel; journey. The tribe made their *trek* farther north that summer in search of game. also V.

**trenchant** ADJ. cutting; keen. With *trenchant* wit, Frank Rich made some highly cutting remarks as he panned another dreadful play.

• **trepidation** N. fear; nervous apprehension. As she entered the office of the dean of admissions, Sharon felt some *trepidation* about how she would do in her interview.

**trifling** ADJ. trivial; unimportant. Why bother going to see a doctor for such a *trifling*, everyday cold?

**trigger** V. set off. John is touchy today; say one word wrong and you'll *trigger* an explosion.

**trite** ADJ. hackneyed; commonplace. The *trite* and predictable situations on many television programs turn off viewers, who respond by turning off their sets.

**trivial** ADJ. trifling; unimportant. Too many magazines ignore newsworthy subjects and feature *trivial* gossip about celebrities.

**trough** N. container for feeding farm animals; lowest point (of a wave, business cycle, etc.). The hungry pigs struggled to get at the fresh swill in the *trough*. The surfer rode her board, coasting along in the *trough* between two waves.

**troupe** N. group of stage performers; touring company. Was Will Kemp a member of Shakespeare's *troupe* of players when they performed at the Globe?

**truism** N. self-evident truth. Many a *truism* is summed up in a proverb; for example, "Marry in haste, repent at leisure."

**turbid** ADJ. muddy; having the sediment disturbed. The water was *turbid* after the children had waded through it.

• **turbulence** N. state of violent agitation. Warned of approaching *turbulence* in the atmosphere, the pilot told the passengers to fasten their seat belts.

**turgid** ADJ. swollen; distended. The *turgid* river threatened to overflow the levees and flood the countryside.

**turmoil** N. great commotion and confusion. Lydia running off with a soldier! Mother fainting at the news! The Bennet household was in *turmoil*.

**typhoon** N. tropical hurricane or cyclone. If you liked *Twister*, you'll love *Typhoon!*

**tyranny** N. oppression; cruel government. Frederick Douglass fought against the *tyranny* of slavery throughout his entire life. tyrant, N.

**ubiquitous** ADJ. being everywhere; omnipresent. That Christmas "The Little Drummer Boy" seemed *ubiquitous*: Justin heard the tune everywhere he went.

**ultimate** ADJ. final; not susceptible to further analysis. Scientists are searching for the *ultimate* truths.

**unanimity** N. complete agreement. We were surprised by the *unanimity* with which members of both parties accepted our proposals. unanimous, ADJ.

**unassuming** ADJ. modest. He is so *unassuming* that some people fail to realize how great a man he really is.

**unbecoming** ADJ. unattractive; improper. What an *unbecoming* dress Mona is wearing! That girl has no color sense. At the court martial the captain was charged with conduct *unbecoming* an officer.

**undermine** V. weaken; sap. The recent corruption scandals have *undermined* many people's faith in the city government.

**underscore** V. emphasize. Addressing the jogging class, Kim *underscored* the importance to runners of good nutrition.

**undulating** ADJ. moving with a wavelike motion. The Hilo Hula Festival was an *undulating* sea of grass skirts.

**unearth** V. dig up. When they *unearthed* the city, the archaeologists found many relics of an ancient civilization.

**unequivocal** ADJ. plain; obvious. My answer to your proposal is an *unequivocal* and absolute "No."

**unfazed** ADJ. not bothered; unworried. Surrounded by armed opponents, Bond nevertheless appeared completely *unfazed* by his danger.

**unfeasible** ADJ. not practical or workable. Roy's plan to enlarge the living room by knocking down a couple of internal walls proved *unfeasible* when he discovered that those walls were holding up the roof.

# Word List 46    unfounded–venerate

**unfounded** ADJ. baseless; not based on fact. Cher feared that her boyfriend was unfaithful; fortunately, her suspicions proved to be *unfounded*.

**ungainly** ADJ. awkward; clumsy; unwieldy. "If you want to know whether Nick's an *ungainly* dancer, check out my bruised feet," said Nora. Anyone who has ever tried to carry a bass fiddle knows it's an *ungainly* instrument.

**uniformity** N. sameness; monotony. At *Persons Magazine*, we strive for *uniformity* of style; as a result, all of our writers wind up sounding exactly alike.

**unintimidating** ADJ. unfrightening. Though Phil had expected to feel overawed when he met Joe Montana, he found the world-famous quarterback friendly and *unintimidating*.

**unique** ADJ. without an equal; single in kind. You have the *unique* distinction of being the only student whom I have had to fail in this course.

**universal** ADJ. characterizing or affecting all; present everywhere. At first, no one shared Christopher's opinions; his theory that the world was round was met with *universal* disbelief.

**unnerve** V. upset; weaken. His wartime experiences left Tom badly shaken; any sudden noise could *unnerve* him, reducing him to a quivering wreck.

**unprecedented** ADJ. novel; unparalleled. Margaret Mitchell's book *Gone with the Wind* was an *unprecedented* success.

**unravel** V. disentangle; solve. With equal ease Miss Marple *unraveled* tangled balls of yarn and baffling murder mysteries.

**unrequited** ADJ. not reciprocated. Suffering the pangs of *unrequited* love, Olivia rebukes Cesario for his hard-heartedness.

**unscathed** ADJ. unharmed. Juan's parents prayed that he would come home from the war *unscathed*.

**unseemly** ADJ. unbecoming; indecent; in poor taste. When he put whoopie cushions on all the seats in the funeral parlor, Seymour's conduct was most *unseemly*.

**unsightly** ADJ. unpleasant to look at; ugly. Although James was an experienced emergency room nurse, he occasionally became queasy when faced with a particularly *unsightly* injury.

**unsullied** ADJ. spotlessly clean; unstained. The reputation of our school is *unsullied*, young ladies; you must conduct yourself modestly and discreetly so that you never disgrace our good name.

**unwarranted** ADJ. unjustified; groundless; undeserved. We could not understand Martin's *unwarranted* rudeness to his mother's guests.

**upbraid** V. severely scold; reprimand. Not only did Miss Minchin *upbraid* Ermengarde for her disobedience, but she hung her up by her braids from a coat rack in the classroom.

**uphold** V. give support; keep from sinking; lift up. Bold Sir Robin was ready to fight to the death to *uphold* the honor of his lady.

**upright** ADJ. honest; ethical; erect; perpendicular. An *upright* person acts straight: he does not cheat. An *upright* post stands straight: it does not lean.

**uproarious** ADJ. marked by commotion; extremely funny; very noisy. The *uproarious* comedy hit *Ace Ventura: Pet Detective* starred Jim Carrey, whose comic mugging provoked gales of *uproarious* laughter from audiences coast to coast.

• **urbane** ADJ. suave; refined; elegant. Country-bred and naïve, Anna felt out of place among her *urbane* and sophisticated new classmates. urbanity, N.

**usurp** V. seize another's power or rank. The revolution ended when the victorious rebel general succeeded in *usurping* the throne.

• **utopia** N. ideal place, state, or society. Fed up with this imperfect universe, Don would have liked to run off to Shangri-la or some other fictitious *utopia*. utopian, ADJ.

• **vacillate** V. waver; fluctuate. Uncertain which suitor she ought to marry, the princess *vacillated*, saying now one, now the other. vacillation, N.

**vacuous** ADJ. empty; lacking in ideas; stupid. The politician's *vacuous* remarks annoyed the audience, who had hoped to hear more than empty platitudes.

**vagabond** N. wanderer; tramp. In summer, college students wander the roads of Europe like carefree *vagabonds*. also ADJ.

**validate** V. confirm; ratify. I will not publish my findings until I *validate* my results.

**vanguard** N. advance guard of a military force; forefront of a movement. When no enemy was in sight, the duke of Plaza Toro marched in the *vanguard* of his troops, but once the bullets flew above, he headed for the rear.

**vantage** N. position giving an advantage. They fired upon the enemy from behind the trees, walls, and any other point of *vantage* they could find.

**vapid** ADJ. dull and unimaginative; insipid and flavorless. "*Bor*-ing!" said Cheryl, as she suffered through yet another *vapid* lecture about Dead White Male Poets.

**vehement** ADJ. forceful; intensely emotional; with marked vigor. Alfred became so *vehement* in describing what was wrong with the Internal Revenue Service that he began jumping up and down and frothing at the mouth. vehemence, N.

**veneer** N. thin layer; cover. Deceived by Victor's *veneer* of sophistication, casual acquaintances failed to perceive his fundamental shallowness.

**venerate** V. revere. In Tibet today, the common people still *venerate* their traditional spiritual leader, the Dalai Lama.

## Word List 47  venturesome–whiff

**venturesome** ADJ. bold. A group of *venturesome* women were the first to scale Mt. Annapurna.

**veracity** N. truthfulness. Asserting his *veracity*, young George Washington proclaimed, "Father, I cannot tell a lie!"

**verbose** ADJ. wordy. Someone mute can't talk; someone *verbose* can hardly stop talking.

**verdant** ADJ. green; lush in vegetation. Monet's paintings of the *verdant* fields were symphonies in green.

**verisimilitude** N. appearance of truth; likelihood. Critics praised her for the *verisimilitude* of her performance as Lady Macbeth. She was completely believable.

• **versatile** ADJ. having many talents; capable of working in many fields. She was a *versatile* athlete, earning varsity letters in basketball, hockey, and track.

**vertigo** N. severe dizziness. When you test potential airplane pilots for susceptibility to spells of *vertigo,* be sure to hand out airsick bags.

**vicarious** ADJ. acting as a substitute; done by a deputy. Though Maud was too meek to talk back to anyone, she got a *vicarious* kick out of Rita's sharp retorts.

**vicissitude** N. change of fortune. Humbled by life's *vicissitudes,* the last emperor of China worked as a lowly gardener in the palace over which he had once ruled.

**vie** V. contend; compete. Politicians *vie* with one another, competing for donations and votes.

**vigor** N. active strength. Although he was over 70 years old, Jack had the *vigor* of a man in his prime. vigorous, ADJ.

**vindicate** V. clear from blame; exonerate; justify or support. The lawyer's goal was to *vindicate* her client and prove him innocent on all charges. The critics' extremely favorable reviews *vindicate* my opinion that *The Madness of King George* is a brilliant movie.

**vindictive** ADJ. out for revenge; malicious. Divorce sometimes brings out a *vindictive* streak in people; when Tony told Tina he wanted a divorce, she poured green Jello into the aquarium and turned his tropical fish into dessert.

**virtuoso** N. highly skilled artist. The promising young cellist Yo-Yo Ma grew into a *virtuoso* whose *virtuosity* on the violin thrilled millions.

**virulent** ADJ. extremely poisonous; hostile; bitter. Laid up with a *virulent* case of measles, Vera blamed her doctors because her recovery took so long. In fact, she became quite *virulent* on the subject of the quality of modern medical care.

**vise** N. tool for holding work in place. Before filing its edges, the keysmith took the blank key and fixed it firmly between the jaws of a *vise*.

**vivacious** ADJ. animated; lively. The hostess on *The Morning News* was a bit too bubbly and *vivacious* for me to take before I'd had my first cup of coffee.

• **volatile** ADJ. changeable; explosive; evaporating rapidly. The political climate today is extremely *volatile*: no one can predict what the electorate will do next. Maria Callas's temper was extremely *volatile*: the only thing you could predict was that she was sure to blow up. Ethyl chloride is an extremely *volatile* liquid: it evaporates instantly.

**voluble** ADJ. fluent; glib; talkative. Excessively *voluble* speakers suffer from logorrhea: they run off at the mouth a lot!

**voluminous** ADJ. extensive; bulky; large. Despite her family burdens, she kept up a *voluminous* correspondence with her friends. A caftan is a *voluminous* garment; most people wearing one look as if they're draped in a small tent.

• **voracious** ADJ. ravenous. The wolf is a *voracious* animal, its hunger never satisfied.

**vulnerable** ADJ. susceptible to wounds. His opponents could not harm Achilles, who was *vulnerable* only in his heel.

**waive** V. give up a claim or right voluntarily; refrain from enforcing; postpone considering. Although technically prospective students had to live in Piedmont to attend high school there, occasionally the school *waived* the residence requirement in order to enroll promising athletes.

**wallow** V. roll in; indulge in; become helpless. The hippopotamus loves to *wallow* in pools of mud. The horror film addict loves to *wallow* in tales of blood.

**wanderlust** N. strong longing to go off traveling. The cowboy had a bad case of *wanderlust;* he could never settle down.

**wane** V. decrease in size or strength; draw gradually to an end. When lit, does a wax candle *wane?*

**wanton** ADJ. unrestrained; willfully malicious; unchaste. Pointing to the stack of bills, Sheldon criticized Sarah for her *wanton* expenditures. In response, Sarah accused Sheldon of making an unfounded, *wanton* attack.

**warble** V. sing; babble. Every morning the birds *warbled* outside her window. also N.

• **wary** ADJ. very cautious. The spies grew *wary* as they approached the sentry.

**wayward** ADJ. ungovernable; unpredictable; contrary. Miss Watson warned Huck that if he didn't mend his ways she would ship him off to a school for *wayward* youths.

**wheedle** V. cajole; coax; deceive by flattery. She knows she can *wheedle* almost anything she wants from her father.

**whet** V. sharpen; stimulate. The odors from the kitchen are *whetting* my appetite; I will be ravenous by the time the meal is served.

**whiff** N. puff or gust (of air, scent, etc.); hint. The slightest *whiff* of Old Spice cologne brought memories of George to her mind.

## Word List 48   whimsical–zephyr

**whimsical** N. capricious; fanciful. In *Mrs. Doubtfire,* the hero is a playful, *whimsical* man who takes a notion to dress up as a woman so that he can look after his children, who are in the custody of his ex-wife. whimsy, N.

**whittle** V. pare; cut off bits. As a present for Aunt Polly, Tom *whittled* some clothespins out of a chunk of wood.

**willful** ADJ. intentional; headstrong. Donald had planned to kill his wife for months; clearly, her death was a case of deliberate, *willful* murder, not a crime of passion committed by a hasty, *willful* youth unable to foresee the consequences of his deeds.

**wile** N. trick intended to deceive; stratagem. At the end of the movie, the hero sees through the temptress's *wiles* and returns to his sweetheart back home.

**wily** ADJ. cunning; artful. If coyotes are supposed to be such sneaky, *wily* creatures, how does Road Runner always manage to outwit Wile E. Coyote?

**winnow** V. sift; separate good parts from bad. This test will *winnow* out the students who study from those who never open a book.

**withdrawn** ADJ. introverted; remote. Rebuffed by his colleagues, the initially outgoing young researcher became increasingly *withdrawn.*

**wither** V. shrivel; decay. Cut flowers are beautiful for a day, but all too soon they *wither.*

**withhold** V. hold back; desist from giving; keep possession of. The tenants decided to *withhold* a portion of the rent until the landlord kept his promise to renovate the building.

**wretch** N. miserable person; vile, despicable person. Tina felt sorry for the poor *wretches* who stood shivering in the rain. However, she was furious with that *wretch* Tony, who stood her up.

**wry** ADJ. twisted; with a humorous twist. We enjoy Dorothy Parker's verse for its *wry* wit.

**zeal** N. eager enthusiasm. Wang's *zeal* was contagious; soon all his fellow students were busily making posters, inspired by his ardent enthusiasm for the cause. zealous, ADJ.

**zenith** N. highest point; culmination. When the film star's career was at its *zenith,* she was in such great demand that producers told her to name her own price.

**zephyr** N. gentle breeze; west wind. When these *zephyrs* blow, it is good to be in an open boat under a full sail.

# High-Frequency Vocabulary Practice Exercises

**Directions:** Briefly review the 30 high-frequency words in each boldfaced grouping. Then tackle the ten sentence completion questions on that group of words. Answer key and explanations are located on page 194.

**absolve–aversion**

1. In the course of the competition, Morgan developed a real respect for the determination and skill of his ---- .
(A) assumption   (B) adversary   (C) apprenticeship
(D) acrimony   (E) ambivalence

2. John preferred working on real-life engineering problems to tackling ---- questions in his theoretical physics class.
(A) accessible   (B) autonomous   (C) altruistic
(D) adverse   (E) abstract

3. It was entirely ---- of Marisa to make an anonymous donation to the Mayor's Disaster Relief Fund; she refused to take credit for her generous act.
(A) ambiguous   (B) aesthetic   (C) affable
(D) altruistic   (E) autonomous

4. The boys' ---- toward one another was so obvious that we feared they might get into a fight.
(A) affinity   (B) antagonism   (C) assumption
(D) apathy   (E) aristocracy

5. Use an ice pack on your swollen knee: it can help ---- the pain and reduce the swelling.
(A) alleviate   (B) acknowledge   (C) appropriate
(D) acclaim   (E) absolve

6. Let us take a moment to ---- the contributions of everyone who helped make this festival such a great event.
(A) aspire   (B) accommodate   (C) absolve
(D) abstract   (E) acknowledge

7. Something that can be easily reached is by definition ---- .
(A) abstract   (B) accessible   (C) aesthetic
(D) ambiguous   (E) ample

8. Before becoming a master woodworker, Karl had to serve an ---- with a member of the woodworkers' guild.
(A) acrimony   (B) affinity   (C) ambivalence
(D) apprenticeship   (E) assumption

9. Tweedledum could not explain the ---- he felt for Tweedledee. Why did he dislike his brother so intensely?
(A) affinity   (B) apathy   (C) apprehension
(D) assumption   (E) aversion

10. The harvest had been plentiful; the farmers were pleased to have an ---- supply of grain stored for the winter.
(A) affable   (B) amenable   (C) ample
(D) authentic   (E) autonomous

**banal–convention**

11. When Bonnie spilled the coffee all over the table-cloth, her bright red blush ---- how embarrassed she felt.
(A) betrayed   (B) compromised   (C) confronted
(D) coalesced   (E) condoned

12. While some doctors assert that taking large doses of vitamin C can be ---- to patients, other medical experts maintain such megadoses are worthless.
(A) banal   (B) beneficial   (C) buoyant
(D) circumspect   (E) contentious

13. Scott enjoyed working at Google because of his friendly coworkers and the ---- surroundings.
(A) conscientious   (B) congenial   (C) brittle
(D) banal   (E) circumspect

14. We were relieved when the disputing parties finally agreed to ---- ; the conflict had gone on far too long, and it was time they reached a settlement.
(A) condone   (B) confront   (C) captivate
(D) confirm   (E) compromise

15. "Strong as an ox" is an example of a ---- , a sadly overused sentence or phrase that has lost its original force.
(A) caricature   (B) chronicle   (C) cliché
(D) component   (E) conformity

**16.** When we remodeled our house, we had to rewire the building to be in ---- with the current building code.
(A) compliance   (B) composure   (C) component
(D) consolidation   (E) convention

**17.** Most bars of soap sink to the bottom of the bathtub. Ivory soap, however, is ---- : it floats.
(A) banal   (B) beneficial   (C) benign
(D) brittle   (E) buoyant

**18.** In his diary, Samuel Pepys attempted to ---- the daily events of his life, faithfully recording them in great detail.
(A) captivate   (B) chronicle   (C) collaborate
(D) coalesce   (E) compromise

**19.** Beat the butter and sugar together until the resulting liquid has the ---- of heavy cream.
(A) candor   (B) composure   (C) compromise
(D) consistency   (E) convention

**20.** John was very ---- about locking up the store when he left work; I never worried that he would forget and leave things unlocked.
(A) banal   (B) benign   (C) brittle
(D) conscientious   (E) contentious

**convoluted–disgruntled**

**21.** The hack writer hadn't had a fresh idea in years. Even the titles of his books were ---- .
(A) convoluted   (B) derivative   (C) detached
(D) diffident   (E) disgruntled

**22.** Quick and active, Mary liked getting places on time; she was always annoyed when her younger sister would ---- and make them late.
(A) dawdle   (B) debilitate   (C) decry
(D) deplete   (E) disclose

**23.** Many educators ---- the over-emphasis on standardized tests today and wish that less importance could be given to the SAT and ACT.
(A) demean   (B) depict   (C) deplete
(D) deplore   (E) digress

**24.** Although the teacher encouraged everyone to participate in class discussions, Martin was too ---- to speak up.
(A) derivative   (B) didactic   (C) diffident
(D) discernible   (E) discordant

**25.** When you make a stupid remark, people are likely to respond to it with ---- .
(A) corrosion   (B) deference   (C) derision
(D) deterrent   (E) discrepancy

**26.** A psychologist cannot afford to get emotionally involved with her patients; she must remain ---- .
(A) degenerate   (B) derisive   (C) derivative
(D) detached   (E) disgruntled

**27.** The ---- of good jobs in rural Arizona convinced Meg to move to Phoenix, where she hoped to find more opportunities of employment.
(A) dearth   (B) defamation   (C) defiance
(D) digression   (E) disclaimer

**28.** Johnny's parents were delighted by his ---- behavior at the dinner party: he conducted himself properly all evening.
(A) decorous   (B) degenerate   (C) discernible
(D) discordant   (E) disgruntled

**29.** The speaker strayed away from the topic from time to time, but nobody minded his ---- .
(A) corrosions   (B) defamations   (C) derisions
(D) deterrents   (E) digressions

**30.** If you do not ---- your uncontrolled shopping sprees, you will be broke in less than a month.
(A) curtail   (B) debilitate   (C) demean
(D) depict   (E) disclose

**disinterested–esoteric**

**31.** It can damage a child's self-esteem if you ---- his first attempts to perform a complex task.
(A) divulge   (B) disparage   (C) dissipate
(D) endorse   (E) entice

**32.** Juanita enjoyed riding spirited horses, but Eva preferred her mounts to be more ---- .
(A) disinterested   (B) docile   (C) dogmatic
(D) ephemeral   (E) esoteric

**33.** Is there a clear ---- between the graphic novel and the conventional comic book? Both are similar in appearance.
(A) dispatch   (B) dissent   (C) distinction
(D) doctrine   (E) enigma

**34.** Because John lacked the data he needed to come up with the correct answer, he leaped to an ---- conclusion.
(A) elated   (B) elusive   (C) eclectic
(D) esoteric   (E) erroneous

35. Monica would never ---- anything that a friend told her in confidence. She was good at keeping secrets.
    (A) dismiss  (B) dispel  (C) disperse
    (D) dissipate  (E) divulge

36. After winning the 5K race, Phil was so ---- that he let out a triumphant cheer.
    (A) disinterested  (B) docile  (C) eclectic
    (D) elated  (E) erroneous

37. Marilyn tried to trap the mouse under a wastebasket, but the small rodent proved too ---- for her to capture.
    (A) docile  (B) dogmatic  (C) elusive
    (D) erroneous  (E) esoteric

38. Supreme Court Justice Ruth Bader Ginsburg would frequently ---- from majority decisions of the court and express her open disagreement with the court's rulings.
    (A) dispatch  (B) dispel  (C) disperse
    (D) dissent  (E) endorse

39. In the months before Christmas, television ads try to ---- viewers to buy lavish gifts for the whole family.
    (A) disparage  (B) dispel  (C) enhance
    (D) entice  (E) enumerate

40. By definition, something ---- does not last very long.
    (A) disinterested  (B) dogmatic  (C) eclectic
    (D) ephemeral  (E) erroneous

**espouse–hypothetical**

41. Tim was always friendly and ---- , happily striking up conversations with strangers on the bus.
    (A) fastidious  (B) gluttonous  (C) gregarious
    (D) hackneyed  (E) hypocritical

42. Although Georgette Heyer wrote several mystery novels, the majority of her works fall under the ---- of historical fiction.
    (A) farce  (B) fervor  (C) excerpt
    (D) genre  (E) hindrance

43. The slender youth looked ---- and vulnerable compared to his robust, muscular opponent.
    (A) fastidious  (B) flippant  (C) frail
    (D) frivolous  (E) garrulous

44. William Lloyd Garrison left the American Anti-Slavery Society (which he had helped found) because its leaders refused to ---- the cause of women's rights.
    (A) espouse  (B) excerpt  (C) exploit
    (D) generate  (E) gratify

45. Because of her ---- behavior during her enlistment, Maya was awarded the Army Good Conduct Medal.
    (A) exemplary  (B) fastidious  (C) feasible
    (D) frivolous  (E) hypothetical

46. Hoping to speed up the delivery of his team's new uniforms, the coach asked the manufacturer to ---- the order.
    (A) esteem  (B) exonerate  (C) expedite
    (D) exploit  (E) hamper

47. In the movie *The Odd Couple*, one roommate is a slob, while the other is a ---- soul, extremely particular about how neat the apartment should be.
    (A) fallacious  (B) fastidious  (C) fawning
    (D) flippant  (E) garrulous

48. Before I purchase a book on Kindle, I like to read the free sample ---- taken from it, so that I can decide whether the book will be worth its purchase price.
    (A) excerpt  (B) exploit  (C) farce
    (D) fervor  (E) genre

49. Is it possible to build a suspension bridge across this river? We need to determine whether such a project is ---- .
    (A) exemplary  (B) fastidious  (C) feasible
    (D) forthright  (E) hypocritical

50. "I hate oatmeal," exclaimed Bobby, viewing his cereal bowl with ---- .
    (A) esteem  (B) excerpt  (C) farce
    (D) hindrance  (E) hostility

**iconoclastic–integrity**

51. Uncle Fred had not expected to be asked to toast the newlyweds at the wedding reception; despite his lack of preparation, he made a fine ---- speech.
    (A) iconoclastic  (B) immutable  (C) implacable
    (D) impromptu  (E) inscrutable

52. Because George was extremely afraid of heights, nothing could ---- him to ride on the Ferris wheel.
    (A) impede  (B) incarcerate  (C) incorporate
    (D) indict  (E) induce

**53.** I cannot trust Edmund: there is an ---- between what he says and what he does.
(A) implement  (B) inconsistency  (C) ineptness
(D) ingrate  (E) integrity

**54.** Although Diane seldom spoke at board meetings, everyone paid attention when she did because her comments were so ---- .
(A) immutable  (B) implacable
(C) inconsequential  (D) insightful
(E) intangible

**55.** The state of California fines people who ---- traffic by driving too slowly, thereby creating hazardous conditions for other drivers.
(A) impede  (B) incarcerate  (C) incorporate
(D) indict  (E) induce

**56.** The counselor warned Brian that his ---- attitude toward his homework assignments would have a negative effect on his chances of graduating from high school.
(A) imperceptible  (B) indifferent  (C) industrious
(D) ingenious  (E) innocuous

**57.** Inspector Javert was the ---- enemy of Jean Valjean, determined to recapture Valjean and send him back to prison.
(A) iconoclastic  (B) imperceptible
(C) implacable  (D) inconsequential
(E) ingenuous

**58.** We called him "Fumblefingers" because he was particularly ---- at tasks that required manual dexterity.
(A) iconclastic  (B) industrious  (C) inept
(D) inherent  (E) insightful

**59.** She was true to her principles and would never compromise them. In other words, she was a model of ---- .
(A) incongruity  (B) inconsistency
(C) implication  (D) inscrutability  (E) integrity

**60.** We all make mistakes: no one is ---- .
(A) iconoclastic  (B) impromptu  (C) infallible
(D) ingenuous  (E) inherent

**intricacy–outmoded**

**61.** Bernice bought only the latest, most trendy fashions; she refused to buy anything the least bit ---- .
(A) outmoded  (B) ostentatious  (C) opaque
(D) nocturnal  (E) meticulous

**62.** Bored by the dull routine of his assembly line job, Mario wished something exciting would happen to break the ---- .
(A) intricacy  (B) larceny  (C) malice
(D) monotony  (E) mutability

**63.** The music department has designed a scholarship program to ---- student musicians by providing them with opportunities to play in the local community orchestra.
(A) loathe  (B) misrepresent  (C) mock
(D) nurture  (E) obscure

**64.** For the most part, owls and bats are both ---- creatures, active primarily at night.
(A) introspective  (B) judicious  (C) meek
(D) mutable  (E) nocturnal

**65.** Michael looked back on his days in the Peace Corps with ---- and longed to visit Malaysia again.
(A) intricacy  (B) malice  (C) monotony
(D) nonchalance  (E) nostalgia

**66.** After soaking in the hot tub, Ming felt ---- and drained of energy.
(A) lethargic  (B) meticulous  (C) notorious
(D) obnoxious  (E) ostentatious

**67.** "Beets!" exclaimed Susan. "I ---- beets. Can't you ever cook a vegetable I like?"
(A) loathe  (B) misrepresent  (C) mock
(D) nurture  (E) obscure

**68.** Frederick Douglass was a famous ---- whose speeches about his days as a slave deeply moved audiences throughout the North.
(A) misconception  (B) monarch
(C) nonchalance  (D) optimist  (E) orator

**69.** Spoiled rotten by his parents, Willy was an ---- little brat.
(A) introspective  (B) obnoxious  (C) opaque
(D) optimistic  (E) outmoded

**70.** Luck comes and goes: that's what we mean when we speak of the ---- of fortune.
(A) larceny  (B) monarchy  (C) monotony
(D) mutability  (E) nonchalance

**pacifist–prosperity**

71. Someone who always expects things to turn out badly is a ---- .
    (A) pacifist  (B) paradox  (C) pessimist
    (D) philanthropist  (E) predator

72. Looking down the darkly menacing alley, Oliver felt a ---- of danger.
    (A) paradox  (B) perjury  (C) potency
    (D) premonition  (E) prosperity

73. Mercedes Lackey is a ---- author, turning out three or four novels every year.
    (A) pedantic  (B) petulant  (C) presumptuous
    (D) prolific  (E) prophetic

74. I used to shop at Walmart, but when I learned how little they paid their workers, I decided not to ---- their stores anymore.
    (A) pacify  (B) patronize  (C) plagiarize
    (D) prevail  (E) proliferate

75. Hunger makes Ira irritable; if he doesn't eat a good breakfast, he starts acting fretful and ---- .
    (A) pervasive  (B) petulant  (C) pragmatic
    (D) profound  (E) prominent

76. Because medications lose strength when they are stored in hot, humid environments, try storing your medications in a dry place to maintain their ---- .
    (A) paradox  (B) pessimism  (C) phenomena
    (D) potency  (E) proliferation

77. Science fiction stories often are based on a puzzling aspect of time travel, in which someone traveling in the past performs an action that would have made the trip back in time impossible (for example, by killing her grandfather at a time before she was born). This is known as the grandfather ---- .
    (A) paradox  (B) perjury  (C) potency
    (D) proliferation  (E) prologue

78. Bribery of city officials was so ---- that it was accepted as the normal cost of doing business in Chicago.
    (A) pedantic  (B) pervasive  (C) pessimistic
    (D) petulant  (E) prophetic

79. An "invalid argument" is an argument that cannot reach any logical or sensible conclusion because the argument's basic assumption or ---- is not based upon real evidence or facts.
    (A) perjury  (B) phenomena  (C) premise
    (D) premonition  (E) proliferation

80. The hungry lion prowled the grassland in search of ---- .
    (A) perjury  (B) predator  (C) premise
    (D) premonition  (E) prey

**provocative–stoic**

81. The housekeeper closely ---- each piece of silverware to make sure that the maids had removed every speck of tarnish.
    (A) refuted  (B) relinquished  (C) rejuvenated
    (D) repudiated  (E) scrutinized

82. Nothing could disturb the monk's ---- ; no matter what happened, he remained calm and undisturbed.
    (A) severity  (B) serenity  (C) renown
    (D) recluse  (E) ramble

83. Josie was too ---- to believe the used car salesman's claim that the automobile had been owned by a little old lady who drove it only once a week to church.
    (A) provocative  (B) random  (C) reprehensible
    (D) reverent  (E) skeptical

84. The poet Seamus Heaney gained worldwide ---- when he received the 1995 Nobel Prize in Literature.
    (A) renown  (B) resignation  (C) resolution
    (D) restraint  (E) severity

85. Because seeing violent acts can negatively affect children's behavior, it is ---- to limit young people's exposure to such violence on television.
    (A) provocative  (B) prudent  (C) reprehensible
    (D) reticent  (E) singular

86. The pirate captain was a ---- killer, showing no mercy as he condemned victim after victim to walk the plank.
    (A) random  (B) reserved  (C) reticent
    (D) reverent  (E) ruthless

87. Wanting to win the debate, Kathryn searched for new evidence that might help ---- her opponent's argument.
    (A) ramble  (B) refute  (C) rejuvenate
    (D) relinquish  (E) retain

88. Nothing could shake Maria's ---- to rebuild her home after the flood had destroyed it.
    (A) recluse  (B) renown  (C) resolution
    (D) seclusion  (E) severity

**89.** Susan had ---- success growing produce this season; she canned so many tomatoes, carrots, and green beans that she ran out of room in her pantry.
(A) reprehensible   (B) reticent   (C) singular
(D) skeptical   (E) stoic

**90.** When I began posting daily quotes on Facebook, I didn't have any particular plan in mind; I just made a ---- selection of quotations.
(A) random   (B) reticent   (C) reverent
(D) reprehensible   (E) ruthless

**stratagem–wary**

**91.** Stacy found proofreading a ---- job and wished she had more exciting work to do.
(A) subversive   (B) susceptible   (C) tedious
(D) transcendent   (E) urbane

**92.** Someone cautious and on the lookout for trouble is by definition ---- .
(A) taciturn   (B) urbane   (C) versatile
(D) volatile   (E) wary

**93.** Martin's ambition was to ---- his big brother's athletic achievements by setting a new school record for the half-mile.
(A) surpass   (B) sustain   (C) temper
(D) vacillate   (E) synthesize

**94.** Warning of severe ---- ahead, the pilot advised the passengers to strap in and prepare for a bumpy ride.
(A) stratagem   (B) symmetry   (C) synthesis
(D) termination   (E) turbulence

**95.** No matter how hard Juan tried to strike up a conversation with the fellow in the next seat, he could not get a word out of the ---- young man.
(A) subversive   (B) superfluous   (C) susceptible
(D) taciturn   (E) voracious

**96.** Fortunately, the wound was only ---- ; the knife failed to cut deep enough to do major damage.
(A) subversive   (B) superficial   (C) superfluous
(D) susceptible   (E) synthetic

**97.** In biology, the modern ---- consolidated the results of various early twentieth-century lines of investigation that supported and reconciled the Darwinian theory of evolution and the Mendelian laws of inheritance.
(A) synthesis   (B) temperament   (C) termination
(D) trepidation   (E) turbulence

**98.** The paint thinner called acetone is a ---- solvent; if you don't keep the container tightly sealed, liquid acetone will evaporate rapidly.
(A) superficial   (B) tedious   (C) toxic
(D) versatile   (E) volatile

**99.** The windstorm had knocked down some of the lampposts lining the avenue, shattering the perfect ---- of the pairs of matched pillars.
(A) stratagem   (B) symmetry   (C) temperament
(D) termination   (E) trepidation

**100.** Make up your mind where you want to go on vacation. Don't just ---- !
(A) surpass   (B) sustain   (C) temper
(D) vacillate   (E) subdue

# Answer Key

| | | | | | | | |
|---|---|---|---|---|---|---|---|
| 1. | B | 21. | B | 41. | C | 61. | A | 81. | E |
| 2. | E | 22. | A | 42. | D | 62. | D | 82. | B |
| 3. | D | 23. | D | 43. | C | 63. | D | 83. | E |
| 4. | B | 24. | C | 44. | A | 64. | E | 84. | A |
| 5. | A | 25. | C | 45. | A | 65. | E | 85. | B |
| 6. | E | 26. | D | 46. | C | 66. | A | 86. | E |
| 7. | B | 27. | A | 47. | B | 67. | A | 87. | B |
| 8. | D | 28. | A | 48. | A | 68. | E | 88. | C |
| 9. | E | 29. | E | 49. | C | 69. | B | 89. | C |
| 10. | C | 30. | A | 50. | E | 70. | D | 90. | A |
| 11. | A | 31. | B | 51. | D | 71. | C | 91. | C |
| 12. | B | 31. | B | 52. | E | 72. | D | 92. | E |
| 13. | B | 33. | C | 53. | B | 73. | D | 93. | A |
| 14. | E | 34. | E | 54. | D | 74. | B | 94. | E |
| 15. | C | 35. | E | 55. | A | 75. | B | 95. | D |
| 16. | A | 36. | D | 56. | B | 76. | D | 96. | B |
| 17. | E | 37. | C | 57. | C | 77. | A | 97. | A |
| 18. | B | 38. | D | 58. | C | 78. | B | 98. | E |
| 19. | D | 39. | D | 59. | E | 79. | C | 99. | B |
| 20. | D | 40. | D | 60. | C | 80. | E | 100. | D |

# Answer Explanations

**absolve–aversion**

1. **(B)** *Adversary* means opponent. Morgan respected his opponent, the person competing against him.

2. **(E)** *Abstract* means theoretical, as opposed to applied or practical. John liked working on practical problems, not theoretical or abstract ones.

3. **(D)** *Altruistic* means unselfishly generous. Because Marisa took no credit for her donation, her generosity was wholly unselfish.

4. **(B)** *Antagonism* means hostility. The boys' obvious hostility made it seem likely that they would get into a fight.

5. **(A)** *Alleviate* means relieve or lessen. The ice pack helps relieve pain and lessen swelling.

6. **(E)** *Acknowledge* means express recognition or appreciation. We recognize people's contributions and thank them.

7. **(B)** *Accessible* means easy to approach, or obtainable.

8. **(D)** An *apprenticeship* is time spent as a novice learning a trade from a skilled worker.

9. **(E)** *Aversion* means strong dislike.

10. **(C)** *Ample* means abundant or plentiful. Thanks to the plentiful harvest, the farmers have ample stores of grain.

**banal–convention**

11. **(A)** *Betray* here means reveal unconsciously or unintentionally. Bonnie's blush reveals or gives away her embarrassment.

12. **(B)** *Beneficial* means helpful or useful. The signal word "While" is your clue that the missing word is an antonym for *worthless*.

13. **(B)** *Congenial* means pleasant or friendly. Scott enjoys his workplace because the surroundings are pleasant.

14. **(E)** To *compromise* is to settle a disagreement by both sides adjusting their demands.

15. **(C)** A *cliché* is by definition a phrase dulled by overuse.

16. **(A)** *Compliance* means the state of being in accordance with requirements. If you follow the requirements of the building code exactly, then your renovation will be in *compliance* with the building code.

17. **(E)** By definition, something *buoyant* is able to float.

18. **(B)** *Chronicle* means to report or record in chronological order. Note the root *chron* here: *chron* means time.

19. **(D)** *Consistency* here means degree of thickness. It can also mean uniformity or dependability.

20. **(D)** *Conscientious* means careful or scrupulous. There's little need to worry about doors being left unlocked if the person in charge of locking up is very careful.

### convoluted–disgruntled

21, **(B)** *Derivative* means unoriginal. A writer without fresh ideas is apt to be unoriginal in his choice of titles.

22. **(A)** *Dawdle* means loiter or waste time.

23. **(D)** *Deplore* means strongly regret. The educators are sorry that standardized tests are overemphasized today.

24. **(C)** *Diffident* means shy or lacking in confidence. Someone so modest would find it difficult to speak up in class.

25. **(C)** *Derision* means mockery or ridicule. People often make fun of stupid remarks.

26. **(D)** *Detached* means emotionally removed and objective. Psychologists need to maintain their detachment.

27. **(A)** A *dearth* is a scarcity or lack. The lack of good jobs in her area motivated Meg to move.

28. **(A)** *Decorous* means proper and dignified.

29. **(E)** *Digressions* by definition are off-topic remarks, comments that wander away from the main subject.

30. **(A)** *Curtail* means cut short or reduce. The shopaholic needs to cut short those shopping sprees.

### disinterested–esoteric

31. **(B)** *Disparage* means belittle or speak mockingly about. Children need encouragement, not disparagement.

32. **(B)** *Docile* means easily managed and obedient. It is an antonym for *spirited* or vigorous and lively.

33. **(C)** A *distinction* is a difference.

34. **(E)** *Erroneous* means mistaken or wrong. If you lack the information you need to come up with a right answer, you are likely to come up with a wrong one.

35. **(E)** *Divulge* means reveal. Someone who is good at keeping secrets is unlikely to divulge something told to her in confidence.

36. **(D)** *Elated* means overjoyed. Winning the race made Phil very, very happy.

37. **(C)** *Elusive* means evasive or hard to grasp. The mouse was too slippery and tricky for her to catch.

38. **(D)** *Dissent* means disagree. Because Justice Ginsburg disagreed with the decision, she expressed her dissent in a minority opinion.

39. **(D)** *Entice* means attract or tempt. The ads tempt viewers to spend more than they possibly should.

40. **(D)** *Ephemeral* means short-lived or fleeting.

### espouse–hypothetical

41. **(C)** *Gregarious* means sociable. Someone who is comfortable chatting with strangers on the bus is by definition gregarious.

42. **(D)** A *genre* is a particular variety of art or literature. Most of Heyer's novels belong to the genre of historical fiction.

43. **(C)** *Frail* means weak. Someone who is slender and who appears easy to wound (vulnerable) might well be described as frail.

44. **(A)** *Espouse* means support or adopt. Garrison left the Anti-Slavery Society because the group would not support the cause of women's rights.

45. **(A)** *Exemplary* means outstandingly good and worth imitating. Maya's exemplary behavior earned her the Good Conduct Medal.

46. **(C)** *Expedite* means hasten or speed up some action. The coach wishes to hasten the delivery of his order.

47. **(B)** *Fastidious* means hard to please or excessively demanding. Felix was fastidious about how neat the apartment should be.

48. **(A)** An *excerpt* is a selected passage taken from a longer work.

49. **(C)** *Feasible* means practical or capable of being done. Major projects often require a preliminary feasibility study.

50. **(E)** *Hostility* means hatred. Bobby hates oatmeal.

## iconoclastic–integrity

51. **(D)** *Impromptu* means off the cuff or unprepared. Uncle Fred had to speak spontaneously without any time for preparation.

52. **(E)** *Induce* means persuade. Ferris wheels take riders high above the ground. Nothing could persuade acrophobic George to ride on one.

53. **(B)** *Inconsistency* is the state of being self-contradictory. What Edmund does contradicts what he says he's going to do.

54. **(D)** *Insightful* means perceptive, full of insights. It makes sense that people would pay attention to insightful comments.

55. **(A)** *Impede* means hinder or delay. Excessively slow drivers impede the flow of traffic.

56. **(B)** *Indifferent* here means unconcerned. Brian is unconcerned about doing his homework; if he doesn't put a little more care and effort into doing his work, he may not graduate.

57. **(C)** *Implacable* means unbending and merciless. An implacable enemy cannot be appeased or mollified.

58. **(C)** *Inept* means lacking skill. Someone called "Fumblefingers" is likely to be physically inept.

59. **(E)** *Integrity* means uprightness and honesty. Someone who remains true to her principles shows integrity.

60. **(C)** *Infallible* means faultless, not capable of making errors.

## intricacy–outmoded

61. **(A)** *Outmoded* means no longer stylish. Bernice refused to buy last year's outmoded fashions.

62. **(D)** *Monotony* means a boring constancy or lack of variety. The dull routine of Mario's assembly line job was sadly monotonous.

63. **(D)** *Nurture* means nourish or foster. The scholarship program fosters or promotes the development of student musicians.

64. **(E)** *Nocturnal* means occurring or active at night.

65. **(E)** *Nostalgia* is a longing for the past. Michael longs for the good old days in the Peace Corps.

66. **(A)** *Lethargic* means drowsy and dull. The hot soak left Ming feeling sleepy and unenergetic.

67. **(A)** *Loathe* means detest or dislike intensely. What vegetables do you loathe?

68. **(E)** An *orator* is a public speaker.

69. **(B)** *Obnoxious* means highly objectionable or annoying. By definition, brats are obnoxious.

70. **(D)** *Mutability* means fickleness or changeableness. The only sure thing about luck is that it's bound to change.

## pacifist–prosperity

71. **(C)** A *pessimist* is by definition someone whose outlook on life is gloomy.

72. **(D)** A *premonition* is a feeling of anxiety about some future event. It is a presentiment or forewarning.

73. **(D)** *Prolific* means highly productive or fruitful. An author who produces three or four novels every year is definitely productive.

74. **(B)** *Patronize* means support or be a customer of. If you disapprove of a business's policies, refuse to patronize that firm.

75. **(B)** *Petulant* means peevish and fussy.

76. **(D)** *Potency* means power or effectiveness. When medications lose their potency, they become ineffective.

77. **(A)** A *paradox* is a self-contradictory situation or statement.

78. **(B)** *Pervasive* means widespread or prevalent. Corruption that is so widespread that it is accepted as normal is definitely pervasive.

79. **(C)** A *premise* by definition is a fundamental assumption upon which one bases an argument.

80. **(E)** *Prey* is, in this case, an animal being hunted by a predator, the carnivorous lion seeking food. *Prey* can also be any victim of muggers, swindlers, and so on.

## provocative–stoic

81. **(E)** *Scrutinized* means examined closely and critically. The housekeeper was making sure the maids had done a good job.

82. **(B)** *Serenity* means calmness and peacefulness. The key words here are "calm and undisturbed."

83. **(E)** *Skeptical* means disbelieving or having doubts. A skeptical buyer would have doubts about a used car salesman's claims.

84. **(A)** *Renown* means fame. Winning the Nobel Prize in Literature earned Heaney great renown.

85. **(B)** *Prudent* means judicious and sensible, cautiously using good judgment. It is prudent to avoid exposing children to influences that can have a bad effect on their behavior.

86. **(E)** *Ruthless* means merciless. The key words here are "showing no mercy."

87. **(B)** *Refute* means disprove. Kathryn hopes to refute the opposing debater's argument.

88. **(C)** *Resolution* means determination. Maria is determined or resolved to rebuild.

89. **(C)** *Singular* means extraordinary, possibly even unique. Susan's bumper crop of vegetables was extraordinary.

90. **(A)** *Random* means haphazard, without a definite plan or purpose. No plan dictated my choice of quotes; I left it to chance.

**stratagem–wary**

91. **(C)** *Tedious* means boring or tiring. It is the opposite of exciting.

92. **(E)** *Wary* means very cautious. If you are wary, you know you need to beware of danger.

93. **(A)** *Surpass* means exceed or do better than.

94. **(E)** *Turbulence* is a state of violent agitation. Turbulent winds often cause plane rides to be bumpy.

95. **(D)** *Taciturn* means habitually silent. It is hard to get someone naturally taciturn to chat.

96. **(B)** *Superficial* means shallow or trivial. A superficial wound cuts the surface of the skin but does not pierce dangerously deep.

97. **(A)** A *synthesis* brings together different, simple parts, combining them into a complex, unified whole.

98. **(E)** *Volatile* means evaporating rapidly, possibly even explosively.

99. **(B)** *Symmetry* is the arrangement of parts to achieve balance among them. When the parts are out of order, the symmetry is destroyed.

100. **(D)** *Vacillate* means waver in mind or dither.

# Basic Word Parts

In addition to reviewing the High-Frequency Word List, what other quick vocabulary-building tactics can you follow when you face a test deadline?

One good approach is to learn how to build up (and tear apart) words. You know that words are made up of other words: the *room* in which you *store* things is the *storeroom;* the person whose job is to *keep* the *books* is the *bookkeeper.*

Just as words are made up of other words, words are also made up of word parts: prefixes, suffixes, and roots. A knowledge of these word parts and their meanings can help you determine the meanings of unfamiliar words.

Most modern English words are derived from Anglo-Saxon (Old English), Latin, and Greek. Because few students nowadays study Latin and Greek (and even fewer study Anglo-Saxon!), the majority of high school juniors and seniors lack a vital tool for unlocking the meaning of unfamiliar words.

Build your vocabulary by mastering basic word parts. Learning thirty key word parts can help you unlock the meaning of over 10,000 words. Learning fifty key word parts can help you unlock the meaning of over 100,000!

## COMMON PREFIXES

*Prefixes* are syllables that precede the root or stem and change or refine its meaning.

| Prefix | Meaning | Illustration |
|---|---|---|
| **ab, abs** | from, away from | *abduct* lead away, kidnap<br>*abjure* renounce<br>*abject* degraded, cast down |
| **ad, ac, af, ag, an, ap, as, as, at** | to, forward | *adit* entrance<br>*adjure* request earnestly<br>*admit* allow entrance<br>*accord* agreement, harmony<br>*affliction* distress<br>*aggregation* collection<br>*annexation* add to<br>*apparition* ghost<br>*arraignment* indictment<br>*assumption* arrogance, the taking for granted<br>*attendance* presence, the persons present |
| **ambi** | both | *ambidextrous* skilled with both hands<br>*ambiguous* of double meaning<br>*ambivalent* having two conflicting emotions |
| **an, a** | without | *anarchy* lack of government<br>*anemia* lack of blood<br>*amoral* without moral sense |
| **ante** | before | *antecedent* preceding event or word<br>*antediluvian* ancient (before the flood)<br>*antenuptial* before the wedding |

| Prefix | Meaning | Illustration |
|---|---|---|
| **anti** | against, opposite | *antipathy* hatred<br>*antiseptic* against infection<br>*antithetical* exactly opposite |
| **arch** | chief, first | *archetype* original<br>*archbishop* chief bishop<br>*archaeology* study of first or ancient times |
| **be** | over, thoroughly | *bedaub* smear over<br>*befuddle* confuse thoroughly<br>*beguile* deceive, charm thoroughly |
| **bi** | two | *bicameral* composed of two houses (Congress)<br>*biennial* every two years<br>*bicycle* two-wheeled vehicle |
| **cata** | down | *catastrophe* disaster<br>*cataract* waterfall<br>*catapult* hurl (throw down) |
| **circum** | around | *circumnavigate* sail around (the globe)<br>*circumspect* cautious (looking around)<br>*circumscribe* limit (place a circle around) |
| **com, co, col, con, cor** | with, together | *combine* merge with<br>*commerce* trade with<br>*communicate* correspond with<br>*coeditor* joint editor<br>*collateral* subordinate, connected<br>*conference* meeting<br>*corroborate* confirm |
| **contra, contro** | against | *contravene* conflict with<br>*controversy* dispute |
| **de** | down, away | *debase* lower in value<br>*decadence* deterioration<br>*decant* pour off |
| **demi** | partly, half | *demigod* partly divine being |
| **di** | two | *dichotomy* division into two parts<br>*dilemma* choice between two bad alternatives |
| **dia** | across | *diagonal* across a figure<br>*diameter* distance across a circle<br>*diagram* outline drawing |
| **dis, dif** | not, apart | *discord* lack of harmony<br>*differ* disagree (carry apart)<br>*disparity* condition of inequality; difference |
| **dys** | faulty, bad | *dyslexia* faulty ability to read<br>*dyspepsia* indigestion |
| **ex, e** | out | *expel* drive out<br>*extirpate* root out<br>*eject* throw out |

| Prefix | Meaning | Illustration |
| --- | --- | --- |
| **extra, extro** | beyond, outside | *extracurricular* beyond the curriculum<br>*extraterritorial* beyond a nation's bounds<br>*extrovert* person interested chiefly in external<br>    objects and actions |
| **hyper** | above; excessively | *hyperbole* exaggeration<br>*hyperventilate* breathe at an excessive rate |
| **hypo** | beneath; lower | *hypoglycemia* low blood sugar |
| **in, il, im, ir** | not | *inefficient* not efficient<br>*inarticulate* not clear or distinct<br>*illegible* not readable<br>*impeccable* not capable of sinning; flawless<br>*irrevocable* not able to be called back |
| **in, il, im, ir** | in, on, upon | *invite* call in<br>*illustration* something that makes clear<br>*impression* effect upon mind or feelings<br>*irradiate* shine upon |
| **inter** | between, among | *intervene* come between<br>*international* between nations<br>*interjection* a statement thrown in |
| **intra, intro** | within | *intramural* within a school<br>*introvert* person who turns within himself |
| **macro** | large, long | *macrobiotic* tending to prolong life<br>*macrocosm* the great world (the entire universe) |
| **mega** | great, million | *megalomania* delusions of grandeur<br>*megaton* explosive force of a million tons of TNT |
| **meta** | involving change | *metamorphosis* change of form |
| **micro** | small | *microcosm* miniature universe<br>*microbe* minute organism<br>*microscopic* extremely small |
| **mis** | bad, improper | *misdemeanor* minor crime; bad conduct<br>*mischance* unfortunate accident<br>*misnomer* wrong name |
| **mis** | hatred | *misanthrope* person who hates mankind<br>*misogynist* woman-hater |
| **mono** | one | *monarchy* government by one ruler<br>*monotheism* belief in one god |
| **multi** | many | *multifarious* having many parts<br>*multitudinous* numerous |
| **neo** | new | *neologism* newly coined word<br>*neophyte* beginner; novice |
| **non** | not | *noncommittal* undecided<br>*nonentity* person of no importance |

| Prefix | Meaning | Illustration |
|---|---|---|
| **ob, oc, of, op** | against | *obloquy* infamy; disgrace<br>*obtrude* push into prominence<br>*occlude* close; block out<br>*offend* insult<br>*opponent* someone who struggles against; foe |
| **olig** | few | *oligarchy* government by a few |
| **pan** | all, every | *panacea* cure-all<br>*panorama* unobstructed view in all directions |
| **para** | beyond, related | *parallel* similar<br>*paraphrase* restate; translate |
| **per** | through, completely | *permeable* allowing passage through<br>*pervade* spread throughout |
| **peri** | around, near | *perimeter* outer boundary<br>*periphery* edge<br>*periphrastic* stated in a roundabout way |
| **poly** | many | *polygamist* person with several spouses<br>*polyglot* speaking several languages |
| **post** | after | *postpone* delay<br>*posterity* generations that follow<br>*posthumous* after death |
| **pre** | before | *preamble* introductory statement<br>*prefix* word part placed before a root/stem<br>*premonition* forewarning |
| **prim** | first | *primordial* existing at the dawn of time<br>*primogeniture* state of being the first born |
| **pro** | forward, in favor of | *propulsive* driving forward<br>*proponent* supporter |
| **proto** | first | *prototype* first of its kind |
| **pseudo** | false | *pseudonym* pen name |
| **re** | again, back | *reiterate* repeat<br>*reimburse* pay back |
| **retro** | backward | *retrospect* looking back<br>*retroactive* effective as of a past date |
| **se** | away, aside | *secede* withdraw<br>*seclude* shut away<br>*seduce* lead astray |
| **semi** | half, partly | *semiannual* every six months<br>*semiconscious* partly conscious |
| **sub, suc, suf, sug, sup, sus** | under, less | *subway* underground road<br>*subjugate* bring under control<br>*succumb* yield; cease to resist<br>*suffuse* spread through<br>*suggest* hint<br>*suppress* put down by force<br>*suspend* delay |

| Prefix | Meaning | Illustration |
|---|---|---|
| **super, sur** | over, above | *supernatural* above natural things<br>*supervise* oversee<br>*surtax* additional tax |
| **syn, sym, syl, sys** | with, together | *synchronize* time together<br>*synthesize* combine together<br>*sympathize* pity; identify with<br>*syllogism* explanation of how ideas relate<br>*system* network |
| **tele** | far | *telemetry* measurement from a distance<br>*telegraphic* communicated over a distance |
| **trans** | across | *transport* carry across<br>*transpose* reverse, move across |
| **ultra** | beyond, excessive | *ultramodern* excessively modern<br>*ultracritical* exceedingly critical |
| **un** | not | *unfeigned* not pretended; real<br>*unkempt* not combed; disheveled<br>*unwitting* not knowing; unintentional |
| **under** | below | *undergird* strengthen underneath<br>*underling* someone inferior |
| **uni** | one | *unison* oneness of pitch; complete accord<br>*unicycle* one-wheeled vehicle |
| **vice** | in place of | *vicarious* acting as a substitute<br>*viceroy* governor acting in place of a king |
| **with** | away, against | *withhold* hold back; keep<br>*withstand* stand up against; resist |

# COMMON ROOTS AND STEMS

*Roots* are basic words which have been carried over into English. *Stems* are variations of roots brought about by changes in declension or conjugation.

| Root or Stem | Meaning | Illustration |
| --- | --- | --- |
| **ac, acr** | sharp | *acrimonious* bitter; caustic<br>*acerbity* bitterness of temper<br>*acidulate* to make somewhat acid or sour |
| **aev, ev** | age, era | *primeval* of the first age<br>*coeval* of the same age or era<br>*medieval or mediaeval* of the middle ages |
| **ag, act** | do | *act* deed<br>*agent* doer |
| **agog** | leader | *demagogue* false leader of people<br>*pedagogue* teacher (leader of children) |
| **agri, agrari** | field | *agrarian* one who works in the field<br>*agriculture* cultivation of fields<br>*peregrination* wandering (through fields) |
| **ali** | another | *alias* assumed (another) name<br>*alienate* estrange (turn away from another) |
| **alt** | high | *altitude* height<br>*altimeter* instrument for measuring height |
| **alter** | other | *altruistic* unselfish, considering others<br>*alter ego* a second self |
| **am** | love | *amorous* loving, especially sexually<br>*amity* friendship<br>*amicable* friendly |
| **anim** | mind, soul | *animadvert* cast criticism upon<br>*unanimous* of one mind<br>*magnanimity* greatness of mind or spirit |
| **ann, enn** | year | *annuity* yearly remittance<br>*biennial* every two years<br>*perennial* present all year; persisting for several years |
| **anthrop** | man | *anthropology* study of man<br>*misanthrope* hater of mankind<br>*philanthropy* love of mankind; charity |
| **apt** | fit | *aptitude* skill<br>*adapt* make suitable or fit |
| **aqua** | water | *aqueduct* passageway for conducting water<br>*aquatic* living in water<br>*aqua fortis* nitric acid (strong water) |

| Root or Stem | Meaning | Illustration |
|---|---|---|
| arch | ruler, first | *archaeology* study of antiquities (study of first things)<br>*monarch* sole ruler<br>*anarchy* lack of government |
| aster | star | *astronomy* study of the stars<br>*asterisk* starlike type character (*)<br>*disaster* catastrophe (contrary star) |
| aud, audit | hear | *audible* able to be heard<br>*auditorium* place where people may be heard<br>*audience* hearers |
| auto | self | *autocracy* rule by one person (self)<br>*automobile* vehicle that moves by itself<br>*autobiography* story of one's own life |
| belli | war | *bellicose* inclined to fight<br>*belligerent* inclined to wage war<br>*rebellious* resisting authority |
| ben, bon | good | *benefactor* one who does good deeds<br>*benevolence* charity (wishing good)<br>*bonus* something extra above regular pay |
| biblio | book | *bibliography* list of books<br>*bibliophile* lover of books<br>*Bible* The Book |
| bio | life | *biography* writing about a person's life<br>*biology* study of living things<br>*biochemist* student of the chemistry of living things |
| breve | short | *brevity* briefness<br>*abbreviate* shorten<br>*breviloquent* marked by brevity of speech |
| cad, cas | to fall | *decadent* deteriorating<br>*cadence* intonation, musical movement<br>*cascade* waterfall |
| cap, capt, cept, cip | to take | *capture* seize<br>*participate* take part<br>*precept* wise saying (originally a command) |
| capit, capt | head | *decapitate* remove (cut off) someone's head<br>*captain* chief |
| carn | flesh | *carnivorous* flesh-eating<br>*carnage* destruction of life<br>*carnal* fleshly |
| ced, cess | to yield, to go | *recede* go back, withdraw<br>*antecedent* that which goes before<br>*process* go forward |
| celer | swift | *celerity* swiftness<br>*decelerate* reduce swiftness<br>*accelerate* increase swiftness |

| Root or Stem | Meaning | Illustration |
|---|---|---|
| cent | one hundred | *century* one hundred years<br>*centennial* hundredth anniversary<br>*centipede* many-footed, wingless animal |
| chron | time | *chronology* timetable of events<br>*anachronism* a thing out of time sequence<br>*chronicle* register events in order of time |
| cid, cis | to cut, to kill | *incision* a cut (surgical)<br>*homicide* killing of a man<br>*fratricide* killing of a brother |
| cit, citat | to call, to start | *incite* stir up, start up<br>*excite* stir up<br>*recitation* a recalling (or repeating) aloud |
| civi | citizen | *civilization* society of citizens, culture<br>*civilian* member of community<br>*civil* courteous |
| clam, clamat | to cry out | *clamorous* loud<br>*declamation* speech<br>*acclamation* shouted approval |
| claud, claus, clos, clud | to close | *claustrophobia* fear of close places<br>*enclose* close in<br>*conclude* finish |
| cognosc, cognit | to learn | *agnostic* lacking knowledge, skeptical<br>*incognito* traveling under assumed name<br>*cognition* knowledge |
| compl | to fill | *complete* filled out<br>*complement* that which completes something<br>*comply* fulfill |
| cord | heart | *accord* agreement (from the heart)<br>*cordial* friendly<br>*discord* lack of harmony |
| corpor | body | *incorporate* organize into a body<br>*corporeal* pertaining to the body, fleshly<br>*corpse* dead body |
| cred, credit | to believe | *incredulous* not believing, skeptical<br>*credulity* gullibility<br>*credence* belief |
| cur | to care | *curator* person who has the care of something<br>*sinecure* position without responsibility<br>*secure* safe |
| curr, curs | to run | *excursion* journey<br>*cursory* brief<br>*precursor* forerunner |
| da, dat | to give | *data* facts, statistics<br>*mandate* command<br>*date* given time |

| Root or Stem | Meaning | Illustration |
|---|---|---|
| **deb, debit** | to owe | *debt* something owed<br>*indebtedness* debt<br>*debenture* bond |
| **dem** | people | *democracy* rule of the people<br>*demagogue* (false) leader of the people<br>*epidemic* widespread (among the people) |
| **derm** | skin | *epidermis* skin<br>*pachyderm* thick-skinned quadruped<br>*dermatology* study of skin and its disorders |
| **di, diurn** | day | *diary* a daily record of activities, feelings, etc.<br>*diurnal* pertaining to daytime |
| **dic, dict** | to say | *abdicate* renounce<br>*diction* speech<br>*verdict* statement of jury |
| **doc, doct** | to teach | *docile* obedient; easily taught<br>*document* something that provides evidence<br>*doctor* learned person (originally, teacher) |
| **domin** | to rule | *dominate* have power over<br>*domain* land under rule<br>*dominant* prevailing |
| **duc, duct** | to lead | *viaduct* arched roadway<br>*aqueduct* artificial waterway |
| **dynam** | power, strength | *dynamic* powerful<br>*dynamite* powerful explosive<br>*dynamo* engine making electrical power |
| **ego** | I | *egoist* person who is self-interested<br>*egotist* selfish person<br>*egocentric* revolving about self |
| **erg, urg** | work | *energy* power<br>*ergatocracy* rule of the workers<br>*metallurgy* science and technology of metals |
| **err** | to wander | *error* mistake<br>*erratic* not reliable, wandering<br>*knight-errant* wandering knight |
| **eu** | good, well, beautiful | *eupeptic* having good digestion<br>*eulogize* praise<br>*euphemism* substitution of pleasant way of saying something blunt |
| **fac, fic, fec, fect** | to make, to do | *factory* place where things are made<br>*fiction* manufactured story<br>*affect* cause to change |
| **fall, fals** | to deceive | *fallacious* misleading<br>*infallible* not prone to error, perfect<br>*falsify* lie |
| **fer, lat** | to bring, to bear | *transfer* bring from one place to another<br>*translate* bring from one language to another<br>*conifer* bearing cones, as pine trees |

| Root or Stem | Meaning | Illustration |
|---|---|---|
| **fid** | belief, faith | *infidel* nonbeliever, heathen<br>*confidence* assurance, belief |
| **fin** | end, limit | *confine* keep within limits<br>*finite* having definite limits |
| **flect, flex** | bend | *flexible* able to bend<br>*deflect* bend away, turn aside |
| **fort** | luck, chance | *fortuitous* accidental, occurring by chance<br>*fortunate* lucky |
| **fort** | strong | *fortitude* strength, firmness of mind<br>*fortification* strengthening<br>*fortress* stronghold |
| **frag, fract** | break | *fragile* easily broken<br>*infraction* breaking of a rule<br>*fractious* unruly, tending to break rules |
| **fug** | flee | *fugitive* someone who flees<br>*refuge* shelter, home for someone fleeing |
| **fus** | pour | *effusive* gushing, pouring out<br>*diffuse* widespread (poured in many directions) |
| **gam** | marriage | *monogamy* marriage to one person<br>*bigamy* marriage to two people at the same time<br>*polygamy* having many wives or husbands at the same time |
| **gen, gener** | class, race | *genus* group of animals with similar traits<br>*generic* characteristic of a class<br>*gender* class organized by sex |
| **grad, gress** | go, step | *digress* go astray (from the main point)<br>*regress* go backwards<br>*gradual* step by step, by degrees |
| **graph, gram** | writing | *epigram* pithy statement<br>*telegram* instantaneous message over great distance<br>*stenography* shorthand (writing narrowly) |
| **greg** | flock, herd | *gregarious* tending to group together, as in a herd<br>*aggregate* group, total<br>*egregious* conspicuously bad; shocking |
| **helio** | sun | *heliotrope* flower that faces the sun<br>*heliograph* instrument that uses the sun's rays to send signals |
| **it, itiner** | journey, road | *exit* way out<br>*itinerary* plan of journey |
| **jac, jact, jec** | to throw | *projectile* missile; something thrown forward<br>*trajectory* path taken by thrown object<br>*ejaculatory* casting or throwing out |
| **jur, jurat** | to swear | *perjure* testify falsely<br>*jury* group of men and women sworn to seek the truth<br>*adjuration* solemn urging |

| Root or Stem | Meaning | Illustration |
|---|---|---|
| **labor, laborat** | to work | *laboratory* place where work is done<br>*collaborate* work together with others<br>*laborious* difficult |
| **leg, lect, lig** | to choose, to read | *election* choice<br>*legible* able to be read<br>*eligible* able to be selected |
| **leg** | law | *legislature* law-making body<br>*legitimate* lawful<br>*legal* lawful |
| **liber, libr** | book | *library* collection of books<br>*libretto* the "book" of a musical play<br>*libel* slander (originally found in a little book) |
| **liber** | free | *liberation* the act of setting free<br>*liberal* generous (giving freely); tolerant |
| **log** | word, study | *entomology* study of insects<br>*etymology* study of word parts and derivations<br>*monologue* speech by one person |
| **loqu, locut** | to talk | *soliloquy* speech by one individual<br>*loquacious* talkative<br>*elocution* speech |
| **luc** | light | *elucidate* enlighten<br>*lucid* clear<br>*translucent* allowing some light to pass through |
| **magn** | great | *magnify* enlarge<br>*magnanimity* generosity, greatness of soul<br>*magnitude* greatness, extent |
| **mal** | bad | *malevolent* wishing evil<br>*malediction* curse<br>*malefactor* evildoer |
| **man** | hand | *manufacture* create (make by hand)<br>*manuscript* written by hand<br>*emancipate* free (let go from the hand) |
| **mar** | sea | *maritime* connected with seafaring<br>*submarine* undersea craft<br>*mariner* seaman |
| **mater, matr** | mother | *maternal* pertaining to motherhood<br>*matriarch* female ruler of a family, group, or state<br>*matrilineal* descended on the mother's side |
| **mit, miss** | to send | *missile* projectile<br>*dismiss* send away<br>*transmit* send across |
| **mob, mot, mov** | move | *mobilize* cause to move<br>*motility* ability to move<br>*immovable* not able to be moved |

| Root or Stem | Meaning | Illustration |
|---|---|---|
| **mon, monit** | to warn | *admonish* warn<br>*premonition* foreboding<br>*monitor* watcher (warner) |
| **mori, mort** | to die | *mortuary* funeral parlor<br>*moribund* dying<br>*immortal* not dying |
| **morph** | shape, form | *amorphous* formless, lacking shape<br>*metamorphosis* change of shape<br>*anthropomorphic* in the shape of man |
| **mut** | change | *immutable* not able to be changed<br>*mutate* undergo a great change<br>*mutability* changeableness, inconstancy |
| **nat** | born | *innate* from birth<br>*prenatal* before birth<br>*nativity* birth |
| **nav** | ship | *navigate* sail a ship<br>*circumnavigate* sail around the world<br>*naval* pertaining to ships |
| **neg** | deny | *negation* denial<br>*renege* deny, go back on one's word<br>*renegade* turncoat, traitor |
| **nomen** | name | *nomenclature* act of naming, terminology<br>*nominal* in name only (as opposed to actual)<br>*cognomen* surname, distinguishing nickname |
| **nov** | new | *novice* beginner<br>*renovate* make new again<br>*novelty* newness |
| **omni** | all | *omniscient* all-knowing<br>*omnipotent* all-powerful<br>*omnivorous* eating everything |
| **oper** | to work | *operate* work<br>*cooperation* working together |
| **pac** | peace | *pacify* make peaceful<br>*pacific* peaceful<br>*pacifist* person opposed to war |
| **pass** | feel | *dispassionate* free of emotion<br>*impassioned* emotion-filled<br>*impassive* showing no feeling |
| **pater, patr** | father | *patriotism* love of one's country (fatherland)<br>*patriarch* male ruler of a family, group, or state<br>*paternity* fatherhood |
| **path** | disease, feeling | *pathology* study of diseased tissue<br>*apathetic* lacking feeling; indifferent<br>*antipathy* hostile feeling |

| Root or Stem | Meaning | Illustration |
|---|---|---|
| **ped, pod** | foot | *impediment* stumbling block; hindrance<br>*tripod* three-footed stand<br>*quadruped* four-footed animal |
| **ped** | child | *pedagogue* teacher of children<br>*pediatrician* children's doctor |
| **pel, puls** | to drive | *compulsion* a forcing to do<br>*repel* drive back<br>*expel* drive out, banish |
| **pet, petit** | to seek | *petition* request<br>*appetite* craving, desire<br>*compete* vie with others |
| **phil** | love | *philanthropist* benefactor, lover of humanity<br>*Anglophile* lover of everything English<br>*philanderer* one involved in brief love affairs |
| **pon, posit** | to place | *postpone* place after<br>*positive* definite, unquestioned (definitely placed) |
| **port, portat** | to carry | *portable* able to be carried<br>*transport* carry across<br>*export* carry out (of country) |
| **poten** | able, powerful | *omnipotent* all-powerful<br>*potentate* powerful person<br>*impotent* powerless |
| **psych** | mind | *psychology* study of the mind<br>*psychosis* mental disorder<br>*psychopath* mentally ill person |
| **put, putat** | to trim, to calculate | *putative* supposed (calculated)<br>*computation* calculation<br>*amputate* cut off |
| **quer, ques, quir, quis** | to ask | *inquiry* investigation<br>*inquisitive* questioning<br>*query* question |
| **reg, rect** | rule | *regicide* murder of a ruler<br>*regent* ruler<br>*insurrection* rebellion; overthrow of a ruler |
| **rid, ris** | to laugh | *derision* scorn<br>*risibility* inclination to laughter<br>*ridiculous* deserving to be laughed at |
| **rog, rogat** | to ask | *interrogate* question<br>*prerogative* privilege |
| **rupt** | to break | *interrupt* break into<br>*bankrupt* insolvent<br>*rupture* a break |
| **sacr** | holy | *sacred* holy<br>*sacrilegious* impious, violating something holy<br>*sacrament* religious act |

| Root or Stem | Meaning | Illustration |
|---|---|---|
| **sci** | to know | *science* knowledge<br>*omniscient* knowing all<br>*conscious* aware |
| **scop** | watch, see | *periscope* device for seeing around corners<br>*microscope* device for seeing small objects |
| **scrib, script** | to write | *transcribe* make a written copy<br>*script* written text<br>*circumscribe* write around, limit |
| **sect** | cut | *dissect* cut apart<br>*bisect* cut into two pieces |
| **sed, sess** | to sit | *sedentary* inactive (sitting)<br>*session* meeting |
| **sent, sens** | to think, to feel | *consent* agree<br>*resent* show indignation<br>*sensitive* showing feeling |
| **sequi, secut, seque** | to follow | *consecutive* following in order<br>*sequence* arrangement<br>*sequel* that which follows<br>*non sequitur* something that does not follow logically |
| **solv, solut** | to loosen | *absolve* free from blame<br>*dissolute* morally lax<br>*absolute* complete (not loosened) |
| **somn** | sleep | *insomnia* inability to sleep<br>*somnolent* sleepy<br>*somnambulist* sleepwalker |
| **soph** | wisdom | *philosopher* lover of wisdom<br>*sophisticated* worldly wise |
| **spec, spect** | to look at | *spectator* observer<br>*aspect* appearance<br>*circumspect* cautious (looking around) |
| **spir** | breathe | *respiratory* pertaining to breathing<br>*spirited* full of life (breath) |
| **string, strict** | bind | *stringent* strict<br>*constrict* become tight<br>*stricture* limit, something that restrains |
| **stru, struct** | build | *constructive* helping to build<br>*construe* analyze (how something is built) |
| **tang, tact, ting** | to touch | *tangent* touching<br>*contact* touching with, meeting<br>*contingent* depending upon |
| **tempor** | time | *contemporary* at same time<br>*extemporaneous* impromptu<br>*temporize* delay |

| Root or Stem | Meaning | Illustration |
|---|---|---|
| **ten, tent** | to hold | *tenable* able to be held<br>*tenure* holding of office<br>*retentive* holding; having a good memory |
| **term** | end | *interminable* endless<br>*terminate* end |
| **terr** | land | *terrestrial* pertaining to earth<br>*subterranean* underground |
| **therm** | heat | *thermostat* instrument that regulates heat<br>*diathermy* sending heat through body tissues |
| **tors, tort** | twist | *distort* twist out of true shape or meaning<br>*torsion* act of twisting<br>*tortuous* twisting |
| **tract** | drag, pull | *distract* pull (one's attention) away<br>*intractable* stubborn, unable to be dragged<br>*attraction* pull, drawing quality |
| **trud, trus** | push, shove | *intrude* push one's way in<br>*protrusion* something sticking out |
| **urb** | city | *urban* pertaining to a city<br>*urbane* polished, sophisticated (pertaining to a city dweller)<br>*suburban* outside of a city |
| **vac** | empty | *vacuous* lacking content, empty-headed<br>*evacuate* compel to empty an area |
| **vad, vas** | go | *invade* enter in a hostile fashion<br>*evasive* not frank; eluding |
| **veni, vent, ven** | to come | *intervene* come between<br>*prevent* stop<br>*convention* meeting |
| **ver** | true | *veracious* truthful<br>*verify* check the truth<br>*verisimilitude* appearance of truth |
| **verb** | word | *verbose* wordy<br>*verbiage* excessive use of words<br>*verbatim* word for word |
| **vers, vert** | turn | *vertigo* turning dizzy<br>*revert* turn back (to an earlier state)<br>*diversion* something causing one to turn aside |
| **via** | way | *deviation* departure from the way<br>*viaduct* roadway (arched)<br>*trivial* trifling (small talk at crossroads) |
| **vid, vis** | to see | *vision* sight<br>*evidence* things seen<br>*vista* view |

| Root or Stem | Meaning | Illustration |
|---|---|---|
| **vinc, vict, vanq** | to conquer | *invincible* unconquerable<br>*victory* winning<br>*vanquish* defeat |
| **viv, vit** | alive | *vivisection* operating on living animals<br>*vivacious* full of life<br>*vitality* liveliness |
| **voc, vocat** | to call | *avocation* calling, minor occupation<br>*provocation* calling or rousing the anger of<br>*invocation* calling in prayer |
| **vol** | wish | *malevolent* wishing someone ill<br>*voluntary* of one's own will |
| **volv, volut** | to roll | *revolve* roll around<br>*evolve* roll out, develop<br>*convolution* coiled state |

# COMMON SUFFIXES

*Suffixes* are syllables that are added to a word. Occasionally, they change the meaning of the word; more frequently, they serve to change the grammatical form of the word (noun to adjective, adjective to noun, noun to verb).

| Suffix | Meaning | Illustration |
|---|---|---|
| **able, ible** | capable of (adjective suffix) | *portable* able to be carried<br>*interminable* not able to be limited<br>*legible* able to be read |
| **ac, ic** | like, pertaining to<br>    (adjective suffix) | *cardiac* pertaining to the heart<br>*aquatic* pertaining to the water<br>*dramatic* pertaining to the drama |
| **acious, icious** | full of (adjective suffix) | *audacious* full of daring<br>*perspicacious* full of mental perception<br>*avaricious* full of greed |
| **al** | pertaining to (adjective or<br>    noun suffix) | *maniacal* insane<br>*final* pertaining to the end<br>*logical* pertaining to logic |
| **ant, ent** | full of (adjective or noun<br>    suffix) | *eloquent* pertaining to fluid, effective speech<br>*suppliant* pleader (person full of requests)<br>*verdant* green |
| **ary** | like, connected with<br>    (adjective or noun suffix) | *dictionary* book connected with words<br>*honorary* with honor<br>*luminary* celestial body |
| **ate** | to make (verb suffix) | *consecrate* to make holy<br>*enervate* to make weary<br>*mitigate* to make less severe |
| **ation** | that which is (noun suffix) | *exasperation* irritation<br>*irritation* annoyance |
| **cy** | state of being (noun suffix) | *democracy* government ruled by the people<br>*obstinacy* stubbornness<br>*accuracy* correctness |
| **eer, er, or** | person who (noun suffix) | *mutineer* person who rebels<br>*lecher* person who lusts<br>*censor* person who deletes improper remarks |
| **escent** | becoming (adjective suffix) | *evanescent* tending to vanish<br>*pubescent* arriving at puberty |
| **fic** | making, doing<br>    (adjective suffix) | *terrific* arousing great fear<br>*soporific* causing sleep |
| **fy** | to make (verb suffix) | *magnify* enlarge<br>*petrify* turn to stone<br>*beautify* make beautiful |
| **iferous** | producing, bearing<br>    (adjective suffix) | *pestiferous* carrying disease<br>*vociferous* bearing a loud voice |

| Suffix | Meaning | Illustration |
|---|---|---|
| **il, ile** | pertaining to, capable of (adjective suffix) | *puerile* pertaining to a boy or child<br>*ductile* capable of being hammered or drawn<br>*civil* polite |
| **ism** | doctrine, belief (noun suffix) | *monotheism* belief in one god<br>*fanaticism* excessive zeal; extreme belief |
| **ist** | dealer, doer (noun suffix) | *fascist* one who believes in a fascist state<br>*realist* one who is realistic<br>*artist* one who deals with art |
| **ity** | state of being (noun suffix) | *annuity* yearly grant<br>*credulity* state of being unduly willing to believe<br>*sagacity* wisdom |
| **ive** | like (adjective suffix) | *expensive* costly<br>*quantitative* concerned with quantity<br>*effusive* gushing |
| **ize, ise** | make (verb suffix) | *victimize* make a victim of<br>*rationalize* make rational<br>*harmonize* make harmonious<br>*enfranchise* make free or set free |
| **oid** | resembling, like (adjective suffix) | *ovoid* like an egg<br>*anthropoid* resembling man<br>*spheroid* resembling a sphere |
| **ose** | full of (adjective suffix) | *verbose* full of words<br>*lachrymose* full of tears |
| **osis** | condition (noun suffix) | *psychosis* diseased mental condition<br>*neurosis* nervous condition<br>*hypnosis* condition of induced sleep |
| **ous** | full of (adjective suffix) | *nauseous* full of nausea<br>*ludicrous* foolish |
| **tude** | state of (noun suffix) | *fortitude* state of strength<br>*beatitude* state of blessedness<br>*certitude* state of sureness |

# PART FOUR

# WRITING SKILLS

Chapter 4: Improving Written Expression

# Improving Written Expression

CHAPTER **4**

---

> You definitely want to study hard when you prepare for the writing skills section of
> the PSAT: a good score on this section of the test may make all the difference between
> your becoming a National Merit finalist and your coming out a runner-up.
>
> There are three different kinds of questions on the writing skills section of the
> PSAT: improving sentences, identifying sentence errors, and improving paragraphs.
> More than half of them, twenty questions out of thirty-nine, involve choosing the best
> of five different versions of a sentence.
>
> The writing skills questions test your ability to recognize clear, correct standard
> written English, the kind of writing your college professors will expect on the papers
> you turn in to them. You'll be expected to know basic grammar, such as subject-verb
> agreement, pronoun-antecedent agreement, correct verb tense, correct sentence
> structure, and correct diction. You'll need to know how to recognize a dangling par-
> ticiple and how to spot when two parts of a sentence are not clearly connected. You'll
> also need to know when a paragraph is (or isn't) properly developed and organized.

## Improving Sentences

The most numerous questions in the Writing Skills section involve spotting the form of
a sentence that works best. In these improving sentences questions, you will be presented
with five different versions of the same sentence; you must choose the *best* one. Here are
the directions:

---

**Improving Sentences Directions:**
Some or all parts of the following sentences are underlined. The first answer choice, (A),
simply repeats the underlined part of the sentence. The other four choices present four
alternative ways to phrase the underlined part. Select the answer that produces the most
effective sentence, one that is clear and exact, and blacken the appropriate space on your
answer sheet. In selecting your choice, be sure that it is standard written English and that
it expresses the meaning of the original sentence.

**EXAMPLE:**

The first biography of author Eudora Welty came out
in 1998, <u>and she was eighty-nine years old at the time.</u>

(A)  and she was eighty-nine years old at the time
(B)  at the time when she was eighty-nine
(C)  upon becoming an eighty-nine year old
(D)  when she was eighty-nine
(E)  at the age of eighty-nine years old

---

**219**

# TIPS FOR HANDLING IMPROVING SENTENCES QUESTIONS

## Tip 1

**If you spot an error in the underlined section, eliminate Choice A and any other answer that contains the same error.** If something in the underlined section of a sentence correction question strikes you as an obvious error, you can immediately ignore Choice A, which is *always* a repetition of the original underlined section, and any other answer choices that repeat the error. Remember, you still don't have to be able to explain what is wrong. You just need to find a correct equivalent. If the error you found in the underlined section is absent from more than one of the answer choices, look over those choices again to see if they add any new errors.

## EXAMPLE 1

See how the first tip works in dealing with the following sentence:

Being as I had studied for the test with a tutor, I was confident.

(A) Being as I had studied for the test
(B) Being as I studied for the test
(C) Since I studied for the test
(D) Since I had studied for the test
(E) Because I studied for the test

*Being as* is unacceptable as a conjunction in standard written English. Therefore, you can eliminate Choices A and B right away. *Since* and *Because* are both acceptable conjunctions, so you have to look more closely at Choices C, D, and E. The only other changes these choices make are in the tense of the verb. Since the studying occurred before the taking of the test, the past perfect tense, *had studied*, is correct, so the answer is Choice D.

## Tip 2

**If you don't spot an error in the underlined section, look at the answer choices to see what is changed.** Sometimes it's hard to spot what's wrong with the underlined section in a sentence correction question. When that happens, turn to the answer choices. Find the changes in the answers. The changes will tell you what kind of error is being tested. When you substitute the answer choices in the original sentence, ask yourself which of these choices makes the sentence seem clearest to you. That may well be the correct answer choice.

## EXAMPLE 2

See how the second tip works in dealing with the following sentence:

Even the play's most minor characters work together with extraordinary skill, <u>their interplay creates a moving theatrical experience</u>.

(A) their interplay creates a moving theatrical experience
(B) a moving theatrical experience is created by their interplay
(C) and their interplay creates a moving theatrical experience
(D) and a moving theatrical experience being the creation of their interplay
(E) with their interplay they create a moving theatrical experience

Look at the underlined section of the sentence. Nothing seems wrong with it. It could stand on its own as an independent sentence: *Their interplay creates a moving theatrical experience*. Choices B and E are similar to it, for both could stand as independent sentences. Choices C and D, however, are not independent sentences; both begin with the linking word *and*. The error needing correction here is the common comma splice, in which two sentences are carelessly linked with only a comma. Choice C corrects this error in the simplest way possible, adding the word *and* to tie these sentences together.

## Tip 3

**Make sure that all parts of the sentence are logically connected.** Not all parts of a sentence are created equal. Some parts should be subordinated to the rest, connected with subordinating conjunctions or relative pronouns, not just added on with *and*. Overuse of *and* frequently makes sentences sound babyish. Compare "We had dinner at the Hard Rock Cafe, and we went to a concert" with "After we had dinner at the Hard Rock Cafe, we went to a concert."

## EXAMPLE 3

See how the third tip works in dealing with the following sentence:

The rock star always had enthusiastic fans <u>and they loved him</u>.

(A) and they loved him
(B) and they loving him
(C) what loved him
(D) who loved him
(E) which loved him

The original version of this sentence doesn't have any grammatical errors, but it is a poor sentence because it doesn't connect its two clauses logically. The second clause ("and they loved him") is merely adding information about the fans, so it should be turned into an adjective clause, introduced by a relative pronoun. Choices D and E both seem to work, but you know that *which* should never be used to refer to people, so Choice D is obviously the correct answer.

## Tip 4

**Make sure that all sentence parts listed as a series are similar in form.** If they are not, the sentence suffers from a lack of parallel structure. The sentence "I'm taking classes in algebra, history, and how to speak French" lacks parallel structure. *Algebra* and *history* are nouns, names of subjects. The third subject should also be a noun: *conversational French*.

## EXAMPLE 4

See how the fourth tip works in dealing with the following sentence:

In this chapter we'll analyze both types of questions, <u>suggest useful techniques for tackling them, providing some sample items for you to try</u>.

(A) suggest useful techniques for tackling them, providing some sample items for you to try
(B) suggest useful techniques for tackling them, providing some sample items which you can try
(C) suggest useful tactics for tackling them, and provide some sample items for you to try
(D) and suggest useful techniques for tackling them by providing some sample items for you to try
(E) having suggested useful techniques for tackling them and provided some sample items for you to try

To answer questions like this correctly, you must pay particular attention to what the sentence means. You must first decide whether *analyzing, suggesting,* and *providing* are logically equal in importance here. Since they are—all are activities that "we" will do— they should be given equal emphasis. Only Choice C provides the proper parallel structure.

## Tip 5

**Pay particular attention to the shorter answer choices.** (This tactic also applies to certain paragraph correction questions.) Good prose is economical. Often the correct answer choice will be the shortest, most direct way of making a point. If you spot no grammatical errors or errors in logic in a concise answer choice, it may well be right.

## EXAMPLE 5

See how the fifth tip works in dealing with the following sentence:

The turning point in the battle of Waterloo probably was <u>Blucher, who was arriving</u> in time to save the day.

(A) Blucher, who was arriving
(B) Blucher, in that he arrived
(C) Blucher's arrival
(D) when Blucher was arriving
(E) that Blucher had arrived

Which answer choice uses the fewest words? Choice C, *Blucher's arrival*. It also happens to be the right answer.

Choice C is both concise in style and correct in grammar. Look back at the original sentence. Strip it of its modifiers, and what is left? "The turning point . . . was Blucher." A turning point is not a person; it is a *thing*. The turning point in the battle was not Blucher, but Blucher's *action*, the thing he did. The correct answer is Choice C, *Blucher's arrival*. Pay particular attention to such concise answer choices. If a concise choice sounds natural when you substitute it for the original underlined phrase, it's a reasonable guess.

# Identifying Sentence Errors

Almost one-third of the Writing Skills questions on the PSAT, fourteen of the thirty-nine, to be exact, are identifying sentence errors questions in which you have to find an error in the underlined section of a sentence. You do *not* have to correct the sentence or explain what is wrong. Here are the directions.

---

**Identifying Sentence Errors Directions:**
The sentences in this section may contain errors in grammar, usage, choice of words, or idioms. There is either just one error per sentence, or the sentence is correct. Some words or phrases are underlined and lettered; everything else in the sentence is correct.

If an underlined word or phrase is incorrect, choose that letter; if the sentence is correct, select <u>No error</u>. Then blacken the appropriate space on your answer sheet.

**EXAMPLE:**

These fields have soil <u>so rich that</u> corn
                A

<u>growing here</u> commonly <u>had stood</u> more
  B              C

than six feet <u>tall</u>. <u>No error</u>.        Ⓐ Ⓑ ● Ⓓ Ⓔ
         D    E

---

## TIPS FOR HANDLING IDENTIFYING SENTENCE ERRORS QUESTIONS

**Tip 6**

**Remember that the error, if there is one, must be in an underlined part of the sentence.** You don't have to worry about improvements that could be made in the rest of the sentence. For example, if you have a sentence in which the subject is plural and the verb is singular, you could call either one the error. But if only the verb is underlined, the error for that sentence is the verb.

## EXAMPLE 6

See how the sixth tip works in dealing with the following sentence:

> If one follows the <u>discipline of Hatha Yoga,</u> <u>you know</u> the critical
>                            A                                B
>
> importance of physical purification <u>to render</u> the body <u>fit</u> for the
>                                   C                D
>
> practice of higher meditation. <u>No error</u>
>                                     E

What's wrong with the sentence above? Look at Choice B. The writer makes an abrupt, unnecessary shift in person, switching from the pronoun one ("one follows") to the pronoun you ("you know"). There are two ways to fix this sentence. You can rewrite it like this:

> If you follow the discipline of Hatha Yoga, you know the critical importance of physical purification to render the body fit for the practice of higher meditation.

You can also rewrite it like this:

> If one follows the discipline of Hatha Yoga, one knows the critical importance of physical purification to render the body fit for the practice of higher meditation.

However, your job is not to rewrite the sentence. Your job is simply to spot the error, and that error *must be in an underlined part*. In answering error identification questions, focus on the underlined portions of the sentence. Don't waste your time thinking of other ways to make the sentence work.

## Tip 7

**Use your ear for the language.** Remember, you don't have to name the error, or be able to explain why it is wrong. All you have to do is recognize that something *is* wrong. On the early, easy questions in the set, if a word or phrase sounds wrong to you, it probably is, even if you don't know why.

## EXAMPLE 7

See how the seventh tip works in dealing with the following sentence:

> <u>In my history class</u> I learned <u>why</u> the American colonies
>              A                         B
>
> opposed the British, <u>how they organized the militia,</u> and
>                               C
>
> <u>the accomplishments of the Continental Congress.</u> <u>No error</u>
>                                  D                    E

When you got to Choice D, the last section of the sentence, did "the accomplishments of the Continental Congress" sound funny to you—awkward, strange, wooden? Even though you didn't know exactly what was wrong, did something feel off there? If so, congratulations: you have a good ear.

If you followed your instincts and chose Choice D as the error, you were right. The error is a lack of parallel structure. The sentence is listing three things you learned, and they should all be in the same form. Your ear expects the pattern to be the same. Since the first two items listed are clauses, the third should be too: "In my history class I learned why the American colonies opposed the British, how they organized the militia, and what the Continental Congress accomplished."

## Tip 8

**Look first for the most common errors. Be systematic: check the underlined sections one by one.** Most of the sentences will have errors. If you are having trouble finding mistakes, check for some of the more common ones: subject-verb agreement, pronoun-antecedent problems, misuse of adjectives and adverbs, dangling modifiers. But look for errors only in the underlined parts of the sentence.

## EXAMPLE 8

See how the eighth tip works in dealing with the following sentence:

Marilyn and I ran as fast as we could, but we missed our train, which
        A      B                                              C

made us late for work. No error
    D                E

Imagine that you have this sentence, and you can't see what is wrong with it. Start at the beginning and check each answer choice. *I* is part of the subject, so it is the right case: after all, you wouldn't say "Me ran fast." *Fast* can be an adverb, so it is being used correctly here. *Which* is a pronoun, and needs a noun for its antecedent. The only available noun is *train*, but that doesn't make sense (the train didn't make us late—*missing* the train made us late.) So there is your error, Choice C.

## Tip 9

**Remember that not every sentence contains an error.** Ten to twenty percent of the time, the sentence is correct as it stands. Do not get so caught up in hunting for errors that you start seeing errors that aren't there. If no obvious errors strike your eye and the sentence sounds natural to your ear, go with Choice E: No error.

# Improving Paragraphs

In the improving paragraphs questions, you will confront a flawed student essay followed by five questions. In some cases, you must select the answer choice that best rewrites and combines portions of two separate sentences. In others, you must decide where in the essay a sentence best fits. In still others, you must choose what sort of additional information would most strengthen the writer's argument. Here are the directions.

> **Improving Paragraphs Directions:**
> The passage below is the unedited draft of a student's essay. Some of the essay needs to be rewritten to make the meaning clearer and more precise. Read the essay carefully.
>
> The essay is followed by five questions about changes that might improve all or part of its organization, development, sentence structure, use of language, appropriateness to the audience, or use of standard written English. Choose the answer that most clearly and effectively expresses the student's intended meaning. Indicate your choice by filling in the corresponding space on the answer sheet.

## TIPS FOR HANDLING IMPROVING PARAGRAPHS QUESTIONS

**Tip 10**

**First read the passage; then read the questions.** Whether you choose to skim the student essay quickly or to read it closely, you need to have a reasonable idea of what the student author is trying to say before you set out to correct this rough first draft.

**Tip 11**

**First tackle the questions that ask you to improve individual sentences; then tackle the ones that ask you to strengthen the passage as a whole.** In the sentence correction questions, you've just been weeding out ineffective sentences and selecting effective ones. Here you're doing more of the same. It generally takes less time to spot an effective sentence than it does to figure out a way to strengthen an argument or link up two paragraphs.

**Tip 12**

**Consider whether the addition of signal words or phrases—transitions—would strengthen the passage or particular sentences within it.** If the essay is trying to contrast two ideas, it might benefit from the addition of a contrast signal.

Contrast Signals: *although, despite, however, in contrast, nevertheless, on the contrary, on the other hand.*

If one portion of the essay is trying to support or continue a thought developed elsewhere in the passage, it might benefit from the addition of a support signal.

Support Signals: *additionally, furthermore, in addition, likewise, moreover.*

If the essay is trying to indicate that one thing causes another, it might benefit from the addition of a cause-and-effect signal.

Cause-and-Effect Signals: *accordingly, as a result of, because, consequently, hence, therefore, thus.*

Pay particular attention to answer choices that contain such signal words.

**Tip 13**

**When you tackle the questions,** *go back to the passage* **to verify each answer choice.** See whether your revised version of a particular sentence sounds right in its context. Ask yourself whether your choice follows naturally from the sentence before.

# Common Grammar and Usage Errors

Some errors are more common than others in this section. Here are a dozen that appear frequently on the examination. Watch out for them when you do the practice exercises and when you take the PSAT.

## The Run-On Sentence

*Mary's party was very exciting, it lasted until 2 A.M.*
*It is raining today, I need a raincoat.*

You may also have heard this error called a comma splice. It can be corrected by making two sentences instead of one:

*Mary's party was very exciting. It lasted until 2 A.M.*

or by using a semicolon in place of the comma:

*Mary's party was very exciting; it lasted until 2 A.M.*

or by proper compounding:

*Mary's party was very exciting and lasted until 2 A.M.*

You can also correct this error with proper subordination. The second example above could be corrected:

*Since it is raining today, I need a raincoat.*
*It is raining today, and so I need a raincoat.*

## The Sentence Fragment

*Since John was talking during the entire class, making it impossible for anyone to concentrate.*

This is the opposite of the first error. Instead of too much in one sentence, here you have too little. Do not be misled by the length of the fragment. It must have a main clause before it can be a complete sentence. All you have in this example is the cause. You still need a result. For example, the sentence could be corrected:

*Since John's talking during the entire class made it impossible for anyone to concentrate, the teacher had him stay after school.*

## Error in the Case of a Noun or Pronoun

*Between you and I, this test is not really very difficult.*

Case problems usually involve personal pronouns, which are in the nominative case (*I, he, she, we, they, who*) when they are used as subjects or predicate nominatives and in the objective case (*me, him, her, us, them, whom*) when they are used as direct objects, indirect objects, and objects of prepositions. In this example, if you realize that *between* is a preposition, you know that *I* should be changed to the objective *me* because it is the object of a preposition.

## Error in Subject-Verb Agreement

*Harvard College, along with several other Ivy League schools, are sending students to the conference.*

Phrases starting with *along with* or *as well as* or *in addition to* that are placed in between the subject and the verb do not affect the verb. The subject of this sentence is *Harvard College,* so the verb should be *is sending.*

*There is three bears living in that house.*

Sentences that begin with *there* have the subject after the verb. The subject of this sentence is *bears,* so the verb should be *are.*

## Error in Pronoun-Number Agreement

*Every one of the girls on the team is trying to do their best.*

Every pronoun must have a specific noun or noun substitute for an antecedent, and it must agree with that antecedent in number (singular or plural). In this example, *their* refers to *one* and must be singular:

*Every one of the girls on the team is trying to do her best.*

## Error in the Tense or Form of a Verb

*After the sun set behind the mountain, a cool breeze sprang up and brought relief from the heat.*

Make sure the verbs in a sentence appear in the proper sequence of tenses, so that it is clear what happened when. Since, according to the sentence, the breeze did not appear until after the sun had finished setting, the setting belongs in the past perfect tense:

*After the sun had set behind the mountain, a cool breeze sprang up and brought relief from the heat.*

## Error in Logical Comparison

*I can go to California or Florida. I wonder which is best.*

When you are comparing only two things, you should use the comparative form of the adjective, not the superlative:

*I wonder which is better.*

Comparisons must also be complete and logical.

*The rooms on the second floor are larger than the first floor.*

It would be a strange building that had rooms larger than an entire floor. Logically, this sentence should be corrected to

*The rooms on the second floor are larger than those on the first floor.*

# Adjective and Adverb Confusion

*She did good on the test.*

*They felt badly about leaving their friends.*

These are the two most common ways that adjectives and adverbs are misused. In the first example, when you are talking about how someone did, you want the adverb *well,* not the adjective *good:*

*She did well on the test.*

In the second example, after a linking verb like *feel,* you want a predicate adjective to describe the subject:

*They felt bad about leaving their friends.*

# Error in Modification and Word Order

*Reaching for the book, the ladder slipped out from under him.*

A participial phrase at the beginning of the sentence should describe the subject of the sentence. Since it doesn't make sense to think of a ladder reaching for a book, this participle is left dangling with nothing to modify. The sentence needs some rewriting:

*When he reached for the book, the ladder slipped out from under him.*

# Error in Parallelism

*In his book on winter sports, the author discusses ice-skating, skiing, hockey, and how to fish in an ice-covered lake.*

Logically, equal and similar ideas belong in similar form. This shows that they are equal. In this sentence, the author discusses four sports, and all four should be presented the same way:

*In his book on winter sports, the author discusses ice skating, skiing, hockey, and fishing in an ice-covered lake.*

# Error in Diction or Idiom

*The affects of the storm could be seen everywhere.*

Your ear for the language will help you handle these errors, especially if you are accustomed to reading standard English. These questions test you on words that are frequently misused, on levels of usage (informal versus formal), and on standard English idioms. In this example, the verb *affect,* meaning "to influence," has been confused with the noun *effect,* meaning "result."

*The effects of the storm could be seen everywhere.*

The exercises that follow will give you practice in answering the three types of questions you'll find on the Identifying Sentence Errors questions, Improving Sentence questions, and Improving Paragraph questions. When you have completed each exercise, check your answers against the answer key. Then, read the answer explanations for any questions you either answered incorrectly or omitted.

# Practice Exercises

The sentences in this section may contain errors in grammar, usage, choice of words, or idioms. There is either just one error per sentence, or the sentence is correct. Some words or phrases are underlined and lettered; everything else in the sentence is correct.

If an underlined word or phrase is incorrect, choose that letter; if the sentence is correct, select <u>No error</u>. Then blacken the appropriate space on your answer sheet.

**EXAMPLE:**

These fields have soil <u>so rich that</u> corn
              A

<u>growing here</u> commonly <u>had stood</u> more
   B               C

than six feet <u>tall</u>. <u>No error</u>
          D     E
       Ⓐ Ⓑ ● Ⓓ Ⓔ

1. We were <u>already</u> <u>to leave for</u> the amusement park
        A      B

   when John's car <u>broke down</u>; we <u>were forced</u> to
              C          D

   postpone our outing. <u>No error</u>
                 E

2. <u>By order of</u> the Student Council, the <u>wearing of</u>
  A                     B

   slacks by <u>we</u> girls in school <u>has been permitted</u>.
         C            D

   <u>No error</u>
     E

3. <u>Each</u> one of the dogs in the show <u>require</u> a <u>special</u>
  A              B    C

   <u>kind of</u> diet. <u>No error</u>
     D      E

4. The major difficulty <u>confronting</u> the authorities
             A

   <u>was</u> the reluctance of the people <u>to talk</u>; they had
    B                C

   been warned not <u>to say nothing</u> to the police.
              D

   <u>No error</u>
     E

5. If I <u>were</u> you, I would never permit <u>him</u>
   A               B

   <u>to take part</u> in such an <u>exhausting and painful</u>
      C            D

   activity. <u>No error</u>
         E

6. Stanford White, <u>who</u> is one of America's
        A

   <u>most notable</u> architects, <u>have designed</u> many
      B          C

   famous buildings, <u>among them</u> the original
              D

   Madison Square Garden. <u>No error</u>
              E

7. The notion <u>of allowing the</u> <u>institution of</u> slavery
          A       B

   <u>to continue to</u> exist in a democratic society had no
     C

   appeal to either the violent followers of John

   Brown <u>nor</u> the peaceful disciples of Sojourner
       D

   Truth. <u>No error</u>
       E

8. Some students <u>prefer</u> watching filmstrips to
         A

   <u>textbooks</u> because they feel <u>uncomfortable with</u>
     B             C

   the presentation <u>of</u> information in a non-oral form.
            D

   <u>No error</u>
     E

9. <u>There</u> was so much conversation <u>in back of</u> me
  A                 B

   that I <u>couldn't</u> hear the actors on the stage.
     C   D

   <u>No error</u>
     E

10. This book is <u>too</u> elementary; <u>it can help</u> neither
        A        B

   you <u>nor</u> <u>I</u>. <u>No error</u>
     C  D   E

11. In a way <u>we</u> may say <u>that</u> we <u>have reached</u> the
             A          B           C

    <u>end of</u> the Industrial Revolution. <u>No error</u>
     D                                           E

12. <u>Although</u> the books are <u>altogether</u> on the shelf,
      A                      B

    <u>they</u> are not arranged in <u>any kind of</u> order.
     C                          D

    <u>No error</u>
     E

13. The <u>reason for</u> my <u>prolonged absence</u> from class
        A              B

    <u>was</u> <u>because</u> I was ill for three weeks. <u>No error</u>
     C    D                        E

14. <u>According to</u> researchers, the weapons and work
      A

    implements <u>used by</u> Cro-Magnon hunters appear
              B

    <u>being</u> <u>actually quite</u> "modern." <u>No error</u>
     C     D              E

15. Since we were caught <u>completely unawares</u>, the
                    A

    <u>affect</u> of Ms. Rivera's remarks <u>was startling</u>; some
     B                      C

    were shocked, <u>but</u> others were angry. <u>No error</u>
              D                   E

16. The committee <u>had intended</u> both <u>you and I</u> to
                A          B

    speak at the assembly; <u>however</u>, <u>only</u> one of us will
                    C    D

    be able to talk. <u>No error</u>
               E

17. The existence of rundown "welfare hotels,"

    <u>in which</u> homeless families <u>reside</u> at enormous
     A                      B

    <u>cost to</u> the taxpayer, provides a shameful
     C

    <u>commentary of</u> America's commitment to house
       D

    the poor. <u>No error</u>
           E

18. We have heard that the <u>principal</u> has decided
                    A

    <u>whom</u> the prizewinners <u>will be</u> <u>and</u> will announce
     B                 C    D

    the names in the assembly today. <u>No error</u>
                           E

19. <u>As soon as</u> the sun <u>had rose</u> <u>over</u> the mountains,
     A               B     C

    the valley became <u>unbearably hot</u> and stifling.
                    D

    <u>No error</u>
     E

20. They are both <u>excellent books</u>, but this one <u>is</u> <u>best</u>.
    A              B                  C D

    <u>No error</u>
     E

21. Although the news <u>had come</u> as a surprise <u>to all</u> in
                  A                 B

    the room, both Jane and Oprah tried to do <u>her</u>
                                   C

    work <u>as though</u> nothing had happened.
        D

    <u>No error</u>
     E

22. Even <u>well-known fashion designers</u> have difficulty
     A

    staying on top <u>from one season to another</u>
                      B

    <u>because of</u> <u>changeable moods</u> and needs in the
     C           D

    marketplace. <u>No error</u>
              E

23. Arms control has been <u>under discussion</u> for
                  A

    decades with the former Soviet Union, <u>but</u>
                             B

    solutions <u>are still</u> <u>alluding</u> the major powers.
             C      D

    <u>No error</u>
     E

24. Perhaps sports enthusiasts are realizing <u>that</u>
                           A

    jogging is <u>not easy on</u> joints and tendons, for the
            B

    <u>latest</u> fad is <u>being walking</u>. <u>No error</u>
     C          D         E

25. Technological advances <u>can cause</u> factual data to
          A

 become obsolete within a <u>short time</u>; <u>yet</u>, students
          B    C

 should concentrate on <u>reasoning skills</u>, not facts.
           D

 <u>No error</u>
   E

26. If anyone cares <u>to join</u> me in this campaign, <u>either</u>
 <u>  </u>     B          C
 A

 now or in the near future, <u>they</u> will be welcomed
           D

 gratefully. <u>No error</u>
      E

27. The poems <u>with which</u> he occasionally
       A

 desired to <u>regale</u> the fashionable world were
     B

 <u>invariably bad</u>—stereotyped, bombastic, and
    C

 <u>even ludicrous</u>. <u>No error</u>
   D    E

28. <u>Ever since</u> the <u>quality of</u> teacher education came
   A     B

 under public scrutiny, suggestions for <u>upgrading</u>
              C

 the profession <u>are abounding</u>. <u>No error</u>
       D    E

29. <u>Because</u> the door was locked and bolted, the police
  A

 <u>were</u> forced <u>to break</u> into the apartment <u>through</u>
  B    C         D

 the bedroom window. <u>No error</u>
        E

30. I <u>will</u> <u>always</u> remember <u>you</u> <u>standing by</u> me
   A  B     C   D

 offering me encouragement. <u>No error</u>
           E

31. With special training, capuchin monkeys

 <u>can enable</u> quadriplegics <u>as well as</u> other
   A        B

 handicapped individuals <u>to become</u>
          C

 increasingly independent. <u>No error</u>
     D     E

32. <u>Contrary to</u> what had previously been reported, the
   A

 conditions <u>governing</u> the truce between Libya and
      B

 Chad <u>arranged by</u> the United Nations <u>has</u> not yet
    C         D

 been revealed. <u>No error</u>
       E

33. Avid readers generally either admire <u>or</u> dislike
            A

 Ernest Hemingway's journalistic <u>style of</u> writing;
            B

 <u>few have</u> no opinion <u>of him</u>. <u>No error</u>
   C     D   E

34. In 1986, the nuclear disaster at Chernobyl

 <u>has aroused</u> intense speculation <u>about</u> the long-
   A         B

 term <u>effects of</u> radiation that continued for
    C

 <u>the better part of</u> a year. <u>No error</u>
    D       E

35. Howard Hughes, <u>who</u> <u>became</u> the subject of
       A  B

 bizarre rumors <u>as a result of</u> his extreme
        C

 reclusiveness, was well-known as an aviator,

 industrialist, and <u>in producing motion pictures</u>.
              D

 <u>No error</u>
   E

Some or all parts of the following sentences are underlined. The first answer choice, (A), simply repeats the underlined part of the sentence. The other four choices present four alternative ways to phrase the underlined part. Select the answer that produces the most effective sentence, one that is clear and exact, and blacken the appropriate space on your answer sheet. In selecting your choice, be sure that it is standard written English and that it expresses the meaning of the original sentence.

**EXAMPLE:**

The first biography of author Eudora Welty came out in 1998, and she was eighty-nine years old at the time.

(A) and she was eighty-nine years old at the time
(B) at the time when she was eighty-nine
(C) upon becoming an eighty-nine year old
(D) when she was eighty-nine
(E) at the age of eighty-nine years old

36. The child is neither encouraged to be critical or to examine all the evidence before forming an opinion.

    (A) neither encouraged to be critical or to examine
    (B) neither encouraged to be critical nor to examine
    (C) either encouraged to be critical or to examine
    (D) encouraged either to be critical nor to examine
    (E) not encouraged either to be critical or to examine

37. The process by which the community influence the actions of its members is known as social control.

    (A) influence the actions of its members
    (B) influences the actions of its members
    (C) had influenced the actions of its members
    (D) influences the actions of their members
    (E) will influence the actions of its members

38. Play being recognized as an important factor improving mental and physical health and thereby reducing human misery and poverty.

    (A) Play being recognized as
    (B) By recognizing play as
    (C) Their recognizing play as
    (D) Recognition of it being
    (E) Play is recognized as

39. To be sure, there would be scarcely any time left over for other things if school children would have been expected to have considered all sides of every matter on which they hold opinions.

    (A) would have been expected to have considered
    (B) should have been expected to have considered
    (C) were expected to consider
    (D) will be expected to have considered
    (E) were expected to be considered

40. Using it wisely, leisure promotes health, efficiency and happiness.

    (A) Using it wisely
    (B) If it is used wisely
    (C) Having used it wisely
    (D) Because of its wise use
    (E) Because of usefulness

41. In giving expression to the play instincts of the human race, new vigor and effectiveness are afforded by recreation to the body and to the mind.

    (A) new vigor and effectiveness are afforded by recreation to the body and to the mind
    (B) recreation affords new vigor and effectiveness to the body and to the mind
    (C) there are afforded new vigor and effectiveness to the body and to the mind
    (D) by recreation the body and the mind are afforded new vigor and effectiveness
    (E) to the body and to the mind afford new vigor and effectiveness to themselves by recreation

42. Depending on skillful suggestion, argument is seldom used in advertising.

    (A) Depending on skillful suggestion, argument is seldom used in advertising.
    (B) Argument is seldom used in advertising, which depends instead on skillful suggestion.
    (C) Skillful suggestion is depended on by advertisers instead of argument.
    (D) Suggestion, which is more skillful, is used in place of argument by advertisers.
    (E) Instead of suggestion, depending on argument is used by skillful advertisers.

43. When this war is over, no nation will either be isolated in war or peace.

   (A) either be isolated in war or peace
   (B) be either isolated in war or peace
   (C) be isolated in neither war nor peace
   (D) be isolated either in war or in peace
   (E) be isolated neither in war or peace

44. Thanks to the prevailing westerly winds, dust blowing east from the drought-stricken plains travels halfway across the continent to fall on the cities of the East Coast.

   (A) blowing east from the drought-stricken plains
   (B) that, blowing east from the drought-stricken plains,
   (C) from the drought-stricken plains and blows east
   (D) that is from the drought-stricken plains blowing east
   (E) blowing east that is from the plains that are drought-stricken

45. Americans are learning that their concept of a research worker toiling alone in a laboratory and who discovers miraculous cures has been highly idealized and glamorized.

   (A) toiling alone in a laboratory and who discovers miraculous cures
   (B) toiling alone in a laboratory and discovers miraculous cures
   (C) toiling alone in a laboratory to discover miraculous cures
   (D) who toil alone in the laboratory and discover miraculous cures
   (E) has toiled alone hoping to discover miraculous cures

46. However many mistakes have been made in our past, the tradition of America, not only the champion of freedom but also fair play, still lives among millions who can see light and hope scarcely anywhere else.

   (A) not only the champion of freedom but also fair play
   (B) the champion of not only freedom but also of fair play
   (C) the champion not only of freedom but also of fair play
   (D) not only the champion but also freedom and fair play
   (E) not the champion of freedom only, but also fair play

47. Examining the principal movements sweeping through the world, it can be seen that they are being accelerated by the war.

   (A) Examining the principal movements sweeping through the world, it can be seen
   (B) Having examined the principal movements sweeping through the world, it can be seen
   (C) Examining the principal movements sweeping through the world can be seen
   (D) Examining the principal movements sweeping through the world, we can see
   (E) It can be seen examining the principal movements sweeping through the world

48. The FCC is broadening its view on what constitutes indecent programming, radio stations are taking a closer look at their broadcasters' materials.

   (A) The FCC is broadening its view on what constitutes indecent programming
   (B) The FCC, broadening its view on what constitutes indecent programming, has caused
   (C) The FCC is broadening its view on what constitutes indecent programming, as a result
   (D) Since the FCC is broadening its view on what constitutes indecent programming
   (E) The FCC, having broadened its view on what constitutes indecent programming

49. As district attorney, Elizabeth Holtzman not only had the responsibility of supervising a staff of dedicated young lawyers but she had the task of maintaining good relations with the police also.

   (A) but she had the task of maintaining good relations with the police also
   (B) but she also had the task of maintaining good relations with the police
   (C) but also had the task of maintaining good relations with the police
   (D) but she had the task to maintain good relations with the police also
   (E) but also she had the task to maintain good relations with the police

50. Many politicians are now trying to take uncontroversial positions on issues; the purpose being to allow them to appeal to as wide a segment of the voting population as possible.

   (A) issues; the purpose being to allow them to appeal
   (B) issues in order to appeal
   (C) issues, the purpose is to allow them to appeal
   (D) issues and the purpose is to allow them to appeal
   (E) issues; that was allowing them to appeal

[1] Throughout history, people have speculated about the future. [2] Will it be a utopia? they wondered. [3] Will injustice and poverty be eliminated? [4] Will people accept ethnic diversity, learning to live in peace? [5] Will the world be clean and unpolluted? [6] Or will technology aid us in creating a trap for ourselves we cannot escape, for example such as the world in *1984*? [7] With the turn of the millennium just around the corner these questions are in the back of our minds.

[8] Science fiction often portrays the future as a technological Garden of Eden. [9] With interactive computers, TVs and robots at our command, we barely need to lift a finger to go to school, to work, to go shopping, and education is also easy and convenient. [10] Yet, the problems of the real twentieth century seem to point in another direction. [11] The environment, far from improving, keeps deteriorating. [12] Wars and other civil conflicts breakout regularly. [13] The world's population is growing out of control. [14] The majority of people on earth live in poverty. [15] Many of them are starving. [16] Illiteracy is a problem in most poor countries. [17] Diseases and malnourishment is very common. [18] Rich countries like the U.S.A. don't have the resources to help the "have-not" countries.

[19] Instead, think instead of all the silly inventions such as tablets you put in your toilet tank to make the water blue, or electric toothbrushes. [20] More money is spent on space and defense than on education and health care. [21] Advancements in agriculture can produce enough food to feed the whole country, yet people in the U.S. are starving.

[22] Although the USSR is gone, the nuclear threat continues from small countries like Iran. [23] Until the world puts its priorities straight, we can't look for a bright future in the twenty-first century, despite the rosy picture painted for us by the science fiction writers.

51. Considering the context of paragraph 1, which of the following is the best revision of sentence 6?
(A) Or will technology create a trap for ourselves from which we cannot escape, for example the world in *1984*?
(B) Or will technology aid people in creating a trap for themselves that they cannot escape; for example, the world in *1984*?
(C) Or will technology create a trap from which there is no escape, as it did in the world in *1984*?
(D) Or will technology trap us in an inescapable world, for example, it did so in the world of *1984*?
(E) Perhaps technology will aid people in creating a trap for themselves from which they cannot escape, just as they did it in the world of *1984*.

52. With regard to the essay as a whole, which of the following best describes the writer's intention in paragraph 1?
(A) to announce the purpose of the essay
(B) to compare two ideas discussed later in the essay
(C) to take a position on the essay's main issue
(D) to reveal the organization of the essay
(E) to raise questions that will be answered in the essay

53. Which of the following is the best revision of the underlined segment of sentence 9 below?
*[9] With interactive computers, TVs and robots at our command, we barely need to lift a finger to go to school, to work, to go shopping, and education is also easy and convenient.*
(A) and to go shopping, while education is also easy and convenient
(B) to go shopping, and getting an education is also easy and convenient
(C) to go shopping as well as educating ourselves are all easy and convenient
(D) to shop, and an easy and convenient education
(E) to shop, and to get an easy and convenient education

**54.** Which of the following is the most effective way to combine sentences 14, 15, 16, and 17?

(A) The majority of people on earth are living in poverty and are starving, with illiteracy, and disease and being malnourished are also a common problems.

(B) Common problems for the majority of people on earth are poverty, illiteracy, diseases, malnourishment, and many are illiterate.

(C) The majority of people on earth are poor, starving, sick, malnourished, and illiterate.

(D) Common among the poor majority on earth is poverty, starvation, disease, malnourishment, and illiteracy.

(E) The majority of the earth's people living in poverty with starvation, disease, malnourishment and illiteracy a constant threat.

**55.** Considering the sentences that precede and follow sentence 19, which of the following is the most effective revision of sentence 19?

(A) Instead they are devoting resources on silly inventions such as tablets to make toilet tank water blue or electric toothbrushes.

(B) Instead, they waste their resources on producing silly inventions like electric toothbrushes and tablets for turning toilet tank water blue.

(C) Think of all the silly inventions: tablets you put in your toilet tank to make the water blue and electric toothbrushes.

(D) Instead, tablets you put in your toilet tank to make the water blue or electric toothbrushes are examples of useless products on the market today.

(E) Instead of spending on useful things, think of all the silly inventions such as tablets you put in your toilet tank to make the water blue or electric toothbrushes.

**56.** Which of the following revisions would most improve the overall coherence of the essay?

(A) moving sentence 7 to paragraph 2

(B) moving sentence 10 to paragraph 1

(C) moving sentence 22 to paragraph 2

(D) deleting sentence 8

(E) deleting sentence 23

## Answer Key

| | | | | | | | | | | |
|---|---|---|---|---|---|---|---|---|---|---|
| 1. | **A** | 11. | **E** | 21. | **C** | 31. | **E** | 41. | **B** | 51. **C** |
| 2. | **C** | 12. | **B** | 22. | **E** | 32. | **D** | 42. | **B** | 52. **E** |
| 3. | **B** | 13. | **D** | 23. | **D** | 33. | **D** | 43. | **D** | 53. **E** |
| 4. | **D** | 14. | **C** | 24. | **D** | 34. | **A** | 44. | **A** | 54. **C** |
| 5. | **E** | 15. | **B** | 25. | **C** | 35. | **D** | 45. | **C** | 55. **B** |
| 6. | **C** | 16. | **B** | 26. | **D** | 36. | **E** | 46. | **C** | 56. **C** |
| 7. | **D** | 17. | **D** | 27. | **E** | 37. | **B** | 47. | **D** | |
| 8. | **B** | 18. | **B** | 28. | **D** | 38. | **E** | 48. | **D** | |
| 9. | **B** | 19. | **B** | 29. | **E** | 39. | **C** | 49. | **C** | |
| 10. | **D** | 20. | **D** | 30. | **C** | 40. | **B** | 50. | **B** | |

## Answer Explanations

1. **(A)** Error in diction. Should be *all ready*. *All ready* means the group is ready; *already* means prior to a given time, previously.

2. **(C)** Error in pronoun case. Should be *us*. The expression *us girls* is the object of the preposition *by*.

3. **(B)** Error in subject-verb agreement. Should be *requires*. Verb should agree with the subject (*each one*).

4. **(D)** Should be *to say anything*. *Not to say nothing* is a double negative.

5. **(E)** Sentence is correct.

6. **(C)** Error in subject-verb agreement. Since the subject is Stanford White (singular), change *have designed* to *has designed*.

7. **(D)** Error in use of correlatives. Change *nor* to *or*. The correct form of the correlative pairs *either* with *or*.

8. **(B)** Error in parallel structure. Change *textbooks* to *reading textbooks*. To have parallel structure, the linked sentence elements must share the same grammatical form.

9. **(B)** Error in diction. Change *in back of* to *behind*.

10. **(D)** Error in pronoun case. Should be *me*. Pronoun is the object of the verb *can help*.

11. **(E)** Sentence is correct.

12. **(B)** Error in diction. Should be *all together*. *All together* means in a group; *altogether* means entirely.

13. **(D)** Improper use of *because*. Change to *that* (*The reason . . . was that . . .* ).

14. **(C)** Incorrect verbal. Change the participle *being* to the infinitive *to be*.

15. **(B)** Error in diction. Change *affect* (a verb meaning to influence or pretend) to *effect* (a noun meaning result).

16. **(B)** Error in pronoun case. Should be *me*. Subjects of infinitives are in the objective case.

17. **(D)** Error in idiom. Change *commentary of* to *commentary on*.

18. **(B)** Error in pronoun case. Should be *who*. The pronoun is the predicate complement of *will be* and is in the nominative case.

19. **(B)** Should be *had risen*. The past participle of the verb *to rise* is *risen*.

20. **(D)** Error in comparison of modifiers. Should be *better*. Do not use the superlative when comparing two things.

21. **(C)** Error in pronoun-number agreement. Should be *their* instead of *her*. The antecedent of the pronoun is *Jane and Oprah* (plural).

22. **(E)** Sentence is correct.

23. **(D)** Error in diction. Change *alluding* (meaning to refer indirectly) to *eluding* (meaning to evade).

24. **(D)** Confusion of verb and gerund (verbal noun). Change *is being walking* to *is walking*.

25. **(C)** Error in coordination and subordination. Change *yet* to *therefore* or another similar connector to clarify the connection between the clauses.

26. **(D)** Error in pronoun-number agreement. Should be *he* or *she*. The antecedent of the pronoun is *anyone* (singular).

27. **(E)** Sentence is correct.

28. **(D)** Error in sequence of tenses. Change *are abounding* to *have abounded*. The present perfect tense talks about an action that occurs at one time, but is seen in relation to another time.

29. **(E)** Sentence is correct.

30. **(C)** Error in pronoun case. Should be *your*. The pronoun modifying a gerund (verbal noun) should be in the possessive case.

31. **(E)** Sentence is correct.

32. **(D)** Error in subject-verb agreement. Since the subject is *conditions* (plural), change *has* to *have*.

33. **(D)** Error in pronoun. Since the sentence speaks about Hemingway's style rather than about Hemingway, the phrase should read *of it,* not *of him.*

34. **(A)** Error in sequence of tenses. Change *has aroused* to *aroused*. The present perfect tense (*has aroused*) is used for indefinite time. In this sentence, the time is defined as *the better part of a year*.

35. **(D)** Lack of parallel structure. Change *in producing motion pictures* to *motion picture producer*.

36. **(E)** This question involves two aspects of correct English. *Neither* should be followed by *nor;* *either* by *or*. Choices A and D are, therefore, incorrect. The words *neither . . . nor* and *either . . . or* should be placed before the two items being discussed—*to be critical* and *to examine*. Choice E meets both requirements.

37. **(B)** This question tests agreement. Errors in subject-verb agreement and pronoun-number agreement are both involved. *Community* (singular) needs a singular verb, *influences*. Also, the pronoun that refers to *community* should be singular *(its)*.

38. **(E)** Error in following conventions. This is an incomplete sentence or fragment. The sentence needs a verb to establish a principal clause. Choice E provides the verb (*is recognized*) and presents the only complete sentence in the group.

39. **(C)** *Would have been expected* is incorrect as a verb in a clause introduced by the conjunction *if*. *Had been expected* or *were expected* is preferable. *To have considered* does not follow correct sequence of tense and should be changed to *to consider*.

40. **(B)** Error in modification and word order. One way of correcting a dangling participle is to change the participial phrase to a clause. Choices B and D substitute clauses for the phrase. However, Choice D changes the meaning of the sentence. Choice B is correct.

41. **(B)** Error in modification and word order. As it stands, the sentence contains a dangling modifier. This is corrected by making *recreation* the subject of the sentence, in the process switching from the passive to the active voice. Choice E also provides a subject for the sentence; however, the meaning of the sentence is changed in Choice E.

42. **(B)** Error in modification and word order. As presented, the sentence contains a dangling parti-ciple, *depending*. Choice B corrects this error. The other choices change the emphasis presented by the author.

43. **(D)** Error in word order. *Either . . . or* should precede the two choices offered (*in war* and *in peace*).

44. **(A)** Sentence is correct.

45. **(C)** Error in parallelism. In the underlined phrase, you will find two modifiers of *worker-toiling* and *who discovers*. The first is a participial phrase, and the second a clause. This results in an error in parallel structure. Choice B also has an error in parallel structure. Choice C corrects this by eliminating one of the modifiers of *worker*. Choice D corrects the error in parallel structure but introduces an error in agreement between subject and verb—*who* (singular) and *toil* (plural). Choice E changes the tense and also the meaning of the original sentence.

46. **(C)** Error in parallelism. Parallel structure requires that *not only* and *but also* immediately precede the words they limit.

47. **(D)** Error in modification and word order. Choices A, B, and E are incorrect because of the dangling participle. Choice C is incoherent. Choice D correctly eliminates the dangling participle by introducing the subject *we*.

48. **(D)** Error in comma splice. The punctuation in Choices A and C creates a run-on sentence. Choices B and E are both ungrammatical. Choice D corrects the run-on sentence by changing the beginning clause into the adverb clause that starts with the subordinating conjunction *since*.

49. **(C)** Error in parallelism. Since the words *not only* immediately precede the verb in the first half of the sentence, the words *but also* should immediately precede the verb in the second half. This error in parallel structure is corrected in Choice C.

50. **(B)** Error in coordination and subordination. The punctuation in Choices A, C, D, and E creates an incomplete sentence or fragment. Choice B corrects the error by linking the elements with *in order to.*

51. **(C)** Choice A is awkward and shifts the pronoun usage in the paragraph from third to first person. Choice B is awkward and contains a semicolon error. A semicolon is used to separate two independent clauses. The material after the semicolon is a sentence fragment. Choice C is succinctly and accurately expressed. It is the best answer. Choice D contains a comma splice between *world* and *for.* A comma may not be used to join two independent clauses. Choice E is awkwardly expressed and contains the pronoun *it,* which lacks a clear referent.

52. **(E)** Choice A indirectly describes the purpose of paragraph 1 but does not identify the writer's main intention. Choices B, C, and D fail to describe the writer's main intention. Choice E accurately describes the writer's main intention. It is the best answer.

53. **(E)** Choice A is grammatically correct but cumbersome. Choice B contains an error in parallel construction. The clause that begins *and getting* is not grammatically parallel to the previous items on the list. Choice C contains a mixed construction. The first and last parts of the sentence are grammatically unrelated. Choice D contains faulty parallel structure. Choice E is correct and accurately expressed. It is the best answer.

54. **(C)** Choice A is wordy and awkwardly expressed. Choice B contains an error in parallel structure. The clause *and many are illiterate* is not grammatically parallel to the previous items on the list of problems. Choice C is concise and accurately expressed. It is the best answer. Choice D is concise, but it contains an error in subject-verb agreement. The subject is *poverty, starvation . . . etc.,* which requires a plural verb; the verb *is* is singular. Choice E is a sentence fragment; it has no main verb.

55. **(B)** Choice A contains an error in idiom. The standard phrase is *devoting to,* not *devoting on.* Choice B ties sentence 19 to the previous sentence and is accurately expressed. It is the best answer. Choice C fails to improve the coherence of the paragraph. Choice D is unrelated to the context of the paragraph. Choice E is insufficiently related to the context of the paragraph.

56. **(C)** Choice A should stay put because it provides a transition between the questions in paragraph 1 and the beginning of paragraph 2. Choice B is a pivotal sentence in paragraph 2 and should not be moved. Choice C fits the topics of paragraph 2; therefore, sentence 22 should be moved to paragraph 2. Choice C is the best answer. Choice D is needed as an introductory sentence in paragraph 2. It should not be deleted. Choice E provides the essay with a meaningful conclusion and should not be deleted.

## WRITING SKILLS WRAP-UP

### Improving Sentences Questions

1. If you spot an error in the underlined section, eliminate any answer that contains the same error.

2. If you don't spot an error in the underlined section, look at the answer choices to see what is changed.

3. Make sure that all parts of the sentence are logically connected.

4. Make sure that all sentence parts listed as a series are similar in form.

5. Pay particular attention to the shorter answer choices.

### Identifying Sentence Errors Questions

6. Remember that the error, if there is one, must be in an underlined part of the sentence.

7. Use your ear for the language.

8. Look first for the most common errors. Be systematic: check the underlined sections one by one.

9. Remember that not every sentence contains an error. Ten to twenty percent of the time, go with Choice E: No error.

### Improving Paragraphs Questions

10. First read the passage; then read the questions.

11. First tackle the questions that ask you to improve individual sentences; then tackle the ones that ask you to strengthen the passage as a whole.

12. Consider whether the addition of signal words or phrases—transitions—would strengthen the passage or particular sentences within it.

13. When you tackle the questions, *go back to the passage to verify each answer choice.*

# PART FIVE

# MATHEMATICS

## CHAPTER 5

# Introduction to the Mathematics Sections

*Part Five consists of three chapters. This first brief chapter serves as an introduction to the mathematics part of the PSAT. Please do not skip it—take the few minutes necessary to carefully read everything in this chapter. It gives some valuable information about the organization of the math part of this book, as well as some important information about the test itself. It discusses the use of calculators on the test and explains the directions for both types of math questions.*

*Chapter 6 includes a discussion of all the essential tactics and strategies that good test takers need to know to do their best on the math part of the PSAT. The explanation of each tactic is followed by sample problems to solve using that particular tactic. The chapter ends with a set of exercises to test your understanding of the tactics discussed. If you master Chapter 6, you will be able to significantly improve your score on the math part of the PSAT.*

*Chapter 7 contains a review of the mathematics you need to know in order to do well on the PSAT, as well as hundreds of sample problems patterned on actual test questions. The chapter is conveniently divided into eighteen short sections (Section A through Section R), each on a different topic—percents, ratios, averages, triangles, circles, and so on.*

## WHEN TO STUDY CHAPTERS 6 AND 7

**H**ow much time you initially devote to Chapter 7 should depend on your math skills. If you are an excellent student who consistently earns A's in math class, you can skip the instructional parts of Chapter 7 for now. If, while doing the practice tests in Part Six, you find that you keep making mistakes on certain types of problems (averages, percents, geometry, for example) or they take you too long, you should study the appropriate sections of Chapter 7. Even if your math skills are excellent and you don't need the review, you should do the sample questions in those sections; they are an excellent source of additional PSAT questions. If you know that your math skills are not very good, it is advisable to review the material in Chapter 7 and work out the problems *before* tackling the practice tests in Part Six.

No matter how good you are in math, *you should carefully read Chapter 6*. In that chapter you will learn techniques for (1) getting the correct answer to problems that you don't know how to solve and (2) getting the correct answer more quickly on those that you do know how to do.

> **SUGGESTED STUDY PLAN**
>
> 1. Review the rules given in Part One of this book on how to pace yourself and when to guess.
>
> 2. Study the rules for the math part of the test that are presented in this chapter, including the use of calculators and the way to handle grid-in questions.
>
> 3. Study the math test-taking strategies presented in Chapter 6.
>
> 4. Take the diagnostic test at the beginning of this book to help you identify your areas of weakness
>
> 5. Study those sections of Chapter 7 that cover the topics you are weak in.
>
> 6. Take the practice tests at the end of this book.

## AN IMPORTANT SYMBOL

Throughout the book, the symbol $\Rightarrow$ is used to indicate that one step in the solution of a problem follows *immediately* from the preceding one and that no explanation is necessary. You should read

$2x = 12 \Rightarrow x = 6$ as
$2x = 12$, *which implies that* $x = 6$, or, *since* $2x = 12$, *then* $x = 6$.

Here is a sample solution to the following problem using $\Rightarrow$:

What is the value of $3x^2 - 7$ when $x = -5$?

$x = -5 \Rightarrow x^2 = (-5)^2 = 25 \Rightarrow 3x^2 = 3(25) = 75 \Rightarrow 3x^2 - 7 = 75 - 7 = 68.$

When the reason for a step is not obvious, $\Rightarrow$ is not used; rather, an explanation is given, often including a reference to a **KEY FACT** from Chapter 7. In many solutions, some steps are explained, while others are linked by the $\Rightarrow$ symbol, as in the following example:

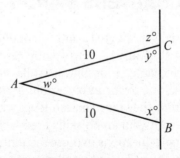

In the diagram above, if $w = 30$, what is the value of $z$?

- By **KEY FACT J1**, $w + x + y = 180$.
- Since $\triangle ABC$ is isosceles, $x = y$ [**KEY FACT J5**].
- Therefore, $w + 2y = 180 \Rightarrow 30 + 2y = 180 \Rightarrow 2y = 150 \Rightarrow y = 75.$
- Finally, since $y + z = 180$ [**KEY FACT I2**], $75 + z = 180 \Rightarrow z = 105.$

## SIX IMPORTANT HEADINGS

In Chapters 6 and 7, you will see six headings that will appear either in the text or in the margins. They will indicate valuable information and will help to guide you as you study this book. Here is a brief explanation of each heading.

-  A useful strategy for attacking a certain type problem. Some TACTICS give you advice on how to handle multiple-choice questions, regardless of the subject matter. Others point out ways to handle specific subject matter, such as finding averages or solving equations, regardless of the type of problem.

-

  **An important mathematical fact that you should commit to memory because it comes up often on the PSAT.**

-  Math Reference Fact

  A basic mathematical fact that is included in the "Reference Information" that appears on the first page of every math section.

-  Helpful Hint

  A useful idea that will help you solve a problem more easily or avoid a pitfall.

-  Caution!

  A warning of a potential danger. Often a Caution points out a common error or a source of careless mistakes.

-  Calculator

  Possible or recommended calculator hints allow you to use your calculator to get answers to questions you would otherwise have to omit or guess at.

You may *not* use the calculator on a cell phone. In fact, you may not have a phone on your desk at any time during the test.

## USE OF THE CALCULATOR

There isn't a single question on the PSAT for which a calculator is required. In fact, for most questions a calculator is completely useless. There are several questions, however, for which a calculator *could* be used, and since calculators are permitted, you should definitely bring one with you when you take the PSAT. As you go through the hundreds of practice math questions in this book, you should have available the calculator you intend to take to the test, and you should use it whenever you think it is appropriate. You will probably use it more at the beginning of your review because, as you go through this book, you will learn more and more strategies to help you solve problems easily without doing tedious calculations.

If you forget to bring a calculator to the actual test, you will not be able to use one, since none will be provided, and you will not be allowed to share one with a friend. For exactly the same reason, be sure that you have new batteries in your calculator or that you bring a spare, because if your calculator fails during the test, you will have to finish without one.

## What Calculator Should You Use?

Almost any four-function, scientific, or graphing calculator is acceptable. Since you don't "need" a calculator at all, you don't "need" any particular type. There is absolutely no advantage to having a graphing calculator, but we do recommend a scientific calculator, since it is occasionally useful to have parentheses keys, ( ); a reciprocal key, $\frac{1}{x}$; and an exponent key, $y^x$ or $\wedge$. All scientific calculators have these features. If you tend to make mistakes working with fractions, you might want to get a calculator that can do fractional arithmetic. With such a calculator, for example, you can add $\frac{1}{3}$ and $\frac{1}{5}$ by entering 1/3 + 1/5; the readout will be 8/15, not the decimal 0.5333333.

Do not buy a new calculator right before you take the PSAT. The best advice is to use a calculator you are completely familiar with—the one you always use in your math class. If you don't have one or want to get a different one, *buy it now* and become familiar with it. Do all the practice exams in this book with the same calculator you intend to bring to the test.

## When Should Calculators Be Used?

If you have strong math skills and are a good test-taker, you will probably use your calculator infrequently, if at all, since, for one thing, strong math students can do a lot of basic arithmetic just as accurately, and faster, in their heads or on paper than with a calculator. A less obvious but more important point is that students who are good test-takers will realize that many problems can be solved without doing any calculations at all (mental, written, or with a calculator); they will solve those problems in less time than it takes to pick a calculator up. On the other hand, if you are less confident about your mathematical ability or your test-taking skills, you will probably find your calculator a useful tool.

**NOTE:** Throughout this book, this icon 📱 will be placed next to a problem where some students may find it useful to use a calculator. As you will see, this judgment is very subjective. Sometimes a question can be answered in a few seconds with no calculations whatsoever, *if* you see the best approach. In that case, the use of a calculator would *not* be recommended. If you don't see the easy way, however, and have to do some arithmetic, you may prefer to use a calculator.

Let's look at two sample questions on which some students would use calculators frequently, others less frequently, and still others not at all.

## EXAMPLE 1

If $16 \times 25 \times 36 = (4a)^2$, what is the value of $a$?

(A) 6    (B) 15    (C) 30    (D) 36    (E) 60

 (i) Heavy calculator use: WITH A CALCULATOR multiply: $16 \times 25 \times 36 = 14400$. Observe that $(4a)^2 = 16a^2$, and so $16a^2 = 14,400$. WITH A CALCULATOR divide: $a^2 = 14,400 \div 16 = 900$. Finally, WITH A CALCULATOR take the square root: $a = \sqrt{900} = 30$. The answer is C.

 (ii) Light calculator use: Immediately notice that you can "cancel" the 16 on the left-hand side with the $4^2$ on the right-hand side. WITH A CALCULATOR: multiply $25 \times 36 = 900$, and WITH A CALCULATOR take the square root of 900.

(iii) No calculator use: Cancel the 16 and the $4^2$. Notice that $25 = 5^2$ and $36 = 6^2$; so $a^2 = 5^2 \times 6^2 = 30^2$, and $a = 30$.

## EXAMPLE 2 (GRID-IN)

If the length of a diagonal of a rectangle is 15, and if one of the sides is 9, what is the perimeter?

Whether or not you intend to use your calculator, the first thing to do is to draw a diagram.

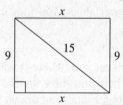

 (i) Heavy calculator use: By the Pythagorean theorem, $x^2 + 9^2 = 15^2$. Observe that $9^2 = 81$, and WITH A CALCULATOR evaluate: $15^2 = 225$. Then WITH A CALCULATOR subtract: $225 - 81 = 144$. So, $x^2 = 144$. Hit the square root key on your calculator to get $x = 12$. Finally, WITH A CALCULATOR add to find the perimeter: $9 + 12 + 9 + 12 = 42$.

 (ii) Light calculator use: Everything is the same as in (i) except *some* of the calculations can be done mentally: finding the square root of 144 and adding to find the perimeter.

(iii) No calculator use: *All of the calculations* are done mentally, or, better yet, *no calculations are done at all*, because you immediately see that each half of the rectangle is a 9-12-15 right triangle (a 3-4-5 right triangle in which each side was multiplied by 3), and you add up the sides in your head.

HELPFUL HINT

In general, you should do very little arithmetic using paper and pencil. If you can't do it mentally, use your calculator. In particular, avoid long division and multiplication in which the factors have two or more digits. If you know that $15^2 = 225$, terrific; if not, it is better to use your calculator than to multiply with paper and pencil.

Here are three final comments on the use of calculators:

1. The reason that calculators are of limited value on the PSAT is that no calculator can *do* mathematics. *You* have to know the mathematics and the way to apply it. A calculator cannot tell you whether to multiply or divide or that on a particular question you should use the Pythagorean theorem.
2. No PSAT problem ever requires tedious calculations. However, if you don't see how to avoid calculating, just do it—*don't spend a lot of time looking for a shortcut that will save you a little time!*
3. Most students use calculators more than they should, but if you can solve a problem with a calculator that you might otherwise miss, use the calculator.

## DIRECTIONS FOR MATHEMATICS SECTIONS

On the first page of Section 2 (the first math section), you will see the following instructions for multiple-choice questions.

---

### Multiple-Choice Directions

For each question in this section, determine which of the five choices is correct and blacken that choice on your answer sheet. You may use any blank space on the page for your work.

NOTES:
- You may use a calculator whenever you believe it will be helpful.
- Use the diagrams provided to help you solve the problems. Unless you see the phrase

  Note: Figure not drawn to scale

  under a diagram, it has been drawn as accurately as possible. Unless it is stated that a figure is three dimensional, you may assume that it lies in a plane.

---

On the first page of Section 4 (the second math section), you will see the same directions for questions 21–28.

In the middle of Section 4 of your PSAT, you will see the following directions for handling questions 29–38, the student-produced response questions, the only questions on the PSAT that are not multiple-choice. Because the answers to these questions are entered in special grids, they are usually referred to as grid-in questions.

## Student-Produced Response Directions

In questions 29–38, first solve the problem, and then enter your answer on the grid provided on the answer sheet. The instructions for entering your answers follow.

- First, write your answer in the boxes at the top of the grid.
- Second, grid your answer in the columns below the boxes.
- Use the fraction bar in the first row or the decimal point in the second row to enter fractions and decimals.

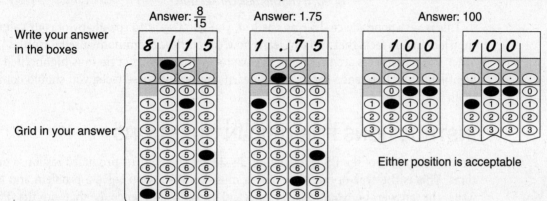

Answer: $\frac{8}{15}$     Answer: 1.75     Answer: 100

Write your answer in the boxes

Grid in your answer

Either position is acceptable

- Grid only one space in each column.
- Entering the answer in the boxes is recommended as an aid in gridding but is not required.
- The machine scoring your exam can read only what you grid, so you **must grid-in your answers correctly to get credit.**
- If a question has more than one correct answer, grid-in only one of them.
- The grid does not have a minus sign; so no answer can be negative.
- A mixed number *must* be converted to an improper fraction or a decimal before it is gridded. Enter $1\frac{1}{4}$ as $\frac{5}{4}$ or 1.25; the machine will interpret 11/4 as $\frac{11}{4}$ and mark it wrong.

- **All decimals must be entered as accurately as possible.** Here are three acceptable ways of gridding

$$\frac{3}{11} = 0.272727\ldots$$

- Note that rounding to .273 is acceptable because you are using the full grid, but you would receive **no credit** for .3 or .27, because they are less accurate.

In addition to the directions for multiple-choice questions, the first page of each math section has a box labeled "Reference" that contains the following mathematical facts:

## Reference

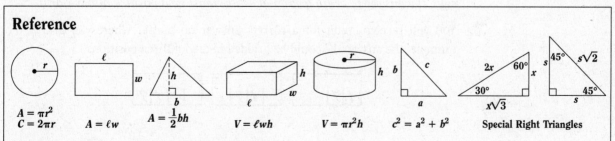

$A = \pi r^2$
$C = 2\pi r$      $A = \ell w$      $A = \frac{1}{2}bh$      $V = \ell wh$      $V = \pi r^2 h$      $c^2 = a^2 + b^2$      **Special Right Triangles**

Number of degrees of arc in a circle: 360
Sum of the measures, in degrees, of the angles of a triangle: 180

Many books advise that since these formulas are printed in the exam booklet, students can always look them up as needed and, therefore, don't have to learn or review them. Even the College Board's official guide, *SAT Preparation Booklet*, states:

> *The test doesn't require you to memorize formulas. Commonly used formulas are provided in the test booklet at the beginning of each mathematical section.*

This is very poor advice. During the test, you don't want to spend any of your valuable time looking up facts that you can learn now. All of these "commonly used formulas" and other important facts are presented in Chapter 7, where each of them is highlighted and identified as a "Reference Fact." As you learn and review these facts, you should commit them to memory.

## INSTRUCTIONS FOR GRID-IN QUESTIONS

On the math part of the PSAT, questions 29–38 are the student-produced response questions. This is the type of question that is most familiar—you solve a problem and then write the answer on your answer sheet. The only difference is that on the PSAT, *after* you write the answer on your answer sheet, you must then enter the answer on a special grid that can be read by a computer. For this reason, these questions are usually referred to as grid-ins.

To be sure you get credit for these questions, you need to know the guidelines for gridding-in your answers. Not all of this information is given in the directions printed in the exam booklet; so you should carefully read each of the ten rules below.

Your answer sheet will have ten grids, one for each question. Each one will look like the grid shown here. After solving a problem, the first step is to write the answer in the four boxes at the top of the grid. You then blacken the appropriate space under each box. For example, if your answer to a question is 2450, you write 2450 at the top of the grid, one digit in each box, and then in each column blacken the space that contains the number you wrote at the top of the column. This is not difficult, but there are some special rules concerning grid-in questions; so let's go over them before you practice gridding-in some numbers.

1. The only symbols that appear in the grid are the digits 0 to 9, a decimal point, and a slash (/), used to write fractions. Keep in mind that, since there is no negative sign, *the answer to every grid-in question must be a positive number or 0.*

2. You will receive credit for a correct answer no matter where you grid it. For example, the answer 17 could be gridded in any of three positions:

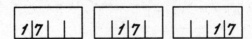

Nevertheless, we suggest that you consistently *write all your answers* the way numbers are usually displayed—*to the right, with blank spaces at the left*.

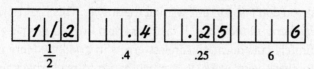

$$\frac{1}{2} \qquad .4 \qquad .25 \qquad 6$$

**3.** *Never round off your answers.* If a decimal answer will fit in the grid and you round it off, your answer will be marked wrong. For example, if the answer is .148 and you rounded it to the nearest hundredth and entered .15, you would receive *no credit*. If a decimal answer will not fit in the grid, enter a decimal point in the first column, followed by the first three digits. For example, if your answer is 0.373737 . . . , enter it as .373. You would receive credit if you rounded it to .374, but don't. You might occasionally make a mistake in rounding, whereas you'll *never* make a mistake if you just copy the first three digits. **Note:** If the correct answer has more than two decimal digits, *you must use all four columns of the grid.*

**4.** *Never write a 0 before the decimal point.* The first column of the grid doesn't even have a 0 in it. If the correct answer is 0.3333 . . . , you must grid it as .333. You can't grid 0.33, and 0.3 is not accurate enough.

**5.** *Never simplify fractions.*
- If your answer is a fraction that will fit in the grid, such as $\frac{2}{3}$ or $\frac{4}{18}$ or $\frac{6}{34}$, *just enter it*. Don't waste time reducing it or converting it to a decimal.
- If your answer is a fraction that won't fit in the grid, do not attempt to reduce it; use your calculator to *convert it to a decimal*. For example, $\frac{24}{65}$ won't fit in a grid; it would require five spaces: 2 4 / 6 5. Do not waste even a few seconds trying to reduce it; just divide on your calculator, and enter .369. Unlike $\frac{24}{65}$, the fraction $\frac{24}{64}$ *can be reduced*—to $\frac{12}{32}$, which doesn't help, or to $\frac{6}{16}$ or $\frac{3}{8}$, both of which could be entered. *Don't do it!* It takes time, and you might make a mistake. You won't make a mistake if you just use your calculator: 24 ÷ 64 = .375.

**6.** *Be aware that you can never enter a mixed number.* If your answer is $2\frac{1}{2}$, you *cannot* leave a space and enter it as 2 1/2. Also if you enter 2 1 / 2, the machine will read it as $\frac{21}{2}$ and mark it wrong. You must enter $2\frac{1}{2}$ as the improper fraction $\frac{5}{2}$ or as the decimal 2.5.

**7.** Sometimes grid-in questions have more than one correct answer. On these questions you are to *grid-in only one of the acceptable answers*. For example, if a question asked for a positive number less than 100 which was divisible by both 5 and 7, you could enter *either* 35 *or* 70, but not both.

**8.** There is no penalty for a wrong answer to a grid-in question. Therefore, you might as well guess.

**9.** Be sure to *grid every answer carefully*. The computer does not read what you have written in the boxes; it reads only the answer in the grid. If the correct answer to a question is 100 and you write 100 in the boxes but accidentally grid-in 200, you get *no* credit.

**10.** If you know that the answer to a question is 100, can you just grid it in and not bother writing it on top? Yes, you will get full credit, and so some books recommend that you don't waste time writing the answer. This is terrible advice. Instead, *write each answer in the boxes.* It takes less than two seconds per answer to do this, and it definitely cuts down on careless errors in gridding. More important, if you go back to check your work, it is much easier to read what's in the boxes than what's in the grid.

Now, check your understanding of these guidelines. Use the empty grids below to enter each of the following numbers.

1. 123

2. $\frac{7}{11}$

3. $2\frac{3}{4}$

4. $\frac{8}{30}$

5. 0

6. $\frac{48}{80}$

7. 1.1111 . . .

8. $\frac{19}{15}$

**Solutions.** Each grid contains the answer we recommend. Other acceptable answers, if any, are written below each grid.

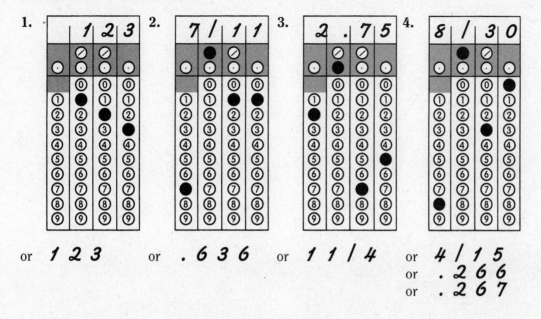

1. or *1 2 3*

2. or *.6 3 6*

3. or *1 1 / 4*

4. or *4 / 1 5*
   or *.2 6 6*
   or *.2 6 7*

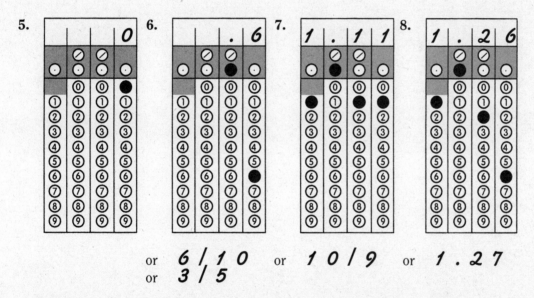

5.

6. or *6 / 1 0*
   or *3 / 5*

7. or *1 0 / 9*

8. or *1 . 2 7*

If you missed even one of these, go back and reread the rules on gridding. *You never want to have a correct answer and get no credit because you didn't grid it properly.* When you do the grid-in problems on the practice PSATs in this book, actually grid in the answers. Make sure you understand all of these rules *now*. When you actually take the PSAT, don't even look at the gridding instructions.

# Tactics and Strategies

## CHAPTER 6

*In this chapter you will learn important strategies to help you answer both the multiple-choice and grid-in questions on the PSAT. However, as invaluable as these tactics are, use them only when you need them.* If you know how to solve a problem and are confident that you can do so accurately and reasonably quickly, JUST DO IT!

## TACTIC
### 6-1  Test the choices, starting with C

**TACTIC 6-1**, often called *backsolving*, is useful when you are asked to solve for an unknown and you understand what needs to be done to answer the question but you want to avoid doing the algebra. The idea is simple: Test the various choices to see which one is correct.

**NOTE:** On the PSAT the answers to virtually all numerical multiple-choice questions are listed in either increasing or decreasing order. Consequently, Choice C is the middle value, and in applying **TACTIC 6-1**, *you should always start with Choice C.* For example, assume that Choices A, B, C, D, and E are given in increasing order. Try Choice C. If it works, you've found the answer. If Choice C doesn't work, you should know whether you need to test a larger number or a smaller one, and that information permits you to eliminate two more choices. If Choice C is too small, you need a larger number, and so Choices A and B are out; if Choice C is too big, eliminate Choices D and E, which are even larger.

Examples 1 and 2 illustrate the proper use of **TACTIC 6-1**.

## EXAMPLE 1

If the average (arithmetic mean) of 5, 6, 7, and $x$ is 10, what is the value of $x$?

(A) 8
(B) 13
(C) 18
(D) 22
(E) 28

**Solution.** Use **TACTIC 6-1**. Test Choice C: $x = 18$.

- Is the average of 5, 6, 7, and 18 equal to 10?
- No: $\frac{5 + 6 + 7 + 18}{4} = \frac{36}{4} = 9$, which is *too small*.
- Eliminate Choice C, and, since for the average to be 10, $x$ must be *greater* than 18, eliminate Choices A and B, as well.

- Try Choice D: $x = 22$. Is the average of 5, 6, 7, and 22, equal to 10?
- Yes: $\frac{5 + 6 + 7 + 22}{4} = \frac{40}{4} = 10$. The answer is Choice D.

Remember that every problem that can be solved using **TACTIC 6-1** can be solved directly, usually in less time. Therefore, we again stress: *If you are confident that you can solve a problem quickly and accurately, just do so.*

Many students would find the following direct solution faster than backsolving:

$$\frac{5 + 6 + 7 + x}{4} = 10 \Rightarrow 5 + 6 + 7 + x = 40 \Rightarrow$$
$$18 + x = 40 \Rightarrow x = 22$$

If you can quickly and accurately do the above algebra, then do so; if you are uncomfortable with the algebra, then just backsolve, and save **TACTIC 6-1** for those problems that you can't easily solve directly.

## EXAMPLE 2

Judy is now twice as old as Adam, but six years ago, she was five times as old as he was. How old is Judy now?

(A) 8
(B) 16
(C) 20
(D) 24
(E) 32

**Solution.** Use **TACTIC 6-1** and backsolve starting with Choice C. If Judy is now 20, Adam is 10, and six years ago, they would have been 14 and 4. Since Judy would have been less than five times as old as Adam, eliminate Choices C, D, and E, and try a smaller value. If Judy is now 16, Adam is 8; six years ago, they would have been 10 and 2. That's it; 10 *is* five times 2. The answer is Choice B. (See Example 4 in Section 7-H on word problems for the correct algebraic solution.)

Some tactics allow you to eliminate a few choices so that you can make an educated guess. On those problems where it can be used, **TACTIC 6-1** *always* gets you the right answer. The only reason not to use it on a particular problem is that you can *easily* solve the problem directly.

TACTIC
6-2    **Replace variables with numbers**

Mastery of **TACTIC 6-2** is critical for anyone developing good test-taking skills. This tactic can be used whenever the five choices involve the variables in the question. There are three steps:

1. Replace each letter with an easy-to-use number.
2. Solve the problem using those numbers.
3. Evaluate each of the five choices with the numbers you chose to see which choice is equal to the answer you obtained.

Examples 3 and 4 illustrate the proper use of **TACTIC 6-2**.

## EXAMPLE 3

If $a$ is equal to the sum of $b$ and $c$, which of the following is equal to the difference of $b$ and $c$?

(A) $a - b - c$
(B) $a - b + c$
(C) $a - c$
(D) $a - 2c$
(E) $a - b - 2c$

**Solution.**

- Choose three easy-to-use numbers that satisfy $a = b + c$: for example, $a = 5$, $b = 3$, $c = 2$.
- Then, solve the problem with these numbers: the difference of $b$ and $c$ is $3 - 2 = 1$.
- Finally, check each of the five choices to see which one is equal to 1:
  - (A) Does $a - b - c = 1$?      No.    $5 - 3 - 2 = 0$
  - (B) Does $a - b + c = 1$?      No.    $5 - 3 + 2 = 4$
  - (C) Does $a - c = 1$?          No.    $5 - 2 = 3$
  - (D) Does $a - 2c = 1$?         Yes!   $5 - 2(2) = 5 - 4 = 1$
  - (E) Does $a - b - 2c = 1$?     No.    $5 - 3 - 2(2) = 2 - 4 = -2$
- The answer is Choice D.

## EXAMPLE 4

If the sum of five consecutive even integers is $t$, then, in terms of $t$, what is the greatest of these integers?

(A) $\frac{t - 20}{5}$

(B) $\frac{t - 10}{5}$

(C) $\frac{t}{5}$

(D) $\frac{t + 10}{5}$

(E) $\frac{t + 20}{5}$

**Solution.**

- Choose five easy-to-use consecutive even integers: 2, 4, 6, 8, 10. Then their sum, $t$, is 30.
- Solve the problem with these numbers: the greatest of these integers is 10.
- When $t = 30$, the five choices are $\frac{10}{5}, \frac{20}{5}, \frac{30}{5}, \frac{40}{5}, \frac{50}{5}$.
- Only $\frac{50}{5}$, Choice E, is equal to 10.

Of course, if your algebra skills are good, Examples 3 and 4 can be solved without using **TACTIC 6-2**. The important point is that if you are uncomfortable with the correct algebraic solution, you don't have to omit these questions. You can use **TACTIC 6-2** and *always* get the correct answer.

Example 5 is somewhat different. You are asked to reason through a word problem involving only variables. Most students find problems like

**HELPFUL HINT** Replace the letters with numbers that are easy to use, not necessarily ones that make sense. It is perfectly OK to ignore reality. A school can have 2 students, apples can cost 10 dollars each, trains can go 5 miles per hour or 1000 miles per hour—it doesn't matter.

this one mind-boggling. Here, the use of **TACTIC 6-2** is essential. Without it, most students would find Example 5 very difficult, if not impossible.

---

### EXAMPLE 5

A vendor sells $h$ hot dogs and $s$ sodas. If a hot dog costs twice as much as a soda, and if the vendor takes in a total of $d$ dollars, how many *cents* does a soda cost?

(A) $\frac{100d}{s+2h}$

(B) $\frac{s+2h}{100d}$

(C) $\frac{100}{d(s+2h)}$

(D) $100d(s+2h)$

(E) $\frac{d}{100(s+2h)}$

**Solution.**

- Replace $h$, $s$, and $d$ with three easy-to-use numbers. Suppose a soda costs 50¢ and a hot dog $1.00. Then if he sold 2 sodas and 3 hot dogs, he took in $4.00.
- Which of the choices equals 50 when $s = 2$, $h = 3$, and $d = 4$?
- Only Choice A: $\frac{100(4)}{2+2(3)} = \frac{400}{8} = 50$.

 Of course, when you check the choices, you should use your calculator whenever necessary. However, you do not need to determine the value of each choice; you only need to know if it is the correct choice. In Example 5, Choices B and E are small fractions and could not possibly equal 50, and Choice D is clearly greater than 50; so don't waste your time evaluating them. Only Choices A and C are even possible.

---

TACTIC

## 6-3    Choose an appropriate number

**TACTIC 6-3** is similar to **TACTIC 6-2**, in that we pick convenient numbers. However, no variable is given in the problem. **TACTIC 6-3** is especially useful in problems involving fractions, ratios, and percents.

---

### EXAMPLE 6

On a certain college committee, $\frac{2}{3}$ of the members are female and $\frac{3}{8}$ of the females are varsity athletes. If $\frac{3}{5}$ of the committee members are not varsity athletes, what fraction of the members of the committee are male varsity athletes?

(A) $\frac{3}{20}$

(B) $\frac{11}{60}$

(C) $\frac{1}{4}$

(D) $\frac{2}{5}$

(E) $\frac{5}{12}$

 In problems involving fractions, the best number to use is the least common denominator of all the fractions. In problems involving percents, the easiest number to use is 100.

**Solution.** Since the lowest common denominator (LCD) of the three fractions is 120, assume that the committee has 120 members. Then there are $\frac{2}{3} \times 120 = 80$ females. Of the 80 females, $\frac{3}{8} \times 80 = 30$ are varsity athletes. Since $\frac{3}{5} \times 120 = 72$ committee members are not varsity athletes, then $120 - 72 = 48$ are varsity athletes; of these, 30 are female and the other 18 are male. Finally, the fraction of the members of the committee who are male varsity athletes is $\frac{18}{120} = \frac{3}{20}$ (Choice A).

## EXAMPLE 7

From 1995 to 2000 the sales of a book decreased by 80%. If the sales in 2005 were the same as in 1995, by what percent did they increase from 2000 to 2005?

(A) 80%
(B) 100%
(C) 120%
(D) 400%
(E) 500%

**Solution.** Since this problem involves percents, assume that 100 copies of the book were sold in 1995 (and 2005). Sales dropped by 80 (80% of 100) to 20 in 2000 and then increased by 80, from 20 back to 100, in 2005. By **KEY FACT C5**, the percent increase was

$$\frac{\text{the actual increase}}{\text{the original amount}} \times 100\% = \frac{80}{20} \times 100\% = 400\% \text{ (Choice D).}$$

**TACTIC**

**6-4**  **Eliminate absurd choices and guess**

When you have no idea how to solve a problem, eliminate all the absurd choices and guess from among the remaining ones.

During the course of a PSAT, you will probably find at least a few multiple-choice questions that you read but have no idea how to solve. *Do not automatically omit these questions!* Often two or three of the answers are absurd. Eliminate them and *guess*. Occasionally, four of the choices are absurd. When this occurs, your answer is no longer a guess.

What makes a choice absurd? Here are a few things to note. Even if you don't know how to solve a problem, you may realize that

- the answer must be positive, but some of the choices are negative.
- the answer must be even, but some of the choices are odd.
- a ratio must be less than 1, but some choices are greater than or equal to 1.

Let's look at five examples. In some of them the information given is intentionally insufficient to solve the problem, but you will still be able to determine that some of the answers are absurd. Even when there is enough information to solve the problem, don't. Rather, see if you can determine which choices are absurd and should therefore be eliminated.

## EXAMPLE 8

A region inside a semicircle of radius $r$ is shaded. What is its area?

(A) $\frac{1}{4}\pi r^2$

(B) $\frac{1}{3}\pi r^2$

(C) $\frac{1}{2}\pi r^2$

(D) $\frac{2}{3}\pi r^2$

(E) $\frac{3}{4}\pi r^2$

**Solution.** Even if you have no idea how to find the area of the shaded region, you should know that since the area of a circle is $\pi r^2$, the area of a semicircle is $\frac{1}{2}\pi r^2$. So the area of the shaded region must be *less than* $\frac{1}{2}\pi r^2$. Eliminate Choices C, D, and E. On an actual problem, if the diagram is drawn to scale, you may be able to make an educated guess between Choices A and B. If not, just choose one or the other.

## EXAMPLE 9

The average of 5, 10, 15, and $x$ is 20. What is $x$?

(A) 0

(B) 20

(C) 25

(D) 45

(E) 50

**Solution.** If the average of four numbers is 20, and three of them are less than 20, the other one must be greater than 20. Eliminate Choices A and B and guess. If you further realize that since 5 and 10 are *a lot* less than 20, $x$ will be *a lot* more than 20, then eliminate Choice C, as well.

## EXAMPLE 10

A prize of $27,000 is to be divided in some ratio among three people. What is the largest share?

(A) $18,900

(B) $13,500

(C) $8100

(D) $5400

(E) $2700

**Solution.** If the prize were divided equally, each share would be worth $9000. If it is divided unequally, the largest share must be *more than* $9000; so eliminate Choices C, D, and E. In an actual question, you would be told what the ratio is, and that information might enable you to eliminate Choice A or Choice B. If not, you would just guess.

## EXAMPLE 11

A jar contains only red and blue marbles. The ratio of the number of red marbles to the number of blue marbles is 5:3. What percent of the marbles are blue?

(A) 37.5%
(B) 50%
(C) 60%
(D) 62.5%
(E) 80%

**Solution.** Since there are 5 red marbles for every 3 blue ones, there are fewer blue ones than red ones. Therefore, *fewer than half* (50%) of the marbles are blue. Eliminate Choices B, C, D, and E. The answer is Choice A.

## EXAMPLE 12

Square *WXYZ* is divided into two unequal regions. If *WX* = 4, which of the following could be the area of the larger region?

(A) $8\pi$
(B) $8\pi - 32$
(C) $16 - 8\pi$
(D) $32 - 8\pi$
(E) $8\pi - 16$

**Solution.** Since the area of the square is 16, the area of the larger region must be more than 8. Since $\pi$ is slightly more than 3, $8\pi$ (which appears in each choice) is somewhat more than 24, approximately 25. Check the choices:

- (A) $8\pi \approx 25$, which is more than the area of the whole square.
- (B) $8\pi - 32$ is negative. Clearly impossible!
- (C) $16 - 8\pi$ is also negative.
- (D) $32 - 8\pi \approx 7$, which is too small.
- (E) $8\pi - 16 \approx 9$. The answer must be E.

## TACTIC
## 6-5   Draw a diagram

On any geometry question for which a figure is not provided, draw one (as accurately as possible) in your test booklet. Often looking at the diagram will lead you to the correct method. Sometimes, as in Example 13 on the following page, a careful examination of the diagram is sufficient to actually determine the correct answer.

## EXAMPLE 13

A rectangle is 7 times as long as it is wide. If the width is *w*, what is the length of a diagonal?

(A) $2w\sqrt{5}$

(B) $5w\sqrt{2}$

(C) $7w$

(D) $8w$

(E) $50w$

**Solution.** First draw a rectangle that is 7 times as large as it is wide. (By marking off 7 widths, you should be able to do this quite accurately.) Then draw in a diagonal.

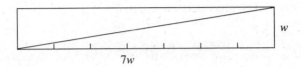

You probably realize that you can use the Pythagorean theorem to find the length of the diagonal, but by looking at the diagram, you should see that the diagonal is just slightly larger than the length, $7w$. Now check each answer choice using your calculator when necessary. Clearly, the answer is not $7w$, and $50w$ is way too big. Eliminate Choices C and E. Even Choice D, $8w$, is probably too big, but don't eliminate it until you use your calculator to test Choices A and B. $2\sqrt{5} \approx 4.5$, which is clearly too small; $5\sqrt{2} \approx 7.07$, which looks just right. Choose Choice B.

**TACTIC**

**6-6**  Use diagrams wisely. If a diagram is drawn to scale, trust it.

Remember that every diagram that appears on the PSAT has been drawn as accurately as possible, *unless* you see "<u>Note</u>: Figure not drawn to scale."

In figures that are drawn to scale, the following are true: line segments that appear to be the same length, *are* the same length; if an angle clearly looks obtuse, it *is* obtuse; and if one angle appears larger than another, you may assume that it *is* larger.

Examples 14, 15, and 16 below all contain diagrams that have been drawn to scale. Of course, each of these relatively easy examples has a correct mathematical solution, but for practice use **TACTIC 6-6** to eliminate as many choices as possible by simply looking at the given diagram.

On the PSAT, if you know how to solve a geometry problem, just do it. However, if you don't know how and if there is a diagram that has been drawn to scale, do not leave it out. Trusting the diagram to be accurate, you can always eliminate some of the choices and make an educated guess.

## EXAMPLE 14

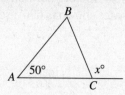

If in the figure above $AB = AC$, what is the value of $x$?

(A) 135
(B) 125
(C) 115
(D) 65
(E) 50

**Solution.** Clearly, the angle is obtuse; so $x$ is greater than 90, and so you can immediately eliminate Choices D and E. You can "measure" $x$ more accurately by drawing a couple of lines in the diagram. Draw in $\overline{DC}$ perpendicular to $\overline{AC}$. Then, $x = 90°$ plus the measure of $\angle DCB$. To estimate the measure of $\angle DCB$, draw in $\overline{EC}$, which bisects $\angle ACD$, a 90° angle. This creates angle $ECD$, a 45° angle, and it is clear that the measure of $\angle DCB$ is about half of that, say 23°. So, $x$ is about $90 + 23 = 113$. The answer must be Choice C, 115.

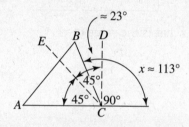

## EXAMPLE 15

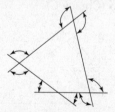

In the figure above, what is the sum of the measures of all the marked angles?

(A) 360°
(B) 540°
(C) 720°
(D) 900°
(E) 1080°

**Solution.** Make your best estimate of each angle and add them up. The five choices are so far apart that even if you're off by 15° or more on some of the angles, you'll get the right answer. The sum of the estimates shown is 690°; so the correct answer *must* be 720° (Choice C).

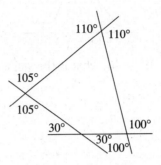

---

## EXAMPLE 16

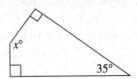

In the figure above, what is the value of *x*?

(A) 120
(B) 130
(C) 145
(D) 160
(E) 175

**Solution.** Since the diagram is drawn to scale, trust it. Look at *x*: it appears to be *about* 90 + 50 = 140; it is *definitely* less than 160. Also, *y* is clearly less than 45; so *x* is greater than 135. The answer must be 145 (Choice C).

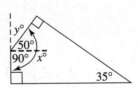

TACTIC
**6-7**
## Use diagrams wisely. If a diagram is not drawn to scale, redraw it to scale.

In figures that are not drawn to scale, make *no* assumptions. Lines that look parallel might not be; an angle that appears to be obtuse, might, in fact, be acute; two line segments might have the same length even though one looks twice as long as the other.

In the examples illustrating **TACTIC 6-6**, all of the diagrams were drawn to scale, and we were able to use the diagrams to our advantage. When diagrams have not been drawn to scale, you must be more careful.

 **HELPFUL HINT** In order to redraw a diagram to scale, ask yourself, "What is wrong with the original diagram?" If an angle is marked 45°, but in the figure it looks like a 75° angle, redraw it. If two line segments appear to be parallel, but you have not been told that they are, redraw them so that they are clearly not parallel. If two segments appear to have the same length, but one is marked 5 and the other 10, redraw them so that the second segment is twice as long as the first.

## EXAMPLE 17

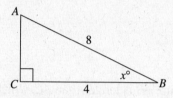

Note: Figure not drawn to scale

In △*ABC*, what is the value of *x*?

(A) 15
(B) 30
(C) 45
(D) 60
(E) 75

**Solution.** In what way is this figure not drawn to scale? $AB = 8$ and $BC = 4$, but in the figure, *AB* is not nearly twice as long as *BC*. Although the figure is not drawn to scale, the square symbol at angle C indicates that angle C is a right angle. So draw a right triangle in which *AB is* twice as long as *BC*. Now you can see that *x* is about 60 (Choice D).

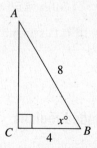

In fact, *x* is exactly 60. If the hypotenuse of a right triangle is twice the length of one of the legs, then the triangle is a 30-60-90 triangle, and the angle formed by the hypotenuse and that leg is 60° (See Section 7-J).

**EXAMPLE 18**

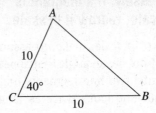

Note: Figure not drawn to scale

In the figure above, which of the following statements *could* be true?

    I.   $AB < AC$
   II.  $AB > AC$
  III.  Area of $\triangle ABC = 50$

  (A) None
  (B) I only
  (C) II only
  (D) I and III only
  (E) II and III only

**Solution.** In the given diagram, *AB* is longer than *AC*, which is 10. But, we know that we *cannot trust the diagram*. Actually, there are two things wrong: angle *C* is labeled 40° but looks much more like 60° or 70°, and *AC* and *BC* are each labeled 10, but *BC* is much longer. Redraw the triangle with a smaller angle and two sides of the same length.

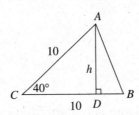

    Now just look: $\overline{AB}$ is clearly shorter than $\overline{AC}$. So I is true and II is false. If you draw in altitude $\overline{AD}$, it is also clear that *h* is less than 10.

$$A = \tfrac{1}{2}bh = \tfrac{1}{2}(10)h = 5h < 5 \times 10 = 50$$

The area must be less than 50. III is false. Only I is true (Choice B).

TACTIC
**6-8**   **Subtract to find shaded regions**

Whenever part of a figure is shaded and part is unshaded, the straightforward way to find the area of the shaded portion is to find the area of the entire figure and subtract from it the area of the unshaded region. Occasionally, you may see an easy way to calculate the shaded area directly, but usually you should subtract.

# EXAMPLE 19

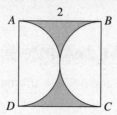

In the figure above, the shaded region is bounded by two semicircles and two sides of square *ABCD*. If $AB = 2$, what is the area of the shaded region?

(A) $4 - 2\pi$
(B) $4 - \pi$
(C) $4 + 2\pi$
(D) $16 - 4\pi$
(E) $4\pi - 16$

**Solution.** The entire region is a square whose area is 4. Since each semicircle has a diameter of 2 (hence a radius of 1), together they form a circle of radius 1. The area of such a circle is $\pi(1)^2 = \pi$. So, the area of the shaded region is $4 - \pi$ (Choice B).

## TACTIC
## 6-9  Add equations

When a question involves two equations, almost always the best strategy is to either add them or subtract. If there are three or more equations, just add them.

# EXAMPLE 20

If $4x + y = 23$ and $x - 2y = 8$, what is the average of $x$ and $y$?

(A) 0
(B) 2.5
(C) 3
(D) 3.5
(E) 5

 Usually, answering a question that involves two or more equations does not require you to solve them.

**Solution.** Add the two equations:

$$\begin{array}{r} 4x + y = 23 \\ + \quad x - 2y = 8 \\ \hline 5x - y = 31 \end{array}$$

This does not appear to help, so try subtracting the two equations:

$$\begin{array}{r} 4x + y = 23 \\ - \quad x - 2y = 8 \\ \hline 3x + 3y = 15 \end{array}$$

Divide each side by 3:

$$x + y = 5$$

The average of $x$ and $y$ is their sum divided by 2:

$$\frac{x + y}{2} = \frac{5}{2} = 2.5$$

The answer is Choice B.

**NOTE:** You *could have* actually solved for $x$ and $y$ [$x = 6, y = -1$] and then taken their average. However, that method would have been more time-consuming and unnecessary.

---
### EXAMPLE 21
---

If $a - b = 1, b - c = 2$, and $c - a = d$, what is the value of $d$?

(A) $-3$
(B) $-1$
(C) $1$
(D) $3$
(E) It cannot be determined from the information given.

**Solution.** Since there are more
than two equations, add them:

$$\begin{aligned} a - b &= 1 \\ b - c &= 2 \\ + \quad c - a &= d \\ \hline 0 &= 3 + d \Rightarrow d = -3 \end{aligned}$$

The answer is Choice A.

**TACTIC**

**6-10**  **Systematically make lists**

When a question asks "how many," often the best strategy is to make a list. If you do this it is important that you make the list in a *systematic* fashion so that you don't inadvertently leave something out. Often, shortly after starting the list, you can see a pattern developing and can figure out how many more entries there will be without writing them all down.

Listing things systematically means writing them in numerical order (if the entries are numbers) or in alphabetical order (if the entries are letters). If the answer to "how many" is a small number (as in Example 22), just list all possibilities. If the answer is a large number (as in Example 23), start the list and write enough entries until you see a pattern.

---
### EXAMPLE 22
---

The sum of three positive integers is 20. If one of them is 5, what is the greatest possible value of the product of the other two?

**Solution.** Since one of the integers is 5, the sum of the other two is 15. Systematically, list all possible pairs, $(a, b)$, of positive integers whose sum is 15, and check their products. First let $a = 1$, then 2, and so on.

| $a$ | $b$ | $ab$ |
|-----|-----|------|
| 1 | 14 | 14 |
| 2 | 13 | 26 |
| 3 | 12 | 36 |
| 4 | 11 | 44 |
| 5 | 10 | 50 |
| 6 | 9 | 54 |
| 7 | 8 | 56 |

The answer is 56.

---

## EXAMPLE 23

A palindrome is a number, such as 74,947, that reads the same forward and backward. How many palindromes are there between 200 and 800?

Don't list *all* the possibilities. STOP as soon as you see the pattern.

**Solution.** First, write down the numbers in the 200s that end in 2:

202, 212, 222, 232, 242, 252, 262, 272, 282, 292

Now write the numbers beginning and ending in 3:

303, 313, 323, 333, 343, 353, 363, 373, 383, 393

By now you should see the pattern: there are ten numbers beginning with a 2, ten beginning with 3, and there will be ten beginning with 4, 5, 6, and 7 for a total of $6 \times 10 = 60$ palindromes.

## TACTIC 6-11 Handle strange symbols properly

On almost all PSATs, there are a few questions that use symbols, such as: ⊕, □, ☺, ✠, or ✦, that you have never before seen in a mathematics problem. How can you answer such a question? Don't panic! It's easy—you are always told exactly what the symbol means! All you have to do is follow the directions carefully.

When there are two questions using the same symbol, the first question is usually easy and involves only numbers; the second is more difficult and usually contains variables.

Examples 24 and 25 refer to the following definition.

If $a$ and $b$ are unequal positive numbers, let the operation ☺ be defined by

$$a ☺ b = \frac{a + b}{a - b}$$

## EXAMPLE 24

What is the value of 6 ☺ 2?

(A) 2
(B) 3
(C) 4
(D) 8
(E) 12

**Solution.** The definition of ☺ tells us that whenever two numbers surround a "happy face," we are to form a fraction in which the numerator is their sum and the denominator is their difference. So, 6 ☺ 2 is the fraction whose numerator is $6 + 2 = 8$ and whose denominator is $6 - 2 = 4$: $\frac{8}{4} = 2$ (Choice A).

**EXAMPLE 25**

If $c \odot d = 3$, which of the following is true?

(A) $c = 3d$
(B) $c = 2d$
(C) $c = d$
(D) $d = 2c$
(E) $d = 3c$

**Solution.** $c \odot d = 3 \Rightarrow \dfrac{c + d}{c - d} = 3 \Rightarrow c + d = 3c - 3d \Rightarrow 4d = 2c \Rightarrow c = 2d$ (Choice B).

# Practice Exercises

None of these exercises *requires* the use of the tactics that you just learned. However, as you try each one, even if you know the correct mathematical solution, before solving it, think about which of the tactics could be used. An answer key follows the questions.

## MULTIPLE-CHOICE QUESTIONS

1. If the average (arithmetic mean) of 10, 20, 30, 40, and $a$ is 50, what is the value of $a$?

   (A) 50
   (B) 60
   (C) 100
   (D) 150
   (E) 250

2. Larry has 250 marbles, all red, white, and blue, in the ratio of $1:3:6$, respectively. How many blue marbles does he have?

   (A) 25
   (B) 75
   (C) 100
   (D) 125
   (E) 150

3. If $w$ whistles cost $c$ cents, how many whistles can you get for $d$ dollars?

   (A) $\frac{100dw}{c}$

   (B) $\frac{dw}{100c}$

   (C) $100cdw$

   (D) $\frac{dw}{c}$

   (E) $cdw$

4. If $x\%$ of $w$ is 10, what is $w$?

   (A) $\frac{10}{x}$

   (B) $\frac{100}{x}$

   (C) $\frac{1000}{x}$

   (D) $\frac{x}{100}$

   (E) $\frac{x}{10}$

5. If 8% of $c$ is equal to 12% of $d$, which of the following is equal to $c + d$?

   (A) $1.5d$
   (B) $2d$
   (C) $2.5d$
   (D) $3d$
   (E) $5d$

6. On a certain legislative committee consisting solely of Republicans and Democrats, $\frac{3}{8}$ of the committee members are Republicans. If $\frac{2}{3}$ of the members are men and $\frac{3}{5}$ of the men are Democrats, what fraction of the members are Democratic women?

   (A) $\frac{3}{20}$

   (B) $\frac{9}{40}$

   (C) $\frac{1}{4}$

   (D) $\frac{2}{5}$

   (E) $\frac{5}{12}$

7. Kim receives a commission of $25 for every $2,000 worth of merchandise she sells. What percent is her commission?

   (A) $1\frac{1}{4}\%$

   (B) $2\frac{1}{2}\%$

   (C) 5%

   (D) 25%

   (E) 125%

8. From 1990 to 1995, the value of one share of stock of *XYZ* corporation increased by 25%. If the value was $D$ dollars in 1995, what was the value in 1990?

   (A) $1.75D$
   (B) $1.25D$
   (C) $1.20D$
   (D) $.80D$
   (E) $.75D$

**9.** What is the value of $p$ if $p$ is positive and
$p \times p \times p = p + p + p$?

(A) $\frac{1}{3}$

(B) $\sqrt{3}$

(C) 3

(D) $3\sqrt{3}$

(E) 9

**10.** What is 4% of 5%?

(A) .09%

(B) .20%

(C) 2.0%

(D) 9%

(E) 20%

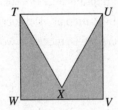

**11.** In the figure above, *TUVW* is a square and *TUX* is an equilateral triangle. If *VW* = 2, what is the area of the shaded region?

(A) $\sqrt{3}$

(B) 2

(C) 3

(D) $4 - 2\sqrt{3}$

(E) $4 - \sqrt{3}$

**12.** If $12a + 3b = 1$ and $7b - 2a = 9$, what is the average (arithmetic mean) of $a$ and $b$?

(A) 0.1

(B) 0.5

(C) 1

(D) 2.5

(E) 5

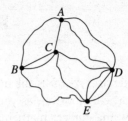

**13.** The map above shows all the roads connecting five towns. How many different ways are there to go from *A* to *E* if you may not return to a town after you leave it and you may not go through both *C* and *D*?

(A) 8

(B) 12

(C) 16

(D) 24

(E) 32

Questions 14–15 refer to the following definition.

For any numbers $a, b, c$  $a \bigstar b \bigstar c = abc - (a + b + c)$.

**14.** What is the value of $3 \bigstar 5 \bigstar 2$?

(A) 0

(B) 5

(C) 10

(D) 20

(E) 30

**15.** For what positive number $x$ is it true that $x \bigstar 2x \bigstar 3x = 0$?

(A) 0

(B) 1

(C) 2

(D) 3

(E) 6

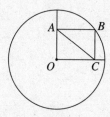

**16.** In the figure above, if the radius of circle $O$ is 10, what is the length of diagonal $AC$ of rectangle $OABC$?

(A) $\sqrt{2}$
(B) $\sqrt{10}$
(C) $5\sqrt{2}$
(D) $10$
(E) $10\sqrt{2}$

## GRID-IN QUESTIONS

**17.** What is the area of a rectangle whose length is twice its width and whose perimeter is equal to the perimeter of a square whose area is 1? _____

**18.** For how many integers between 1 and 1000 is at least one of the digits a 9? _____

## Answer Key

Next to the answer for each question is the number of the tactic that would be most helpful in answering the question, in the event that you do not see the direct solution.

**1.** D (TACTIC 6-1)

**2.** E (TACTIC 6-1)

**3.** A (TACTIC 6-2)

**4.** C (TACTIC 6-2)

**5.** C (TACTIC 6-3)

**6.** B (TACTIC 6-3)

**7.** A (TACTIC 6-4)

**8.** D (TACTIC 6-4)

**9.** B (TACTIC 6-1)

**10.** B (TACTIC 6-4)

**11.** E (TACTIC 6-8)

**12.** B (TACTIC 6-9)

**13.** B (TACTIC 6-10)

**14.** D (TACTIC 6-11)

**15.** B (TACTIC 6-11)

**16.** D (TACTIC 6-6)

**17.** $\frac{8}{9}$ (TACTIC 6-5)

**18.** 271 (TACTIC 6-10)

# Review of PSAT Mathematics

---

## Arithmetic

*To do well on the PSAT, you need to feel comfortable with most topics of basic arithmetic. The first five sections of Chapter 7 provide you with a review of the basic arithmetic operations, signed numbers, fractions and decimals, ratios, percents, and averages. Because you will have a calculator with you at the test, you will not have to do long division, multiply three-digit numbers, or perform any other tedious calculations using paper and pencil. If you use a calculator with fraction capabilities, you can even avoid finding least common denominators and reducing fractions.*

*The solutions to more than one-third of the math questions on the PSAT depend on your knowing the **KEY FACTS** in these sections. Be sure to review them all.*

## 7-A  BASIC ARITHMETIC CONCEPTS

A **set** is a collection of "things" that have been grouped together in some way. Those "things" are called the **elements** or **members**. For example:

If $A$ is the set of states in the United States, then California is an element of $A$.
If $B$ is the set of letters in the English alphabet, then $z$ is a member of $B$.
If $C$ is the set of even integers, then 46 is in $C$.

The **union** of two sets, $A$ and $B$, is the set consisting of all the elements that are in $A$ or $B$ or both. Note that this includes those elements that are in $A$ and $B$. The union is represented as $A \cup B$.

The **intersection** of two sets, $A$ and $B$, is the set consisting only of those elements that are in both $A$ and $B$. The intersection is represented as $A \cap B$.

In describing a set of numbers, we usually list the elements inside a pair of braces. For example, let A be the set of prime numbers less than 10, and let $B$ be the set of even positive integers less than 10.

$$A = \{2, 3, 5, 7\} \qquad B = \{2, 4, 6, 8\}$$
$$A \cup B = \{2, 3, 4, 5, 6, 7, 8\}$$
$$A \cap B = \{2\}$$

The **solution set** of an equation is the set of all numbers that satisfy the equation.

## EXAMPLE 1

If $C = \{-2, -1, 0, 1, 2\}$ and $D$ is the set that consists of the squares of each of the elements of $C$, how many numbers are elements of $D$?

**Solution.** 0 is in $D$ (since $0^2 = 0$); 1 is in $D$ (since $1^2 = 1$); and 4 is in $D$ (since $2^2 = 4$). These are the only elements of $D$; so $D$ has 3 elements. Note that $(-1)^2 = 1$ and $(-2)^2 = 4$, but we have already listed 1 and 4. $D = \{0, 1, 4\}$.

Let's start our review of arithmetic by reviewing the most important sets of numbers and their properties. On the PSAT the word *number* always means *real number*, a number that can be represented by a point on the number line.

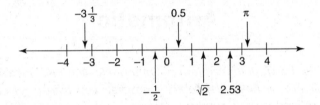

## Signed Numbers

The numbers to the right of 0 on the number line are called **positive** and those to the left of 0 are called **negative**. Note that 0 is neither positive nor negative. Negative numbers must be written with a *negative sign* ($-3$); positive numbers can be written with a *plus sign* ($+3$) but are usually written without a sign (3). All numbers can be called *signed numbers*.

The **absolute value** of a number $a$, denoted $|a|$, is the distance between $a$ and 0 on the number line. Since 5 is 5 units to the right of 0 on the number line and $-5$ is 5 units to the left of 0, both have an absolute value of 5:

$$|5| = 5 \quad \text{and} \quad |-5| = 5$$

## EXAMPLE 2

How many integers are solutions of the inequality $|x| < 5$?

(A) 0
(B) 4
(C) 8
(D) 9
(E) infinitely many

**Solution.** There are infinitely many *numbers* whose absolute value is less than 5, but only 9 of them are *integers*.

$$-4, -3, -2, -1, 0, 1, 2, 3, 4 \quad \text{(Choice D)}.$$

In arithmetic we are basically concerned with the addition, subtraction, multiplication, and division of numbers. The table below gives the terms for the results of these operations.

| Operation | Symbol | Result | Example | |
|---|---|---|---|---|
| Addition | + | *Sum* | 16 is the sum of 12 and 4 | $12 + 4 = 16$ |
| Subtraction | − | *Difference* | 8 is the difference of 12 and 4 | $12 - 4 = 8$ |
| Multiplication* | × | *Product* | 48 is the product of 12 and 4 | $12 \times 4 = 48$ |
| Division | ÷ | *Quotient* | 3 is the quotient of 12 and 4 | $12 \div 4 = 3$ |

*In certain situations, multiplication can also be indicated by a dot, parentheses, or the juxtaposition of symbols without any sign: $2^2 \cdot 2^4$, 3(4), 3(x + 2), 3a, 4abc.

Given any two numbers *a* and *b*, you can *always* find their sum, difference, product, and quotient (with a calculator, if necessary), but you can *never divide by zero.*

$$0 \div 7 = 0, \quad \text{but} \quad 7 \div 0 \text{ is meaningless}$$

## EXAMPLE 3

What is the sum of the product and quotient of 8 and 8?

**Solution.** Product: $8 \times 8 = 64$. Quotient: $8 \div 8 = 1$. Sum: $64 + 1 = 65$.

## Key Fact A1

For any number *a*: $a \times 0 = 0$. Conversely, if the product of two or more numbers is 0, *at least one* of them must be 0.

If $ab = 0$, then $a = 0$ or $b = 0$.
If $rst = 0$, then $r = 0$ or $s = 0$ or $t = 0$.

## EXAMPLE 4

What is the product of all the integers from −5 to 5, inclusive?

**Solution.** Before reaching for your calculator, look and think. You are asked for the product of eleven numbers, one of which is 0. So, by **KEY FACT A1**, the product is 0.

## Key Fact A2

The product and quotient of two positive numbers or two negative numbers is positive; the product and quotient of a positive number and a negative number is negative.

| | | | |
|---|---|---|---|
| $12 \times 2 = 24$ | $12 \times (-2) = -24$ | $(-12) \times 2 = -24$ | $(-12) \times (-2) = 24$ |
| $12 \div 2 = 6$ | $12 \div (-2) = -6$ | $(-12) \div 2 = -6$ | $(-12) \div (-2) = 6$ |

To determine whether a product of more than two numbers is positive or negative, count the number of negative factors.

### Key Fact A3

- The product of an *even* number of negative factors is positive.
- The product of an *odd* number of negative factors is negative.

### EXAMPLE 5

Which of the following are equal to $(-1)^{25}$?

  I. $(-1)^{100}$
 II. $-(1)^{100}$
III. $-(-1)^{100}$

(A) I only
(B) II only
(C) III only
(D) II and III only
(E) I, II, and III

**Solution.** Since 25 is odd and 100 is even, $(-1)^{25} = -1$, whereas $(-1)^{100} = 1$. (I is false.) Since $1^{100} = 1$, $-(1)^{100} = -1$. II is true. Since $(-1)^{100} = 1$, $-(-1)^{100} = -1$. III is true. Only II and III are true (Choice D).

### Key Fact A4

- The sum of two positive numbers is positive.
- The sum of two negative numbers is negative.

$$6 + 2 = 8 \quad (-6) + (-2) = -8$$

- To find the sum of a positive and a negative number, find the difference of their absolute values and use the sign of the number with the larger absolute value.

To calculate $6 + (-2)$ or $(-6) + 2$, take the *difference*, $6 - 2 = 4$, and use the sign of the number whose absolute value is 6:

$$6 + (-2) = 4 \quad (-6) + 2 = -4$$

### Key Fact A5

To subtract signed numbers, change the problem to an addition problem, by changing the sign of what is being subtracted, and use **KEY FACT A4**.

$$2 - 6 = 2 + (-6) = -4 \qquad 2 - (-6) = 2 + (6) = 8$$

$$(-2) - (-6) = (-2) + (6) = 4 \qquad (-2) - 6 = (-2) + (-6) = -8$$

In each case, the minus sign was changed to a plus sign, and either the 6 was changed to $-6$ or the $-6$ was changed to 6.

All arithmetic involving signed numbers can be accomplished on *any* calculator, but not all calculators handle negative numbers the same way. Be sure you know how to enter negative numbers and how to use them on *your* calculator. It is a good idea to always put negative numbers in parentheses.

## Integers

| | |
|---|---|
| The *integers* are | $\{\ldots, -4, -3, -2, -1, 0, 1, 2, 3, 4, \ldots\}$ |
| The *positive integers* are | $\{1, 2, 3, 4, 5, \ldots\}$ |
| The *negative integers* are | $\{\ldots, -5, -4, -3, -2, -1\}$ |

*Consecutive integers* are two or more integers written in sequence in which each integer is 1 more than the preceding one. For example:

 **CAUTION:** Never assume that *number* means *integer*: 3 is not the only number between 2 and 4—there are infinitely many,

$$22, 23 \qquad 6, 7, 8, 9$$

$$-2, -1, 0, 1 \qquad n, n + 1, n + 2, n + 3, \ldots$$

## EXAMPLE 6

If $0 < x < 3$ and $2 < y < 8$, what is the largest integer value of $x + y$?

**Solution.** If $x$ and $y$ are integers, the largest value of $x + y$ is $2 + 7 = 9$. However, even though $x + y$ is to be an integer, neither $x$ nor $y$ must be. If $x = 2.5$ and $y = 7.5$, then $x + y = 10$, which must be the largest integer value, since clearly $x + y < 11$.

The sum, difference, and product of two integers is *always* an integer; the quotient of two integers may be an integer, but not necessarily. The quotient $37 \div 10$ can be expressed as $\frac{37}{10}$ or $3\frac{7}{10}$ or 3.7. If the quotient is to be an integer, you can also say that the quotient is 3 and there is a *remainder* of 7. It depends upon your point of view. For example, if 37 pounds of rice is to be divided into 10 bags, each bag will hold 3.7 pounds; but if 37 books are to be divided among 10 people, each one will get 3 books and there will be 7 left over (the remainder).

To find the remainder when 100 is divided by 7, divide on your calculator: $100 \div 7 = 14.285714\ldots$ This tells you that the quotient is 14. Ignore everything to the right of the decimal point. To find the remainder, multiply: $14 \times 7 = 98$, and then subtract: $100 - 98 = 2$.

 The standard way to find quotients and remainders is to use long division. But on the PSAT, you should *never* do long division; you should use your calculators.

## EXAMPLE 7

If the remainder when $a$ is divided by 7 is 2 and the remainder when $b$ is divided by 7 is 4, what is the remainder when $ab$ is divided by 7?

(A) 0
(B) 1
(C) 3
(D) 6
(E) 8

**Solution.** *a* can be any number that is 2 more than a multiple of 7: 9, 16, 23, . . . . *b* can be any number that is 4 more than a multiple of 7: 11, 18, 25, . . . .

For simplicity, let *a* = 9 and *b* = 11. Then *ab* = 99, and when 99 is divided by 7, the quotient is 14 and the remainder is 1 (Choice B).

If *a* and *b* are integers, the following four terms are synonymous:

|                          |                        |
|--------------------------|------------------------|
| *a* is a **divisor** of *b* | *a* is a **factor** of *b* |
| *b* is **divisible** by *a* | *b* is a **multiple** of *a* |

All these statements mean that, when *b* is divided by *a*, there is no remainder (or, more precisely, the remainder is 0). For example:

|                          |                        |
|--------------------------|------------------------|
| 3 is a divisor of 12.    | 3 is a factor of 12.   |
| 12 is divisible by 3.    | 12 is a multiple of 3. |

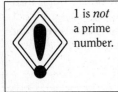

1 is *not* a prime number.

The only positive divisor of 1 is 1. All other positive integers have at least two positive divisors: 1 and itself, and possibly many more. For example, 6 is divisible by 1 and 6, as well as 2 and 3, whereas 7 is divisible only by 1 and 7. Positive integers, such as 7, which have *exactly two* positive divisors are called **prime numbers** or **primes**. Here are the first few primes:

$$2, 3, 5, 7, 11, 13, 17, 19, 23.$$

Memorize this list—it will come in handy. Note that 1 is *not* a prime.

### EXAMPLE 8

What is the sum of the largest prime factor of 26 and the largest prime factor of 28?

**Solution.**
The factors of 26 are 1, 2, 13, and 26. The largest *prime* factor is 13.
The factors of 28 are 1, 2, 4, 7, 14, and 28. The largest *prime* factor is 7.
The sum of 13 and 7 is 20.

The **even numbers** are all the integer multiples of 2: $\{\ldots, -4, -2, 0, 2, 4, 6, \ldots\}$
The **odd numbers** are the integers not divisible by 2: $\{\ldots, -5, -3, -1, 1, 3, 5, \ldots\}$

**NOTE**

0 is an even integer.

### Key Fact A6

1. If two integers are both even or both odd, their sum and difference are even.
2. If one integer is even and the other odd, their sum and difference are both odd.
3. The product of two integers is even unless both of them are odd.

## Exponents and Roots

Repeated addition of the same number is indicated by multiplication:

$$11 + 11 + 11 + 11 + 11 + 11 + 11 = 7 \times 11$$

Repeated multiplication of the same number is indicated by an exponent:

$$11 \times 11 \times 11 \times 11 \times 11 \times 11 \times 11 = 11^7$$

In the expression $11^7$, 11 is called the **base** and 7 is the **exponent**.

Although most of the exponents you will encounter on the PSAT are positive integers, you may occasionally see 0, negative integers, and rational numbers used as exponents. All of these are defined in the next **KEY FACT**.

### Key Fact A7

For any number $b$ and positive integer $n$:

- $b^0 = 1$
- $b^1 = b$
- $b^n = b \times b \times \ldots \times b$, where $b$ is used as a factor $n$ times
- $b^{-n} = \dfrac{1}{b^n}$
- $b^{\frac{1}{n}} = \sqrt[n]{b}$

For example,

$2^0 = 1$ $\qquad\qquad 2^1 = 2 \qquad\qquad 2^4 = 2 \times 2 \times 2 \times 2 = 16$

$2^{-4} = \dfrac{1}{2^4} = \dfrac{1}{16} \qquad 16^{\frac{1}{4}} = \sqrt[4]{16} = 2$

Now consider the following four calculations.

(i) $\quad 5^4 \times 5^3 = (5 \times 5 \times 5 \times 5) \times (5 \times 5 \times 5) = 5^7 = 5^{4+3}$

(ii) $\quad \dfrac{5^6}{5^4} = \dfrac{\cancel{5} \times \cancel{5} \times \cancel{5} \times \cancel{5} \times 5 \times 5}{\cancel{5} \times \cancel{5} \times \cancel{5} \times \cancel{5}_{\,1}} = 5 \times 5 = 5^2 = 5^{6-4}$

(iii) $\quad (5^2)^3 = (5 \times 5)^3 = (5 \times 5) \times (5 \times 5) \times (5 \times 5) = 5^6 = 5^{2 \times 3}$

(iv) $\quad 5^3 \times 6^3 = (5 \times 5 \times 5) \times (6 \times 6 \times 6) = (5 \times 6)(5 \times 6)(5 \times 6) = (5 \times 6)^3$

These four examples illustrate the following important laws of exponents.

### Key Fact A8

For any numbers $b$, $c$, $m$, and $n$:

(i) $b^m b^n = b^{m+n}$ $\quad$ (ii) $\dfrac{b^m}{b^n} = b^{m-n}$ $\quad$ (iii) $(b^m)^n = b^{mn}$ $\quad$ (iv) $b^m c^m = (bc)^m$

### EXAMPLE 9

If $5^a \times 5^b = 5^{50}$, what is the average (arithmetic mean) of $a$ and $b$?

**Solution.** Since $5^a \times 5^b = 5^{a+b}$, we see that $a + b = 50 \Rightarrow \dfrac{a+b}{2} = 25$.

### EXAMPLE 10

What is the value of $16^{\frac{3}{4}}$?

**Solution.** By **KEY FACT A8** (iii), $16^{\frac{3}{4}} = (16^{\frac{1}{4}})^3 = (\sqrt[4]{16})^3 = 2^3 = 8$.

## Squares and Square Roots

The exponent that appears most often on the PSAT is 2. It is used to form the square of a number, as in $\pi r^2$ (the area of a circle), $a^2 + b^2 = c^2$ (Pythagorean theorem), or $x^2 - y^2$ (the difference of two squares). Therefore, it is helpful to recognize the **perfect squares**, numbers that are the squares of integers. The squares of the integers from 0 to 15 are as follows:

| $x$ | 0 | 1 | 2 | 3 | 4 | 5 | 6 | 7 | 8 | 9 | 10 | 11 | 12 | 13 | 14 | 15 |
|-----|---|---|---|---|----|----|----|----|----|----|-----|-----|-----|-----|-----|-----|
| $x^2$ | 0 | 1 | 4 | 9 | 16 | 25 | 36 | 49 | 64 | 81 | 100 | 121 | 144 | 169 | 196 | 225 |

There are two numbers that satisfy the equation $x^2 = 4$: $x = 2$ and $x = -2$. The positive number, 2, is called the **principal square root** of 4 and is denoted by the symbol $\sqrt{4}$. Clearly, each perfect square has a square root: $\sqrt{0} = 0$, $\sqrt{16} = 4$, $\sqrt{49} = 7$, and $\sqrt{121} = 11$. It is an important fact, however, that *every* positive number has a square root.

### Key Fact A9

For any positive number $a$, there is a positive number $b$ that satisfies the equation $b^2 = a$. That number is called the principal square root of $a$ and is written $b = \sqrt{a}$. Therefore, for any positive number $a$: $\sqrt{a} \times \sqrt{a} = (\sqrt{a})^2 = a$.

The only difference between $\sqrt{4}$ and $\sqrt{5}$ is that $\sqrt{4}$ is an integer, whereas $\sqrt{5}$ is not. Since 5 is greater than 4, we know that $\sqrt{5}$ is greater than $\sqrt{4} = 2$. In fact, $(2.2)^2 = 4.84$, which is close to 5, and $(2.23)^2 = 4.9729$, which is very close to 5. So, $\sqrt{5} \approx 2.23$. Using the square root key on your calculator, you can find the value of any square root to several decimal places of accuracy, much more than you need for the PSAT.

### EXAMPLE 11

What is the circumference of a circle whose area is $10\pi$?

(A) $5\pi$

(B) $10\pi$

(C) $\pi\sqrt{10}$

(D) $2\pi\sqrt{10}$

(E) $\pi\sqrt{20}$

**Solution.** Since the area of a circle is given by the formula $A = \pi r^2$, we have

$$\pi r^2 = 10\pi \Rightarrow r^2 = 10 \Rightarrow r = \sqrt{10}.$$

The circumference is given by the formula $C = 2\pi r$, so $C = 2\pi\sqrt{10}$ (Choice D). (See Section 7-L on circles.)

# PEMDAS

When a calculation requires performing more than one operation, it is important to carry out the operations in the correct order. For decades students have memorized the sentence, "<u>P</u>lease <u>E</u>xcuse <u>M</u>y <u>D</u>ear <u>A</u>unt <u>S</u>ally," or just the first letters, PEMDAS, to remember the proper order of operations. The letters stand for:

 Every scientific and graphing calculator automatically follows PEMDAS, but to be sure of getting the right answer, you must enter the numbers carefully, always using parentheses around negative numbers, fractions, and even around numerators and denominators that are not single numbers.

- <u>P</u>arentheses: First do whatever appears in parentheses, following PEMDAS within the parentheses also, if necessary.
- <u>E</u>xponents: Next evaluate all terms with exponents.
- <u>M</u>ultiplication and <u>D</u>ivision: Do all multiplications and divisions *in order from left to right*—do not necessarily multiply first and then divide.
- <u>A</u>ddition and <u>S</u>ubtraction: Finally, do all additions and subtractions *in order from left to right*—do not necessarily add first and then subtract.

Here are some worked-out examples.

1.  $10 + 4 \times 2 = 10 + 8 = 18$      [Multiply before you add.]
    $(10 + 4) \times 2 = 14 \times 2 = 28$      [First add in the parentheses.]

2.  $16 \div 2 \times 4 = 8 \times 4 = 32$      [Just go from left to right.]
    $16 \div (2 \times 4) = 16 \div 8 = 2$      [First multiply in the parentheses.]

3.  $5 \times 2^3 = 5 \times 8 = 40$      [Do exponents first.]
    $(5 \times 2)^3 = 10^3 = 1000$      [First multiply in the parentheses.]

4.  $10 + 15 \div (2 + 3) = 10 + 15 \div 5 = 10 + 3 = 13$      [Do parentheses first, then divide.]

5.  $100 - 2^2(3 + 4 \times 5) = 100 - 2^2(23) = 100 - 4(23) = 100 - 92 = 8$
    [Do parentheses first (using PEMDAS), then the exponent, then multiplication.]

## Key Fact A10

**(The distributive law)** For any real numbers $a$, $b$, and $c$:

$$a(b + c) = ab + ac \qquad a(b - c) = ab - ac$$

and if $a \neq 0$

$$\frac{b + c}{a} = \frac{b}{a} + \frac{c}{a} \qquad \frac{b - c}{a} = \frac{b}{a} - \frac{c}{a}$$

 Be sure you use the distributive law with both multiplication and division whenever you can.

## EXAMPLE 12

Which of the following is equivalent to $\dfrac{x^5 + x^4}{x^4}$ for all nonzero numbers $x$?

(A) $x + 1$
(B) $x^5$
(C) $x^5 + 1$
(D) $x + x^4$
(E) $x^{16}$

**Solution.** $\dfrac{x^5 + x^4}{x^4} = \dfrac{x^5}{x^4} + \dfrac{x^4}{x^4} = x + 1$ (Choice A).

# Practice Exercises

## MULTIPLE-CHOICE QUESTIONS

1. For how many integers $n$, is it true that $n^2 = n^3$?

   (A) None
   (B) 1
   (C) 2
   (D) 4
   (E) More than 4

2. If $x \blacklozenge y$ represents the number of integers greater than $x$ and less than $y$, what is the value of $-\pi \blacklozenge \pi$?

   (A) 0
   (B) 3
   (C) 4
   (D) 6
   (E) 7

3. Which of the following is equal to $(5^8 \times 5^9)^{10}$?

   (A) $5^{27}$
   (B) $5^{82}$
   (C) $5^{170}$
   (D) $5^{720}$
   (E) $25^{720}$

4. If $p$ and $q$ are primes greater than 100, which of the following must be true?

   I. $p + q$ is even
   II. $pq$ is odd
   III. $p^2 - q^2$ is even

   (A) I only
   (B) II only
   (C) I and II only
   (D) I and III only
   (E) I, II, and III

5. If $(5^a)(5^b) = \frac{5^c}{5^d}$, what is $d$ in terms of $a$, $b$, and $c$?

   (A) $\frac{c}{ab}$
   (B) $c - a - b$
   (C) $a + b - c$
   (D) $c - ab$
   (E) $\frac{c}{a + b}$

## GRID-IN QUESTIONS

6. A number is "nifty" if it is a multiple of 2 or 3. How many nifty numbers are there between $-11$ and 11?

7. If for any positive integer $n$, $\tau(n)$ represents the number of positive divisors of $n$, what is the value of $\tau(\tau(\tau(12)))$?

8. If the product of four consecutive integers is equal to one of the integers, what is the largest possible value of one of the integers?

**9.** At Ben's Butcher Shop, 199 pounds of chopped meat is being divided into packages, each weighing 2.5 pounds. How many pounds of meat are left when there isn't enough to make another whole package?

**10.** What is the largest number, *x*, that can be entered in the grid such that $\sqrt{x}$ is an integer?

## Answer Key

**1.** C

**2.** E

**3.** C

**4.** E

**5.** B

**6.** `15`

**7.** `3`

**8.** `3`

**9.** `1.5`

**10.** `9801`

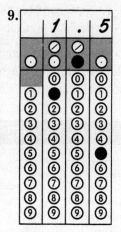

## 7-B FRACTIONS AND DECIMALS

Several questions on the PSAT involve fractions or decimals. In this section we will present all of the important facts you need to know for the PSAT. Even if you are using a calculator that has fraction capabilities, it is essential that you review all of this material thoroughly.

## Comparing Fractions and Decimals

### Key Fact B1

To compare two decimals, follow these rules:

- Whichever number has the greater number to the left of the decimal point is greater: since $10 > 9$, $10.001 > 9.896$ and since $1 > 0$, $1.234 > 0.8$.
- If the numbers to the left of the decimal point are equal (or if there are no numbers to the left of the decimal point), proceed as follows:

   1. If the numbers do not have the same number of digits to the right of the decimal point, add zeros to make the number of digits equal.
   2. Now, compare the numbers to the right of the decimal point (*ignoring* the decimal point itself).

   For example, to compare 1.83 and 1.823, add a zero to the end of 1.83, forming 1.830. Now, thinking of them as whole numbers, compare the numbers to the right of the decimal point: $830 > 823 \Rightarrow 1.830 > 1.823$.

### Key Fact B2

 On the PSAT, *never* do long division to convert a fraction to a decimal (or for any other reason). Use your calculator.

To compare two fractions, use your calculator to convert them to decimals. Then apply **KEY FACT B1**. This *always* works.

 To compare $\frac{1}{3}$ and $\frac{3}{8}$, use your calculator: $\frac{1}{3} = .333\ldots$ and $\frac{3}{8} = .375$. Since $.375 > .333$, $\frac{3}{8} > \frac{1}{3}$.

### Key Fact B3

**KEY FACTS B1** and **B2** apply to *positive* decimals and fractions. Clearly, any positive number is greater than any negative number. For negative decimals and fractions, note that if $a > b$, then $-a < -b$.

$$\frac{3}{8} > \frac{1}{3} \Rightarrow -\frac{1}{3} > -\frac{3}{8} \quad \text{and} \quad .83 > .829 \Rightarrow -.83 < -.829$$

# Arithmetic Operations with Decimals and Fractions

Using a calculator saves time and avoids careless errors. If you know that $12 \times 12 = 144$ and that $1.2 \times 1.2 = 1.44$, fine, but if you're not sure, use your calculator rather than paper and pencil. You should even use your calculator to multiply $.2 \times .2$ if there's any chance that you would write 0.4 instead of 0.04 as the answer.

 On the PSAT, *all* decimal arithmetic (including whole numbers) that you can't easily do mentally should be done on your calculator.

## Key Fact B4

To multiply two fractions, multiply their numerators and multiply their denominators:

$$\frac{3}{5} \times \frac{4}{7} = \frac{3 \times 4}{5 \times 7} = \frac{12}{35}.$$

## Key Fact B5

To multiply a fraction by any other number, write that number as a fraction whose denominator is 1:

$$\frac{3}{5} \times 7 = \frac{3}{5} \times \frac{7}{1} = \frac{21}{5} \qquad \frac{3}{4} \times \pi = \frac{3}{4} \times \frac{\pi}{1} = \frac{3\pi}{4}$$

 TACTIC

**B1** **Reduce fractions before multiplying (divide the numerator and the denominator by a common factor).**

### EXAMPLE 1

Express the product, $\frac{3}{4} \times \frac{8}{9} \times \frac{15}{16}$, in lowest terms.

**Solution.** If you just multiply the numerators and denominators (with a calculator, of course), you get $\frac{360}{576}$, which is a nuisance to reduce. Also, dividing on your calculator won't help, since your answer is supposed to be a fraction in lowest terms. It is better to use **TACTIC B1** and reduce first:

$$\frac{{}^1\cancel{3}}{4} \times \frac{{}^1\cancel{8}}{\cancel{9}_{\,3}} \times \frac{{}^5\cancel{15}}{\cancel{16}_{\,2}} = \frac{1 \times 1 \times 5}{4 \times 1 \times 2} = \frac{5}{8}.$$

 TACTIC

**B2** **When a problem requires you to find a fraction of a number, multiply.**

### EXAMPLE 2

If $\frac{5}{8}$ of the 320 seniors at Central High School are girls, and $\frac{4}{5}$ of the senior girls are taking a science course, how many senior girls are NOT taking a science course?

(A) 40
(B) 70
(C) 160
(D) 200
(E) It cannot be determined from the information given.

**Solution.** There are $\frac{5}{18} \times \overset{40}{\cancel{320}} = 200$ senior girls. Of these, $\frac{4}{15} \times \overset{40}{\cancel{200}} = 160$ are taking science. Then, $200 - 160 = 40$ are not taking science (Choice A).

> **CALCULATOR HINT**
>
> If you are going to use your calculator, enter the numbers without reducing. Given the choice of multiplying $\frac{48}{128} \times 80$ or $\frac{3}{8} \times 80$, *you* would prefer the second option, but with *your calculator*, the first one is just as easy.

The ***reciprocal*** of any nonzero number *x*, is the number $\frac{1}{x}$. The reciprocal of the fraction $\frac{a}{b}$ is the fraction $\frac{b}{a}$.

## Key Fact B6

To divide any number by a fraction, multiply that number by the reciprocal of the fraction:

$$20 \div \frac{2}{3} = \frac{20}{1} \times \frac{3}{2} = 30 \qquad \frac{3}{5} \div \frac{2}{3} = \frac{3}{5} \times \frac{3}{2} = \frac{9}{10}$$

## EXAMPLE 3

A certain real estate course takes 36 hours to complete. If the course is divided into 40-minute classes, how many times does the class meet?

**Solution.** First, note that 40 minutes $= \frac{40}{60}$ hour $= \frac{2}{3}$ hour. Then, $36 \div \frac{2}{3} = \frac{36}{1} \times \frac{3}{2} = 54$.

**NOTE:** In this problem, you could have avoided fractions by changing 36 hours to $36 \times 60 = 2,160$ minutes and then dividing: $2,160 \div 40 = 54$.

## Key Fact B7

To add or subtract fractions with the same denominator, add or subtract the numerators and keep the denominator:

$$\frac{4}{9} + \frac{1}{9} = \frac{5}{9} \quad \text{and} \quad \frac{4}{9} - \frac{1}{9} = \frac{3}{9} = \frac{1}{3}$$

To add or subtract fractions with different denominators, first rewrite the fractions as equivalent fractions with the same denominators:

$$\frac{1}{6} + \frac{3}{4} = \frac{2}{12} + \frac{9}{12} = \frac{11}{12}$$

**NOTE:** The *easiest* denominator to get is the product of the denominators ($6 \times 4 = 24$, in this example), but the *best* denominator to use is the *least common denominator*, which is the *least common multiple* (LCM) of the denominators (12 in this case). Using the least common denominator minimizes the amount of reducing that is necessary to express the answer in lowest terms.

## EXAMPLE 4

Michael had a baseball card collection. Sally took $\frac{1}{3}$ of his cards and Heidi took $\frac{1}{4}$ of them. What fraction of his cards did Michael have left?

## EXAMPLE 5

Michael had a baseball card collection. Sally took $\frac{1}{3}$ of his cards and Heidi took $\frac{1}{4}$ of what was left. What fraction of his cards did Michael have left?

**Solution 4.** $\frac{1}{3} + \frac{1}{4} = \frac{4}{12} + \frac{3}{12} = \frac{7}{12}$ of the cards were taken; so Michael had $\frac{5}{12}$ of them left.

**Solution 5.** $\frac{1}{3} + \frac{1}{6} = \frac{2}{6} + \frac{1}{6} = \frac{3}{6} = \frac{1}{2}$ of the cards were taken; so Michael had $\frac{1}{2}$ of them left.

 **CAUTION:** Be sure to read questions carefully. In Example 4, Heidi took $\frac{1}{4}$ of the cards. In Example 5, however, she took only $\frac{1}{4}$ of the $\frac{2}{3}$ that were left after Sally took her cards: she took $\frac{1}{4} \times \frac{2}{3} = \frac{1}{6}$ of the cards.

# Arithmetic Operations with Mixed Numbers

A ***mixed number*** is a number such as $3\frac{1}{2}$, which consists of an integer followed by a fraction. It is an abbreviation for the *sum* of the number and the fraction; so, $3\frac{1}{2}$ is an abbreviation for $3 + \frac{1}{2}$. Every mixed number can be written as an improper fraction, and every improper fraction can be written as a mixed number:

$$3\frac{1}{2} = 3 + \frac{1}{2} = \frac{3}{1} + \frac{1}{2} = \frac{6}{2} + \frac{1}{2} = \frac{7}{2} \quad \text{and} \quad \frac{7}{2} = \frac{6}{2} + \frac{1}{2} = 3 + \frac{1}{2} = 3\frac{1}{2}$$

### Key Fact B8

To write a mixed number as an improper fraction or an improper fraction as a mixed number, follow these rules:

1. To write a mixed number $(3\frac{1}{2})$ as an improper fraction, multiply the whole number (3) by the denominator (2), add the numerator (1), and write the sum over the denominator (2): $\frac{3 \times 2 + 1}{2} = \frac{7}{2}$.

2. To write an improper fraction $(\frac{7}{2})$ as a mixed number, divide the numerator by the denominator; the quotient (3) is the whole number. Place the remainder (1) over the denominator to form the fractional part $\left(\frac{1}{2}\right)$: $3\frac{1}{2}$.

 **CAUTION:** You can *never* grid-in a mixed number. You must change it to an improper fraction or a decimal.
(See Chapter 5.)

### Key Fact B9

To add mixed numbers, add the integers and add the fractions:

- $5\frac{1}{4} + 3\frac{2}{3} = (5 + 3) + \left(\frac{1}{4} + \frac{2}{3}\right) = 8 + \left(\frac{3}{12} + \frac{8}{12}\right) = 8 + \frac{11}{12} = 8\frac{11}{12}$

- $5\frac{3}{4} + 3\frac{2}{3} = (5 + 3) + \left(\frac{3}{4} + \frac{2}{3}\right) = 8 + \left(\frac{9}{12} + \frac{8}{12}\right) = 8 + \frac{17}{12} = 8 + 1\frac{5}{12} =$

  $8 + 1 + \frac{5}{12} = 9\frac{5}{12}$

## Key Fact B10

To subtract mixed numbers, subtract the integers and also subtract the fractions. If, however, the fraction in the second number is greater than the fraction in the first number, you first have to borrow 1 from the integer part. For example, since $\frac{2}{3} > \frac{1}{4}$, you can't subtract $5\frac{1}{4} - 3\frac{2}{3}$ until you borrow 1 from the 5:

$$5\frac{1}{4} = 5 + \frac{1}{4} = (4 + 1) + \frac{1}{4} = 4 + \left(1 + \frac{1}{4}\right) = 4 + \frac{5}{4}.$$

Now, you have

$$5\frac{1}{4} - 3\frac{2}{3} = 4\frac{5}{4} - 3\frac{2}{3} = (4 - 3) + \left(\frac{5}{4} - \frac{2}{3}\right) =$$
$$1 + \left(\frac{15}{12} - \frac{8}{12}\right) = 1\frac{7}{12}.$$

 All arithmetic operations on mixed numbers can be done directly on your calculator. There is no need to change the mixed numbers to improper fractions or to borrow.

## Key Fact B11

To multiply or divide mixed numbers, change them to improper fractions:

$$1\frac{2}{3} \times 3\frac{1}{4} = \frac{5}{3} \times \frac{13}{4} = \frac{65}{12} = 5\frac{5}{12}$$

 Remember that on the PSAT, if you ever get stuck on a fraction problem, you can always convert the fractions to decimals and do all the work on your calculator.

# Practice Exercises

## MULTIPLE-CHOICE QUESTIONS

1. The school band has 24 boys and 16 girls. What fraction of the band members are girls?

   (A) $\frac{2}{5}$

   (B) $\frac{3}{5}$

   (C) $\frac{2}{3}$

   (D) $\frac{3}{4}$

   (E) $\frac{3}{2}$

2. Adam had a baseball card collection. One day he gave Noah $\frac{1}{5}$ of cards; the following day he gave Pete $\frac{3}{8}$ of the cards he had left. What fraction of his original collection did Adam still have?

   (A) $\frac{3}{10}$

   (B) $\frac{17}{40}$

   (C) $\frac{1}{2}$

   (D) $\frac{23}{40}$

   (E) $\frac{7}{10}$

3. For how many integers $n$ between 20 and 30 is it true that $\frac{3}{n}$, $\frac{5}{n}$, and $\frac{7}{n}$ are all in lowest terms?

   (A) 2
   (B) 3
   (C) 4
   (D) 5
   (E) 6

4. What fractional part of a week is 63 hours?

   (A) $\frac{7}{24}$

   (B) $\frac{3}{8}$

   (C) $\frac{24}{63}$

   (D) $\frac{4}{7}$

   (E) $\frac{7}{9}$

5. If $\frac{3}{7}$ of a number is 35, what is $\frac{6}{7}$ of that number?

   (A) 6
   (B) 15
   (C) 17.5
   (D) 30
   (E) 70

## GRID-IN QUESTIONS

6. $\frac{5}{8}$ of 24 is equal to $\frac{15}{7}$ of what number?

7. If $5a = 3$ and $3b = 5$, what is the value of $\frac{a}{b}$?

8. What is a possible value of $x$ if $\frac{2}{3} < \frac{1}{x} < \frac{7}{9}$?

10. Let $A = \{1, 2, 3\}$ and $B = \{2, 3, 4\}$, and let $C$ be the set consisting of the 9 fractions whose numerators are in $A$ and whose denominators are in $B$. What is the product of all of the numbers in $C$?

9. Michael gave $\frac{1}{12}$ of his money to Sally and $\frac{1}{5}$ of his remaining money to Heidi. If he still had $704, how much money did he have originally?

## Answer Key

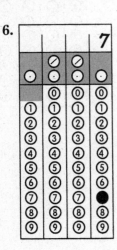

# 7-C PERCENTS

The word *percent* means hundredth. We use the symbol % to express the word "percent." For example, "15 percent" means "15 hundredths" and can be written with a % symbol, as a fraction, or as a decimal: $15\% = \frac{15}{100} = .15$.

### Key Fact C1

To convert a percent to a decimal or a percent to a fraction, follow these rules:

1. To convert a percent to a decimal, drop the % symbol and move the decimal point two places to the left, adding zeros if necessary. (Remember that we assume that there is a decimal point to the right of any whole number.)
2. To convert a percent to a fraction, drop the % symbol, write the number over 100, and reduce.

$$25\% = .25 = \frac{25}{100} = \frac{1}{4} \qquad 100\% = 1.00 = \frac{100}{100}$$

$$12.5\% = .125 = \frac{12.5}{100} = \frac{125}{1000} = \frac{1}{8}$$

$$1\% = .01 = \frac{1}{100} \qquad \frac{1}{2}\% = .5\% = .005 = \frac{.5}{100} = \frac{1}{200}$$

$$250\% = 2.50 = \frac{250}{100} = \frac{5}{2}$$

### Key Fact C2

To convert a decimal to a percent or a fraction to a percent, follow these rules:

1. To convert a decimal to a percent, move the decimal point two places to the right, adding zeros if necessary, and add the % symbol.
2. To convert a fraction to a percent, first convert the fraction to a decimal, and then complete step 1.

$$.375 = 37.5\% \quad .3 = 30\% \qquad 1.25 = 125\% \quad 10 = 1000\%$$

$$\frac{3}{4} = .75 = 75\% \qquad \frac{1}{3} = .33333... = 33.333...\% = 33\frac{1}{3}\%$$

You should be familiar with the following basic conversions.

$$\frac{1}{4} = 25\% \qquad \frac{1}{3} = 33\frac{1}{3}\% \qquad \frac{1}{2} = 50\% \qquad \frac{2}{3} = 66\frac{2}{3}\% \qquad \frac{3}{4} = 75\%$$

 Any problem involving percents can be done on your calculator (even if your calculator doesn't have a % key): to find 25% of 32, write 25% as a decimal and multiply: $32 \times .25 = 8$. Consider these three questions:

(i) What is 35% of 200?
(ii) 70 is 35% of what number?
(iii) 70 is what percent of 200?

Each question can be answered easily by using your calculator, but you must first set up the question properly so that you know what to multiply or divide. In each case, there is one unknown; call it *x*. Now, just translate each sentence, replacing "is" with "=" and the unknown by *x*.

(i) $x = 35\%$ of $200 \Rightarrow x = .35 \times 200 = 70$.

(ii) $70 = 35\%$ of $x \Rightarrow 70 = .35x \Rightarrow x = 70 \div .35 = 200$.

(iii) $70 = x\%$ of $200 \Rightarrow 70 = \frac{x}{100}(200) \Rightarrow x = 35$.

Another way to handle questions such as these is to set up the proportion $\frac{is}{of} = \frac{\%}{100}$. To use this method, think of "is," "of," and "%" as variables.

In each percent problem you are given two of them and need to find the third, which you label *x*. Of course, you then solve such equations by cross-multiplying. For example, the three problems we just solved could be handled as follows:

(i) <u>What</u> <u>is</u> 35% of 200? (Let *x* = the "is" number.)

$$\frac{x}{200} = \frac{35}{100} \Rightarrow 100x = 35(200) = 7000 \Rightarrow x = 70$$

(ii) 70 is 35% <u>of what</u> number? (Let *x* = the "of" number.)

$$\frac{70}{x} = \frac{35}{100} \Rightarrow 7000 = 35x \Rightarrow x = 200$$

(iii) 70 is <u>what</u> <u>%</u> of 200? (Let *x* = the %.)

$$\frac{70}{200} = \frac{x}{100} \Rightarrow 200x = 7000 \Rightarrow x = 35$$

## EXAMPLE 1

Justin gave 30% of his baseball cards to Judy and 25% to Lior. If he still had 540 cards, how many did he have originally?

**Solution.** Originally, Justin had 100% of the cards (all of them). Since he gave away 55% of them, he had $100\% - 55\% = 45\%$ of them left. So, 540 is 45% of what number? $540 = .45x \Rightarrow x = 540 \div .45 = 1200$.

## EXAMPLE 2

After Sharon gave 157 baseball cards to Zach and 95 to Samir, she still had 348 left. What percent of her cards did Sharon give away?

**Solution.** Sharon gave away a total of 252 cards and had 348 left. Therefore, she started with $252 + 348 = 600$ cards. So, 252 is what percent of 600?

$$252 = \frac{x}{\cancel{100}}(\cancel{600})^{6} \Rightarrow 6x = 252 \Rightarrow x = 252 \div 6 = 42.$$

Sharon gave away 42% of her cards.

### Key Fact C3

For any positive number *a*: *a*% of 100 is *a*. For example: 17.2% of 100 is 17.2; 600% of 100 is 600; and $\frac{1}{5}\%$ of 100 $= \frac{1}{5}$.

TACTIC

**C1**

**In any problem involving percents, try to use the number 100.**

## EXAMPLE 3

In 1980 the populations of Madison and Monroe were the same. From 1980 to 1990, however, the population of Madison increased by 25% while the population of Monroe decreased by 25%. In 1990, the population of Monroe was what percent of the population of Madison?

(A) 25%
(B) 50%
(C) 60%
(D) $66\frac{2}{3}\%$
(E) $166\frac{2}{3}\%$

**Solution.** Assume that in 1980 the population of each town was 100. Then, since 25% of 100 is 25, in 1990, the populations were $100 + 25 = 125$ (Madison) and $100 - 25 = 75$ (Monroe). Then, in 1990, Monroe's population was $\frac{75}{125} = \frac{3}{5} = 60\%$ of Madison's.

### Key Fact C4

For any positive numbers $a$ and $b$: $a\%$ of $b = b\%$ of $a$.

## Percent Increase and Percent Decrease

### Key Fact C5

The *percent increase* of a quantity is

$$\frac{\text{the actual increase}}{\text{the original amount}} \times 100\%.$$

The *percent decrease* of a quantity is

$$\frac{\text{the actual decrease}}{\text{the original amount}} \times 100\%.$$

For example:

- If the price of a radio goes from \$60 to \$75, the actual increase is \$15, and the percent increase is $\frac{15}{60} \times 100\% = \frac{1}{4} \times 100\% = 25\%$.
- If a \$75 radio is on sale for \$60, the actual decrease in price is \$15, and the percent decrease is $\frac{\overset{1}{15}}{\underset{5}{75}} \times 100\% = \frac{1}{5} \times 100\% = 20\%$.

**CAUTION:** Percents over 100%, which come up most often on questions involving percent increases, are often confusing for many students. Be sure you understand that 100% of a particular number is that number, 200% of a number is 2 times the number, and 1000% of a number is 10 times the number.

Notice that the percent increase in going from 60 to 75 is *not* the same as the percent decrease in going from 75 to 60.

If the value of an investment rises from $1000 to $5000, the investment is now worth 5 times, or 500%, as much as it was originally, but there has been only a 400% increase in value:

$$\frac{\text{the actual increase}}{\text{the original amount}} \times 100\% =$$

$$\frac{4000}{1000} \times 100\% = 4 \times 100\% = 400\%.$$

## EXAMPLE 4

The value of an investment doubled every 5 years from 1980 to 1995. What was the percent increase in the value during this time?

**Solution.** The value doubled 3 times from, say, $100 in 1980 to $200 in 1985, to $400 in 1990, and to $800 in 1995. So the value in 1995 was 8 times the value in 1980, but this was an increase of $700 or 700%.

# Practice Exercises

## MULTIPLE-CHOICE QUESTIONS

**1.** Ron bought a $60 sweater on sale at 10% off. How much did he pay, including 5% sales tax?

(A) $51.00
(B) $53.50
(C) $55.00
(D) $56.70
(E) $57.00

**2.** What is 5% of 10% of 40%?

(A) 0.002%
(B) 0.2%
(C) 2%
(D) 20%
(E) 2,000%

**3.** What percent of 25 is $b$?

(A) $\frac{b}{25}$

(B) $\frac{b}{4}$

(C) $\frac{25}{b}$

(D) $\frac{4}{b}$

(E) $4b$

**4.** 10 is $\frac{1}{10}$% of what number?

(A) .01
(B) 1
(C) 100
(D) 1,000
(E) 10,000

**5.** On a test consisting of 80 questions, Susan answered 75% of the first 60 questions correctly. What percent of the other 20 questions does she need to answer correctly for her grade on the entire exam to be 80%?

(A) 85%
(B) 87.5%
(C) 90%
(D) 95%
(E) 100%

## GRID-IN QUESTIONS

**6.** A supermarket reduced the price per pound of whole chickens by 20%. How many pounds of chicken can now be purchased for the amount of money that used to buy 20 pounds of chicken?

**7.** If $c$ is a positive number, 300% of $c$ is what percent of $300c$?

**8.** If 25 students took an exam and 7 of them failed, what percent of them passed?

**9.** A college has 3000 students. If 23.5% of them are freshmen, 29.2% of them are sophomores, and 27% of them are juniors, how many are seniors?

**10.** There are twice as many girls as boys in a science class. If 30% of the girls and 45% of the boys have already completed their lab reports, what percent of the students have not yet finished their reports?

## Answer Key

**1.** D    **2.** B    **3.** E    **4.** E    **5.** D

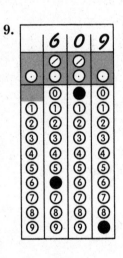

**6.** 25   **7.** 1   **8.** 72   **9.** 609   **10.** 65

## 7-D RATIOS AND PROPORTIONS

A *ratio* is a fraction that compares two quantities that are measured in the *same* units. One quantity is the numerator of the fraction, and the other quantity is the denominator.

For example, if there are 6 boys and 16 girls in the chess club, we say that the ratio of the number of boys to the number of girls in the club is 6 to 16, or $\frac{6}{16}$, often written as 6:16. Since a ratio is just a fraction, it can be reduced or converted to a decimal or a percent. The following are all different ways to express the same ratio:

$$6 \text{ to } 16 \qquad 6:16 \qquad \frac{6}{16} \qquad 3 \text{ to } 8 \qquad 3:8 \qquad \frac{3}{8} \qquad .375 \qquad 37.5\%$$

### Key Fact D1

If a set of objects is divided into two groups in the ratio of *a:b*, then the first group contains $\frac{a}{a+b}$ of the objects and the second group contains $\frac{b}{a+b}$ of the objects.

### EXAMPLE 1

A jar contains only red and blue marbles. If the ratio of the number of blue marbles to the number of red marbles in the jar is 2:3, what percent of the marbles are red?

**Solution.**  The red marbles constitute $\frac{3}{2+3} = \frac{3}{5} = 60\%$ of the total number.

### EXAMPLE 2

If 35% of the students in the honor society are male, what is the ratio of male students to female students in the society?

**Solution.**  Assume that there are 100 students in the society; then 35 of them are male, and $100 - 35 = 65$ of them are female. So, the ratio of males to females is $\frac{35}{65} = \frac{7}{13}$.

In problems involving percents, the best number to use is 100.

If we know a ratio, we *cannot* determine from that fact alone how many objects there are. In Example 1 above, since the ratio of blue marbles to red marbles is 2:3, there *might be* 2 blue marbles and 3 red ones, but *not necessarily*—there might be 200 blue marbles and 300 red ones, since the ratio 200:300 clearly reduces to 2:3. In the same way, all of the following are possibilities for the distribution of marbles.

| Blue | 4 | 6 | 8 | 20 | 400 | 8,000 | **2x** |
|------|---|---|----|----|-----|--------|--------|
| Red  | 6 | 9 | 12 | 30 | 600 | 12,000 | **3x** |

The important thing to observe is that the number of red marbles can be *any* multiple of 3, as long as the number of blue marbles is the *same* multiple of 2.

### Key Fact D2

If two numbers are in the ratio of *a:b*, then for some number *x*, the first number is *ax* and the second number is *bx*.

TACTIC

**In any ratio problem, write the letter *x* after each number and use some given information to solve for *x*.**

## EXAMPLE 3

If the ratio of boys to girls at a pep rally is 4:5, which of the following CANNOT be the number of children at the pep rally?

(A) 27
(B) 45
(C) 108
(D) 120
(E) 360

**Solution.** If $4x$ and $5x$ are the number of boys and girls at the pep rally, respectively, then the number of children present is $4x + 5x = 9x$. Therefore, the number of children must be a multiple of 9. Only 120 (Choice D), is not divisible by 9.

Ratios can be extended to three or four or more terms. For example, we can say that the ratio of freshmen to sophomores to juniors to seniors in the school play is 2:3:5:3, which means that for every 2 freshmen in the play, there are 3 sophomores, 5 juniors, and 2 seniors.

## EXAMPLE 4

If the measures of the three angles in a triangle are in the ratio of 5:6:7, what is the measure of the largest angle?

**Solution.** Let the measures of the three angles be $5x$, $6x$, and $7x$. Since in any triangle the sum of the measures of the three angles is 180° (**KEY FACT J1**):

$$5x + 6x + 7x = 180 \Rightarrow 18x = 180 \Rightarrow x = 10.$$

Therefore, the measure of the largest angle is $7 \times 10 = 70°$.

A *proportion* is an equation that states that two ratios are equivalent. Since ratios are just fractions, any equation such as $\frac{4}{6} = \frac{10}{15}$, in which each side is a single fraction, is a proportion. Usually, the proportions you encounter on the PSAT involve one or more variables.

TACTIC

**Solve proportions by cross-multiplying: if $\dfrac{a}{b} = \dfrac{c}{d}$, then *ad* = *bc*.**

## EXAMPLE 5

If $\frac{2}{7} = \frac{x}{91}$, what is the value of $x$?

 **Solution.** Cross-multiply: $2(91) = 7x \Rightarrow 182 = 7x \Rightarrow x = 26$.

A *rate* is a fraction that compares two quantities measured in *different* units. The word *per* often appears in rate problems: miles per hour, dollars per week, cents per ounce, children per classroom, and so on.

**TACTIC**
**D3**

**Set up rate problems just like ratio problems.**
**Solve the proportions by cross-multiplying.**

## EXAMPLE 6

Susan completed 25 math exercises in 35 minutes. At this rate, how many exercises can she do in 42 minutes?

**Solution.** Handle this rate problem exactly like a ratio problem. Set up a proportion and cross-multiply:

$$\frac{\text{exercises}}{\text{minutes}} = \frac{25}{35} = \frac{x}{42} \Rightarrow 35x = 25 \times 42 = 1050 \Rightarrow x = 30.$$

On the PSAT, many rate problems involve only variables. These problems are handled in exactly the same way.

## EXAMPLE 7

If *a* apples cost *c* cents, how many apples can be bought for *d* dollars?

(A) $100acd$

(B) $\frac{100d}{ac}$

(C) $\frac{ad}{100c}$

(D) $\frac{c}{100ad}$

(E) $\frac{100ad}{c}$

**Solution.** First change *d* dollars to $100d$ cents, and set up a proportion:
$\frac{\text{apples}}{\text{cents}} = \frac{a}{c} = \frac{x}{100d}$. Now cross-multiply:

$$100ad = cx \Rightarrow x = \frac{100ad}{c} \text{ (Choice E).}$$

Rate problems are examples of *direct variation*. We say that one variable *varies directly* with a second variable or that the two variables are *directly proportional* if their quotient is a constant. So if *y* is directly proportional to *x*, there is a constant *k*, such that $\frac{y}{x} = k$. The constant is the rate of increase or decrease. In Example 6, the number of math exercises Susan does varies directly with the number of minutes she spends on them. Susan's rate of solving is $\frac{5}{7}$ exercises per minute.

$$\text{The quotient } \frac{\text{exercises}}{\text{minutes}} \text{ is constant: } \frac{25}{35} = \frac{5}{7} \text{ and } \frac{30}{42} = \frac{5}{7}.$$

Notice that when two quantities vary directly, as the first quantity increases or decreases, so does the other. In Example 6 as the number of exercises increases, the number of minutes it takes Susan to do them also increases.

## EXAMPLE 8

If $x$ and $y$ are directly proportional and $x = 12$ when $y = 3$, what is $x$ when $y = 12$?

**Solution.** Since $x$ and $y$ are directly proportional, their quotient is a constant. So $\frac{12}{3} = 4 = \frac{x}{12} \Rightarrow x = 48$.

Occasionally on the PSAT you will encounter problems in which as one quantity increases, the other decreases. Problems such as these are usually examples of ***inverse variation***. We say that one variable ***varies inversely*** with a second variable or that the two variables are ***inversely proportional*** if their product is a constant. So if $y$ is inversely proportional to $x$, there is a constant $k$ such that $xy = k$.

## EXAMPLE 9

If $x$ and $y$ are inversely proportional and $x = 12$ when $y = 3$, what is $x$ when $y = 12$?

**Solution.** Since $x$ and $y$ are inversely proportional, their product is a constant. Since $xy = 12 \times 3 = 36$, if $y = 12$, then $x(12) = 36$, and so $x = 3$.

## EXAMPLE 10

A landscaper has enough money on hand to hire six workers for ten days. Assuming each worker earns the same amount of money per day, for how many days could the landscaper meet his payroll if he hires fifteen workers?

(A) 4
(B) 6
(C) 12
(D) 15
(E) 25

**Solution.** As the number of workers increases, the number of days the money will last decreases. So this is an example of inverse variation. The product (workers) $\times$ (days) remains constant.

(6 workers) $\times$ (10 days) = 60 worker-days = (15 workers) $\times$ ($d$ days) $\Rightarrow d = 4$.

# Practice Exercises

## MULTIPLE-CHOICE QUESTIONS

1. If the ratio of boys to girls in the French Club is 2:3, what percent of the club members are girls?

    (A) $33\frac{1}{3}\%$

    (B) 40%

    (C) 60%

    (D) $66\frac{2}{3}\%$

    (E) It cannot be determined from the information given.

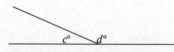

Note: Figure not drawn to scale.

2. In the diagram above, $c{:}d = 5{:}7$. What is $d - c$?

    (A) 15

    (B) 30

    (C) 75

    (D) 105

    (E) 165

3. The measures of the three angles in a triangle are in the ratio of 1:1:2. Which of the following must be true?

    I. The triangle is isosceles.
    II. The triangle is a right triangle.
    III. The triangle is equilateral.

    (A) None

    (B) I only

    (C) II only

    (D) I and II only

    (E) I and III only

4. Gilda can grade $t$ tests in $\frac{1}{x}$ hours. At this rate, how many tests can she grade in $x$ hours?

    (A) $tx$

    (B) $tx^2$

    (C) $\frac{1}{t}$

    (D) $\frac{x}{t}$

    (E) $\frac{1}{tx}$

5. Kerry can polish $i$ inches of a railing in $m$ minutes. At this rate, how many feet can he polish in $h$ hours?

    (A) $\frac{5hi}{m}$

    (B) $\frac{60hi}{m}$

    (C) $\frac{hi}{12m}$

    (D) $\frac{5m}{hi}$

    (E) $5him$

## GRID-IN QUESTIONS

6. If $\frac{a}{9} = \frac{9}{2a}$, what is the value of $a^2$?

7. Roselle can read 36 pages per hour. At this rate, how many pages can she read in 36 minutes?

**8.** If $3a = 2b$ and $3b = 5c$, what is the ratio of $a$ to $c$?

**9.** In a quadrilateral, the ratio of the measures of the four angles is 5:6:6:7. What is the degree measure of the largest angle?

**10.** If $a$ varies directly with $b^2$, and if $b = 4$ when $a = 3$, what is the value of $a$ when $b = 8$?

## Answer Key

**1.** C   **2.** B   **3.** D   **4.** B   **5.** A

**6.** 40.5   **7.** 21.6   **8.** 10/9   **9.** 105   **10.** 12

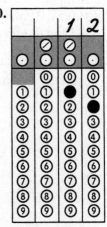

# 7-E AVERAGES

The **average** of a set of $n$ numbers is the sum of those numbers divided by $n$.

$$\text{Average} = \frac{\text{the sum of the } n \text{ numbers}}{n} \quad \text{or simply} \quad A = \frac{\text{sum}}{n}.$$

If you took three math tests so far this year and your grades were 81, 93, and 78, to calculate your average, you would add the three grades and divide by 3:

$$\frac{81 + 93 + 78}{3} = \frac{252}{3} = 84.$$

The technical name for this is *arithmetic mean*, and on the PSAT those words always appear in parentheses—for example, "What is the average (arithmetic mean) of 81, 93, and 78?"

Very often on the PSAT, you are *not* asked to find an average; rather, you are given the average of a set of numbers and asked to provide some other information. The key to solving all of these problems is to first find the sum of the numbers. Since $A = \frac{\text{sum}}{n}$, multiplying both sides by $n$ yields this equation: sum $= nA$.

### Key Fact E1

If the average of a set of $n$ numbers is $A$, the sum of those numbers is $nA$.

**TACTIC**

**E1**    **Whenever you know the average $A$ of a set of $n$ numbers, multiply $A$ by $n$ to get their sum.**

## EXAMPLE 1

The average (arithmetic mean) of Carol's grades on the 6 French tests that she has taken this year is 86. If her average after the first 4 tests was 83, what was the average of her fifth and sixth tests?

(A) 84.5
(B) 87.5
(C) 89
(D) 90
(E) 92

**Solution.**

- Use **TACTIC E1**: Carol has earned a total of $6 \times 86 = 516$ points.
- Use **TACTIC E1** again: On her first 4 tests she earned $4 \times 83 = 332$ points.
- Subtract: On her last 2 tests Carol earned $516 - 332 = 184$ points.
- So, Carol's average on her last 2 tests is $\frac{184}{2} = 92$ (Choice E).

## EXAMPLE 2

In Mr. Walsh's biology class, the average (arithmetic mean) of the grades earned by the 15 girls was 90, and the average grade earned by the 10 boys was 80. What was the class average?

**Solution.**

- The 15 girls earned a total of $15 \times 90 = 1350$ points.
- The 10 boys earned a total of $10 \times 80 = 800$ points.
- Together the 25 students earned a total of $1350 + 800 = 2150$ points.
- The class average was $2150 \div 25 = 86$.

Notice that the answer to Example 2 is *not* 85. When we combine two or more averages to form a single average, we cannot take the average of the averages. We must assign each average its proper *weight*. In this case, more students earned 90 then 80, so the class average is closer to 90 than to 80. This is called a *weighted average*.

The solution to Example 2 can be expressed as a single fraction:

$$\frac{15(90) + 10(80)}{25} = \frac{1350 + 800}{25} = \frac{2150}{25} = 86.$$

Two other terms that are associated with averages are ***median*** and ***mode***. In a set of $n$ numbers that are arranged in increasing order, the ***median*** is the middle number (if $n$ is odd) or the average of the two middle numbers (if $n$ is even). The ***mode*** is the number in the set that occurs most often.

## EXAMPLE 3

In 1998, Judith sold 9 paintings. The selling prices were: $500, $1100, $1200, $500, $1200, $5000, $700, $500, $4000. What is the average (arithmetic mean) of the median and mode of this set of data?

**Solution.** The first step is to write the data in increasing order:

$$500, 500, 500, 700, \underline{1100}, 1200, 1200, 4000, 5000.$$

The median is 1100, the middle number. The mode is 500, the number that appears more times than any other. The average of the median and the mode is

$$\frac{1100 + 500}{2} = \frac{1600}{2} = 800.$$

# Practice Exercises

## MULTIPLE-CHOICE QUESTIONS

1. If the average (arithmetic mean) of 15, 16, 17, and $w$ is 18, what is the value of $w$ ?

    (A) 16.5
    (B) 18
    (C) 24
    (D) 48
    (E) 72

2. Linda's average (arithmetic mean) on 4 tests is 80. What does she need on her fifth test to raise her average to 84?

    (A) 82
    (B) 84
    (C) 92
    (D) 96
    (E) 100

3. If $x + y = 5$, $y + z = 8$, and $z + x = 9$, what is the average (arithmetic mean) of $x$, $y$, and $z$?

    (A) $\frac{11}{3}$

    (B) $\frac{11}{2}$

    (C) $\frac{22}{3}$

    (D) 11

    (E) 22

4. If $a + b = 3(c + d)$, which of the following is the average (arithmetic mean) of $a$, $b$, $c$, and $d$ ?

    (A) $\frac{c + d}{4}$

    (B) $\frac{3(c + d)}{8}$

    (C) $\frac{c + d}{2}$

    (D) $\frac{3(c + d)}{4}$

    (E) $c + d$

5. Which of the following is the average (arithmetic mean) of $x^2 - 10$, $30 - x^2$, and $6x + 10$?

    (A) $2x + 10$
    (B) $2x + 30$
    (C) $3x + 15$
    (D) $2x^2 + 6x + 30$
    (E) $6x + 10$

## GRID-IN QUESTIONS

6. What is the average (arithmetic mean) of the positive integers from 1 to 50, inclusive?

7. If $20a + 20b = 70$, what is the average (arithmetic mean) of $a$ and $b$?

8. What is the average (arithmetic mean), in degrees, of the measures of the five angles in a pentagon?

9. Jason's average (arithmetic mean) on 4 tests is 80. Assuming he can earn no more than 100 on any test, what is the least he can earn on his fifth test and still have a chance for an 85 average after 7 tests?

10. Let $M$ be the median and $m$ the mode of the following set of numbers: 20, 80, 30, 50, 80, 100. What is the average (arithmetic mean) of $M$ and $m$?

## Answer Key

1. C        2. E        3. A        4. E        5. A

6. 25.5     7. 1.75     8. 108     9. 75     10. 72.5

# Algebra

> *For the PSAT you need to know only a small part of the algebra normally taught in a high school elementary algebra course and none of the material taught in an intermediate or advanced algebra course. In Sections 7-F, 7-G, and 7-H, we will review only those topics that you absolutely need for the PSAT.*

## 7-F POLYNOMIALS

Even though the terms *monomial*, *binomial*, *trinomial*, and *polynomial* are not used on the PSAT, you need to be able to work with simple polynomials, and these terms will make it easy to discuss the important concepts.

- A ***monomial*** is any number or variable or product of numbers and variables. Each of the following are monomials:

$$3 \quad -4 \quad x \quad y \quad 3x \quad -4xyz \quad 5x^3 \quad 1.5xy^2 \quad a^3b^4$$

The number that appears in front of the variables in a monomial is called the ***coefficient***. The coefficient of $5x^3$ is 5. If there is no number, the coefficient is 1 or $-1$, because $x$ means $1x$ and $-ab^2$ means $-1ab^2$.

- A ***polynomial*** is a monomial or the sum of two or more monomials. Each monomial that makes up the polynomial is called a ***term*** of the polynomial.

Polynomials that have two terms are called **binomials**, and polynomials that have three terms are called **trinomials**. The table below gives examples of each type.

| Monomials | Binomials | Trinomials |
|-----------|-----------|------------|
| $x^2$ | $2x^2 + 3$ | $x^2 + 5x - 1$ |
| $3abc$ | $3x^2 - 7$ | $w^2 - 2w + 1$ |
| $-a^2b^3$ | $a^2b + b^2a$ | $a^2 + 2ab + b^2$ |

Two terms are called *like terms* if they have exactly the same variables and exponents; they can differ only in their coefficients: $5a^2b$ and $-3a^2b$ are like terms, whereas $a^2b$ and $b^2a$ are not.

On the PSAT, you are often asked to evaluate a polynomial for specific values of the variables.

## EXAMPLE 1

What is the value of $-2a^2b + ab$ when $a = -6$ and $b = 0.5$?

**Solution.** Rewrite the expression, replacing the letters $a$ and $b$ by the numbers $-6$ and $0.5$, respectively. First, write each number in parentheses and then evaluate:

$$-2(-6)^2(0.5) + (-6)(0.5) =$$
$$-2(36)(0.5) + (-3) =$$
$$-36 - 3 = -39.$$

 **CAUTION:** Be sure you follow PEMDAS: Handle exponents before the other operations. For example, in Example 1, you cannot multiply $-2$ by $-6$, get 12, and then square 12. You must first square $-6$, and then multiply by $-2$.

### Key Fact F1

The only terms of a polynomial that can be combined are like terms.

### Key Fact F2

To add two polynomials, put a plus sign between them, erase the parentheses, and combine like terms.

## EXAMPLE 2

What is the sum of $5x^2 + 10x - 7$ and $3x^2 - 4x + 2$?

To add, subtract, multiply, and divide polynomials, use the usual laws of arithmetic. To avoid careless errors, write each polynomial in parentheses before performing any arithmetic operations.

**Solution.**
$(5x^2 + 10x - 7) + (3x^2 - 4x + 2) =$
$5x^2 + 10x - 7 + 3x^2 - 4x + 2 =$
$(5x^2 + 3x^2) + (10x - 4x) + (-7 + 2) =$
$8x^2 + 6x - 5.$

### Key Fact F3

To subtract two polynomials, change the minus sign between them to a plus sign and change the sign of every term in the second parentheses. Then use **KEY FACT F2** to add them: erase the parentheses and combine like terms.

## EXAMPLE 3

**CAUTION:** Make sure you get the order right in a subtraction problem.

Subtract $3x^2 - 4x + 2$ from $5x^2 + 10x - 7$.

**Solution.** Be careful. Start with the second polynomial and subtract the first:
$(5x^2 + 10x - 7) - (3x^2 - 4x + 2) =$
$(5x^2 + 10x - 7) + (-3x^2 + 4x - 2) =$
$2x^2 + 14x - 9$

### Key Fact F4

To multiply monomials, first multiply their coefficients and then multiply their variables, by adding the exponents (see Section 7-A).

## EXAMPLE 4

What is the product of $5xy^3z^5$ and $-2x^3y$?

**Solution.** $(5xy^3z^5)(-2x^2y) = 5(-2)(x)(x^3)(y^3)(y)(z^5) = -10x^4y^4z^5.$

All other polynomials are multiplied by using the distributive property.

## Key Fact F5

To multiply a monomial by any polynomial, just multiply each term of the polynomial by the monomial.

## EXAMPLE 5

What is the product of $2a$ and $3a^2 - 6ab + b^2$?

**Solution.** $2a(3a^2 - 6ab + b^2) = 6a^3 - 12a^2b + 2ab^2$.

On the PSAT, the only other polynomials that you could be asked to multiply are two binomials.

## Key Fact F6

To multiply two binomials, use the so-called FOIL method, which is really nothing more than the distributive law. Multiply each term in the first parentheses by each term in the second parentheses and simplify by combining terms, if possible.

$$(2x - 7)(3x + 2) = \underset{\text{First terms}}{(2x)(3x)} + \underset{\text{Outer terms}}{(2x)(2)} + \underset{\text{Inner terms}}{(-7)(3x)} + \underset{\text{Last terms}}{(-7)(2)} = 6x^2 + 4x - 21x - 14 = 6x^2 - 17x - 14$$

## EXAMPLE 6

What is the value of $(x - 3)(x + 4) - (x - 5)(x + 6)$?

**Solution.** First, multiply both pairs of binomials:

$(x - 3)(x + 4) = x^2 + 4x - 3x - 12 = x^2 + x - 12$
$(x - 5)(x + 6) = x^2 + 6x - 5x - 30 = x^2 + x - 30$

Now, subtract: $(x^2 + x - 12) - (x^2 + x - 30) = x^2 + x - 12 - x^2 - x + 30 = 18$.

## Key Fact F7

The three most important binomial products on the PSAT are

- $(x - y)(x + y) = x^2 - y^2$
- $(x - y)^2 = x^2 - 2xy + y^2$
- $(x + y)^2 = x^2 + 2xy + y^2$

 If you memorize these products, you won't have to multiply the binomials out each time you need them.

## EXAMPLE 7

If $a - b = 9.2$ and $a + b = 5$, what is the value of $a^2 - b^2$?

**Solution.** The moment you see $a^2 - b^2$, you should think $(a - b)(a + b)$. So, $a^2 - b^2 = (a - b)(a + b) = (9.2)(5) = 46$.

On the PSAT, the only division of polynomials you will have to do is to divide a polynomial by a monomial. You will *not* have to do long division of polynomials.

## Key Fact F8

To divide a polynomial by a monomial, use the distributive property.

## EXAMPLE 8

What is the quotient when $24a^2b + 9ab^3c$ is divided by $6ab$?

**Solution.** By the distributive property, $\frac{24a^2b + 9ab^3c}{6\,ab} = \frac{24a^2b}{6ab} + \frac{9ab^3c}{6ab}$.

Now simplify each fraction: $4a + \frac{3}{2}b^2c$.

Occasionally on the PSAT you will be asked to simplify an algebraic expression. To do so, you will probably have to do some simple factoring.

## Key Fact F9

To factor a polynomial, the first step is *always* to use the distributive property to remove the greatest common factor of all the terms.

For example:

$$6xy + 8yz = 2y(3x + 4z)$$
$$x^3 + x^2 + x = x(x^2 + x + 1)$$

## Key Fact F10

To factor a trinomial, use trial and error to find the binomials whose product is that trinomial.

For example:

$$x^2 - 4x + 4 = (x - 2)(x - 2)$$
$$x^2 - 2x - 15 = (x - 5)(x + 3)$$
$$2x^2 + 12x + 16 = 2(x^2 + 6x + 8) = 2(x + 4)(x + 2)$$

## EXAMPLE 9

Which of the following is equivalent to $\frac{2x^2 - 8}{x^2 - 4x + 4}$ ?

(A) $2$

(B) $\frac{2(x + 2)}{x - 2}$

(C) $\frac{2(x + 4)}{x - 4}$

(D) $\frac{2x + 2}{x - 2}$

(E) $\frac{6}{4x - 4}$

**Solution.**

$$\frac{2x^2-8}{x^2-4x+4}=\frac{2\left(x^2-4\right)}{(x-2)(x-2)}=\frac{2\cancel{(x-2)}(x+2)}{\cancel{(x-2)}(x-2)}=\frac{2(x+2)}{x-2}\quad\text{(Choice B)}.$$

In Example 9, when $x = 3$, the value of $\dfrac{2x^2-8}{x^2-4x+4}$ is

 If you ever get stuck trying to simplify an algebraic expression, you can plug in a number and test the answers.

$$\frac{2(3)^2-8}{3^2-4(3)+4}=\frac{18-8}{9-12+4}=\frac{10}{1}=10.$$

Only Choice B is 10 when $x = 3$: $\dfrac{2(3+2)}{3-2}=\dfrac{2(5)}{1}=10.$

Note that this does not depend on the choice of $x$. You can verify, for example, that if $x = 6$, the original expression and the correct answer choice are both equal to 4.

# Practice Exercises

## MULTIPLE-CHOICE QUESTIONS

**1.** If $x^2 + y^2 = 36$ and $(x + y)^2 = 64$, what is the value of $xy$?

(A) 7
(B) 14
(C) 28
(D) 100
(E) It cannot be determined from the information given.

**2.** What is the value of $(500,001)^2 - (499,999)^2$?

(A) 2
(B) 4
(C) 1,000,000
(D) 2,000,000
(E) 1,000,000,000,000

**3.** If $\frac{1}{x} + \frac{1}{y} = \frac{1}{z}$ and $xy = z$, what is the average of $x$ and $y$?

(A) 0
(B) $\frac{1}{2}$
(C) 1
(D) $\frac{z}{2}$
(E) $\frac{x+y}{2z}$

**4.** What is the average (arithmetic mean) of $x^2 + 2x - 3$, $3x^2 - 2x - 3$, and $30 - 4x^2$?

(A) $\frac{8x^2 + 4x + 24}{3}$

(B) $\frac{8x^2 + 24}{3}$

(C) $\frac{24 - 4x}{3}$

(D) $-12$

(E) 8

**5.** What is the value of $x^2 - 10x + 25$ when $x = 95$?

(A) 90
(B) 100
(C) 950
(D) 8,100
(E) 10,000

## GRID-IN QUESTIONS

**6.** If $a^2 + b^2 = 4$ and $(a - b)^2 = 2$, what is the value of $ab$?

**7.** What is the value of $\frac{c^2 - d^2}{c - d}$ when $c = 23.4$ and $d = 34.5$?

**8.** If $x^2 - y^2 = 80$ and $x - y = 16$, what is the average of $x$ and $y$ ?

9. What is the value of
(2x + 3)(x + 6) −
(2x − 5)(x + 10)?

10. If $\left(\frac{1}{a} + a\right)^2 = 144$, what is the value of $\frac{1}{a^2} + a^2$?

## Answer Key

1. B   2. D   3. B   4. E   5. D

6. *1*   7. *57.9*   8. *2.5*   9. *68*   10. *142*

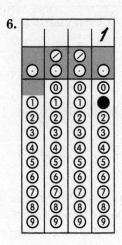
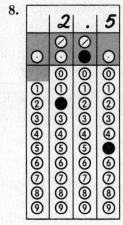
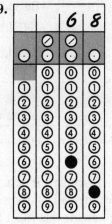
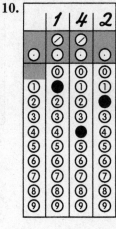

## 7-G  SOLVING EQUATIONS AND INEQUALITIES

Most of the equations and inequalities that you will have to solve on the PSAT have only one variable and no exponents. A simple six-step method, illustrated below, can be used on all of them.

### EXAMPLE 1

If $\frac{1}{2}x + 3(x - 2) = 2(x + 1) + 1$, what is the value of $x$?

**Solution.** Follow the steps outlined in the following table.

| Step | What to Do | Example |
|------|------------|---------|
| 1 | Remove fractions and decimals by multiplying both sides by the Lowest Common Denominator (LCD). | Multiply each term by 2: $x + 6(x - 2) = 4(x + 1) + 2$ |
| 2 | Remove all parentheses by using the distributive property. | $x + 6x - 12 = 4x + 4 + 2$ |
| 3 | Combine like terms on each side. | $7x - 12 = 4x + 6$ |
| 4 | By adding or subtracting, get all the variables on one side. | Subtract $4x$ from each side: $3x - 12 = 6$ |
| 5 | By adding or subtracting, get all the plain numbers on the other side. | Add 12 to each side: $3x = 18$ |
| 6 | Divide both sides by the coefficient of the variable. | Divide both sides by 3: $x = 6$ |

**Note:** If you start with an inequality and in Step 6 you divide by a negative number, remember to reverse the inequality.

Example 1 *is actually much more difficult than any equation on the PSAT,* because it requires all six steps. This never happens on the PSAT. Think of the six steps as a list of questions that must be answered. Ask whether each step is necessary. If it isn't, move on to the next one; if it is, do it.

Let's look at Example 2, which does not require all six steps.

### EXAMPLE 2

For what real number $x$ is it true that $4(2x - 7) = x$?

(A) $-4$
(B) $-1$
(C) $0$
(D) $1$
(E) $4$

**Solution.** Do whichever of the six steps are necessary.

| Step | Question | Yes/No | What to Do |
|------|----------|--------|------------|
| 1 | Are there any fractions or decimals? | No | |
| 2 | Are there any parentheses? | Yes | Get rid of them: $8x - 28 = x$. |
| 3 | Are there any like terms to combine? | No | |
| 4 | Are there variables on both sides? | Yes | Subtract $x$ from each side: $7x - 28 = 0$ |
| 5 | Is there a plain number on the same side as the variable? | Yes | Add 28 to each side: $7x = 28$ |
| 6 | Does the variable have a coefficient? | Yes | Divide both sides by 7: $x = 4$ |

**TACTIC**

**G1**   Memorize these six steps in order, and use this method whenever you have to solve this type of equation or inequality.

Sometimes on the PSAT, you are given an equation with several variables and asked to solve for one of them in terms of the others.

**TACTIC**

**G2**   When you have to solve for one variable in terms of the others, treat all of the others as if they were numbers, and apply the six-step method.

## EXAMPLE 3

If $r = 5s - 2t$, what is the value of $s$ in terms of $r$ and $t$?

**Solution.** To solve for $s$, treat $r$ and $t$ as numbers, and use the six-step method with $s$ as the only variable.

| Step | Question | Yes/No | What to Do |
|------|----------|--------|-----------|
| 1 | Are there any fractions or decimals? | No | |
| 2 | Are there any parentheses? | No | |
| 3 | Are there any like terms to combine? | No | |
| 4 | Are there variables on both sides? | No | Remember: The only variable is *s*. |
| 5 | Is there a plain number on the same side as the variable? | Yes | Remember: We're considering *t* as a number, and it is on the same side as *s*, the variable. Add $2t$ to both sides: $r + 2t = 5s$ |
| 6 | Does the variable have a coefficient? | Yes | Divide both sides by 5: $s = \frac{r + 2t}{5}$ |

HELPFUL HINT

In applying the six-step method, you should not actually make a table, as we did in Examples 1–3, since it would be too time consuming. Instead, use the method as a guideline and mentally go through each step, doing only those that are required.

The six-step method can also be used if a variable is in a denominator. Just be sure to start with Step 1 and get rid of the fraction.

## EXAMPLE 4

If $\frac{1}{2x} + \frac{2}{3} = \frac{4}{3x}$, then $x =$

**Solution.** Multiply each term by $6x$, the LCD,

$$6x\left(\frac{1}{2x}\right) + 6x\left(\frac{2}{3}\right) = 6x\left(\frac{4}{3x}\right) \Rightarrow 3 + 4x = 8 \Rightarrow 4x = 5 \Rightarrow x = \frac{5}{4} \text{ (or 1.25)}$$

Occasionally, on the PSAT you will have to solve an equation, such as $2\sqrt{x} - 7 = 5$, that involves a square root. Proceed normally, treating the square root as your variable, using whichever of the six steps are necessary until you have that square root equal to a number. Then square both sides.

## EXAMPLE 5

If $2\sqrt{x} - 7 = 5$, then $x =$

**Solution.**

Add 7 to each side: $\qquad 2\sqrt{x} = 12$
Divide each side by 2: $\qquad \sqrt{x} = 6$
Now square each side: $\qquad (\sqrt{x})^2 = 6^2 \Rightarrow x = 36$

## Systems of Linear Equations

The equations $x + y = 10$ and $x - y = 2$ each have infinitely many solutions. However, there is only one pair of numbers, $x = 6$ and $y = 4$, which satisfy both equations simultaneously: $6 + 4 = 10$ and $6 - 4 = 2$. These numbers are the only solution of the *system of equations*: $x + y = 10$ and $x - y = 2$.

A system of equations is a set of two or more equations involving two or more variables. To solve such a system, you must find values for each of the variables that will make each equation true. On the PSAT, the most useful method is to add or subtract the equations (usually add).

TACTIC

**G3** | To solve a system of equations, add or subtract them. If there are more than two equations, add them.

### EXAMPLE 6

If $2x + y = 10$ and $x - y = 2$, then what is the value of $xy$?

**Solution.** Add the two equations:

$$2x + y = 10$$
$$+ \quad x - y = 2$$
$$\overline{3x \qquad = 12} \quad \text{so, } x = 4$$

Replacing $x$ by 4 in $x - y = 2$ yields $y = 2$. So, $xy = (4)(2) = 8$.

### EXAMPLE 7

If $3a + 5b = 10$ and $5a + 3b = 30$, what is the average (arithmetic mean) of $a$ and $b$?

(A) 2.5
(B) 4
(C) 5
(D) 20
(E) It cannot be determined from the information given.

**Solution.** Add the two equations:

$$3a + 5b = 10$$
$$+ \quad 5a + 3b = 30$$
$$\overline{8a + 8b = 40}$$

Divide both sides by 8: $\qquad a + b = 5$

The average of $a$ and $b$ is: $\qquad \dfrac{a+b}{2} = \dfrac{5}{2} = 2.5$ (Choice A)

 On the PSAT, most problems involving systems of equations do not require you to solve the system. These problems usually ask for something other than the value of each variable. Read the questions very carefully, circle what you need, and do not do more than is required.

**NOTE:** It is not only unnecessary to first solve for $a$ and $b$ ($a = 7.5$ and $b = -2.5$), but because it is so much more time consuming, it would be foolish to do so.

# Practice Exercises

## MULTIPLE-CHOICE QUESTIONS

1. If $5x + 12 = 5 - 2x$, what is the value of $x$?

   (A) $-\frac{17}{7}$

   (B) $-3$

   (C) $-1$

   (D) $1$

   (E) $\frac{17}{7}$

2. If $\frac{1}{a-b} = 6$, then $a =$

   (A) $b + 6$

   (B) $b - 6$

   (C) $b + \frac{1}{6}$

   (D) $b - \frac{1}{6}$

   (E) $\frac{1 - 6b}{6}$

3. If $\frac{1}{3}x + \frac{1}{6}x + \frac{1}{9}x = 33$, what is the value of $x$?

   (A) $3$

   (B) $18$

   (C) $27$

   (D) $54$

   (E) $72$

4. If $ax - b = c - dx$, what is the value of $x$ in terms of $a$, $b$, $c$, and $d$?

   (A) $\frac{b+c}{a+d}$

   (B) $\frac{c-b}{a-d}$

   (C) $\frac{b+c-d}{a}$

   (D) $\frac{c-b}{a+d}$

   (E) $\frac{c}{b} - \frac{d}{a}$

5. If $\frac{a + 2b + 3c}{3} = \frac{a + 2b}{2}$, then $c =$

   (A) $\frac{a+2b}{6}$

   (B) $\frac{a+2b}{3}$

   (C) $\frac{a+2b}{2}$

   (D) $a + 2b$

   (E) $\frac{1}{2}$

## GRID-IN QUESTIONS

6. If $9x + 10 = 32$, what is the value of $9x - 10$?

7. If $7x - 3 = 11$, what is the value of $(7x - 3)^2$?

8. If $a = 2b$, $3b = 4c$, and $5c = 6a - 7$, what is the value of $c$?

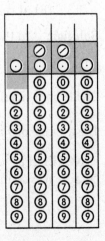

**9.** If $7y - 5x = 3$, what is the smallest integer value of $x$ for which $y > 75$?

**10.** If $x^2 + 5 < 6$ and $2x^2 + 7 > 8$, what is one possible value of $x$?

## Answer Key

**1.** C   **2.** C   **3.** D   **4.** A   **5.** A

**6.**  1 2

**7.**  1 2 1

**8.**  7 / 1 1

**9.**  1 0 5

**10.**  3 / 4

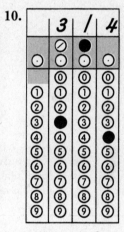

or any number satisfying $.71 < x < 1$

## 7-H WORD PROBLEMS

A typical PSAT has several word problems. In this chapter you have already seen word problems on consecutive integers in Section 7-A, fractions in Section 7-B, percents in Section 7-C, ratios and proportions in Section 7-D, and averages in Section 7-E. Later in this chapter you will see word problems involving probability, circles, triangles, and other geometric figures. A few of these problems can be solved with just arithmetic, but most of them require basic algebra.

In problems involving ages, remember that "years ago" means you need to subtract, and "years from now" means you need to add.

## Age Problems

Example 1 below is the same as Example 2 in Chapter 6. In Chapter 6 you were shown how to solve it by backsolving; now we will show you the correct algebraic solution.

### EXAMPLE 1

Judy is now twice as old as Adam, but six years ago, she was five times as old as he was. How old is Judy now?

(A) 8
(B) 16
(C) 20
(D) 24
(E) 32

**Solution.** Let $x$ = Adam's age now, and fill in the table below.

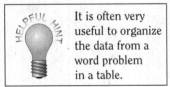

It is often very useful to organize the data from a word problem in a table.

|             | Judy     | Adam    |
|-------------|----------|---------|
| Now         | $2x$     | $x$     |
| 6 years ago | $2x - 6$ | $x - 6$ |

Now translate: Judy's age six years ago was five times Adam's age:

$$2x - 6 = 5(x - 6)$$
$$2x - 6 = 5x - 30 \Rightarrow 24 = 3x \Rightarrow x = 8.$$

Adam is now 8. However, 8 is *not* the answer. The question could have asked for Adam's age now or six years ago or at any time. It could have asked for Judy's age at any time or for their combined ages. What it did ask for is Judy's age now, which is 16, twice Adam's age (Choice B).

In all word problems on the PSAT, circle what you're looking for in your exam booklet. Don't answer the wrong question!

## Distance Problems

All distance problems involve one of three variations of the same formula:

$$\text{distance} = \text{rate} \times \text{time} \quad \text{rate} = \frac{\text{distance}}{\text{time}}$$

$$\text{time} = \frac{\text{distance}}{\text{rate}}$$

These are usually abbreviated, $d = rt$, $r = \frac{d}{t}$, and $t = \frac{d}{r}$.

### EXAMPLE 2

Justin drove 1 mile, from Exit 10 to Exit 11 on the thruway, at 50 miles per hour. Adam drove the same distance at 60 miles per hour. How many *seconds* longer did it take Justin than Adam to drive that mile?

**Solution.** The time to drive 1 mile at 50 miles per hour is given by

$$t = \frac{1 \text{ mile}}{50 \text{ miles per hour}} = \frac{1}{50} \text{ hour} = \frac{1}{50} \times 60 \text{ minutes} =$$

$$\frac{6}{5} \text{ minutes} = 1\frac{1}{5} \text{ minutes}$$

The time to drive 1 mile at 60 miles per hour is given by

$$t = \frac{1 \text{ mile}}{60 \text{ miles per hour}} = \frac{1}{60} \text{ hour} = 1 \text{ minute.}$$

The difference is $\frac{1}{5}$ minute $= \frac{1}{5}$ (60 seconds) $= 12$ seconds.

Note that the solution to Example 2 used the time formula but required only arithmetic, not algebra. Example 3 requires an algebraic solution.

### EXAMPLE 3

Eve drove from her home to college at an average speed of 60 miles per hour. Returning over the same route, due to construction delays, she was able to average only 45 miles per hour. If the return trip took 30 minutes longer, how many miles did she drive each way?

(A) 1.5
(B) 2
(C) 2.5
(D) 90
(E) 180

**Solution.** Let $x =$ the number of hours it took to go. Then to return, it took $x + 0.5$ hours (*not* $x + 30$). Now make a table.

|          | Rate | Time    | Distance   |
|----------|------|---------|------------|
| going    | 60   | $x$     | $60x$      |
| returning| 45   | $x + 0.5$ | $45(x + 0.5)$ |

Since she drove the same distance going and returning:

$$60x = 45(x + 0.5) \Rightarrow 60x = 45x + 22.5 \Rightarrow 15x = 22.5 \Rightarrow x = 1.5.$$

Now be sure to answer the correct question. Choices A, B, and C are the time, in hours, for going, returning, and the round-trip; Choices D and E are the distances each way and round-trip. You could have been asked for any of the five. If you circled what you're looking for, you won't make a careless mistake. Eve drove 60(1.5) = 90 miles each way, and so the correct answer is Choice D.

The $d$ in $d = rt$ stands for "distance," but it could represent any type of work that is performed at a certain rate $r$ for a certain amount of time $t$. Example 3 did not have to be about distance. Instead of driving 90 miles at 45 miles per hour for 2 hours, Eve could have read 90 pages at a rate of 45 pages per hour for 2 hours or planted 90 flowers at the rate of 45 flowers per hour for 2 hours or typed 90 words at a rate of 45 words per minute for 2 minutes.

Most algebraic word problems on the PSAT are not too difficult. If you get stuck on one, however, don't despair. Use one or more of the tactics that you learned in Chapter 6, especially backsolving, to eliminate choices and, if necessary, guess.

# Practice Exercises

## MULTIPLE-CHOICE QUESTIONS

**1.** In 7 years Danielle will be twice as old as she was 8 years ago. How old is Danielle now?

(A) 7
(B) 15
(C) 23
(D) 30
(E) 37

**2.** In the morning, Alan drove 100 miles at the rate of 60 miles per hour; in the afternoon, he drove another 100 miles at the rate of 40 miles per hour. What was his average rate of speed, in miles per hour, for the day?

(A) 45
(B) 48
(C) 50
(D) 52
(E) 55

**3.** In a family of three, the father weighed 5 times as much as the child, and the mother weighed $\frac{3}{4}$ as much as the father. If the three of them weighed a total of 390 pounds, how much did the mother weigh?

(A) 40
(B) 100
(C) 125
(D) 150
(E) 200

**4.** At 7:00 P.M., the hostess of the party remarked that only $\frac{1}{4}$ of her guests had arrived so far but that as soon as 10 more showed up, $\frac{1}{3}$ of the guests would be there. How many people were invited?

(A) 20
(B) 32
(C) 80
(D) 120
(E) 144

**5.** If the sum of 5 consecutive integers is $S$, what is the largest of those integers in terms of $S$?

(A) $\frac{S-10}{5}$

(B) $\frac{S+4}{4}$

(C) $\frac{S+5}{4}$

(D) $\frac{S-5}{2}$

(E) $\frac{S+10}{5}$

## GRID-IN QUESTIONS

**6.** A box contains only red, yellow, and green jelly beans. The number of red jelly beans is $\frac{4}{5}$ the number of green ones, and the number of green ones is $\frac{3}{4}$ the number of yellow ones. If there are 470 jelly beans in all, how many of them are yellow?

**7.** On a certain project the only grades awarded were 75 and 100. If 85 students completed the project and the average of their grades was 85, how many earned 100?

**8.** Since 1953, when Frank graduated from high school, he has gained two pounds every year. In 1983 he was 40% heavier than in 1953. What percent of his 1998 weight was his 1983 weight?

**9.** The number of baseball cards in Neil's collection is 80% of the number in Larry's collection. If Neil has 80 fewer baseball cards than Larry, how many do they have altogether?

**10.** What is the greater of two numbers whose product is 700, if the sum of the two numbers exceeds their difference by 20?

## Answer Key

1. C    2. B    3. D    4. D    5. E

6. 200    7. 34    8. 87.5    9. 720    10. 70

# Geometry

> *Although about 30 percent of the math questions on the PSAT involve geometry, you need to know only a relatively small number of facts—far fewer than you would learn in a geometry course—and, of course, you don't need to provide proofs. In the next six sections we will review all of the geometry that you need to know to do well on the PSAT. Also, we will present the material exactly as it appears on the PSAT, using the same vocabulary and notation, which may be slightly different from the terminology you have used in your math classes.*

## 7-I  LINES AND ANGLES

An *angle* is formed by the intersection of two line segments, rays, or lines. The point of intersection is called the *vertex*. On the PSAT, angles are always measured in degrees.

### Key Fact I1

Angles are classified according to their degree measures.

- An *acute* angle measures less than 90° (Figure 1).
- A *right* angle measures 90° (Figure 2).
- An *obtuse* angle measures more than 90° but less than 180° (Figure 3).
- A *straight* angle measures 180° (Figure 4).

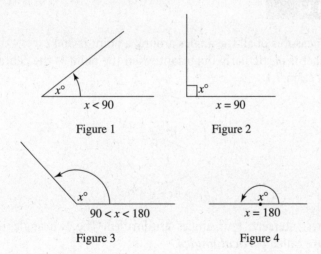

| | |
|---|---|
| $x < 90$ | $x = 90$ |
| Figure 1 | Figure 2 |
| $90 < x < 180$ | $x = 180$ |
| Figure 3 | Figure 4 |

> **NOTE**
>
> A small square like the one in Figure 2 at left *always* means that the angle is a right angle. On the PSAT, if an angle has a square in it, it must be a 90° angle, *even if the figure has not been drawn to scale.*

### Key Fact I2

If two or more angles form a straight angle, the sum of their measures is 180°.

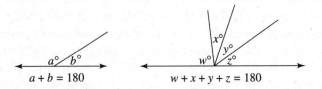

$a + b = 180$

$w + x + y + z = 180$

### EXAMPLE 1

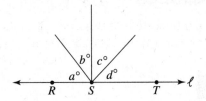

In the figure above, $R$, $S$, and $T$ are all on line $\ell$. What is the average of $a$, $b$, $c$, and $d$?

**Solution.** Since $\angle RST$ is a straight angle, by **KEY FACT I2**, $a + b + c + d = 180$, and so their average is $\frac{180}{4} = 45$.

### Key Fact I3

The sum of the measures of all the angles around a point is 360°.

**NOTE:** This fact is particularly important when the point is the center of a circle, as we shall see in Section 7-L.

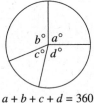

$a + b + c + d = 360$

When two lines intersect, four angles are formed. The two angles in each pair of opposite angles are called *vertical angles*.

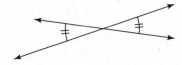

### Key Fact I4

Vertical angles have equal measures.

## EXAMPLE 2

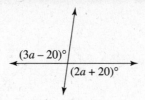

In the figure above, what is the value of *a*?

**Solution.** Because vertical angles are equal, $3a - 20 = 2a + 20 \Rightarrow a = 40$.

Two lines that intersect to form right angles are called **perpendicular**.
Two lines that never intersect are said to be **parallel**. So, parallel lines form no angles. However, if a third line, called a **transversal**, intersects a pair of parallel lines, eight angles are formed; the relationships among these angles are very important.

### Key Fact I5

If a pair of parallel lines is cut by a transversal that is not perpendicular to the parallel lines,

- Four of the angles are acute, and four are obtuse.
- All four acute angles are equal: $a = c = e = g$.
- All four obtuse angles are equal: $b = d = f = h$.
- The sum of any acute angle and any obtuse angle is 180°; for example, $d + e = 180, c + f = 180, b + g = 180, \ldots$

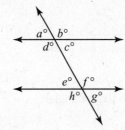

 You must know **KEY FACT I5**—almost every PSAT has questions based on it. However, you do *not* need to know the special terms you learned in your geometry class for these pairs of angles; those terms are not used on the PSAT.

## EXAMPLE 3

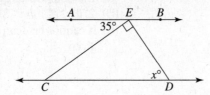

In the figure above, $\overleftrightarrow{AB}$ is parallel to $\overleftrightarrow{CD}$. What is the value of *x*?

**Solution.** Let *y* be the measure of $\angle BED$. Then, by **KEY FACT I2**,

$$35 + 90 + y = 180 \Rightarrow 125 + y = 180 \Rightarrow y = 55.$$

Since $\overleftrightarrow{AB}$ and $\overleftrightarrow{CD}$ are parallel, by **KEY FACT I5**, $x = y \Rightarrow x = 55$.

# Practice Exercises

## MULTIPLE-CHOICE QUESTIONS

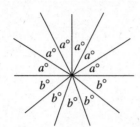

1. In the figure above, what is the value of $\frac{b+a}{b-a}$?

   (A) 6
   (B) 11
   (C) 30
   (D) 36
   (E) 66

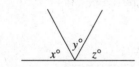

Note: Figure not drawn to scale

2. In the figure above, $x:y = 3:5$ and $z:y = 2:1$. What is the measure of the largest angle?

   (A) 60
   (B) 90
   (C) 100
   (D) 120
   (E) 150

3. What is the measure of the smaller angle formed by the minute and hour hands of a clock at 1:40?

   (A) 120°
   (B) 135°
   (C) 150°
   (D) 170°
   (E) 180°

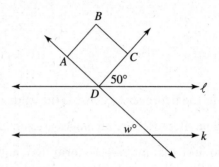

4. In the figure above, lines $k$ and $\ell$ are parallel, and line $\ell$ passes through $D$, one of the vertices of square $ABCD$. What is the value of $w$?

   (A) 30
   (B) 40
   (C) 45
   (D) 50
   (E) 60

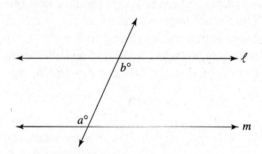

Note: Figure not drawn to scale

5. In the figure above, $\ell \parallel m$. Which of the following statements about $a + b$ is true?

   (A) $a + b < 180$
   (B) $a + b = 180$
   (C) $180 < a + b \le 270$
   (D) $270 < a + b \le 360$
   (E) It cannot be determined from the information given.

## GRID-IN QUESTIONS

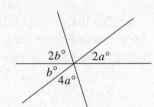

**6.** In the figure above, what is the value of *b*?

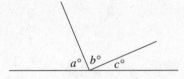

**7.** In the figure above, if *a:b:c* = 3:4:1, what is the value of *a*?

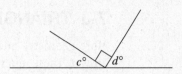

**8.** In the figure above, what is the value of *c* if *d:c* = 3:2?

**9.** *A*, *B*, and *C* are points on a line with *B* between *A* and *C*. Let *M* and *N* be the midpoints of $\overline{AB}$ and $\overline{BC}$, respectively. If *AB* = 3*BC*, what is $\frac{AB}{MN}$?

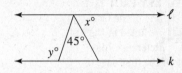

**10.** In the figure above, lines *k* and *l* are parallel. What is the value of *y* − *x*?

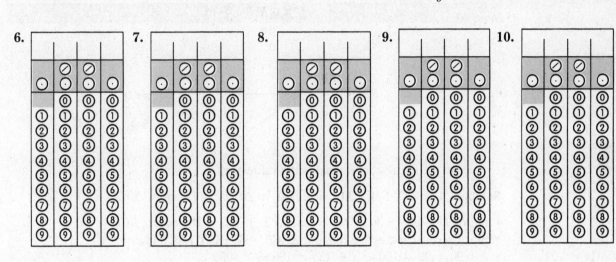

## Answer Key

**1.** B     **2.** C     **3.** D     **4.** B     **5.** E

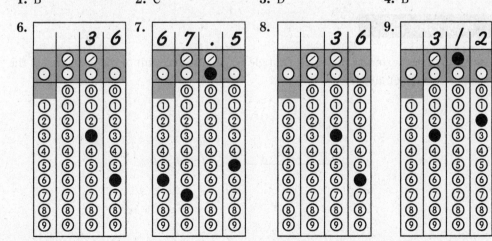

## 7-J  TRIANGLES

More geometry questions on the PSAT pertain to triangles than to any other topic. To answer these questions correctly, you need to know several important facts about the angles and sides of triangles. The **KEY FACTS** in this section are extremely useful. *Be sure you learn them all.*

### Key Fact J1

In any triangle, the sum of the measures of the three angles is 180°.

**KEY FACT J1** is one of the facts included in the Reference Information box on the first page of each math section of the PSAT.

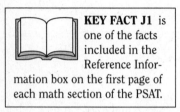

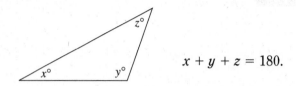

$x + y + z = 180.$

### EXAMPLE 1

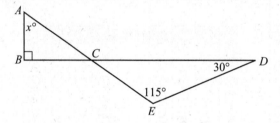

In the figure above, what is the value of $x$?

**Solution.** Use **KEY FACT J1** twice: first, in $\triangle CDE$ and then in $\triangle ABC$.

• m$\angle DCE + 115 + 30 = 180 \Rightarrow$ m$\angle DCE + 145 = 180 \Rightarrow$ m$\angle DCE = 35$
• Since vertical angles are equal, m$\angle ACB = 35$ [**KEY FACT I4**]
• $x + 90 + 35 = 180 \Rightarrow x + 125 = 180 \Rightarrow x = 55$

An ***exterior angle*** of a triangle is an angle formed by one side of the triangle and the extension of another side.

### Key Fact J2

The measure of an exterior angle of a triangle is equal to the sum of the measures of the two opposite interior angles.

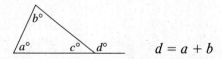

$d = a + b$

## EXAMPLE 2

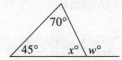

In the figure above, what is the value of $w$?

**Solution.** By **KEY FACT J2**: $w = 45 + 70 = 115$.

### Key Fact J3

In any triangle

- the longest side is opposite the largest angle.
- the shortest side is opposite the smallest angle.
- sides with the same length are opposite angles with the same measure.

A triangle with two equal sides is called **isosceles**; the angles opposite the two equal sides have the same measure. A triangle with three equal sides is called **equilateral**; it has three equal angles, each of which measures $60°$.

## EXAMPLE 3

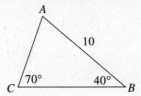

Note: Figure not drawn to scale

Which of the following statements about $\triangle ABC$ in the figure above must be true?

   I.  $m\angle A = 70°$
  II.  $BC = 10$
 III.  Perimeter of $\triangle ABC = 30$

(A) I only
(B) II only
(C) I and II only
(D) I and III only
(E) I, II, and III

**Solution.**

- By **KEY FACT J1**, $m\angle A + 70 + 40 = 180 \Rightarrow m\angle A = 70$. (I is true.)
- Therefore, $m\angle A = m\angle C$, and by **KEY FACT J3**, $BC = 10$. (II is true.)
- Since $\angle B$ is the smallest angle, $AC$ is the smallest side. In particular, it is less than 10.
- Therefore, the perimeter is less than 30. (III is false.)
- Only I and II are true (Choice C).

*Right triangles* are triangles that have one right angle and two acute ones. The side opposite the 90° angle is called the **hypotenuse**, and by **KEY FACT J3**, it is the longest side. The other two sides are called the *legs*.

## EXAMPLE 4

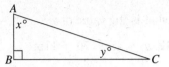

In the figure above, what is the average (arithmetic mean) of $x$ and $y$?

**Solution.** Since the diagram indicates that $\triangle ABC$ is a right triangle, then, by **KEY FACT J1**, $90 + x + y = 180 \Rightarrow x + y = 90$. The average of $x$ and $y$ is $\frac{x+y}{2} = \frac{90}{2} = 45$.

The most important facts concerning right triangles are the **Pythagorean theorem** and its converse, which are given in **KEY FACT J4**.

### Key Fact J4

If $a$, $b$, and $c$ are the lengths of the sides of a triangle, with $a \leq b \leq c$, then the triangle is a right triangle if and only if $a^2 + b^2 = c^2$.

**KEY FACT J4** is one of the facts included in the Reference Information box on the first page of each math section of the PSAT.

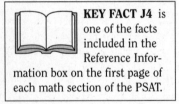

$$a^2 + b^2 = c^2$$

Consider the following two triangles.

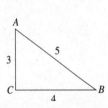

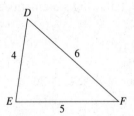

Since $3^2 + 4^2 = 5^2$, $\triangle ABC$ is a right triangle, whereas $\triangle DEF$ is not a right triangle, since $4^2 + 5^2 \neq 6^2$.

## EXAMPLE 5

Which of the following are *not* the sides of a right triangle?
(A) 6, 8, 10
(B) 1, 1, $\sqrt{2}$
(C) 1, $\sqrt{3}$, 2
(D) $\sqrt{3}$, $\sqrt{4}$, $\sqrt{5}$
(E) 5, 12, 13

**Solution.** Just check each of the choices.

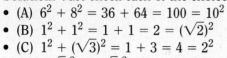

- (A) $6^2 + 8^2 = 36 + 64 = 100 = 10^2$     These *are* the sides of a right triangle.
- (B) $1^2 + 1^2 = 1 + 1 = 2 = (\sqrt{2})^2$     These *are* the sides of a right triangle.
- (C) $1^2 + (\sqrt{3})^2 = 1 + 3 = 4 = 2^2$     These *are* the sides of a right triangle.
- (D) $(\sqrt{3})^2 + (\sqrt{4})^2 = 3 + 4 = 7 \neq (\sqrt{5})^2$     These *are not* the sides of a right triangle.

Stop. The answer is Choice D. There is no need to check Choice E.

On the PSAT, the most common right triangles whose sides are *integers* are the 3-4-5 triangle and its multiples, such as 6-8-10 and 30-40-50.

Let $x$ = length of each leg, and $h$ = length of the hypotenuse, of an isosceles right triangle. By the Pythagorean theorem (**KEY FACT J4**).

$$x^2 + x^2 = h^2 \Rightarrow 2x^2 = h^2 \Rightarrow h = \sqrt{2x^2} = x\sqrt{2}$$

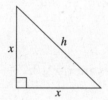

## Key Fact J5

In a 45-45-90 right triangle, the sides are $x$, $x$, and $x\sqrt{2}$.

In a 45-45-90 right triangle:

- Multiply the length of a leg by $\sqrt{2}$ to find the length of the hypotenuse.
- Divide the hypotenuse by $\sqrt{2}$ to find the length of each leg.

**KEY FACT J5** is one of the facts included in the Reference Information box on the first page of each math section of the PSAT.

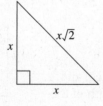 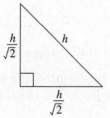

## Key Fact J6

A diagonal of a square divides the square into two isosceles right triangles.

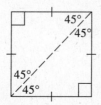

An ***altitude*** of a triangle is a line segment drawn from a vertex, perpendicular to the opposite side.

### Key Fact J7

An altitude divides an equilateral triangle into two 30-60-90 right triangles.

Let $2x$ be the length of each side of equilateral triangle $ABC$, in which altitude $\overline{AD}$ is drawn. Then $\triangle ABD$ is a 30-60-90 right triangle, and its sides are $x$, $2x$, and $h$. By the Pythagorean theorem,

$$x^2 + h^2 = (2x)^2 = 4x^2, \text{ so } h^2 = 3x^2,$$
$$\text{and } h = \sqrt{3x^2} = x\sqrt{3}.$$

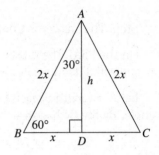

### Key Fact J8

In a 30-60-90 right triangle the sides are $x$, $x\sqrt{3}$, and $2x$.

In a 30-60-90 right triangle:

If you know the length of the shorter leg ($x$),

- multiply it by $\sqrt{3}$ to get the length of the longer leg, and
- multiply it by 2 to get the length of the hypotenuse.

**KEY FACT J8** is one of the facts included in the Reference Information box on the first page of each math section of the PSAT.

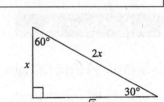

If you know the length of the longer leg ($a$),

- divide it by $\sqrt{3}$ to get the length of the shorter leg, and
- multiply the shorter leg by 2 to get the length of the hypotenuse.

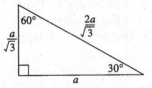

If you know the length of the hypotenuse ($h$),

- divide it by 2 to get the length of the shorter leg, and
- multiply the shorter leg by $\sqrt{3}$ to get the length of the longer leg.

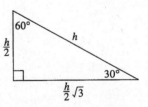

## EXAMPLE 6

What is the area of a square whose diagonal is 4?

(A) 4
(B) 8
(C) 16
(D) $4\sqrt{3}$
(E) $16\sqrt{3}$

**Solution.** Draw a diagonal in a square, creating two 45-45-90 right triangles. Label the diagonal 4 and each side *s*.

By **KEY FACT J6**,

$$s = \frac{4}{\sqrt{2}} \text{ and } A = s^2 = \left(\frac{4}{\sqrt{2}}\right)^2 = \frac{16}{2} = 8. \text{ The answer is Choice B.}$$

## EXAMPLE 7

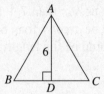

In equilateral triangle *ABC*, the length of altitude *AD* is 6. What is the perimeter of △*ABC*?

(A) 18

(B) $6\sqrt{3}$

(C) $12\sqrt{3}$

(D) $18\sqrt{3}$

(E) 36

**Solution.** Use **KEY FACT J8**.

• Divide the longer leg, *AD*, of right triangle *ADB* by $\sqrt{3}$ to get the shorter leg, *BD*:

$$\frac{6}{\sqrt{3}} = \frac{6}{\sqrt{3}} \times \frac{\sqrt{3}}{\sqrt{3}} = \frac{6\sqrt{3}}{3} = 2\sqrt{3}.$$

• Multiply *BD* by 2 to get side *BC*. Then $BC = 2\left(2\sqrt{3}\right) = 4\sqrt{3}$.

• Finally, multiply *BC* by 3 to get the perimeter of △*ABC*: $3\left(4\sqrt{3}\right) = 12\sqrt{3}$.
• The answer is Choice C.

## Key Fact J9

**(Triangle Inequality)**

• The sum of the lengths of any two sides of a triangle is greater than the length of the third side.
• The difference of the lengths of any two sides of a triangle is less than the length of the third side.

## EXAMPLE 8

If the lengths of two of the sides of a triangle are 7 and 8, which of the following could be the length of the third side?

   I. 1
  II. 2
 III. 15

(A) None
(B) I only
(C) II only
(D) I and II only
(E) I, II, and III

**Solution.** Use **KEY FACT J9**.

- The length of the third side must be *less* than 7 + 8 = 15. So III is false.
- The length of the third side must be *greater* than 8 − 7 = 1. So I is false.
- *Any* number between 1 and 15 could be the length of the third side. So II is true.
- The answer is Choice C.

## Key Fact J10

The area of a triangle is given by $A = \frac{1}{2}bh$, where $b$ is the base and $h$ is the height.

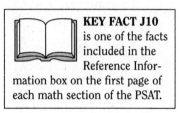

**KEY FACT J10** is one of the facts included in the Reference Information box on the first page of each math section of the PSAT.

**Note:**

**1.** *Any* side of the triangle can be taken as the base.
**2.** The height is the altitude drawn to the base from the opposite vertex.
**3.** In a right triangle, either leg can be the base and the other the height.
**4.** The height may be outside the triangle. [See the figure below.]

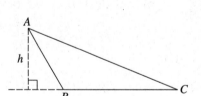

In the figure below:

If *AC* is the base, *BD* is the height. If *AB* is the base, *CE* is the height. If *BC* is the base, *AF* is the height.

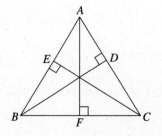

## EXAMPLE 9

What is the area of an equilateral triangle whose sides are 10?

(A) 30
(B) $25\sqrt{3}$
(C) 50
(D) $50\sqrt{3}$
(E) 100

**Solution.** Draw an equilateral triangle and one of its altitudes.

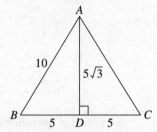

- By **KEY FACT J7**, $\triangle ABD$ is a 30-60-90 right triangle.
- By **KEY FACT J8**, $BD = 5$ and $AD = 5\sqrt{3}$.
- The area of $\triangle ABC = \frac{1}{2}(10)(5\sqrt{3}) = 25\sqrt{3}$ (Choice B).

Replacing 10 by $s$ in Example 10 yields a very useful result.

### Key Fact J11

If $A$ represents the area of an equilateral triangle with side $s$, then $A = \frac{s^2\sqrt{3}}{4}$.

For example, the area of an equilateral triangle whose sides are each 6 is

$$A = \frac{6^2\sqrt{3}}{4} = \frac{36\sqrt{3}}{4} = 9\sqrt{3}$$

Memorize the formula in KEY FACT J11: it is quite useful.

# Practice Exercises

## MULTIPLE-CHOICE QUESTIONS

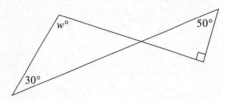

**1.** In the figure above, what is the value of $w$?

(A) 90
(B) 100
(C) 110
(D) 120
(E) 130

**2.** Two sides of a right triangle are 5 and 7. Which of the following could be the length of the third side?

  I. $\sqrt{24}$
  II. $\sqrt{54}$
  III. $\sqrt{74}$

(A) I only
(B) II only
(C) I and II
(D) I and III
(E) I, II, and III

Questions 3 and 4 refer to the following figure.

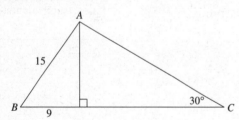

**3.** What is the perimeter of $\triangle ABC$?

(A) 48
(B) $48 + 12\sqrt{2}$
(C) $48 + 12\sqrt{3}$
(D) 72
(E) It cannot be determined from the information given.

**4.** What is the area of $\triangle ABC$?

(A) 108
(B) $54 + 72\sqrt{2}$
(C) $54 + 72\sqrt{3}$
(D) 198
(E) It cannot be determined from the information given.

**5.** Which of the following expresses a true relationship between $x$ and $y$ in the figure above?

(A) $y = 60 - x$
(B) $y = x$
(C) $x + y = 90$
(D) $y = 180 - 3x$
(E) $x = 90 - 3y$

## GRID-IN QUESTIONS

**6.** If the difference between the measures of the two smaller angles of a right triangle is 6°, what is the measure, in degrees, of the smallest angle?

**7.** What is the smallest integer $x$ for which $x$, $x + 5$, and $2x - 15$ could be the lengths of the sides of a triangle?

**8.** If the measures of the angles of a triangle are in the ratio of $1:2:3$ and if the length of the smallest side is 10, what is the length of the longest side?

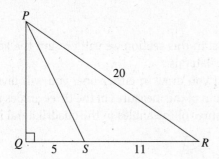

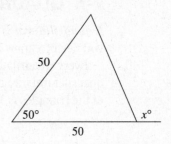

**9.** In the figure above, what is the value of *PS*?

**10.** In the figure above, what is the value of *x*?

6.
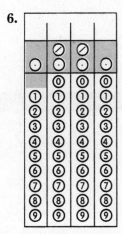

7.
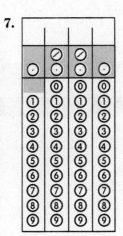

8.
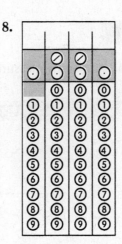

9.
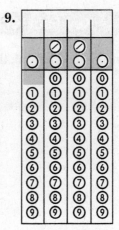

10.
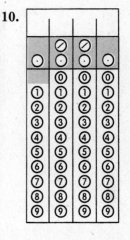

## Answer Key

**1.** C     **2.** D     **3.** C     **4.** C     **5.** A

6.
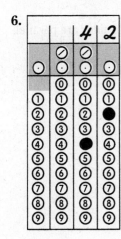

7.
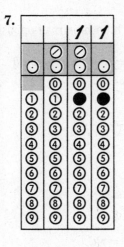

8.
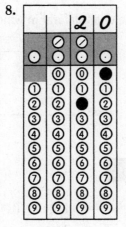

## 7-K QUADRILATERALS

A *quadrilateral* is a polygon with four sides. In this section we will present the key facts you need to know about three special quadrilaterals.

Every quadrilateral has two diagonals. If you draw in either one, you will divide the quadrilateral into two triangles. Since the sum of the measures of the three angles in each of the triangles is 180°, the sum of the measures of the angles in the quadrilateral is 360°.

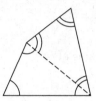

### Key Fact K1

In any quadrilateral, the sum of the measures of the four angles is 360°.

### EXAMPLE 1

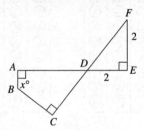

In the figure above, what is the value of $x$?

**Solution.** Since $\triangle DEF$ is an isosceles right triangle, m$\angle EDF = 45°$; also, since the two angles at vertex $D$ are vertical angles, their measures are equal. Therefore, the measure of $\angle ADC$ is 45°. Finally, since the sum of the measures of all four angles of $ABCD$ is 360°:

$$45 + 90 + 90 + x = 360 \Rightarrow 225 + x = 360 \Rightarrow x = 135.$$

A *parallelogram* is a quadrilateral in which both pairs of opposite sides are parallel.

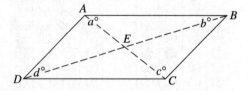

### Key Fact K2

Parallelograms have the following properties:

* Opposite sides are equal: $AB = CD$ and $AD = BC$.
* Opposite angles are equal: $a = c$ and $b = d$.
* Adjacent angles add up to 180°: $a + b = b + c = c + d = a + d = 180$.
* The diagonals bisect each other: $AE = EC$ and $DE = EB$.

## EXAMPLE 2

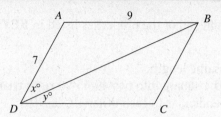

In the figure above, *ABCD* is a parallelogram. Which of the following statements must be true?

(A) $x < y$
(B) $x = y$
(C) $x > y$
(D) $x + y < 90$
(E) $x + y > 90$

**Solution.** Since $\overline{AB}$ and $\overline{CD}$ are parallel line segments cut by transversal $\overline{BD}$, m$\angle ABD = y°$. In $\triangle ABD$ $AB > AD$, so by **KEY FACT J3**, the measure of the angle opposite $\overline{AB}$ is greater than the measure of the angle opposite $\overline{AD}$. Therefore, $x > y$ (Choice C).

A **rectangle** is a parallelogram in which all four angles are right angles. Two adjacent sides of a rectangle are usually called the **length** (*l*) and the **width** (*w*).

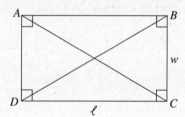

## Key Fact K3

Since a rectangle is a parallelogram, all of the properties listed in **KEY FACT K2** hold for rectangles. In addition,

- The measure of each angle in a rectangle is 90°.
- The diagonals of a rectangle have the same length: $AC = BD$.

A **square** is a rectangle in which all four sides have the same length.

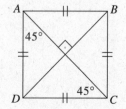

## Key Fact K4

Since a square is a rectangle, all of the properties listed in **KEY FACTS K2** and **K3** hold for squares. In addition,

- All four sides have the same length.
- Each diagonal divides the square into two 45-45-90 right triangles.
- The diagonals are perpendicular to each other: $AC \perp BD$.

## EXAMPLE 3

What is the length of each side of a square if its diagonals are 8?

**Solution.** Draw a diagram. In square *ABCD*, diagonal *AC* is the hypotenuse of a 45-45-90 right triangle, and side *AB* is a leg of that triangle. By **KEY FACT J5**,

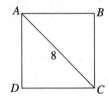

$$AB = \frac{AC}{\sqrt{2}} = \frac{8}{\sqrt{2}} \times \frac{\sqrt{2}}{\sqrt{2}} = \frac{8\sqrt{2}}{2} = 4\sqrt{2}.$$

The *perimeter* (*P*) of any polygon is the sum of the lengths of all its sides.

## Key Fact K5

In a rectangle, $P = 2(\ell + w)$, and in a square, $P = 4s$.

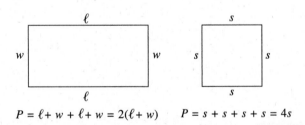

$$P = \ell + w + \ell + w = 2(\ell + w) \qquad P = s + s + s + s = 4s$$

## EXAMPLE 4

A rectangle is divided into two squares, each with a perimeter of 10. What is the perimeter of the rectangle?

(A) 10
(B) 12.5
(C) 15
(D) 17.5
(E) 20

**Solution.** Don't do anything until you have drawn a diagram.

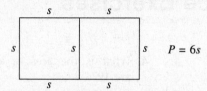

Since the perimeter of each square is 10, the length of each side is $10 \div 4 = 2.5$. Therefore, the perimeter of the rectangle is $6 \times 2.5 = 15$ (Choice C).

In Section 9-J we reviewed the formula for the ***area*** of a triangle. You also need to know the area formulas for a parallelogram, rectangle, and square.

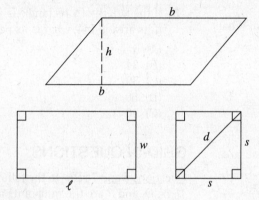

### Key Fact K6

Here are the area formulas you need to know:

- For a parallelogram: $A = bh$
- For a rectangle: $A = \ell w$
- For a square: $A = s^2$ or $A = \frac{1}{2}d^2$

> The formula for the area of a rectangle, given in **KEY FACT K6** is one of the facts included in the Reference Information box on the first page of each math section of the PSAT.

## EXAMPLE 5

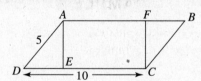

In the figure above, the area of parallelogram *ABCD* is 40. What is the area of rectangle *AFCE*?

(A) 20
(B) 24
(C) 28
(D) 32
(E) 36

**Solution.** Since the base *CD*, is 10 and the area of *ABCD* is 40, the height *AE* must be 4. Then $\triangle AED$ must be a 3-4-5 right triangle with *DE* = 3, which implies that *EC* = 7. The area of the rectangle is $7 \times 4 = 28$ (Choice C).

# Practice Exercises

## MULTIPLE-CHOICE QUESTIONS

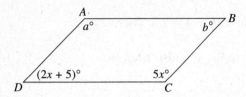

1. In the figure above, *ABCD* is a parallelogram. What is the value of $a - b$?

   (A) 25
   (B) 55
   (C) 70
   (D) 90
   (E) 125

2. What is the perimeter of a rectangle whose area is 21?

   (A) 10
   (B) 20
   (C) 21
   (D) 44
   (E) It cannot be determined from the information given.

3. The length of a rectangle is 10 more than the side of a square, and the width of the rectangle is 10 less than the side of the square. If the area of the square is 125, what is the area of the rectangle?

   (A) 25
   (B) 115
   (C) 125
   (D) 135
   (E) 225

4. What is the area of a square whose diagonals are 12?

   (A) $5\sqrt{2}$
   (B) $50\sqrt{2}$
   (C) 72
   (D) 144
   (E) $144\sqrt{2}$

5. If the length of a rectangle is 4 times its width, and if its area is 144, what is its perimeter?

   (A) 6
   (B) 24
   (C) 30
   (D) 60
   (E) 96

## GRID-IN QUESTIONS

Questions 6 and 7 refer to the following figure, in which *M*, *N*, *O*, and *P* are the midpoints of the sides of rectangle *ABCD*.

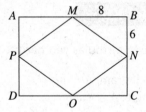

6. What is the perimeter of quadrilateral *MNOP*?

7. What is the area of quadrilateral *MNOP*?

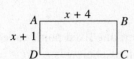 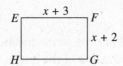 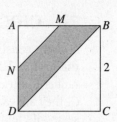

**8.** If in the figures above, the area of rectangle *ABCD* is 100, what is the area of rectangle *EFGH*?

**9.** In quadrilateral *PQRS*, the measure of angle *S* is 20 more than the average of the measures of the other three. What is the measure of angle *S*?

**10.** If in the figure above, *M* and *N* are the midpoints of two of the sides of square *ABCD*, what is the area of the shaded region?

6.  7.  8.  9.  10.

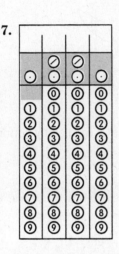 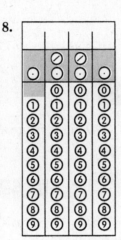 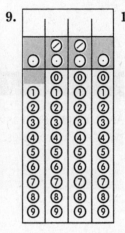 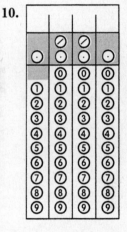

## Answer Key

1. C  2. E  3. A  4. C  5. D

6. 40  7. 96  8. 102  9. 105  10. 1.5

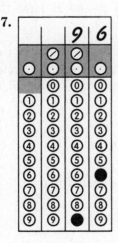

## 7-L CIRCLES

A *circle* consists of all the points that are the same distance from one fixed point called the *center*. That distance is called the *radius* of the circle. The figure below is a circle of radius 1 unit whose center is at the point *O*. Since *A*, *B*, *C*, *D*, and *E* are all points on circle *O*, they are each 1 unit from *O*. The word *radius* is also used to represent any of the line segments joining the center and a point on the circle. The plural of *radius* is *radii*. In circle *O*, $\overline{OA}$, $\overline{OB}$, $\overline{OC}$, $\overline{OD}$, and $\overline{OE}$ are all radii. If a circle has radius *r*, each of the radii is *r* units long.

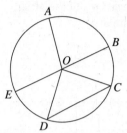

### Key Fact L1

Any triangle, such as $\triangle COD$ in the figure above, formed by connecting the endpoints of two radii, is isosceles.

### EXAMPLE 1

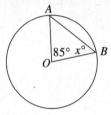

If *A* and *B* are points on circle *O*, what is the value of *x*?

**Solution.** Since $\triangle AOB$ is isosceles, angles *A* and *B* have the same measure. So $85 + x + x = 180 \Rightarrow 2x = 95 \Rightarrow x = 47.5$.

A line segment, such as $\overline{CD}$ in circle *O* at the beginning of this section, whose endpoints are on a circle, is called a *chord*. A chord such as $\overline{BE}$ in circle *O* that passes through the center is called a *diameter*. Since $\overline{BE}$ is made up of two radii, $\overline{OB}$ and $\overline{OE}$, a diameter is twice as long as a radius.

### Key Fact L2

If *d* is the diameter and *r* the radius of a circle, then $d = 2r$.

### Key Fact L3

A diameter is the longest chord that can be drawn in a circle.

## EXAMPLE 2

*A*, *B*, and *C*, the three vertices of right triangle *ABC*, all lie on a circle whose radius is 4. Which of the following statements *could* be true?

   I.  The hypotenuse of △*ABC* is 10
  II.  The perimeter of △*ABC* is 25
 III.  The area of △*ABC* is 35

(A)  None
(B)  I only
(C)  II only
(D)  III only
(E)  I, II, and III

**Solution.** Since the radius is 4, the diameter is 8. Since each side of △*ABC* is a chord, none of the sides can be greater than 8; so *AC* cannot be 10 (I is false), and the perimeter can surely not exceed 24 (II is false). Since the area of a right triangle can be calculated using one of the legs as the base and the other as the height, the area cannot exceed $\frac{1}{2}(8)(8) = 32$ and so cannot equal 35 (III is false). None of the statements is true (Choice A).

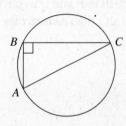

The total length around a circle is called the ***circumference*** of the circle. In every circle the ratio of the circumference to the diameter is exactly the same and is denoted by the symbol π (the Greek letter pi).

### Key Fact L4

For every circle,

$$\pi = \frac{\text{circumference}}{\text{diameter}} = \frac{C}{d} \quad \text{or} \quad C = \pi d \quad \text{or} \quad C = 2\pi r$$

 $C = 2\pi r$ is one of the facts included in the Reference Information box on the first page of each math section of the PSAT.

### Key Fact L5

The value of π is *approximately* 3.14.

## EXAMPLE 3

If the circumference of a circle is equal to the perimeter of a square whose sides are π, what is the radius of the circle?

 On almost every question on the PSAT that involve circles, you are expected to leave your answer in terms of π; so don't multiply by 3.14 unless you need to. If you need an approximation—to test a choice, for example—then use the π-key on your calculator.

**Solution.** If each side of the square is π, then its perimeter is 4π. Since the circumference of the circle is equal to the perimeter of the square, $C = 4\pi$. But $C = 2\pi r$, and so $2\pi r = 4\pi \Rightarrow r = 2$.

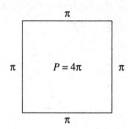

An *arc* consists of two points on a circle and all the points between them. If two points, such as *P* and *Q* in circle *O*, are the endpoints of a diameter, they divide the circle into two arcs called *semicircles*. On the PSAT, *arc AB* always refers to the small arc joining *A* and *B*.

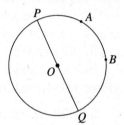

An angle whose vertex is at the center of a circle is called a *central angle*.

Key Fact L6

The degree measure of a complete circle is 360°.

**KEY FACT L6** is one of the facts included in the Reference Information box on the first page of each math section of the PSAT.

Key Fact L7

The degree measure of an arc equals the degree measure of the central angle that intercepts it.

**CAUTION:** Degree measure is *not* a measure of length. In these circles, arcs *AB* and *CD* each measure 72°, even though arc *CD* is much longer.

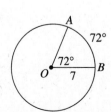

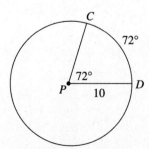

How long *is* arc *CD*? Since the radius of circle *P* is 10, its diameter is 20, and its circumference is $20\pi$. Since there are 360° in a circle, arc *CD* is $\frac{72}{360}$, or $\frac{1}{5}$, of the circumference: $\frac{1}{5}(20\pi) = 4\pi$.

### Key Fact L8

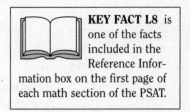

**KEY FACT L8** is one of the facts included in the Reference Information box on the first page of each math section of the PSAT.

The formula for the area of a circle of radius *r* is $A = \pi r^2$.

The area of circle *P*, above, is $\pi(10)^2 = 100\pi$ square units. The area of sector *CPD* is $\frac{1}{5}$ of the area of the circle: $\frac{1}{5}(100\pi) = 20\pi$.

### Key Fact L9

If an arc measures $x°$, the length of the arc is $\frac{x}{360}(2\pi r)$, and the area of the sector formed by the arc and two radii is $\frac{x}{360}(\pi r^2)$.

Examples 4 and 5 refer to the figure below, in which the radius of the inner circle is 4 and the radius of the outer circle is 6.

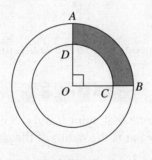

### EXAMPLE 4

What is the area of the shaded region, *ABCD*?

(A) $4\pi$
(B) $5\pi$
(C) $9\pi$
(D) $16\pi$
(E) $20\pi$

**Solution.** To find the area of *ABCD*, subtract the area of sector *DOC* from the area of sector *AOB*. Since m∠*AOB* is 90°, each sector is a quarter-circle.

The area of $AOB = \frac{1}{4}\pi(6)^2 = \frac{1}{4}(36\pi) = 9\pi$.

The area of $COD = \frac{1}{4}\pi(4)^2 = \frac{1}{4}(16\pi) = 4\pi$.

So the area of $ABCD = 9\pi - 4\pi = 5\pi$ (Choice B).

## EXAMPLE 5

What is the perimeter of the shaded region, *ABCD*?

(A) $5\pi$

(B) $2 + 5\pi$

(C) $4 + 5\pi$

(D) $4 + 20\pi$

(E) $4 + 24\pi$

**Solution.** Arcs *AB* and *CD* are each quarter-circles, and so their lengths are $\frac{1}{4}$ of the circumferences of circles whose diameters are 8 and 12.

$$AB = \frac{1}{4}(12\pi) = 3\pi \qquad CD = \frac{1}{4}(8\pi) = 2\pi$$

The lengths of line segments *AD* and *BC* are each $6 - 4 = 2$. So the perimeter is $2 + 2 + 3\pi + 2\pi = 4 + 5\pi$ (Choice C).

A line that touches a circle at exactly one point is called a ***tangent***. In the figure below, line *l* is ***tangent*** to circle *O* at point *P*.

### Key Fact L10

A line tangent to a circle is perpendicular to the radius drawn to the point of contact.

## EXAMPLE 6

If line *l* is tangent to circle *O* at point *P* and if *B* is a point on *l* such that $PB = 8$ and $OB = 10$, what is the radius of the circle?

**Solution.** Draw a diagram and label it. By **KEY FACT L10**, radius $\overline{OP}$ is perpendicular to *l*. Therefore, $\triangle OPB$ is a right triangle.

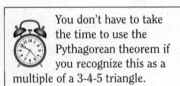

You don't have to take the time to use the Pythagorean theorem if you recognize this as a multiple of a 3-4-5 triangle.

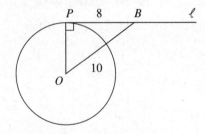

By the Pythagorean theorem,

$$OP^2 + 8^2 = 10^2 \Rightarrow OP^2 + 64 = 100 \Rightarrow OP^2 = 36 \Rightarrow OP = 6.$$

# Practice Exercises

## MULTIPLE-CHOICE QUESTIONS

Questions 1 and 2 refer to the following figure.

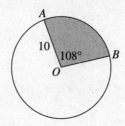

1. What is the length of arc *AB*?

   (A) $3\pi$
   (B) $6\pi$
   (C) $12\pi$
   (D) $18\pi$
   (E) $30\pi$

2. What is the area of the shaded sector?

   (A) $3\pi$
   (B) $6\pi$
   (C) $12\pi$
   (D) $18\pi$
   (E) $30\pi$

3. What is the circumference of a circle whose area is $100\pi$?

   (A) 10
   (B) 20
   (C) $10\pi$
   (D) $20\pi$
   (E) $25\pi$

4. What is the area of a circle whose circumference is $\pi$?

   (A) $\frac{\pi}{4}$
   (B) $\frac{\pi}{2}$
   (C) $\pi$
   (D) $2\pi$
   (E) $4\pi$

5. What is the area of a circle whose radius is the diagonal of a square whose area is 4?

   (A) $2\pi$
   (B) $2\pi\sqrt{2}$
   (C) $4\pi$
   (D) $8\pi$
   (E) $16\pi$

## GRID-IN QUESTIONS

6. The circumferences of two circles are in the ratio of 3:5. What is the ratio of the area of the smaller circle to the area of the larger circle?

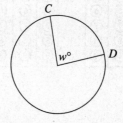

7. In the figure above, the ratio of the length of arc *CD* to the circumference of the circle is 2:9. What is the value of *w*?

**8.** The circumference of a circle is $a\pi$ units, and the area of the circle is $b\pi$ square units. If $a = b$, what is the radius of the circle?

**10.** If the area of a circle whose diameter is $\pi$, is written as $a\pi^b$, what is the value of $ab$?

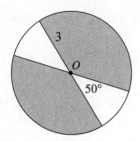

**9.** In the figure above, the radius of circle $O$ is 3, and the area of the shaded region is $k\pi$. What is the value of $k$?

## Answer Key

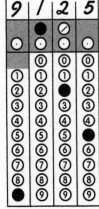

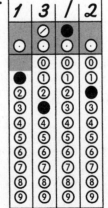

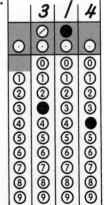

# 7-M SOLID GEOMETRY

There is very little solid geometry on the PSAT. Basically, all you need to know are the formulas for the volume and surface areas of rectangular solids (including cubes) and cylinders.

A **rectangular solid** or **box** is a solid formed by six rectangles, called **faces**. The sides of the rectangles are called **edges**. As shown in the diagram below, the edges are called the **length**, **width**, and **height**. A **cube** is a rectangular solid in which the length, width, and height are equal, so all the edges are the same length.

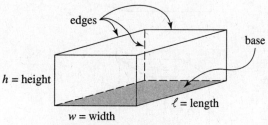

**RECTANGULAR SOLID**

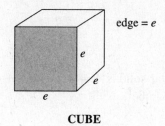

**CUBE**

> **KEY FACT M1**
> is one of the facts included in the Reference Information box on the first page of each math section of the PSAT.

## Key Fact M1

- The formula for the volume of a rectangular solid is $V = \ell wh$.
- In a cube, all the edges are equal. Therefore, if $e$ is the edge, the formula for the volume is $V = e^3$.

## EXAMPLE 1

The base of a rectangular tank is 3 feet wide and 4 feet long; the height of the tank is 10 inches. If water is pouring into the tank at the rate of 3 cubic feet per hour, how many *minutes* will be required to fill the tank?

**Solution.** Draw a picture. Change all units to feet. Then the volume of the tank is $3 \times 4 \times \frac{5}{6} = 10$ cubic feet. At 3 cubic feet per hour, the required time is $\frac{10}{3}$ hours = $\frac{10}{3}(60) = 200$ minutes.

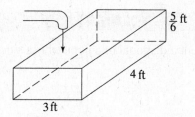

To find the ***surface area*** of a rectangular solid, add the area of the six rectangular faces. Since the top and bottom faces are equal, the front and back faces are equal, and the left and right faces are equal, we can calculate the area of one face from each pair and then double the sum. In a cube, each of the six faces has the same area.

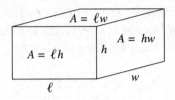

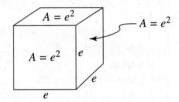

### Key Fact M2

- The surface area of a rectangular solid is $A = 2(lw + lh + wh)$.
- The surface area of a cube is $A = 6e^2$.

## EXAMPLE 2

The volume of a cube is $v$ cubic yards, and its surface area is $a$ square feet. If $v = a$, what is the length in inches of each edge?

**Solution.** Draw a diagram. If $e$ is the length of the edge in yards, then $3e$ is the length in feet, and $36e$ is the length in inches. Therefore, $v = e^3$ and $a = 6(3e)^2 = 6(9e^2) = 54e^2$.

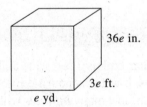

Since $v = a$, $e^3 = 54e^2 \Rightarrow e = 54$; the length of each edge is $36(54) = 1944$ inches.

A ***diagonal*** of a box is a line segment joining a vertex on the top of the box to the opposite vertex on the bottom.

## EXAMPLE 3

What is the length of a diagonal of a cube whose sides are 1?

**Solution.** Draw a diagram and label it. Since the base is a $1 \times 1$ square, the length of diagonal $\overline{AC}$ is $\sqrt{2}$. Then $\overline{AD}$, a diagonal of the cube, is the hypotenuse of right triangle $ACD$ whose legs are 1 and $\sqrt{2}$; so

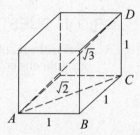

$$(AD)^2 = 1^2 + (\sqrt{2})^2 = 1 + 2 = 3, \text{ and } AD = \sqrt{3}.$$

A **cylinder** is similar to a rectangular solid except that the base is a circle instead of a rectangle. The volume of a cylinder is the area of its circular base ($\pi r^2$) times its height ($h$).

> **KEY FACT M3** is one of the facts included in the Reference Information box on the first page of each math section of the PSAT.

### Key Fact M3

The formula for the volume, $V$, of a cylinder whose circular base has radius $r$ and whose height is $h$ is $V = \pi r^2 h$.

### EXAMPLE 4

What is the height of a cylinder whose diameter is 10 and whose volume is $100\pi$?

**Solution.** Since the diameter is 10, the radius is 5.

$$V = 100\pi = \pi r^2 h = \pi(5^2)h = 25\pi h \Rightarrow h = 4.$$

# Practice Exercises

## MULTIPLE-CHOICE QUESTIONS

1. What is the volume, in cubic feet, of a rectangular solid whose length, width, and height are 1 foot 3 inches, 1 foot 4 inches, and 1 foot 6 inches?

   (A) 2.5
   (B) 2.912
   (C) 3.375
   (D) 49
   (E) 4320

2. The volume of a cube is $a$ cubic feet and its surface area is $b$ square feet. If $a = b$, what is the length, in feet, of each edge?

   (A) 1
   (B) 2
   (C) 6
   (D) 12
   (E) 36

3. What is the volume of a cube whose surface area is 150?

   (A) 25
   (B) 100
   (C) 125
   (D) 1000
   (E) 15,625

4. What is the surface area of a cube whose volume is 64?

   (A) 16
   (B) 64
   (C) 96
   (D) 128
   (E) 384

5. The height and radius of a cylinder are each equal to the edge of a cube. What is the ratio of the volume of the cube to the volume of the cylinder?

   (A) $\frac{1}{\pi}$
   (B) $\pi$
   (C) $\pi^2$
   (D) $\pi^3$
   (E) It cannot be determined from the information given.

## GRID-IN QUESTIONS

6. What is the number of cubic inches in one cubic foot?

7. What is the volume, in cubic centimeters, of a cube in which the sum of the lengths of all the edges is 6 centimeters?

8. A solid metal cube with sides of 3 inches is placed in a rectangular tank whose length, width, and height are 3, 4, and 5 inches, respectively. What is the volume, in cubic inches, of water that the tank can now hold?

**9.** A rectangular tank has a base that is 16 inches by 5 inches and a height of 18 inches. If the tank is half full of water, by how many inches will the water level rise if 260 cubic inches of water are poured into it?

**10.** The base of a rectangular tank is 2 feet wide and 4 feet long; the height of the tank is 20 inches. If water is pouring into the tank at the rate of 2 cubic inches per second, how many *hours* will be required to fill the tank?

## Answer Key

**1.** A          **2.** C          **3.** C          **4.** C          **5.** A

**6.** 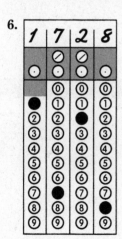          **7.**          **8.**          **9.**          **10.**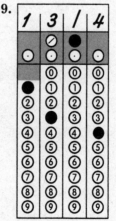

## 7-N COORDINATE GEOMETRY

The PSAT has very few questions on coordinate geometry. Most often they deal with the coordinates of points and occasionally with the slope of a line. You are *never* required to draw a graph.

In coordinate geometry, each point in the plane is assigned two numbers, an **x-coordinate** and a **y-coordinate**, which are written as an ordered pair, **(x, y)**.

- Points to the right of the *y*-axis have positive *x*-coordinates, and those to the left have negative *x*-coordinates.
- Points above the *x*-axis have positive *y*-coordinates, and those below it have negative *y*-coordinates.
- If a point is on the *x*-axis, its *y*-coordinate is 0.
- If a point is on the *y*-axis, its *x*-coordinate is 0.

For example, point *A* in the figure below is labeled (2, 3) since it is 2 units to the right of the *y*-axis and 3 units above the *x*-axis. Similarly, *B*(−3, −5) is 3 units to the left of the *y*-axis and 5 units below the *x*-axis.

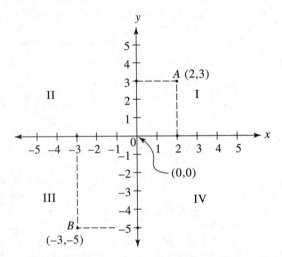

## EXAMPLE 1

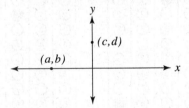

In the diagram above, which of the following must be true?

   I. $a + b < ab$
  II. $c + d < cd$
 III. $a + b < c + d$

(A) I only

(B) II only

(C) III only

(D) I and III only

(E) I, II, and III

**Solution.** Since $(a, b)$ is on the $x$-axis, $b = 0$. Therefore, $ab = 0$ and $a + b = a$, which is negative, since $(a, b)$ is to the left of the $y$-axis. Since any negative number is less than 0, $a + b < ab$ (I is true). Since $(c, d)$ is on the $y$-axis, $c = 0$. Therefore, $cd = 0$ and $c + d = d$, which is positive since $(c, d)$ is above the $x$-axis. So $cd < c + d$ (II is false). Since $a + b$ is negative and $c + d$ is positive, $a + b < c + d$ (III is true). Only statements I and III are true (Choice D).

Often a question requires you to calculate the distance between two points. This is easiest when the points lie on the same horizontal or vertical line.

If two points have been plotted on a graph and if they have the same $x$-coordinates or $y$-coordinates, you can find the distance between them by counting boxes.

### Key Fact N1

- All the points on a horizontal line have the same $y$-coordinate. To find the distance between any two of them, subtract the smaller $x$-coordinate from the larger $x$-coordinate.
- All the points on a vertical line have the same $x$-coordinate. To find the distance between any two of them, subtract the smaller $y$-coordinate from the larger $y$-coordinate.

### Key Fact N2

The distance $d$, between two points, $A(x_1, y_1)$ and $B(x_2, y_2)$, can be calculated using the distance formula:

$$d = \sqrt{(x_2 - x_1)^2 + (y_2 - y_1)^2}.$$

**CAUTION:** To find the distance between two points that do *not* lie on the same horizontal or vertical line, you cannot count boxes and you cannot subtract; you *must* use the distance formula or the Pythagorean theorem.

## EXAMPLE 2

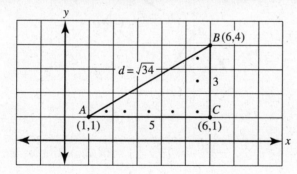

What is the perimeter of $\triangle ABC$, in the figure above?

(A) 13
(B) 16
(C) $8 + \sqrt{34}$
(D) $10 + \sqrt{34}$
(E) $8 + \sqrt{74}$

**Solution.** By counting boxes or subtracting, you find that the distance from $A$ to $C$ is $6 - 1 = 5$, and the distance from $B$ to $C$ is $4 - 1 = 3$. To find the distance from $A$ to $B$, use the distance formula:

$$AB = \sqrt{(6-1)^2 + (4-1)^2} = \sqrt{(5)^2 + (3)^2} = \sqrt{25+9} = \sqrt{34}$$

So the perimeter is $5 + 3 + \sqrt{34} = 8 + \sqrt{34}$  (Choice C).

### Key Fact N3

If $P\,(x_1, y_1)$ and $Q\,(x_2, y_2)$ are any two points, then the midpoint, $M$, of segment $\overline{PQ}$ is the point whose coordinates are $\left(\frac{x_1+x_2}{2}, \frac{y_1+y_2}{2}\right)$.

### EXAMPLE 3

$ABCD$ is a rectangle whose vertices are at $A\,(2, 0)$, $B\,(0, 3)$, $C\,(6, 7)$, and $D\,(8, 4)$. If the diagonals intersect at $E$, what are the coordinates of $E$?

(A) $(2, 3.5)$
(B) $(3, 5)$
(C) $(4, 0.5)$
(D) $(4, 3.5)$
(E) $(8, 7)$

**Solution.** Since, by **KEY FACT K2**, the diagonals of a parallelogram (and, hence, a rectangle) bisect each other, $E$ is the midpoint of diagonal $AC$:

You should make a quick sketch. This often allows you to see the correct answer and always allows you to eliminate choices that are clearly wrong.

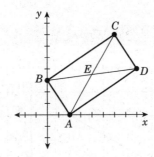

$$E = \left(\frac{2+6}{2}, \frac{7+0}{2}\right) = \left(\frac{8}{2}, \frac{7}{2}\right) = (4, 3.5) \text{ (Choice D)}.$$

The *slope* of a line is a number that indicates how steep the line is.

### Key Fact N4

• Vertical lines do not have slopes.
• To find the slope of any nonvertical line, proceed as follows:

1. Choose any 2 points $A(x_1, y_1)$ and $B(x_2, y_2)$ on the line.
2. Take the differences of the $y$-coordinates, $y_2 - y_1$, and the $x$-coordinates, $x_2 - x_1$.
3. Divide. Slope $= \frac{y_1-y_2}{x_1-x_2}$.

## EXAMPLE 4

What is the slope of the line that passes through (0, 3) and (4, 0)?

**Solution.** Use the slope formula: $\frac{0-3}{4-0} = \frac{-3}{4} = -\frac{3}{4}$.

### Key Fact N5

- The slope of any horizontal line is 0.
- The slope of any line that goes up as you move from left to right is positive.
- The slope of any line that goes down as you move from left to right is negative.

## EXAMPLE 5

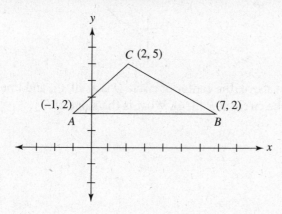

In the figure above, let $r$, $s$, and $t$ represent the slopes of line segments $\overline{AB}$, $\overline{BC}$, and $\overline{AC}$, respectively. Which of the following is true?

(A) $r < s < t$
(B) $r < t < s$
(C) $s < r < t$
(D) $s < t < r$
(E) $t < r < s$

**Solution.** Since $\overline{AB}$ is horizontal, its slope is 0: $r = 0$; since $\overline{BC}$ goes down as you move from left to right, its slope is negative: $s < 0$; and since $\overline{AC}$ goes up as you move from left to right, its slope is positive: $t > 0$. Therefore,

$$s < r < t \text{ (Choice C)}.$$

Note that you *could have* calculated the slopes of $\overline{AC}$ and $\overline{BC}$, but it was unnecessary to do so.

### Key Fact N6

- If two nonvertical lines are parallel, their slopes are equal.
- If two nonvertical lines are perpendicular, the product of their slopes is $-1$.

If the product of two numbers, $a$ and $b$, is $-1$, then $ab = -1 \Rightarrow a = -\frac{1}{b}$. So another way to express the second part of **KEY FACT N6** is to say that *if two nonvertical lines are perpendicular, then the slope of one is the negative reciprocal of the slope of the other.*

## EXAMPLE 6

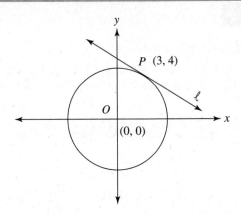

In the figure above, the center of circle $O$ is at $(0, 0)$, and line $l$ is tangent to the circle at $P$ $(3, 4)$. What is the slope of $l$?

(A) $-\frac{4}{3}$

(B) $-\frac{3}{4}$

(C) $0$

(D) $\frac{3}{4}$

(E) $\frac{4}{3}$

**Solution.** From the diagram, it is clear that the slope of $l$ is negative; so the answer must be (A) or (B). In fact, the slope of radius $\overline{OP}$ is $\frac{4-0}{3-0} = \frac{3}{4}$. By **KEY FACT L10**, $\overline{OP} \perp l$, and so, by **KEY FACT N6**, the slope of $l$ is the negative reciprocal of $\frac{4}{3}$. The slope of $l$ is $-\frac{3}{4}$ (Choice B).

On the PSAT you won't have to graph a straight line (or anything else), but you should recognize the equations of straight lines.

## Key Fact N7

For any real numbers $a, b, m$:

- The equation of a vertical line can be written as $x = a$.
- The equation of any nonvertical line can be written as $y = mx + b$.
- In the equation $y = mx + b$, $m$ is the slope of the line, and $b$ is the $y$-intercept.
- If $m = 0$, the line is horizontal, and its equation is $y = b$.

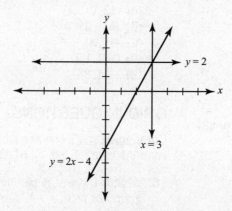

## EXAMPLE 7

Which of the following is an equation of a line that is parallel to the line whose equation is $y = 2x - 3$?

(A) $y = 2x + 3$

(B) $y = -2x - 3$

(C) $y = \frac{1}{2}x + 3$

(D) $y = -\frac{1}{2}x + 3$

(E) $y = -\frac{1}{2}x - 3$

**Solution.** By **KEY FACT N7**, the slope of the line $y = 2x - 3$ is 2. By **KEY FACT N6**, parallel lines have equal slopes. Only Choice A, $y = 2x + 3$, is also the equation of a line whose slope is 2.

# Practice Exercises

## MULTIPLE-CHOICE QUESTIONS

1. What is the area of the rectangle, three of whose vertices are the points $A(2, 2)$, $B(6, 4)$, and $C(7, 2)$?

   (A) 10
   (B) 25
   (C) 40
   (D) 50
   (E) 100

2. A circle whose center is at $(2, -3)$ passes through the point $(4, 4)$. What is the area of the circle?

   (A) $5\pi$
   (B) $37\pi$
   (C) $53\pi$
   (D) $85\pi$
   (E) It cannot be determined from the information given.

3. $B(7, -7)$ is a point on a circle whose center is at $(3, 5)$. If $AB$ is a diameter of the circle, what is the slope of $AB$?

   (A) $-3$
   (B) $-\frac{1}{3}$
   (C) $\frac{1}{3}$
   (D) $3$
   (E) It cannot be determined from the information given.

4. What is the slope of the line that passes through $(0, a)$ and $(b, 0)$, where $b \neq 0$?

   (A) $\frac{a}{b}$
   (B) $-\frac{a}{b}$
   (C) $\frac{b}{a}$
   (D) $-\frac{b}{a}$
   (E) It cannot be determined from the information given.

5. A circle whose center is at $(6, 8)$ passes through the origin. Which of the following points is NOT on the circle?

   (A) $(12, 0)$
   (B) $(6, -2)$
   (C) $(16, 8)$
   (D) $(-2, 12)$
   (E) $(-4, 8)$

## GRID-IN QUESTIONS

Questions 6 and 7 concern parallelogram $ABCD$, whose coordinates are $A(-6, 2)$, $B(-3, 6)$, $C(4, 6)$, $D(1, 2)$.

6. What is the area of parallelogram $ABCD$?

7. What is the perimeter of parallelogram $ABCD$?

**8.** If the coordinates of △*JKL* are *J*(0, 0), *K*(8, 0), and *L*(2, 6), what is the sum of the slopes of the three sides of the triangle?

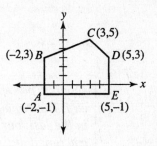

**10.** What is the area of pentagon *ABCDE*?

**9.** If *P*(−3, 3) and *Q*(1, −2) are the endpoints of one side of square *PQRS*, what is the area of the square?

# Answer Key

**1.** A    **2.** C    **3.** A    **4.** B    **5.** D

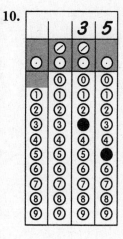

6. | | | 2 | 8 |
7. | | | 2 | 4 |
8. | | | | 2 |
9. | | | 4 | 1 |
10. | | | 3 | 5 |

# Miscellaneous Topics

> *About 90 percent of the questions on the PSAT are on arithmetic, algebra, and geometry. The remaining 10 percent of the questions are on miscellaneous topics covered in the last four sections of this chapter: probability, sequences, data interpretation, and functions.*

## 7-O  BASIC PROBABILITY

The **probability** that an **event** will occur is a number between 0 and 1, usually written as a fraction, which indicates how likely it is that the event will happen. For example, if you spin the spinner at the right, there are four possible outcomes: it is equally likely that the spinner will stop in any of the four regions. There is one chance in four that it will stop in the region marked 2. So we say that the probability of spinning a 2 is one-fourth and write $P(2) = \frac{1}{4}$. Since 2 is the only even number on the spinner we could also say $P(\text{even}) = \frac{1}{4}$. There are three chances in four that the spinner will land in a region with an odd number in it, so $P(\text{odd}) = \frac{3}{4}$.

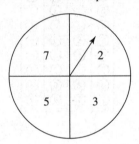

### Key Fact O1

If $E$ is any event, the probability that $E$ will occur is given by

$$P(E) = \frac{\text{the number of favorable outcomes}}{\text{the total number of possible outcomes}}$$

assuming that all of the possible outcomes are equally likely.

In the preceding example, each of the four regions is the same size; so it is equally likely that the spinner will land on the 2, 3, 5, or 7. Therefore,

$$P(\text{odd}) = \frac{\text{the number of ways of getting an odd number}}{\text{the total number of possible outcomes}} = \frac{3}{4}.$$

Let's look at some other probabilities associated with spinning this spinner once:

$$P(\text{number} > 8) = \frac{\text{the number of ways of getting a number} > 8}{\text{the total number of possible outcomes}} = \frac{0}{4} = 0$$

$$P(\text{prime number}) = \frac{\text{the number of ways of getting a prime number}}{\text{the total number of possible outcomes}} = \frac{4}{4} = 1$$

$$P(\text{number} < 5) = \frac{\text{the number of ways of getting a number} < 5}{\text{the total number of possible outcomes}} = \frac{2}{4} = \frac{1}{2}$$

## Key Fact O2

Let $E$ be an event and $P(E)$ the probability it will occur.

**CAUTION:** The answer to a probability question can *never* be negative and can *never* be greater than 1.

Then with reference to the example above:

- If $E$ is *impossible* (such as getting a number greater than 8), $P(E) = 0$.
- If it is *certain* that $E$ will occur (such as getting a prime number), $P(E) = 1$.
- In all cases $0 \le P(E) \le 1$.
- The probability that event $E$ will *not* occur is $1 - P(E)$.
- If 2 or more events constitute all the outcomes, the sum of their probabilities is 1.

$$\text{[For example, } P(\text{even}) + P(\text{odd}) = \tfrac{1}{4} + \tfrac{3}{4} = 1].$$

- The more likely it is that an event will occur, the higher its probability (the closer to 1 it is); the less likely it is that an event will occur, the lower its probability (the closer to 0 it is).

## EXAMPLE 1

A two-digit number is chosen at random. What is the probability that the number chosen is a multiple of 9?

**Solution.** There are 90 two-digit numbers (all of the integers between 10 and 99, inclusive). Of these 90 numbers, 10 of them (18, 27, 36, . . . , 99) are multiples of 9. Therefore,

$$\text{probability} = \frac{\text{the number of favorable outcomes}}{\text{the total number of possible outcomes}} = \frac{10}{90} = \frac{1}{9}.$$

## Key Fact O3

If an experiment is done two (or more) times, the probability that first one event will occur and then a second event will occur is the product of the probabilities.

## EXAMPLE 2

The spinner at the beginning of this section is spun three times. What is the probability that it never lands on the 2?

(A) $\frac{1}{64}$

(B) $\frac{1}{4}$

(C) $\frac{27}{64}$

(D) $\frac{3}{4}$

(E) $\frac{9}{4}$

**Solution.** We want the probability that on each of the three spins the spinner lands on one of the three odd numbers. Since $P(\text{odd}) = \frac{3}{4}$, by **KEY FACT O3**, the probability of three consecutive odd numbers is

$$P(\text{odd 1st time}) \times P(\text{odd 2nd time}) \times P(\text{odd 3rd time}) = \frac{3}{4} \times \frac{3}{4} \times \frac{3}{4} = \frac{27}{64}.$$

Occasionally, on a PSAT there will be a question that relates to probability and geometry. The next **KEY FACT** will help you deal with that type of question.

### Key Fact O4

If a point is chosen at random inside a geometrical figure, the probability that the chosen point lies in a particular region is

$$\frac{\text{the area of that region}}{\text{the area of the whole figure}}$$

### EXAMPLE 3

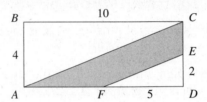

If a point is chosen at random inside rectangle *ABCD*, what is the probability that the point lies in the shaded region?

**Solution.** The area of rectangle *ABCD* is $4 \times 10 = 40$. The area of right triangle *ABC* is $\frac{1}{2}(4 \times 10) = 20$, and the area of right triangle *EDF* is $\frac{1}{2}(2 \times 5) = 5$. So the total area of the white region is $20 + 5 = 25$, and the area of the shaded region is $40 - 25 = 15$. The probability that the chosen point lies inside the shaded region is $\frac{15}{40} = \frac{3}{8}$.

# Practice Exercises

## MULTIPLE-CHOICE QUESTIONS

Questions 1–3 refer to a jar that contains 5 marbles, 1 of each of the colors red, white, blue, green, and yellow.

1. If four marbles are removed from the jar, what is the probability that the yellow one was removed?

    (A) $\frac{1}{20}$

    (B) $\frac{1}{5}$

    (C) $\frac{1}{4}$

    (D) $\frac{4}{5}$

    (E) $\frac{5}{4}$

2. If one marble is removed from the jar, what is the probability that it is red, white, or blue?

    (A) $\frac{1}{15}$

    (B) $\frac{1}{5}$

    (C) $\frac{2}{5}$

    (D) $\frac{3}{5}$

    (E) $\frac{5}{3}$

3. If two marbles are removed from the jar, what is the probability that each of them is red, white, or blue?

    (A) $\frac{6}{25}$

    (B) $\frac{3}{10}$

    (C) $\frac{9}{25}$

    (D) $\frac{2}{3}$

    (E) $\frac{6}{5}$

4. The Smiths have two children. If their older child is a boy, what is the probability that their younger child is also a boy?

    (A) $\frac{1}{4}$

    (B) $\frac{1}{3}$

    (C) $\frac{1}{2}$

    (D) $\frac{2}{3}$

    (E) $\frac{3}{4}$

5. The Kleins have two children. What is the probability that both of their children are boys?

    (A) $\frac{1}{4}$

    (B) $\frac{1}{3}$

    (C) $\frac{1}{2}$

    (D) $\frac{2}{3}$

    (E) $\frac{3}{4}$

## GRID-IN QUESTIONS

6. If three coins are flipped, what is the probability that there are more heads than tails?

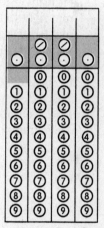

7. A box contains 10 slips of paper, each with a different number from 1 to 10 written on it. If one slip is removed at random, what is the probability that the number selected is a multiple of 2 or 3?

**8.** If two people are chosen at random, what is the probability that they were born on different days of the week?

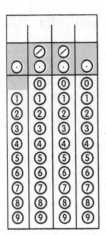

**9.** A number is a *palindrome* if it reads exactly the same from right to left as it does from left to right. For example, 66, 818, and 2552 are all palindromes. If a three-digit number is chosen at random, what is the probability that it is a palindrome?

**10.** In the diagram above, the radius of the large circle is 5 and the radius of the small circle is 3. If a point is chosen at random inside the large circle, what is the probability that the point lies inside the small white circle?

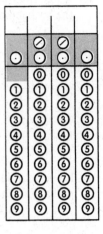

## Answer Key

**1.** D    **2.** D    **3.** B    **4.** C    **5.** A

**6.** 1/2 or .5

**7.** 7/10 or .7

**8.** 6/7

**9.** 1/10

**10.** 9/25 or .36

# 7-P SEQUENCES

There are three types of sequences that occasionally appear on the PSAT: *arithmetic sequences*, *geometric sequences*, and *repeating sequences*.

An **arithmetic sequence** is a sequence in which the *difference* between any two consecutive terms is the same. For example, the sequence 8, 11, 14, 17, 20, ... is an arithmetic sequence in which the common difference is 3. An easy way to find the $n$th term of such a sequence is to start with the first term and add the common difference $n-1$ times. In this example, the fifth term is 20, which can be obtained by taking the first term, 8, and adding the common difference, 3, four times: $8 + 4(3) = 8 + 12 = 20$.

**KEY FACT P1** gives the formula for finding the $n$th term of any arithmetic sequence.

### Key Fact P1

If $a_1, a_2, a_3, \ldots$ is an arithmetic sequence whose common difference is $d$, then $a_n = a_1 + (n-1)\, d$.

## EXAMPLE 1

What is the 100th term of the sequence 8, 11, 14, 17, 20, ... ?

**Solution.** This is an arithmetic sequence whose first term is 8 and whose comman difference is 3. So by **KEY FACT P1**

$$a_{100} = a_1 + 99d = 8 + 99(3) = 8 + 297 = 305.$$

A **geometric sequence** is a sequence in which the *ratio* between any two consecutive terms is the same. For example, the sequence 2, 8, 32, 128, 512, ... is a geometric sequence: the ratios $\frac{8}{2}, \frac{32}{8}, \frac{128}{32}$ are all equal to 4.

An easy way to find the $n$th term of a geometric sequence is to start with the first term and multiply it by the common ratio $n-1$ times. For example, in the sequence 2, 8, 32, 128, 512, ... the fourth term is 128, which can be obtained by taking the first term, 2, and multiplying it by the common ratio, 4, three times: $2 \times 4 \times 4 \times 4 = 2 \times 4^3 = 2 \times 64 = 128$. The next **KEY FACT** gives the formula for finding the $n$th term of a geometric sequence.

### Key Fact P2

If $a_1, a_2, a_3, \ldots$ is a geometric sequence whose common ratio is $r$, then $a_n = a_1\, (r)^{n-1}$.

## EXAMPLE 2

What is the 100th term of the sequence 2, 8, 32, 128, 512, ... ?

(A) $2^{99}$
(B) $2^{100}$
(C) $2 \times 4^{99}$
(D) $2 \times 4^{100}$
(E) $2 \times 4^{101}$

**Solution.** This is a geometric series whose first term is 2 and whose common ratio is 4. So by **KEY FACT P2**,

$$a_{100} = a_1(r)^{99} = 2 \times 4^{99} \text{ (Choice C)}.$$

A ***repeating sequence*** is a sequence in which a certain number of terms repeat indefinitely. Each of the following is a repeating sequence

(i)  $-1, 0, 1, -1, 0, 1, -1, 0, 1, \ldots$

(ii)  $1, 4, 2, 8, 5, 7, 1, 4, 2, 8, 5, 7, \ldots$

(iii)  red, white, blue, green, red, white, blue, green, $\ldots$

On the PSAT, questions concerning repeating sequences usually ask you to find a particular term of the sequence, such as the 100th term or 1000th term. So you need to have a procedure for finding the term you want. For example, let's find the 500th term of the sequence 1, 4, 2, 8, 5, 7, 1, 4, 2, 8, 5, 7, . . . Think of this as a sequence in which the set {1, 4, 2, 8, 5, 7} of 6 numbers keeps repeating. Since the last number in the set is 7, if we write down 1 set or 2 sets or 3 sets or 10 sets, the last number will be 7. So the 6th, 12th, 18th, and 60th terms are all 7. In general, if $n$ is a multiple of 6, the $n$th term is 7. So the 30th term, the 666th term, and the 6,000,000th terms are all 7. To answer the question, "What is the 500th term?" the first thing you should do is divide 500 by 6. If 500 is a multiple of 6, the answer will be 7. Using your calculator, you find that $500 \div 6 = 83.333$. So 500 is not a multiple of 6. When 500 is divided by 6, the *integer* quotient is 83 (ignore the decimal portion). This means that in the first 500 terms of the sequence, the set {1, 4, 2, 8, 5, 7} repeats 83 times. Since $83 \times 6 = 498$, the 498th term is 7. The 499th term starts the next set; it is 1 and the 500th term is 4.

TACTIC

## P1

To find the $n$th term of a repeating sequence, divide $n$ by the number of terms that repeat. If $r$ is the integer remainder, then the $n$th term is the same as the $r$th term.

In the worked-out example preceding **TACTIC P1**, we found the 500th term of the sequence 1, 4, 2, 8, 7, 1, 4, 2, 8, 7, . . . Using **TACTIC P1**, we would proceed as follows:

$500 \div 6 = 83.333 \Rightarrow$ the quotient is 83. Then $83 \times 6 = 498$ and $500 - 498 = 2$. The remainder is 2, and so the 500th term is the same as the 2nd term, namely 4.

# Practice Exercises

## MULTIPLE-CHOICE QUESTIONS

1. What is the 100th term of the sequence 4, 9, 14, 19, 24, . . . ?

   (A) 494
   (B) 499
   (C) 504
   (D) 509
   (E) 514

2. Consider the sequence 2, 6, 18, 54, 162, . . . What is the 25th term?

   (A) $3^{24}$
   (B) $3^{25}$
   (C) $2 \times 3^{24}$
   (D) $2 \times 3^{25}$
   (E) $6^{24}$

3. If today is Saturday, what day will it be 500 days from today?

   (A) Saturday
   (B) Sunday
   (C) Tuesday
   (D) Wednesday
   (E) Friday

4. If it is now September, what month will it be 555 months from now?

   (A) April
   (B) June
   (C) September
   (D) November
   (E) December

5. The first term of sequence I is 2 and each subsequent term is 2 more than the preceding term. The first term of sequence II is 2 and each subsequent term is 2 times the preceding term. What is the ratio of the 32nd term of sequence II to the 32nd term of sequence I?

   (A) 1
   (B) 2
   (C) $2^{26}$
   (D) $2^{27}$
   (E) $2^{32}$

## GRID-IN QUESTIONS

6. The first term of a sequence is 1 and every term after the first one is 1 more than the square of the preceding term. What is the fifth term?

7. The first two terms of a sequence are 5 and 7. Each term after the second one is found by taking the average (arithmetic mean) of all the preceding terms. What is the 50th term of this sequence?

8. Consider the sequence 2, 6, 18, 54, 162, . . . If the 77th term is $a$ and the 80th term is $b$, what is the value of $\frac{b}{a}$?

**9.** Consider the sequence 1, 2, 3, 1, 2, 3, 1, 2, 3, . . . What is the sum of the first 100 terms?

**10.** In a certain sequence the difference between any two consecutive terms is 4. If the 20th term is 100, what is the 2nd term?

## Answer Key

**1.** B

**2.** C

**3.** C

**4.** E

**5.** C

**6.** 6 7 7

**7.** 6

**8.** 2 7

**9.** 1 9 9

**10.** 2 8

## 7-Q INTERPRETATION OF DATA

On the PSAT it is likely that there will be one or two questions that will require you to interpret the data that appear in some type of table or graph. Occasionally you will be asked two questions based on the same set of data. In this case, the first question is usually quite easy, requiring only that you *read* the information in the table or graph. The second question is usually a little more challenging and may ask you to *interpret* the data or *manipulate* them or *make a prediction* based on them.

On the PSAT, charts and graphs are *always* drawn to scale.

The data can be presented in the columns of a table or displayed graphically. The graphs that appear most often are circle graphs, bar graphs, line graphs, and scatter-plot graphs. In this section, we will illustrate each of these and give examples of the types of questions that may be asked.

## Line Graphs

A *line graph* indicates how one or more quantities change over time. The horizontal axis is usually marked off in units of time; the units on the vertical axis can represent almost any type of numerical data: dollars, weights, exam grades, number of people, and so on.

Here is a typical line graph:

Before reading even one of the questions based on the above graph, you should have acquired *at least* the following information: (i) the graph gives the values of two different stocks; (ii) the graph covers the period from January 1, 2005, to January 1, 2010; (iii) during that time, both stocks rose in value. There are several questions that could be asked about the data in this graph. Here are two examples.

## EXAMPLE 1

On January 1 of what year was the ratio of the value of a share of stock *A* to the value of a share of stock *B* the greatest?

(A) 2005
(B) 2006
(C) 2007
(D) 2008
(E) 2010

**Solution.** From 2008 to 2010, the values of the two stocks were fairly close; so those years are not candidates. In 2007 the ratio was $40:10$ or $4:1$ or 4. In 2006 the ratio was $35:15$ or $7:3$ or 2.33. In 2005 the ratio was $30:10$ or $3:1$ or 3. The ratio was greatest in 2007 (Choice C).

## EXAMPLE 2

What was the average yearly increase in the value of a share of stock *A* from 2005 to 2010?

**Solution.** Over the five-year period from January 1, 2005, to January 1, 2010, the value of a share of stock *A* rose from $30 to $45, an increase of $15. The average yearly increase was $15 ÷ 5 years, or $3 per year.

## Tables and Bar Graphs

The same information that was given in the preceding line graph could have been presented in a *table* or in a *bar graph*.

In a bar graph, the taller the bar, the greater the value of the quantity. Bar graphs can also be drawn horizontally; in this case the longer the bar, the greater the quantity.

**PRICE PER SHARE OF STOCKS *A* AND *B***
**ON JANUARY 1 OF 6 YEARS**

|  | Prices (dollars) | | | | | |
|---|---|---|---|---|---|---|
| Stock | 2005 | 2006 | 2007 | 2008 | 2009 | 2010 |
| Stock *A* | 30 | 35 | 40 | 25 | 40 | 45 |
| Stock *B* | 10 | 20 | 15 | 35 | 40 | 40 |

**PRICE PER SHARE OF STOCKS *A* AND *B* ON**
**JANUARY 1 OF 6 YEARS**

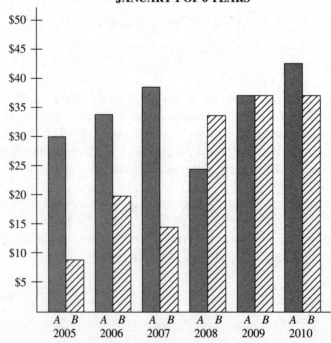

In a slight variation of the horizontal bar graph, the bars are replaced by a string of icons, or symbols. For example, the graph on the following page, in which each picture of a person represents 100 students, conveys information about the languages studied by the students at State College in 2010.

**NUMBERS OF STUDENTS ENROLLED IN
LANGUAGE COURSES AT STATE COLLEGE IN 2010**

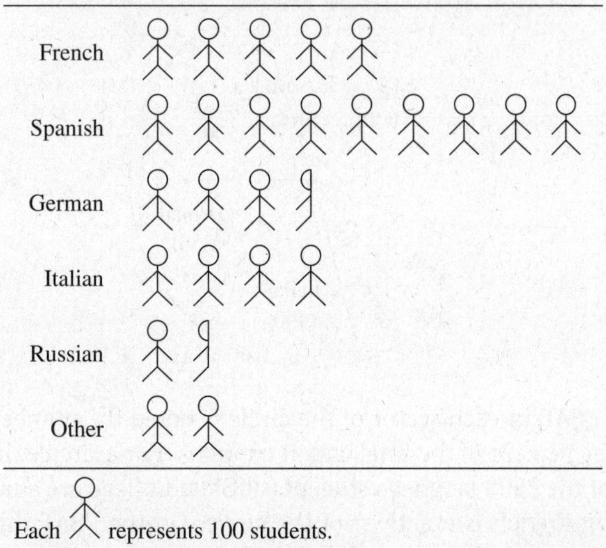

Each represents 100 students.

---

## EXAMPLE 3

If the "Other" category includes five languages, what is the average (arithmetic mean) number of students studying each language offered at the college?

**Solution.** First determine the total number of students taking a language course. Either get the number for each language and add or just count the number of icons: there are 24 full icons and 2 half icons for a total of 25 icons, representing 2500 students. The 2500 students are divided among 10 languages (the 5 languages listed plus the 5 in the "Other" category): 2500 ÷ 10 = 250.

---

## EXAMPLE 4

If the number of students studying Italian next year is the same as the number taking Spanish this year, by what percent will the number of students taking Italian increase?

**Solution.** The number of students taking Italian would increase by 500 from 400 to 900. This represents a $\frac{500}{400} \times 100\% = 125\%$ increase.

## Circle Graphs

A *circle graph* is another way to present data. In a circle graph, which is sometimes called a *pie chart*, the circle is divided into sectors, with the size of each sector exactly proportional to the quantity it represents. For example, the information included in the previous graph is presented in the circle graph below.

**NUMBERS OF STUDENTS ENROLLED IN
LANGUAGE COURSES AT STATE COLLEGE IN 2010**

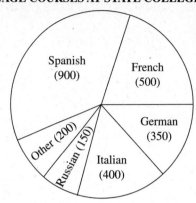

Usually on the PSAT, in each sector of the circle is noted the number of degrees of its central angle or the percent of the total data it contains. For example, in the circle graph above, since 500 of the 2500 language students at State College are studying French, the sector representing French is exactly $\frac{1}{5}$ of the circle. On the PSAT this sector could be marked either 72° ($\frac{1}{5}$ of 360°) or 20% ($\frac{1}{5}$ of 100%), as in the graphs below.

**DISTRIBUTION OF THE 2500 STUDENTS
ENROLLED IN LANGUAGE COURSES**

**DISTRIBUTION OF THE 2500 STUDENTS
ENROLLED IN LANGUAGE COURSES**

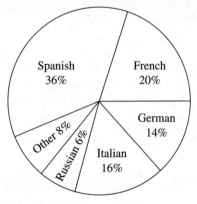

# Practice Exercises

## MULTIPLE-CHOICE QUESTIONS

Questions 1 and 2 refer to the following graph.

BAKER FAMILY HOUSEHOLD BUDGET IN 2010

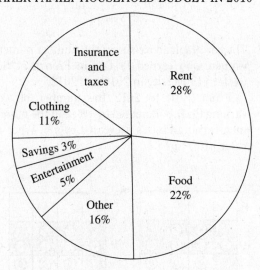

1. If the Baker's income in 2010 was $40,000, how much more did they spend on insurance and taxes than they did on clothing?

   (A) $1600
   (B) $2000
   (C) $3200
   (D) $4400
   (E) $6000

2. What is the degree measure of the central angle of the sector representing insurance and taxes?

   (A) 45
   (B) 54
   (C) 60
   (D) 72
   (E) 90

Questions 3 and 4 refer to the following graph.

MATH SAT SCORES OF JUNIORS AT WESTSIDE HIGH SCHOOL

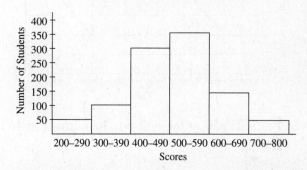

3. How many juniors at Westside High School took the SAT?

   (A) 1000
   (B) 1100
   (C) 1200
   (D) 1250
   (E) 1300

4. To the nearest 5%, what percent of the juniors had Math SAT scores of less than 600?

   (A) 70
   (B) 75
   (C) 80
   (D) 85
   (E) It cannot be determined from the information given.

Questions 5 and 6 refer to the following graph.

SPEEDS AT WHICH TOM DROVE BETWEEN
8:00 A.M. AND 10:30 A.M. ON SUNDAY MORNING

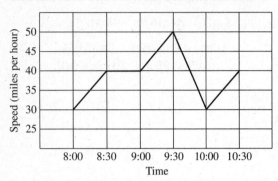

5. For what part of the time was Tom driving at 40 miles per hour or faster?

(A) 20%
(B) 25%
(C) $33\frac{1}{3}$%
(D) 40%
(E) 50%

6. How far, in miles, did Tom drive between 8:30 and 9:00?

(A) 0
(B) 20
(C) 30
(D) 40
(E) It cannot be determined from the information given.

## GRID-IN QUESTIONS

DISTRIBUTION OF GRADES ON
THE FINAL EXAM IN PHYSICS

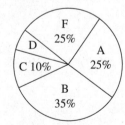

7. On the basis of the data in the graph above, if 300 students took the physics exam, how many earned a grade of D?

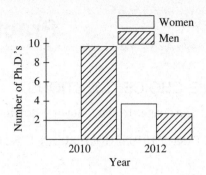

8. The bar graph above shows the number of men and women who earned Ph.D.'s in French at Southwestern University in 2010 and 2012.

From 2010 to 2012 the number of women earning Ph.D.'s increased by $x$%, and the number of men earning Ph.D.'s decreased by $y$%. What is the value of $x - y$?

7.                                  8.

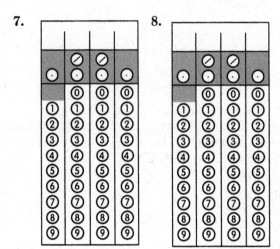

## Answer Key

# 7-R FUNCTIONS

Very little of what is taught about functions in high school math classes is tested on the PSAT. In this section we will review only those basic facts about functions and their graphs that you need to know for the PSAT.

As used on the PSAT, a ***function*** is a rule that assigns to each number in one set a number in another set. The function is usually designated by the letter $f$, although other letters, such as $g$ and $h$, are sometimes used. The numbers in the first set are labeled $x$, and the number in the second set to which $x$ is assigned by the function is designated by the letter $y$ or by $f(x)$.

For example, the function that assigns to each real number $x$, the number $2x + 3$, can be written $y = 2x + 3$ or $f(x) = 2x + 3$.

The number assigned to 5 is $2(5) + 3 = 10 + 3 = 13$, and the number assigned to $-5$ is $2(-5) + 3 = -10 + 3 = -7$.

To express these facts, we write

$f(5) = 13$  and  $f(-5) = -7$.

The proper way to think of the function $f(x) = 2x + 3$ is that $f$ takes *anything* and assigns to it 2 times *that thing* plus 3:

$$f(anything) = 2(that\ thing) + 3$$

- $f(100) = 2(100) + 3 = 203$
- $f(a) = 2a + 3$
- $f(x^2) = 2x^2 + 3$

- $f(0) = 2(0) + 3 = 0 + 3 = 3$
- $f(a + b) = 2(a + b) + 3$
- $f(2x^2 + 3) = 2(2x^2 + 3) + 3 = 4x^2 + 9$

## EXAMPLE 1

If $f(x) = x^2 + 2x$, what is $f(3) + f(-3)$?

**Solution.**          $f(3) = 3^2 + 2(3) = 9 + 6 = 15$
$f(-3) = (-3)^2 + 2(-3) = 9 - 6 = 3$
Therefore,          $f(3) + f(-3) = 15 + 3 = 18$.

## EXAMPLE 2

If $f(x) = x^2 + 2x$, what is $f(x + 2)$?

(A) $x^2 + 2x + 4$
(B) $x^2 + 2x + 8$
(C) $x^2 + 6x + 4$
(D) $x^2 + 6x + 8$
(E) $x^3 + 4x^2 + 4x$

**Solution.** $f(x + 2) = (x + 2)^2 + 2(x + 2) = (x^2 + 4x + 4) + (2x + 4) = x^2 + 6x + 8$ (Choice D).

## EXAMPLE 3

Let $f(x) = x^2 + 2x$ and $g(x) = x^2 - 2x$. If $g(4) = a$ and $f(a) = b$, what is the value of $b$?

**Solution.** $g(4) = 4^2 - 2(4) = 16 - 8 = 8$; so $a = 8$. Then

$$f(a) = f(8) = 8^2 + 2(8) = 64 + 16 = 80.\ \text{So } b = 80.$$

The graph of a function, *f*, is a certain set of points in the coordinate plane. The point $(x, y)$ is on the graph of *f* if and only if $y = f(x)$. So, for example, the graph of $f(x) = 2x + 3$ consists of all points $(x, y)$ such that $y = 2x + 3$. Since $f(5) = 13$ and $f(-5) = -7$, then $(5, 13)$ and $(-5, -7)$ are both points on the graph of $f(x) = 2x + 3$. On the PSAT you may have to know whether a certain point is on the graph of a given function, but you won't have to actually graph the function.

## EXAMPLE 4

Which of the following is NOT a point on the graph of $f(x) = x^2 + \dfrac{4}{x^2}$?

(A)  $(1, 5)$
(B)  $(-1, 5)$
(C)  $(2, 5)$
(D)  $(-2, -5)$
(E)  $(4, 16.25)$

**Solution.**

$f(1) = 1^2 + \dfrac{4}{1^2} = 1 + 4 = 5 \Rightarrow (1, 5)$ *is* a point on the graph.

$f(-1) = (-1)^2 + \dfrac{4}{(-1)^2} = 1 + 4 = 5 \Rightarrow (-1, 5)$ *is* a point on the graph.

$f(2) = 2^2 + \dfrac{4}{2^2} = 4 + 1 = 5 \Rightarrow (2, 5)$ *is* a point on the graph.

$f(-2) = (-2)^2 + \dfrac{4}{(-2)^2} = 4 + 1 = 5 \neq -5 \Rightarrow (-2, -5)$ is *NOT* a point on the graph.

The answer is Choice D.

# Practice Exercises

## MULTIPLE-CHOICE QUESTIONS

**1.** If $f(x) = 2x - x^2$, what is the value of $f(-2)$?

(A) $-8$
(B) $-4$
(C) $0$
(D) $4$
(E) $8$

**2.** If $f(x) = 3x + 5$ and $f(2) = a$, what is $f(a)$?

(A) $11$
(B) $13$
(C) $25$
(D) $38$
(E) $121$

**3.** If $f(x) = 3x + 5$ and $g(x) = 5x + 3$, what is $g(6) - f(6)$?

(A) $0$
(B) $6$
(C) $10$
(D) $26$
(E) $56$

**4.** Let $f(x) = 3x + 5$ and $g(x) = 5x + 3$. If $f(2) = a$ and $g(a) = b$, what is $b$?

(A) $11$
(B) $24$
(C) $44$
(D) $58$
(E) $143$

**5.** If $f(x) = 3x - 5$ and $(2, b)$ is a point on the graph of $y = f(x)$, then $b =$

(A) $-1$
(B) $1$
(C) $3$
(D) $5$
(E) $11$

## GRID-IN QUESTIONS

**6.** If $f(x) = 3x + 5$ and $(a, 20)$ is a point on the graph of $y = f(x)$, then what is the value of $a$?

**7.** If $f(x) = 2^x + x^2$, what is $f(1)$?

**8.** Let $f(x) = x^2 + 1$ and $g(x) = 1 - x^2$. If $g(3) = a$ and $f(a) = b$, what is $b$?

**9.** If $f(x) = x^2 + 1$ and $f(3) = a$, what is $f(a)$?

**10.** If $f(x) = 4 - x^2$ and $(a, b)$ is a point on the graph of $y = f(x)$, what is the greatest possible value of $b$?

## Answer Key

**1.** A    **2.** D    **3.** C    **4.** D    **5.** B

**6.**    **7.**    **8.**

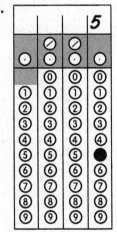

**9.**    **10.**

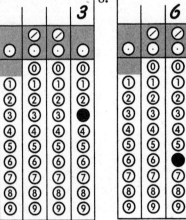

# PART SIX

## TEST YOURSELF

Four Practice Tests

# Four Practice Tests

A two-hour and ten-minute test can be exhausting. Here are some tips that will help you cope on the day of the test:

- Build up your stamina. You have to get used to answering tough questions for more than two hours straight. Take these four practice tests under timed conditions. Try to stay focused the entire time. This practice will pay off when you take the actual test.

- Be well rested on the day of the test. Last-minute cramming will only tire you out. Try to organize your study plan so that you can quit prepping a few days before you take the test. Above all, get a good night's sleep the night before the test.

- Bring a timepiece, preferably the same one you have been using while you have been taking your practice exams. Remember, no beeps or rings! You are not allowed to use a watch or timer with an audible alarm.

- Wear layers. You don't want to be too hot or too cold.

- As you take the test, use the short breaks to stretch and get out the kinks. Breathe in deeply, and let go of the tension as you breathe out. You've done a good job preparing, so think positive, and relax.

# Answer Sheet—Practice Test 1

Each mark should completely fill the appropriate space, and should be as dark as all other marks. Make all erasures complete. Traces of an erasure may be read as an answer.

## Section 1 – Critical Reading
### 25 minutes

1 Ⓐ Ⓑ Ⓒ Ⓓ Ⓔ
2 Ⓐ Ⓑ Ⓒ Ⓓ Ⓔ
3 Ⓐ Ⓑ Ⓒ Ⓓ Ⓔ
4 Ⓐ Ⓑ Ⓒ Ⓓ Ⓔ
5 Ⓐ Ⓑ Ⓒ Ⓓ Ⓔ
6 Ⓐ Ⓑ Ⓒ Ⓓ Ⓔ
7 Ⓐ Ⓑ Ⓒ Ⓓ Ⓔ
8 Ⓐ Ⓑ Ⓒ Ⓓ Ⓔ
9 Ⓐ Ⓑ Ⓒ Ⓓ Ⓔ
10 Ⓐ Ⓑ Ⓒ Ⓓ Ⓔ
11 Ⓐ Ⓑ Ⓒ Ⓓ Ⓔ
12 Ⓐ Ⓑ Ⓒ Ⓓ Ⓔ
13 Ⓐ Ⓑ Ⓒ Ⓓ Ⓔ
14 Ⓐ Ⓑ Ⓒ Ⓓ Ⓔ
15 Ⓐ Ⓑ Ⓒ Ⓓ Ⓔ
16 Ⓐ Ⓑ Ⓒ Ⓓ Ⓔ
17 Ⓐ Ⓑ Ⓒ Ⓓ Ⓔ
18 Ⓐ Ⓑ Ⓒ Ⓓ Ⓔ
19 Ⓐ Ⓑ Ⓒ Ⓓ Ⓔ
20 Ⓐ Ⓑ Ⓒ Ⓓ Ⓔ
21 Ⓐ Ⓑ Ⓒ Ⓓ Ⓔ
22 Ⓐ Ⓑ Ⓒ Ⓓ Ⓔ
23 Ⓐ Ⓑ Ⓒ Ⓓ Ⓔ
24 Ⓐ Ⓑ Ⓒ Ⓓ Ⓔ

## Section 2 – Math
### 25 minutes

1 Ⓐ Ⓑ Ⓒ Ⓓ Ⓔ
2 Ⓐ Ⓑ Ⓒ Ⓓ Ⓔ
3 Ⓐ Ⓑ Ⓒ Ⓓ Ⓔ
4 Ⓐ Ⓑ Ⓒ Ⓓ Ⓔ
5 Ⓐ Ⓑ Ⓒ Ⓓ Ⓔ
6 Ⓐ Ⓑ Ⓒ Ⓓ Ⓔ
7 Ⓐ Ⓑ Ⓒ Ⓓ Ⓔ
8 Ⓐ Ⓑ Ⓒ Ⓓ Ⓔ
9 Ⓐ Ⓑ Ⓒ Ⓓ Ⓔ
10 Ⓐ Ⓑ Ⓒ Ⓓ Ⓔ
11 Ⓐ Ⓑ Ⓒ Ⓓ Ⓔ
12 Ⓐ Ⓑ Ⓒ Ⓓ Ⓔ
13 Ⓐ Ⓑ Ⓒ Ⓓ Ⓔ
14 Ⓐ Ⓑ Ⓒ Ⓓ Ⓔ
15 Ⓐ Ⓑ Ⓒ Ⓓ Ⓔ
16 Ⓐ Ⓑ Ⓒ Ⓓ Ⓔ
17 Ⓐ Ⓑ Ⓒ Ⓓ Ⓔ
18 Ⓐ Ⓑ Ⓒ Ⓓ Ⓔ
19 Ⓐ Ⓑ Ⓒ Ⓓ Ⓔ
20 Ⓐ Ⓑ Ⓒ Ⓓ Ⓔ

## Section 3 – Critical Reading
### 25 minutes

25 Ⓐ Ⓑ Ⓒ Ⓓ Ⓔ
26 Ⓐ Ⓑ Ⓒ Ⓓ Ⓔ
27 Ⓐ Ⓑ Ⓒ Ⓓ Ⓔ
28 Ⓐ Ⓑ Ⓒ Ⓓ Ⓔ
29 Ⓐ Ⓑ Ⓒ Ⓓ Ⓔ
30 Ⓐ Ⓑ Ⓒ Ⓓ Ⓔ
31 Ⓐ Ⓑ Ⓒ Ⓓ Ⓔ
32 Ⓐ Ⓑ Ⓒ Ⓓ Ⓔ
33 Ⓐ Ⓑ Ⓒ Ⓓ Ⓔ
34 Ⓐ Ⓑ Ⓒ Ⓓ Ⓔ
35 Ⓐ Ⓑ Ⓒ Ⓓ Ⓔ
36 Ⓐ Ⓑ Ⓒ Ⓓ Ⓔ
37 Ⓐ Ⓑ Ⓒ Ⓓ Ⓔ
38 Ⓐ Ⓑ Ⓒ Ⓓ Ⓔ
39 Ⓐ Ⓑ Ⓒ Ⓓ Ⓔ
40 Ⓐ Ⓑ Ⓒ Ⓓ Ⓔ
41 Ⓐ Ⓑ Ⓒ Ⓓ Ⓔ
42 Ⓐ Ⓑ Ⓒ Ⓓ Ⓔ
43 Ⓐ Ⓑ Ⓒ Ⓓ Ⓔ
44 Ⓐ Ⓑ Ⓒ Ⓓ Ⓔ
45 Ⓐ Ⓑ Ⓒ Ⓓ Ⓔ
46 Ⓐ Ⓑ Ⓒ Ⓓ Ⓔ
47 Ⓐ Ⓑ Ⓒ Ⓓ Ⓔ
48 Ⓐ Ⓑ Ⓒ Ⓓ Ⓔ

## Section 4 – Math
### 25 minutes

21 Ⓐ Ⓑ Ⓒ Ⓓ Ⓔ
22 Ⓐ Ⓑ Ⓒ Ⓓ Ⓔ
23 Ⓐ Ⓑ Ⓒ Ⓓ Ⓔ
24 Ⓐ Ⓑ Ⓒ Ⓓ Ⓔ
25 Ⓐ Ⓑ Ⓒ Ⓓ Ⓔ
26 Ⓐ Ⓑ Ⓒ Ⓓ Ⓔ
27 Ⓐ Ⓑ Ⓒ Ⓓ Ⓔ
28 Ⓐ Ⓑ Ⓒ Ⓓ Ⓔ

29

30

31

32

33

34

35

36

37

38

## Section 5 – Writing
### 30 minutes

1 Ⓐ Ⓑ Ⓒ Ⓓ Ⓔ
2 Ⓐ Ⓑ Ⓒ Ⓓ Ⓔ
3 Ⓐ Ⓑ Ⓒ Ⓓ Ⓔ
4 Ⓐ Ⓑ Ⓒ Ⓓ Ⓔ
5 Ⓐ Ⓑ Ⓒ Ⓓ Ⓔ
6 Ⓐ Ⓑ Ⓒ Ⓓ Ⓔ
7 Ⓐ Ⓑ Ⓒ Ⓓ Ⓔ
8 Ⓐ Ⓑ Ⓒ Ⓓ Ⓔ
9 Ⓐ Ⓑ Ⓒ Ⓓ Ⓔ
10 Ⓐ Ⓑ Ⓒ Ⓓ Ⓔ
11 Ⓐ Ⓑ Ⓒ Ⓓ Ⓔ
12 Ⓐ Ⓑ Ⓒ Ⓓ Ⓔ
13 Ⓐ Ⓑ Ⓒ Ⓓ Ⓔ
14 Ⓐ Ⓑ Ⓒ Ⓓ Ⓔ
15 Ⓐ Ⓑ Ⓒ Ⓓ Ⓔ
16 Ⓐ Ⓑ Ⓒ Ⓓ Ⓔ
17 Ⓐ Ⓑ Ⓒ Ⓓ Ⓔ
18 Ⓐ Ⓑ Ⓒ Ⓓ Ⓔ
19 Ⓐ Ⓑ Ⓒ Ⓓ Ⓔ
20 Ⓐ Ⓑ Ⓒ Ⓓ Ⓔ
21 Ⓐ Ⓑ Ⓒ Ⓓ Ⓔ
22 Ⓐ Ⓑ Ⓒ Ⓓ Ⓔ
23 Ⓐ Ⓑ Ⓒ Ⓓ Ⓔ
24 Ⓐ Ⓑ Ⓒ Ⓓ Ⓔ
25 Ⓐ Ⓑ Ⓒ Ⓓ Ⓔ
26 Ⓐ Ⓑ Ⓒ Ⓓ Ⓔ
27 Ⓐ Ⓑ Ⓒ Ⓓ Ⓔ
28 Ⓐ Ⓑ Ⓒ Ⓓ Ⓔ
29 Ⓐ Ⓑ Ⓒ Ⓓ Ⓔ
30 Ⓐ Ⓑ Ⓒ Ⓓ Ⓔ
31 Ⓐ Ⓑ Ⓒ Ⓓ Ⓔ
32 Ⓐ Ⓑ Ⓒ Ⓓ Ⓔ
33 Ⓐ Ⓑ Ⓒ Ⓓ Ⓔ
34 Ⓐ Ⓑ Ⓒ Ⓓ Ⓔ
35 Ⓐ Ⓑ Ⓒ Ⓓ Ⓔ
36 Ⓐ Ⓑ Ⓒ Ⓓ Ⓔ
37 Ⓐ Ⓑ Ⓒ Ⓓ Ⓔ
38 Ⓐ Ⓑ Ⓒ Ⓓ Ⓔ
39 Ⓐ Ⓑ Ⓒ Ⓓ Ⓔ

# SECTION 1/CRITICAL READING

TIME: 25 MINUTES
24 QUESTIONS (1–24)

**Directions:** For each question in this section, select the best answer from among the choices given and fill in the corresponding circle on the answer sheet.

---

Each sentence below has one or two blanks, each blank indicating that something has been omitted. Beneath the sentence are five words or sets of words labeled A through E. Choose the word or set of words that, when inserted in the sentence, best fits the meaning of the sentence as a whole.

**EXAMPLE:**

Medieval kingdoms did not become constitutional republics overnight; on the contrary, the change was ----.

(A) unpopular   (B) unexpected
(C) advantageous   (D) sufficient   (E) gradual

---

1. Nothing anyone could say was able to alter North's ---- that his attempt to lie to Congress was justified.

   (A) demand   (B) conviction   (C) maxim
   (D) fear   (E) ambivalence

2. Excessive use of coal and oil eventually may ---- the earth's supply of fossil fuels, leaving us in need of a new source of energy.

   (A) replenish   (B) magnify   (C) merge
   (D) deplete   (E) redirect

3. Contemporary authorities have come to ---- the use of "healthy" in place of "healthful"; however, they still reject the use of "disinterested" in place of "uninterested."

   (A) condone   (B) evaluate   (C) imitate
   (D) disdain   (E) repudiate

4. Michael's severe bout of the flu ---- him so much that he was too tired to go to work for a week.

   (A) recuperated   (B) diagnosed
   (C) incarcerated   (D) captivated
   (E) debilitated

5. Though Alec Guinness was determined to make a name for himself on the stage, when he considered the uncertainties of an actor's life, his ---- wavered.

   (A) resolution   (B) reverence   (C) affectation
   (D) theatricality   (E) skepticism

6. In *Gulliver's Travels*, Swift's intent is ----; he exposes the follies of English society by ridiculing the follies of the Lilliputians.

   (A) elegiac   (B) prophetic   (C) satirical
   (D) questionable   (E) derivative

7. Even the threat of sudden death could not ---- the intrepid pilot and explorer Beryl Markham; a true ----, she risked her life countless times to set records for flying small planes.

   (A) intimidate..patrician
   (B) divert..renegade
   (C) interest..dilettante
   (D) daunt..daredevil
   (E) survive..firebrand

8. As an indefatigable consumer advocate, Ralph Nader is constantly engaged in ---- the claims of unscrupulous merchandisers and cautioning the public to exercise a healthy ----.

   (A) asserting..autonomy
   (B) deflating..prodigality
   (C) debunking..skepticism
   (D) affirming..indifference
   (E) exaggerating..optimism

**GO ON TO NEXT PAGE ▶**

**Directions:** The passages below precede questions based on their content or the relationship between the passages. Answer the questions that follow on the basis of what is stated or implied in the passage.

**Questions 9–12 are based on the following passages.**

**Passage 1**

Spiders, and in particular hairy spiders, possess a highly developed sense of touch. Tarantulas, for example, perceive three distinct types of touch:
Line  a light whisper that flutters the sensitive leg hairs;
5   a smooth rubbing of the body hair; a steady pressure against the body wall. Press a pencil against the tarantula's body wall and it will back away cautiously without reacting defensively. However, if the tarantula sees the pencil approaching from
10  above, the motion will excite a defensive reaction: it will rear up, lifting its front legs and baring its fangs, maintaining this attack stance until the pencil stops moving.

**Passage 2**

"The eensy-weensy spider climbed up the
15  waterspout..."
Tarantulas are the world's largest spiders. The very largest live in the jungles of South America, and, in the days when bananas were transported as large bunches on stalks, tarantulas
20  often were accidentally imported with the fruit. Stout-bodied and hairy, tarantulas can create great panic among arachnophobes (people who fear spiders). Actually, these large spiders are gentle giants, whose temperaments do not match
25  their intimidating appearance. Docile and non-aggressive, tarantulas do not bite unless they are severely provoked. Even if they do bite, their bites are not particularly dangerous; they are about as painful as bee stings, and should be
30  treated similarly.

9. In Passage 1, the author's attitude toward tarantulas can best be described as
(A) apprehensive   (B) sentimental
(C) approving   (D) objective   (E) defensive

10. In line 10, "excite" most nearly means
(A) irritate   (B) delight   (C) stimulate
(D) exhilarate   (E) discompose

11. Which statement best expresses the relationship between the two passages?
(A) Passage 1 describes its subject by supplying details with which the author of Passage 2 would disagree.
(B) Passage 1 provides scientific observations of the subject, while Passage 2 offers a popular introduction to the subject.
(C) Passage 1 presents its subject in highly figurative terms, while Passage 2 is more technical in nature.
(D) Both Passage 1 and Passage 2 assume readers will have an automatically negative response to the subject under discussion.
(E) Passage 2 is objective in its presentation, while Passage 1 is more personal in tone.

12. Which generalization about tarantulas is supported by both passages?
(A) They have a marked degree of intelligence.
(B) Their gentleness belies their frightening looks.
(C) They have been unfairly maligned by arachnophobes.
(D) They are capable of acting to defend themselves.
(E) They are easily intimidated by others.

**GO ON TO NEXT PAGE ▶**

**Directions:** Each passage below is followed by questions based on its content. Answer the questions following each passage on the basis of what is <u>stated</u> or <u>implied</u> in that passage and in any introductory material that may be provided.

**Questions 13–24 are based on the following passage.**

*In this excerpt, the novelist Mary McCarthy shares her memories of her Catholic grandmother, who raised McCarthy and her brother after their parents' death.*

Luckily, I am writing a memoir and not a work of fiction, and therefore I do not have to account for my grandmother's unpleasing character
Line and look for the Oedipal fixation or the traumatic
5 experience which would give her that clinical authenticity that is nowadays so desirable in portraiture. I do not know how my grandmother got the way she was; I assume, from family photographs and from the inflexibility of her habits, that she
10 was always the same, and it seems as idle to inquire into her childhood as to ask what was ailing Iago or look for the error in toilet-training that was responsible for Lady Macbeth. My grandmother's sexual history, bristling with infant
15 mortality in the usual style of her period, was robust and decisive: three tall, handsome sons grew up, and one attentive daughter. Her husband treated her kindly. She had money, many grandchildren, and religion to sustain her. White hair,
20 glasses, soft skin, wrinkles, needlework—all the paraphernalia of motherliness were hers; yet it was a cold, grudging, disputatious old woman who sat all day in her sunroom making tapestries from a pattern, scanning religious periodicals, and setting
25 her iron jaw against any infraction of her ways.
Combativeness was, I suppose, the dominant trait in my grandmother's nature. An aggressive churchgoer, she was quite without Christian feeling; the mercy of the Lord Jesus had never entered
30 her heart. Her piety was an act of war against the Protestant ascendancy. The religious magazines on her table furnished her not with food for meditation but with fresh pretexts for anger; articles attacking birth control, divorce, mixed marriages,
35 Darwin, and secular education were her favorite reading. The teachings of the Church did not interest her, except as they were a rebuke to others; "Honor thy father and thy mother," a command-

ment she was no longer called upon to practice,
40 was the one most frequently on her lips. The extermination of Protestantism, rather than spiritual perfection, was the boon she prayed for. Her mind was preoccupied with conversion; the capture of a soul for God much diverted her fancy—it
45 made one less Protestant in the world. Foreign missions, with their overtones of good will and social service, appealed to her less strongly; it was not a *harvest* of souls that my grandmother had in mind.
50 This pugnacity of my grandmother's did not confine itself to sectarian enthusiasm. There was the defense of her furniture and her house against the imagined encroachments of visitors. With her, this was not the gentle and tremulous
55 protectiveness endemic in old ladies, who fear for the safety of their possessions with a truly touching anxiety, inferring the fragility of all things from the brittleness of their old bones and hearing the crash of mortality in the perilous tinkling of a
60 tea-cup. My grandmother's sentiment was more autocratic: she hated having her chairs sat in or her lawns stepped on or the water turned on in her basins, for no reason at all except pure officiousness; she even grudged the mailman his daily
65 promenade up her sidewalk. Her home was a center of power, and she would not allow it to be derogated by easy or democratic usage. Under her jealous eye, its social properties had atrophied, and it functioned in the family structure simply
70 as a political headquarters. The family had no friends, and entertaining was held to be a foolish and unnecessary courtesy as between blood relations. Holiday dinners fell, as a duty, on the lesser members of the organization: the daughters and
75 daughters-in-law (converts from the false religion) offered up Baked Alaska on a platter like the head of John the Baptist, while the old people sat enthroned at the table, and only their digestive processes acknowledged, with rumbling,
80 enigmatic salvos, the festal day.

**GO ON TO NEXT PAGE** ▶

13. The passage primarily conveys the author's

    (A) open admiration of her grandmother's spiritual discipline
    (B) grudging respect for her grandmother's ability to dominate others
    (C) marked regret for her grandmother's unfulfilled promise
    (D) bitter alienation from her cold and aggressive grandmother
    (E) unwarranted skepticism about her grandmother's piety

14. McCarthy's attitude toward her grandmother is best described as

    (A) tolerant
    (B) appreciative
    (C) indifferent
    (D) nostalgic
    (E) sardonic

15. According to McCarthy, a portrait of a character in a work of modern fiction must have

    (A) photographic realism
    (B) psychological validity
    (C) sympathetic attitudes
    (D) religious qualities
    (E) historical accuracy

16. Lines 1–7 suggest that McCarthy views character portrayals in modern novels with

    (A) approbation
    (B) outrage
    (C) wistfulness
    (D) disdain
    (E) trepidation

17. In line 10, "idle" most nearly means

    (A) slothful
    (B) passive
    (C) fallow
    (D) pointless
    (E) unoccupied

18. McCarthy refers to Iago and Lady Macbeth in order to

    (A) demonstrate her grandmother's familiarity with Shakespearean drama
    (B) emphasize the folly of speculating about what formed her grandmother's character
    (C) explore the nature of early childhood influences on their villainous behavior
    (D) contrast Iago's medical history with the childhood traumas inflicted on Lady Macbeth
    (E) illustrate the dramatic conventions of Shakespeare's period

19. In lines 13–19, McCarthy mentions her grandmother's large, supportive family and material comfort in order to support the claim that

    (A) her grandmother's character would have been far worse without these props to support her
    (B) her grandmother had suffered no traumas or deprivation that might explain her unpleasantness
    (C) overcoming adversity helped build her grandmother's strong character
    (D) her grandmother deserved all the good fortune that came her way
    (E) one had to understand her grandmother's family background to appreciate her generosity

20. McCarthy's primary point in describing her grandmother's physical appearance (lines 19–25) is best summarized by which of the following axioms?

    (A) Familiarity breeds contempt.
    (B) You can't judge a book by its cover.
    (C) One picture is worth more than ten thousand words.
    (D) There's no smoke without fire.
    (E) Blood is thicker than water.

21. In line 27, "aggressive" most directly emphasizes which aspect of the grandmother's approach to religion?

    (A) Her perseverance in prayer
    (B) Her dedication to performing good works
    (C) Her antagonism towards other faiths
    (D) Her willingness to support foreign missions
    (E) Her sense of spirituality

**GO ON TO NEXT PAGE ▶**

**22.** By describing the typical old woman's fear for the safety of her possessions (lines 53–60), McCarthy emphasizes that

(A) her grandmother feared the approach of death
(B) old women have dangerously brittle bones
(C) her grandmother possessed considerable wealth
(D) her grandmother had different reasons for her actions
(E) visitors were unwelcome in her grandmother's house

**23.** In line 68, "properties" most nearly means

(A) belongings
(B) attributes
(C) holdings
(D) titles
(E) acreage

**24.** According to the passage, all of the following were important to McCarthy's grandmother EXCEPT

(A) governing the actions of others
(B) contributing to religious organizations
(C) surrounding herself with a circle of friends
(D) combating the spread of Protestantism
(E) guarding her possessions from outsiders

IF YOU FINISH IN LESS THAN 25 MINUTES, YOU MAY CHECK YOUR WORK ON THIS SECTION ONLY. DO NOT TURN TO ANY OTHER SECTION IN THE TEST.

**STOP**

## SECTION 2 /MATHEMATICS

TIME: 25 MINUTES
20 QUESTIONS (1–20)

### Directions:

For each question in this section, determine which of the five choices is correct, and blacken that choice on your answer sheet. You may use any blank space on the page for your work.

NOTES:
- You may use a calculator whenever you believe it will be helpful.
- Use the diagrams provided to help you solve the problems. Unless you see the phrase
  <u>Note:</u> Figure not drawn to scale
  under a diagram, it has been drawn as accurately as possible. Unless it is stated that a figure is three dimensional, you may assume that it lies in a plane.

### Reference

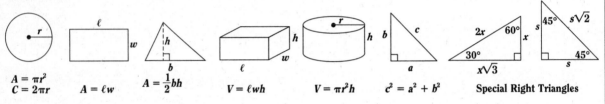

$A = \pi r^2$
$C = 2\pi r$

$A = \ell w$

$A = \frac{1}{2}bh$

$V = \ell w h$

$V = \pi r^2 h$

$c^2 = a^2 + b^2$

**Special Right Triangles**

Number of degrees in a circle: 360
Sum of the measures, in degrees, of the three angles of a triangle: 180

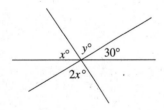

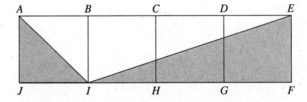

**1.** In the figure above, what is the value of $y$?

(A) 50
(B) 70
(C) 90
(D) 100
(E) 140

**2.** If $(a + 12) - 12 = 12$, then $a =$

(A) −12
(B) 0
(C) 12
(D) 24
(E) 36

**3.** In the figure above, rectangle *AEFJ* is divided into four equal squares. What is the ratio of the area of the shaded region to the area of the white region?

(A) 1:2
(B) 3:5
(C) 5:8
(D) 1:1
(E) 5:3

**GO ON TO NEXT PAGE ▶**

**4.** The Albertville Little League raised some money. They used 72% of the money to buy uniforms, 19% for equipment, and the remaining $243 for a team party. How much money did the team raise?

(A) $2400
(B) $2450
(C) $2500
(D) $2600
(E) $2700

**5.** If it is now 1:30, what time will it be when the hour hand has moved through an angle of 20°?

(A) 1:45
(B) 1:50
(C) 2:00
(D) 2:10
(E) 2:15

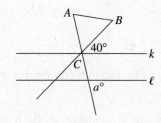

**6.** In the figure above, lines $k$ and $\ell$ are parallel, and line $k$ passes through $C$, one of the vertices of equilateral triangle $ABC$. What is the value of $a$?

(A) 40
(B) 50
(C) 60
(D) 80
(E) 90

**7.** If the difference of two numbers is less than the sum of the numbers, which of the following must be true?

(A) Neither number is positive.
(B) At least one of the numbers is positive.
(C) Exactly one of the numbers is positive.
(D) Both numbers are positive.
(E) None of these statements must be true.

**8.** 20 is what percent of $C$?

(A) $20C\%$
(B) $\frac{1}{20C}\%$
(C) $\frac{20}{C}\%$
(D) $\frac{200}{C}\%$
(E) $\frac{2000}{C}\%$

**9.** Two sides of a right triangle are 5 and 9. Which of the following could be the length of the third side?

I. $\sqrt{56}$
II. $\sqrt{76}$
III. $\sqrt{106}$

(A) I only
(B) III only
(C) I and II only
(D) I and III only
(E) I, II, and III

**10.** Which of the following is an equation of a line that is parallel to the line whose equation is $y = 2x - 3$?

(A) $y = 2x + 3$
(B) $y = -2x - 3$
(C) $y = \frac{1}{2}x - 3$
(D) $y = -\frac{1}{2}x + 3$
(E) $y = -\frac{1}{2}x - 3$

**11.** If $n$ is an integer and $n$, $n + 1$, and $n + 2$ are the lengths of the sides of a triangle, which of the following could be the value of $n$?

I. 1
II. 3
III. 13

(A) I only
(B) II only
(C) III only
(D) II and III only
(E) I, II, and III

**GO ON TO NEXT PAGE ▶**

12. A bank raised the minimum payment on its charge accounts from $10 to $20 per month. What was the percent increase in the minimum monthly pament?

(A) 10%
(B) 20%
(C) 50%
(D) 100%
(E) 200%

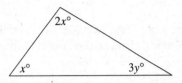

13. For the figure above, which of the following is an expression for $y$ in terms of $x$?

(A) $x$
(B) $60 - x$
(C) $x - 60$
(D) $180 - 3x$
(E) $90 - x$

**Questions 14 and 15 refer to the following definition.**

For any number $x$, $\|x\| = \frac{2}{3}x^2$.

14. What is the value of $\|6^2\|$?

(A) 16
(B) 24
(C) 144
(D) 576
(E) 864

15. If $y = \frac{2}{3}x$, which of the following is an expression for $\|y\|$ in terms of $x$?

(A) $\frac{2}{3}x^3$
(B) $\frac{4}{9}x^2$
(C) $\frac{4}{9}x^3$
(D) $\frac{8}{27}x^2$
(E) $\frac{8}{27}x^3$

16. If $f(x) = 9x + 9^x$, what is the value of $f\left(\frac{1}{2}\right)$?

(A) 3
(B) 6
(C) 7.5
(D) 9
(E) 9.9

17. The road from Jack's house to Jill's is exactly 10 kilometers. At different times, Jack and Jill each left home and walked toward the other's house. They walked at the same rate, and they met at noon, 4 kilometers from Jill's house. If Jack left at 10:00, at what time did Jill leave?

(A) 9:40
(B) 10:00
(C) 10:40
(D) 11:00
(E) 11:20

18. The Northport High School French Club has twice as many female members as male members. One day, the percentage of female members attending a meeting of the club was twice the percentage of male members. What percent of those attending the meeting were males?

(A) 20%
(B) 25%
(C) $33\frac{1}{3}$%
(D) 50%
(E) It cannot be determined from the information given.

19. If $a$ and $b$ are the lengths of the legs of a right triangle whose hypotenuse is 10 and whose area is 20, what is the value of $(a + b)^2$?

(A) 100
(B) 120
(C) 140
(D) 180
(E) 200

20. A lottery prize worth $d$ dollars was to be divided equally among 4 winners. It was subsequently discovered that there were 2 additional winners, and the prize would now be divided equally among all the winners. How much more money, in dollars, would each original winner have received if the additional winners were not discovered?

(A) $\frac{d}{12}$
(B) $\frac{d}{6}$
(C) $\frac{d}{4}$
(D) $\frac{12}{d}$
(E) $\frac{6}{d}$

IF YOU FINISH IN LESS THAN 25 MINUTES, YOU MAY CHECK YOUR WORK ON THIS SECTION ONLY. DO NOT TURN TO ANY OTHER SECTION IN THE TEST.

**STOP**

# SECTION 3/CRITICAL READING

TIME: 25 MINUTES
24 QUESTIONS (25–48)

**Directions:** For each question in this section, select the best answer from among the choices given and fill in the corresponding circle on the answer sheet.

Each sentence below has one or two blanks, each blank indicating that something has been omitted. Beneath the sentence are five words or sets of words labeled A through E. Choose the word or set of words that, when inserted in the sentence, best fits the meaning of the sentence as a whole.

**EXAMPLE:**

Medieval kingdoms did not become constitutional republics overnight; on the contrary, the change was ----.

(A) unpopular  (B) unexpected
(C) advantageous  (D) sufficient  (E) gradual

25. Unhappily, the psychology experiment was ---- by the subjects' awareness of the presence of observers in their midst.

(A) muted  (B) palliated  (C) marred
(D) clarified  (E) concluded

26. Until James learned to be more ---- about writing down his homework assignments, he seldom knew when any assignment was due.

(A) obdurate  (B) contrary  (C) opportunistic
(D) methodical  (E) literate

27. Despite all the advertisements singing the ---- of the new product, she remained ---- its merits, wanting to see what *Consumer Reports* had to say about its claims.

(A) virtues..an optimist about
(B) praises..a skeptic about
(C) joys..a convert to
(D) defects..a cynic about
(E) advantages..a believer in

28. After working on the project night and day for two full months, Sandy felt that she had earned a ----.

(A) penalty  (B) scolding  (C) degree
(D) chore  (E) respite

29. Even though the basic organization of the brain does not change after birth, details of its structure and function remain ---- for some time, particularly in the cerebral cortex.

(A) plastic  (B) immutable  (C) essential
(D) unknown  (E) static

**GO ON TO NEXT PAGE ▶**

**Directions:** Each of the passages below precedes two questions based on its content. Answer the questions following each passage on the basis of what is <u>stated</u> or <u>implied</u> in that passage.

**Questions 30 and 31 are based on the following passage.**

Can prison reform people, positively transforming their lives? Some who answer yes to this question point to the example of Malcolm Little,
Line later known as Malcolm X. *The Autobiography of*
5 *Malcolm X* describes how Malcolm, a high school dropout, in prison set himself the task of reading straight through the dictionary; to him, reading was purposeful, not aimless, and he plowed his way through its hundreds of pages, from A for
10 *aardvark* to Z for *zymurgy*.

**30.** The author's attitude toward Malcolm's activities in prison can best be described as

(A) nostalgic   (B) pessimistic
(C) condescending   (D) approving
(E) apologetic

**31.** In line 8, "plowed" most nearly means

(A) harrowed   (B) cultivated
(C) plunged recklessly   (D) prepared hastily
(E) proceeded steadily

**Questions 32 and 33 are based on the following passage.**

Many primates live together in an organized troop or social group that includes members of all ages and both sexes. Such troops always move
Line compactly together in a stable social unit. A
5 typical primate troop characteristically exhibits a ranking hierarchy among the males in the troop. This ranking hierarchy serves to alleviate conflict within the troop. The highest-ranking male or males defend, control, and lead the troop; the
10 strong social bond among members and their safety is maintained.

**32.** According to the passage, primate societies are

(A) generally unstable
(B) hierarchically flexible
(C) extremely competitive
(D) dominated by adult males
(E) frequently in conflict with each other

**33.** According to the passage, the hierarchic structure within a troop serves to

(A) protect the members of the troop
(B) facilitate food gathering
(C) establish friendships within the group
(D) keep members of other troops from joining
(E) teach the youngest members how to survive

**GO ON TO NEXT PAGE ▶**

**Directions:** The passage below is followed by questions on its content. Answer the questions on the basis of what is stated or implied in the passage and in any introductory material that may be provided.

**Questions 34–42 are based on the following passage.**

*The passage below, taken from a museum bulletin, discusses tapestry making as an art form.*

Tapestries are made on looms. Their distinctive weave is basically simple: the colored weft threads interface regularly with the monochrome warps, as in darning or plain cloth, but as they do
5 so, they form a design by reversing their direction when a change of color is needed. The wefts are beaten down to cover the warps completely. The result is a design or picture that is the fabric itself, not one laid upon a ground like an embroidery, a
10 print, or brocading. The back and front of a tapestry show the same design. The weaver always follows a preexisting model, generally a drawing or painting, known as the cartoon, which in most cases he reproduces as exactly as he can. Long
15 training is needed to become a professional tapestry weaver. It can take as much as a year to produce a yard of very finely woven tapestry.

Tapestry-woven fabrics have been made from China to Peru and from very early times to the
20 present day, but large wall hangings in this technique, mainly of wool, are typically Northern European. Few examples predating the late fourteenth century have survived, but from about 1400 tapestries were an essential part of aristo-
25 cratic life. The prince or great nobleman sent his plate and his tapestries ahead of him to furnish his castles before his arrival as he traveled through his domains; both had the same function, to display his wealth and social position. It has frequently
30 been suggested that tapestries helped to heat stone-walled rooms, but this is a modern idea; comfort was of minor importance in the Middle Ages. Tapestries were portable grandeur, instant splendor, taking the place, north of the Alps, of
35 painted frescoes further south. They were hung without gaps between them, covering entire walls and often doors as well. Only very occasionally were they made as individual works of art such as altar frontals. They were usually commissioned or
40 bought as sets, or "chambers," and constituted the most important furnishings of any grand room, except for the display of plate, throughout the

Middle Ages and the sixteenth century. Later, woven silks, ornamental wood carving, stucco
45 decoration, and painted leather gradually replaced tapestry as expensive wall coverings, until at last wallpaper was introduced in the late eighteenth century and eventually swept away almost everything else.

50 By the end of the eighteenth century, the "tapestry-room" [a room with every available wall surface covered with wall hangings] was no longer fashionable: paper had replaced wall coverings of wool and silk. Tapestries, of course, were still
55 made, but in the nineteenth century they often seem to have been produced mainly as individual works of art that astonish by their resemblance to oil paintings, tours de force woven with a remarkably large number of wefts per inch. In England
60 during the second half of the century, William Morris attempted to reverse this trend and to bring tapestry weaving back to its true principles, those he considered to have governed it in the Middle Ages. He imitated medieval tapestries in
65 both style and technique, using few warps to the inch, but he did not make sets; the original function for which tapestry is so admirably suited—completely covering the walls of a room and providing sumptuous surroundings for a life
70 of pomp and splendor—could not be revived. Morris's example has been followed, though with less imitation of medieval style, by many weavers of the present century, whose coarsely woven cloths hang like single pictures and can be
75 admired as examples of contemporary art.

**GO ON TO NEXT PAGE ▶**

34. Tapestry weaving may be characterized as which of the following?

   I. Time-consuming
   II. Spontaneous in concept
   III. Faithful to an original

   (A) I only
   (B) III only
   (C) I and II only
   (D) I and III only
   (E) II and III only

35. In lines 1–2, "distinctive" most nearly means
   (A) characteristic   (B) stylish
   (C) discriminatory   (D) eminent
   (E) articulate

36. Renaissance nobles carried tapestries with them to demonstrate their
   (A) piety   (B) consequence
   (C) aesthetic judgment   (D) need for privacy
   (E) dislike for cold

37. In line 9, "ground" most nearly means
   (A) terrain   (B) dust   (C) thread   (D) base
   (E) pigment

38. The statement in line 31 ("but this . . . idea") is best described as an example of
   (A) a definition of a central concept
   (B) an acknowledgment of a principle
   (C) a dismissal of a common view
   (D) an emotional refutation
   (E) a moral proclamation

39. In line 40, the quotation marks around the word "chambers" serve to
   (A) emphasize the inadequacy of the particular choice of words
   (B) point out the triteness of the term
   (C) indicate the use of a colloquialism
   (D) illustrate the need for the word to be stressed when spoken aloud
   (E) indicate the word is being used in a special sense

40. The author regards William Morris (lines 60–64) as
   (A) a bold innovator
   (B) an uninspired hack
   (C) a medieval nobleman
   (D) a cartoonist
   (E) a traditionalist

41. In contrast to nineteenth-century tapestries, contemporary tapestries
   (A) are displayed in sets of panels
   (B) echo medieval themes
   (C) faithfully copy oil paintings
   (D) have a less fine weave
   (E) indicate the owner's social position

42. The primary purpose of the passage is to
   (A) explain the process of tapestry making
   (B) contrast Eastern and Western schools of tapestry
   (C) analyze the reasons for the decline in popularity of tapestries
   (D) provide a historical perspective on tapestry making
   (E) advocate a return to a more colorful way of life

**GO ON TO NEXT PAGE ▶**

**Questions 43–48 are based on the following passages.**

*These passages present two perspectives on the behavior of European jackdaws, members of the crow family. Passage 1 was written by the Austrian naturalist Konrad Lorenz in 1949. Passage 2 was written by a Dutch colleague late in the twentieth century.*

**Passage 1**

In the chimney the autumn wind sings the song of the elements, and the old firs before my study window wave excitedly with their arms and
Line sing so loudly in chorus that I can hear their
5 sighing melody through the double panes. Suddenly, from above, a dozen black, streamlined projectiles shoot across the piece of clouded sky for which my window forms a frame. Heavily as stones they fall, fall to the tops of the firs where
10 they suddenly sprout wings, become birds and then light feather rags that the storm seizes and whirls out of my line of vision, more rapidly than they were borne into it.

I walk to the window to watch this extraordi-
15 nary game that the jackdaws are playing with the wind. A game? Yes, indeed, it is a game, in the most literal sense of the word: practiced movements, indulged in and enjoyed for their own sake and not for the achievement of a special object.
20 And rest assured, these are not merely inborn, purely instinctive actions, but movements that have been carefully learned. All these feats that the birds are performing, their wonderful exploitation of the wind, their amazingly exact assessment of
25 distances and, above all, their understanding of local wind conditions, their knowledge of all the up-currents, air pockets and eddies—all this proficiency is no inheritance, but, for each bird, an individually acquired accomplishment.
30 And look what they do with the wind! At first sight, you, poor human being, think that the storm is playing with the birds, like a cat with a mouse, but soon you see, with astonishment, that it is the fury of the elements that here plays the
35 role of the mouse and that the jackdaws are treating the storm exactly as the cat its unfortunate victim. Nearly, but only nearly, do they give the storm its head, let it throw them high, high into the heavens, till they seem to fall upwards, then,
40 with a casual flap of a wing, they turn themselves

over, open their pinions for a fraction of a second from below against the wind, and dive—with an acceleration far greater than that of a falling stone—into the depths below. Another tiny jerk of
45 the wing and they return to their normal position and, on close-reefed sails, shoot away with breathless speed into the teeth of the gale, hundreds of yards to the west: this all playfully and without effort, just to spite the stupid wind that tries to
50 drive them towards the east. The sightless monster itself must perform the work of propelling the birds through the air at a rate of well over 80 miles an hour; the jackdaws do nothing to help beyond a few lazy adjustments of their black wings. Sover-
55 eign control over the power of the elements, intoxicating triumph of the living organism over the pitiless strength of the inorganic!

**Passage 2**

In the Netherlands the jackdaw is a sedentary species. They breed in holes that they do not exca-
60 vate themselves, and territorial defense is limited to the nest-hole. Both mates share the duties related to the defense of the nest-site, the building of the nest, and the rearing of the young. However, only the female incubates. During this
65 time, she is fed by her mate. The mated pair remains together throughout the year and from year to year. Within the jackdaw population in the study area, two social categories can be distinguished, based on seasonal differences in nest-site
70 defense: resident pairs and non-resident birds.

The resident pairs defend at least one nesthole continuously from early fall (September) until the end of the breeding season (July), usually year after year. Only adult, mated jackdaws
75 belong to this group.

Unlike the resident pairs, non-resident birds do not defend a nest-site in the winter. The nonresident component of the population is rather heterogeneous. It contains birds of all ages, mated
80 and non-mated, breeders and non-breeders. During their first year of life, all jackdaws belong to the non-resident category. At the end of their first year of life, pairs are formed and some of these juvenile pairs obtain a nest-site, breed, and
85 may become residents in fall. Adult jackdaws may belong to the non-resident category for several

**GO ON TO NEXT PAGE ▶**

reasons. For instance, non-mated jackdaws do not
defend a nest-site, and hence all non-mated birds,
including residents remaining behind after their
90 mate died or disappeared, become non-residents.
Furthermore, jackdaws depend on natural holes
for breeding. Hollow trees may fall, chimneys may
be swept and provided with an "anti-jackdaw" cap,
and church towers may be restored and made
95 unavailable for jackdaw nesting. The loss of their
nest-site probably is a common event in the life
of a jackdaw pair.

**43.** Compared to Passage 1, Passage 2 is

(A) more eloquent and less poetic
(B) more detailed and less ambivalent
(C) more objective and less lyrical
(D) more metaphorical and less realistic
(E) more ambiguous and less literal

**44.** According to Passage 1, the bird's skill in adapting
to wind conditions is

(A) genetically determined
(B) limited
(C) undependable
(D) dependent on the elements
(E) gained through practice

**45.** In line 20, "rest assured" most nearly means

(A) sleep securely
(B) others are convinced
(C) be confident
(D) remain poised
(E) in their certain leisure

**46.** Throughout Passage 1, the author is most
impressed by

(A) the direction-finding skills employed by the
birds
(B) the jackdaws' superhuman strength
(C) his inability to join the jackdaws in their game
(D) the jackdaws' mastery of the forces of nature
(E) the fleeting nature of his encounter with the
birds

**47.** The author of Passage 1 does all of the following
EXCEPT

(A) use a metaphor
(B) argue a cause
(C) clarify a term
(D) describe a sequence of actions
(E) dismiss a notion

**48.** The author of Passage 2 makes significant use of
which of the following?

(A) Personal anecdotes
(B) Observational data
(C) Figurative language
(D) Statistical correlations
(E) Rhetorical questions

IF YOU FINISH IN LESS THAN 25 MINUTES, YOU MAY CHECK YOUR WORK ON
THIS SECTION ONLY. DO NOT TURN TO ANY OTHER SECTION IN THE TEST.

**STOP**

# SECTION 4/MATHEMATICS

TIME: 25 MINUTES

18 QUESTIONS (21–38)

## Directions:

For questions 21–28, determine which of the five choices is correct, and blacken that choice on your answer sheet. You may use any blank space on the page for your work.

NOTES:
- You may use a calculator whenever you believe it will be helpful.
- Use the diagrams provided to help you solve the problems. Unless you see the phrase
<u>Note:</u> Figure not drawn to scale
under a diagram, it has been drawn as accurately as possible. Unless it is stated that a figure is three dimensional, you may assume that it lies in a plane.

## Reference

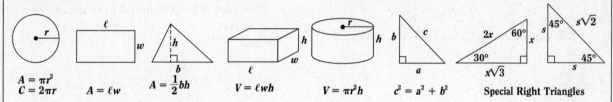

$A = \pi r^2$
$C = 2\pi r$    $A = \ell w$    $A = \frac{1}{2}bh$    $V = \ell w h$    $V = \pi r^2 h$    $c^2 = a^2 + b^2$    **Special Right Triangles**

Number of degrees in a circle: 360
Sum of the measures, in degrees, of the three angles of a triangle: 180

---

**21.** If the ratio of the number of boys to girls in a club is 2:3, what percent of the club members are girls?

(A) $33\frac{1}{3}\%$

(B) 40%

(C) 50%

(D) 60%

(E) $66\frac{2}{3}\%$

**22.** The Salem Soccer League is divided into $d$ divisions. Each division has $t$ teams, and each team has $p$ players. How many players are there in the entire league?

(A) $\frac{pt}{d}$

(B) $\frac{dt}{p}$

(C) $\frac{d}{pt}$

(D) $d + t + p$

(E) $dtp$

**23.** Which of the following is *NOT* a solution of $3x^2 + 2y = 5$?

(A) $x = 1$ and $y = 1$
(B) $x = -1$ and $y = 1$
(C) $x = 1$ and $y = -1$
(D) $x = 3$ and $y = -11$
(E) $x = -3$ and $y = -11$

**24.** Sally wrote the number 1 on 1 slip of paper, the number 2 on 2 slips of paper, the number 3 on 3 slips of paper, the number 4 on 4 slips of paper, the number 5 on 5 slips of paper, and the number 6 on 6 slips of paper. All the slips of paper were placed in a bag, and Lana drew one slip at random. What is the probability that the number on the slip Lana drew was odd?

(A) $\frac{1}{9}$

(B) $\frac{1}{7}$

(C) $\frac{3}{7}$

(D) $\frac{1}{2}$

(E) $\frac{4}{7}$

**GO ON TO NEXT PAGE ▶**

25. If $|x| = |y|$, which of the following must be true?

   I. $-x = -y$
   II. $x^2 = y^2$
   III. $x^3 = y^3$

   (A) I only
   (B) II only
   (C) I and II only
   (D) II and III only
   (E) I, II, and III

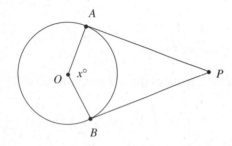

26. In the figure above, $\overline{PA}$ and $\overline{PB}$ are tangent to circle $O$. If $m\angle P = 50°$, what is the value of $x$?

   (A) 50
   (B) 90
   (C) 120
   (D) 130
   (E) 150

27. Which of the following expressions is equal to $2^{3x} + 2^{3x} + 2^{3x} + 2^{3x}$?

   (A) $2^{3x+2}$
   (B) $2^{3x+4}$
   (C) $2^{6x}$
   (D) $2^{12x}$
   (E) $2^{9x^2}$

28. The circumference of circle II is 4 feet longer than the circumference of circle I. How many feet longer is the radius of circle II than the radius of circle I?

   (A) $\frac{1}{4\pi}$

   (B) $\frac{2}{\pi}$

   (C) $\frac{1}{\pi}$

   (D) 2

   (E) It cannot be determined from the information given.

**GO ON TO NEXT PAGE ▶**

# Student-Produced Response Directions

In questions 29–38, first solve the problem, and then enter your answer on the grid provided on the answer sheet. The instructions for entering your answers follow.

- First, write your answer in the boxes at the top of the grid.
- Second, grid your answer in the columns below the boxes.
- Use the fraction bar in the first row or the decimal point in the second row to enter fractions and decimals.

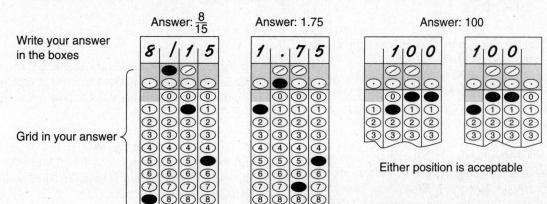

Answer: $\frac{8}{15}$    Answer: 1.75    Answer: 100

Write your answer in the boxes

Grid in your answer

Either position is acceptable

- Grid only one space in each column.
- Entering the answer in the boxes is recommended as an aid in gridding but is not required.
- The machine scoring your exam can read only what you grid, so you **must grid-in your answers correctly to get credit.**
- If a question has more than one correct answer, grid-in only one of them.
- The grid does not have a minus sign; so no answer can be negative.
- A mixed number *must* be converted to an improper fraction or a decimal before it is gridded. Enter $1\frac{1}{4}$ as $\frac{5}{4}$ or 1.25; the machine will interpret 11/4 as $\frac{11}{4}$ and mark it wrong.

- **All decimals must be entered as accurately as possible.** Here are three acceptable ways of gridding
$$\frac{3}{11} = 0.272727\ldots$$

- Note that rounding to .273 is acceptable because you are using the full grid, but you would receive **no credit** for .3 or .27, because they are less accurate.

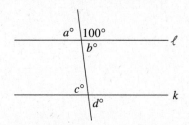

Lines $\ell$ and $k$ are parallel.

**29.** In the figure above, what is the value of $a + b + c + d$?

**30.** If $a = 6$ and $b = -6$, what is the value of $2a - 3b$?

**31.** If $A$ is the median of {1, 2, 3, 4, 5, 6} and $B$ is the median of {1, 2, 3, 4, 5, 6, 7}, what is the average (arithmetic mean) of $A$ and $B$?

**GO ON TO NEXT PAGE ▶**

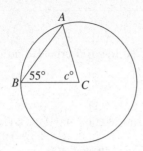

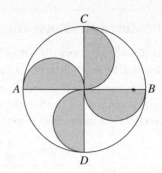

**32.** In the figure above, $C$ is the center of the circle. What is the value of $c$?

**33.** If Elaine drove 190 kilometers between 12:00 noon and 3:20 P.M., what was her average speed, in kilometers per hour?

**34.** From 2000 until 2010 the value of an investment increased by 10% every year. The value of that investment on January 1, 2006, was how many times greater than the value on January 1, 2004?

**35.** How many two-digit numbers do not contain the digit 9?

**36.** If the average (arithmetic mean) of five numbers is 95 and the average of three of them is 100, what is the average of the other two?

**37.** In the circle above, diameters $AB$ and $CD$ are perpendicular, and each of the four shaded regions is a semicircle. The shaded area is how many times the white area?

**38.** When a group of people were tested for a rare disease, 99.6% of them were found not to have the disease. If 10 people did have the disease, how many people were tested?

IF YOU FINISH IN LESS THAN 25 MINUTES, YOU MAY CHECK YOUR WORK ON THIS SECTION ONLY. DO NOT TURN TO ANY OTHER SECTION IN THE TEST.

**STOP**

# SECTION 5/WRITING SKILLS

TIME: 30 MINUTES

39 QUESTIONS (1–39)

**Directions:** For each question in this section, select the best answer from among the choices given and fill in the corresponding circle on the answer sheet.

---

Some or all parts of the following sentences are underlined. The first answer choice, (A), simply repeats the underlined part of the sentence. The other four choices present four alternative ways to phrase the underlined part. Select the answer that produces the most effective sentence, one that is clear and exact, and blacken the appropriate space on your answer sheet. In selecting your choice, be sure that it is standard written English and that it expresses the meaning of the original sentence.

**EXAMPLE:**

The first biography of author Eudora Welty came out in 1998, and she was eighty-nine years old at the time.

(A) and she was eighty-nine years old at the time
(B) at the time when she was eighty-nine
(C) upon becoming an eighty-nine year old
(D) when she was eighty-nine
(E) at the age of eighty-nine years old

Ⓐ Ⓑ Ⓒ ● Ⓔ

---

1. Although serfs were lucky to drink their ale from cracked wooden bowls, nobles customarily drunk their wine from elaborately chased drinking horns.

(A) drunk their wine from
(B) have drinked their wine from
(C) drank their wine from
(D) had drunken their wine from
(E) drinking their wine from

2. Before the search party reached the scene of the accident, the rain began to fall, making rescue efforts more difficult.

(A) the rain began to fall
(B) the rain had began to fall
(C) it began to rain
(D) the rain had begun to fall
(E) it started to rain

3. For many students, keeping a journal during college seems satisfying their need for self-expression.

(A) keeping a journal during college seems satisfying their need
(B) keeping a journal during college seems to satisfy their need
(C) keeping a journal during college seeming satisfying their need
(D) to keep a journal during college seems satisfying their need
(E) the keeping of a journal during college seems to satisfy their need

4. Peter Martins began to develop his own choreographic style, but he was able to free himself from the influence of Balanchine.

(A) style, but he was able to
(B) style; but he was able to
(C) style only when he was able to
(D) style only when he is able to
(E) style: only when he was able to

5. Irregardless of the outcome of this dispute, our two nations will remain staunch allies.

(A) Irregardless of the outcome
(B) Regardless of how the outcome
(C) With regard to the outcome
(D) Regardless of the outcome
(E) Disregarding the outcome

**GO ON TO NEXT PAGE ▶**

6. With the onset of winter, the <u>snows began to fall, we were soon forced to remain indoors</u> most of the time.

   (A) the snows began to fall, we were soon forced to remain indoors
   (B) the snows began to fall; we were soon forced to remain indoors
   (C) the snows began to fall; we are soon forced to remain indoors
   (D) the snows began to fall, having forced us to remain indoors
   (E) the snows begin to fall; we were soon forced to remain indoors

7. "Araby," along with several other stories from Joyce's *Dubliners*, <u>are going to be read</u> at Town Hall by the noted Irish actor Brendan Coyle.

   (A) are going to be read
   (B) were going to be read
   (C) are gone to be read
   (D) is going to be read
   (E) is gone to be read

8. In 1980 the Democrats <u>lost not only the executive branch, but also their majority</u> in the United States Senate.

   (A) lost not only the executive branch but also their majority
   (B) lost not only the executive branch but also its majority
   (C) not only lost the executive branch but also their majority
   (D) lost the executive branch but also their majority
   (E) lost not only the executive branch but their majority also

9. <u>Before considering an applicant for this job, he must have</u> a degree in electrical engineering as well as three years in the field.

   (A) Before considering an applicant for this job, he must have
   (B) Before considering an applicant for this job, he should have
   (C) We will not consider an applicant for this job without
   (D) To consider an applicant for this job, he must have
   (E) We will not consider an applicant for this job if he does not have

10. <u>To invest intelligently for the future, mutual funds</u> provide an excellent opportunity for the average investor.

    (A) To invest intelligently for the future, mutual funds
    (B) As an intelligent investment for the future, mutual funds
    (C) Investing intelligently for the future, mutual funds
    (D) To invest with intelligence, mutual funds
    (E) Having invested intelligently, you must determine that mutual funds

11. When you remodel your home, your renovations <u>must be in compliance to the local building code.</u>

    (A) must be in compliance to the local building code
    (B) must be in compliance with the local building code
    (C) must comply to the local building code
    (D) must have been in compliance to the local building code
    (E) must have been in compliance with the local building code

12. Although bothered by constant heckling from their traditional rivals, <u>the home team's response was to stick to the coach's game plan and defeat their opponents.</u>

    (A) the home team's response was to stick to the coach's game plan and defeat their opponents
    (B) the home team's response was to stick to the coach's game plan and defeat its opponents
    (C) the home team's response is about sticking to the coach's game plan and defeating their opponents
    (D) the home team responded with sticking to the coach's game plan and they defeated their opponents
    (E) the home team responded by sticking to the coach's game plan and defeating their opponents

13. Mary is <u>as fast as, if not faster than, anyone</u> in her class and should be on the team.

    (A) as fast as, if not faster than, anyone
    (B) as fast, if not faster than, anyone else
    (C) as fast as, if not more fast than, anyone
    (D) as fast as, if not faster than, anyone else
    (E) as swift as, if not faster than, anyone

**14.** Senator Schumer is <u>one of the legislators who are going</u> to discuss the budget with the president.

(A) one of the legislators who are going

(B) one of the legislators who is going

(C) one of the legislators who has gone

(D) one of the legislators who is gone

(E) one of the legislators who were gone

**15.** New research studies show that alcohol and tobacco <u>are as harmful to elderly women as elderly men.</u>

(A) are as harmful to elderly women as elderly men

(B) are so harmful to elderly women as elderly men

(C) being as harmful to elderly women as elderly men

(D) are as harmful to elderly women as to elderly men

(E) are as harmful to elderly women as to men being elderly

**16.** Chronic fatigue syndrome is not a normal <u>condition; rather, it is an abnormal response to stress factors such as</u> anxiety or infection.

(A) condition; rather, it is an abnormal response to stress factors such as

(B) condition, it is a rather abnormal response to stress factors such as

(C) condition; but it is an abnormal response to stress factors such as

(D) condition rather, it is an abnormal response to stress factors like

(E) condition, rather it is a way of responding abnormally to such stress factors as

**17.** <u>A cynic is when someone has a tendency to disbelieve that any actions can have wholly unselfish motivations.</u>

(A) A cynic is when someone has a tendency to disbelieve that any actions can have wholly unselfish motivations.

(B) Someone who has a tendency to disbelieve that any actions can have wholly unselfish motivations, and he is a cynic.

(C) A cynic is when someone tends not to believe that any actions might have had wholly unselfish motivations.

(D) A cynic is someone which has a tendency to disbelieve that any actions can be wholly unselfishly motivated.

(E) A cynic is someone who tends to disbelieve that any actions can have wholly unselfish motivations.

**18.** <u>When NASA has been informed of the dangerous weather conditions,</u> the head of the space agency decided to postpone the shuttle launch.

(A) When NASA has been informed of the dangerous weather conditions

(B) Because NASA having been informed of the dangerous weather conditions

(C) Although NASA was informed with the dangerous weather conditions

(D) When NASA was informed of the dangerous weather conditions

(E) When NASA has been informed with the dangerous weather conditions

**19.** Henry James wrote the play *Guy Domville* primarily because <u>he hoped revitalizing of his waning literary career.</u>

(A) he hoped revitalizing of his waning literary career

(B) he hoped revitalizing of his literary career that was waning

(C) his hoping was the revitalizing of his waning literary career

(D) he hoped to revitalize his waning literary career

(E) he hoped revitalizing of his literary career that had waned

**20.** While strolling in Golden Gate Park one day, <u>seeing the carousel with its elegantly carved horses delighted the young couple.</u>

(A) seeing the carousel with its elegantly carved horses delighted the young couple

(B) the sight of the carousel with its elegantly carved horses delighted the young couple

(C) the young couple was delighted by the sight of the carousel with its elegantly carved horses

(D) the carousel delighted the young couple with its elegantly carved horses when they saw it

(E) to have seen the carousel's elegantly carved horses delighted the young couple

**GO ON TO NEXT PAGE ▶**

The sentences in this section may contain errors in grammar, usage, choice of words, or idioms. There is either just one error per sentence, or the sentence is correct. Some words or phrases are underlined and lettered; everything else in the sentence is correct.

If an underlined word or phrase is incorrect, choose that letter; if the sentence is correct, select <u>No error</u>. Then blacken the appropriate space on your answer sheet.

**EXAMPLE:**

The region has a climate <u>so severe that</u> plants
                              A

<u>growing there</u> rarely <u>had been</u> more than twelve
        B                    C

inches <u>high.</u> <u>No error</u>
        D        E

Ⓐ Ⓑ ● Ⓓ Ⓔ

21. <u>Being that</u> my car is getting <u>its</u> annual tune-up, I
        A                              B

<u>will not be able</u> <u>to pick you up</u> tomorrow morning.
        C                    D

<u>No error</u>
    E

22. The average taxpayer <u>can't hardly</u> believe that
                              A

income tax fraud is <u>so widespread as</u> <u>to justify</u>
                          B              C

the precautions that the authorities <u>have taken.</u>
                                          D

<u>No error</u>
    E

23. No one <u>but</u> <u>he</u> knew <u>what</u> questions
           A    B        C

<u>were going</u> to be asked on this test. <u>No error</u>
        D                                    E

24. You are being <u>quite</u> cynical when you say
                      A

<u>that the reason</u> we have <u>such a large</u> turnout
        B                        C

<u>is because</u> we are serving refreshments.
        D

<u>No error</u>
    E

25. <u>Although</u> I <u>am playing</u> golf for more <u>than</u> three
        A              B                    C

years, I cannot manage <u>to break</u> 90. <u>No error</u>
                            D              E

26. Studies <u>have found</u> that a mild salt solution is
                A

more <u>affective</u> <u>than</u> the commercial preparations
        B          C

available in drug stores <u>in the treatment of</u> this
                              D

ailment. <u>No error</u>
            E

27. If I have to make a choice <u>between</u> John, Henry
    A                              B

and <u>her</u>, I think I'll select Henry because of his
        C

self-control <u>during</u> moments of stress. <u>No error</u>
                D                              E

28. <u>In order to</u> raise public consciousness concerning
        A

environmental problems, <u>you</u> should distribute
                              B

leaflets, write to <u>your representative</u> in Congress,
                          C

<u>as well as signing</u> the necessary petitions.
        D

<u>No error</u>
    E

**GO ON TO NEXT PAGE** ▶

**29.** Members of a scientific expedition discovered the

Titanic, <u>which</u> sank after <u>it</u> struck an iceberg,
     A             B

<u>furthermore</u> it was not possible for them to
  C

<u>raise it</u>. <u>No error</u>
 D     E

**30.** Scientists <u>show</u> that change, <u>whether</u> good or bad,
        A         B

leads to stress <u>and</u> that the <u>accumulation from</u>
           C         D

stress-related changes can cause major illness.

<u>No error</u>
 E

**31.** We have spent <u>all together</u> <u>too much</u> money on
           A       B

this project; we have <u>exceeded</u> our budget and
              C

<u>can expect</u> no additional funds until the beginning
 D

of the new year. <u>No error</u>
         E

**32.** Between thirty <u>and</u> forty students <u>seem willing</u> to
            A          B

volunteer; <u>the rest</u> are not <u>planning to</u> participate
        C        D

in the program. <u>No error</u>
        E

**33.** The horse <u>that</u> won the trophies <u>differed with</u> the
        A             B

<u>other</u> horses in <u>overall appearance</u> as well as
 C        D

ability. <u>No error</u>
    E

**34.** The business executive, <u>planning</u> to attend the
              A

conference in New Orleans, <u>could not decide</u>
               B

whether to travel on or <u>remaining at</u> the hotel was
           C

the <u>better</u> choice. <u>No error</u>
   D       E

**GO ON TO NEXT PAGE ▶**

## Improving Paragraphs Directions

The passage below is the unedited draft of a student's essay. Some of the essay needs to be rewritten to make the meaning clearer and more precise. Read the essay carefully.

The essay is followed by questions about changes that might improve all or part of its organization, development, sentence structure, use of language, appropriateness to the audience, or use of standard written English. Choose the answer that most clearly and effectively expresses the student's intended meaning. Indicate your choice by filling in the corresponding space on the answer sheet.

[1] In the modern era, women have held a major part in influencing social change and social status. [2] In such developing countries as Saudi Arabia, restrictions on women are gradually being lifted, and they have gained the right to be in public without your head covered.

[3] In the area of social status, women have fought for better treatment and more respect. [4] An example of this is the fight for women in the workplace. [5] Not long ago most women stayed at home and took care of their families, while their husbands worked at white collar and blue collar jobs. [6] But now many women work as doctors, lawyers, and other established positions. [7] Women are finally out in the work force competing with men for the same jobs.

[8] In the area of politics and government, many women have attained high positions. [9] Hillary Rodham Clinton became a role model for many young women in this country. [10] Two women are now members of the U.S. Supreme Court. [11] Several women also are governors, senators and representatives. [12] There will never again be an all-male cabinet. [13] Ever since women's suffrage, women have won the rights reserved for men. [14] The result was that women now have a voice in the actions of our country.

[15] In the areas of health, medicine, sciences, and the military, women have also come into their own. [16] Although the world still has a long way to go before women achieve total equality with men, the modern era may long be remembered as the time when the first steps were taken.

35. Considering the essay as a whole, which revision of sentence 1 would serve best as the essay's opening sentence?

(A) The social status of women has undergone a major change during the modern era.
(B) Modern era women will have a major influence in changing their social status.
(C) As a major influence in the modern era, women have had their social status changed.
(D) Under the influence of modern era women, their status has changed.
(E) Being influenced by social change in the modern era, the status of women has changed.

36. Which is the most effective revision of the underlined segment of sentence 2 below?

*In such developing countries as Saudi Arabia, restrictions on women are gradually being lifted, and they have gained the right to be in public without your head covered.*

(A) for example, women are gaining rights like the one to be in public bareheaded
(B) which means that they have gained the right to be in public with their heads uncovered
(C) and they have the right, for example, for you to go barehaded in public
(D) and women now have gained the right to be bareheaded in public
(E) to the extent that women can exercise the right of going into public with their head uncovered

**37.** Which revision of sentence 8 provides the best transition between the second and the third paragraphs?

(A) The competition has extended into politics and government, where many women have replaced men in high positions.

(B) Irregardless, in the field of politics and government many women have attained high positions.

(C) High positions in government and politics have been attained by women.

(D) Among the jobs that women have attained are in politics and government.

(E) The world of politics and government has changed because women have attained high positions.

**38.** Sentence 8 is the topic sentence of the third paragraph. Which of the following is the best revision of sentence 9?

(A) The wife of the president, Hillary Rodham Clinton, made herself a role model for many young American women.

(B) In the 1992 national election, Hillary Rodham Clinton helped her husband win the presidency of the United States.

(C) After seven years as prime minister of England, Margaret Thatcher was finally defeated by a male, John Major.

(D) While she was the leader of India, Indira Ghandi was assassinated.

(E) In recent years both Margaret Thatcher of England and Indira Ghandi of India, for example, served as leaders of their countries.

**39.** Which sentence in the third paragraph should be revised or deleted because it contributes least to the development of the main idea of the paragraph?

(A) Sentence 10    (B) Sentence 11
(C) Sentence 12    (D) Sentence 13
(E) Sentence 14

IF YOU FINISH IN LESS THAN 30 MINUTES, YOU MAY CHECK YOUR WORK ON THIS SECTION ONLY. DO NOT TURN TO ANY OTHER SECTION IN THE TEST.

**STOP**

# Answer Key

## Section 1    Critical Reading

| | | | | | | | | |
|---|---|---|---|---|---|---|---|---|
| 1. | B | 6. | C | 11. | B | 16. | D | 21. | C |
| 2. | D | 7. | D | 12. | D | 17. | D | 22. | D |
| 3. | A | 8. | C | 13. | D | 18. | B | 23. | B |
| 4. | E | 9. | D | 14. | E | 19. | B | 24. | C |
| 5. | A | 10. | C | 15. | B | 20. | B | | |

## Section 2    Mathematics

| | | | | | | | | |
|---|---|---|---|---|---|---|---|---|
| 1. | D | 5. | D | 9. | D | 13. | B | 17. | C |
| 2. | C | 6. | D | 10. | A | 14. | E | 18. | A |
| 3. | D | 7. | B | 11. | D | 15. | D | 19. | D |
| 4. | E | 8. | E | 12. | D | 16. | C | 20. | A |

## Section 3    Critical Reading

| | | | | | | | | |
|---|---|---|---|---|---|---|---|---|
| 25. | C | 30. | D | 35. | A | 40. | E | 45. | C |
| 26. | D | 31. | E | 36. | B | 41. | D | 46. | D |
| 27. | B | 32. | D | 37. | D | 42. | D | 47. | B |
| 28. | E | 33. | A | 38. | C | 43. | C | 48. | B |
| 29. | A | 34. | D | 39. | E | 44. | E | | |

## Section 4    Mathematics

| | | | | | | | | |
|---|---|---|---|---|---|---|---|---|
| 21. | D | 23. | C | 25. | B | 27. | A |
| 22. | E | 24. | C | 26. | D | 28. | B |

29. 3 2 0

30. 3 0

31. 3 . 7 5   or *1 5 / 4*

32. 7 0

33. 57

34. 1.21

35. 72

36. 87.5

37. 1

38. 2500

## Section 5    Writing Skills

| | | | | |
|---|---|---|---|---|
| 1. **C** | 9. **E** | 17. **E** | 25. **B** | 33. **B** |
| 2. **D** | 10. **B** | 18. **D** | 26. **B** | 34. **C** |
| 3. **B** | 11. **B** | 19. **D** | 27. **B** | 35. **A** |
| 4. **C** | 12. **E** | 20. **C** | 28. **D** | 36. **A** |
| 5. **D** | 13. **D** | 21. **A** | 29. **C** | 37. **A** |
| 6. **B** | 14. **A** | 22. **A** | 30. **D** | 38. **E** |
| 7. **D** | 15. **D** | 23. **B** | 31. **A** | 39. **E** |
| 8. **A** | 16. **A** | 24. **D** | 32. **E** | |

## Scoring Chart—Practice Test 1

### Critical Reading Sections

**Section 1: 24 Questions (1–24)**

| | | |
|---|---|---|
| Number correct | _____ | (A) |
| Number omitted | _____ | (B) |
| Number incorrect | _____ | (C) |
| $\frac{1}{4}$ (C) | _____ | (D) |
| (A) − (D) | _____ | Raw Score I |

**Section 3: 24 Questions (25–48)**

| | | |
|---|---|---|
| Number correct | _____ | (A) |
| Number omitted | _____ | (B) |
| Number incorrect | _____ | (C) |
| $\frac{1}{4}$ (C) | _____ | (D) |
| (A) − (D) | _____ | Raw Score II |

**Total Critical Reading Raw Score**

Raw Scores I + II     _____

### Mathematics Sections

**Section 2: 20 Questions (1–20)**

| | | |
|---|---|---|
| Number correct | _____ | (A) |
| Number omitted | _____ | (B) |
| Number incorrect | _____ | (C) |
| $\frac{1}{4}$ (C) | _____ | (D) |
| (A) − (D) | _____ | Raw Score I |

**Section 4: First 8 Questions (21–28)**

| | | |
|---|---|---|
| Number correct | _____ | (A) |
| Number omitted | _____ | (B) |
| Number incorrect | _____ | (C) |
| $\frac{1}{4}$ (C) | _____ | (D) |
| (A) − (D) | _____ | Raw Score II |

**Section 4: Next 10 Questions (29–38)**

| | | |
|---|---|---|
| Number correct | _____ | Raw Score III |

**Total Mathematics Raw Score**

Raw Scores I + II + III     _____

**NOTE: In each section (A) + (B) + (C) should equal the number of questions in that section.**

### Writing Skills Section

**Section 5: 39 Questions (1–39)**

| | | |
|---|---|---|
| Number correct | _____ | (A) |
| Number omitted | _____ | (B) |
| Number incorrect | _____ | (C) |
| $\frac{1}{4}$ (C) | _____ | (D) |

**Writing Skills Raw Score**

(A) − (D)     _____

## Evaluation Chart

Study your score. Your raw score is an indication of your probable achievement on the PSAT/NMSQT. As a guide to the amount of work you need or want to do with this book, study the following.

| Raw Score | | | Self-Rating |
|---|---|---|---|
| *Critical Reading* | *Mathematics* | *Writing Skills* | |
| 42–48 | 35–38 | 33–39 | Superior |
| 37–41 | 30–34 | 28–32 | Very good |
| 32–36 | 25–29 | 23–27 | Good |
| 26–31 | 21–24 | 17–22 | Above average |
| 20–25 | 17–20 | 12–16 | Average |
| 12–19 | 10–16 | 7–11 | Below average |
| less than 12 | less than 10 | less than 7 | Inadequate |

# ANSWER EXPLANATIONS

## Section 1  Critical Reading

1. **(B)** Remember to think of your own answer before looking at the choices. North clearly had a strong belief; no one's words could convince him otherwise. This would guide you to choose *conviction*, one meaning of which is belief.

   Choice A is incorrect. *Demand* means requirement or forceful request. It is not the *best* word in the context of the sentence. Choice C is incorrect. A *maxim* is a proverbial saying or rule of conduct. It is not the *best* word in the context of the sentence. Choice D is incorrect. *Fear* makes no sense in the context of the sentence.

   Choice E is incorrect. *Ambivalence* means uncertainty or conflict of ideas. It makes no sense in the context of the sentence.

2. **(D)** If we are likely to be in need of a new source of energy, we must be about to run out of the old source of fuel. This would happen if we *deplete* or exhaust our supply. The phrase "excessive use" is also a clue that we may be running out, through using too much. Excessive use of fossil fuels clearly would not *replenish* (refill; restock) or *magnify* (enlarge) the supply of coal and oil. Likewise, it would not *merge* (combine) or *redirect* (reroute; send elsewhere) the supply of fossil fuels.

3. **(A)** The word "however" signals a contrast. The sentence says the authorities reject the use of "disinterested." Therefore, *in contrast*, they accept or *condone* the use of "healthy." You are looking for a word that is opposite in meaning to *reject*. None of the remaining choices—*evaluate* (assess), *imitate* (copy), *disdain* (look down on; scorn), *repudiate* (disown; deny)—have that meaning.

4. **(E)** The flu weakened or *debilitated* Michael, leaving him too tired to return to work. *Recuperated* (regained health), *diagnosed* (identified an illness), *incarcerated* (imprisoned; confined), and *captivated* (enchanted; enthralled) all make no sense in this context.

5. **(A)** The word "though" also signals a contrast. Although Alec Guinness had his mind set on becoming an actor, his determination or *resolution* wavered. Note that *resolution* is not just a statement of intent; it can mean firmness of intent as well. It was Guinness's determination to become an actor that momentarily wavered, not his *reverence* (awed respect; veneration), *affectation* (artificiality of manner), *theatricality* (staginess), or *skepticism* (unbelief; doubting attitude).

6. **(C)** The key word here is "ridiculing," meaning making fun of or mocking. In writing *Gulliver's Travels*, Swift means to mock or make fun of his society: his intent is *satirical* (sarcastic and cutting). It is not *elegiac* (expressing sorrow), *prophetic* (visionary; oracular), or *derivative* (imitative; unoriginal). It certainly is not *questionable* (dubious or disputable).

7. **(D)** Someone who risks his or her life frequently is a *daredevil*. Since the threat of death does not keep Markham from such activities, the first missing word must be *daunt*, meaning to frighten or lessen one's courage.

   Choice A is incorrect. Remember, *both* words of your answer choice must fit the meaning of the sentence as a whole. *Intimidate* means frighten or threaten. It is a good choice for the first blank. However, a *patrician* is an aristocrat, a person of high rank. Such persons are not by definition people who customarily risk their lives. Choice B is incorrect. Neither *divert* (redirect; distract) nor *renegade* (turncoat; traitor) complete the sentence properly. Choice C is incorrect. A *dilettante* is a dabbler or casual participant in an activity. In risking her life countless times to set records, clearly Markham was no dabbler at flying small planes. Choice E is incorrect. A *firebrand* is an agitator or troublemaker. Markham was a risk taker, not a troublemaker.

8. **(C)** "Unscrupulous merchandisers" make false claims. *Debunking* means exposing falseness in something. Nader, who is an advocate or protector of the consumer, teaches people to be suspicious and to exercise *skepticism*. Note that "exercising skepticism" is a cliché, a very commonly used phrase.

---

**Note the following icons, used throughout this book:**

 Time saver

 Look it up; math reference fact

 Helpful Hint

 Educated guess

 Prefixes, roots, and suffixes

 Caution!

 Did you notice?

 Positive or negative?

A calculator might be useful.

Choice A is incorrect. A consumer advocate would not be engaged in *asserting* (insisting on; affirming) the claims of dishonest merchandisers. Choice B is incorrect. While a consumer advocate might become involved in *deflating* (belittling; puncturing) the claims of dishonest merchandisers, there's no way he or she would have warned the public to exercise a healthy *prodigality* (wastefulness). Choice D is incorrect. A consumer advocate would not be engaged in *affirming* (supporting; confirming) the claims of dishonest merchandisers. Choice E is incorrect. A consumer advocate would not be engaged in *exaggerating* (overstating) the claims of dishonest merchandisers, nor would he or she warn the public to exercise a healthy *optimism* (hopefulness).

9. **(D)** The author's presentation of factual information about tarantulas is scientifically *objective* (impartial).

10. **(C)** To excite a defensive response is to *stimulate* or arouse that reaction.

11. **(B)** Passage 1 describes what you would see if you subjected a tarantula to various forms of stimuli (pressing a pencil against its body-wall, holding a pencil above it, etc.). In other words, it *provides scientific observations of the subject* (the tarantula). Passage 2, in contrast, offers highly general, chatty information about tarantulas, providing *a popular introduction to the subject*.

12. **(D)** You can answer this question by using the process of elimination.
Do both passages indicate that tarantulas have a marked degree of intelligence? Nothing in either passage suggests this. You can eliminate Choice A.

Do both passages indicate that the tarantulas' gentleness belies (contradicts) their frightening looks? No. Although Passage 2 states that tarantulas are gentler creatures than their appearance suggests, Passage 1 says nothing about their being gentle. You can eliminate Choice B.
Do both passages indicate that tarantulas have been maligned (slandered; bad-mouthed) by arachnophobes? No. Passage 1 says nothing at all about arachnophobes. You can eliminate Choice C.
Do both passages indicate that tarantulas are capable of acting to defend themselves? Yes. Passage 1 portrays a tarantula's defensive reaction to a perceived threat: the spider immediately goes into its attack stance. Passage 2 indicates that tarantulas will bite if they are severely provoked; thus, they *are capable of acting to defend themselves*. The correct answer is most likely Choice D.

Confirm your answer choice by checking Choice E. Do both passages indicate that tarantulas are easily intimidated (frightened) by others? No. Nothing in either passage indicates this. You can eliminate Choice E.
Only Choice D is left. It is the correct answer.

13. **(D)** Throughout the passage the author depicts her grandmother's character as unpleasing. She was "a cold, grudging, disputatious old woman." The entire passage conveys McCarthy's *bitter alienation* (unfriendly estrangement) from her cold and aggressive grandmother.

14. **(E)** In candidly exposing her grandmother's flaws, the author exhibits a *sardonic* or scornful and sarcastic attitude.

15. **(B)** The author states (somewhat ironically) that modern fictional characters must have "clinical authenticity." In other words, they must appear to be genuine or *valid* in *psychological* terms.

16. **(D)** McCarthy sneers at the need to look for Oedipal fixations and traumatic experiences in literary characters. She views such clinically authentic character portrayals in modern fiction with *disdain* (scorn).

17. **(D)** McCarthy sees as little point in speculating about her grandmother's childhood as she does in wondering about the toilet training of a fictional character like Lady Macbeth. Such speculations are, in McCarthy's mind, idle or *pointless*.

18. **(B)** McCarthy makes her point about the foolishness of making guesses about her grandmother's childhood by comparing it to making (pointless) guesses about the (nonexistent) childhoods of Iago and Lady Macbeth. In doing so, she *emphasizes the folly of speculating about what formed her grandmother's character*.

19. **(B)** Just as McCarthy refuses to speculate about possible traumas in childhood that might have soured her grandmother, she also rejects the notion that any hardships of old age might excuse her offensiveness. Thus, McCarthy cites her grandmother's large, supportive family and financial prosperity in order to support the claim that *her grandmother had suffered no traumas or deprivation that might explain her unpleasantness*.

20. **(B)** Although the grandmother's outward appearance was soft and motherly, her essential nature was hard as nails. Clearly, you cannot judge a book (person) by its cover (outward appearance).

21. **(C)** McCarthy's aggressive grandmother engages in prayer as an "act of war" against the dominant Protestant culture; her goal is the extermination of Protestantism. In describing her grandmother as "(a)n aggressive churchgoer," McCarthy underscores her grandmother's *antagonism towards other faiths.*

22. **(D)** McCarthy is building up a portrait of her grandmother as a pugnacious, autocratic person. She describes the fear old ladies have for their belongings as a very human (and understandable) reaction: aware of their own increasing fragility (and eventual death), old ladies identify with their fragile possessions and are protective of them. McCarthy's grandmother was also protective of her belongings, but she was not the typical "gentle and tremulous" elderly woman. She was a petty tyrant and had decidedly *different reasons for her actions.*

23. **(B)** Because her grandmother was more interested in maintaining her power than in being hospitable, the social properties or *attributes* (qualities) of the family home had withered and decayed until no real sociability existed.

24. **(C)** Lines 70–71 state clearly that "(t)he family had no friends." McCarthy's grandmother had no interest in *surrounding herself with a circle of friends.* She surrounded herself with cowed relatives instead.

## Section 2 Mathematics

For many problems, the explanation provides a reference to one or more **KEY FACTS** from Chapter 7. These are the mathematical facts that you need to solve that problem. If a solution refers to **KEY FACT J2**, for example, the solution depends on the second **KEY FACT** discussed in Section J of Chapter 7.

For some problems, an alternative solution, indicated by two asterisks (**), follows the first solution. When this occurs, usually one of the solutions is the direct mathematical one and the other is based on one of the tactics discussed in Chapters 6 and 7.

See page 244 for an explanation of the symbol ⇒, which is used in several answer explanations.

1. **(D)** Since $x + y + 30 = 180$ and $y = 2x$, we get
$$x + 2x + 30 = 180 \Rightarrow 3x = 150 \Rightarrow$$
$$x = 50 \Rightarrow y = 2x = 100.$$

2. **(C)** The left-hand side of $(a + 12) - 12 = 12$ is just $a$. So, $a = 12$.
**Of course, you can use **TACTIC 6-1**: backsolve, starting (and ending) with C.

3. **(D)** Let each side of the small squares be 1. Then each square has area 1, and the area of rectangle *AEFJ* is 4. The shaded area consists of $\triangle AJI$ and $\triangle EFI$. The white region is $\triangle AEI$, whose area is $\frac{1}{2}(4)(1) = 2$. The area of the shaded region is $4 - 2 = 2$, and so the ratio of the areas is $2:2 = 1:1$.
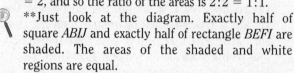
**Just look at the diagram. Exactly half of square *ABIJ* and exactly half of rectangle *BEFI* are shaded. The areas of the shaded and white regions are equal.

4. **(E)** Since 72% + 19% = 91%, the $243 spent on the party represents the other 9% of the money raised. Then $.09m = 243 \Rightarrow m = 243 \div .09 = 2700$.

5. **(D)** Every hour the hour hand moves through 30° ($\frac{1}{12}$ of 360°). So it will move through 20° in $\frac{2}{3}$ of an hour or 40 minutes; 40 minutes after 1:30 is 2:10.

6. **(D)** Since *ABC* is an equilateral triangle, $x = 60$. So, $60 + 40 + y = 180 \Rightarrow y = 80$. Then by **KEY FACT I6** (when parallel lines are cut by a transversal, the four acute angles have the same measure), $y = a$. So, $a = 80$.

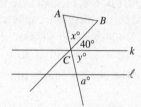

**Use **TACTIC 6-6** (trust the diagram)—*a* appears to be slightly less than a 90° angle.

7. **(B)** Let $x$ and $y$ be the two numbers: $x < y < x + y \Rightarrow -y < y \Rightarrow 0 < 2y \Rightarrow y$ is positive. Therefore, at least one of the numbers is positive. (Note that there are no restrictions on $x$.)

8. **(E)** Solve the equation $20 = \frac{x}{100}C$:
$$2000 = xC \Rightarrow x = \frac{2000}{C}\%.$$
**Use **TACTIC 6-3**: substitute an easy-to-use number: 20 is 100% of 20. Which of the choices is equal to 100% when $C = 20$? Only $\frac{2000}{C}\%$.

9. **(D)** Whenever we know two of the three sides of a right triangle, we can find the third side by using the Pythagorean theorem. First, assume that the two given sides are both legs, and let $x$ represent the hypotenuse. Then
$$x^2 = 5^2 + 9^2 = 25 + 81 = 106 \Rightarrow x = \sqrt{106}$$
and III is true. Now assume that one side is a leg and that the longer side is the hypotenuse; let $y$ represent the other leg. Then
$$5^2 + y^2 = 9^2 \Rightarrow 25 + y^2 = 81 \Rightarrow$$
$$y^2 = 56 \Rightarrow y = \sqrt{56}$$
and I is true. Therefore, I and III only are true.

10. **(A)** By **KEY FACT N7**, the slope of the line $y = 2x - 3$ is 2. By **KEY FACT N6**, parallel lines have equal slopes. Only Choice A, $y = 2x + 3$, also has a slope equal to 2.

11. **(D)** Just check each choice. Is there a triangle whose sides are 1, 2, 3? No, the sum of any two sides of a triangle must be *greater* than the third side (**KEY FACT J12**). (I is false.) Are there triangles whose sides are 3, 4, 5 and 13, 14, 15. Yes. (II and III are true.) Statements II and III only are true.

12. **(D)** By **KEY FACT C5**, the percent increase in the bank's charge is $\frac{\text{the actual increase}}{\text{the original amount}} \times 100\%$. The charge was originally $10 and the actual increase was $10. So, the percent increase is

$$\frac{10}{10} \times 100 = 100\%.$$

13. **(B)** Since the sum of the three measures is 180°:
$$180 = x + 2x + 3y = 3x + 3y = 3(x + y)$$
So, $x + y = 60$ and $y = 60 - x$.
**Use TACTIC 6-3**: pick an easy-to-use value for $x$. Note that in the diagram $x$ appears to be about 50, but you can pick any value: say 10. Then
$$10 + 20 + 3y = 180 \Rightarrow 3y = 150 \Rightarrow y = 50.$$
Which of the choices equals 10 when $y$ is 50? Only $60 - x$.

14. **(E)** $\|6^2\| = \frac{2}{3}(6^2)^2 = \frac{2}{3}(36)^2 = \frac{2}{3}(1296) = 864.$

15. **(D)** $\|y\| = \|\frac{2}{3}x\| = \frac{2}{3}(\frac{2}{3}x)^2 = \frac{2}{3}(\frac{4}{9}x^2) = \frac{8}{27}x^2.$

   **Use TACTIC 6-2**: replace the variables with numbers. Let $x = 3$. Then $y = \frac{2}{3}(3) = 2$, and $\|2\| = \frac{2}{3}(2)^2 = \frac{2}{3}(4) = \frac{8}{3}$. Which of the choices is equal to $\frac{8}{3}$ when $x = 3$? Only $\frac{8}{27}x^2$.

16. **(C)** $f(\frac{1}{2}) = 9(\frac{1}{2}) + 9^{\frac{1}{2}} = 4.5 + \sqrt{9} = 4.5 + 3 = 7.5.$

17. **(C)** Jill walked 4 kilometers and Jack walked 6 kilometers; so Jill walked $\frac{4}{6} = \frac{2}{3}$ the distance that Jack walked. Since their rates were the same, she did it in $\frac{2}{3}$ the time: $\frac{2}{3}$ of 2 hours is $\frac{4}{3}$ of an hour, or 1 hour and 20 minutes. She left at 10:40.
   **Jack walked 6 kilometers in exactly 2 hours; so, he was walking at a rate of 3 kilometers per hour. Jill walked 4 kilometers, also at 3 kilometers per hour; so her walking time was $4 \div 3$ or $1\frac{1}{3}$ hours ($t = d \div r$: See Section 7-H). Therefore, Jill left $1\frac{1}{3}$ hours, or 1 hour and 20 minutes, before noon—at 10:40.

18. **(A)** Even if you can do the algebra, this type of problem is easier by using **TACTIC 6-3**: choose easy-to-use numbers. Assume that there are 100 females and 50 males in the club and that 20% of the females and 10% of the males attended the meeting. Then, 20 females and 5 males were there, and 5 is 20% of 25, the total number attending.

19. **(D)** $(a + b)^2 = a^2 + 2ab + b^2 = (a^2 + b^2) + 2ab$. By the Pythagorean theorem, $a^2 + b^2 = 10^2 = 100$; and since the area is 20, $\frac{1}{2}ab = 20 \Rightarrow ab = 40$, and $2ab = 80$. Then
$$(a^2 + b^2) + 2ab = 100 + 80 = 180.$$

20. **(A)** Originally the fund of $d$ dollars was to be divided among 4 winners, in which case each of them would have received $\frac{d}{4}$ dollars. Instead, the fund was divided among 6 winners, and each received $\frac{d}{6}$ dollars. This represents a loss to each of the original winners of $\frac{d}{4} - \frac{d}{6} = \frac{3d}{12} - \frac{2d}{12} = \frac{d}{12}$ dollars.

   **Unless you are comfortable with the algebra, plug in a number for $d$; say $d = 24$. Then the 4 winners would have received $24 \div 4 = 6$ dollars each. Now the 6 winners will receive $24 \div 6 = 4$ dollars each, a difference of $2. Which of the choices is equal to 2 when $d = 24$? Only $\frac{d}{12}$.

## Section 3 Critical Reading

25. **(C)** The use of "unhappily" tells us that the experiment was somehow damaged or *marred* by the presence of observers. It makes no sense for the psychology experiment to have been *muted* (hushed), *palliated* (mitigated; alleviated), or *clarified* (made clear) by the subjects becoming aware of the presence of observers around them. Likewise, while the subjects' awareness of the presence of observers in their midst might have caused the experiment to be hastily *concluded* (ended), that is not the best possible answer choice.

26. **(D)** James didn't know when assignments were due because there was something wrong with the way he wrote them down. He was not orderly or *methodical* about it. Basically, James was careless about writing down his assignments. That is the reason he seldom knew when they were due. It would not have helped him to be more *obdurate* (stubborn and unyielding), more *contrary* (stubbornly willful or opposed), or more *literate* (well read). To be *opportunistic* is to base one's actions on effectiveness or expediency rather than on ethical principles. The word makes no sense in the context.

27. **(B)** The word "despite" signals a contrast. Despite the advertised *praises*, she had doubts—she remained *a skeptic* about the product. Note also that "singing the praises of" is a cliché, a customary phrase. Choice A is incorrect. It makes no sense to say that *despite* ads expressing admiration for a product's *virtues* (good qualities) the woman still was *optimistic* or hopeful about its merits. Choice C is incorrect. It makes no sense to say that *despite* ads expressing admiration for a product's *joys* the woman still was *converted to* a belief in its merits. Choice D is incorrect. *Defects* are flaws. Note that the first missing word must be positive in nature. No advertisers would sing (express admiration for) the bad points of a product they were trying to sell. Choice E is incorrect. It makes no sense to say that *despite* ads expressing admiration for a product's *advantages* (favorable qualities) the woman still was *a believer in* its merits.

28. **(E)** Again, think of your own answer before looking at the choices. What would you need after two full months of solid work? A rest, or *respite*. It makes no sense for Sandy to feel that she had earned a *penalty* (punishment), *scolding* (rebuke), *degree* (academic award), or *chore* (unpleasant task). She felt she had earned a rest.

29. **(A)** The phrase "even though" tells us that there will be a contrast. This requires a word that is opposite in meaning to "does not change." *Plastic* can mean adaptable or pliable when used as an adjective, as it is here. Choice B is incorrect. *Immutable* means unchangeable. For some time after birth, the details of the brain's structure and function *are* able to change or adapt. Choice C is incorrect. *Essential* (absolutely necessary) makes no sense in the context. Choice D is incorrect. *Unknown* (not discovered or identified; obscure) makes no sense in the context. Choice E is incorrect. *Static* means showing little or no change. For some time after birth, the details of the brain's structure and function *do* change or adapt.

30. **(D)** The author's attitude is clearly *approving*: she notes that some commentators cite Malcolm's change in prison as an example of positive transformation; she also uses words with positive connotations ("purposeful") to describe Malcolm's method of tackling his task.

31. **(E)** In plowing his way through the dictionary, Malcolm *proceeded steadily* and purposefully from the beginning to the end.

32. **(D)** Lines 8–9 of the passage say that in primate troops, males "defend, control and lead the troop."

Therefore, the troops are *dominated by adult males*.

33. **(A)** The passage says that the ranking hierarchy lessens conflict within the troop. Therefore, it is meant to *protect the members of the troop* from internal strife.

34. **(D)** Tapestry weaving is time-consuming, taking "as much as a year to produce a yard." In addition, it is faithful to the original ("The weaver always follows a preexisting model."). It is not, however, spontaneous in concept.

35. **(A)** The author mentions tapestry's distinctive or *characteristic* weave as something that distinguishes tapestry-woven materials from other fabrics (prints, brocades, etc.).

36. **(B)** By using tapestries "to display his wealth and social position," the nobleman is using them to demonstrate his *consequence* or importance.

37. **(D)** The "ground" upon which embroidery is laid is the cloth *base* upon which the embroiderer stitches a design.

38. **(C)** The author refers to the suggestion that tapestries served primarily as a source of warmth only to *dismiss* or reject the idea. To prove his point he asserts that comfort had little importance in medieval times.

39. **(E)** Here the word "chambers" *is being used in a special sense* to mean a set of wall hangings made to fit a specific room.

40. **(E)** In describing Morris as someone who attempted to bring back tapestry making to its true, medieval principles, the author depicts him as a *traditionalist*, someone who attempts to preserve or restore ancient cultural practices or beliefs.

41. **(D)** In comparison to the tightly-woven tapestries of the nineteenth-century, present-day wall hangings are described as "coarsely woven cloths." Thus, they *have a less fine weave* than their predecessors.

42. **(D)** Although the passage explains the process of tapestry making and mentions that large wall hangings are Western rather than Eastern in origin, Choices A and B do not reflect the passage's primary purpose. This purpose is to *provide a historical perspective on tapestry making*.

43. **(C)** Compared with Passage 1, Passage 2 is far *less lyrical* or poetic. As part of a scientific study, it is appropriately *more objective* (based on observable facts; impartial) than Lorenz's loving account of the jackdaws' flight.

44. **(E)** The author of Passage 1 states that the jack-daw's proficiency is not inherited or innate, but "an individually acquired accomplishment." In other words, it has been *gained through practice*.

45. **(C)** The author is stressing that you can *be sure* or *confident* of the truth about what he says.

46. **(D)** The concluding sentence of the passage celebrates the birds' "Sovereign control over the power of the elements," in other words, their *mastery of the forces of nature*. Though Choice B may seem tempting, you can rule it out. Lorenz emphasizes the storm's strength ("the pitiless strength of the inorganic"), not the strength of the birds. Choices A, C, and E are unsupported by the passage.

47. **(C)** The author uses several metaphors ("close-reefed sails," "the teeth of the gale," etc.) and clarifies what he means by the term *game*. He describes the jackdaws' behavior in detail and dismisses the notion that their behavior is purely instinctive. However, he never *argues* or presents reasons in favor of *a cause*.

48. **(B)** The author of Passage B neither relates personal anecdotes nor makes use of figurative language such as metaphors and similes. He cites no statistics and asks no rhetorical questions. However, he provides a great deal of *observational data* from his ongoing study of jackdaw behavior.

## Section 4  Mathematics

For many problems, the explanation provides a reference to one or more **KEY FACTS** from Chapter 7. These are the mathematical facts that you need to solve that problem. If a solution refers to **KEY FACT J2**, for example, the solution depends on the second **KEY FACT** discussed in Section J of Chapter 7.

For some problems, an alternative solution, indicated by two asterisks (**), follows the first solution. When this occurs, usually one of the solutions is the direct mathematical one and the other is based on one of the tactics discussed in Chapters 6 and 7.

See page 244 for an explanation of the symbol ⇒, which is used in several answer explanations.

21. **(D)** Since the ratio of the number of boys to girls is 2:3, the number of boys is $2x$, the number of girls is $3x$, and the total number of members is $2x + 3x = 5x$. So the girls make up $\frac{3x}{5x} = \frac{3}{5} = 60\%$ of the members.

22. **(E)** Since $d$ divisions each have $t$ teams, multiply to get $dt$ teams, and since each team has $p$ players, multiply the number of teams $(dt)$ by $p$ to get the total number of players: $dtp$.

**Use **TACTIC 6-2**. Choose easy-to-use numbers for $t$, $d$, and $p$. For example, assume that there are 2 divisions, each with 4 teams So, there are $2 \times 4 = 8$ teams. Then assume that each of the teams has 10 players, for a total of $8 \times 10 = 80$ players. Now check the five choices. Which one is equal to 80 when $d = 2$, $t = 4$, and $p = 10$? Only $dtp$.

23. **(C)** Test each set of values to see which one does not work. Only Choice C, $x = 1$ and $y = -1$ does not work: $3(1)^2 + 2(-1) = 3 - 2 = 1$, not 5. The other choices all work.

24. **(C)** There is a total of $1 + 2 + 3 + 4 + 5 + 6 = 21$ slips of paper. Since odd numbers are written on $1 + 3 + 5 = 9$ of them, the probability of drawing an odd number is $\frac{9}{21} = \frac{3}{7}$.

25. **(B)** If $|x| = |y|$, then $x = y$ or $x = -y$. So $x^2 = y^2$ or $x^2 = (-y)^2 = y^2$. (II is true.) If $x = 1$ and $y = -1$, then both I and III are false. Only statement II is true.

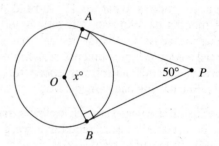

26. **(D)** Since $\overline{OA}$ and $\overline{OB}$ are radii drawn to the points of contact of two tangents, by **KEY FACT L10**, $\overline{OA} \perp \overline{PA}$ and $\overline{OB} \perp \overline{PB}$. So angles $A$ and $B$ are right angles. Finally, by **KEY FACT K1**, the sum of the measures of the four angles in any quadrilateral is 360; so, $90 + 90 + 50 + x = 360$. Therefore, $230 + x = 360$, and $x = 130$.

27. **(A)** $2^{3x} + 2^{3x} + 2^{3x} + 2^{3x} = 4(2^{3x}) = 2^2(2^{3x}) = 2^{3x+2}$.
**Let $x = 1$; then $2^{3x} = 2^3 = 8$, and
$$2^{3x} + 2^{3x} + 2^{3x} + 2^{3x} = 8 + 8 + 8 + 8 = 32.$$
Which of the choices equals 32 when $x = 1$? Only $2^{3x+2}$ ($2^5 = 32$).

28. **(B)** Let $r$ and $R$ be the radii of circle I and circle II, respectively.

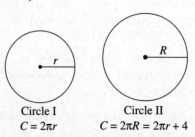

Circle I
$C = 2\pi r$

Circle II
$C = 2\pi R = 2\pi r + 4$

Since the circumference of circle I is $2\pi r$, the circumference of circle II is $2\pi r + 4 = 2(\pi r + 2)$. But, of course, the circumference of circle II is also $2\pi R$. Therefore, $2\pi R = 2(\pi r + 2)$. Dividing by 2, we get $\pi R = \pi r + 2$. Now, dividing by $\pi$, we get $R = r + \frac{2}{\pi}$.

29. **(320)** Since $a + 100 = 180$, $a = 80$. But since $\ell$ and $k$ are parallel, the four acute angles are all equal: $80 = a = b = c = d$, so their sum is $4 \times 80 = 320$.

30. **(30)** Evaluate: $2(6) - 3(-6) = 12 + 18 = 30$.

31. $\left(\textbf{3.75 or } \frac{\textbf{15}}{\textbf{4}}\right)$ The median of the 7 numbers 1, 2, 3, 4, 5, 6, 7 is the middle one: 4. The median of the 6 numbers 1, 2, 3, 4, 5, 6 is the average of the two middle ones: $\frac{3+4}{2} = 3.5$. Finally, the average of 4 and 3.5 is 3.75 or $\frac{15}{4}$.

32. **(70)** Since all of the radii of a circle have the same length, $CA = CB$. Therefore,
$$m\angle A = m\angle B = 55°, \text{ and}$$
$$c = 180 - (55 + 55) = 180 - 110 = 70.$$

33. **(57)** To find Elaine's average speed in kilometers per hour, divide the distance she went, in kilometers (190), by the time it took, in hours. Elaine drove for 3 hours and 20 minutes, which is $3\frac{1}{3}$ hours (20 minutes $= \frac{20}{60}$ hour $= \frac{1}{3}$ hour). Elaine's average speed is

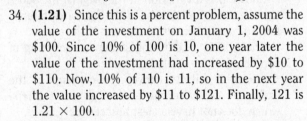

34. **(1.21)** Since this is a percent problem, assume the value of the investment on January 1, 2004 was $100. Since 10% of 100 is 10, one year later the value of the investment had increased by $10 to $110. Now, 10% of 110 is 11, so in the next year the value increased by $11 to $121. Finally, 121 is $1.21 \times 100$.

35. **(72)** There are 90 two-digit numbers (the integers from 10 to 99 inclusive). To find out how many of them do not contain the digit 9, calculate how many of them *do* contain the digit 9, and subtract that number from 90. There are a total of 18 two-digit numbers that contain the digit 9—the 10 numbers from 90 to 99 plus the 8 other numbers that end in 9: 19, 29, . . . , 89. Finally, there are $90 - 18 = 72$ two-digit numbers that do not contain the digit 9.

36. **(87.5)** If the average of 5 numbers is 95, the sum of those numbers is $5 \times 95 = 475$. Similarly, the sum of the 3 numbers whose average is 100 is 300, leaving 175 $(475 - 300)$ as the sum of the 2 remaining numbers. The average of these 2 numbers is their sum divided by 2: $175 \div 2 = 87.5$.

**Assume that the five numbers are 100, 100, 100, $x$, and $y$. Then we have $\frac{100+100+100+x+y}{5} = 95$. So, $300 + x + y = 475$. So, $x + y = 175$, and $\frac{x+y}{2} = \frac{175}{2} = 87.5$.

37. **(1)** Assume that the radius of the large circle is 2. Then the area of the circle is $4\pi$. The radius of each semicircle is 1, and since the area of a circle of radius 1 is $\pi$, the area of each semicircle is $\frac{1}{2}\pi$, and the total shaded area is $4\left(\frac{1}{2}\pi\right) = 2\pi$. Since the shaded area is exactly one-half of the circle, the white area is also one-half of the circle. The areas are equal, and so the shaded area is 1 times the white area.

38. **(2500)** If 99.6% of the people tested did not have the disease, then 0.4% of them did have the disease. If $x =$ the number of people tested, then $10 = 0.004x \Rightarrow x = 10 \div .004 = 2500$.

## Section 5 Writing Skills

1. **(C)** Choice C uses *drank*, the correct form of the irregular verb *drink*.

2. **(D)** Error in tense. Change *began* to *had begun*.

3. **(B)** Error in idiom. *Seems satisfying their need* is unidiomatic. *Seems to satisfy their need* is correct.

4. **(C)** Error in coordination and subordination. Choice C corrects the error in conjunction use.

5. **(D)** Error in following conventions. *Irregardless* is a nonstandard use of *regardless*.

6. **(B)** Comma splice. The run-on sentence is corrected in Choice B.

7. **(D)** Errors in subject-verb agreement. The phrase *along with several other stories* is not part of the subject of the sentence. The subject is *"Araby"* (singular); the verb should be *is going to be read* (singular).

8. **(A)** Sentence is correct. Choice B introduces an error in agreement. Choices C, D, and E misuse the *not only . . . but also* construction.

9. **(E)** Error in modification and word order. The dangling modifier is corrected in Choice E.

10. **(B)** Error in modification and word order. The dangling construction is corrected in Choices B and E. However, only Choice B retains the meaning of the original sentence.

11. **(B)** Error in idiom. Choice B properly replaces the incorrect preposition *to* with the correct preposition, *with*. Although Choice E also properly replaces the incorrect preposition, it introduces a new error involving the sequence of tenses.

12. **(E)** Dangling participle. A participial phrase modifies or describes a noun. Was the *response* bothered by the rival team's heckling? No. The *home team* was bothered by the heckling. Choice E corrects the dangling participle without introducing any fresh errors.

13. **(D)** Error in logical comparison. The faulty comparison is corrected in Choice D.

14. **(A)** The original sentence is correct. The subject of *are going* is *legislators* (plural). Therefore, Choices B, C, and D are incorrect. Choice E changes the meaning of the original sentence.

15. **(D)** Incomplete comparison. They are as harmful *to* women as they are *to* men.

16. **(A)** Sentence is correct.

17. **(E)** Error in usage. Do not use *when* or *where* after *is* in making a definition.

18. **(D)** Error in sequence of tenses. The present perfect tense ("has been informed") indicates some vague time before now, or a time that lasts up to the present. NASA, however, was told about the dangerous weather conditions at a definite time in the past. Therefore, you should use either the simple past tense ("was informed") or the past perfect tense ("had been informed") here.

19. **(D)** Error in idiom. Either James hoped *for* the revitalization of his career, or he hoped *to* revitalize it. In this case, the verbal *to revitalize* is correct.

20. **(C)** Dangling modifier. Ask yourself who are strolling in the park. Choice C rearranges the words in the sentence to make "While strolling in Golden Gate Park one day" clearly refer to "the young couple."

21. **(A)** Error in diction. Change *Being that* to *Since.*

22. **(A)** Error in following conventions. Double negative. Change *can't* to *can.*

23. **(B)** Error in pronoun case. *But,* as used in this sentence, is a preposition meaning *except.* Change *he* to *him.*

24. **(D)** Error in following conventions. Change *reason . . . is because* to *reason . . . is that.*

25. **(B)** Error in tense. Change *am playing* to *have been playing.*

26. **(B)** Error in diction. Change *affective* to *effective.*

27. **(B)** Error in diction. Use *among* rather than *between* when you are dealing with three or more items.

28. **(D)** Error in parallelism. Change *as well as signing* to *and sign* in order to match the other items in the list.

29. **(C)** Error in coordination and subordination. Incorrect sentence connector. Change *furthermore* to the coordinating conjunction *but* to clarify the relationship between the clauses.

30. **(D)** Error in idiom. Change *accumulation from* to *accumulation of.*

31. **(A)** Error in diction. *Altogether* is correct.

32. **(E)** Sentence is correct.

33. **(B)** Error in idiom. Change *differ with* (which indicates a difference of opinion) to *differ from* (which indicates a difference in appearance).

34. **(C)** Error in parallelism. Change *remaining at* to the infinitive *to remain at* in order to match *to travel on.*

35. **(A)** Choice A accurately describes the content of the essay. The original introductory sentence is misleading. The essay is about changes in the status of women, not about the role women played in causing the changes. It is the best answer.

Choice B is a variation of the original introductory sentence but the use of the future verb tense fails to convey the actual content of the essay.

Choice C is a confusing sentence consisting of two illogically unrelated clauses.

Choice D fails to convey the contents of the essay. It also contains the pronoun *their,* which does not have a clear antecedent.

Choice E is virtually meaningless. It also contains a dangling participle. The phrase that begins *Being influenced . . .* should modify *women,* not *status.*

36. **(D)** Choice A inserts a comma splice between *lifted* and *for example.* Two independent clauses should be separated by a period or semicolon.

Choice B contains the pronoun *they,* which lacks a specific reference.

Choice C improperly shifts pronouns from third person to second person.

Choice D is effectively expressed. It is the best answer.

Choice E is cumbersome and awkwardly worded. The phrase *the right of going into public* contains an idiom error. The correct phrase is *right to go into public.*

37. **(A)** Choice A provides a smooth transition by alluding to the discussion of competition in the second paragraph and introducing the main topic of the third. A is the best answer.

Choice B uses a nonstandard transitional word *irregardless*, which in the context makes no sense.

Choice C contains no specifically transitional material.

Choice D would be a decent transition were it not for its mixed construction. The first half of the sentence doesn't fit grammatically with the second half.

Choice E introduces a new idea that is unrelated to the content of the third paragraph.

38. **(E)** Choice A is illogical; becoming a role model is not an example of attaining a high position in politics and government.

Choice B is not a good example of attaining a high position in politics.

Choice C is irrelevant. Margaret Thatcher's defeat is not an example of an achievement in politics and government.

Choice D is slightly off the mark. The sentence emphasizes Indira Ghandi's assassination instead of her leadership.

Choice E gives two examples of women who have attained a high position in politics and government. It is the best answer.

39. **(E)** All the sentences except sentence 14 support the idea stated in the topic sentence, that women have made gains in politics and government. Threfore, Choice E is the best answer.

# Answer Sheet—Practice Test 2

Each mark should completely fill the appropriate space, and should be as dark as all other marks. Make all erasures complete. Traces of an erasure may be read as an answer.

## Section 1 – Critical Reading
### 25 minutes

1 Ⓐ Ⓑ Ⓒ Ⓓ Ⓔ
2 Ⓐ Ⓑ Ⓒ Ⓓ Ⓔ
3 Ⓐ Ⓑ Ⓒ Ⓓ Ⓔ
4 Ⓐ Ⓑ Ⓒ Ⓓ Ⓔ
5 Ⓐ Ⓑ Ⓒ Ⓓ Ⓔ
6 Ⓐ Ⓑ Ⓒ Ⓓ Ⓔ
7 Ⓐ Ⓑ Ⓒ Ⓓ Ⓔ
8 Ⓐ Ⓑ Ⓒ Ⓓ Ⓔ
9 Ⓐ Ⓑ Ⓒ Ⓓ Ⓔ
10 Ⓐ Ⓑ Ⓒ Ⓓ Ⓔ
11 Ⓐ Ⓑ Ⓒ Ⓓ Ⓔ
12 Ⓐ Ⓑ Ⓒ Ⓓ Ⓔ
13 Ⓐ Ⓑ Ⓒ Ⓓ Ⓔ
14 Ⓐ Ⓑ Ⓒ Ⓓ Ⓔ
15 Ⓐ Ⓑ Ⓒ Ⓓ Ⓔ
16 Ⓐ Ⓑ Ⓒ Ⓓ Ⓔ
17 Ⓐ Ⓑ Ⓒ Ⓓ Ⓔ
18 Ⓐ Ⓑ Ⓒ Ⓓ Ⓔ
19 Ⓐ Ⓑ Ⓒ Ⓓ Ⓔ
20 Ⓐ Ⓑ Ⓒ Ⓓ Ⓔ
21 Ⓐ Ⓑ Ⓒ Ⓓ Ⓔ
22 Ⓐ Ⓑ Ⓒ Ⓓ Ⓔ
23 Ⓐ Ⓑ Ⓒ Ⓓ Ⓔ
24 Ⓐ Ⓑ Ⓒ Ⓓ Ⓔ

## Section 2 – Math
### 25 minutes

1 Ⓐ Ⓑ Ⓒ Ⓓ Ⓔ
2 Ⓐ Ⓑ Ⓒ Ⓓ Ⓔ
3 Ⓐ Ⓑ Ⓒ Ⓓ Ⓔ
4 Ⓐ Ⓑ Ⓒ Ⓓ Ⓔ
5 Ⓐ Ⓑ Ⓒ Ⓓ Ⓔ
6 Ⓐ Ⓑ Ⓒ Ⓓ Ⓔ
7 Ⓐ Ⓑ Ⓒ Ⓓ Ⓔ
8 Ⓐ Ⓑ Ⓒ Ⓓ Ⓔ
9 Ⓐ Ⓑ Ⓒ Ⓓ Ⓔ
10 Ⓐ Ⓑ Ⓒ Ⓓ Ⓔ
11 Ⓐ Ⓑ Ⓒ Ⓓ Ⓔ
12 Ⓐ Ⓑ Ⓒ Ⓓ Ⓔ
13 Ⓐ Ⓑ Ⓒ Ⓓ Ⓔ
14 Ⓐ Ⓑ Ⓒ Ⓓ Ⓔ
15 Ⓐ Ⓑ Ⓒ Ⓓ Ⓔ
16 Ⓐ Ⓑ Ⓒ Ⓓ Ⓔ
17 Ⓐ Ⓑ Ⓒ Ⓓ Ⓔ
18 Ⓐ Ⓑ Ⓒ Ⓓ Ⓔ
19 Ⓐ Ⓑ Ⓒ Ⓓ Ⓔ
20 Ⓐ Ⓑ Ⓒ Ⓓ Ⓔ

## Section 3 – Critical Reading
### 25 minutes

25 Ⓐ Ⓑ Ⓒ Ⓓ Ⓔ
26 Ⓐ Ⓑ Ⓒ Ⓓ Ⓔ
27 Ⓐ Ⓑ Ⓒ Ⓓ Ⓔ
28 Ⓐ Ⓑ Ⓒ Ⓓ Ⓔ
29 Ⓐ Ⓑ Ⓒ Ⓓ Ⓔ
30 Ⓐ Ⓑ Ⓒ Ⓓ Ⓔ
31 Ⓐ Ⓑ Ⓒ Ⓓ Ⓔ
32 Ⓐ Ⓑ Ⓒ Ⓓ Ⓔ
33 Ⓐ Ⓑ Ⓒ Ⓓ Ⓔ
34 Ⓐ Ⓑ Ⓒ Ⓓ Ⓔ
35 Ⓐ Ⓑ Ⓒ Ⓓ Ⓔ
36 Ⓐ Ⓑ Ⓒ Ⓓ Ⓔ
37 Ⓐ Ⓑ Ⓒ Ⓓ Ⓔ
38 Ⓐ Ⓑ Ⓒ Ⓓ Ⓔ
39 Ⓐ Ⓑ Ⓒ Ⓓ Ⓔ
40 Ⓐ Ⓑ Ⓒ Ⓓ Ⓔ
41 Ⓐ Ⓑ Ⓒ Ⓓ Ⓔ
42 Ⓐ Ⓑ Ⓒ Ⓓ Ⓔ
43 Ⓐ Ⓑ Ⓒ Ⓓ Ⓔ
44 Ⓐ Ⓑ Ⓒ Ⓓ Ⓔ
45 Ⓐ Ⓑ Ⓒ Ⓓ Ⓔ
46 Ⓐ Ⓑ Ⓒ Ⓓ Ⓔ
47 Ⓐ Ⓑ Ⓒ Ⓓ Ⓔ
48 Ⓐ Ⓑ Ⓒ Ⓓ Ⓔ

## Section 4 – Math
### 25 minutes

21 Ⓐ Ⓑ Ⓒ Ⓓ Ⓔ
22 Ⓐ Ⓑ Ⓒ Ⓓ Ⓔ
23 Ⓐ Ⓑ Ⓒ Ⓓ Ⓔ
24 Ⓐ Ⓑ Ⓒ Ⓓ Ⓔ
25 Ⓐ Ⓑ Ⓒ Ⓓ Ⓔ
26 Ⓐ Ⓑ Ⓒ Ⓓ Ⓔ
27 Ⓐ Ⓑ Ⓒ Ⓓ Ⓔ
28 Ⓐ Ⓑ Ⓒ Ⓓ Ⓔ

29 [grid-in answer grid]
30 [grid-in answer grid]
31 [grid-in answer grid]
32 [grid-in answer grid]
33 [grid-in answer grid]
34 [grid-in answer grid]
35 [grid-in answer grid]
36 [grid-in answer grid]
37 [grid-in answer grid]
38 [grid-in answer grid]

## Section 5 – Writing
### 30 minutes

1 Ⓐ Ⓑ Ⓒ Ⓓ Ⓔ
2 Ⓐ Ⓑ Ⓒ Ⓓ Ⓔ
3 Ⓐ Ⓑ Ⓒ Ⓓ Ⓔ
4 Ⓐ Ⓑ Ⓒ Ⓓ Ⓔ
5 Ⓐ Ⓑ Ⓒ Ⓓ Ⓔ
6 Ⓐ Ⓑ Ⓒ Ⓓ Ⓔ
7 Ⓐ Ⓑ Ⓒ Ⓓ Ⓔ
8 Ⓐ Ⓑ Ⓒ Ⓓ Ⓔ
9 Ⓐ Ⓑ Ⓒ Ⓓ Ⓔ
10 Ⓐ Ⓑ Ⓒ Ⓓ Ⓔ
11 Ⓐ Ⓑ Ⓒ Ⓓ Ⓔ
12 Ⓐ Ⓑ Ⓒ Ⓓ Ⓔ
13 Ⓐ Ⓑ Ⓒ Ⓓ Ⓔ
14 Ⓐ Ⓑ Ⓒ Ⓓ Ⓔ
15 Ⓐ Ⓑ Ⓒ Ⓓ Ⓔ
16 Ⓐ Ⓑ Ⓒ Ⓓ Ⓔ
17 Ⓐ Ⓑ Ⓒ Ⓓ Ⓔ
18 Ⓐ Ⓑ Ⓒ Ⓓ Ⓔ
19 Ⓐ Ⓑ Ⓒ Ⓓ Ⓔ
20 Ⓐ Ⓑ Ⓒ Ⓓ Ⓔ
21 Ⓐ Ⓑ Ⓒ Ⓓ Ⓔ
22 Ⓐ Ⓑ Ⓒ Ⓓ Ⓔ
23 Ⓐ Ⓑ Ⓒ Ⓓ Ⓔ
24 Ⓐ Ⓑ Ⓒ Ⓓ Ⓔ
25 Ⓐ Ⓑ Ⓒ Ⓓ Ⓔ
26 Ⓐ Ⓑ Ⓒ Ⓓ Ⓔ
27 Ⓐ Ⓑ Ⓒ Ⓓ Ⓔ
28 Ⓐ Ⓑ Ⓒ Ⓓ Ⓔ
29 Ⓐ Ⓑ Ⓒ Ⓓ Ⓔ
30 Ⓐ Ⓑ Ⓒ Ⓓ Ⓔ
31 Ⓐ Ⓑ Ⓒ Ⓓ Ⓔ
32 Ⓐ Ⓑ Ⓒ Ⓓ Ⓔ
33 Ⓐ Ⓑ Ⓒ Ⓓ Ⓔ
34 Ⓐ Ⓑ Ⓒ Ⓓ Ⓔ
35 Ⓐ Ⓑ Ⓒ Ⓓ Ⓔ
36 Ⓐ Ⓑ Ⓒ Ⓓ Ⓔ
37 Ⓐ Ⓑ Ⓒ Ⓓ Ⓔ
38 Ⓐ Ⓑ Ⓒ Ⓓ Ⓔ
39 Ⓐ Ⓑ Ⓒ Ⓓ Ⓔ

# SECTION 1/CRITICAL READING

TIME: 25 MINUTES
24 QUESTIONS (1–24)

**Directions:** For each question in this section, select the best answer from among the choices given and fill in the corresponding circle on the answer sheet.

Each sentence below has one or two blanks, each blank indicating that something has been omitted. Beneath the sentence are five words or sets of words labeled A through E. Choose the word or set of words that, when inserted in the sentence, best fits the meaning of the sentence as a whole.

**EXAMPLE:**

Medieval kingdoms did not become constitutional republics overnight; on the contrary, the change was ----.

(A) unpopular   (B) unexpected
(C) advantageous   (D) sufficient   (E) gradual

Ⓐ Ⓑ Ⓒ Ⓓ ●

1. Impressed by the extraordinary potential of the new superconductor, scientists predict that its use will ---- the computer industry, creating new products overnight.

   (A) justify   (B) alienate   (C) nullify
   (D) revolutionize   (E) overestimate

2. No matter how ---- the revelations of the coming year may be, they will be hard put to match those of the past decade, which have ---- transformed our view of the emergence of Mayan civilization.

   (A) minor..dramatically
   (B) profound..negligibly
   (C) striking..radically
   (D) bizarre..nominally
   (E) questionable..possibly

3. Few other plants can grow beneath the canopy of the sycamore tree, whose leaves and pods produce a natural herbicide that leaches into the soil, ---- other plants that might compete for water and nutrients.

   (A) inhibiting   (B) distinguishing
   (C) nourishing   (D) encouraging
   (E) refreshing

4. Black women authors such as Zora Neale Hurston, originally ---- by both white and black literary establishments to obscurity as minor novelists, are being rediscovered by black feminist critics today.

   (A) inclined   (B) relegated   (C) subjected
   (D) diminished   (E) characterized

5. Critics of the movie version of *The Color Purple* ---- its saccharine, overoptimistic mood as out of keeping with the novel's more ---- tone.

   (A) applauded..somber
   (B) condemned..hopeful
   (C) acclaimed..positive
   (D) denounced..sanguine
   (E) decried..acerbic

**GO ON TO NEXT PAGE** ▶

**Directions:** The passages below precede questions based on their content or the relationship between the passages. Answer the questions that follow on the basis of what is stated or implied in the passage.

### Questions 6–9 are based on the following passages.

**Passage 1**

There was a time when poetry mattered in America—a time when T. S. Eliot could fill a football stadium with poetry fans, when literature
Line enjoyed a central place in our culture, and young
5   men and women dreamed about becoming writers. That time is long gone. Today if young people dream of writing at all, they dream of writing rap songs or sitcom scripts, pop lit, not enduring works of art.

**Passage 2**

10   Recently a children's book about writing poetry came out. It was called *Poetry Matters*. In essence, that's the question poets face today. Does poetry matter? As Billy Collins wrote, "One of the ridiculous aspects of being a poet is the huge gulf
15   between how seriously we take ourselves and how generally we are ignored by everybody else." We think that what we write matters, but for the most part, in America no one cares. It may be different elsewhere on the globe—Ossip Mandelstam
20   once maintained that only in Russia was poetry respected because there it got people killed. Here, we don't get killed, but we're dying anyway.

6. In Passage 1, the reference to the football stadium (line 3) serves primarily to
   (A) demonstrate the connection between sports and poetry
   (B) show Eliot's deep appreciation of football
   (C) emphasize the popularity of poetry in the period
   (D) suggest a potential site for poetry readings today
   (E) point out Eliot's enduring vision

7. In line 4, "enjoyed" most nearly means
   (A) fancied
   (B) relished
   (C) possessed
   (D) appreciated
   (E) flourished

8. In Passage 2, the statement "we're dying anyway" (line 22) is an example of
   (A) an apology
   (B) a metaphor
   (C) a euphemism
   (D) a hypothesis
   (E) an understatement

9. The authors of Passage 1 and Passage 2 agree that
   (A) poetry plays a significant role in modern culture
   (B) poets must take themselves seriously if poetry is to survive
   (C) rap songs are a valid form of poetic expression
   (D) poetry is more appealing to children than to adults
   (E) the climate for poetry in America is inauspicious

**GO ON TO NEXT PAGE** ▶

**Directions:** Each passage below is followed by questions based on its content. Answer the questions following each passage on the basis of what is <u>stated</u> or <u>implied</u> in that passage and in any introductory material that may be provided.

**Questions 10–15 are based upon the following passage.**

*In the following passage from Jane Austen's novel* Pride and Prejudice, *the heroine Elizabeth Bennet faces an unexpected encounter with her father's cousin (and prospective heir), the clergyman Mr. Collins.*

It was absolutely necessary to interrupt him now.

"You are too hasty, Sir," she cried. "You forget
Line that I have made no answer. Let me do it without
5  further loss of time. Accept my thanks for the
compliment you are paying me. I am very sensible
of the honour of your proposals, but it is impossible for me to do otherwise than decline them."

"I am not now to learn," replied Mr. Collins
10  with a formal wave of the hand, "that it is usual
with young ladies to reject the addresses of the
man whom they secretly mean to accept, when he
first applies for their favour; and that sometimes
the refusal is repeated a second or even a third
15  time. I am therefore by no means discouraged by
what you have just said, and shall hope to lead
you to the altar ere long."

"Upon my word, Sir," cried Elizabeth, "your
hope is rather an extraordinary one after my
20  declaration. I do assure you that I am not one of
those young ladies (if such young ladies there are)
who are so daring as to risk their happiness on the
chance of being asked a second time. I am perfectly serious in my refusal. You could not make
25  *me* happy, and I am convinced that I am the last
woman in the world who would make *you* so. Nay,
were your friend Lady Catherine to know me, I
am persuaded she would find me in every respect
ill qualified for the situation."

30  "Were it certain that Lady Catherine would
think so," said Mr. Collins very gravely—"but I
cannot imagine that her ladyship would at all disapprove of you. And you may be certain that when
I have the honour of seeing her again I shall speak
35  in the highest terms of your modesty, economy,
and other amiable qualifications."

"Indeed, Mr. Collins, all praise of me will be
unnecessary. You must give me leave to judge for
myself, and pay me the compliment of believing
40  what I say. I wish you very happy and very rich,
and by refusing your hand, do all in my power to

prevent your being otherwise. In making me the
offer, you must have satisfied the delicacy of your
feelings with regard to my family, and may take
45  possession of Longbourn estate whenever it falls,
without any self-reproach. This matter may be
considered, therefore, as finally settled." And rising as she thus spoke, she would have quitted the
room, had not Mr. Collins thus addressed her.

50  "When I do myself the honour of speaking to
you next on this subject I shall hope to receive a
more favourable answer than you have now given
me; though I am far from accusing you of cruelty
at present, because I know it to be the established
55  custom of your sex to reject a man on the first
application, and perhaps you have even now said as
much to encourage my suit as would be consistent
with the true delicacy of the female character."

"Really, Mr. Collins," cried Elizabeth
60  with some warmth, "you puzzle me exceedingly. If
what I have hitherto said can appear to you in the
form of encouragement, I know not how to
express my refusal in such a way as may convince
you of its being one."

**10.** It can be inferred that in the paragraphs immediately preceding this passage

(A) Elizabeth and Mr. Collins quarreled
(B) Elizabeth met Mr. Collins for the first time
(C) Mr. Collins asked Elizabeth to marry him
(D) Mr. Collins gravely insulted Elizabeth
(E) Elizabeth discovered that Mr. Collins was a fraud

**11.** In line 6, "sensible" most nearly means

(A) logical
(B) perceptible
(C) sound in judgment
(D) keenly aware
(E) appreciable

**12.** Instead of having the intended effect, Elizabeth's initial refusal of Mr. Collins (lines 3–8)

(A) causes her to rethink rejecting him
(B) makes him less inclined to wed
(C) gives her the opportunity to consider other options
(D) persuades him she dislikes him intensely
(E) fails to put an end to his suit

**GO ON TO NEXT PAGE ▶**

**13.** It can be inferred from lines 30–33 that Mr. Collins

(A) will take Elizabeth's words seriously
(B) admires Elizabeth's independence
(C) is very disappointed by her decision
(D) would accept Lady Catherine's opinion
(E) means his remarks as a joke

**14.** The reason Elizabeth insists all praise of her "will be unnecessary" (lines 37–38) is that she

(A) feels sure Lady Catherine will learn to admire her in time
(B) is too shy to accept compliments readily
(C) has no intention of marrying Mr. Collins
(D) believes a clergyman should be less effusive
(E) values her own worth excessively

**15.** On the basis of his behavior in this passage, Mr. Collins may best be described as

(A) malicious in intent
(B) both obtuse and obstinate
(C) unsure of his acceptance
(D) kindly and understanding
(E) sensitive to Elizabeth's wishes

**Questions 16–24 are based on the following passage.**

*African elephants now are an endangered species. The following passage, taken from a newspaper article written in 1989, discusses the potential ecological disaster that might occur if the elephant were to become extinct.*

The African elephant—mythic symbol of a
continent, keystone of its ecology and the largest
land animal remaining on earth—has become the
Line object of one of the biggest, broadest international
5 efforts yet mounted to turn a threatened species
off the road to extinction. But it is not only the
elephant's survival that is at stake, conservationists say. Unlike the endangered tiger, unlike even
the great whales, the African elephant is in great
10 measure the architect of its environment. As a
voracious eater of vegetation, it largely shapes the
forest-and-savanna surroundings in which it lives,
thereby setting the terms of existence for millions
of other storied animals—from zebras to gazelles
15 to giraffes and wildebeests—that share its habitat.
And as the elephant disappears, scientists and conservationists say, many other species will also disappear from vast stretches of forest and savanna,
drastically altering and impoverishing whole
20 ecosystems.

Just as the American buffalo was hunted
almost to extinction a century ago, so the African
elephant is now the victim of an onslaught of commercial killing, stimulated in this case by soaring
25 global demand for ivory. Most of the killing is illegal, and conservationists say that although the
pressure of human population and development
contributes to the elephants' decline, poaching is
by far the greatest threat. The elephant may or
30 may not be on the way to becoming a mere zoological curiosity like the buffalo, but the trend is
clear.

In an atmosphere of mounting alarm among
conservationists, a new international coordinating
35 group backed by 21 ivory-producing and ivory-
consuming countries has met and adopted an
ambitious plan of action. Against admittedly long
odds, the multinational rescue effort is aimed both
at stopping the slaughter of the elephants in the
40 short term and at nurturing them as a vital "keystone species" in the long run.

It is the elephant's metabolism and appetite
that make it a disturber of the environment and
therefore an important creator of habitat. In a
45 constant search for the 300 pounds of vegetation it
must have every day, it kills small trees and under-
brush and pulls branches off big trees as high as
its trunk will reach. This creates innumerable
open spaces in both deep tropical forests and in
50 the woodlands that cover part of the African savannas. The resulting patchwork, a mosaic of vegetation in various stages of regeneration, in turn
creates a greater variety of forage that attracts a
greater variety of other vegetation-eaters than
55 would otherwise be the case.

In studies over the last 20 years in southern
Kenya near Mount Kilimanjaro, Dr. David Western
has found that when elephants are allowed to
roam the savannas naturally and normally, they
60 spread out at "intermediate densities." Their foraging creates a mixture of savanna woodlands
(what the Africans call bush) and grassland. The
result is a highly diverse array of other plant-
eating species: those like the zebra, wildebeest and
65 gazelle, that graze; those like the giraffe, bushbuck
and lesser kudu, that browse on tender shoots,
buds, twigs and leaves; and plant-eating primates
like the baboon and vervet monkey. These herbi-
vores attract carnivores like the lion and cheetah.

**GO ON TO NEXT PAGE ▶**

70     When the elephant population thins out, Dr. Western said, the woodlands become denser and the grazers are squeezed out. When pressure from poachers forces elephants to crowd more densely onto reservations, the woodlands there are
75 knocked out and the browsers and primates disappear.

    Something similar appears to happen in dense tropical rain forests. In their natural state, because the overhead forest canopy shuts out sunlight and
80 prevents growth on the forest floor, rain forests provide slim pickings for large, hoofed plant-eaters. By pulling down trees and eating new growth, elephants enlarge natural openings in the canopy, allowing plants to regenerate on the forest
85 floor and bringing down vegetation from the canopy so that smaller species can get at it.

    In such situations, the rain forest becomes hospitable to large plant-eating mammals such as bongos, bush pigs, duikers, forest hogs, swamp
90 antelopes, forest buffaloes, okapis, sometimes gorillas and always a host of smaller animals that thrive on secondary growth. When elephants disappear and the forest reverts, the larger animals give way to smaller, nimbler animals like
95 monkeys, squirrels and rodents.

**16.** The passage is primarily concerned with

(A) explaining why elephants are facing the threat of extinction
(B) explaining difficulties in providing sufficient forage for plant eaters
(C) explaining how the elephant's impact on its surroundings affects other species
(D) distinguishing between savannas and rain forests as habitats for elephants
(E) contrasting elephants with members of other endangered species

**17.** In line 5, "mounted" most nearly means

(A) ascended
(B) increased
(C) launched
(D) attached
(E) exhibited

**18.** In the opening paragraph, the author mentions tigers and whales in order to emphasize which point about the elephant?

(A) Like them, it faces the threat of extinction.
(B) It is herbivorous rather than carnivorous.
(C) It moves more ponderously than either the tiger or the whale.
(D) Unlike them, it physically alters its environment.
(E) It is the largest extant land mammal.

**19.** A necessary component of the elephant's ability to transform the landscape is its

(A) massive intelligence
(B) fear of predators
(C) ravenous hunger
(D) lack of grace
(E) ability to regenerate

**20.** It can be inferred from the passage that

(A) the lion and the cheetah commonly prey upon elephants
(B) the elephant is dependent upon the existence of smaller plant-eating mammals for its survival
(C) elephants have an indirect effect on the hunting patterns of certain carnivores
(D) the floor of the tropical rain forest is too overgrown to accommodate larger plant-eating species
(E) the natural tendency of elephants is to crowd together in packs

**21.** In lines 40 and 41, the quotation marks around the phrase "keystone species" serve to

(A) emphasize the triteness of the phrase
(B) contradict the literal meaning of the term
(C) indicate the author's desire to write colloquially
(D) imply the phrase has ironic connotations
(E) indicate the phrase is being used in a special or technical sense

22. The passage contains information that would answer which of the following questions?

    I. How does the elephant's foraging affect its surroundings?

    II. How do the feeding patterns of gazelles and giraffes differ?

    III. What occurs in the rain forest when the elephant population dwindles?

    (A) I only
    (B) II only
    (C) I and II only
    (D) II and III only
    (E) I, II, and III

23. In line 91, "host" most nearly means

    (A) food source for parasites
    (B) very large number
    (C) provider of hospitality
    (D) military force
    (E) angelic company

24. Which of the following statements best expresses the author's attitude toward the damage to vegetation caused by foraging elephants?

    (A) It is a regrettable by-product of the feeding process.
    (B) It is a necessary but undesirable aspect of elephant population growth.
    (C) It fortuitously results in creating environments suited to diverse species.
    (D) It has the unexpected advantage that it allows scientists access to the rain forest.
    (E) It reinforces the impression that elephants are a disruptive force.

IF YOU FINISH IN LESS THAN 25 MINUTES, YOU MAY CHECK YOUR WORK ON THIS SECTION ONLY. DO NOT TURN TO ANY OTHER SECTION IN THE TEST.

**STOP**

# SECTION 2 /MATHEMATICS

TIME: 25 MINUTES
20 QUESTIONS (1–20)

---

**Directions:**

For each question in this section, determine which of the five choices is correct, and blacken that choice on your answer sheet. You may use any blank space on the page for your work.

NOTES:
- You may use a calculator whenever you believe it will be helpful.
- Use the diagrams provided to help you solve the problems. Unless you see the phrase
  <u>Note:</u> Figure not drawn to scale
  under a diagram, it has been drawn as accurately as possible. Unless it is stated that a figure is three dimensional, you may assume that it lies in a plane.

## Reference

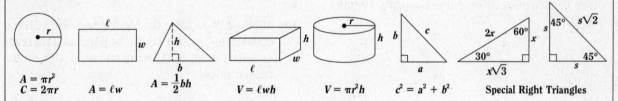

$A = \pi r^2$
$C = 2\pi r$      $A = \ell w$      $A = \frac{1}{2} bh$      $V = \ell wh$      $V = \pi r^2 h$      $c^2 = a^2 + b^2$      **Special Right Triangles**

Number of degrees in a circle: 360
Sum of the measures, in degrees, of the three angles of a triangle: 180

---

**1.** If $b - 8 = 0$, what is the value of $b + 8$?

(A) $-16$
(B) $-8$
(C) $0$
(D) $8$
(E) $16$

**2.** Isaac has twice as many toys as Sidney. If Isaac has $t$ toys, how many does Sidney have?

(A) $2t$
(B) $t^2$
(C) $\frac{t}{2}$
(D) $\frac{2}{t}$
(E) $t + 2$

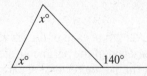

**3.** In the figure above, what is the value of $x$?

(A) 40
(B) 60
(C) 70
(D) 80
(E) 140

**4.** What is the value of $n$ if $10^{2n + 1} = 1,000,000$?

(A) 2
(B) 2.5
(C) 3
(D) 5
(E) 6

**GO ON TO NEXT PAGE** ▶

**5.** What is the product of 1.5 and 1.7 rounded to the nearest tenth?

(A) 2.2
(B) 2.5
(C) 2.6
(D) 3.0
(E) 3.2

**6.** A square has the same area as a circle of diameter 4. What is the length of each side of the square?

(A) $2\sqrt{\pi}$
(B) $4\sqrt{\pi}$
(C) $2\pi$
(D) $4\pi$
(E) $8\pi$

**7.** On a map, $\frac{1}{3}$ inch represents 14 miles. What is the length, in inches, of the line segment drawn on the map between two cities that are actually 30 miles apart?

(A) $\frac{7}{15}$

(B) $\frac{5}{7}$

(C) $\frac{3}{4}$

(D) $1\frac{2}{5}$

(E) 10

**8.** What is the length of each of the six equal sides of a regular hexagon, if the perimeter of the hexagon is equal to the perimeter of a square whose area is 36?

(A) 4
(B) 6
(C) 12
(D) 24
(E) 36

**9.** If for any number $b$, the operations $\diamond$ and $\blacklozenge$ are defined by $b\diamond = b + 1$ and $\blacklozenge b = b - 1$, which of the following is NOT equal to $(3\diamond)(\blacklozenge 5)$?

(A) $(1\diamond)(\blacklozenge 9)$
(B) $7\diamond + \blacklozenge 9$
(C) $(4\diamond)(\blacklozenge 4)$
(D) $(7\diamond)(\blacklozenge 3)$
(E) $15\diamond \div \blacklozenge 2$

**10.** If $\frac{n+2}{5}$ is an integer, what is the remainder when $n$ is divided by 5?

(A) 1
(B) 2
(C) 3
(D) 4
(E) It cannot be determined from the information given.

**11.** The day of a quiz, only Michelle was absent. The average (arithmetic mean) grade of the other students was 85. When Michelle took a makeup quiz, her grade was 30, which lowered the class's average to 80. How many students are in the class?

(A) 8
(B) 9
(C) 10
(D) 11
(E) 12

**12.** At Music Warehouse the regular price for a CD is $d$ dollars. How many CDs can be purchased there for $m$ dollars when the CDs are on sale at 20% off the regular price?

(A) $\frac{4d}{5m}$
(B) $\frac{4m}{5d}$
(C) $\frac{5d}{4m}$
(D) $\frac{5m}{4d}$
(E) $\frac{md}{20}$

**13.** In a group of 40 people, 13 own dogs and 18 own cats. If 16 have neither a dog nor a cat, how many people have both?

(A) 0
(B) 3
(C) 6
(D) 7
(E) 11

**14.** How many integers are solutions of the inequality $3|x| + 1 < 16$?

(A) 0
(B) 4
(C) 8
(D) 9
(E) Infinitely many

**GO ON TO NEXT PAGE ▶**

**15.** Each of the 15 members of a club owns a certain number of teddy bears. The following chart shows the number of teddy bears owned.

| Number of Teddy Bears | Number of Members |
|:---:|:---:|
| 6 | 2 |
| 8 | 5 |
| 10 | 4 |
| 13 | 4 |

What is the average (arithmetic mean) of the median and the mode of this set of data?

(A) 4.5
(B) 8
(C) 8.5
(D) 9
(E) 9.5

**16.** What is the value of $3^{\frac{1}{2}} \times 3^{\frac{1}{3}} \times 3^{\frac{1}{6}}$?

(A) $3^{\frac{1}{36}}$

(B) $3^{\frac{1}{11}}$·

(C) $27^{\frac{1}{36}}$

(D) $27^{\frac{1}{11}}$

(E) $3$

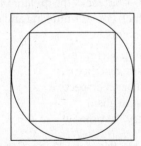

**17.** In the figure above, the small square is inscribed in the circle, which is inscribed in the large square. What is the ratio of the area of the large square to the area of the small square?

(A) $\sqrt{2}$:1
(B) $\sqrt{3}$:1
(C) 2:1
(D) $2\sqrt{2}$:1
(E) It cannot be determined from the information given.

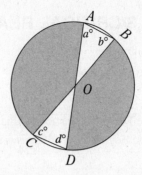

**18.** In the figure above, $O$ is the center of the circle and $AD = 10$. If the area of the shaded region is $20\pi$, what is the value of $a + b + c + d$?

(A) 144
(B) 216
(C) 240
(D) 270
(E) 288

**19.** If $r + 2s = a$ and $r - 2s = b$, which of the following is an expression for $rs$?

(A) $ab$
(B) $\frac{a + b}{2}$
(C) $\frac{a - b}{2}$
(D) $\frac{a^2 - b^2}{4}$
(E) $\frac{a^2 - b^2}{8}$

**20.** If $a$ is increased by 25% and $b$ is decreased by 25%, the resulting numbers will be equal. What is the ratio of $a$ to $b$?

(A) $\frac{3}{5}$
(B) $\frac{3}{4}$
(C) $\frac{1}{1}$
(D) $\frac{4}{3}$
(E) $\frac{5}{3}$

IF YOU FINISH IN LESS THAN 25 MINUTES, YOU MAY CHECK YOUR WORK ON THIS SECTION ONLY. DO NOT TURN TO ANY OTHER SECTION IN THE TEST.

**STOP**

*Practice Test 2*

# SECTION 3/CRITICAL READING

TIME: 25 MINUTES
24 QUESTIONS (25–48)

Each sentence below has one or two blanks, each blank indicating that something has been omitted. Beneath the sentence are five words or sets of words labeled A through E. Choose the word or set of words that, when inserted in the sentence, best fits the meaning of the sentence as a whole.

**EXAMPLE:**

Medieval kingdoms did not become constitutional republics overnight; on the contrary, the change was ----.

(A) unpopular   (B) unexpected
(C) advantageous   (D) sufficient   (E) gradual

25. In order that they may be able to discriminate wisely among the many conflicting arguments put before them, legislators must be trained to ---- the truth.

(A) confuse   (B) condemn   (C) ignore
(D) condone   (E) discern

26. In their new collections of lighthearted, provocative dresses, French fashion designers are gambling that even ---- professional women are ready for a bit of ---- in style.

(A) strict..reticence
(B) serious..frivolity
(C) elegant..tradition
(D) modern..harmony
(E) unsentimental..propriety

27. The airline customer service representative tried to ---- the ---- passenger by offering her a seat in first class.

(A) pacify..placid
(B) thwart..irate
(C) divert..grateful
(D) authorize..listless
(E) mollify..angry

28. People who find themselves unusually ---- and ready to drowse off at unexpected moments may be suffering from a hormonal imbalance.

(A) lethargic   (B) distracted   (C) obdurate
(D) benign   (E) perfunctory

29. The expression "he passed away" is ---- for "he died."

(A) a reminder   (B) a commiseration
(C) a simile   (D) a euphemism
(E) an exaggeration

30. Despite the enormous popularity and influence of his book, *Thunder Out of China*, White's career ----.

(A) soared   (B) endured   (C) accelerated
(D) revived   (E) foundered

31. Written just after Martin Luther King's assassination, Lomax's book has all the virtues of historical ---- but lacks the greater virtue of historical ----, which comes from long and mature reflection upon events.

(A) precision..accuracy
(B) criticism..distance
(C) immediacy..perspective
(D) outlook..realism
(E) currency..testimony

32. Relishing his triumph, Kevin Costner especially ---- the chagrin of the critics who had predicted his ----.

(A) regretted..success
(B) acknowledged..comeback
(C) understated..bankruptcy
(D) distorted..mortification
(E) savored..failure

**GO ON TO NEXT PAGE ▶**

**Directions:** Each of the passages below precedes two questions based on its content. Answer the questions following each passage on the basis of what is <u>stated</u> or <u>implied</u> in that passage.

**Questions 33 and 34 are based on the following passage.**

Little vegetation grows in the vast South African tableland known as the Nama Karroo. The open plateau, home to springboks and other
Line members of the antelope family, seems a rocky,
5 inhospitable place. Yet the springboks find sustenance, searching among the rocks and pebbles, and coming up with mouthfuls of "stones" which they munch contentedly. These stones are in actuality plants, members of the genus Lithops, some
10 of the strangest succulents in the world. Nature has camouflaged these stone plants so well that even trained botanists have trouble telling them apart from the rocks surrounding them.

**33.** The quotation marks around the word "stones" (line 7) primarily serve to emphasize that the plants

(A) are extraordinarily hard
(B) are inedible by humans
(C) are not literally stones
(D) can be recognized by antelopes
(E) survive in an arid environment

**34.** The context suggests that a succulent (line 10) is most likely

(A) a rock form
(B) an antelope
(C) a desert insect
(D) a type of camouflage
(E) a kind of plant

**Questions 35 and 36 are based on the following passage.**

Echoing leaders in the field such as Noam Chomsky, many linguists argue that the capacity for language is a uniquely human property. They
Line contend that chimpanzees and related primates
5 are incapable of using language because their brains lack the human brain structures that make language. Other researchers, however, disagree, citing experiments in which apes have been taught to use symbolic communication systems, such as
10 American Sign Language. In one study, for example, Georgia State professor E. Sue Savage-Rambaugh has worked with a "keyboard" consisting of 400 symbols to communicate with bonobos (also known as pygmy chimpanzees).

**35.** In line 3, "property" most nearly means

(A) trait   (B) wealth   (C) ownership
(D) oddity   (E) affliction

**36.** Savage-Rambaugh and Chomsky disagree in their evaluations of

(A) primates' value in experimental research
(B) primates' abilities in language acquisition
(C) primates' abilities to manipulate artifacts
(D) researchers' knowledge of American Sign Language
(E) researchers' impartiality in primate studies

**GO ON TO NEXT PAGE ▶**

**Directions:** The passages below are followed by questions on their content; questions following a pair of related passages may also be based on the relationship between the paired passages. Answer the questions on the basis of what is <u>stated</u> or <u>implied</u> in the passages and in any introductory material that may be provided.

**Questions 37–48 are based on the following passages.**

*The following passages are excerpted from two recent essays that relate writing to sports. The author of Passage 1 deals with having had a novel rejected by his publisher. The author of Passage 2 explores how his involvement in sports affected his writing career.*

**Passage 1**

In consigning this manuscript to a desk drawer, I am comforted by the behavior of baseball players. There are *no* pitchers who do not give up home runs, there are *no* batters who do not strike
Line out. There are *no* major league pitchers or batters
5    who have not somehow learned to survive giving up home runs and striking out. That much is obvious.

What seems to me less obvious is how
10   these "failures" must be digested, or put to use, in the overall experience of the player. A jogger once explained to me that the nerves of the ankle are so sensitive and complex that each time a runner sets his foot down, hundreds of messages are conveyed
15   to the runner's brain about the nature of the terrain and the requirements for weight distribution, balance, and muscle-strength. I'm certain that the ninth-inning home run that Dave Henderson hit off Donny Moore registered complexly and
20   permanently in Moore's mind and body and that the next time Moore faced Henderson, his pitching was informed by his awful experience of October 1986. Moore's continuing baseball career depended to some extent on his converting that
25   encounter with Henderson into something useful for his pitching. I can also imagine such an experience destroying an athlete, registering in his mind and body in such a negative way as to produce a debilitating fear.
30      Of the many ways in which athletes and artists are similar, one is that, unlike accountants or plumbers or insurance salesmen, to succeed at all they must perform at an extraordinary level of excellence. Another is that they must be willing to
35   extend themselves irrationally in order to achieve that level of performance. A writer doesn't have to write all-out all the time, but he or she must be ready to write all-out any time the story requires it. Hold back and you produce what just about any

40   literate citizen can produce, a "pretty good" piece of work. Like the cautious pitcher, the timid writer can spend a lifetime in the minor leagues.

And what more than failure—the strike out, the crucial home run given up, the manuscript
45   criticized and rejected—is more likely to produce caution or timidity? An instinctive response to painful experience is to avoid the behavior that produced the pain. To function at the level of excellence required for survival, writers like
50   athletes must go against instinct, must absorb their failures and become stronger, must endlessly repeat the behavior that produced the pain.

**Passage 2**

The athletic advantages of this concentration, particularly for an athlete who was making up for
55   the absence of great natural skill, were considerable. Concentration gave you an edge over many of your opponents, even your betters, who could not isolate themselves to that degree. For example, in football if they were ahead (or behind) by several
60   touchdowns, if the game itself seemed to have been settled, they tended to slack off, to ease off a little, certainly to relax their own concentration. It was then that your own unwavering concentration and your own indifference to the larger point of
65   view paid off. At the very least you could deal out surprise and discomfort to your opponents.

But it was more than that. Do you see? The ritual of physical concentration, of acute engagement in a small space while disregarding all the
70   clamor and demands of the larger world, was the best possible lesson in precisely the kind of selfish intensity needed to create and to finish a poem, a story, or a novel. This alone mattered while all the world going on, with and without you, did not.
75      I was learning first in muscle, blood, and bone, not from literature and not from teachers of literature or the arts or the natural sciences, but from coaches, in particular this one coach who paid me enough attention to influence me to teach
80   some things to myself. I was learning about art and life through the abstraction of athletics in much the same way that a soldier is, to an extent, prepared for war by endless parade ground drill. His body must learn to be a soldier before heart,
85   mind, and spirit can.

**GO ON TO NEXT PAGE ▶**

Ironically, I tend to dismiss most comparisons of athletics to art and to "the creative process." But only because, I think, so much that is claimed for both is untrue. But I have come to believe—in-
90 deed I have to believe it insofar as I believe in the validity and efficacy of art—that what comes to us first and foremost through the body, as a sensuous affective experience, is taken and transformed by mind and self into a thing of the spirit. Which is
95 only to say that what the body learns and is taught is of enormous significance—at least until the last light of the body fails.

**37.** Why does the author of Passage 1 consign his manuscript to a desk drawer?

(A) to protect it from the inquisitive eyes of his family
(B) to prevent its getting lost or disordered
(C) because his publisher wishes to take another look at it
(D) because he chooses to watch a televised baseball game
(E) to set it aside as unmarketable in its current state

**38.** Why is the author of Passage 1 "comforted by the behavior of baseball players" (lines 1–8)?

(A) He treasures the timeless rituals of America's national pastime.
(B) He sees he is not alone in having to confront failure and move on.
(C) He enjoys watching the frustration of the batters who strike out.
(D) He looks at baseball from the viewpoint of a behavioral psychologist.
(E) He welcomes any distraction from the task of revising his novel.

**39.** What function in the passage is served by the discussion of the nerves in the ankle in lines 11–17?

(A) It provides a momentary digression from the overall narrative flow.
(B) It emphasizes how strong a mental impact Henderson's home run must have had on Moore.
(C) It provides scientific confirmation of the neuromuscular abilities of athletes.
(D) It illustrates that the author's interest in sports is not limited to baseball alone.
(E) It conveys a sense of how confusing it is for the mind to deal with so many simultaneous messages.

**40.** In line 19, "registered" most nearly means

(A) enrolled formally
(B) expressed without words
(C) corresponded exactly
(D) made an impression
(E) qualified officially

**41.** The attitude of the author of Passage 1 to accountants, plumbers, and insurance salesmen (lines 30–36) can best be described as

(A) respectful
(B) cautious
(C) superior
(D) cynical
(E) hypocritical

**42.** In the concluding paragraphs of Passage 1, the author appears to

(A) romanticize the writer as someone heroic in his or her accomplishments
(B) deprecate athletes for their inability to react to experience instinctively
(C) minimize the travail that artists and athletes endure to do their work
(D) advocate the importance of literacy to the common citizen
(E) suggest a cautious approach would reduce the likelihood of future failure

**43.** The author of Passage 2 prizes

(A) his innate athletic talent
(B) the respect of his peers
(C) his ability to focus
(D) the gift of relaxation
(E) winning at any cost

**44.** In line 61, "settled" most nearly means

(A) judged
(B) decided
(C) reconciled
(D) pacified
(E) inhabited

**45.** What does the author mean by "indifference to the larger point of view" (lines 64–65)?

(A) inability to see the greater implications of the activity in which you were involved
(B) hostility to opponents coming from larger, better trained teams
(C) reluctance to look beyond your own immediate concerns
(D) refusing to care how greatly you might be hurt by your opponents
(E) being more concerned with the task at hand than with whether you win or lose

**GO ON TO NEXT PAGE ▶**

**46.** What is the function of the phrase "to an extent" in line 82?

(A) It denies a situation.
(B) It conveys a paradox.
(C) It qualifies a statement.
(D) It represents a metaphor.
(E) It minimizes a liability.

**47.** The author finds it ironic that he tends to "dismiss most comparisons of athletics to art" (lines 86–87) because

(A) athletics is the basis for great art
(B) he finds comparisons generally unhelpful
(C) he is making such a comparison
(D) he typically is less cynical
(E) he rejects the so-called creative process

**48.** The authors of both passages would agree that

(A) the lot of the professional writer is more trying than that of the professional athlete
(B) athletics has little to do with the actual workings of the creative process
(C) both artists and athletes learn hard lessons in the course of mastering their art
(D) it is important to concentrate on the things that hurt us in life
(E) participating in sports provides a distraction from the isolation of a writer's life

IF YOU FINISH IN LESS THAN 25 MINUTES, YOU MAY CHECK YOUR WORK ON THIS SECTION ONLY. DO NOT TURN TO ANY OTHER SECTION IN THE TEST.

**STOP**

# SECTION 4/MATHEMATICS

TIME: 25 MINUTES

18 QUESTIONS (21–38)

---

**Directions:**

For questions 21–28, determine which of the five choices is correct, and blacken that choice on your answer sheet. You may use any blank space on the page for your work.

NOTES:

• You may use a calculator whenever you believe it will be helpful.

• Use the diagrams provided to help you solve the problems. Unless you see the phrase

<u>Note:</u> Figure not drawn to scale

under a diagram, it has been drawn as accurately as possible. Unless it is stated that a figure is three dimensional, you may assume that it lies in a plane.

**Reference**

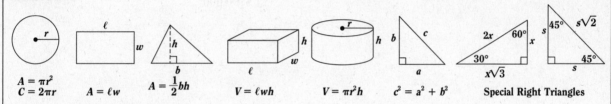

$A = \pi r^2$
$C = 2\pi r$     $A = \ell w$     $A = \frac{1}{2}bh$     $V = \ell wh$     $V = \pi r^2 h$     $c^2 = a^2 + b^2$     **Special Right Triangles**

Number of degrees in a circle: 360

Sum of the measures, in degrees, of the three angles of a triangle: 180

---

**21.** If a basket of fruit contains 5 pounds of apples, 3 pounds of oranges, and 1 pound of pears, by weight, what fraction of the fruit is oranges?

(A) $\frac{1}{9}$

(B) $\frac{1}{5}$

(C) $\frac{1}{3}$

(D) $\frac{3}{8}$

(E) $\frac{1}{2}$

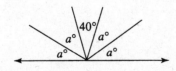

**22.** In the figure above, what is the value of $a$?

(A) 30

(B) 35

(C) 36

(D) 45

(E) 80

**23.** If $\frac{5}{8}$ of the members of a chess club are boys, what is the ratio of girls to boys in the club?

(A) $\frac{3}{13}$

(B) $\frac{5}{13}$

(C) $\frac{3}{5}$

(D) $\frac{5}{3}$

(E) $\frac{8}{5}$

**24.** A rectangle has a perimeter equal to the circumference of a circle of radius 3. If the width of the rectangle is 3, what is its length?

(A) $3\pi - 3$

(B) $4.5\pi - 3$

(C) $6\pi - 3$

(D) $9\pi - 3$

(E) $3\pi + 3$

**GO ON TO NEXT PAGE ▶**

**25.** If $p$, $q$, and $r$ are prime numbers greater than 5, which of the following could be true?

   I. $p - q$ is prime

  II. $p + q$ is prime

 III. $p + q + r$ is prime

(A) I only
(B) II only
(C) I and II only
(D) I and III only
(E) I, II, and III

**26.** If $A$ (3, −2) and $B$ (7, 2) are the endpoints of a diameter of a circle, what is the area of the circle?

(A) $2\sqrt{2}\,\pi$
(B) $4\sqrt{2}\,\pi$
(C) $8\pi$
(D) $16\pi$
(E) $32\pi$

**27.** If $13 - 2\sqrt{x} = 7$, then what is the value of $x$?

(A) −9
(B) 6
(C) 9
(D) 16
(E) There is no value of $x$ that satisfies the equation.

**28.** The estate of a wealthy man was distributed as follows: 10% to his wife, 5% divided equally among his 3 children, 5% divided equally among his 5 grandchildren, and the balance to a charitable trust. If the trust received $1,000,000, how much did each grandchild inherit?

(A) $10,000
(B) $12,500
(C) $20,000
(D) $62,500
(E) $100,000

## Student-Produced Response Directions

In questions 29–38, first solve the problem, and then enter your answer on the grid provided on the answer sheet. The instructions for entering your answers follow.

- First, write your answer in the boxes at the top of the grid.
- Second, grid your answer in the columns below the boxes.
- Use the fraction bar in the first row or the decimal point in the second row to enter fractions and decimals.

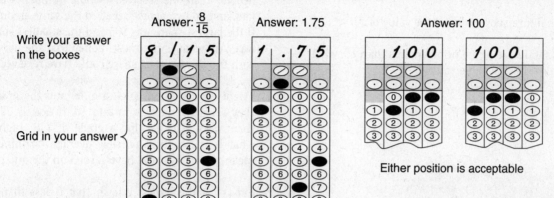

Write your answer in the boxes

Grid in your answer

Answer: $\frac{8}{15}$    Answer: 1.75    Answer: 100

Either position is acceptable

- Grid only one space in each column.
- Entering the answer in the boxes is recommended as an aid in gridding but is not required.
- The machine scoring your exam can read only what you grid, so you **must grid-in your answers correctly to get credit.**
- If a question has more than one correct answer, grid-in only one of them.
- The grid does not have a minus sign; so no answer can be negative.
- A mixed number *must* be converted to an improper fraction or a decimal before it is gridded. Enter $1\frac{1}{4}$ as $\frac{5}{4}$ or 1.25; the machine will interpret 11/4 as $\frac{11}{4}$ and mark it wrong.

- **All decimals must be entered as accurately as possible.** Here are three acceptable ways of gridding

$$\frac{3}{11} = 0.272727\ldots$$

- Note that rounding to .273 is acceptable because you are using the full grid, but you would receive **no credit** for .3 or .27, because they are less accurate.

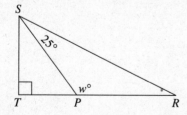

**29.** In the figure above, if *PS* bisects $\angle RST$, what is the value of *w*?

**30.** There are 150 people in line outside a ballpark. If Peter is the 10th person from the front and Wendy is the 110th person from the front, how many people are there between Peter and Wendy?

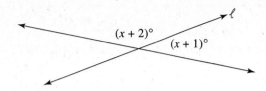

Note: Figure not drawn to scale

**31.** In the figure above, what is the value of $x$?

**32.** If $r$, $s$, and $t$ are prime numbers less than 15, what is the greatest possible value of $\frac{r-s}{t}$?

**33.** If $\frac{2}{x} + \frac{3}{4} = \frac{4}{5}$, then $x =$

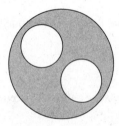

Note: Figure not drawn to scale

**34.** In the figure above, the radius of the large circle is 3 and the radius of each of the small white circles is 1. If a point, $P$, is chosen at random inside the big circle, what is the probability that $P$ lies in the shaded region?

**35.** Two circles have diameters of 12 inches and 10 inches, respectively. The area of the larger circle is what percent *more* than the area of the smaller circle? (Grid-in your answer without a percent sign.)

**36.** One hundred dollars has been divided among five people. Each one received a whole number of dollars, and no two people received the same amount. If the largest share was $35 and the smallest share was $10, what is the most money that the person with the third largest share could have received?

**37.** Twenty-five students took a quiz, and the grades they earned ranged from 2 to 10. If exactly 22 of them passed by earning a grade of 7 or higher, what is the highest possible average (arithmetic mean) the class could have earned on the quiz?

**38.** Let $[x]$ = the largest integer that is less than or equal to $x$. For example, $[2.66] = 2$ and $[5] = 5$. What is the value of $[2\pi] - [-2\pi]$?

IF YOU FINISH IN LESS THAN 25 MINUTES, YOU MAY CHECK YOUR WORK ON THIS SECTION ONLY. DO NOT TURN TO ANY OTHER SECTION IN THE TEST.

**STOP**

# SECTION 5/WRITING SKILLS

TIME: 30 MINUTES
39 QUESTIONS (1–39)

**Directions:** For each question in this section, select the best answer from among the choices given and fill in the corresponding circle on the answer sheet.

Some or all parts of the following sentences are underlined. The first answer choice, (A), simply repeats the underlined part of the sentence. The other four choices present four alternative ways to phrase the underlined part. Select the answer that produces the most effective sentence, one that is clear and exact, and blacken the appropriate space on your answer sheet. In selecting your choice, be sure that it is standard written English and that it expresses the meaning of the original sentence.

**EXAMPLE:**

The first biography of author Eudora Welty came out in 1998, and she was eighty-nine years old at the time.

(A) and she was eighty-nine years old at the time
(B) at the time when she was eighty-nine
(C) upon becoming an eighty-nine year old
(D) when she was eighty-nine
(E) at the age of eighty-nine years old

1. Fifty-three thousand shouting enthusiasts filled the stadium, they had come to watch the first game of the season and to cheer the home team.

   (A) enthusiasts filled the stadium, they had come
   (B) enthusiasts filled the stadium to come
   (C) enthusiasts, filling the stadium, had come
   (D) enthusiasts filled the stadium; and had come
   (E) enthusiasts filling the stadium, who had come

2. Cecil Sharp wrote the initial volume of *The Country Dance Book* because he wanted preserving of Britain's traditional dances before they were totally forgotten.

   (A) he wanted preserving of
   (B) he had wanted the preserving of
   (C) he wanted to preserve
   (D) his desire was the preservation of
   (E) he has wanted to preserve

3. Finally reviewing the extensive evidence against the defendant, he was found guilty.

   (A) Finally reviewing the extensive evidence against the defendant,
   (B) Reviewing the extensive evidence against the defendant,
   (C) The jury finally reviewed the extensive evidence against the defendant,
   (D) When the jury finally reviewed the extensive evidence against the defendant,
   (E) The jury finally reviewed the evidence against the defendant,

4. Paul Gauguin was married and had family responsibilities and he ran away to the South Seas to paint.

   (A) Paul Gauguin was married and had family responsibilities and he
   (B) Although being married and having family responsibilities, Paul Gauguin
   (C) Although Paul Gauguin was married and had family responsibilities, he
   (D) Being married, and therefore having family responsibilities, Paul Gauguin
   (E) Despite the fact that Paul Gauguin was married and had family responsibilities, he

**GO ON TO NEXT PAGE ▶**

5. A key difference between mice and voles is tail length, <u>a mouse's tail</u> is twice as long as the tail of a vole.

   (A) length, a mouse's tail is
   (B) length; a mouse's tail is
   (C) length, the tail of a mouse is
   (D) length; a mouse's tail, it is
   (E) length, mice's tails are

6. As a retired executive, he is now busier than ever; he makes his living <u>by speaking before business and philanthropic groups, writing books and articles, and he is a director of</u> three major corporations.

   (A) by speaking before business and philanthropic groups, writing books and articles, and he is a director of
   (B) by speaking before business and philanthropic groups, and he writes books and articles as well as being a director of
   (C) by speaking before business and philanthropic groups, and he writes books and articles, and directs
   (D) by speaking before business and philanthropic groups, writing books and articles, and directing
   (E) by speaking before business and philanthropic groups, in addition to writing books and articles, and he is a director of

7. President Reagan established a special commission for the space <u>program; the purpose being to</u> investigate the causes of the *Challenger* disaster.

   (A) program; the purpose being to
   (B) program; whose purpose being to
   (C) program, the purpose was to
   (D) program to
   (E) program; in order to

8. <u>When Harriet Tubman decided to help runaway slaves escape</u> to the North, she knew that her mission would bring her into danger in both South and North.

   (A) When Harriet Tubman decided to help runaway slaves escape
   (B) When Harriet Tubman decides to help runaway slaves escape
   (C) When Harriet Tubman decided about helping runaway slaves escape
   (D) After the decision by Harriet Tubman to help runaway slaves escape
   (E) After Harriet Tubman's making of the decision to help runaway slaves escape

9. The growing impoverishment of women and children in American society <u>distresses Senator Feinstein, and she is also infuriated.</u>

   (A) distresses Senator Feinstein, and she is also infuriated
   (B) distresses Senator Feinstein, infuriating her
   (C) distresses and infuriates Senator Feinstein
   (D) is distressing Senator Feinstein, making her infuriated
   (E) is a cause of distress to Senator Feinstein, and of a fury

10. <u>Being a successful reporter demands</u> powers of observation, fluency, and persistence.

   (A) Being a successful reporter demands
   (B) Being a successful reporter who demands
   (C) To be a successful reporter who demands
   (D) Being a successful reporter demanding
   (E) To be a successful reporter demanding

11. <u>Had I been at the scene of the accident,</u> I could have administered first aid to the victims.

   (A) Had I been at the scene of the accident
   (B) If I were at the scene of the accident
   (C) If I was at the scene of the accident
   (D) I should have been at the scene of the accident
   (E) I should have been at the scene of the accident, and

12. The Northern Lights, or Aurora Borealis, is so named <u>because it is a light display that takes place</u> in the northern skies.

   (A) because it is a light display that takes place
   (B) as a light display taking place
   (C) because of taking place
   (D) due to the fact that it is a light display
   (E) contrary to the fact of taking place

13. It is not for you to assume responsibility; it is rather <u>me who is</u> the guilty person in this matter.

   (A) me who is
   (B) me who am
   (C) I who is
   (D) I who are
   (E) I who am

**GO ON TO NEXT PAGE ▶**

14. Brightly colored birds soared to and fro, indifferent with the ships that traversed the blue Caribbean waters.

(A) Brightly colored birds soared to and fro, indifferent with the ships that traversed
(B) Brightly colored birds soared to and from, indifferent with the ships which traversed
(C) Brightly colored birds soared to and fro, indifferent to the ships that traversed
(D) Bright colored birds soared to and fro, indifferently with the ships, they traversed
(E) Brighly colored birds soaring to and fro, indifferent with the ships that traversed

15. The Metropolitan Museum of Art's collection of medieval sculptures, like so many other aspects of the museum, have benefited significantly from the generosity of J. Pierpont Morgan, the financier.

(A) sculptures, like so many other aspects of the museum, have benefited significantly from
(B) sculptures, like so many other aspects of the museum, have significant benefits from
(C) sculptures, like so many other aspects of the museum, has benefited significantly from
(D) sculptures, similar to many other aspects of the museum, have benefited significantly from
(E) sculptures, like so many other aspects of the museum, have benefited significantly through

16. Native Americans did not fare well in the mission system, perishing in vast numbers from measles and other diseases introduced by the Spanish.

(A) fare well in the mission system, perishing
(B) fare good in the mission system, perishing
(C) fare well in the mission system, they perished
(D) fare well from the mission system, perishing
(E) fare well in the mission system, despite perishing

17. Standoffish and reserved, Charles Lindbergh was uncomfortable with the applause he received from the crowds which have cheered his historic flight.

(A) received from the crowds which have cheered his historic flight
(B) receives from the crowds which cheer his historic flight
(C) received from the cheering crowds about his historic flight
(D) received from the crowds when they cheer his historic flight
(E) received from the crowds that cheered his historic flight

18. Study-abroad programs can enhance students' acquisition of a foreign language, improve their knowledge of the host culture, and even their world views can be transformed.

(A) culture, and even their world views can be transformed
(B) culture, and even can transform their world views
(C) culture, and their world views can even be transformed
(D) culture, and even transform their world views
(E) culture, and even transforming their world views

19. Once dried and pinned as specimens, dragonflies lose most of their color and become increasing fragile.

(A) Once dried and pinned as specimens, dragonflies lose most of their color and become increasing fragile.
(B) Once dried and pinned as a specimen, dragonflies lose most of their color and become increasing fragile.
(C) Once they have been dried and pinned as specimens, dragonflies lose most of their color, becoming increasing fragile.
(D) They were once dried and pinned as specimens, and then dragonflies lose most of their color and become increasingly fragile.
(E) Once dried and pinned as specimens, dragonflies lose most of their color and become increasingly fragile.

20. By the time Jews began to arrive in the United States in significant numbers in the early twentieth century, they already have established an affinity with political liberalism in Europe.

(A) they already have established an affinity with
(B) they all ready have established an affinity with
(C) they already have established an affinity for
(D) an affinity had already been established by them toward
(E) they already had established an affinity with

Practice Test 2

The sentences in this section may contain errors in grammar, usage, choice of words, or idioms. There is either just one error per sentence, or the sentence is correct. Some words or phrases are underlined and lettered; everything else in the sentence is correct.

If an underlined word or phrase is incorrect, choose that letter; if the sentence is correct, select No error. Then blacken the appropriate space on your answer sheet.

**EXAMPLE:**

The region has a climate so severe that plants
                                    A

growing there rarely had been more than twelve
        B                    C

inches high. No error
         D        E

21. After his heart attack, he was ordered to lay in bed
    A                          B           C
    and rest for two weeks. No error
             D              E

22. While my aunt and I were traveling through our
                         A       B          C
    national parks, my aunt was frightened by a bear.
                                 D
    No error
    E

23. Only recently, the newly organized football
    A                    B
    association added two new teams to their league.
                 C                      D
    No error
    E

24. In view of the controversy with the school board,
    A
    neither the teachers nor the principal are being
                         B              C
    considered for salary increases at this time.
                                      D
    No error
    E

25. While we have rummaged through the attic, we
                  A         B
    found not only an album of our trip to Europe
          C
    but also a multitude of old news clippings.
                        D
    No error
    E

26. Of all the members of the United States team,
    A           B
    Greg Lemond was the first to win the prestigious
                C           D
    Tour de France bike race. No error
                              E

27. Before we adopt this legislation, we ought to
                A                       B
    consider the affect the new law will have on our
                 C                               D
    retired and disabled citizens. No error
                                   E

28. The legendary Mark McGwire has established
                                A
    an enviable record, and it probably will not
       B        C
    be broken during the next fifty years. No error
    D                                      E

29. Toni Cade Bambara, who is a black American
                        A
    writer, has been active in civil rights and women's
            B
    issues, nor is she attuned to Afro-American
            C          D
    relationships. No error
                   E

30. The boom in sales of video cassette recorders can
                                                   A
    be attributed to numerous things, including being
       B              C                   D
    price reduction and the growth of rental stores.

    No error
    E

**GO ON TO NEXT PAGE** ▶

**31.** <u>After</u> a six-month study semester abroad, she <u>was</u>
     A                                                B

happy to get home to <u>comfortable familiar</u>
     C                        D

surroundings and appetizing food. <u>No error</u>
                                        E

**32.** The conductor's <u>uncompromising</u> manner at the
                        A

podium sometimes created <u>friction with</u>
                              B

orchestral players, <u>who</u> saw him as <u>dictatorial</u>.
                        C                    D

<u>No error</u>
   E

**33.** Because he <u>has been warned</u> <u>only</u> about the
                        A               B

danger of <u>walking</u> on the railroad trestle, he dared
              C

<u>several of</u> his friends to walk on the tracks.
   D

<u>No error</u>
   E

**34.** Where is it possible to find <u>if</u> it <u>was</u> James Russell
                                    A        B

Lowell <u>or</u> Henry Wadsworth Longfellow <u>who</u>
          C                                      D

wrote "Hiawatha"? <u>No error</u>
                      E

Practice Test 2

## Improving Paragraphs Directions

The passage below is the unedited draft of a student's essay. Some of the essay needs to be rewritten to make the meaning clearer and more precise. Read the essay carefully.

The essay is followed by questions about changes that might improve all or part of its organization, development, sentence structure, use of language, appropriateness to the audience, or use of standard written English. Choose the answer that most clearly and effectively expresses the student's intended meaning. Indicate your choice by filling in the corresponding space on the answer sheet.

[1] Although some people believe that certain celebrations have no point, celebrations are one of the few things that all people have in common. [2] They take place everywhere. [3] Listing all of them would be an impossible task. [4] People of all kinds look forward to celebrations for keeping traditions alive for generation after generation. [5] Those who criticize celebrations do not understand the human need to preserve tradition and culture.

[6] In the Muslim religion, the Ead is a celebration. [7] It begins as soon as Ramadan (the fasting month) is over. [8] During the Ead, families gather together. [9] New clothes are bought for children, and they receive money from both family and friends. [10] Also, each family, if they can afford it, slaughters a sheep or a cow. [11] They keep a small fraction of the meat, and the rest they must give to the poor. [12] They also donate money to a mosque.

[13] Many celebrations involve eating meals. [14] In the United States, people gather together on Thanksgiving to say thank you for their blessings by having a huge feast with turkey, sweet potatoes, and cranberry sauce. [15] Christmas and Easter holiday dinners are a custom in the Christian religion. [16] They have a roast at Christmas. [17] At Easter they serve ham. [18] The Jewish people celebrate Passover with a big meal called a seder. [19] They say prayers, drink wine, and sing songs to remember how Jews suffered centuries ago when they escaped from slavery in Egypt.

[20] A celebration is held each year to honor great people like Dr. Martin Luther King. [21] His birthday is celebrated because of this man's noble belief in equality of all races. [22] People wish to remember not only his

famous speeches, including "I Have A Dream," but also about him being assassinated in Memphis in 1968. [23] He died while fighting for the equality of minorities. [24] Unlike religious celebrations, celebrations for great heroes like Martin Luther King are for all people everywhere in the world. [25] He is a world-class hero and he deserved the Nobel Prize for Peace that he won.

35. To improve the unity of the first paragraph, which of the following is the best sentence to delete?
    (A) sentence 1
    (B) sentence 2
    (C) sentence 3
    (D) sentence 4
    (E) sentence 5

36. In the context of the third paragraph, which is the best way to combine sentences 15, 16, and 17?
    (A) A roast at Christmas, ham at Easter—that's what Christians eat.
    (B) Christians customarily serve a roast for Christmas dinner, at Easter ham is eaten.
    (C) At customary holiday dinners, Christians eat a roast at Christmas and ham is for Easter dinner.
    (D) Christians often celebrate the Christmas holiday with a roast for dinner and Easter with a traditional ham.
    (E) Christmas and Easter dinners are the custom in the Christian religion, where they have a roast at Christmas and ham at Easter.

**37.** In an effort to provide a more effective transition between paragraphs 3 and 4, which of the following would be the best revision of sentence 20 below?

*A celebration is held each year to honor great people like Dr. Martin Luther King.*

(A) There are also some celebrations to honor great people like Dr. Martin Luther King.

(B) Martin Luther King is also celebrated in the United States.

(C) In the United States, celebrating to honor great people like Dr. Martin Luther King has become a tradition.

(D) In addition to observing religious holidays, people hold celebrations to honor great leaders like Dr. Martin Luther King.

(E) Besides holding religion-type celebrations, celebrations to honor great people like Dr. Martin Luther King are also held.

**38.** Which is the best revision of the underlined segment of sentence 22 below?

*People wish to remember not only his famous speeches, including "I Have A Dream," but also about him being assassinated in Memphis in 1968.*

(A) that his assassination occurred

(B) about his being assassination

(C) the fact that he was assassinated

(D) about the assassination, too,

(E) his assassination

**39.** Considering the essay as a whole, which one of the following best explains the main function of the last paragraph?

(A) to summarize the main idea of the essay

(B) to refute a previous argument stated in the essay

(C) to give an example

(D) to provide a solution to a problem

(E) to evaluate the validity of the essay's main idea

IF YOU FINISH IN LESS THAN 30 MINUTES, YOU MAY CHECK YOUR WORK ON THIS SECTION ONLY. DO NOT TURN TO ANY OTHER SECTION IN THE TEST.    **STOP**

# Answer Key

## Section 1    Critical Reading

| | | | | | | | | | |
|---|---|---|---|---|---|---|---|---|---|
| 1. | **D** | 6. | **C** | 11. | **D** | 16. | **C** | 21. | **E** |
| 2. | **C** | 7. | **C** | 12. | **E** | 17. | **C** | 22. | **E** |
| 3. | **A** | 8. | **B** | 13. | **D** | 18. | **D** | 23. | **B** |
| 4. | **B** | 9. | **E** | 14. | **C** | 19. | **C** | 24. | **C** |
| 5. | **E** | 10. | **C** | 15. | **B** | 20. | **C** | | |

## Section 2    Mathematics

| | | | | | | | | | |
|---|---|---|---|---|---|---|---|---|---|
| 1. | **E** | 5. | **C** | 9. | **C** | 13. | **D** | 17. | **C** |
| 2. | **C** | 6. | **A** | 10. | **C** | 14. | **D** | 18. | **E** |
| 3. | **C** | 7. | **B** | 11. | **D** | 15. | **D** | 19. | **E** |
| 4. | **B** | 8. | **A** | 12. | **D** | 16. | **E** | 20. | **A** |

## Section 3    Critical Reading

| | | | | | | | | | |
|---|---|---|---|---|---|---|---|---|---|
| 25. | **E** | 30. | **E** | 35. | **A** | 40. | **D** | 45. | **E** |
| 26. | **B** | 31. | **C** | 36. | **B** | 41. | **C** | 46. | **C** |
| 27. | **E** | 32. | **E** | 37. | **E** | 42. | **A** | 47. | **C** |
| 28. | **A** | 33. | **C** | 38. | **B** | 43. | **C** | 48. | **C** |
| 29. | **D** | 34. | **E** | 39. | **B** | 44. | **B** | | |

## Section 4    Mathematics

| | | | | | | | | |
|---|---|---|---|---|---|---|---|---|
| 21. | **C** | 23. | **C** | 25. | **D** | 27. | **C** |
| 22. | **B** | 24. | **A** | 26. | **C** | 28. | **B** |

29. 1 1 5

30. 9 9

31. 8 8 . 5

32. 1 1 / 2   or **5.5**

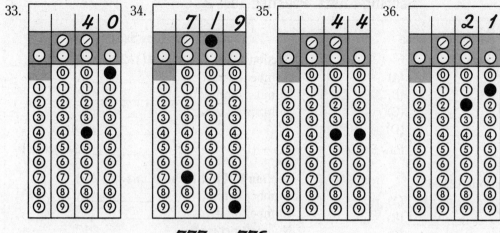

33. `4 0`

34. `7 / 9`
or **.777** or **.778**

35. `4 4`

36. `2 1`

37. `9 . 3 6`

38. `1 3`

# Section 5    Writing Skills

| | | | | | | | | | |
|---|---|---|---|---|---|---|---|---|---|
| 1. | C | 9. | C | 17. | E | 25. | A | 33. | A |
| 2. | C | 10. | A | 18. | D | 26. | E | 34. | A |
| 3. | D | 11. | A | 19. | E | 27. | C | 35. | C |
| 4. | C | 12. | A | 20. | E | 28. | C | 36. | D |
| 5. | B | 13. | E | 21. | C | 29. | C | 37. | D |
| 6. | D | 14. | C | 22. | E | 30. | D | 38. | E |
| 7. | D | 15. | C | 23. | D | 31. | D | 39. | C |
| 8. | A | 16. | A | 24. | C | 32. | E | | |

# Scoring Chart—Practice Test 2

Critical Reading Sections

**Section 1: 24 Questions (1–24)**

| | | |
|---|---|---|
| Number correct | _____ | (A) |
| Number omitted | _____ | (B) |
| Number incorrect | _____ | (C) |
| $\frac{1}{4}$ (C) | _____ | (D) |
| (A) − (D) | _____ | Raw Score I |

**Section 3: 24 Questions (25–48)**

| | | |
|---|---|---|
| Number correct | _____ | (A) |
| Number omitted | _____ | (B) |
| Number incorrect | _____ | (C) |
| $\frac{1}{4}$ (C) | _____ | (D) |
| (A) − (D) | _____ | Raw Score II |

**Total Critical Reading Raw Score**

Raw Scores I + II _____

Mathematics Sections

**Section 2: 20 Questions (1–20)**

| | | |
|---|---|---|
| Number correct | _____ | (A) |
| Number omitted | _____ | (B) |
| Number incorrect | _____ | (C) |
| $\frac{1}{4}$ (C) | _____ | (D) |
| (A) − (D) | _____ | Raw Score I |

**Section 4: First 8 Questions (21–28)**

| | | |
|---|---|---|
| Number correct | _____ | (A) |
| Number omitted | _____ | (B) |
| Number incorrect | _____ | (C) |
| $\frac{1}{4}$ (C) | _____ | (D) |
| (A) − (D) | _____ | Raw Score II |

**Section 4: Next 10 Questions (29–38)**

| | | |
|---|---|---|
| Number correct | _____ | Raw Score III |

**Total Mathematics Raw Score**

Raw Scores I + II + III _____

**NOTE: In each section (A) + (B) + (C) should equal the number of questions in that section.**

Writing Skills Section

**Section 5: 39 Questions (1–39)**

| | | |
|---|---|---|
| Number correct | _____ | (A) |
| Number omitted | _____ | (B) |
| Number incorrect | _____ | (C) |
| $\frac{1}{4}$ (C) | _____ | (D) |

**Writing Skills Raw Score**

(A) − (D) _____

# Evaluation Chart

Study your score. Your raw score is an indication of your probable achievement on the PSAT/NMSQT. As a guide to the amount of work you need or want to do with this book, study the following.

| Raw Score | | | Self-Rating |
|---|---|---|---|
| *Critical Reading* | *Mathematics* | *Writing Skills* | |
| 42–48 | 35–38 | 33–39 | Superior |
| 37–41 | 30–34 | 28–32 | Very good |
| 32–36 | 25–29 | 23–27 | Good |
| 26–31 | 21–24 | 17–22 | Above average |
| 20–25 | 17–20 | 12–16 | Average |
| 12–19 | 10–16 | 7–11 | Below average |
| less than 12 | less than 10 | less than 7 | Inadequate |

# ANSWER EXPLANATIONS

## Section 1 Critical Reading

1. **(D)** Such an extraordinarily useful material would *revolutionize* or make radical changes in an industry. The key word here is "Impressed." This tells you that the missing word must be positive in nature. You can immediately eliminate *alienate* (estrange; make unfriendly) and *nullify* (invalidate; make futile). Likewise, *justify* (warrant; show to be just or right) and *overestimate* (overrate; give excessive importance to) make no sense in the context.

2. **(C)** A contrast is set up here by the expression "no matter how." It tells us that, although future "revelations" (surprising news) may be *striking*, they will not equal past ones. These past revelations *radically* transformed or thoroughly changed our view.

   Choice A is incorrect. *Minor* means unimportant. It makes no sense in the context. Choice B is incorrect. *Profound* (very deep; great) revelations would make great changes in our view of the emergence of Mayan civilization. It makes no sense to say such revelations would have transformed it *negligibly* (insignificantly; only in a minor way). Choice D is incorrect. It makes no sense to say that truly *bizarre* (strange; weird) revelations would have transformed our view of the emergence of Mayan civilization only *nominally* (minimally; in name only). Choice E is incorrect. *Questionable* means dubious or debatable. It makes no sense in the context.

3. **(A)** Since "few other plants can grow beneath the canopy of the sycamore," it must be *inhibiting* or restraining the other plants. What is an herbicide? It is something that kills plants. It definitely does not *nourish* (feed; nurture), *encourage*, or *refresh* them. It makes no sense to say that it *distinguishes* (recognizes differences between; perceives) them.

4. **(B)** Certain authors have been *relegated* or sent off to "obscurity," a state of being hidden or forgotten. There they must be "rediscovered."

   Choice A is incorrect. *Inclined* means mentally disposed or apt to do something. It makes no sense

in this context. Choice C is incorrect. *Subjected* means made vulnerable to or exposed to. Although it is a possible answer choice, it is not the word that *best* fits the meaning of the sentence as a whole. Choice D is incorrect. *Diminished* means lessened or made smaller. It would be unidiomatic to describe someone or something as being "diminished to obscurity." Choice E is incorrect. *Characterized* means described. It makes no sense to describe someone or something as being "characterized to obscurity."

5. **(E)** Critics sometimes praise but more often *decry* or condemn things. Here the critics see the "saccharine" (too sweet) mood of the movie as inconsistent with the *acerbic* (sour, bitter) tone of the book. The key phrase here is "out of keeping." It signals a contrast. The movie's tone is overly optimistic. The book's tone, therefore, cannot be optimistic. *Hopeful* and *sanguine* are synonyms for *optimistic*. Therefore, you can eliminate Choices B and D. Similarly, critics of the movie dislike its being so sugary and overoptimistic. The critics condemn the change of tone; they do not *applaud* or *acclaim* (praise) it.

6. **(C)** If poetry fans can fill an entire football stadium, there must be a lot of them. Thus, the reference to the football stadium suggests the size of the audience for poetry and thus *emphasizes the popularity of poetry in the period*.

7. **(C)** To say that literature enjoyed a central place in the culture is to say that literature *possessed* or occupied such a place.

8. **(B)** The statement "we're dying anyway" is an example of a *metaphor* or implicit comparison. The author does not mean that he and his fellow poets are literally dying; they are dying metaphorically (figuratively), for their poetry does not matter to anyone, and to be ignored feels like death.

9. **(E)** The time when poetry mattered "is long gone." In America "no one cares." Clearly the authors of Passage 1 and Passage 2 agree that *the climate for poetry in America is inauspicious* (unfavorable).

---

**Note the following icons, used throughout this book:**

 Time saver      Look it up; math reference fact     Helpful Hint

 Educated guess      Prefixes, roots, and suffixes      Caution!

 Did you notice?      Positive or negative?      A calculator might be useful.

10. **(C)** Among other clues, Mr. Collins states that he hopes to lead Elizabeth "to the altar ere long."

11. **(D)** Elizabeth is "sensible of the honour" Mr. Collins is paying her by proposing. She is all too *keenly aware* of his intentions and wants nothing to do with them.

12. **(E)** Elizabeth expects that by refusing Mr. Collins's proposal, she will *put an end to his suit*; that is the result she desires. However, her rejection *fails* to have this intended effect. Instead, Mr. Collins in his stubbornness and conceit continues to pursue her and even takes her refusal as an encouraging sign.

13. **(D)** Mr. Collins breaks off in the middle of a sentence that begins, "Were it certain that Lady Catherine would think so—." He then finishes it awkwardly by saying, "but I cannot imagine that her ladyship would at all disapprove of you." By implication, his unspoken thought was that, if Lady Catherine *didn't* approve of Elizabeth, then Mr. Collins wouldn't want to marry her after all.

14. **(C)** Mr. Collins plans to praise Elizabeth to Lady Catherine in order to ensure Lady Catherine's approval of his bride. Elizabeth insists all such praise will be unnecessary because she *has no intention of marrying Mr. Collins* and thus has no need of Lady Catherine's approval.

15. **(B)** *Obtuse* means thickheaded, and *obstinate* means stubborn. Both apply to Mr. Collins, who can't seem to understand that Elizabeth is telling him "no."

16. **(C)** The author's emphasis is on the elephant as an important "creator of habitat" for other creatures.

17. **(C)** To mount an effort to rescue an endangered species is to *launch* or initiate a campaign.

18. **(D)** The elephant is the architect of its environment in that it *physically alters its environment*, transforming the landscape around it.

19. **(C)** The author states that it is the elephant's metabolism and appetite—in other words, its voracity or *ravenous hunger*—that leads to its creating open spaces in the woodland and transforming the landscape.

20. **(C)** Since the foraging of elephants creates a varied landscape that attracts a diverse group of plant-eating animals and since the presence of these plant eaters in turn attracts carnivores, it follows that elephants *have an indirect effect on the hunting patterns of carnivores.*

21. **(E)** Here the phrase "keystone species" *is being used in a special or technical sense* to mean a species whose very presence contributes to a diversity of life and whose extinction would consequently lead to the extinction of other forms of life.

22. **(E)** You can arrive at the correct answer choice through the process of elimination.

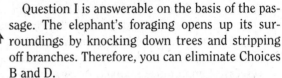

Question I is answerable on the basis of the passage. The elephant's foraging opens up its surroundings by knocking down trees and stripping off branches. Therefore, you can eliminate Choices B and D.

Question II is answerable on the basis of the passage. Gazelles are grazers; giraffes are browsers. Therefore, you can eliminate Choice A.

Question III is answerable on the basis of the passage. The concluding sentence states that when elephants disappear, the forest reverts. Therefore, you can eliminate Choice C.

Only Choice E is left. It is the correct answer.

23. **(B)** The author is listing the many species that depend on the elephant as a creator of habitat. Thus, the host of smaller animals is the *very large number* of these creatures that thrive in the elephant's wake.

24. **(C)** The author is in favor of the effect of elephants on the environment; he feels an accidental or *fortuitous result* of their foraging is that it allows a greater variety of creatures to exist in mixed-growth environments.

## Section 2  Mathematics

For many problems, the explanation provides a reference to one or more **KEY FACTS** from Chapter 7. These are the mathematical facts that you need to solve that problem. If a solution refers to **KEY FACT J2**, for example, the solution depends on the second **KEY FACT** discussed in Section J of Chapter 7.

For some problems, an alternative solution, indicated by two asterisks (**), follows the first solution. When this occurs, usually one of the solutions is the direct mathematical one and the other is based on one of the tactics discussed in Chapters 6 and 7.

See page 244 for an explanation of the symbol ⇒, which is used in several answer explanations.

1. **(E)** $b - 8 = 0 \Rightarrow b = 8 \Rightarrow b + 8 = 16.$

2. **(C)** If Isaac has twice as many toys as Sydney, then Sydney has half as many as Isaac: $\frac{t}{2}$. This is so easy that you shouldn't have to plug in a number, but you could: If Isaac has 10 toys, then Sydney has 5, and only Choice C equals 5 when $t$ is 10.

3. **(C)** By **KEY FACT J2**, the measure of an exterior angle of a triangle is equal to the sum of the measures of the two opposite interior angles; so

$$140 = x + x = 2x \Rightarrow x = 70.$$

\*\*Let the third angle in the triangle be $y$. Then $140 + y = 180 \Rightarrow y = 40$; and

$$40 + x + x = 180 \Rightarrow x = 70.$$

4. **(B)** Since $1{,}000{,}000 = 10^6$, then

$$2n + 1 = 6 \Rightarrow 2n = 5 \Rightarrow n = 2.5.$$

5. **(C)** Use your calculator: $1.5 \times 1.7 = 2.55$, which, to the nearest tenth, is 2.6.

6. **(A)** Since the circle's diameter is 4, its radius is 2, and by **KEY FACT L8** its area is $\pi(2)^2 = 4\pi$. Since the area of the square is also $4\pi$, the length of each side is $\sqrt{4\pi} = 2\sqrt{\pi}$.

7. **(B)** Set up a proportion and cross-multiply:

$$\frac{\text{inches}}{\text{miles}} = \frac{\frac{1}{3}}{14} = \frac{x}{30}.$$

Then, $14x = 30\left(\dfrac{1}{3}\right) = 10$, and $x = \dfrac{10}{14} = \dfrac{5}{7}$.

8. **(A)** Since the area of the square is 36, its sides are 6, and its perimeter is 24. Since the perimeter of the hexagon is also 24, each of its six sides is 4.

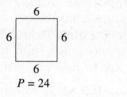  

9. **(C)** The first step is to calculate $(3\diamond)(\blacklozenge 5)$:

$$(3\diamond)(\blacklozenge 5) = (3 + 1)(5 - 1) = 4 \times 4 = 16.$$

Now check each answer until you find one that is NOT equal to 16.

A: $(1\diamond)(\blacklozenge 9) = (1 + 1)(9 - 1) = (2)(8) = 16.$
B: $(7\diamond)(\blacklozenge 9) = (7 + 1) + (9 - 1) = 8 + 8 = 16.$
C: $(4\diamond)(\blacklozenge 4) = (4 + 1)(4 - 1) = 5 \times 3 \neq 16.$

10. **(C)** Pick an integer for $\dfrac{n+2}{5}$, say 2. Then

$$\frac{n+2}{5} = 2 \Rightarrow n + 2 = 10 \Rightarrow n = 8,$$

and 5 goes into 8 once with a remainder of 3.

11. **(D)** Let $n$ represent the number of students in the class other than Michelle. These $n$ students earned a total of $85n$ points (**TACTIC E1**). When Michelle was included, there were $n + 1$ students who earned a total of $85n + 30$ points. Since the class average was then 80:

$$80 = \frac{85n + 30}{n + 1} \Rightarrow$$
$$85n + 30 = 80(n + 1) = 80n + 80 \Rightarrow$$
$$5n = 50 \Rightarrow n = 10, \text{ and so } n + 1 = 11.$$

  \*\*Use **TACTIC 6-1**: backsolve, starting with Choice C. If there were 10 children in the class, the 9 students other than Michelle would have earned $9 \times 85 = 765$ points, and so including Michelle, the total number of points earned would have been $765 + 30 = 795$ points. The class average, then, would have been $\dfrac{795}{10} = 79.5$, which is just a little too low. Eliminate Choices A, B, and C, and try Choice D, which works.

12. **(D)** At the regular price, a CD costs $d$ dollars; at 20% off, each one costs 80% of $d$ dollars:

$$\frac{80}{100}(d) = \frac{80d}{100} = \frac{4d}{5} \text{ dollars.}$$

To find out how many you can buy, divide the amount of money, $m$, by the price per CD, $\dfrac{4d}{5}$:

$$m \div \frac{4d}{5} = m\left(\frac{5}{4d}\right) = \frac{5m}{4d}.$$

\*\*Use **TACTIC 6-3** and plug in easy-to-use numbers. If CDs regularly cost \$10, then on sale at 20% off, they cost \$8 each. How many can be purchased on sale for \$40? The answer is 5. Which of the choices equals 5 when $d = 10$ and $m = 40$? Only $\dfrac{5m}{4d}$.

13. **(D)** Since 16 of the 40 people have neither a dog nor a cat, 24 people have at least one, possibly both. Since 18 of those 24 have cats, 6 of them have dogs, but no cat. But since 13 have dogs, it must be that 7 dog owners also have cats.

\*\*A Venn diagram may make this easier.

Let $x$ = the number of people who have both a cat and a dog.

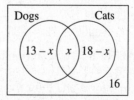

$$(13 - x) + x + (18 - x) = 24 \Rightarrow$$
$$31 - x = 24 \Rightarrow x = 7.$$

14. **(D)** $3|x| + 1 < 16 \Rightarrow 3|x| < 15 \Rightarrow |x| < 5$. There are 9 integers whose absolute value is less than 5: $-4, -3, -2, -1, 0, 1, 2, 3, 4$.

15. **(D)** The mode is 8, since more people have 8 teddy bears than any other number. Since there are 15 members, the median is the eighth piece of data when arranged in increasing order; so the median is 10. Finally, the average of 8 and 10 is 9.

16. **(E)** By **KEY FACT A21**,

$$3^{\frac{1}{2}} \times 3^{\frac{1}{3}} \times 3^{\frac{1}{6}} = 3^{\left(\frac{1}{2} + \frac{1}{3} + \frac{1}{6}\right)} = 3^1 = 3$$

\*\*Just enter the given expression into your calculator.

17. **(C)** Label the diagram as shown below, letting $s$ and $S$ be the sides of squares $ABCD$ and $EFGH$, respectively.

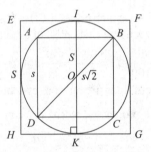

Since $\triangle DAB$ is a 45-45-90 right triangle, $BD = s\sqrt{2}$. Draw line segment $\overline{IK}$ through center $O$ and perpendicular to $\overline{GH}$. Then $IK = HE = S$. Notice that $BD$ and $IK$ are each diameters of circle $O$, so $BD = IK$, which means that

$$S = s\sqrt{2} \Rightarrow \frac{S}{s} = \sqrt{2} \Rightarrow \frac{S^2}{s^2} = 2.$$

Since $s^2$ and $S^2$ are the areas of the squares, the desired ratio is $2:1$.

18. **(E)** Since the diameter of the circle is 10, the radius is 5 and the area is $25\pi$. Also, since the area of the shaded region is $20\pi$, it is $\frac{20}{25} = \frac{4}{5}$ of the circle, and the white area is $\frac{1}{5}$ of the circle. Then the sum of the measures of the two white central angles is $\frac{1}{5}$ of 360°, or 72°. The sum of the measures of all six angles in the two triangles is $2 \times 180° = 360°$; so

$$a + b + c + d = 360 - 72 = 288.$$

19. **(E)** Use **TACTIC 6-3**: plug in numbers for $r$ and $s$. Let $r = 2$ and $s = 1$. So $2s = 2$, $a = 4$ and $b = 0$. Now, plug in 4 for $a$ and 0 for $b$ and see which of the five choices is equal to 2. Only E works:

$$\frac{a^2 - b^2}{8} = \frac{4^2 - 0^2}{8} = \frac{16}{8} = 2.$$

\*\*Here is the correct algebraic solution.

Add the two equations:

$$\begin{array}{r} r + 2s = a \\ + \underline{r - 2s = b} \\ 2r = a + b \end{array}$$

Divide by 2: $\qquad r = \frac{a + b}{2}$

Now, multiply the second equation by $-1$ and add it to the first:

$$\begin{array}{r} r + 2s = a \\ + \underline{-r + 2s = -b} \\ 4s = a - b \end{array}$$

Divide by 4: $\qquad s = \frac{a - b}{4}$

So, $rs = \frac{a + b}{2} \cdot \frac{a - b}{4} = \frac{a^2 - b^2}{8}$.

This is the type of algebra you want to avoid.

20. **(A)** $a + 25\%(a) = 1.25a$, and $b - 25\%(b) = 0.75b$.

So, $1.25a = .75b$, and $\frac{a}{b} = \frac{.75}{1.25} = \frac{75}{125} = \frac{3}{5}$.

\*\*If after increasing $a$ and decreasing $b$, the results are equal, $a$ must be smaller than $b$. So, *the ratio of a to b must be less than 1*. Eliminate Choices C, D, and E. Now, either test Choices A and B, or just guess. To test Choice B, pick two numbers in the ratio of 3 to 4—30 and 40, for example. Then, 30 increased by 25% is 37.5, and 40 decreased by 25% is 30. The results are not equal; so eliminate Choice B. The answer is $\frac{3}{5}$. (Note that 50 decreased by 25% *is* 37.5.)

## Section 3  Critical Reading

25. **(E)** To make the correct decisions, the lawmakers must be able to *discern* or recognize the truth. It would be counterproductive to have lawmakers *confuse* (bewilder), *condemn* (blame), or *ignore* (pay no attention to) the truth. To have them *condone* (excuse or overlook) the truth would not make them better able to make wise decisions.

26. **(B)** There is a chance that *serious* women may not be attracted by an inappropriate *frivolity* or light-heartedness in style—hence the gamble. Lighthearted, provocative dresses are unlikely examples of *reticence* (restraint; reserve), *tradition* (established custom), *harmony* (friendly agreement), or *propriety* (socially appropriate behavior).

27. **(E)** A customer service agent would try to *mollify* or soothe an *angry* passenger by giving her an upgrade to a better class of service.
    Choice A is incorrect. *Placid* means calm. The customer service representative would have no need to *pacify* (calm) an already placid passenger. Choice B is incorrect. *Thwart* means frustrate. Offering the passenger a seat in first class would not thwart her. Choice C is incorrect. *Divert* means distract or entertain. The passenger is grateful; the customer service representative does not need to divert her. Choice D is incorrect. *Authorize* means approve or give permission. *Listless* means weary and uninterested. Neither word makes sense in the context.

28. **(A)** If falling asleep at times you wouldn't normally wish to, you clearly would strike yourself as unusually *lethargic* (drowsily slow to respond; sluggish; listless). The key phrase here is "ready to drowse off." *Distracted* means preoccupied. *Obdurate* means pig-headedly stubborn. *Benign* means kindly; it can also mean harmless. *Perfunctory* means done routinely and without enthusiasm. None of these words conveys a sense of drowsiness.

29. **(D)** A *euphemism* is by definition a mild expression used in place of a more unpleasant or distressing one. The blunt expression "he died" is unpleasantly direct for some people, who substitute the vague euphemism "he passed away."

    Choice A is incorrect. A *reminder* is a memory aid. Choice B is incorrect. A *commiseration* is an expression of sympathy. Choice C is incorrect. A *simile* is a figure of speech drawing a comparison between two things. "My love is like a red, red rose" is an example of a simile. Choice E is incorrect. An *exaggeration* is an overstatement. "I could eat a horse" is an example of an exaggeration.

30. **(E)** *Despite* signals a contrast. If someone writes an enormously popular book, you would expect his career to prosper. Instead, White's career *foundered* or came to grief. Contrary to expectations, White's career did not do well. The missing word clearly must be negative. *Soared* (flew high; ascended to new heights), *endured* (survived; lasted through hardships), *accelerated* (gathered speed; progressed faster), and *revived* (flourished again) all are positive terms.

31. **(C)** Because it was written immediately after the assassination, the book has *immediacy*, but it lacks *perspective*; the author had not had enough time to distance himself from his immediate reactions to the event and think about it. The key phrases here are "just after Martin Luther King's assassination" and "long and mature reflection upon events."

    Choice A is incorrect. *Precision* (exactness) and *accuracy* (correctness) are synonyms. The author is drawing a contrast between the virtues the book has and the virtues it lacks. The missing words must be antonyms or near-antonyms. Choice B is incorrect. *Criticism* or assessment makes no sense in the context. Choice D is incorrect. Neither *outlook* (viewpoint; attitude) nor *realism* (theory of representing real life accurately without idealizing it) makes sense in the context. Choice E is incorrect. *Currency* is the quality of being prevalent or current. *Testimony* is the solemn declaration made by a witness under oath. Neither word makes sense in the context.

32. **(E)** The key word here is "chagrin." Because Costner has triumphed, the critics who predicted his *failure* feel chagrin (great annoyance mixed with disappointment or humiliation). Costner, for his part, greatly enjoys his success and especially enjoys or *savors* their embarrassment and vexation. Costner enjoys his critics' mortification. He does not *regret* (feel sorry for) it, *understate* (minimize) it, or *distort* (misrepresent or twist) it. He does more than merely *acknowledge* it (grant that it exists).

33. **(C)** The next sentence says that these stones in actuality are plants. Thus, the quotation marks around the word "stones" serve to underscore that these stonelike objects *are not literally stones*.

34. **(E)** Examine the context: "These stones are in actuality *plants*, members of the genus Lithops, some of the strangest succulents in the world." A succulent is clearly *a kind of plant*.

35. **(A)** Chomsky and others contend that the capacity for language is a uniquely human property or *trait*.

36. **(B)** Where Chomsky and Savage-Rambaugh differ has to do with the primates' capacity to use language, in other words, their *abilities in language acquisition*.

37. **(E)** The italicized introduction states that the author has had his manuscript rejected by his publisher. He is consigning or committing it to a desk drawer *to set it aside as unmarketable*.

38. **(B)** The rejected author identifies with these baseball players, who constantly must face "failure." *He sees he is not alone in having to confront failure and move on.*

39. **(B)** The author uses the jogger's comment to make a point about the *mental impact Henderson's home run must have had on Moore*. He reasons that, if each step a runner takes sends so many complex messages to the brain, then Henderson's ninth-inning home run must have flooded Moore's brain with messages, impressing its image indelibly in Moore's mind.

40. **(D)** The author is talking of the impact of Henderson's home run on Moore's mind. Registering in Moore's mind, the home run *made an impression* on him.

41. **(C)** The author looks on himself as someone who "to succeed at all . . . must perform at an extraordinary level of excellence." This level of excellence, he maintains, is not demanded of accountants, plumbers, and insurance salesmen, and he seems to pride himself on belonging to such a demanding profession. Thus, his attitude to members of less demanding professions can best be described as *superior*.

42. **(A)** The description of the writer defying his pain and extending himself irrationally to create a "masterpiece" despite the rejections of critics and publishers is a highly romantic one that elevates *the writer as someone heroic in his or her accomplishments.*

43. **(C)** The author of Passage 2 discusses the advantages of his ability to concentrate. Clearly, he prizes *his ability to focus* on the task at hand.

44. **(B)** When one football team is ahead of another by several touchdowns and there seems to be no way for the second team to catch up, the outcome of the game appears *decided* or settled.

45. **(E)** The "larger point of view" focuses on what to most people is the big question: the outcome of the game. The author is indifferent to this larger point of view. Concentrating on his own performance, he is *more concerned with the task at hand than with* winning or losing the game.

46. **(C)** Parade ground drill clearly does not entirely prepare a soldier for the reality of war. It only does so "to an extent." By using this phrase, the author is *qualifying his statement*, making it less absolute.

47. **(C)** One would expect someone who dismisses or rejects most comparisons of athletics to art to avoid making such comparisons. The author, however, *is making such a comparison*. This reversal of what would have been expected is an instance of irony.

48. **(C)** To learn to overcome failure, to learn to give one's all in performance, to learn to focus on the work of the moment, to learn "the selfish intensity needed to create and to finish a poem, a story, or a novel"—these are hard lessons that *both athletes and artists learn.*

## Section 4  Mathematics

For many problems, the explanation provides a reference to one or more **KEY FACTS** from Chapter 7. These are the mathematical facts that you need to solve that problem. If a solution refers to **KEY FACT J2**, for example, the solution depends on the second **KEY FACT** discussed in Section J of Chapter 7.

For some problems, an alternative solution, indicated by two asterisks (**), follows the first solution. When this occurs, usually one of the solutions is the direct mathematical one and the other is based on one of the tactics discussed in Chapters 6 and 7.

See page 244 for an explanation of the symbol ⇒, which is used in several answer explanations.

21. **(C)** The weight of the fruit is $5 + 3 + 1 = 9$ pounds, of which 3 pounds are oranges. Hence, the desired fraction is $\frac{3}{9} = \frac{1}{3}$.

22. **(B)** Since the sum of the five angles is 180°:

$$4a + 40 = 180 \Rightarrow 4a = 140 \Rightarrow a = 35.$$

23. **(C)** Use **TACTIC 6-3** and choose an easy-to-use number. Since $\frac{5}{8}$ of the members are boys, assume there are 8 members, 5 of whom are boys. Then the other 3 are girls, and the ratio of girls to boys is 3 to 5, or $\frac{3}{5}$.

24. **(A)** Refer to the figures below.

$3$  $C = 6\pi$  $3$ $\boxed{\phantom{xxxx}}$ $3$  $P = 2(\ell + 3)$

with $\ell$ labeled on the top and bottom of the rectangle.

The circumference of a circle of radius 3 is $6\pi$ (**KEY FACT L4**). By **KEY FACT K5**, the perimeter of a rectangle is $2(\ell + w)$, so $6\pi = 2(\ell + 3)$. So, $\ell + 3 = 3\pi$ and $\ell = 3\pi - 3$.

25. **(D)** $13 - 11 = 2$, so I could be true. Since $5 + 7 + 11 = 23$, III could be true. Since all primes greater than 5 are odd, $p + q$ must be even and so cannot be a prime. (Statement II is false.) Statements I and III only are true.

26. **(C)** Use the distance formula, **KEY FACT N2**, to calculate the length of diameter $\overline{AB}$:

$$AB = \sqrt{(7-3)^2 + (2-(-2))^2} = \sqrt{4^2 + 4^2} = \sqrt{32}.$$

So the diameter is $\sqrt{32}$ and the radius is $\frac{\sqrt{32}}{2}$.
Then, by **KEY FACT L8**, the area is

$$A = \pi r^2 = \pi\left(\frac{\sqrt{32}}{2}\right)^2 = \pi\left(\frac{32}{4}\right) = 8\pi.$$

Note: You do not need to simplify $\sqrt{32}$. You also don't need to use your calculator to evaluate $\sqrt{32}$, but if you do, don't round off. Take whatever appears in your calculator's window, divide it by 2 and then square it—you will get exactly 8. Of course, *do not* multiply by 3.14.

27. **(C)** $13 - 2\sqrt{x} = 7 \Rightarrow -2\sqrt{x} = -6 \Rightarrow \sqrt{x} = 3.$ So, $x = 9$.

**You can use **TACTIC 6-1** and backsolve. Choice C, 9, works.

28. **(B)** The trust received 80% of the estate (10% went to the man's wife, 5% to his children, and 5% to his grandchildren). If $E$ represents the value of the estate, then $0.80E = 1,000,000$. Therefore,

$$E = 1,000,000 \div .80 = 1,250,000.$$

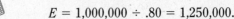

Each grandchild received 1% (one fifth of 5%) of the estate: $.01 \times \$1,250,000 = \$12,500$.

29. **(115)** We can find any or all of the angles in the figure. One way to get $w$ is to note that since $\overline{PS}$ is an angle bisector, the measure of $\angle PST = 25$ and so, by **KEY FACT J2**, $w = 25 + 90 = 115$.

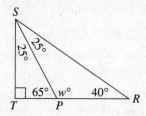

30. **(99)** From the 109 people in front of Wendy, remove Peter plus the 9 people in front of Peter: $109 - 10 = 99$.

31. **(88.5)** $(x + 1) + (x + 2) = 180 \Rightarrow 2x + 3 = 180$. So, $2x = 177 \Rightarrow x = 88.5$.

32. $\left(\frac{11}{2} \text{ or } 5.5\right)$ To make the fraction $\frac{r - s}{t}$ as large as possible, make the numerator, $r - s$, as large as you can, and the denominator $t$, as small as you can. So let $t$ be 2, the smallest prime. In order for the difference $r - s$ to be as large as possible, let $r$ be large, and subtract as little as possible. Therefore, let $r$ be 13, the largest prime less than 15, and let $s$ be 2, the smallest prime. (Note that the question did not say that $s$ and $t$ had to be different, only that they had to be primes.) Finally,

$$\frac{r - s}{t} = \frac{13 - 2}{2} = \frac{11}{2} \text{ or } 5.5.$$

33. **(40)** To solve the equation $\frac{2}{x} + \frac{3}{4} = \frac{4}{5}$, subtract $\frac{3}{4}$ from each side:

$$\frac{2}{x} + \frac{3}{4} = \frac{4}{5} \Rightarrow \frac{2}{x} = \frac{1}{20} \Rightarrow x = 40$$

Note: Do not waste time getting a common denominator; just use your calculator.

34. $\left(\frac{7}{9} \text{ or } .777 \text{ or } .778\right)$ Since the radius of the large circle is 3 by **KEY FACT L8**, its area is $9\pi$. Each of the small circles has a radius of 1 and an area of $\pi$. So the total area of the white region is $2\pi$, leaving $7\pi$ for the area of the shaded region. Therefore, the probability that $P$ lies in the shaded region is $\frac{7\pi}{9\pi} = \frac{7}{9}$.

35. **(44)** Since the diameters of the circles are in the ratio of 12:10 or 6:5, the ratio of their areas is $6^2:5^2 = 36:25$. Convert the ratio to a percent:

$$36:25 = \frac{36}{25} = \frac{144}{100} = 144\%.$$

So, the area of the large circle is 144% of the area of the small one, or is 44% *more* than the area of the small one.

 **With your calculator, actually calculate the areas. The radius of the large circle is 6, so its area is $\pi(6)^2 = 36\pi$. Similarly, the radius of the small circle is 5 and its area is $\pi(5)^2 = 25\pi$. The difference in the areas is $36\pi - 25\pi = 11\pi$, and $11\pi$ is 44% of $25\pi$ $\left(\frac{11\pi}{25\pi} = \frac{11}{25} = \frac{44}{100}\right)$.

36. **(21)** For the third place share to be as large as possible, the fourth place share must be as small as possible. However, it must be more than 10, so let it be 11. Then the amount, in dollars, left for second and third place is $100 - (35 + 11 + 10) = 100 - 56 = 44$. So, the second place share could be $23 and the third place share $21.

37. **(9.36)** For the average to be as high as possible, each student needs to have scored the maximum number of points. Therefore, assume that each of the 22 students who passed earned a grade of 10, that only one student earned a 2, and that the other two students who failed each earned a 6, the highest possible failing grade. Then the average is

 $\frac{10(22) + 2 + 2(6)}{25} = \frac{234}{25} = 9.36$.

38. **(13)** Since $\pi$ is approximately 3.14, $2\pi$ is approximately 6.28, and $[2\pi] = 6$. Now, be careful: $-2\pi$ is approximately $-6.28$, and the largest integer less than $-6.28$ is $-7$. Finally,

$$[2\pi] - [-2\pi] = 6 - (-7) = 6 + 7 = 13.$$

## Section 5  Writing Skills

1. **(C)** Comma splice. Choices A, D, and E are run-on sentences. Choice B is constructed awkwardly.

2. **(C)** The verb *want* (meaning wish or desire) customarily is followed by the infinitive. Sharp wished *to preserve* or save the old folk dances.

3. **(D)** This choice corrects the dangling modifier.

4. **(C)** Error in coordination and subordination. The subordinating conjunction *Although* best connects the sentence's two clauses.

5. **(B)** Comma splice. Choices A, C, and E are run-on sentences; Choice D is unidiomatic.

6. **(D)** Error in parallelism. Parallel structure is maintained in Choice D.

7. **(D)** Choices A, B, and E contain sentence fragments; Choice C creates a comma splice.

8. **(A)** Sentence is correct. The past tense and the subordinating conjunction *when* are correctly used in Choice A.

9. **(C)** Choice C expresses the author's meaning directly and concisely. All other choices are either indirect or ungrammatical.

10. **(A)** Choices B, C, D, and E are sentence fragments.

11. **(A)** Sentence is correct.

12. **(A)** Sentence is correct.

13. **(E)** The errors in pronoun case and subject-verb agreement are corrected in Choice E. *I* should be used instead of *me* because it is the predicate nominative of the verb *is*. *Who*, having as its antecedent the pronoun *I*, is a first-person singular pronoun. The first-person singular verb *am* should be used.

14. **(C)** Error in idiomatic usage. The birds are indifferent *to* the ships.

15. **(C)** Error in subject-verb agreement. The subject of the sentence, *collection*, is singular; the verb should be singular as well.

16. **(A)** Sentence is correct.

17. **(E)** Error in sequence of tenses. *Was* and *received* are in the simple past tense. Both indicate a definite time in the past. *Have cheered* is in the present perfect tense. It indicates sometime before now but not a definite time. The sequence is illogical.

18. **(D)** Error in parallelism. Choice D corrects the lack of parallel structure.

19. **(E)** Adjective-adverb confusion. The dragonflies become *increasingly* fragile.

20. **(E)** Error in sequence of tenses. The *had* before *established* indicates a time prior to *began to arrive*.

21. **(C)** Error in diction. Use *lie* instead of *lay*.

22. **(E)** Sentence is correct.

23. **(D)** Error in pronoun number agreement. Since antecedent is *association*, change *their* to *its*.

24. **(C)** Error in subject-verb agreement. In a neither-nor construction the verb agrees with the noun or pronoun that comes immediately before the verb. *Principal is being considered* is correct.

25. **(A)** Error in tense. Change *have rummaged* to *were rummaging*.

26. **(E)** Sentence is correct.

27. **(C)** Error in diction. Use *effect* instead of *affect*.

28. **(C)** Error in coordination and subordination. Delete the comma and substitute *that* for *and it*. The second clause describes McGwire's record.

29. **(C)** Error in coordination and subordination. Change *nor is she* to *and she is* to clarify the relationship between the clauses.

30. **(D)** Error in diction. The word *being* is unnecessary. Change *including being* to *including*.

31. **(D)** Adjective and adverb confusion. Change *comfortable* to *comfortably*.

32. **(E)** Sentence is correct.

33. **(A)** Error in tense. Change *has been warned* to *had been warned*.

34. **(A)** Error in diction. Use *if* to indicate a condition. Substitute *whether*.

35. **(C)** All sentences except sentence 3 contribute to the paragraph's main point, that celebrations help to unite people and keep traditions alive. Therefore, Choice C is the best answer.

36. **(D)** Choice A is fresh, but its tone is not consistent with the rest of the essay.

    Choice B contains a comma splice between *dinner* and *at*.

    Choice C emphasizes the idea properly but contains an error in parallel construction.

    Choice D places the emphasis where it belongs and expresses the idea effectively. It is the best answer.

    Choice E is repetitious, and it contains an error in pronoun reference. The pronoun *they* has no specific referent.

37. **(D)** Choice A does not provide a significantly better transition.

    Choice B does nothing to improve the relationship between paragraphs 3 and 4.

    Choice C is awkwardly worded and does not include transitional material.

    Choice D provides an effective transition between paragraphs. It is the best answer.

    Choice E tries to provide a transition, but it is wordy and it contains a dangling participle.

38. **(E)** Choice A places emphasis on the location of the assassination instead of on the event itself, an emphasis that the writer did not intend.

    Choice B contains a nonstandard usage. The phrase *to remember about* is not standard.

    Choice C is grammatically correct but wordy.

    Choice D is the same as B.

    Choice E is a succinct and proper revision. It is the best answer.

39. **(C)** The main purpose of the last paragraph is to provide an example of a celebration that unites people and preserves tradition. Therefore, Choice C is the best answer.

# Answer Sheet–Practice Test 3

Each mark should completely fill the appropriate space, and should be as dark as all other marks. Make all erasures complete. Traces of an erasure may be read as an answer.

## Section 1 – Critical Reading
### 25 minutes

1. Ⓐ Ⓑ Ⓒ Ⓓ Ⓔ
2. Ⓐ Ⓑ Ⓒ Ⓓ Ⓔ
3. Ⓐ Ⓑ Ⓒ Ⓓ Ⓔ
4. Ⓐ Ⓑ Ⓒ Ⓓ Ⓔ
5. Ⓐ Ⓑ Ⓒ Ⓓ Ⓔ
6. Ⓐ Ⓑ Ⓒ Ⓓ Ⓔ
7. Ⓐ Ⓑ Ⓒ Ⓓ Ⓔ
8. Ⓐ Ⓑ Ⓒ Ⓓ Ⓔ
9. Ⓐ Ⓑ Ⓒ Ⓓ Ⓔ
10. Ⓐ Ⓑ Ⓒ Ⓓ Ⓔ
11. Ⓐ Ⓑ Ⓒ Ⓓ Ⓔ
12. Ⓐ Ⓑ Ⓒ Ⓓ Ⓔ
13. Ⓐ Ⓑ Ⓒ Ⓓ Ⓔ
14. Ⓐ Ⓑ Ⓒ Ⓓ Ⓔ
15. Ⓐ Ⓑ Ⓒ Ⓓ Ⓔ
16. Ⓐ Ⓑ Ⓒ Ⓓ Ⓔ
17. Ⓐ Ⓑ Ⓒ Ⓓ Ⓔ
18. Ⓐ Ⓑ Ⓒ Ⓓ Ⓔ
19. Ⓐ Ⓑ Ⓒ Ⓓ Ⓔ
20. Ⓐ Ⓑ Ⓒ Ⓓ Ⓔ
21. Ⓐ Ⓑ Ⓒ Ⓓ Ⓔ
22. Ⓐ Ⓑ Ⓒ Ⓓ Ⓔ
23. Ⓐ Ⓑ Ⓒ Ⓓ Ⓔ
24. Ⓐ Ⓑ Ⓒ Ⓓ Ⓔ

## Section 2 – Math
### 25 minutes

1. Ⓐ Ⓑ Ⓒ Ⓓ Ⓔ
2. Ⓐ Ⓑ Ⓒ Ⓓ Ⓔ
3. Ⓐ Ⓑ Ⓒ Ⓓ Ⓔ
4. Ⓐ Ⓑ Ⓒ Ⓓ Ⓔ
5. Ⓐ Ⓑ Ⓒ Ⓓ Ⓔ
6. Ⓐ Ⓑ Ⓒ Ⓓ Ⓔ
7. Ⓐ Ⓑ Ⓒ Ⓓ Ⓔ
8. Ⓐ Ⓑ Ⓒ Ⓓ Ⓔ
9. Ⓐ Ⓑ Ⓒ Ⓓ Ⓔ
10. Ⓐ Ⓑ Ⓒ Ⓓ Ⓔ
11. Ⓐ Ⓑ Ⓒ Ⓓ Ⓔ
12. Ⓐ Ⓑ Ⓒ Ⓓ Ⓔ
13. Ⓐ Ⓑ Ⓒ Ⓓ Ⓔ
14. Ⓐ Ⓑ Ⓒ Ⓓ Ⓔ
15. Ⓐ Ⓑ Ⓒ Ⓓ Ⓔ
16. Ⓐ Ⓑ Ⓒ Ⓓ Ⓔ
17. Ⓐ Ⓑ Ⓒ Ⓓ Ⓔ
18. Ⓐ Ⓑ Ⓒ Ⓓ Ⓔ
19. Ⓐ Ⓑ Ⓒ Ⓓ Ⓔ
20. Ⓐ Ⓑ Ⓒ Ⓓ Ⓔ

## Section 3 – Critical Reading
### 25 minutes

25. Ⓐ Ⓑ Ⓒ Ⓓ Ⓔ
26. Ⓐ Ⓑ Ⓒ Ⓓ Ⓔ
27. Ⓐ Ⓑ Ⓒ Ⓓ Ⓔ
28. Ⓐ Ⓑ Ⓒ Ⓓ Ⓔ
29. Ⓐ Ⓑ Ⓒ Ⓓ Ⓔ
30. Ⓐ Ⓑ Ⓒ Ⓓ Ⓔ
31. Ⓐ Ⓑ Ⓒ Ⓓ Ⓔ
32. Ⓐ Ⓑ Ⓒ Ⓓ Ⓔ
33. Ⓐ Ⓑ Ⓒ Ⓓ Ⓔ
34. Ⓐ Ⓑ Ⓒ Ⓓ Ⓔ
35. Ⓐ Ⓑ Ⓒ Ⓓ Ⓔ
36. Ⓐ Ⓑ Ⓒ Ⓓ Ⓔ
37. Ⓐ Ⓑ Ⓒ Ⓓ Ⓔ
38. Ⓐ Ⓑ Ⓒ Ⓓ Ⓔ
39. Ⓐ Ⓑ Ⓒ Ⓓ Ⓔ
40. Ⓐ Ⓑ Ⓒ Ⓓ Ⓔ
41. Ⓐ Ⓑ Ⓒ Ⓓ Ⓔ
42. Ⓐ Ⓑ Ⓒ Ⓓ Ⓔ
43. Ⓐ Ⓑ Ⓒ Ⓓ Ⓔ
44. Ⓐ Ⓑ Ⓒ Ⓓ Ⓔ
45. Ⓐ Ⓑ Ⓒ Ⓓ Ⓔ
46. Ⓐ Ⓑ Ⓒ Ⓓ Ⓔ
47. Ⓐ Ⓑ Ⓒ Ⓓ Ⓔ
48. Ⓐ Ⓑ Ⓒ Ⓓ Ⓔ

## Section 4 – Math

25 minutes

21 Ⓐ Ⓑ Ⓒ Ⓓ Ⓔ
22 Ⓐ Ⓑ Ⓒ Ⓓ Ⓔ
23 Ⓐ Ⓑ Ⓒ Ⓓ Ⓔ
24 Ⓐ Ⓑ Ⓒ Ⓓ Ⓔ
25 Ⓐ Ⓑ Ⓒ Ⓓ Ⓔ
26 Ⓐ Ⓑ Ⓒ Ⓓ Ⓔ
27 Ⓐ Ⓑ Ⓒ Ⓓ Ⓔ
28 Ⓐ Ⓑ Ⓒ Ⓓ Ⓔ

Grid-in answer boxes for items 29, 30, 31, 32, 33, 34, 35, 36, 37 and 38 each print the following grid:

| | | | |
|---|---|---|---|
| | / | / | |
| . | . | . | . |
| | 0 | 0 | 0 |
| 1 | 1 | 1 | 1 |
| 2 | 2 | 2 | 2 |
| 3 | 3 | 3 | 3 |
| 4 | 4 | 4 | 4 |
| 5 | 5 | 5 | 5 |
| 6 | 6 | 6 | 6 |
| 7 | 7 | 7 | 7 |
| 8 | 8 | 8 | 8 |
| 9 | 9 | 9 | 9 |

## Section 5 – Writing

30 minutes

1 Ⓐ Ⓑ Ⓒ Ⓓ Ⓔ
2 Ⓐ Ⓑ Ⓒ Ⓓ Ⓔ
3 Ⓐ Ⓑ Ⓒ Ⓓ Ⓔ
4 Ⓐ Ⓑ Ⓒ Ⓓ Ⓔ
5 Ⓐ Ⓑ Ⓒ Ⓓ Ⓔ
6 Ⓐ Ⓑ Ⓒ Ⓓ Ⓔ
7 Ⓐ Ⓑ Ⓒ Ⓓ Ⓔ
8 Ⓐ Ⓑ Ⓒ Ⓓ Ⓔ
9 Ⓐ Ⓑ Ⓒ Ⓓ Ⓔ
10 Ⓐ Ⓑ Ⓒ Ⓓ Ⓔ
11 Ⓐ Ⓑ Ⓒ Ⓓ Ⓔ
12 Ⓐ Ⓑ Ⓒ Ⓓ Ⓔ
13 Ⓐ Ⓑ Ⓒ Ⓓ Ⓔ
14 Ⓐ Ⓑ Ⓒ Ⓓ Ⓔ
15 Ⓐ Ⓑ Ⓒ Ⓓ Ⓔ
16 Ⓐ Ⓑ Ⓒ Ⓓ Ⓔ
17 Ⓐ Ⓑ Ⓒ Ⓓ Ⓔ
18 Ⓐ Ⓑ Ⓒ Ⓓ Ⓔ
19 Ⓐ Ⓑ Ⓒ Ⓓ Ⓔ
20 Ⓐ Ⓑ Ⓒ Ⓓ Ⓔ
21 Ⓐ Ⓑ Ⓒ Ⓓ Ⓔ
22 Ⓐ Ⓑ Ⓒ Ⓓ Ⓔ
23 Ⓐ Ⓑ Ⓒ Ⓓ Ⓔ
24 Ⓐ Ⓑ Ⓒ Ⓓ Ⓔ
25 Ⓐ Ⓑ Ⓒ Ⓓ Ⓔ
26 Ⓐ Ⓑ Ⓒ Ⓓ Ⓔ
27 Ⓐ Ⓑ Ⓒ Ⓓ Ⓔ
28 Ⓐ Ⓑ Ⓒ Ⓓ Ⓔ
29 Ⓐ Ⓑ Ⓒ Ⓓ Ⓔ
30 Ⓐ Ⓑ Ⓒ Ⓓ Ⓔ
31 Ⓐ Ⓑ Ⓒ Ⓓ Ⓔ
32 Ⓐ Ⓑ Ⓒ Ⓓ Ⓔ
33 Ⓐ Ⓑ Ⓒ Ⓓ Ⓔ
34 Ⓐ Ⓑ Ⓒ Ⓓ Ⓔ
35 Ⓐ Ⓑ Ⓒ Ⓓ Ⓔ
36 Ⓐ Ⓑ Ⓒ Ⓓ Ⓔ
37 Ⓐ Ⓑ Ⓒ Ⓓ Ⓔ
38 Ⓐ Ⓑ Ⓒ Ⓓ Ⓔ
39 Ⓐ Ⓑ Ⓒ Ⓓ Ⓔ

# SECTION 1/CRITICAL READING

TIME: 25 MINUTES

24 QUESTIONS (1–24)

---

**Directions:** For each question in this section, select the best answer from among the choices given and fill in the corresponding circle on the answer sheet.

---

Each sentence below has one or two blanks, each blank indicating that something has been omitted. Beneath the sentence are five words or sets of words labeled A through E. Choose the word or set of words that, when inserted in the sentence, best fits the meaning of the sentence as a whole.

**EXAMPLE:**

Medieval kingdoms did not become constitutional republics overnight; on the contrary, the change was ----.

(A) unpopular   (B) unexpected
(C) advantageous   (D) sufficient   (E) gradual

 Ⓐ Ⓑ Ⓒ Ⓓ ●

---

1. The dean tried to retain control of the situation on campus, but her attempt was ---- by the board of trustees.

   (A) endorsed   (B) frustrated   (C) disclosed
   (D) witnessed   (E) justified

2. The extended heat wave left many people ----, lacking their usual energy and interest in life.

   (A) isolated   (B) fervid   (C) intemperate
   (D) listless   (E) nomadic

3. Disliking sudden changes in plans when she traveled abroad, Ethel refused to make any alterations to her ----.

   (A) manuscript   (B) itinerary   (C) residence
   (D) detour   (E) wardrobe

4. Though Mark had reservations about many of the fraternity's policies, he diplomatically kept them to himself and allowed his fellow members to interpret his ---- as a sign of ---- on his part.

   (A) complaints..reluctance
   (B) silence..acquiescence
   (C) arguments..pugnacity
   (D) comments..inarticulateness
   (E) selfishness..wisdom

5. Just as avarice is the mark of the miser, indulgence is the mark of the ----.

   (A) pauper   (B) philanthropist   (C) coward
   (D) martinet   (E) glutton

6. Given the many areas of conflict still awaiting ----, the outcome of the peace talks remains ----.

   (A) justification..pragmatic
   (B) settlement..permanent
   (C) resolution..problematic
   (D) compromise..plausible
   (E) arbitration..pacific

7. While some people take satisfaction from a religious or mystical explanation of human intelligence, for Bonner, the more ---- and ---- the explanation, the better she likes it.

   (A) rational..materialistic
   (B) logical..spiritual
   (C) pragmatic..dubious
   (D) theoretical..rudimentary
   (E) occult..viable

8. Unfortunately, the book comes down so firmly on the nature side of the nature-nurture debate that it tends to ---- many of the subtleties of the argument, leaving the reader with a highly ---- view of the issue.

   (A) carry through..lucid
   (B) skim over..simplistic
   (C) go beyond..dogmatic
   (D) sidestep..cerebral
   (E) highlight..arbitrary

**GO ON TO NEXT PAGE ▶**

**Directions:** Each of the passages below precedes two questions based on its content. Answer the questions following each passage on the basis of what is <u>stated</u> or <u>implied</u> in that passage.

**Questions 9 and 10 are based on the following passage.**

To students today, continental drift is a commonplace. They cheerfully talk about supercontinents that break apart or about shifts in the
Line earth's crust as if everyone has always known that
5 this solid earth beneath our feet is seated on large, rigid plates that float on a soft, partly molten layer of the earth's mantle. Not so. It was not quite a century ago that Alfred Wegener first proposed the theory that the components making
10 up the supercontinent Pangaea had slowly moved thousands of miles apart over lengthy periods of geologic time.

9. In lines 1–2, "a commonplace" most nearly means

(A) a customary location
(B) a traditional rank
(C) an accepted concept
(D) a vulgar saying
(E) an inexpensive property

10. The passage's final sentence (lines 7–12) primarily serves to emphasize the

(A) definitive nature of an experiment
(B) recent origin of a theory
(C) sudden end to a controversy
(D) limited possibilities for research
(E) stubborn character of a scientist

**Questions 11 and 12 are based on the following passage.**

The morning after the battle of Fredericksburg, the ground before the stone wall was covered with wounded, dead, and dying Northerners. Hours
Line passed by as soldiers from both sides listened to
5 the cries for water and pleas for help. Finally, Richard Kirkland, a young Confederate sergeant, could bear it no more. Receiving permission from his general to help the wounded, he ventured over the wall. Under Northern fire, he reached the
10 nearest sufferer and gave him water. As soon as they understood his intent, the enemy ceased fire, and for an hour and a half Kirkland tended the wounded unharmed.

11. The primary function of the passage is to

(A) establish that Kirkland sought his commander's approval before taking action
(B) indicate the young sergeant's eagerness to be seen as a hero
(C) dramatize the degree of suffering experienced during the Civil War
(D) depict an instance of heroism under fire
(E) analyze the military importance of the battle of Fredericksburg

12. In line 7, "bear" most nearly means

(A) carry   (B) endure   (C) produce
(D) conduct   (E) warrant

**Directions:** The passages below are followed by questions based on their content; questions following a pair of related passages may also be based on the relationship between the paired passages. Answer the questions on the basis of what is stated or implied in the passages and in any introductory material that may be provided.

**Questions 13–24 are based on the following passages.**

*In the following passages, the novelist Virginia Woolf and a contemporary literary critic separately discuss the relationship between women and fiction.*

**Passage 1**

The most superficial inquiry into women's writing instantly raises a host of questions. Why, we ask at once, was there no continuous writing
Line done by women before the eighteenth century?
5 Why did they then write almost habitually as men, and in the course of that writing produce, one after another, some of the classics of English fiction? And why did their art then, and why to some extent does their art still, take the form of fiction?
10 A little thought will show us that we are asking questions to which we shall get, as answer, only further fiction. The answer lies at present locked in old diaries, stuffed away in old drawers, half obliterated in the memories of the aged. It is
15 to be found in the lives of the obscure—in those almost unlit corridors of history where the figures of generations of women are so dimly, so fitfully perceived. For very little is known about women. The history of England is the history of the male
20 line, not of the female. Of our fathers we know always some fact, some distinction. They were soldiers or they were sailors; they filled that office or they made that law. But of our mothers, our grandmothers, our great-grandmothers, what
25 remains? Nothing but a tradition. One was beautiful; one was red-haired; one was kissed by a Queen. We know nothing of them except their names and the dates of their marriages and the number of children they bore.
30 Thus, if we wish to know why at any particular time women did this or that, why they wrote nothing, why on the other hand they wrote masterpieces, it is extremely difficult to tell. Anyone who should seek among those old papers, who should
35 turn history wrong side out and so construct a faithful picture of the daily life of the ordinary woman in Shakespeare's time, in Milton's time, in Johnson's time, would not only write a book of astonishing interest, but would furnish the critic
40 with a weapon which he now lacks. The extraordi-

nary woman depends on the ordinary woman. It is only when we know what were the conditions of the average woman's life—the number of her children, whether she had money of her own, if she
45 had a room to herself, whether she had help in bringing up her family, if she had servants, whether part of the housework was her task—it is only when we can measure the way of life and the experience of life made possible to the ordinary
50 woman that we can account for the success or failure of the extraordinary woman as writer.

**Passage 2**

As the works of dozens of women writers have been rescued from what E.P. Thompson calls "the enormous condescension of posterity," and consid-
55 ered in relation to each other, the lost continent of the female tradition has risen like Atlantis from the sea of English literature. It is now becoming clear that, contrary to Mill's theory, women have had a literature of their own all along. The woman novel-
60 ist, according to Vineta Colby, was "really neither single nor anomalous," but she was also more than a "register and spokesman for her age." She was part of a tradition that had its origins before her age, and has carried on through our own.
65 Many literary historians have begun to reinterpret and revise the study of women writers. Ellen Moers sees women's literature as an international movement, "apart from, but hardly subordinate to the mainstream: an undercurrent, rapid
70 and powerful. This 'movement' began in the late eighteenth century, was multinational, and produced some of the greatest literary works of two centuries, as well as most of the lucrative potboilers." Other critics are beginning to agree that
75 when we look at women writers collectively we can see an imaginative continuum, the recurrence of certain patterns, themes, problems, and images from generation to generation.
This book is an effort to describe the female
80 literary tradition in the English novel from the generation of the Brontes to the present day, and to show how the development of this tradition is similar to the development of any literary subculture. It is important to see the female literary tra-
85 dition in these broad terms, in relation to the

**GO ON TO NEXT PAGE ▶**

wider evolution of women's self-awareness and to
the ways any minority group finds its direction of
self-expression relative to a dominant society,
because we cannot show a pattern of deliberate
90  progress and accumulation. It is true, as Ellen
Moers writes, that "women studied with a special
closeness the works written by their own sex"; in
terms of influences, borrowings, and affinities, the
tradition is strongly marked. But it is also full of
95  holes and hiatuses, because of what Germaine
Greer calls the "phenomenon of the transience of
female literary fame"; "almost uninterruptedly
since the Interregnum, a small group of women
have enjoyed dazzling literary prestige during
100  their own lifetimes, only to vanish without trace
from the records of posterity." Thus each generation of women writers has found itself, in a sense,
without a history, forced to rediscover the past
anew, forging again and again the consciousness
105  of their sex. Given this perpetual disruption, and
also the self-hatred that has alienated women
writers from a sense of collective identity, it does
not seem possible to speak of a movement.

**13.** The questions in lines 2–9 chiefly serve to

(A) suggest how the author defines women's
writing
(B) outline the direction of the author's research
(C) underscore how little is known about the
subject
(D) divert the reader's attention from the central
issue
(E) express the author's reluctance to appear
dogmatic

**14.** In line 22, "filled" most nearly means

(A) inflated   (B) blocked   (C) furnished
(D) held   (E) pervaded

**15.** Woolf's point in lines 23–29 about how little is
known about women is made primarily through

(A) case histories   (B) examples   (C) statistics
(D) metaphors   (E) repeated quotations

**16.** The individual women mentioned in lines 25–29
are presented primarily as instances of people who

(A) encountered royalty
(B) gave birth to children
(C) observed family traditions
(D) sought to become writers
(E) lived largely unrecorded lives

**17.** The "conditions" of the average woman's life to
which the author refers (line 42) include all of the
following EXCEPT the woman's

(A) financial circumstances
(B) medical problems
(C) maternal obligations
(D) social position
(E) housing arrangements

**18.** In the first paragraph of Passage 2, the author
makes use of all the following techniques EXCEPT

(A) extended metaphor
(B) enumeration and classification
(C) classical allusion
(D) direct quotation
(E) comparison and contrast

**19.** The metaphor of the newly arisen "lost continent"
(lines 55–57) is used primarily to convey

(A) the vast degree of effort involved in reinterpreting women's literature
(B) the number of works of literature that have
been created by women
(C) the way forgotten literary works have resur-
faced after many years
(D) the extent to which books written by women
appeared unrelated
(E) the overwhelming size of the problem con-
fronting the author

20. In the second paragraph of Passage 2, the author's attitude toward the literary critics cited can best be described as one of

    (A) irony   (B) ambivalence   (C) disparagement
    (D) receptiveness   (E) awe

21. In line 92, "closeness" most nearly means

    (A) proximity in space
    (B) narrow margin of victory
    (C) disposition to secrecy
    (D) cautiousness about expenditures
    (E) minute attention to details

22. Which of the following words could best be substituted for "forging" (line 104) without substantially changing the author's meaning?

    (A) counterfeiting   (B) creating   (C) exploring
    (D) diverting   (E) straining

23. It can be inferred from Passage 2 that the author considers Moers's work to be

    (A) fallacious and misleading
    (B) scholarly and definitive
    (C) admirable but inaccurate in certain of its conclusions
    (D) popular but irrelevant to mainstream female literary criticism
    (E) idiosyncratic but of importance historically

24. Compared with the author of Passage 2, the author of Passage 1 is

    (A) more academic and less colloquial
    (B) less effusive and more detached
    (C) less didactic and more dogmatic
    (D) less scholarly and more descriptive
    (E) more radical and less entertaining

IF YOU FINISH IN LESS THAN 25 MINUTES, YOU MAY CHECK YOUR WORK ON
THIS SECTION ONLY. DO NOT TURN TO ANY OTHER SECTION IN THE TEST.

**STOP**

Practice Test 3

# SECTION 2 /MATHEMATICS

TIME: 25 MINUTES
20 QUESTIONS (1–20)

---

**Directions:**

For each question in this section, determine which of the five choices is correct, and blacken that choice on your answer sheet. You may use any blank space on the page for your work.

NOTES:
- You may use a calculator whenever you believe it will be helpful.
- Use the diagrams provided to help you solve the problems. Unless you see the phrase

<u>Note:</u> Figure not drawn to scale

under a diagram, it has been drawn as accurately as possible. Unless it is stated that a figure is three dimensional, you may assume that it lies in a plane.

**Reference**

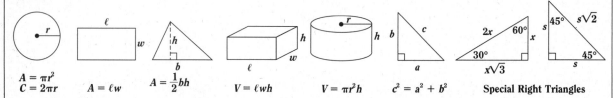

$A = \pi r^2$
$C = 2\pi r$

$A = \ell w$

$A = \frac{1}{2}bh$

$V = \ell wh$

$V = \pi r^2 h$

$c^2 = a^2 + b^2$

**Special Right Triangles**

Number of degrees in a circle: 360
Sum of the measures, in degrees, of the three angles of a triangle: 180

---

**1.** If Mr. Beck earns $16 per hour, how many hours will he have to work in order to earn $88?

(A) 5
(B) 5.5
(C) 6.5
(D) 23.5
(E) 1408

**2.** Sarah saves $8 every day. If 11 days ago she had $324, how many dollars will she have 11 days from now?

(A) 148
(B) 236
(C) 412
(D) 500
(E) 566

**3.** Which of the following is an expression for "the product of 7 and the average (arithmetic mean) of $a$ and $b$?"

(A) $\frac{7a + b}{2}$

(B) $\frac{7a + 7b}{2}$

(C) $\frac{7 + a + b}{3}$

(D) $7 + \frac{a + b}{2}$

(E) $\frac{7 + 7a + 7b}{3}$

**4.** If $\frac{3}{4}$ of a number is 7 more than $\frac{1}{6}$ of the number, what is $\frac{5}{3}$ of the number?

(A) 12
(B) 15
(C) 18
(D) 20
(E) 24

**GO ON TO NEXT PAGE ▶**

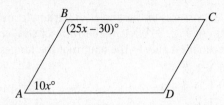

**5.** In parallelogram *ABCD* above, what is the value of *x*?

(A) 2
(B) 4
(C) 6
(D) 20
(E) 60

**6.** An operation, $*$, is defined as follows: for any positive numbers *a* and *b*, $a*b = \sqrt{a} + \sqrt{b}$. Which of the following is an integer?

(A) $11*5$
(B) $4*9$
(C) $4*16$
(D) $7*4$
(E) $9*9$

**7.** A factory that is open exactly 25 days each month produces 64 engines each day it is open. How many years will it take to produce 96,000 engines?

(A) fewer than 5
(B) 5
(C) more than 5 but less than 10
(D) 10
(E) more than 10

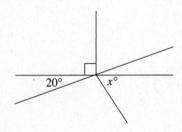

**8.** In the figure above, what is the value of *x*?

(A) 20
(B) 70
(C) 60
(D) 110
(E) It cannot be determined from the information given.

**9.** If $x - y = 5$, and $x^2 - y^2 = 75$, what is the value of *y*?

(A) $-10$
(B) $-5$
(C) 5
(D) 10
(E) $5\sqrt{2}$

**10.** Julie inherited 40% of her father's estate. After paying a tax equal to 30% of her inheritance, what percent of her father's estate did she own?

(A) 10%
(B) 12%
(C) 18%
(D) 28%
(E) 30%

**11.** For any positive integer $n > 1$: $n!$ represents the product of the first *n* positive integers. For example, $3! = 1 \times 2 \times 3 = 6$. Which of the following are equal to $(3!)(4!)$?

 I. 7!
 II. 12!
III. $4! + 5!$

(A) None
(B) I only
(C) III only
(D) I and III
(E) I, II, and III

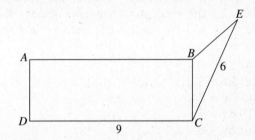

**12.** In the figure above, $BC = BE$. If *R* represents the perimeter of rectangle *ABCD* and *T* represents the perimeter of triangle *CBE*, what is the value of $R - T$?

(A) 3
(B) 12
(C) 30
(D) $18 - 6\sqrt{2}$
(E) $12 - 3\sqrt{2}$

**GO ON TO NEXT PAGE ▶**

13. There are 12 men on a basketball team, and in a game 5 of them play at any one time. If the game is one hour long and if each man plays exactly the same amount of time, how many minutes does each man play?

    (A) 10
    (B) 12
    (C) 24
    (D) 25
    (E) 30

14. Which of the following expresses the circumference of a circle in terms of $A$, its area?

    (A) $2A$

    (B) $2A\sqrt{\pi}$

    (C) $2\pi\sqrt{A}$

    (D) $2\sqrt{\pi A}$

    (E) $2\pi A$

15. What is the value of $k$ if the line that passes through $(3, -3)$ and $(k, 5)$ has a slope of $\frac{2}{3}$?

    (A) 0
    (B) 6
    (C) $8\frac{1}{3}$
    (D) 15
    (E) 18

16. If $x$ is an odd number, what is the difference between the smallest odd number greater than $5x + 4$ and the largest odd number less than $3x + 7$?

    (A) $2x$
    (B) $2x - 3$
    (C) $2x + 3$
    (D) $8x + 7$
    (E) $8x + 8$

17. The measures of the angles of a triangle are in the ratio of $1:2:3$. What is the ratio of the length of the smallest side to the length of the longest side?

    (A) $1:\sqrt{2}$
    (B) $1:\sqrt{3}$
    (C) $1:2$
    (D) $1:3$
    (E) It cannot be determined from the information given.

18. A car going 50 miles per hour set out on a 200-mile trip at 12:00 P.M. Exactly 20 minutes later, a second car left from the same place and followed the same route. How fast, in miles per hour, was the second car going if it caught up with the first car at 2:00 P.M.?

    (A) 55
    (B) 60
    (C) 65
    (D) 70
    (E) 75

19. If $a$ is inversely proportional to $b$ and $b = 5$ when $a = 3$, what is the value of $b$ when $a = 10$?

    (A) $\frac{1}{2}$

    (B) $\frac{3}{2}$

    (C) 2

    (D) $\frac{50}{3}$

    (E) 30

20. If 12% of $a$ equals 60% of $b$, then $b$ is equal to what percent of $a$?

    (A) 20%
    (B) 25%
    (C) 50%
    (D) 200%
    (E) 500%

IF YOU FINISH IN LESS THAN 25 MINUTES, YOU MAY CHECK YOUR WORK ON THIS SECTION ONLY. DO NOT TURN TO ANY OTHER SECTION IN THE TEST.

**STOP**

# SECTION 3/CRITICAL READING

TIME: 25 MINUTES
24 QUESTIONS (25–48)

**Directions:** For each question in this section, select the best answer from among the choices given and fill in the corresponding circle on the answer sheet.

---

Each sentence below has one or two blanks, each blank indicating that something has been omitted. Beneath the sentence are five words or sets of words labeled A through E. Choose the word or set of words that, when inserted in the sentence, best fits the meaning of the sentence as a whole.

**EXAMPLE:**

Medieval kingdoms did not become constitutional republics overnight; on the contrary, the change was ----.

(A) unpopular   (B) unexpected
(C) advantageous   (D) sufficient   (E) gradual

---

25. Though he was reputedly a skilled craftsman, the judging committee found his work ---- and lacking in polish.

    (A) crude   (B) accomplished
    (C) distinguished   (D) adequate
    (E) conceptual

26. Taxonomy—the branch of biology that describes and classifies living creatures—has ---- for approximately 1.4 million creatures.

    (A) need   (B) names   (C) sanctions
    (D) relevance   (E) scope

27. During the height of the mating season, disputes often erupt in the small rookery where space is ---- and male egrets must ---- a patch on which to build their nests.

    (A) inadequate..mull over
    (B) circumscribed..rule out
    (C) unavailable..pick through
    (D) unconditional..seek out
    (E) limited..vie for

28. Because he could not support the cures he obtained with scientific data, he was accused by some skeptics of being ----.

    (A) a zealot   (B) an artist   (C) a mendicant
    (D) a charlatan   (E) a dilettante

29. Critics have been misled by Tennessee Williams's obvious ---- exaggerated theatrical gestures into ---- his plays as mere melodramas, "full of sound and fury, signifying nothing."

    (A) disinclination for..disparaging
    (B) repudiation of..misrepresenting
    (C) indulgence in..acclaiming
    (D) propensity for..denigrating
    (E) indifference to..lauding

**GO ON TO NEXT PAGE** ▶

**Directions:** The passages below are followed by questions based on their content; questions following a pair of related passages may also be based on the relationship between the paired passages. Answer the questions on the basis of what is stated or implied in the passages and in any introductory material that may be provided.

**Questions 30–33 are based on the following passages.**

**Passage 1**

True scientists are no strangers to hard work. To prove a hypothesis or confirm a discovery, they conduct test after test, examining their subject
Line from every possible angle that might cast fresh
5 light upon it. They never jump to conclusions, but inch by methodical inch creep up upon them, slowly, unerringly, surely. This is the essence of modern scientific method, the method championed by Boyle and Hooke and other seventeenth
10 century experimental scientists.

**Passage 2**

According to the naturalist Donald Culross Peattie, many scientists reject the idea of scientific intuition. In Peattie's words, they "rely utterly on the celebrated inductive method of
15 reasoning: the facts are to be exposed, and we have to conclude from them only what we must." Peattie acknowledges the soundness of this rule for ordinary researchers (minds "that can do no better"), but nevertheless derides this step-by-
20 step, fact-by-fact method as plodding. He points to Einstein, who, working in a patent office, suddenly, out of the blue, had his famous insight $e = mc^2$. "First he dreamed it; then he knew it; then, rather for others' sake, he proved it." This is
25 how the really great advances in science are made.

30. The author of Passage 1 characterizes true scientists as all of the following EXCEPT

(A) systematic  (B) deliberate  (C) accurate
(D) diligent  (E) inspired

31. In lines 8–9, "championed" most nearly means

(A) challenged  (B) triumphed  (C) espoused
(D) overpowered  (E) defeated

32. Unlike the author of Passage 1, the author of Passage 2 makes use of

(A) scientific data
(B) direct citation
(C) historical references
(D) first person narration
(E) positive assertions

33. The author of Passage 1 would most likely respond to the first three sentences of Passage 2 (lines 11–20) by arguing that Peattie

(A) refuses to acknowledge any contributions to scientific knowledge by ordinary researchers
(B) minimizes the value of intuition to the advancement of science
(C) fails to appreciate the virtues of the inductive method sufficiently
(D) misunderstands the way in which scientists apply the inductive method
(E) fails to distinguish between the inductive and deductive methods of reasoning

**Directions:** Each passage below is followed by questions based on its content. Answer the questions following each passage on the basis of what is <u>stated</u> or <u>implied</u> in that passage and in any introductory material that may be provided.

**Questions 34–39 are based on the following passage.**

*Noted for their destructiveness, tornadoes have long fascinated both scientists and the public at large. The following passage is from a magazine article on tornadoes written in 1984.*

A tornado is the product of a thunderstorm, specifically of the interaction of a strong thunderstorm with winds in the troposphere (the active
Line layer of the atmosphere that extends nine to 17
5 kilometers up from the ground). The process by which a tornado is formed is one in which a small fraction of the tremendous energy of the thunderstorm, whose towering cumulonimbus cloud can be 10 to 20 kilometers across and more than 17
10 kilometers high, is concentrated in an area no more than several hundred meters in diameter. Before going into the process in detail let me first describe the phenomenon itself.

A tornado is a vortex; air rotates around the
15 tornado's axis about as fast as it moves toward and along the axis. Drawn by greatly reduced atmospheric pressure in the central core, air streams into the base of the vortex from all directions through a shallow layer a few tens of meters deep
20 near the ground. In the base the air turns abruptly to spiral upward around the core and finally merges, at the hidden upper end of the tornado, with the airflow in the parent cloud. The pressure within the core may be as much as 10 percent less
25 than that of the surrounding atmosphere; about the same difference as that between sea level and an altitude of one kilometer. Winds in a tornado are almost always cyclonic, which in the Northern Hemisphere means counterclockwise.
30 The vortex frequently—not always—becomes visible as a funnel cloud hanging part or all of the way to the ground from the generating storm. A funnel cloud forms only if the pressure drop in the core exceeds a critical value that depends on the
35 temperature and the humidity of the inflowing air. As air flows into the area of lower pressure, it expands and cools; if it cools enough, the water vapor in it condenses and forms droplets. The warmer and drier the inflowing air is, the greater
40 the pressure drop must be for condensation to

occur and a cloud to form. Sometimes no condensation funnel forms, in which case the tornado reveals itself only through the dust and debris it carries aloft.
45 A funnel can be anywhere from tens of meters to several kilometers long, and where it meets the parent cloud its diameter ranges from a few meters to hundreds of meters. Usually it is coneshaped, but short, broad, cylindrical pillars are
50 formed by very strong tornadoes, and long, ropelike tubes that trail off horizontally are also common. Over a tornado's brief lifetime (never more than a few hours) the size and shape of the funnel may change markedly, reflecting changes in the
55 intensity of the winds or in the properties of the inflowing air. Its color varies from a dirty white to gray to dark blue gray when it consists mostly of water droplets, but if the core fills with dust, the funnel may take on a more exotic hue, such as the
60 red of west Oklahoma clay. Tornadoes can also be noisy, often roaring like a freight train or a jet engine. This may result from the interaction of the concentrated high winds with the ground.

**34.** Tornadoes are characterized by which of the following?

I. Brevity of duration
II. Intense concentration of energy
III. Uniformity of shape

(A) I only
(B) II only
(C) I and II only
(D) II and III only
(E) I, II, and III

**35.** The sentence in lines 12–13 ("Before . . . itself") functions in the passage primarily as

(A) a transition
(B) a concession
(C) an apology
(D) a criticism
(E) a refutation

**GO ON TO NEXT PAGE ▶**

**36.** In line 16, "Drawn" most nearly means

(A) elongated  (B) sketched  (C) drained
(D) inferred  (E) pulled

**37.** The passage suggests that which of the following is true of a tornado?

(A) Its winds are invariably counterclockwise.
(B) It can last for days at a time.
(C) Its funnel cloud will not form if the air is cool and dry.
(D) It exceeds its parent cloud in size.
(E) It responds to changes in temperature and humidity.

**38.** According to the author, a direct relation may exist between the color a tornado takes on and

(A) the composition of the terrain it passes over
(B) the intensity of the winds it concentrates
(C) the particular shape of funnel it forms
(D) the direction in which its winds rotate
(E) the degree of noise involved

**39.** In the final paragraph the author does all of the following EXCEPT

(A) suggest a hypothesis
(B) provide a concrete example
(C) indicate a time span
(D) argue a viewpoint
(E) use a simile

**Questions 40–48 are based on the following passage.**

*The following passage is an excerpt from* "An American Childhood," *the autobiography of the writer Annie Dillard published in 1987.*

Outside in the neighborhoods, learning our way around the streets, we played among the enormous stone monuments of the millionaires—both
Line those tireless Pittsburgh founders of the heavy
5 industries from which the nation's wealth derived (they told us at school) and the industrialists' couldn't-lose bankers and backers, all of whom began as canny boys, the stories of whose rises to riches adults still considered inspirational to
10 children.

We were unthinkingly familiar with the moguls' immense rough works as so much weird scenery on long drives. We saw the long, low-slung stripes of steel factories by the rivers; we
15 saw pyramidal heaps of yellow sand at glassworks by the shining railroad tracks; we saw rusty slag heaps on the outlying hilltops, and coal barges tied up at the docks. We recognized, on infrequent trips downtown, the industries' smooth corporate
20 headquarters, each to its own soaring building—Gulf Oil, Alcoa, U.S. Steel, Koppers Company, Pittsburgh Plate Glass, Mellon Bank. Our classmates' fathers worked in these buildings, or at nearby corporate headquarters for Westinghouse
25 Electric, Jones & Laughlin Steel, Allegheny Ludlum, Westinghouse Air Brake, and H. J. Heinz.

The nineteenth-century industrialists' institutions—galleries, universities, hospitals, churches, Carnegie libraries, the Carnegie Museum, Frick
30 Park, Mellon Park—were, many of them, my stomping grounds. These absolute artifacts of philanthropy littered the neighborhoods with marble. Millionaires' encrusted mansions, now obsolete and turned into parks or art centers, weighed on
35 every block. They lent their expansive, hushed moods to the Point Breeze neighborhoods where we children lived and where those fabulous men had lived also, or rather had visited at night in order to sleep. Everywhere I looked, it was the
40 Valley of the Kings, their dynasty just ended, and their monuments intact but already out of fashion.

All these immensities wholly dominated the life of the city. So did their several peculiar social legacies: their powerful Calvinist mix of piety and
45 acquisitiveness, which characterized the old and

new Scotch-Irish families and the nation they
helped found; the wall-up hush of what was, by my
day, old money—amazing how fast it ages if you
let it alone—and the clang and roar of making
50 that money; the owners' Presbyterian churches,
their anti-Catholicism, anti-Semitism,
Republicanism, and love of continuous work; their
dogmatic practicality; their easy friendliness; their
Pittsburgh-centered innocence, and, paradoxically,
55 their egalitarianism.

　　For all the insularity of the old guard,
Pittsburgh was always an open and democratic
town. "Best-natured people I ever went among," a
Boston visitor noted two centuries earlier. In colo-
60 nial days, everybody went to balls, regardless of
rank. No one had any truck with aristocratic pretensions—hadn't they hated the British lords in
Ulster? People who cared to rave about their
bloodlines, Mother told us, had stayed in Europe,
65 which deserved them. We were vaguely proud of
living in a city so full of distinctive immigrant
groups, among which we never thought to number ourselves. We had no occasion to visit the
steep hillside neighborhoods—Polish, Hungarian,
70 Rumanian, Italian, Slav—of the turn-of-the-
century immigrants who poured the steel and
stirred the glass and shoveled the coal.

　　We children played around the moguls' enormous pale stone houses, restful as tombs, set back
75 just so on their shaded grounds. Henry Clay
Frick's daughter, unthinkably old, lived alone in
her proud, sinking mansion; she had lived alone
all her life. No one saw her. Men mowed the wide
lawns and seeded them, and pushed rollers over
80 them, over the new grass seed and musket balls
and arrowheads, over the big trees' roots, bones,
shale, coal.

　　We knew bits of this story, and we knew none
of it. We knew that before big industry there had
85 been small industry here—H. J. Heinz setting up a
roadside stand to sell horseradish roots from his
garden. There were the makers of cannonballs for
the Civil War. There were the braggart and rowdy
flatboat men and keelboat men, and the honored
90 steamboat builders and pilots. There were local
men getting rich in iron and glass manufacturing
and trade downriver. There was a whole continent-
ful of people passing through, native-born and
immigrant men and women who funneled down
95 Pittsburgh, where two rivers converged to make a
third river. It was the gateway to the West; they
piled onto flatboats and launched out into the

Ohio River singing, to head for new country. There
had been a Revolutionary War, and before that the
100 French and Indian War. And before that, and first
of all, had been those first settlers come walking
bright-eyed in, into nowhere from out of nowhere,
the people who, as they said, "broke wilderness,"
the pioneers. This was the history.

**40.** The opening paragraph suggests the author
regards the inspirational tales of the lives of the
industrialists with a sense of

(A) optimism　(B) reverence　(C) discomfort
(D) irony　(E) envy

**41.** The author and her fellow children regarded the
enormous buildings as

(A) unnatural phenomena to observe
(B) a backdrop to their lives
(C) a challenge to the imagination
(D) signs of excessive consumption
(E) intimations of immortality

**42.** The author calls the moguls fabulous (line 37)
because they were

(A) fictitious　(B) celebrated　(C) wonderful
(D) startling　(E) affluent

**43.** The author's remark in lines 48 and 49 ("amazing
how fast . . . alone") can best be described as

(A) an extended metaphor
(B) an ironic aside
(C) a faulty hypothesis
(D) a concrete example
(E) a personal reminiscence

**44.** By "People who cared to rave about their bloodlines . . . had stayed in Europe, which deserved
them" (lines 63–65), the author's mother means

(A) only Europe was worthy enough to have citizens descended from noble blood
(B) aristocrats tended to be disinclined to travel
(C) Americans were ashamed of their lack of
noble birth, and therefore avoided Europe
(D) it served Europe right if all those snobs who
boasted about their lineage stayed right there
(E) it was madness for an American to try to
trace his bloodlines; only a European could
succeed

**GO ON TO NEXT PAGE ▶**

**45.** The author uses the description of the Frick lawns in lines 78–82 chiefly to help

(A) indicate the opulence of the moguls' lifestyle
(B) counteract the isolation of Henry Clay Frick's daughter
(C) convey a sense of Pittsburgh's buried past
(D) highlight the distinction between the moguls and their employees
(E) argue in favor of preserving open spaces in cities

**46.** The opening sentence of the last paragraph (lines 83–84) presents the reader with

(A) a euphemism   (B) an epitaph   (C) a simile
(D) a paradox   (E) a reminiscence

**47.** In the phrase "broke wilderness" (line 103), "broke" most likely means

(A) shattered   (B) bankrupted   (C) unraveled
(D) interrupted   (E) penetrated

**48.** The passage's closing paragraph is organized according to

(A) geographical principles
(B) reverse chronological order
(C) cause and effect
(D) personal recollections
(E) extensive quotations

IF YOU FINISH IN LESS THAN 25 MINUTES, YOU MAY CHECK YOUR WORK ON THIS SECTION ONLY. DO NOT TURN TO ANY OTHER SECTION IN THE TEST.

**STOP**

Practice Test 3

# SECTION 4/MATHEMATICS

TIME: 25 MINUTES

18 QUESTIONS (21–38)

---

**Directions:**

For questions 21–28, determine which of the five choices is correct, and blacken that choice on your answer sheet. You may use any blank space on the page for your work.

NOTES:
- You may use a calculator whenever you believe it will be helpful.
- Use the diagrams provided to help you solve the problems. Unless you see the phrase
  <u>Note: Figure not drawn to scale</u>
  under a diagram, it has been drawn as accurately as possible. Unless it is stated that a figure is three dimensional, you may assume that it lies in a plane.

**Reference**

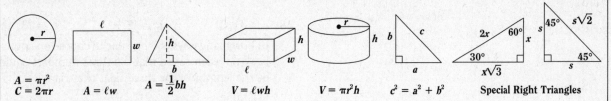

$A = \pi r^2$
$C = 2\pi r$      $A = \ell w$      $A = \frac{1}{2}bh$      $V = \ell wh$      $V = \pi r^2 h$      $c^2 = a^2 + b^2$      **Special Right Triangles**

Number of degrees in a circle: 360
Sum of the measures, in degrees, of the three angles of a triangle: 180

---

**21.** What is the value of $2x^2 - 4x - 3$ when $x = -5$?

(A) 27
(B) 67
(C) 73
(D) 87
(E) 117

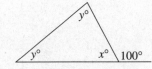

Note: Figure not drawn to scale

**22.** In the figure above, what is the value of $y$?

(A) 20
(B) 40
(C) 50
(D) 80
(E) It cannot be determined from the information given.

**23.** If $\frac{1}{b} + \frac{1}{b} + \frac{1}{b} + \frac{1}{b} = 12$, then $b =$

(A) $\frac{1}{12}$

(B) $\frac{1}{4}$

(C) $\frac{1}{3}$

(D) 3

(E) 4

**24.** Lucy had to unpack $c$ cartons. After unpacking $d$ of them, what percent of the cartons were not yet unpacked?

(A) $100(c - d)\%$

(B) $\frac{c-d}{100}\%$

(C) $\frac{c-d}{100c}\%$

(D) $\frac{100(c-d)}{d}\%$

(E) $\frac{100(c-d)}{c}\%$

**GO ON TO NEXT PAGE ▶**

25. In the figure above, $\triangle ABC$ is a right triangle. What is the value of $a + b + c + d$?

    (A) 180
    (B) 240
    (C) 270
    (D) 300
    (E) 360

26. If $\dfrac{1}{x} + \dfrac{1}{3} + \dfrac{1}{4} = 1$, then $x =$

    (A) $\dfrac{5}{12}$

    (B) $\dfrac{7}{5}$

    (C) 2

    (D) $\dfrac{12}{5}$

    (E) 5

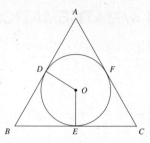

Note: Figure not drawn to scale

27. In the figure above, $AB = AC$ and the sides of triangle $ABC$ are tangent to circle $O$, at points $D, E,$ and $F$. If $m\angle A = 30°$, what is $m\angle DOE$?

    (A) 75
    (B) 90
    (C) 105
    (D) 120
    (E) 150

28. $A = \{1, 2\}$  $\qquad$ $B = \{2, 3\}$  $\qquad$ $C = \{3, 4\}$

    In how many ways is it possible to choose one number from each set so that the three numbers could be the lengths of the three sides of a triangle?

    (A) None
    (B) 1
    (C) 4
    (D) 6
    (E) 8

## Student-Produced Response Directions

In questions 29–38, first solve the problem, and then enter your answer on the grid provided on the answer sheet. The instructions for entering your answers follow.

- First, write your answer in the boxes at the top of the grid.
- Second, grid your answer in the columns below the boxes.
- Use the fraction bar in the first row or the decimal point in the second row to enter fractions and decimals.

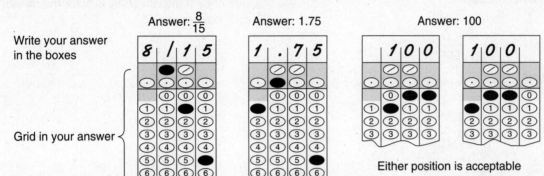

Answer: $\frac{8}{15}$     Answer: 1.75     Answer: 100

Write your answer in the boxes

Grid in your answer

Either position is acceptable

- Grid only one space in each column.
- Entering the answer in the boxes is recommended as an aid in gridding but is not required.
- The machine scoring your exam can read only what you grid, so you **must grid-in your answers correctly to get credit.**
- If a question has more than one correct answer, grid-in only one of them.
- The grid does not have a minus sign; so no answer can be negative.
- A mixed number *must* be converted to an improper fraction or a decimal before it is gridded. Enter $1\frac{1}{4}$ as $\frac{5}{4}$ or 1.25; the machine will interpret 11/4 as $\frac{11}{4}$ and mark it wrong.

- **All decimals must be entered as accurately as possible.** Here are three acceptable ways of gridding

$$\frac{3}{11} = 0.272727\ldots$$

- Note that rounding to .273 is acceptable because you are using the full grid, but you would receive **no credit** for .3 or .27, because they are less accurate.

---

**29.** If $a * b = (a + b)^2 - (a - b)^2$, what is the value of $7 * 11$?

**30.** If $3x - 11 = 11 - 3x$, what is the value of $x$?

**31.** Jim, Kim, Ben, and Len divided $1000 as follows: Kim got twice as much as Jim, Ben got 3 times as much as Jim, and Len got $100. How much, in dollars, did Jim get?

**32.** If $x$, $y$, and $z$ are different positive integers less than 10, what is the greatest possible value of $\frac{x^2 - y}{z}$?

**33.** $A$ $(-3, 2)$ and $B$ $(5, -1)$ are the endpoints of a diameter of a circle whose center is at $(x, y)$. What is the value of $x + y$?

34. $\frac{3}{7} = 0.428571428571\dots$, with the digits 4, 2, 8, 5, 7, 1 repeating indefinitely in that order. What digit is in the 200th place to the right of the decimal point?

35. In the addition problem below, each letter represents a different digit.

$$\begin{array}{r} AB \\ +CD \\ \hline AAA \end{array}$$

What is the value of $A + B + C + D$?

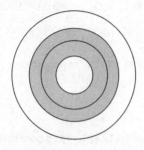

36. The figure above consists of 4 circles with the same center. The radii of the 4 circles are 1, 2, 3, and 4.

If $a$ and $b$ are the areas in the figure above of the shaded region and white region, respectively, what is the value of $\frac{a}{b}$?

37. In a jar containing only red and blue marbles, 40% of the marbles are red. If the average weight of a red marble is 40 grams and the average weight of a blue marble is 60 grams, what is the average weight, in grams, of all the marbles in the jar?

38. How many sides does a polygon have if the measure of each interior angle is twice the measure of each exterior angle?

IF YOU FINISH IN LESS THAN 25 MINUTES, YOU MAY CHECK YOUR WORK ON
THIS SECTION ONLY. DO NOT TURN TO ANY OTHER SECTION IN THE TEST.

**STOP**

# SECTION 5/WRITING SKILLS

TIME: 30 MINUTES

39 QUESTIONS (1–39)

> **Directions:** For each question in this section, select the best answer from among the choices given and fill in the corresponding circle on the answer sheet.

Some or all parts of the following sentences are underlined. The first answer choice, (A), simply repeats the underlined part of the sentence. The other four choices present four alternative ways to phrase the underlined part. Select the answer that produces the most effective sentence, one that is clear and exact, and blacken the appropriate space on your answer sheet. In selecting your choice, be sure that it is standard written English and that it expresses the meaning of the original sentence.

**EXAMPLE:**

The first biography of author Eudora Welty came out in 1998, and she was eighty-nine years old at the time.

(A) and she was eighty-nine years old at the time
(B) at the time when she was eighty-nine
(C) upon becoming an eighty-nine year old
(D) when she was eighty-nine
(E) at the age of eighty-nine years old

1. The police officer refused to permit us to enter the apartment, saying that he had orders to stop him going into the building.

   (A) stop him going   (B) prevent him going
   (C) stop his going   (D) stop us going
   (E) stop our going

2. After conducting the orchestra for six concerts, Beethoven's *Ninth Symphony* was scheduled.

   (A) After conducting
   (B) After his conducting
   (C) While conducting
   (D) Although he conducted
   (E) After he had conducted

3. Jackie Robinson became the first black player in major league baseball, he paved the way for black athletes to be accepted on the field.

   (A) Jackie Robinson became the first black player in major league baseball, he
   (B) Jackie Robinson, in becoming the first black player in major league baseball, he
   (C) Jackie Robinson became the first black player in major league baseball; he
   (D) Jackie Robinson, the first black player in major league baseball; he
   (E) Jackie Robinson had become the first black player in major league baseball and he

4. Sitting in the Coliseum, the music couldn't hardly be heard because of the cheering and yelling of the spectators.

   (A) the music couldn't hardly be heard because of
   (B) the music couldn't hardly be heard due to
   (C) the music could hardly be heard due to
   (D) we could hardly be heard because of
   (E) we could hardly hear the music because of

5. The contents of the examination came as a shock to the student, everything on it having no resemblance to what she had studied.

   (A) as a shock to the student, everything on it having
   (B) to the student as a shock, being that everything on it had
   (C) to the student as a shock, with everything on it having
   (D) as a shock to the student, everything on it has
   (E) as a shock to the student; everything on it had

**GO ON TO NEXT PAGE ▶**

6. Across the nation, curricular changes sweeping the universities as schools reassess the knowledge that educated people should have.

(A) curricular changes sweeping the universities as schools
(B) curricular changes are sweeping the universities as schools
(C) changes are sweeping the curricular since schools
(D) curricular changes sweeping the universities causing schools to
(E) curricular changes sweep the universities, but schools

7. If you have enjoyed these kind of programs, write to your local public television station and ask for more.

(A) these kind of programs
(B) those kind of programs
(C) these kinds of programs
(D) these kind of a program
(E) these kind of a program

8. In her critique of the newly opened restaurant, the reviewer discussed the elaborate menu, the impressive wine list, and how the waiters functioned.

(A) list, and how the waiters functioned
(B) list and how the waiters functioned
(C) list, and the excellent service
(D) list, and even the excellent service
(E) list, and how the waiters usually function

9. Contemporary poets are not abandoning rhyme, but some avoiding it.

(A) but some avoiding it
(B) but it is avoided by some of them
(C) but it is being avoided
(D) but some are avoiding it
(E) but it has been being avoided by some

10. Your complaint is no different from the last customer who expected a refund.

(A) Your complaint is no different from the last customer
(B) Your complaint is no different from that of the last customer
(C) Your complaint is similar to the last customer
(D) Your complaint is no different then that of the last customer
(E) Your complaint is the same as the last customer

11. According to the review board, many laboratory tests were ordered by the staff of the hospital that had no medical justification.

(A) many laboratory tests were ordered by the staff of the hospital that
(B) many laboratory tests were ordered by the staff of the hospital who
(C) the staff of the hospital ordered many laboratory tests that
(D) the staff of the hospital, who ordered many laboratory tests that
(E) the ordering of many laboratory tests by the staff of the hospital which

12. Confident about the outcome, President Obama, along with his staff, are traveling to the conference.

(A) Confident about the outcome, President Obama, along with his staff, are traveling
(B) Confident about the outcome, President Obama's party are traveling
(C) Confident about the outcome, President Obama, along with his staff, is traveling
(D) With confidence about the outcome, President Obama, along with his staff, are traveling
(E) President Obama, along with his staff, is traveling confidently about the outcome

13. Helen Keller was blind and deaf from infancy and she learned to communicate using both sign language and speech.

    (A) Helen Keller was blind and deaf from infancy and she
    (B) Although blind and deaf from infancy, Helen Keller
    (C) Although being blind and deaf from the time she was an infant, Helen Keller
    (D) Being blind and deaf from infancy, Helen Keller
    (E) Helen Keller, being blind and deaf from infancy, she

14. Standing alone beside her husband's grave, grief overwhelmed the widow and she wept inconsolably.

    (A) grief overwhelmed the widow and she wept inconsolably
    (B) grief overwhelmed the widow, who wept inconsolably
    (C) grief overwhelmed the widow that wept inconsolably
    (D) the widow, overwhelmed by grief, wept inconsolably
    (E) the widow was overwhelmed by grief, she wept inconsolably

15. Survivors of a major catastrophe are likely to exhibit aberrations of behavior because of the trauma they have experienced.

    (A) likely to exhibit aberrations of behavior because of the trauma they have experienced
    (B) likely to exhibit aberrations of behavior because of them having experienced a trauma
    (C) liable to exhibit aberrations from behavior due to the trauma they experienced
    (D) liable to exhibit aberrations of behavior, the reason being that they have experienced a trauma
    (E) likely for exhibiting aberrations of behavior due to the trauma they had experienced

16. Because the warranty on the defective toaster has expired, the store manager cannot do nothing about the problem.

    (A) has expired, the store manager cannot do nothing about the problem
    (B) has expired, the store manager cannot do anything against the problem
    (C) has expired, the store manager can do nothing about the problem
    (D) had expired, the store manager cannot do nothing about the problem
    (E) has expired, the store manager cannot do nothing for the problem

17. In 1940, during the Battle of Britain, German bombs severely have damaged Holy Trinity Church in London, but the two bronze angels on the altar rail survived the bombardment unscathed.

    (A) In 1940, during the Battle of Britain, German bombs severely have damaged Holy Trinity Church
    (B) In 1940, during the Battle of Britain, German bombs severe have damaged Holy Trinity Church
    (C) In 1940, during the Battle of Britain, German bombs severely damaging Holy Trinity Church
    (D) During the Battle of Britain in 1940, German bombs severely have damaged Holy Trinity Church
    (E) In 1940, during the Battle of Britain, German bombs severely damaged Holy Trinity Church

18. Not surprising, given the popularity of the spectacles in which they appeared, gladiators captured the public imagination.

    (A) Not surprising, given the popularity of the spectacles in which they appeared
    (B) Not surprising, because they were given the popularity of the spectacles in which they appeared
    (C) Not surprisingly, given the popularity of the spectacles in which they appeared
    (D) Not surprisingly, giving the popularity of the spectacles in which they appeared
    (E) Not surprising, given the popularity of the spectacles where they appeared

19. Whether we admit it or not, biomedical <u>research is currently supported on the backs of postdoctoral fellows, who make the industry possible by providing</u> cheap labor.

(A) research is currently supported on the backs of postdoctoral fellows, who make the industry possible by providing

(B) research are currently supported on the backs of postdoctoral fellows, who make possible the industry for providing

(C) research is currently supported in back of postdoctoral fellows, who have made the industry possible by providing

(D) research is currently supported on the backs of postdoctoral fellows, with them making the industry possible by the provision of

(E) research is currently being supported on the backs of postdoctoral fellows, being that they make the industry possible by providing

20. Because the insect order Odonata, to which drag-onflies <u>belong, is not well studied, authoritative manuals on dragonflies that could be read and understood by the untrained observer were scarce until recently.</u>

(A) belong, is not well studied, authoritative manuals on dragonflies that could be read and understood by the untrained observer were scarce until recently

(B) belong, are not well studied, authoritative manuals on dragonflies, which could be read and understood by the untrained observer were scarce until recently

(C) belong, is not well studied, until recently there were not scarcely any authoritative manuals on dragonflies that the untrained observer could read and understand

(D) belonged, was not well studied, authoritarian manuals on dragonflies that observers could have read and understood without being trained until recently were scarce

(E) belong, is not well studied, authoritative manuals on the dragonfly that could be read and understood by the untrained observer was scarcely until recently

The sentences in this section may contain errors in grammar, usage, choice of words, or idioms. There is either just one error per sentence, or the sentence is correct. Some words or phrases are underlined and lettered; everything else in the sentence is correct.

If an underlined word or phrase is incorrect, choose that letter; if the sentence is correct, select <u>No error</u>. Then blacken the appropriate space on your answer sheet.

**EXAMPLE:**

The region has a climate <u>so severe that</u> plants
                 A

<u>growing there</u> rarely <u>had been</u> more than twelve
    B             C

inches <u>high</u>. <u>No error</u>
    D    E

21. Notice the <u>immediate</u> <u>affect</u> <u>this</u> drug has on the
           A     B   C

    <u>behavior</u> of the rats in the cage. <u>No error</u>
      D                     E

22. <u>In spite of</u> official denials, news sources reported
    A

    <u>that</u> the bombs that hit Tripoli in 1986 were <u>really</u>
    B                               C

    <u>intended</u> to kill Muammar al-Qaddafi. <u>No error</u>
    D                           E

23. <u>Neither</u> the teacher nor her pupils <u>were</u> <u>enthused</u>
    A                        B   C

    about <u>going on</u> the field trip. <u>No error</u>
         D                  E

24. <u>While</u> the Egyptian president Anwar El-Sadat was
    A

    reviewing a military parade in 1981, <u>a band of</u>
                                B

    commandos <u>had shot</u> him and others
               C

    <u>in the vicinity</u>. <u>No error</u>
        D      E

25. Please do not be <u>aggravated</u> by his <u>bad manners</u>
                  A             B

    <u>since</u> he is <u>merely</u> trying to attract attention.
    C         D

    <u>No error</u>
      E

26. Neither the opera singers <u>or</u> the general public
                         A

    <u>had seen</u> <u>as much glitter</u> in years as they did
    B         C

    during *Turandot*, the <u>finale</u> of the opera season.
                     D

    <u>No error</u>
      E

27. His story about having been abducted by

    <u>strange beings</u> in a spaceship was <u>so</u> <u>incredulous</u>
    A                          B    C

    <u>that</u> no one believed him. <u>No error</u>
    D                 E

28. The hot air balloon had burst as they

    <u>were preparing</u> <u>for launch</u>, and the platform
    A          B

    <u>had broke</u> <u>as a result</u>. <u>No error</u>
    C      D        E

29. Ann Landers, <u>whose</u> name was a household word
              A

    <u>to millions</u> of readers, <u>are</u> <u>well-known</u> for family
    B               C    D

    advice. <u>No error</u>
         E

30. Child custody in surrogate mother cases is just

    one of the many controversial issues that are
    ‾‾‾‾‾‾‾‾‾‾‾                            A            ‾‾‾‾ ‾‾‾
                                                       B    C

    currently being decided upon in the courts.
                     ‾‾‾‾‾‾‾‾‾‾‾
                          D

    No error
    ‾‾‾‾‾‾‾
       E

31. If you continue to drive so recklessly, you
    ‾‾                        ‾‾‾‾‾‾‾‾‾‾
    A                               B

    are likely to have a serious accident in the very
    ‾‾‾‾‾‾‾                                      ‾‾‾‾
       C                                           D

    near future. No error
               ‾‾‾‾‾‾‾
                  E

32. The general, along with the members of
                 ‾‾‾‾‾‾‾‾‾
                     A

    his general staff, seem to favor
        ‾‾‾‾‾‾‾‾‾‾‾‾‾  ‾‾‾‾
             B           C

    immediate retaliation . No error
    ‾‾‾‾‾‾‾‾‾‾‾‾‾‾‾‾‾‾‾‾‾   ‾‾‾‾‾‾‾
              D                E

33. The rescue workers resented him criticizing their
                                ‾‾‾ ‾‾‾‾‾‾‾‾‾‾
                                 A       B

    efforts because he had ignored their requests for
                      ‾‾‾‾‾‾‾‾‾‾‾‾
                           C

    assistance up to that time. No error
              ‾‾‾‾‾‾‾‾‾‾‾‾‾‾   ‾‾‾‾‾‾‾
                   D              E

34. Casey Jones, who was killed in the line of duty,
               ‾‾‾                    ‾‾‾‾
                A                      B

    became a hero to fellow railroad workers and
    ‾‾‾‾‾‾
      C

    was to be immortalized  by a ballad. No error
    ‾‾‾‾‾‾‾‾‾‾‾‾‾‾‾‾‾‾‾‾‾                 ‾‾‾‾‾‾‾
              D                             E

[1] Members of our community have objected to the inclusion of various pieces of art in the local art exhibit. [2] They say that these pieces offend community values. [3] The exhibit in its entirety should be presented.

[4] The reason for this is that people have varied tastes, and those who like this form of art have a right to see the complete exhibit. [5] An exhibit like this one gives the community a rare chance to see the latest modern art nearby, and many people have looked forward to it with great anticipation. [6] It would be an unfortunate blow to those people for it not to be shown.

[7] The exhibit may contain pieces of art that tend to be slightly erotic, but what is being shown that most people haven't already seen? [8] So, give it an R or an X rating and don't let small children in. [9] But how many small children voluntarily go to see an art exhibit? [10] The exhibit includes examples of a new style of modern art. [11] The paintings show crowds of nude people. [12] The exhibit is at the library's new art gallery. [13] For centuries artists have been painting and sculpting people in the nude. [14] Why are these works of art different? [15] Perhaps they are more graphic in some respects, but we live in a entirely different society than from the past. [16] It is strange indeed for people in this day and age to be offended by the sight of the human anatomy.

[17] If people don't agree with these pieces, they simply should just not go. [18] But they should not be allowed to prevent others from seeing it.

**35.** Taking into account the sentences that precede and follow sentence 3, which of the following is the best revision of sentence 3?

(A) On the other hand, the whole exhibit should be presented.
(B) The exhibit, however, should be presented in its entirety.
(C) The exhibit should be entirely presented regardless of what the critics say.
(D) But another point of view is that the exhibit should be presented in its entirety.
(E) Still other members also say the whole exhibit should be presented in its entirety.

**36.** In the context of paragraph 3, which of the following is the best revision of sentences 10, 11, and 12?

(A) Paintings on exhibit at the library showing crowds of nude people and done in a new style of modern art.
(B) The exhibit, on display at the library, includes paintings of crowds of nude people done in a new style of modern art.
(C) The exhibit includes paintings in a new style of modern art, which shows crowds of nude people at the library.
(D) The library is the site of the exhibit which shows a new style of modern art, with paintings showing crowds of nude people.
(E) The new style of modern art includes examples of paintings showing crowds of nude people on exhibit in the library.

**GO ON TO NEXT PAGE ▶**

**37.** To improve the clarity and coherence of the whole essay, where is the best place to relocate the ideas contained in sentences 10, 11, and 12?

(A) before sentence 1
(B) between sentences 1 and 2
(C) between sentences 8 and 9
(D) between sentences 15 and 16
(E) after sentence 18

**38.** Which of the following is the best revision of the underlined segment of sentence 15 below?

*Perhaps they are more graphic in some respects, but we live in a entirely different society than from the past.*

(A) an entirely different society than of the past
(B) a completely different society than the past
(C) a society completely different than from past societies
(D) a society which is entirely different from the way societies have been in the past
(E) an entirely different society from that of the past

**39.** Which of the following revisions of sentence 17 provides the best transition between paragraphs 3 and 4?

(A) If anyone doesn't approve of these pieces, they simply should not go to the exhibit.
(B) Anyone disagreeing with the pieces in the exhibit shouldn't go to it.
(C) Anyone who disapproves of nudity in art simply shouldn't go to the exhibit.
(D) If anyone dislikes the sight of nudes in art, this show isn't for them.
(E) Don't go if you disapprove of nudity in art.

IF YOU FINISH IN LESS THAN 30 MINUTES, YOU MAY CHECK YOUR WORK ON THIS SECTION ONLY. DO NOT TURN TO ANY OTHER SECTION IN THE TEST.

**STOP**

# Answer Key

## Section 1 Critical Reading

| | | | | |
|---|---|---|---|---|
| 1. B | 6. C | 11. D | 16. E | 21. E |
| 2. D | 7. A | 12. B | 17. B | 22. B |
| 3. B | 8. D | 13. C | 18. B | 23. C |
| 4. B | 9. C | 14. D | 19. C | 24. D |
| 5. E | 10. B | 15. B | 20. D | |

## Section 2 Mathematics

| | | | | |
|---|---|---|---|---|
| 1. B | 5. C | 9. C | 13. D | 17. C |
| 2. D | 6. D | 10. D | 14. D | 18. B |
| 3. B | 7. B | 11. C | 15. D | 19. B |
| 4. D | 8. E | 12. B | 16. A | 20. A |

## Section 3 Critical Reading

| | | | | |
|---|---|---|---|---|
| 25. A | 30. E | 35. A | 40. D | 45. C |
| 26. B | 31. C | 36. E | 41. B | 46. D |
| 27. E | 32. B | 37. E | 42. B | 47. E |
| 28. D | 33. C | 38. A | 43. B | 48. B |
| 29. D | 34. C | 39. D | 44. D | |

## Section 4 Mathematics

| | | | |
|---|---|---|---|
| 21. B | 23. C | 25. C | 27. C |
| 22. C | 24. E | 26. D | 28. C |

29. 308  30. 22/6 or 11/3, 3.66  31. 150  32. 79

33. **3 / 2**

or *1.5*

34. **2**

35. **2 1**

36. **1**

37. **5 2**

38. **6**

## Section 5    Writing Skills

| | | | | | | | | | |
|---|---|---|---|---|---|---|---|---|---|
| 1. | E | 9. | D | 17. | E | 25. | A | 33. | A |
| 2. | E | 10. | B | 18. | C | 26. | A | 34. | D |
| 3. | C | 11. | C | 19. | A | 27. | C | 35. | D |
| 4. | E | 12. | C | 20. | A | 28. | C | 36. | B |
| 5. | E | 13. | B | 21. | B | 29. | C | 37. | A |
| 6. | B | 14. | D | 22. | E | 30. | D | 38. | E |
| 7. | C | 15. | A | 23. | C | 31. | E | 39. | C |
| 8. | C | 16. | C | 24. | C | 32. | C | | |

## Scoring Chart—Practice Test 3

### Critical Reading Sections

**Section 1: 24 Questions (1–24)**

Number correct _____ (A)
Number omitted _____ (B)
Number incorrect _____ (C)
$\frac{1}{4}$ (C) _____ (D)
(A) − (D) _____ Raw Score I

**Section 3: 24 Questions (25–48)**

Number correct _____ (A)
Number omitted _____ (B)
Number incorrect _____ (C)
$\frac{1}{4}$ (C) _____ (D)
(A) − (D) _____ Raw Score II

**Total Critical Reading Raw Score**
Raw Scores I + II _____

### Mathematics Sections

**Section 2: 20 Questions (1–20)**

Number correct _____ (A)
Number omitted _____ (B)
Number incorrect _____ (C)
$\frac{1}{4}$ (C) _____ (D)
(A) − (D) _____ Raw Score I

**Section 4: First 8 Questions (21–28)**

Number correct _____ (A)
Number omitted _____ (B)
Number incorrect _____ (C)
$\frac{1}{4}$ (C) _____ (D)
(A) − (D) _____ Raw Score II

**Section 4: Next 10 Questions (29–38)**

Number correct _____ Raw Score III

**Total Mathematics Raw Score**
Raw Scores I + II + III _____

**NOTE: In each section (A) + (B) + (C) should equal the number of questions in that section.**

### Writing Skills Section

**Section 5: 39 Questions (1–39)**

Number correct _____ (A)
Number omitted _____ (B)
Number incorrect _____ (C)
$\frac{1}{4}$ (C) _____ (D)

**Writing Skills Raw Score**
(A) − (D) _____

## Evaluation Chart

Study your score. Your raw score is an indication of your probable achievement on the PSAT/NMSQT. As a guide to the amount of work you need or want to do with this book, study the following.

| Raw Score | | | Self-Rating |
| --- | --- | --- | --- |
| *Critical Reading* | *Mathematics* | *Writing Skills* | |
| 42–48 | 35–38 | 33–39 | Superior |
| 37–41 | 30–34 | 28–32 | Very good |
| 32–36 | 25–29 | 23–27 | Good |
| 26–31 | 21–24 | 17–22 | Above average |
| 20–25 | 17–20 | 12–16 | Average |
| 12–19 | 10–16 | 7–11 | Below average |
| less than 12 | less than 10 | less than 7 | Inadequate |

Practice Test 3

# ANSWER EXPLANATIONS

## Section 1  Critical Reading

1. **(B)** The use of *but* indicates that the dean's attempt to keep control failed. It did so because it was *frustrated* by the board of trustees. None of the other possible actions of the board of trustees would necessarily have caused the dean's attempt to fail.

2. **(D)** To lack one's usual energy and interest in life is by definition to be *listless* (languid, spiritless). Note how the phrase following the comma serves to define the missing word.

3. **(B)** A plan for a journey is by definition an *itinerary*.

4. **(B)** Mark keeps his reservations or reluctance to go along with his fraternity's policies to himself: he says nothing. By saying nothing, he lets his fraternity brothers assume his *silence* is a sign of *acquiescence* or agreement.

5. **(E)** A *glutton* is by definition a person who eats or drinks excessively, someone who indulges his or her appetites without restraint.

6. **(C)** The phrase "given the . . ." signals cause and effect. *Because* many areas of conflict are still in need of *resolution* or settlement, we do not know what the outcome of the peace talks will be. In other words, the end result of the talks remains *problematic* (unclear and unsettled; perplexing).

7. **(A)** *While* signals a contrast. Bonner does not like religious or mystical (spiritual; not apparent to the senses) explanations of intelligence. Instead she likes *rational* (logical) and *materialistic* ones that define reality as explainable only in terms of physical matter.

8. **(D)** It would be unfortunate for a book to come down very firmly on one side of a debate if, in the process, it *skimmed over* (examined superficially or missed entirely) tricky spots in the argument and gave the reader a *simplistic*, oversimplified picture of the subject.

9. **(C)** If students talk about continental drift as if everyone has always known about the concept, then it is an *accepted concept* or commonplace.

10. **(B)** The author is denying that everyone has always known about the theory of continental drift. ("Not so.") He states that it was "not quite" a century ago that the theory was proposed. Thus, he is emphasizing the relatively *recent origin* of the theory.

11. **(D)** The passage serves simply to portray or *depict an instance of heroism under fire*.

12. **(B)** Kirkland could no longer bear or *endure* the cries of the dying.

13. **(C)** Repetition often is used rhetorically for emphasis. By asking question after question about why women's writing has taken the shape it has, the author *underscores* or emphasizes *how little is known about* a significant subject.

14. **(D)** To fill an office is to work in or *hold* that job.

15. **(B)** To make her point, Woolf gives *examples* of three women about whom little is known.

16. **(E)** "One was beautiful; one was red-haired; one was kissed by a Queen." What did these women have in common? They all led *largely unrecorded lives*: their grandchildren know only stray fragments about the history of these women's lives.

17. **(B)** You can answer this question by using the process of elimination. The author includes among the conditions of the average woman's life the question of whether she had money of her own, in other words, her *financial circumstances*. Therefore, you can eliminate Choice A. Likewise, the author wishes to know the number of the average woman's children in order to assess her *maternal obligations*. You can eliminate Choice C. In inquiring whether the average woman had servants or other household help, the author seeks information about her *social position* or rank. You can eliminate Choice D. Finally, in asking whether the average woman had a room to herself, the author seeks information about her *housing arrangements*. You can eliminate Choice E. Only Choice B

---

is left. It is the correct answer. The author never specifically inquires about the average woman's illnesses or *medical problems*.

18. **(B)** The writer neither lists (*enumerates*) nor sorts (*classifies*) anything in the opening paragraph.

    Choice A is incorrect. The writer likens the female tradition to a lost continent and develops the metaphor by describing the continent "rising . . . from the sea of English literature." Choice C is incorrect. The author refers or *alludes* to the classical legend of Atlantis. Choice D is incorrect. The author quotes Colby and Thompson. Choice E is incorrect. The author contrasts the revised view of women's literature with Mill's view.

19. **(C)** The legend of Atlantis tells of a continent that sank beneath the sea, only to rise again. The author uses the metaphor of the newly arisen lost continent to give the reader a sense of how an enormous body of *literary works written by women* has once more come to public attention, *resurfacing after many years*.

20. **(D)** The author opens the paragraph by stating that many literary critics have begun reinterpreting the study of women's literature. She then goes on to cite individual comments that support her assertion. Clearly, she is *receptive* or open to the ideas of these writers, for they and she share a common sense of the need to reinterpret their common field.

    Choices A and B are incorrect. The author cites the literary critics straightforwardly, presenting their statements as evidence supporting her thesis. Choice C is incorrect. The author does not *disparage* or belittle these critics. By quoting them respectfully she implicitly acknowledges their competence. Choice E is incorrect. The author quotes the critics as acknowledged experts in the field. However, she is quite ready to disagree with their conclusions (as she disagrees with Moers's view of women's literature as an international movement). Clearly, she does not look on these critics with *awe*.

21. **(E)** To study something with a special closeness is to pay *minute attention to details*.

22. **(B)** If women writers have no history, they have to rediscover the past. In the process, they *create* or forge their consciousness of what their sex has achieved. Here *forge* is used with its meaning of *fashion* or *make*, as blacksmiths forge metal by hammering it into shape. It is in this sense that James Joyce used *forge* in *A Portrait of the Artist as a Young Man*, whose hero goes forth to "forge in

the smithy of (his) soul the uncreated conscience of (his) race."

23. **(C)** The author both cites Moers's work in support of her own assertions and argues against the validity of Moers's conclusion that women's literature is an international movement. Thus, while she finds Moers's work basically *admirable* and worthy of respect, she considers it *inaccurate* in some of the conclusions it draws.

    Choice A is incorrect. The author would not cite Moers as she does in the second paragraph if she believed Moers to be wholly *misleading*. Choice B is incorrect. Since the author disagrees with at least one of Moers's conclusions, she obviously does not find Moers's work the *definitive* or final word. Choices D and E are incorrect. Neither is supported by the author's mentions of Moers.

24. **(D)** Woolf does not document her argument with extensive quotations from literary critics. Instead, she uses telling examples ("One was beautiful; one was red-haired; one was kissed by a Queen") to show how little we know about our grandmothers' actual lives. She is *less scholarly and more descriptive* in her approach to the subject.

## Section 2 Mathematics

For many problems, the explanation provides a reference to one or more **KEY FACTS** from Chapter 7. These are the mathematical facts that you need to solve that problem. If a solution refers to **KEY FACT J2**, for example, the solution depends on the second **KEY FACT** discussed in Section J of Chapter 7.

For some problems, an alternative solution, indicated by two asterisks (**), follows the first solution. When this occurs, usually one of the solutions is the direct mathematical one and the other is based on one of the tactics discussed in Chapters 6 and 7.

See page 244 for an explanation of the symbol $\Rightarrow$, which is used in several answer explanations.

1. **(B)** $\$88 \div \$16$ per hour $= 5.5$ hours.

    **If you prefer, set up a ratio and cross-multiply:

    $$\frac{16 \text{ dollars}}{1 \text{ hour}} = \frac{88 \text{ dollars}}{x \text{ hours}}.$$

2. **(D)** In 11 days Sarah saves $88. If 11 days ago she had $324, she now has $324 + $88 = $412, and 11 days from now will have $412 + $88 = $500.

    **From 11 days ago to 11 days from now is 22 days. In 22 days Sarah saves 22 × $8 = $176, and $176 + $324 = $500.

\*\*Remember, even on easy questions, some of the choices are absurd. Clearly, 11 days from now Sarah will have much more money than she did 11 days ago. So the answer has to be much more than $324. You can eliminate choices A and B and almost certainly C.

3. **(B)** The average of $a$ and $b$ is $\frac{a+b}{2}$, and the product of that with 7 is $7\left(\frac{a+b}{2}\right) = \frac{7a+7b}{2}$.

\*\*It is easier and quicker to do this directly. So substitute for $a$ and $b$, only if you get stuck or confused. If $a = 2$ and $b = 4$, their average is 3, and the product of 7 and their average is 21. Only Choice B is equal to 21 when $a = 2$ and $b = 4$.

4. **(D)** Let the number be $x$, and write the equation

$$\frac{3}{4}x = 7 + \frac{1}{6}x.$$

Multiply both sides by 12:  $\qquad 9x = 84 + 2x$

Subtract $2x$ from each side and divide by 7:

$$7x = 84 \Rightarrow x = 12$$

Be careful: 12 is *not* the answer. You were asked for $\frac{5}{3}$ of the number. $\frac{5}{3}(12) = 20$.

5. **(C)** By **KEY FACT K2**, the sum of the measures of two adjacent angles of a parallelogram is 180°. Therefore,

$$180 = 10x + 25x - 30 = 35x - 30,$$

which implies that $35x = 210$ and $x = 6$.

6. **(D)** There's nothing to do except check the choices, although it is often faster to start with E and work toward A.

E: $9*9 = \sqrt{9 + \sqrt{9}} = \sqrt{9 + 3} = \sqrt{12}$, which is not an integer.

D: $7*4 = \sqrt{7 + \sqrt{4}} = \sqrt{7 + 2} = \sqrt{9} = 3$, an integer. The answer is D. Once you find the answer, do not waste any time trying the other choices—they won't work.

7. **(B)** The factory produces 64 engines per day × 25 days per month × 12 months per year = 19,200 engines per year, and $96,000 \div 19,200 = 5$.

8. **(E)** Label each angle in the diagram.

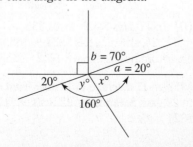

Since vertical angles are equal, $a = 20$, and so $x + y = 160$. We can see that $b = 70$, but there are no other vertical angles, and it is impossible to determine $x$ or $y$ from the information given.

9. **(C)** Since $x^2 - y^2 = (x - y)(x + y)$, then

$$75 = x^2 - y^2 = (x - y)(x + y) = 5(x + y).$$

Therefore, $x + y = 15$. Adding the equations

$$x + y = 15 \text{ and } x - y = 5, \text{ we get}$$
$$2x = 20 \Rightarrow x = 10 \Rightarrow y = 5.$$

\*\*Use **TACTIC 6-1**: backsolve. Choice C works.

10. **(D)** If Julie had to pay 30% of the value of her inheritance in taxes, she still owned 70% of her inheritance: 70% of 40% is 28% ($0.70 \times 0.40 = 0.28$).

\*\*Use **TACTIC 6-3**. Assume the estate was worth $100. Julie received 40% or $40. Her tax was 30% of $40, or $12. She still had $28, or 28% of the $100 estate.

11. **(C)** The given expression $(3!)(4!) = 6(24) = 144$. Now, evaluate the three choices.

I: $7! = 5040$, which is much too big (false).
II: $12!$ is even bigger (false).
III: $4! + 5! = 24 + 120 = 144$ (true).

III only is true.

12. **(B)** It is given that $BE = BC$; also $BC = AD$, since they are opposite sides of a rectangle. Label each of them $w$, as shown in the diagram.

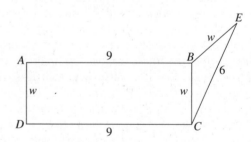

Then $R = 18 + 2w$ and $T = 6 + 2w$. So,
$$R - T = (18 + 2w) - (6 + 2w) = 18 - 6 = 12.$$

13. **(D)** Since the game takes one hour, or 60 minutes, and there are always 5 men playing, the game consists of $5 \times 60 = 300$ player-minutes. If that is evenly divided among the 12 players, each one plays $300 \div 12 = 25$ minutes.

\*\*If you get stuck, test the choices. Eliminate the choices that can't be right, and guess. If 5 men played the first 10 or 12 minutes and 5 other men played the next 10 or 12 minutes, there wouldn't be 5 men available to play the rest of the game. So 10

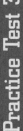

and 12 are much too small. Eliminate A and B. If 5 men played for 30 minutes and 5 other men played the next 30 minutes, the game would be over, and 2 men wouldn't have played at all. Eliminate E since 30 is too large. The answer must be 24 or 25.

14. **(D)** Since $A = \pi r^2$, $r^2 = \frac{A}{\pi}$ and $r = \sqrt{\frac{A}{\pi}} = \frac{\sqrt{A}}{\sqrt{\pi}}$.

The circumference, $C$, equals $2\pi r$. So,

$$C = 2\pi \frac{\sqrt{A}}{\sqrt{\pi}} = 2\sqrt{\pi}\sqrt{A} = 2\sqrt{\pi A}$$

**Let $r$, the radius of the circle, be 2. Then the circumference, $C$, is $2\pi r = 4\pi$ and the area, $A$, is $\pi r^2 = 4\pi$. Only choice D is equal to $4\pi$ when $A = 4\pi$.

15. **(D)** By **KEY FACT N4**, the slope $= \frac{y_2 - y_1}{x_2 - x_1}$.

Then $\frac{2}{3} = \frac{5 - (-3)}{k - 3} = \frac{8}{k - 3}$.

Cross-multiply:

$$24 = 2k - 6 \Rightarrow 2k = 30 \Rightarrow k = 15.$$

**If you don't remember the formula, make a quick sketch:

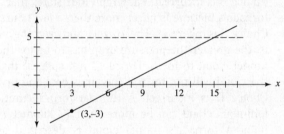

Since the slope is positive, $k$ is greater than 3, and since the slope is less than 1, the line is going up too slowly for $k$ to be 6 or 8. Guess 15.

16. **(A)** If $x$ is odd, so are $5x$ and $5x + 4$. To get the smallest odd number greater than $5x + 4$, add 2: $5x + 6$. On the other hand, $3x + 7$ is even, and the largest odd number smaller than it is 1 less than $3x + 7$, namely $3x + 6$. The required difference is $(5x + 6) - (3x + 6) = 2x$.

**Use **TACTIC 6-2** and let $x = 3$. The smallest odd number greater than 19 is 21; the largest odd number less than 16 is 15; and $21 - 15 = 6$.

Which answer equals 6 when $x = 3$? Only A.

17. **(C)** It's worth remembering that when the three angles of a triangle are in the ratio of 1:2:3, the triangle is a 30-60-90 right triangle. (If you don't remember that, then solve the equation $x + 2x + 3x = 180$.) In a 30-60-90 right triangle

the sides are $a$, $a\sqrt{3}$, and $2a$; so the desired ratio is $a:2a = 1:2$.

18. **(B)** At 2:00, the first car had been going 50 miles per hour for 2 hours and so had gone 100 miles. The second car covered the same 100 miles in 1 hour and 40 minutes, or $1\frac{2}{3} = \frac{5}{3}$ hours. Therefore, its rate was $100 \div \frac{5}{3} = 100 \times \frac{3}{5} = 60$ miles per hour.

19. **(B)** Since $a$ is inversely proportional to $b$, there is a constant $k$ such that $ab = k$. (See Section 7-D.)

So $k = (3)(5) = 15$.

Therefore, $10b = 15 \Rightarrow b = \frac{15}{10} = \frac{3}{2}$.

20. **(A)** If 12% of $a$ = 60% of $b$, then

$$.12a = .60b \Rightarrow 12a = 60b \Rightarrow b = \frac{12a}{50} = \frac{a}{5}.$$

So, $b$ is $\frac{1}{5}$ or 20% of $a$.

**Let $b = 100$. Then, since 12% of $a$ = 60% of $b$, we have $0.12a = 60$. So, $a = 60 \div 0.12 = 500$. Finally, 100 is $\frac{1}{5}$ or 20% of 500.

## Section 3 Critical Reading

25. **(A)** *Though* calls for a contrast. From someone with the reputation of a skilled craftsman, we expect fine work; instead, the work here is not polished but *crude*.

26. **(B)** According to the definition set off by dashes, the science of taxonomy is to classify or categorize living creatures, sorting them into groups with individual *names*.

27. **(E)** Why would fights break out in a small rookery? They would do so because there is not enough room to accommodate all the birds that need to build a nest. Because space is *limited*, each bird therefore must *vie for* (struggle or fight) its own patch of land.

28. **(D)** A person who could not support his claims for alleged cures with hard scientific data might as a consequence be called a *charlatan* (a faker or quack) by skeptics or disbelievers in his powers.

29. **(D)** It is Williams's *propensity* or liking for theatricality that causes critics to *denigrate* or belittle his plays as mere melodrama. Note how the use of *mere* and the sense of the Shakespearean quotation convey the idea that Williams's plays have been sullied or belittled.

30. **(E)** You can arrive at the correct answer by the process of elimination.

True scientists do not jump to conclusions but methodically work their way toward them. Therefore, they are *systematic* and *deliberate*. You can eliminate Choices A and B.

True scientists work toward their conclusions unerringly, that is, without making errors. Therefore, they are *accurate*. You can eliminate Choice C.

True scientists are not strangers to hard work. Instead, they are *diligent* or hard-working. You can eliminate Choice D.

Only Choice E is left. It is the correct answer. The author never characterizes true scientists as *inspired* in their approach to science.

31. **(C)** To champion a method or cause is to *espouse* (adopt or embrace) it.

32. **(B)** Unlike the author of Passage 1, the author of Passage 2 directly quotes a scientist, the naturalist Donald Culross Peattie. Thus, the author of Passage 2 makes use of *direct citation*. (Be on the lookout for quotation marks. They signal a direct quote or citation. While the author of Passage 1 refers to Boyle and Hooke by name, he does not quote them *directly*.)

33. **(C)** The author of Passage 1 wholeheartedly believes in the inductive method of reasoning, the modern scientific method advocated by Boyle and Hooke. Peattie, however, makes fun of this method and calls it plodding (poky and slow). It is therefore likely that the author of Passage 1 would respond to Peattie's mocking comments by arguing that Peattie *fails to appreciate the virtues of the inductive method sufficiently*.

34. **(C)** You can arrive at the correct answer by the process of elimination.

Statement I is true. The passage states that the tornado's lifetime is never more than a few hours. Therefore, you can eliminate Choices B and D.

Statement II is true. The first paragraph indicates that a fraction of the thunderstorm's tremendous energy "is concentrated into an area no more than several hundred meters in diameter." A later portion of the passage refers to the tornado's "concentrated high winds." Therefore, you can eliminate Choice A.

Statement III is untrue. The passage indicates that tornadoes may vary markedly in size and shape. Therefore, you can eliminate Choice E.

Only Choice C is left. It is the correct answer.

35. **(A)** The opening paragraph's concluding sentence serves as a *transition* or linking sentence connecting one part of the lengthy discussion to another. In this case, it introduces several paragraphs that describe tornadoes. The sentence is not a *concession* (acknowledgment; yielding a point in an argument). It is not an *apology* (expression of regret; formal defense). Neutral in tone, it is neither a *criticism* (serious judgment, often pointing out faults) nor a *refutation* (disproof of an argument).

36. **(E)** The reduced atmospheric pressure in the core region *pulls* or draws air to the base of the tornado.

37. **(E)** Paragraph three states that the "warmer and drier the inflowing air is, the greater the pressure drop must be for condensation to occur and a cloud to form." This suggests that temperature and humidity affect the tornado and that it *responds to changes in temperature and humidity*.

Choice A is incorrect. The passage indicates that in the Northern Hemisphere a tornado's winds may be counterclockwise; it never suggests that a tornado's winds are *invariably* counterclockwise. Choice B is incorrect. Paragraph four states that a tornado's lifetime is never more than a few hours. Choice C is incorrect. The *warmer* and *drier* the air is, the greater the pressure drop has to be for the funnel cloud to form. This does not suggest that the cloud will not form if the air is cool and dry. Choice D is incorrect. A thunderstorm's cumulonimbus cloud can be more than 17 kilometers high. A tornado's funnel cloud is described as smaller than this.

38. **(A)** The author states that "if the core fills with dust, the funnel may take on a more exotic hue, such as the red of west Oklahoma clay." The hue or color of the funnel thus depends on what the soil in that region is made of.

39. **(D)** The author suggests a hypothesis (tornado noise "may result from the interaction of the concentrated high winds with the ground"). He provides a concrete example ("the red of west Oklahoma clay"). He indicates a time span ("never more than a few hours"). He uses similes ("roaring like a freight train"). He does not, however, argue a particular point of view.

40. **(D)** The author calls the industrialists and their "couldn't-lose" bankers and backers "canny boys" (shrewd fellows) and says the adults considered stories about these wheelers and dealers "inspirational to children." Clearly, she finds neither the stories nor the men inspirational: she looks on both with *irony*.

**41. (B)** In stating that she and the other children were "unthinkingly familiar" with the moguls' enormous buildings "as so much weird scenery on long drives," the author reveals that the children viewed these buildings as an accepted *backdrop to their lives*, something they saw in passing without giving it much thought.

**42. (B)** The moguls were fabulous men in being *celebrated* or famed for their wealth and philanthropy.

**43. (B)** The author's remark here can best be described as *an ironic aside*, a parenthetic comment that digresses from the theme or topic under discussion.

**44. (D)** The mother's tone in this comment is highly sardonic. Clearly, she is not someone who cares to rave or talk boastfully about her good birth and noble connections. Instead, she dismisses such people as snobs and dismisses Europe as a fit home for snobs.

**45. (C)** Beneath the lawns lie musket balls and arrowheads and bones, all relics of *Pittsburgh's buried past*. Note that in the paragraph that immediately follows this description the author cites details from Pittsburgh's history.

**46. (D)** To say that one knows something and does not know it is to state a *paradox*, an apparently self-contradictory declaration.

**47. (E)** In breaking the wilderness, the first white settlers *penetrated* the forest, bursting through the undergrowth into territory known only to the Native Americans.

**48. (B)** Summing up Pittsburgh's history, the author starts with modern big industry and works her way back in time till she concludes citing the pioneers who were the first white settlers in the region. Thus, she organizes the paragraph in *reverse chronological order*.

## Section 4  Mathematics

For many problems, the explanation provides a reference to one or more **KEY FACTS** from Chapter 7. These are the mathematical facts that you need to solve that problem. If a solution refers to **KEY FACT J2**, for example, the solution depends on the second **KEY FACT** discussed in Section J of Chapter 7.

For some problems, an alternative solution, indicated by two asterisks (**), follows the first solution. When this occurs, usually one of the solutions is the direct mathematical one and the other is based on one of the tactics discussed in Chapters 6 and 7.

See page 244 for an explanation of the symbol $\Rightarrow$, which is used in several answer explanations.

**21. (B)** If $x = -5$, then
$$2x^2 - 4x - 3 = 2(-5)^2 - 4(-5) - 3 =$$
$$2(25) + 20 - 3 = 67.$$

**22. (C)** Since $x + 100 = 180$, $x = 80$; also,
$$y + y + x = 180 \Rightarrow$$
$$2y + 80 = 180 \Rightarrow$$
$$2y = 100 \Rightarrow y = 50.$$

**Since by **KEY FACT J2** the measure of an exterior angle of a triangle is equal to the sum of the measures of the two opposite interior angles, $100 = y + y$. So, $y = 50$.

**23. (C)** $12 = \frac{1}{b} + \frac{1}{b} + \frac{1}{b} + \frac{1}{b} = \frac{4}{b} \Rightarrow 12b = 4$

So, $b = \frac{4}{12} = \frac{1}{3}$.

**24. (E)** If $d$ of the cartons were unpacked, $c - d$ were still full, so the fraction of the cartons that were not yet unpacked was $\frac{c-d}{c}$. To get the percent, multiply the fractional part by 100%: $\frac{100\,(c-d)}{c}$%.

**Use **TACTIC 8-2**. If Lucy had 10 cartons to unpack, then after unpacking 2 of them, 8 of the 10 (80%) still had to be unpacked. Only $\frac{100(c-d)}{c}$% equals 80% when $c = 10$ and $d = 2$.

**25. (C)** Since the sum of the measures of the two acute angles of a right triangle is $90°$, $a + d = 90$. Also, $b + c = 180$. Therefore,
$$a + b + c + d = 90 + 180 = 270.$$

**26. (D)** First add $\frac{1}{3} + \frac{1}{4}$ and then subtract that sum from both sides:
$$\frac{1}{x} + \left(\frac{1}{3} + \frac{1}{4}\right) = \frac{1}{x} + \frac{7}{12} = 1 \Rightarrow \frac{1}{x} = \frac{5}{12}.$$

Finally, take the reciprocal of each side (or cross-multiply): $x = \frac{12}{5}$.

27. **(C)** Since $AB = AC$, by **KEY FACT J2**, $m\angle B = m\angle C$. So, by **KEY FACT J1**,

$$30 + m\angle B + m\angle C = 180 \Rightarrow$$
$$m\angle B + m\angle C = 150 \Rightarrow m\angle B = 75.$$

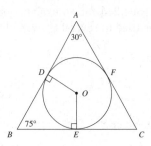

Also, since $\overline{AB}$ and $\overline{BC}$ are tangents, then, by **KEY FACT L10**, the radii $\overline{OD}$ and $\overline{OE}$ are perpendicular to $\overline{AB}$ and $\overline{BC}$, respectively, and hence form 90° angles. Finally, by **KEY FACT K1**, the sum of the four angles in quadrilateral *ODBE* is 360:

$$75 + 90 + 90 + m\angle DOE = 360 \Rightarrow$$
$$255 + m\angle DOE = 360 \Rightarrow m\angle DOE = 105.$$

28. **(C)** According to the triangle inequality **(KEY FACT J9)**, the sum of the lengths of two sides of a triangle must be greater than the length of the third. Now use **TACTIC 6-10**: systematically test each possibility. Try choosing 1 from *A*: you can't choose 2 from *B*, because $1 + 2 = 3$, which is not greater than any number in *C*; you can, however, choose 3 from *B* and 3 from *C*. So one way is (1,3,3). The other ways are (2,2,3), (2,3,3), and (2,3,4), a total of 4 ways.

29. **(308)** Don't do any algebra. Just replace *a* and *b* by 7 and 11 in the original expression:

$$(7 + 11)^2 - (7 - 11)^2 =$$
$$18^2 - (-4)^2 = 324 - 16 = 308.$$

30. $\left(\dfrac{22}{6} \textbf{ or } \dfrac{11}{3} \textbf{ or } \textbf{3.66}\right)$ Notice that the left-hand side of the equation is the negative of the right-hand side, meaning that each side is equal to 0. Therefore,

$$3x - 11 = 0 \Rightarrow 3x = 11 \Rightarrow x = \frac{11}{3}.$$

**Just solve the equation

$$3x - 11 = 11 - 3x \Rightarrow 6x = 22 \Rightarrow x = \frac{22}{6}.$$

Note that it is *not* necessary to reduce $\frac{22}{6}$. (It's not even advisable.)

31. **(150)** Since Len got $100, the other three shared the remaining $900. If *x* represents Jim's share, then Kim got 2*x* and Ben got 3*x*. Then

$$900 = x + 2x + 3x = 6x \Rightarrow x = 150.$$

32. **(79)** For a fraction to be large, the numerator should be as large as possible and the denominator as small as possible. The greatest value that $x^2 - y$ could have is 80, by letting $x = 9$ and $y = 1$. Since $x, y$, and $z$ are different, the least that $z$ could be is 2, and the value of the fraction would be $\frac{80}{2}$, or 40. However, if you interchange $x$ and $y$, you get 79 for the numerator ($9^2 - 2$) and 1 for the denominator: $\frac{79}{1}$ or 79.

33. $\left(\dfrac{3}{2} \textbf{ or } \textbf{1.5}\right)$ The center of a circle is the midpoint of any diameter. Therefore, by the midpoint formula **(KEY FACT N3)**

$$(x,y) = \left(\frac{-3+5}{2}, \frac{2+(-1)}{2}\right) = \left(\frac{2}{2}, \frac{1}{2}\right) = \left(1, \frac{1}{2}\right).$$

So $x + y = 1 + \frac{1}{2} = 1\frac{1}{2}.$

Note: Since you cannot grid-in a mixed number, you *must* enter $1\frac{1}{2}$ as $\frac{3}{2}$ or 1.5.

34. **(2)** Since the repeating portion of this decimal number is 6 digits long, divide 200 by 6 to determine how many times the sequence 4, 2, 8, 5, 7, 1 repeats in the first 200 digits. When 200 is divided by 6, the quotient is 33.333 . . . Ignore the decimal portion. There are 33 complete repetitions, and since $33 \times 6 = 198$, the 198th digit ends the 33rd group and so is a 1. Then the 199th digit is 4, and the 200th digit is 2.

35. **(21)** The sum of 2 two-digit numbers must be less than 200; so $A = 1$, and the sum is 111. If $B + D$ were 1, either $B$ or $D$ would be 0 and the other would be 1; but $A = 1$ and each letter represents a different digit. So $B + D$ must be 11, which means that 1 is carried into the tens column. In the tens column we must add 1 (for $A$), the 1 we carried, and $C$, and the sum is 11. Then $1 + 1 + C = 11$, and $C = 9$.

So, $A = 1$, $C = 9$, and $B + D = 11$. Therefore, $A + B + C + D = 1 + 9 + 11 = 21$.

36. **(1)** Since the entire region is a circle of radius 4, its area is $\pi(4)^2 = 16\pi$. The shaded region is a circle of radius 3 minus the small white circle of radius 1; so its area is $9\pi - \pi = 8\pi$ ($a = 8\pi$). The area of the white region can be found by subtracting the area of the shaded region ($8\pi$) from the total area ($16\pi$). So $b = 16\pi - 8\pi = 8\pi$. Finally, $\frac{a}{b} = \frac{8\pi}{8\pi} = 1.$

37. **(52)** This is a weighted average:

$$\frac{40\%(40) + 60\%(60)}{100\%} = \frac{16 + 36}{1} = 52.$$

\*\*If you prefer, assume there are 100 marbles, 40 of which are red and 60 of which are blue:

$$\frac{40(40) + 60(60)}{100} = \frac{1600 + 3600}{100} = 52.$$

38. **(6)** Let $x$ represent the degree measure of each exterior angle, and then $2x$ is the degree measure of each interior angle. Since the sum of the measures of an interior and exterior angle is 180°: $x + 2x = 180 \Rightarrow 3x = 180 \Rightarrow x = 60$. Since the sum of the measures of all the exterior angles of a polygon is 360°, there are $360 \div 60 = 6$ angles and, of course, 6 sides.

## Section 5  Writing Skills

1. **(E)** Error in pronoun case. The noun or pronoun preceding a gerund (*going*) should be in the possessive case.

2. **(E)** Error in modification. The dangling modifier is best corrected in Choice E.

3. **(C)** Comma splice. Choices A and B are run-on sentences. Choices D and E are ungrammatical.

4. **(E)** Error in modification and double negative. Both are corrected in Choice E.

5. **(E)** Error in coordination and subordination. By changing *having* to *had* and connecting the two main clauses with a semicolon, you tighten the sentence and eliminate wordiness.

6. **(B)** Sentence fragment. Choice B expresses the author's meaning directly and concisely. All other choices are indirect, ungrammatical, or fail to retain the meaning of the original statement.

7. **(C)** Error in agreement. *Kind* should be modified by *this* or *that*; *kinds*, by *these* or *those*.

8. **(C)** Error in parallelism. *New, list,* and *service* are all nouns. Thus, parallel structure is retained in Choice C.

9. **(D)** This corrects the sentence fragment smoothly.

10. **(B)** Error in logical comparison. Compare *complaints* with *complaints*, not with *customers*. The faulty comparison is corrected in Choice B.

11. **(C)** Error in modification. Choice C corrects the misplaced modifier and eliminates the unnecessary use of the passive voice.

12. **(C)** Error in subject-verb agreement. The phrase *along with his staff* is not part of the subject of the sentence. The subject is *President Obama* (singular); the verb should be *is traveling* (singular).

13. **(B)** Error in coordination and subordination. The use of the subordinating conjunction *Although* and the deletion of unnecessary words strengthen this sentence.

14. **(D)** Choices A, B, and C have dangling modifiers; Choice E creates a run-on sentence.

15. **(A)** Sentence is correct.

16. **(C)** Double negative. Change *cannot do nothing* to *can do nothing*.

17. **(E)** Error in sequence of tenses. The present perfect tense (*have damaged*) refers to some unspecified time in the past. Here, however, the author is telling about something that occurred at a definite time in the past: "In 1940, during the Battle of Britain." In this context, the simple past tense (*damaged*) is correct.

18. **(C)** Adjective-adverb confusion. The adverb phrase *Not surprisingly* modifies (describes or limits) the rest of the sentence.

19. **(A)** Sentence is correct.

20. **(A)** Sentence is correct.

21. **(B)** Error in diction. *Affect* is a verb and should not be used in place of *effect*.

22. **(E)** Sentence is correct.

23. **(C)** Error in diction. There is no such verb as *enthuse*. Change *enthused* to *enthusiastic*.

24. **(C)** Error in tense. Change *had shot* to *shot*.

25. **(A)** Error in diction. Use *irritated* instead of *aggravated*.

26. **(A)** Error in idiom. Change *neither . . . or* to *neither . . . nor*.

27. **(C)** Error in diction. Change *incredulous* to *incredible*.

28. **(C)** Error in tense. Change *had broke* to *had broken*.

29. **(C)** Error in subject-verb agreement. The subject, *Ann Landers*, is singular; the verb should be singular—*is*.

30. **(D)** Error in diction. Issues are *decided* or settled. The actual choice made is what is *decided upon*. Delete *upon*.

31. **(E)** Sentence is correct.

32. **(C)** Error in subject-verb agreement. The subject, *general*, is singular; the verb should be singular—*seems*.

33. **(A)** Error in pronoun case. The possessive pronoun precedes a gerund. Change *him* to *his*.

34. **(D)** Error in tense. Change *was to be immortalized* to *was immortalized*.

35. **(D)** Choices A, B, and C abruptly state the contrasting point of view without regard to the context.

    Choice D takes the context into account and provides for a smooth progression of thought. It is the best answer.

    Choice E is confusing. It is unclear until the end of the sentence whether the *other members* support or oppose the exhibit.

36. **(B)** Choice A lacks a main verb; therefore, it is a sentence fragment.

    Choice B accurately combines the sentences. It is the best answer.

    Choice C expresses the idea in a way that the writer could not have intended.

    Choice D subordinates important ideas and emphasizes a lesser one.

    Choice E restates the idea in a manner that changes the writer's intended meaning.

37. **(A)** Choice A is the best choice because the sentences contain basic information about the topic. Readers are left in the dark unless the information appears as early as possible in the essay.

38. **(E)** Choice A contains faulty idiom; the phrase *than of the past* is nonstandard usage. Choice B contains a faulty comparison; *society* and *the past* cannot be logically compared. Choice C contains an error in idiom; the phrase *than from* is redundant. Choice D is correct but excessively wordy. Choice E is the best answer.

39. **(C)** Choice A provides a reasonable transition, but it contains an error in pronoun-antecedent agreement. The pronoun *they* is plural; its antecedent *anyone* is singular.

    Choice B contains an error in diction. One can *disapprove of* but not *disagree with* a piece of art.

    Choice C alludes to the content of the previous paragraph and is clearly and succinctly expressed. It is the best answer.

    Choice D contains an error in pronoun-antecedent agreement. The pronoun *them* is plural; the antecedent *anyone* is singular.

    Choice E is inconsistent in tone and mood with the rest of the essay.

# Answer Sheet—Practice Test 4

Each mark should completely fill the appropriate space, and should be as dark as all other marks. Make all erasures complete. Traces of an erasure may be read as an answer.

### Section 1 – Critical Reading
#### 25 minutes

1 Ⓐ Ⓑ Ⓒ Ⓓ Ⓔ
2 Ⓐ Ⓑ Ⓒ Ⓓ Ⓔ
3 Ⓐ Ⓑ Ⓒ Ⓓ Ⓔ
4 Ⓐ Ⓑ Ⓒ Ⓓ Ⓔ
5 Ⓐ Ⓑ Ⓒ Ⓓ Ⓔ
6 Ⓐ Ⓑ Ⓒ Ⓓ Ⓔ
7 Ⓐ Ⓑ Ⓒ Ⓓ Ⓔ
8 Ⓐ Ⓑ Ⓒ Ⓓ Ⓔ
9 Ⓐ Ⓑ Ⓒ Ⓓ Ⓔ
10 Ⓐ Ⓑ Ⓒ Ⓓ Ⓔ
11 Ⓐ Ⓑ Ⓒ Ⓓ Ⓔ
12 Ⓐ Ⓑ Ⓒ Ⓓ Ⓔ
13 Ⓐ Ⓑ Ⓒ Ⓓ Ⓔ
14 Ⓐ Ⓑ Ⓒ Ⓓ Ⓔ
15 Ⓐ Ⓑ Ⓒ Ⓓ Ⓔ
16 Ⓐ Ⓑ Ⓒ Ⓓ Ⓔ
17 Ⓐ Ⓑ Ⓒ Ⓓ Ⓔ
18 Ⓐ Ⓑ Ⓒ Ⓓ Ⓔ
19 Ⓐ Ⓑ Ⓒ Ⓓ Ⓔ
20 Ⓐ Ⓑ Ⓒ Ⓓ Ⓔ
21 Ⓐ Ⓑ Ⓒ Ⓓ Ⓔ
22 Ⓐ Ⓑ Ⓒ Ⓓ Ⓔ
23 Ⓐ Ⓑ Ⓒ Ⓓ Ⓔ
24 Ⓐ Ⓑ Ⓒ Ⓓ Ⓔ

### Section 2 – Math
#### 25 minutes

1 Ⓐ Ⓑ Ⓒ Ⓓ Ⓔ
2 Ⓐ Ⓑ Ⓒ Ⓓ Ⓔ
3 Ⓐ Ⓑ Ⓒ Ⓓ Ⓔ
4 Ⓐ Ⓑ Ⓒ Ⓓ Ⓔ
5 Ⓐ Ⓑ Ⓒ Ⓓ Ⓔ
6 Ⓐ Ⓑ Ⓒ Ⓓ Ⓔ
7 Ⓐ Ⓑ Ⓒ Ⓓ Ⓔ
8 Ⓐ Ⓑ Ⓒ Ⓓ Ⓔ
9 Ⓐ Ⓑ Ⓒ Ⓓ Ⓔ
10 Ⓐ Ⓑ Ⓒ Ⓓ Ⓔ
11 Ⓐ Ⓑ Ⓒ Ⓓ Ⓔ
12 Ⓐ Ⓑ Ⓒ Ⓓ Ⓔ
13 Ⓐ Ⓑ Ⓒ Ⓓ Ⓔ
14 Ⓐ Ⓑ Ⓒ Ⓓ Ⓔ
15 Ⓐ Ⓑ Ⓒ Ⓓ Ⓔ
16 Ⓐ Ⓑ Ⓒ Ⓓ Ⓔ
17 Ⓐ Ⓑ Ⓒ Ⓓ Ⓔ
18 Ⓐ Ⓑ Ⓒ Ⓓ Ⓔ
19 Ⓐ Ⓑ Ⓒ Ⓓ Ⓔ
20 Ⓐ Ⓑ Ⓒ Ⓓ Ⓔ

### Section 3 – Critical Reading
#### 25 minutes

25 Ⓐ Ⓑ Ⓒ Ⓓ Ⓔ
26 Ⓐ Ⓑ Ⓒ Ⓓ Ⓔ
27 Ⓐ Ⓑ Ⓒ Ⓓ Ⓔ
28 Ⓐ Ⓑ Ⓒ Ⓓ Ⓔ
29 Ⓐ Ⓑ Ⓒ Ⓓ Ⓔ
30 Ⓐ Ⓑ Ⓒ Ⓓ Ⓔ
31 Ⓐ Ⓑ Ⓒ Ⓓ Ⓔ
32 Ⓐ Ⓑ Ⓒ Ⓓ Ⓔ
33 Ⓐ Ⓑ Ⓒ Ⓓ Ⓔ
34 Ⓐ Ⓑ Ⓒ Ⓓ Ⓔ
35 Ⓐ Ⓑ Ⓒ Ⓓ Ⓔ
36 Ⓐ Ⓑ Ⓒ Ⓓ Ⓔ
37 Ⓐ Ⓑ Ⓒ Ⓓ Ⓔ
38 Ⓐ Ⓑ Ⓒ Ⓓ Ⓔ
39 Ⓐ Ⓑ Ⓒ Ⓓ Ⓔ
40 Ⓐ Ⓑ Ⓒ Ⓓ Ⓔ
41 Ⓐ Ⓑ Ⓒ Ⓓ Ⓔ
42 Ⓐ Ⓑ Ⓒ Ⓓ Ⓔ
43 Ⓐ Ⓑ Ⓒ Ⓓ Ⓔ
44 Ⓐ Ⓑ Ⓒ Ⓓ Ⓔ
45 Ⓐ Ⓑ Ⓒ Ⓓ Ⓔ
46 Ⓐ Ⓑ Ⓒ Ⓓ Ⓔ
47 Ⓐ Ⓑ Ⓒ Ⓓ Ⓔ
48 Ⓐ Ⓑ Ⓒ Ⓓ Ⓔ

## Section 4 – Math
### 25 minutes

21 Ⓐ Ⓑ Ⓒ Ⓓ Ⓔ
22 Ⓐ Ⓑ Ⓒ Ⓓ Ⓔ
23 Ⓐ Ⓑ Ⓒ Ⓓ Ⓔ
24 Ⓐ Ⓑ Ⓒ Ⓓ Ⓔ
25 Ⓐ Ⓑ Ⓒ Ⓓ Ⓔ
26 Ⓐ Ⓑ Ⓒ Ⓓ Ⓔ
27 Ⓐ Ⓑ Ⓒ Ⓓ Ⓔ
28 Ⓐ Ⓑ Ⓒ Ⓓ Ⓔ

29

30

31

32

33

34

35

36

37

38

## Section 5 – Writing
### 30 minutes

1 Ⓐ Ⓑ Ⓒ Ⓓ Ⓔ
2 Ⓐ Ⓑ Ⓒ Ⓓ Ⓔ
3 Ⓐ Ⓑ Ⓒ Ⓓ Ⓔ
4 Ⓐ Ⓑ Ⓒ Ⓓ Ⓔ
5 Ⓐ Ⓑ Ⓒ Ⓓ Ⓔ
6 Ⓐ Ⓑ Ⓒ Ⓓ Ⓔ
7 Ⓐ Ⓑ Ⓒ Ⓓ Ⓔ
8 Ⓐ Ⓑ Ⓒ Ⓓ Ⓔ
9 Ⓐ Ⓑ Ⓒ Ⓓ Ⓔ
10 Ⓐ Ⓑ Ⓒ Ⓓ Ⓔ
11 Ⓐ Ⓑ Ⓒ Ⓓ Ⓔ
12 Ⓐ Ⓑ Ⓒ Ⓓ Ⓔ
13 Ⓐ Ⓑ Ⓒ Ⓓ Ⓔ
14 Ⓐ Ⓑ Ⓒ Ⓓ Ⓔ
15 Ⓐ Ⓑ Ⓒ Ⓓ Ⓔ
16 Ⓐ Ⓑ Ⓒ Ⓓ Ⓔ
17 Ⓐ Ⓑ Ⓒ Ⓓ Ⓔ
18 Ⓐ Ⓑ Ⓒ Ⓓ Ⓔ
19 Ⓐ Ⓑ Ⓒ Ⓓ Ⓔ
20 Ⓐ Ⓑ Ⓒ Ⓓ Ⓔ
21 Ⓐ Ⓑ Ⓒ Ⓓ Ⓔ
22 Ⓐ Ⓑ Ⓒ Ⓓ Ⓔ
23 Ⓐ Ⓑ Ⓒ Ⓓ Ⓔ
24 Ⓐ Ⓑ Ⓒ Ⓓ Ⓔ
25 Ⓐ Ⓑ Ⓒ Ⓓ Ⓔ
26 Ⓐ Ⓑ Ⓒ Ⓓ Ⓔ
27 Ⓐ Ⓑ Ⓒ Ⓓ Ⓔ
28 Ⓐ Ⓑ Ⓒ Ⓓ Ⓔ
29 Ⓐ Ⓑ Ⓒ Ⓓ Ⓔ
30 Ⓐ Ⓑ Ⓒ Ⓓ Ⓔ
31 Ⓐ Ⓑ Ⓒ Ⓓ Ⓔ
32 Ⓐ Ⓑ Ⓒ Ⓓ Ⓔ
33 Ⓐ Ⓑ Ⓒ Ⓓ Ⓔ
34 Ⓐ Ⓑ Ⓒ Ⓓ Ⓔ
35 Ⓐ Ⓑ Ⓒ Ⓓ Ⓔ
36 Ⓐ Ⓑ Ⓒ Ⓓ Ⓔ
37 Ⓐ Ⓑ Ⓒ Ⓓ Ⓔ
38 Ⓐ Ⓑ Ⓒ Ⓓ Ⓔ
39 Ⓐ Ⓑ Ⓒ Ⓓ Ⓔ

# SECTION 1/CRITICAL READING

TIME: 25 MINUTES

24 QUESTIONS (1–24)

**Directions:** For each question in this section, select the best answer from among the choices given and fill in the corresponding circle on the answer sheet.

---

Each sentence below has one or two blanks, each blank indicating that something has been omitted. Beneath the sentence are five words or sets of words labeled A through E. Choose the word or set of words that, when inserted in the sentence, best fits the meaning of the sentence as a whole.

**EXAMPLE:**

Medieval kingdoms did not become constitutional republics overnight; on the contrary, the change was ----.

(A) unpopular   (B) unexpected
(C) advantageous   (D) sufficient   (E) gradual

Ⓐ Ⓑ Ⓒ Ⓓ ●

---

1. The traditional French café is slowly becoming ----, a victim to the growing popularity of *le fast food*.

   (A) celebrated   (B) indispensable
   (C) prevalent   (D) extinct   (E) fashionable

2. Although we expected the women's basketball coach to be ---- over the recent victory of the team, we found her surprisingly ----.

   (A) ecstatic..gleeful
   (B) ambivalent..devious
   (C) triumphant..responsive
   (D) elated..naive
   (E) jubilant..disheartened

3. The debate coach suggested that he eliminate his ---- remarks in his otherwise serious speech because they were ----.

   (A) bantering..inappropriate
   (B) jesting..accurate
   (C) solemn..irrelevant
   (D) tacit..digressive
   (E) perfunctory..inconsiderate

4. Many young people and adults, uncomfortable with math, feel it is a subject best ---- engineers, scientists, and that small, elite group endowed at birth with a talent for the ---- world of numbers.

   (A) ignored by..abstract
   (B) suited to..accessible
   (C) studied by..interminable
   (D) left to..esoteric
   (E) avoided by..abstruse

5. Her novel published to universal acclaim, her literary gifts acknowledged by the chief figures of the Harlem Renaissance, her reputation as yet ---- by envious slights, Hurston clearly was at the ---- of her career.

   (A) undamaged..ebb
   (B) untarnished..zenith
   (C) untainted..end
   (D) blackened..mercy
   (E) unmarred..whim

**GO ON TO NEXT PAGE ▶**

**Directions:** The passages below are followed by questions based on their content; questions following a pair of related passages may also be based on the relationship between the paired passages. Answer the questions on the basis of what is stated or implied in the passages and in any introductory material that may be provided.

**Questions 6–9 are based on the following passages.**

**Passage 1**

Although commonly held up as a cornerstone of American democracy, the Mayflower Compact had little impact on the growth of freedom in
Line America. Indeed, the compact limited its signers'
5  liberty. That was its intent. Of the *Mayflower*'s 100 emigrants, less than half were Pilgrims. The rest were "strangers," non-Pilgrims who, finding themselves hundreds of miles north of their planned destination in Virginia, believed them-
10  selves outside the bounds of governmental authority. Rather than respect the rules of the Pilgrims, these strangers wanted to go their own way. By signing the compact, both Pilgrims and non-Pilgrims agreed to accept whatever form of
15  government was established after landing.

**Passage 2**

What is the Mayflower Compact? It is a social contract that established a system of government by voluntary agreement. Forty-one men of differ-ent social classes, some Pilgrims, some not, all
20  committed to a new life in a new land, were equal signers of this remarkable document. At a time when the liberties of Englishmen were still con-strained by the remains of the feudal system, this compact laid a sound foundation for the principle
25  of government by mutual consent of the gov-erned. Let others belittle its importance if they will. To me, the Mayflower Compact will always be a cornerstone of American democracy.

**6.** In line 1, "held up" most nearly means

(A) delayed   (B) cited   (C) accommodated
(D) waylaid   (E) carried

**7.** The author of the Passage 1 can best be described as

(A) a debunker   (B) an atheist
(C) a mythmaker   (D) an elitist
(E) an authoritarian

**8.** Unlike the author of Passage 1, the author of Passage 2 makes use of

(A) historical data
(B) direct quotation
(C) personal voice
(D) specific details
(E) literary anecdotes

**9.** The author of Passage 2 would most likely argue that the opening assertion of Passage 1 (lines 1–4) was

(A) meant to be taken literally
(B) accurate and to the point
(C) unnecessarily cautious
(D) taken out of context
(E) of dubious validity

**Directions:** Each passage below is followed by questions based on its content. Answer the questions following each passage on the basis of what is <u>stated</u> or <u>implied</u> in that passage and in any introductory material that may be provided.

**Questions 10–15 are based on the following passage.**

*The following passage is excerpted from a book on prominent black Americans during Franklin Delano Roosevelt's presidency.*

Like her white friends Eleanor Roosevelt and Aubrey Williams, Mary Bethune believed in the fundamental commitment of the New Deal to
Line  assist the black American's struggle and in the
5    need for blacks to assume responsibilities to help win that struggle. Unlike those of her white liberal associates, however, Bethune's ideas had evolved out of a long experience as a "race leader." Founder of a small black college in Florida, she
10   had become widely known by 1935 as an organizer of black women's groups and as a civil and political rights activist. Deeply religious, certain of her own capabilities, she held a relatively uncluttered view of what she felt were the New Deal's
15   and her own people's obligations to the cause of racial justice. Unafraid to speak her mind to powerful whites, including the President, or to differing black factions, she combined faith in the ultimate willingness of whites to discard their
20   prejudice and bigotry with a strong sense of racial pride and commitment to Negro self-help.
     More than her liberal white friends, Bethune argued for a strong and direct black voice in initiating and shaping government policy. She pursued
25   this in her conversations with President Roosevelt, in numerous memoranda to Aubrey Williams, and in her administrative work as head of the National Youth Administration's Office of Negro Affairs. With the assistance of Williams, she was successful in
30   having blacks selected to NYA posts at the national, state, and local levels. But she also wanted a black presence throughout the federal government. At the beginning of the war she joined other black leaders in demanding appointments to the Selective Service
35   Board and to the Department of the Army; and she was instrumental in 1941 in securing Earl Dickerson's membership on the Fair Employment Practices Committee. By 1944, she was still making appeals for black representation in "all public pro-
40   grams, federal, state, and local," and "in policy-making posts as well as rank and file jobs."

Though recognizing the weakness in the Roosevelt administration's response to Negro needs, Mary Bethune remained in essence a black
45   partisan champion of the New Deal during the 1930s and 1940s. Her strong advocacy of administration policies and programs was predicated on a number of factors: her assessment of the low status of black Americans during the Depression; her
50   faith in the willingness of some liberal whites to work for the inclusion of blacks in the government's reform and recovery measures; her conviction that only massive federal aid could elevate the Negro economically; and her belief that the thir-
55   ties and forties were producing a more self-aware and self-assured black population. Like a number of her white friends in government, Bethune assumed that the preservation of democracy and black people's "full integration into the benefits
60   and the responsibilities" of American life were inextricably tied together. She was convinced that, with the help of a friendly government, a militant, aggressive "New Negro" would emerge out of the devastation of depression and war, a "New Negro"
65   who would "save America from itself," who would lead America toward the full realization of its democratic ideas.

**10.** The author's primary goal in the passage is to do which of the following?
(A) criticize Mary Bethune for adhering too closely to New Deal policies
(B) argue that Mary Bethune was too optimistic in her assessment of race relations
(C) explore Mary Bethune's convictions and her influence on black progress in the Roosevelt years
(D) point out the weaknesses of the white liberal approach to black needs during Roosevelt's presidency
(E) summarize the attainments of blacks under the auspices of Roosevelt's New Deal

**GO ON TO NEXT PAGE** ▶

11. It can be inferred from the passage that Aubrey Williams was which of the following?

   I. A man with influence in the National Youth Administration
   II. A white liberal
   III. A man of strong religious convictions

(A) I only
(B) II only
(C) I and II only
(D) II and III only
(E) I, II, and III

12. The author mentions Earl Dickerson (lines 36–37) primarily in order to

(A) cite an instance of Bethune's political impact
(B) contrast his career with that of Bethune
(C) introduce the subject of a subsequent paragraph
(D) provide an example of Bethune's "New Negro"
(E) show that Dickerson was a leader of his fellow blacks

13. In line 36, "instrumental" most nearly means

(A) subordinate  (B) triumphant  (C) musical
(D) gracious  (E) helpful

14. It can be inferred from the passage that Bethune believed the "New Negro" would "save America from itself" (lines 61–67) by

(A) joining the Army and helping America overthrow its Fascist enemies
(B) helping America accomplish its egalitarian ideals
(C) voting for administration antipoverty programs
(D) electing other blacks to government office
(E) expressing a belief in racial pride

15. The author uses all the following techniques in the passage EXCEPT

(A) comparison and contrast
(B) development of an extended metaphor
(C) direct quotation
(D) general statement and concrete examples
(E) repetition of central ideas

**Questions 16–24 are based upon the following passage.**

*In this excerpt from the novel* Hard Times *by Charles Dickens, the reader is introduced to Thomas Gradgrind, headmaster of a so-called model school.*

Thomas Gradgrind, sir. A man of realities. A man of facts and calculations. A man who proceeds upon the principle that two and two are
Line four, and nothing over, and who is not to be
5 talked into allowing for anything over. Thomas Gradgrind, sir—peremptorily Thomas—Thomas Gradgrind. With a rule and a pair of scales, and the multiplication table always in his pocket, sir, ready to weigh and measure any parcel of human
10 nature, and tell you exactly what it comes to. It is a mere question of figures, a case of simple arithmetic. You might hope to get some other nonsensical belief into the head of George Gradgrind, or Augustus Gradgrind, or John Gradgrind, or
15 Joseph Gradgrind (all suppositions, non-existent persons), but into the head of Thomas Gradgrind— no, sir!

Mr. Gradgrind walked homeward from the school in a state of considerable satisfaction. It was
20 his school, and he intended it to be a model. He intended every child in it to be a model—just as the young Gradgrinds were all models.

There were five young Gradgrinds, and they were models every one. They had been lectured at
25 from their tenderest years; coursed, like little hares. Almost as soon as they could run alone, they had been made to run to the lecture-room. The first object with which they had an association, or of which they had a remembrance, was a
30 large blackboard with a dry Ogre chalking ghastly white figures on it.

Not that they knew, by name or nature, anything about an Ogre. Fact forbid! I only use the word to express a monster in a lecturing castle,
35 with Heaven knows how many heads manipulated into one, taking childhood captive, and dragging it into gloomy statistical dens by the hair.

No little Gradgrind had ever seen a face in the moon; it was up in the moon before it could speak
40 distinctly. No little Gradgrind had ever learnt the silly jingle, Twinkle, twinkle, little star; how I wonder what you are! No little Gradgrind had ever known wonder on the subject of the stars, each little Gradgrind having at five years old dissected

45 the Great Bear like a Professor Owen, and driven
Charles's Wain like a locomotive engine-driver. No
little Gradgrind had ever associated a cow in a field
with that famous cow with the crumpled horn
who tossed the dog who worried the cat who killed
50 the rat who ate the malt, or with that yet more
famous cow who swallowed Tom Thumb: it had
never heard of those celebrities, and had only
been introduced to a cow as a graminivorous
ruminating quadruped with several stomachs.

**16.** The phrase "peremptorily Thomas" in line 6
emphasizes Gradgrind's

(A) absolute insistence upon facts
(B) dislike of the name Augustus
(C) need to remind himself of the simplest details
(D) desire to be on a first-name basis with others
(E) inability to introduce himself properly

**17.** In line 7, "rule" most nearly means

(A) legal regulation
(B) academic custom
(C) scientific principle
(D) dominion over schoolchildren
(E) straight edge used in measuring

**18.** Gradgrind's mood as he marches homeward (lines
18–19) can best be characterized as one of

(A) uncertainty  (B) complacency
(C) boredom  (D) relief  (E) cynicism

**19.** The author's tone in describing Thomas
Gradgrind's educational methodology is

(A) openly admiring
(B) acutely concerned
(C) bitterly scornful
(D) broadly satirical
(E) warmly nostalgic

**20.** The passage suggests that Gradgrind rejects from
his curriculum anything that is in the least

(A) analytical  (B) mechanical  (C) fanciful
(D) dogmatic  (E) pragmatic

**21.** The passage is narrated from the point of view of

(A) Thomas Gradgrind
(B) an observer who does not know Gradgrind at
first but who comes to know about him in the
course of the passage
(C) an observer whose understanding of
Gradgrind is necessarily incomplete
(D) an observer who knows all about Gradgrind's
thoughts and feelings
(E) an instructor at Gradgrind's model school

**22.** It can be inferred from the passage that the Great
Bear and Charles's Wain most likely are

(A) subjects of nursery rhymes
(B) groupings of stars
(C) zoological phenomena
(D) themes of popular songs
(E) popular toys for children

**23.** Which of the following axioms is closest to
Gradgrind's view of education as presented in the
passage?

(A) Experience keeps a dear school, but fools will
learn in no other.
(B) Let early education be a sort of amusement,
that you may be better able to find out the
natural bent.
(C) Education is what you have left over after you
have forgotten everything you have learned.
(D) A teacher who can arouse a feeling for one
single good action accomplishes more than
one who fills our memory with rows on rows
of natural objects, classified with name and
form.
(E) Modern science, as training the mind to an
exact and impartial analysis of fact, is an
education specially fitted to promote sound
citizenship.

**24.** In line 52, the word "celebrities" refers to

(A) the little Gradgrinds
(B) famous professors
(C) heavenly bodies
(D) locomotive engine-drivers
(E) fictional characters

IF YOU FINISH IN LESS THAN 25 MINUTES, YOU MAY CHECK YOUR WORK ON
THIS SECTION ONLY. DO NOT TURN TO ANY OTHER SECTION IN THE TEST.

**STOP**

## SECTION 2/MATHEMATICS

TIME: 25 MINUTES

20 QUESTIONS (1–20)

---

**Directions:**

For each question in this section, determine which of the five choices is correct, and blacken that choice on your answer sheet. You may use any blank space on the page for your work.

NOTES:
- You may use a calculator whenever you believe it will be helpful.
- Use the diagrams provided to help you solve the problems. Unless you see the phrase
    <u>Note:</u> Figure not drawn to scale
    under a diagram, it has been drawn as accurately as possible. Unless it is stated that a figure is three dimensional, you may assume that it lies in a plane.

**Reference**

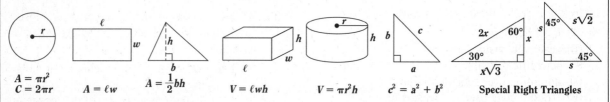

$A = \pi r^2$
$C = 2\pi r$      $A = \ell w$      $A = \frac{1}{2}bh$      $V = \ell w h$      $V = \pi r^2 h$      $c^2 = a^2 + b^2$      **Special Right Triangles**

Number of degrees in a circle: 360
Sum of the measures, in degrees, of the three angles of a triangle: 180

---

**1.** What is the value of $m$ if $(7 - 2)(7 - m) = 35$?

(A) $-7$
(B) $-5$
(C) 0
(D) 5
(E) 7

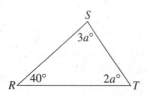

**2.** In the figure above, what is the value of $a$?

(A) 10
(B) 20
(C) 28
(D) 36
(E) 45

**3.** Samir studied for exactly 225 minutes. If he began studying at 10:05 A.M., at what time did he stop studying?

(A) 12:30 P.M.
(B) 1:00 P.M.
(C) 1:30 P.M.
(D) 1:50 P.M.
(E) 2:00 P.M.

**4.** What positive number $n$ satisfies the equation,
$(9)(9)(9)n = \frac{(27)(27)}{n}$?

(A) $\frac{1}{3}$
(B) 1
(C) 3
(D) 9
(E) 27

**GO ON TO NEXT PAGE ▶**

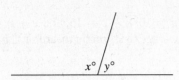

Note: Figure not drawn to scale

**5.** In the figure above, if $x$ is 140 more than $y$, what is the value of $y$?

(A) 10
(B) 15
(C) 20
(D) 30
(E) 40

**6.** If $x^2 = 10$, what is $x^6$?

(A) $10\sqrt{10}$
(B) 100
(C) $100\sqrt{10}$
(D) 1000
(E) $1000\sqrt{10}$

**7.** If $a$, $b$, $c$, and $d$ are four consecutive integers, which of the following could be their average (arithmetic mean)?

  I. 99
 II. 99.5
III. 100

(A) I only
(B) II only
(C) I and II only
(D) II and III only
(E) I, II, and III

**8.** What is the diameter of a circle whose area is $A$?

(A) $2\sqrt{\dfrac{A}{\pi}}$

(B) $\sqrt{\dfrac{A}{\pi}}$

(C) $\dfrac{A}{2\pi}$

(D) $\dfrac{A}{\pi}$

(E) $\dfrac{2\sqrt{A}}{\pi}$

**9.** The following chart lists the monthly salaries in 2010 of five people and the percent change in their salaries from 2010 to 2012.

| Name | 2010 Salary | % change |
|------|-------------|----------|
| Ann | $4200 | +6% |
| Ben | $4000 | +11% |
| Dan | $3500 | +25% |
| Ken | $5000 | −12% |
| Len | $3200 | +35% |

Who had the highest salary in 2012?

(A) Ann
(B) Ben
(C) Dan
(D) Ken
(E) Len

**10.** If the measures of the angles of a triangle are in the ratio of 1:1:2, what is the ratio of the lengths of the sides?

(A) 1:1:2
(B) 1:1:3
(C) 1:1:$\sqrt{2}$
(D) 2:2:3
(E) 1:$\sqrt{3}$:2

**11.** $A$, $B$, and $C$ are points with $AC = 2AB$. Which of the following could be true?

  I. $A$, $B$, and $C$ are the vertices of a right triangle.
 II. $A$, $B$, and $C$ are three of the vertices of a square.
III. $A$, $B$, and $C$ all lie on the circumference of a circle.

(A) I only
(B) III only
(C) I and II only
(D) I and III only
(E) I, II, and III

**GO ON TO NEXT PAGE ▶**

12. Last year Ross bought two paintings. Last week he sold them for $1200 each. He had a 20% profit on one painting and a 20% loss on the other. What was his net loss or profit?

    (A) He lost exactly $100.
    (B) He lost less than $100.
    (C) He lost more than $100.
    (D) He earned less than $100.
    (E) He earned more than $100.

13. What is the measure in degrees of the smaller angle formed by the hour hand and the minute hand of a clock at 3:30?

    (A) 15
    (B) 60
    (C) 70
    (D) 75
    (E) 90

14. If $m$ is an integer, which of the following could be true?

    I. $\frac{15}{m}$ is an even integer
    II. $\frac{m}{15}$ is an even integer
    III. $15m$ is a prime

    (A) I only
    (B) II only
    (C) III only
    (D) I and II only
    (E) II and III only

Questions 15–16 refer to the following definition.

For any integers $m$ and $n$: $m*n$ represents the remainder when $m$ is divided by $n$.

15. What is the value of

    $$6*1 + 6*2 + 6*3 + 6*4 + 6*5 + 6*6?$$

    (A) 0
    (B) 3
    (C) 6
    (D) 9
    (E) 14

16. If $a < b$, what is the maximum possible value of $a*b + b*a$?

    (A) $a + b$
    (B) $ab - 1$
    (C) $2a - 1$
    (D) $2b - 1$
    (E) $a + b - 1$

17. If $x + y = 10$, $y + z = 15$, and $x + z = 17$, what is the average (arithmetic mean) of $x$, $y$, and $z$?

    (A) 7
    (B) 14
    (C) 15
    (D) 21
    (E) It cannot be determined from the information given.

18. If $x$ is a positive integer, which of the following CANNOT be an integer?

    (A) $\sqrt{x-1}$
    (B) $\sqrt{x^2-1}$
    (C) $\frac{1}{x}$
    (D) $\frac{x+2}{x+1}$
    (E) $\frac{7}{x+1}$

19. Which of the following CANNOT be expressed as the sum of two or more consecutive positive integers?

    (A) 12
    (B) 13
    (C) 14
    (D) 15
    (E) 16

20. If $p$ painters can complete a job in $d$ days, how long will it take $q$ painters, all working at the same rate, to complete 25% of the job?

    (A) $\frac{pd}{4q}$
    (B) $\frac{q}{4pd}$
    (C) $\frac{4pd}{q}$
    (D) $\frac{pq}{4d}$
    (E) $\frac{pqd}{4}$

IF YOU FINISH IN LESS THAN 25 MINUTES, YOU MAY CHECK YOUR WORK ON THIS SECTION ONLY. DO NOT TURN TO ANY OTHER SECTION IN THE TEST.

**STOP**

# SECTION 3/CRITICAL READING

TIME: 25 MINUTES
24 QUESTIONS (25–48)

> **Directions:** For each question in this section, select the best answer from among the choices given and fill in the corresponding circle on the answer sheet.

Each sentence below has one or two blanks, each blank indicating that something has been omitted. Beneath the sentence are five words or sets of words labeled A through E. Choose the word or set of words that, when inserted in the sentence, best fits the meaning of the sentence as a whole.

**EXAMPLE:**

Medieval kingdoms did not become constitutional republics overnight; on the contrary, the change was ----.

(A) unpopular   (B) unexpected
(C) advantageous   (D) sufficient   (E) gradual

Ⓐ Ⓑ Ⓒ Ⓓ ●

25. Once known only to importers of exotic foreign delicacies, the kiwi fruit has been transplanted successfully to America and is now ---- a much wider market.

(A) accessible to
(B) unknown to
(C) perplexing to
(D) comparable to
(E) uncultivated by

26. Continuously looking for new ways of presenting her material, for fresh methods of capturing her students' attention, she has been ---- in the classroom.

(A) a pedant   (B) a misfit   (C) an innovator
(D) a stoic   (E) a martinet

27. This coming trip to France should provide me with ---- test of the value of my conversational French class.

(A) an intimate   (B) an uncertain
(C) a pragmatic   (D) a pretentious
(E) an arbitrary

28. Allowing women a voice in tribal government did not ---- Cherokee custom, for traditional Cherokee society was matrilineal, granting women the right to own property and to divorce their husbands.

(A) violate   (B) emulate   (C) retrace
(D) preclude   (E) fulfill

29. In a shocking instance of ---- research, one of the most influential researchers in the field of genetics reported on experiments that were never carried out and published deliberately ---- scientific papers on his nonexistent work.

(A) comprehensive..abstract
(B) theoretical..challenging
(C) erroneous..impartial
(D) derivative..authoritative
(E) fraudulent..deceptive

30. Many of the characters portrayed by Clint Eastwood are strong but ---- types, rugged men of few words.

(A) ruthless   (B) equivocal   (C) laconic
(D) stingy   (E) vociferous

31. Like sauces, without a certain amount of spice, conversations grow ----.

(A) eloquent   (B) heated   (C) elaborate
(D) straightforward   (E) insipid

32. Both ---- and ----, Scrooge seldom smiled and never gave away a halfpenny.

(A) sanguine..miserly
(B) acerbic..magnanimous
(C) morose..munificent
(D) crabbed..parsimonious
(E) sullen..philanthropic

**GO ON TO NEXT PAGE ▶**

**Directions:** Each of the passages below precedes two questions based on its content. Answer the questions following each passage on the basis of what is <u>stated</u> or <u>implied</u> in that passage.

**Questions 33 and 34 are based on the following passage.**

"The very first requirement in a hospital (is) that it should do the sick no harm." So wrote Florence Nightingale, nursing pioneer. Most peo-
Line ple picture Nightingale as the brave "Lady with the
5 Lamp" who journeyed to the Crimea to nurse British soldiers wounded in the war. It was after the war, however, that Nightingale came into her own as the world's most renowned authority on hospital reform. In *Notes on Hospitals*, Nightingale
10 addressed every aspect of hospital construction and management, from replacing wooden bedsteads with iron ones, to minimizing infection by dividing hospitals into airy, self-contained pavilions.

33. Which statement best expresses the author's central point about Florence Nightingale?

   (A) She deserved great praise for her work with wounded soldiers in the Crimea.
   (B) She worried about the effects of infection on mortality rates.
   (C) Her greatest accomplishments were in improving hospital planning and administration.
   (D) She preferred airy, separate hospital units to large wards.
   (E) Her change of focus to hospital administration represented a loss to the nursing profession.

34. In line 10, "addressed" most nearly means

   (A) orated   (B) labeled   (C) set apart
   (D) dealt with   (E) averted

**Questions 35 and 36 are based on the following passage.**

Critics call Edgar Allan Poe the father of detective fiction. Whom then should we call detective fiction's mother? Agatha Christie, say some mystery readers. Dorothy Sayers, say others.
Line
5 Well before Christie and Sayers wrote their classic British whodunits, however, an American named Anna Katharine Green wrote a best-seller about the murder of a Fifth Avenue millionaire. *The Leavenworth Case*, which sold over 150,000
10 copies, marked the initial appearance of Inspector Ebenezer Gryce, the first serial detective in genre history. Today, with two novels back in print after nearly a century, Gryce's long-neglected creator is finally beginning to receive the recognition she
15 deserves.

35. The author's purpose in writing this passage is most likely to

   (A) relegate a writer to obscurity
   (B) contrast the careers of Poe and Green
   (C) introduce the concept of the serial detective
   (D) dismiss the contributions of British authors
   (E) reclaim a forgotten literary pioneer

36. In line 10, "marked" most nearly means

   (A) graded   (B) noticed   (C) denoted
   (D) branded   (E) disfigured

**GO ON TO NEXT PAGE ▶**

**Directions:** The passages below are followed by questions on their content; questions following a pair of related passages may also be based on the relationship between the paired passages. Answer the questions on the basis of what is <u>stated</u> or <u>implied</u> in the passages and in any introductory material that may be provided.

**Questions 37–48 are based on the following passages.**

*The following passages are excerpted from recent essays about flying.*

**Passage 1**

Flying alone in an open plane is the purest experience of flight possible. That pure experience is felt at its most intense in acrobatic flying, when

Line  you are upside down, or pointed at the sky or at
5   the earth, and moving in ways that you can only in the unsubstantial medium of the air. Acrobatic flying is a useless skill in its particulars—nobody *needs* to do a loop or a roll, not even a fighter pilot—but this skill extends your control of the
10  plane and yourself and makes extreme actions in the sky comfortable. When you reach the top of a loop, upside down and engine at full throttle, and tilt your head back to pick up the horizon line behind you, you are as far outside instinctive
15  human behavior as you can go—hanging in space, the sky below you and the earth above, inscribing a circle on emptiness. And then the nose drops across the horizon; your speed increases and the plane scoops through into normal flight, and you
20  are back in the normal world, with the earth put back in its place. The going out and coming back are what makes a loop so satisfying.

After a while, that is. At first it was terrifying, like being invited to a suicide that you didn't want
25  to commit. "This is a loop," my instructor said casually. He lowered the plane's nose to gain airspeed, and then pulled sharply up. The earth, and my stomach, fell away from me; and we were upside down, and I could feel gravity clawing at
30  me, pulling me out into the mile of empty space between me and the ground. I grabbed at the sides of the cockpit and hung on until gravity was on my side again.

"You seemed a little nervous that time," the
35  instructor said when the plane was right side up again. "You've got to have confidence in that seat belt, or you'll never do a decent loop. So this time, when we get on top, I want you to put both arms out of the cockpit." And I did it. It was like step-
40  ping off a bridge, but I did it, and the belt held, and the plane came round. And after that I could fly a loop. It was, as I said, satisfying.

**Passage 2**

The black plane dropped spinning, and flattened out spinning the other way; it began to
45  carve the air into forms that built wildly and musically on each other and never ended. Reluctantly, I started paying attention. Rahm drew high above the world an inexhaustibly glorious line; it piled over our heads in loops and arabesques. The plane
50  moved every way a line can move, and it controlled three dimensions, so the line carved massive and subtle slits in the air like sculptures. The plane looped the loop, seeming to arch its back like a gymnast; it stalled, dropped, and spun out of it
55  climbing; it spiraled and knifed west on one side's wings and back east on another; it turned cartwheels, which must be physically impossible; it played with its own line like a cat with yarn. How did the pilot know where in the air he was? If he
60  got lost, the ground would swat him.

His was pure energy and naked spirit. I have thought about it for years. Rahm's line unrolled in time. Like music, it split the bulging rim of the future along its seam. It pried out the present. We
65  watchers waited for the split-second curve of beauty in the present to reveal itself. The human pilot, Dave Rahm, worked in the cockpit right at the plane's nose; his very body tore into the future for us and reeled it down upon us like a curling peel.

70  Like any fine artist, he controlled the tension of the audience's longing. You desired, unwittingly, a certain kind of roll or climb, or a return to a certain portion of the air, and he fulfilled your hope slantingly, like a poet, or evaded it until
75  you thought you would burst, and then fulfilled it surprisingly, so you gasped and cried out.

The oddest, most exhilarating and exhausting thing was this: he never quit. The music had no periods, no rests or endings; the poetry's beautiful
80  sentence never ended; the line had no finish; the sculptured forms piled overhead, one into another without surcease. Who could breathe, in a world where rhythm itself had no periods?

I went home and thought about Rahm's per-
85  formance that night, and the next day, and the next.

**GO ON TO NEXT PAGE** ▶

I had thought I knew my way around beauty a
little bit. I knew I had devoted a good part of my
life to it, memorizing poetry and focusing my
90 attention on complexity of rhythm in particular,
on force, movement, repetition, and surprise, in
both poetry and prose. Now I had stood among
dandelions between two asphalt runways in
Bellingham, Washington, and begun learning
95 about beauty. Even the Boston Museum of Fine
Arts was never more inspiring than this small
northwestern airport on this time-killing Sunday
afternoon in June. Nothing on earth is more glad-
dening than knowing we must roll up our sleeves
100 and move back the boundaries of the humanly
possible once more.

**37.** According to the author of Passage 1, training in
acrobatic flying

(A) has only theoretical value
(B) expands a pilot's range of capabilities
(C) is an essential part of general pilot training
(D) comes naturally to most pilots
(E) should be required only of fighter pilots

**38.** In line 6, "medium" most nearly means

(A) midpoint
(B) appropriate occupation
(C) method of communication
(D) environment
(E) compromise

**39.** To "pick up the horizon line" (line 13) is to

(A) lift it higher
(B) spot it visually
(C) measure its distance
(D) choose it eagerly
(E) increase its visibility

**40.** Passage 1 suggests that the author's grabbing at
the sides of the cockpit (lines 31–33) was

(A) instinctive   (B) terrifying   (C) essential
(D) habit forming   (E) life threatening

**41.** In line 40, the word "held" most nearly means

(A) carried   (B) detained   (C) accommodated
(D) remained valid   (E) maintained its grasp

**42.** By putting both arms out of the cockpit (lines
38–40), the author

(A) chooses the path of least resistance
(B) enables himself to steer the plane more freely
(C) relies totally on his seat belt to keep him safe
(D) allows himself to give full expression to his
nervousness
(E) is better able to breathe deeply and relax

**43.** The author's use of the word "satisfying" (line 42)
represents

(A) a simile   (B) an understatement
(C) a fallacy   (D) a euphemism
(E) a hypothesis

**44.** The author of Passage 2 mentions her initial
reluctance to watch the stunt flying (lines 46–47)
in order to

(A) demonstrate her hostility to commercial
entertainment
(B) reveal her fear of such dangerous enterprises
(C) minimize her participation in aerial
acrobatics
(D) indicate how captivating the demonstration
was
(E) emphasize the acuteness of her perceptions

**45.** By fulfilling "your hope slantingly, like a poet"
(line 74), the author means that

(A) the pilot flew the plane on a diagonal
(B) Rahm was a writer of popular verse
(C) the pilot had a bias against executing certain
kinds of rolls
(D) Rahm refused to satisfy your expectations
directly
(E) the pilot's sense of aesthetic judgment was
askew

**46.** At the end of Passage 2, the author is left feeling

(A) empty in the aftermath of the stunning performance she has seen
(B) jubilant at the prospect of moving from Boston to Washington
(C) exhilarated by her awareness of new potentials for humanity
(D) glad that she has not wasted any more time memorizing poetry
(E) surprised by her response to an art form she had not previously believed possible

**47.** Compared with Passage 2, Passage 1 is

(A) less informative
(B) more tentative
(C) more argumentative
(D) more speculative
(E) less lyrical

**48.** How would the author of Passage 2 most likely react to the assessment of acrobatic flying in lines 6–11?

(A) She would consider it too utilitarian an assessment of an aesthetic experience.
(B) She would reject it as an inaccurate description of the pilot's technique.
(C) She would admire it as a poetic evocation of the pilot's art.
(D) She would criticize it as a digression from the author's main point.
(E) She would regard it as too effusive to be appropriate to its subject.

IF YOU FINISH IN LESS THAN 25 MINUTES, YOU MAY CHECK YOUR WORK ON THIS SECTION ONLY. DO NOT TURN TO ANY OTHER SECTION IN THE TEST.

**STOP**

## SECTION 4/MATHEMATICS

TIME: 25 MINUTES
18 QUESTIONS (21–38)

---

### Directions:

For questions 21–28, determine which of the five choices is correct, and blacken that choice on your answer sheet. You may use any blank space on the page for your work.

NOTES:
- You may use a calculator whenever you believe it will be helpful.
- Use the diagrams provided to help you solve the problems. Unless you see the phrase
Note: Figure not drawn to scale
  under a diagram, it has been drawn as accurately as possible. Unless it is stated that a figure is three dimensional, you may assume that it lies in a plane.

### Reference

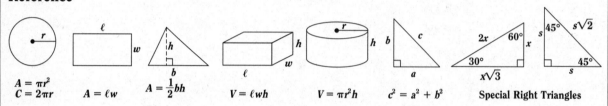

$A = \pi r^2$
$C = 2\pi r$
$A = \ell w$
$A = \frac{1}{2}bh$
$V = \ell wh$
$V = \pi r^2 h$
$c^2 = a^2 + b^2$
**Special Right Triangles**

Number of degrees in a circle: 360
Sum of the measures, in degrees, of the three angles of a triangle: 180

---

**21.** If $2x - 1 = 9$, what is $20x - 1$?

(A) 19
(B) 80
(C) 90
(D) 99
(E) 100

**22.** If $8 - (8 + w) = 8$, then $w =$

(A) −16
(B) −8
(C) 0
(D) 8
(E) 16

**23.** One positive number is $\frac{1}{5}$ of another number. If the product of the numbers is 20, what is their sum?

(A) 4
(B) 8
(C) 10
(D) 12
(E) 20

**24.** Mr. Riccardo wrote a number on the chalkboard. When he added 3 to the number, he got the same result as when he multiplied the number by 3. What is the number he wrote?

(A) −3
(B) 0
(C) 1.5
(D) $\sqrt{3}$
(E) 3

---

**GO ON TO NEXT PAGE ▶**

**25.** If a team played *g* games and lost *l* of them, what fraction of the games played did the team win?

(A) $\frac{l-g}{l}$

(B) $\frac{l-g}{g}$

(C) $\frac{g-l}{g}$

(D) $\frac{g}{g-l}$

(E) $\frac{g-l}{l}$

**26.** If Steven was born on Friday, August 13, 2010, and Daniel was born exactly 200 days later, on what day of the week was Daniel born?

(A) Monday
(B) Tuesday
(C) Friday
(D) Saturday
(E) Sunday

**27.** In the figure above, the shaded region is bounded by two semicircles and two sides of a square. If the area of the square is 20, what is the area of the shaded region?

(A) $20 - \pi$
(B) $5(4 - \pi)$
(C) $4\pi$
(D) $\sqrt{20}(2 + \pi)$
(E) $2\sqrt{20} + 10\pi$

**28.** If $a - b = 10$, $b - c = 20$ and $c - d = 30$, what is the value of $a - d$?

(A) 40
(B) 50
(C) 60
(D) 80
(E) 100

## Student-Produced Response Directions

In questions 29–38, first solve the problem, and then enter your answer on the grid provided on the answer sheet. The instructions for entering your answers follow.

- First, write your answer in the boxes at the top of the grid.
- Second, grid your answer in the columns below the boxes.
- Use the fraction bar in the first row or the decimal point in the second row to enter fractions and decimals.

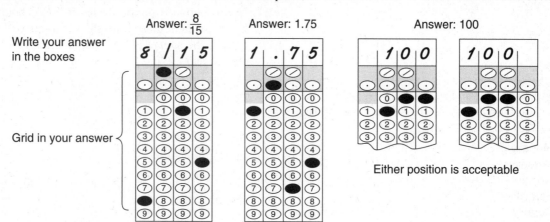

- Grid only one space in each column.
- Entering the answer in the boxes is recommended as an aid in gridding but is not required.
- The machine scoring your exam can read only what you grid, so you **must grid-in your answers correctly to get credit.**
- If a question has more than one correct answer, grid-in only one of them.
- The grid does not have a minus sign; so no answer can be negative.
- A mixed number *must* be converted to an improper fraction or a decimal before it is gridded. Enter $1\frac{1}{4}$ as $\frac{5}{4}$ or 1.25; the machine will interpret 11/4 as $\frac{11}{4}$ and mark it wrong.

- **All decimals must be entered as accurately as possible.** Here are three acceptable ways of gridding $\frac{3}{11} = 0.272727\ldots$

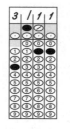 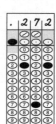 

- Note that rounding to .273 is acceptable because you are using the full grid, but you would receive **no credit** for .3 or .27, because they are less accurate.

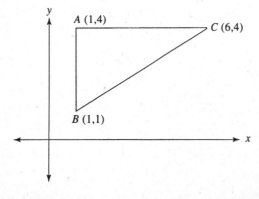

**29.** In the figure above, what is the area of △*ABC*?

**30.** In the figure above, what is the value of *a* if *b* = 60?

**GO ON TO NEXT PAGE ▶**

**31.** If the average (arithmetic mean) of 20, 30, 40, 50 and $y$ is 100, what is the value of $y$?

**32.** At Central High School, 40% of the members of the Spanish club are boys. How many members does the club have if 30 of the members are girls?

**33.** Line $l$ passes through the points (1, 3) and (4, 7). Line $m$ passes through (7, 5) parallel to $l$, and line $n$ passes through (7, 5) perpendicular to $l$. What is the sum of the slopes of lines $m$ and $n$?

**34.** The first two terms of a sequence are 1 and 2. Every other term in the sequence is the sum of the two terms immediately preceding it. For example, the third term is $1 + 2 = 3$ and the fourth term is $2 + 3 = 5$. How many of the first 100 terms are odd?

**35.** If $5(\sqrt{x} - 3) = 3\sqrt{x} - 5$, then $x =$

**36.** If 3 bangs = 2 clangs and 4 bangs = 5 tangs, then 1 clang is equal to how many tangs?

**37.** There are 25 students in a class, 40% of whom are girls. If the average (arithmetic mean) weight of the girls is 120 pounds and the average weight of the boys in the class is 150 pounds, what is the average weight of the children in the class?

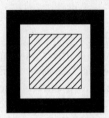

**38.** In the figure above, the diagonals of the three squares are 3, 4, and 5. What is the ratio of the black area to the striped area?

IF YOU FINISH IN LESS THAN 25 MINUTES, YOU MAY CHECK YOUR WORK ON
THIS SECTION ONLY. DO NOT TURN TO ANY OTHER SECTION IN THE TEST.

**STOP**

# SECTION 5/WRITING SKILLS

TIME: 30 MINUTES
39 QUESTIONS (1–39)

---

**Directions:** For each question in this section, select the best answer from among the choices given and fill in the corresponding circle on the answer sheet.

---

Some or all parts of the following sentences are underlined. The first answer choice, (A), simply repeats the underlined part of the sentence. The other four choices present four alternative ways to phrase the underlined part. Select the answer that produces the most effective sentence, one that is clear and exact, and blacken the appropriate space on your answer sheet. In selecting your choice, be sure that it is standard written English and that it expresses the meaning of the original sentence.

**EXAMPLE:**

The first biography of author Eudora Welty came out in 1998, and she was eighty-nine years old at the time.

(A) and she was eighty-nine years old at the time
(B) at the time when she was eighty-nine
(C) upon becoming an eighty-nine year old
(D) when she was eighty-nine
(E) at the age of eighty-nine years old

1. Maya Angelou is almost as talented a performer as she is a poet.
   (A) almost as talented a performer as she is a poet
   (B) almost equally talented, whether a performer or a poet
   (C) of the same talent as a performer and a poet, almost
   (D) a talented poet, and almost so talented in performing
   (E) talented as a poet, with almost as much talent in performing

2. The imminent historian stood in bed, recuperating from a viral infection, while his paper was being read at the convention.
   (A) imminent historian stood
   (B) imminent historian remained
   (C) eminent historian stayed
   (D) eminent historian stood
   (E) eminent historian had remained

3. At the zoo, the brightly plumaged birds that fluttered overhead like tropical flowers in a breeze.
   (A) birds that fluttered    (B) birds fluttering
   (C) birds which fluttered    (D) birds fluttered
   (E) birds aflutter

4. When the National Association for the Advancement of Colored People examined discrimination in the music business, its report concentrating on offstage employment opportunities.
   (A) its report concentrating on offstage employment opportunities
   (B) its report having concentrated on offstage employment opportunities
   (C) its report concentrated on offstage employment opportunities
   (D) its report concentrating in offstage employment opportunities
   (E) its report concentrated in offstage employment opportunities

5. Some doctors volunteer to serve the poor in addition to their regular practices, they find healing the poor provides different insights than healing the rich.
   (A) Some doctors volunteer to serve the poor in addition to their regular practices, they find
   (B) Besides their regular practices, some doctors serve the poor to find
   (C) In addition to running their regular practices, some doctors volunteer to serve the poor; they find that
   (D) Some doctors, in volunteering to serve the poor, find
   (E) Running their regular practices and serving the poor help some doctors realize that

**GO ON TO NEXT PAGE ▶**

6. In India, Mahatma Gandhi was more than a politi-cal leader he was the enlightened one embodying the soul of the nation.

   (A) political leader he was
   (B) political leader; he was
   (C) political leader, he was
   (D) political leader which was
   (E) political leader, although he was

7. Because of a teacher shortage in the math and science disciplines, educators are encouraging retired scientists and engineers to pursue a second career in teaching.

   (A) Because of a teacher shortage in the math and science disciplines, educators are encouraging
   (B) Educators, faced with a teacher shortage in technical disciplines have encouraged
   (C) In addition to a teacher shortage in the math and science areas, educators encourage
   (D) Teacher shortages in the math and science disciplines have forced educators to hire
   (E) Because there is a teacher shortage in the math and science disciplines, educators encourage

8. Neither the principal or the teachers had been satisfied with the addition of a crossing guard, and wanted a traffic light installed at the street crossing.

   (A) Neither the principal or the teachers had been satisfied with the addition of a crossing guard, and
   (B) Neither the principal nor the teachers were satisfied with the addition of a crossing guard; they
   (C) Because neither the principal or the teachers had been satisfied with the addition of a cross-ing guard, they
   (D) As the result of the addition of a crossing guard, the principal and the teachers
   (E) Neither the principal nor the teachers feels the crossing guard is sufficient; and they

9. Most of the students like to read these kind of detective stories as recreational reading.

   (A) these kind of detective stories
   (B) these kind of detective story
   (C) this kind of detective story
   (D) this kinds of detective story
   (E) those kind of detective story

10. Because of his now chronic throat ailment, the tenor recently has not and apparently never will sing again.

    (A) has not and apparently never will sing
    (B) had not sung and apparently never would sing
    (C) has not and apparently never would sing
    (D) has not sung and apparently never will sing
    (E) had not and apparently never will sing

11. Having the best record for attendance, the school awarded him a medal at graduation.

    (A) the school awarded him a medal
    (B) the school awarded a medal to him
    (C) he was awarded a medal by the school
    (D) a medal was awarded to him by the school
    (E) a school medal was awarded to him

12. Several regulations were proposed by the president of the university that had a sexist bias, according to women students.

    (A) Several regulations were proposed by the president of the university that
    (B) Several regulations were proposed by the president of the university who
    (C) The proposal of several regulations by the president of the university which
    (D) The president of the university, who proposed several regulations that
    (E) The president of the university proposed several regulations that

13. The difference between the candidates is that one is radical; the other, conservative.

    (A) one is radical; the other, conservative
    (B) one is radical; the other being conservative
    (C) while one is radical; the other, conservative
    (D) one is radical, the other, conservative
    (E) one is radical, although the other is more conservative

14. Police academies, on seeing as how new recruits lack basic driving skills, are teaching recruits the basics on test fields and neighborhood streets.

    (A) Police academies, on seeing as how new recruits lack basic driving skills, are teaching
    (B) Since new police recruits lack basic driving skills, police academies are teaching
    (C) Police academies, because new recruits are lacking basic driving skills, teach
    (D) As a result of new recruits lacking basic driving skills, police academies are teaching
    (E) Even though new recruits lack basic driving skills, police academies are teaching

**GO ON TO NEXT PAGE ▶**

15. Although the babysitter had expected the twins to protest being told to go to bed, they went to their room without scarcely a murmur.

   (A) being told to go to bed, they went to their room without scarcely a murmur
   (B) being told to go to bed, they had gone off to their room without scarcely a murmur
   (C) being told that they should go to bed, they went to their room without scarcely a murmur
   (D) being told to go to bed, however, they went to their room without scarcely a murmur
   (E) being told to go to bed, they went to their room with scarcely a murmur

16. Although hydroponics is unsuitable for growing root vegetables and trees, which require soil and space, the system is ideal for cultivating a wide variety of plants such as tomatoes and beans.

   (A) Although hydroponics is unsuitable for growing root vegetables and trees, which require
   (B) Although hydroponics being unsuitable for growing root vegetables and trees, which require
   (C) Although hydroponics is unsuitable for growing root vegetables and trees, being that they require
   (D) Although hydroponics is unsuited to grow root vegetables and trees, these require
   (E) Although hydroponics is unsuitable for growing root vegetables and trees, and they require

17. Acutely aware of how much he owed to the generosity of Mr. Fezziwig, young Ebenezer addressed his benefactor respectively.

   (A) Acutely aware of how much he owed to the generosity of Mr. Fezziwig, young Ebenezer addressed his benefactor respectively.
   (B) Being that he was acutely aware of how much he owed to the generosity of Mr. Fezziwig, young Ebenezer addressed his benefactor respectively.
   (C) Young Ebenezer was acutely aware of how much he owed to the generosity of Mr. Fezziwig, so he addressed his benefactor respectively.
   (D) Acutely aware of how much he owed to the generosity of Mr. Fezziwig, young Ebenezer addressed his benefactor respectfully.
   (E) Acutely aware of how much he owed to the generosity of Mr. Fezziwig, young Ebenezer addressed his respective benefactor.

18. Although the suspect resolutely maintained his innocence, the jury found his story entirely incredulous.

   (A) the jury found his story entirely incredulous
   (B) the jury found his entire story incredulous
   (C) his story was found by the jury to be entirely incredulous
   (D) the jury found his story entirely incredible
   (E) the jury had found his story entirely incredulous

19. Many studies of new drugs are funded by major pharmaceutical firms, which suggests the possibility of bias in their conclusions.

   (A) which suggests the possibility of bias in their conclusions
   (B) thus the possibility of bias to their conclusions is suggested
   (C) a state of affairs that suggests the possibility of bias in their conclusions
   (D) and the possibility of bias in their conclusions being suggested
   (E) this fact suggests the possibility of bias in their conclusions

20. Intended to promote safety in the workplace, the regulation stipulates that protective goggles must be worn while welding.

   (A) that protective goggles must be worn while welding
   (B) that protective goggles while welding must be worn
   (C) that, while welding, protective goggles must be worn
   (D) that one must wear protective goggles while you weld
   (E) that you must wear protective goggles when you are welding

**GO ON TO NEXT PAGE ▶**

The sentences in this section may contain errors in grammar, usage, choice of words, or idioms. There is either just one error per sentence, or the sentence is correct. Some words or phrases are underlined and lettered; everything else in the sentence is correct.

If an underlined word or phrase is incorrect, choose that letter; if the sentence is correct, select <u>No error</u>. Then blacken the appropriate space on your answer sheet.

**EXAMPLE:**

The region has a climate <u>so severe that</u> plants
                         A

<u>growing there</u> rarely <u>had been</u> more than twelve
     B                    C

inches <u>high</u>. <u>No error</u>
       D        E

---

**21.** As <u>some</u> of the conglomerates gain more power,
       A    B

the legal codes <u>regarding</u> bankruptcy and
                    C

monopoly <u>will need</u> further consideration.
              D

<u>No error</u>
    E

**22.** In 1777, the Second Continental Congress

<u>has adopted</u> a resolution <u>to designate</u> the design
     A                              B

for the American flag, <u>but</u> no flags were issued
                          C

<u>until</u> 1783. <u>No error</u>
   D              E

**23.** He <u>dashed into</u> the burning building, <u>irregardless</u>
         A                                      B

of the risk <u>involved</u>, to warn the
                 C

<u>sleeping occupants</u>. <u>No error</u>
        D                    E

**24.** <u>According to</u> Ms. Lynch's portfolio, <u>there</u> is
           A                                    B

little doubt that she and her staff <u>is</u>
                                     C

<u>eminently qualified</u> for the assignment.
        D

<u>No error</u>
    E

**25.** Neither the Republican members of the

committee <u>who</u> supported the proposed
              A

legislation <u>or</u> the Democratic members who
                B

opposed it controlled a <u>clear majority</u>; the votes of
                            C

the independents <u>were</u> crucial. <u>No error</u>
                    D                    E

**26.** <u>No one</u> can predict <u>what</u> the <u>affect</u> of the
           A                B             C

government investigations <u>will be</u> on American
                              D

politics in the near future. <u>No error</u>
                                 E

**27.** <u>In order to</u> give adequate attention to all students,
           A

many teachers <u>prefer</u> team teaching, <u>which</u> divides
                  B                          C

students according to <u>his and her</u> abilities.
                          D

<u>No error</u>
    E

**GO ON TO NEXT PAGE ▶**

28. I was <u>irritated by</u> <u>you</u> coming into the room <u>as</u>
        A          B                        C
    you did—<u>shouting</u> and screaming. <u>No error</u>
              D                              E

29. Just <u>like</u> prehistoric man, some <u>groups of</u>
         A                              B
    southwestern Indians <u>have dwelled</u> in caves along
                              C
    <u>steep, rocky</u> ledges. <u>No error</u>
         D                    E

30. I <u>find</u> that sculpture <u>more unusual</u> <u>than</u> any
       A                    B              C
    of the other sculptures exhibited <u>during</u> this
                                          D
    special exhibit. <u>No error</u>
                        E

31. <u>One</u> of the basic economic reactions is <u>that</u> as
     A                                          B
    bond prices fall, stock prices <u>rise</u>, and
                                      C
    <u>an increase in interest rates</u> . <u>No error</u>
                   D                       E

32. <u>Some</u> of the major networks <u>have created</u>
     A                                  B
    <u>special prepared</u> news stories about life on city
            C
    streets <u>to publicize</u> the plight of the homeless.
                 D
    <u>No error</u>
        E

33. <u>Some women</u> have made a <u>clear-cut choice</u>
         A                          B
    between a career and motherhood; others have

    <u>been creating</u> a <u>balance between</u> the two.
         C                    D
    <u>No error</u>
        E

34. The renter of the car <u>initialed</u> the clause in the
                              A
    contract <u>to indicate</u> <u>his</u> awareness that he
                   B           C
    <u>was liable</u> for any damage to the automobile.
         D
    <u>No error</u>
        E

## Improving Paragraphs Directions

The passage below is the unedited draft of a student's essay. Some of the essay needs to be rewritten to make the meaning clearer and more precise. Read the essay carefully.

The essay is followed by questions about changes that might improve all or part of its organization, development, sentence structure, use of language, appropriateness to the audience, or use of standard written English. Choose the answer that most clearly and effectively expresses the student's intended meaning. Indicate your choice by filling in the corresponding space on the answer sheet.

[1] For two hundred years United States citizens have taken for granted their right to life, liberty, and the pursuit of happiness. [2] From the experiences in the former Yugoslavia to the repressive regime in the People's Republic of China, Americans should know, however, that human rights are always in danger.

[3] During the period of the conquistadores and Spanish colonial rule of Latin America, for example. [4] Latin American natives were often violated and repressed by European settlers, an example of this is the fact that the land formerly owned by the native Latin Americans was taken away from them so the people lost the right to own land. [5] Secondly, the Latin American people were forced to work this land as slaves on their own land. [6] These human rights violations were overcome by the independence movements led by such freedom fighters as Bolivar and San Martin in the late 1800s.

[7] In the Soviet Union, the extremely repressive Stalinist regime after WW II violated the rights of the Russian peasants, known as kulaks. [8] Collectivizing their farmlands by force, their rights were violated by Stalin. [9] Therefore, their private possessions were lost. [10] Another way by which they had their human rights violated was by forcing political opponents to remain silent, to work in labor camps, or to be killed. [11] After Stalin's death in 1953, one of his successors, Nikita Khrushchev, attempted to denounce the Stalinist regime. [12] However, it took another thirty years and the collapse of the Soviet Union to bring about basic human rights in Russia.

[13] About the history of human rights violations, the Serbs in the former Yugoslavia and the leaders of Communist China should know that they can't go on forever. [14] Eventually, their power will be usurped, or the people will rise up to claim their God-given human rights.

35. Taking into account the sentences that precede and follow sentence 3, which of the following is the best revision of sentence 3?

(A) As an example, the time that the Spanish were expanding their empire and searching for gold.

(B) Take, for example, during the era of the conquistadores and Spanish colonial rule in Latin America.

(C) Consider, for example, the period of the conquistadores and Spanish colonial rule in Latin America.

(D) The Spanish expanded their empire into Latin America in the 16th century.

(E) For instance, the period of Spanish colonialism in Latin America, for example.

36. Which of the following is the best revision of sentence 4?

(A) The land of Latin American natives was confiscated by European settlers. In fact, the rights of the natives to own land was violated and repressed.

(B) European settlers in Latin America have seized the land and the natives had repressed the right to own property.

(C) The colonial rulers confiscated the natives' property and denied them the right to own land.

(D) Having their rights violated, the natives of Latin America had their land taken away. Then the European settlers repress their right to own any land at all.

(E) The rights of the Latin American natives were violated and repressed. For example, they took their land and they prohibited them from owning land.

**37.** In the context of paragraph 3, which is the best revision of sentences 8 and 9?

(A) Forcing them to collectivize their farmlands, Stalin confiscated their private property.

(B) One of the ways by which Stalin violated their rights was by forcing people to collectivize their farmlands, thus causing them to lose their right to hold private possessions.

(C) One way in which the kulaks had their rights violated was Stalin forcing them to collectivize their farmlands and therefore, surrender private property.

(D) Having lost the right to own private property, Stalin collectivized the kulaks' farmland.

(E) The loss of private property and the collectivization of farmland was one way by which Stalin violated their rights.

**38.** Considering the content of the entire essay, which revision of the underlined segment of sentence 13 below provides the best transition between paragraphs 3 and 4?

*About the history of human rights violations, the Serbs in the former Yugoslavia and the leaders of Communist China should know that they can't go on forever.*

(A) In conclusion,

(B) Finally,

(C) Last but not least,

(D) Based on the history of international agreements on human rights,

(E) If the experience of Latin America and the Soviet Union means anything,

**39.** On the basis of the essay as a whole, which of the following describes the writer's intention in the last paragraph?

(A) To draw a conclusion based on the evidence in the passage

(B) To prepare readers for the future

(C) To instruct readers about the past

(D) To offer solutions to the problem posed by the essay

(E) To give an example

IF YOU FINISH IN LESS THAN 30 MINUTES, YOU MAY CHECK YOUR WORK ON THIS SECTION ONLY. DO NOT TURN TO ANY OTHER SECTION IN THE TEST.

**STOP**

# Answer Key

## Section 1   Critical Reading

| | | | |
|---|---|---|---|
| 1. D | 6. B | 11. C | 16. A | 21. D |
| 2. E | 7. A | 12. A | 17. E | 22. B |
| 3. A | 8. C | 13. E | 18. B | 23. E |
| 4. D | 9. E | 14. B | 19. D | 24. E |
| 5. B | 10. C | 15. B | 20. C | |

## Section 2   Mathematics

| | | | | |
|---|---|---|---|---|
| 1. C | 5. C | 9. A | 13. D | 17. A |
| 2. C | 6. D | 10. C | 14. B | 18. D |
| 3. D | 7. B | 11. D | 15. B | 19. E |
| 4. B | 8. A | 12. A | 16. C | 20. A |

## Section 3   Critical Reading

| | | | | |
|---|---|---|---|---|
| 25. A | 30. C | 35. E | 40. A | 45. D |
| 26. C | 31. E | 36. C | 41. E | 46. C |
| 27. C | 32. D | 37. B | 42. C | 47. E |
| 28. A | 33. C | 38. D | 43. B | 48. A |
| 29. E | 34. D | 39. B | 44. D | |

## Section 4   Mathematics

| | | | |
|---|---|---|---|
| 21. D | 23. D | 25. C | 27. B |
| 22. B | 24. C | 26. B | 28. C |

29. 7.5 or 15/2
30. 52.5
31. 360
32. 50

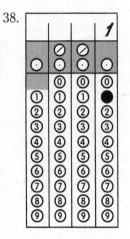

33. `7 / 1 2`

34. ` 6 7`

35. ` 2 5`

36. `1 5 / 8`

or *1.87*
or *1.88*

37. ` 1 3 8`

38. ` 1`

## Section 5    Writing Skills

| | | | | |
|---|---|---|---|---|
| 1. **A** | 9. **C** | 17. **D** | 25. **B** | 33. **C** |
| 2. **C** | 10. **D** | 18. **D** | 26. **C** | 34. **E** |
| 3. **D** | 11. **C** | 19. **C** | 27. **D** | 35. **C** |
| 4. **C** | 12. **E** | 20. **E** | 28. **B** | 36. **C** |
| 5. **C** | 13. **A** | 21. **E** | 29. **E** | 37. **A** |
| 6. **B** | 14. **B** | 22. **A** | 30. **E** | 38. **E** |
| 7. **A** | 15. **E** | 23. **B** | 31. **D** | 39. **A** |
| 8. **B** | 16. **A** | 24. **C** | 32. **C** | |

# Scoring Chart—Practice Test 4

## Critical Reading Sections

### Section 1: 24 Questions (1–24)

| | | |
|---|---|---|
| Number correct | _____ | (A) |
| Number omitted | _____ | (B) |
| Number incorrect | _____ | (C) |
| $\frac{1}{4}$ (C) | _____ | (D) |
| (A) − (D) | _____ | Raw Score I |

### Section 3: 24 Questions (25–48)

| | | |
|---|---|---|
| Number correct | _____ | (A) |
| Number omitted | _____ | (B) |
| Number incorrect | _____ | (C) |
| $\frac{1}{4}$ (C) | _____ | (D) |
| (A) − (D) | _____ | Raw Score II |

### Total Critical Reading Raw Score

Raw Scores I + II _____

## Mathematics Sections

### Section 2: 20 Questions (1–20)

| | | |
|---|---|---|
| Number correct | _____ | (A) |
| Number omitted | _____ | (B) |
| Number incorrect | _____ | (C) |
| $\frac{1}{4}$ (C) | _____ | (D) |
| (A) − (D) | _____ | Raw Score I |

### Section 4: First 8 Questions (21–28)

| | | |
|---|---|---|
| Number correct | _____ | (A) |
| Number omitted | _____ | (B) |
| Number incorrect | _____ | (C) |
| $\frac{1}{4}$ (C) | _____ | (D) |
| (A) − (D) | _____ | Raw Score II |

### Section 4: Next 10 Questions (29–38)

| | | |
|---|---|---|
| Number correct | _____ | Raw Score III |

### Total Mathematics Raw Score

Raw Scores I + II + III _____

**NOTE: In each section (A) + (B) + (C) should equal the number of questions in that section.**

## Writing Skills Section

### Section 5: 39 Questions (1–39)

| | | |
|---|---|---|
| Number correct | _____ | (A) |
| Number omitted | _____ | (B) |
| Number incorrect | _____ | (C) |
| $\frac{1}{4}$ (C) | _____ | (D) |

### Writing Skills Raw Score

(A) − (D) _____

# Evaluation Chart

Study your score. Your raw score is an indication of your probable achievement on the PSAT/NMSQT. As a guide to the amount of work you need or want to do with this book, study the following.

| Raw Score | | | Self-Rating |
|---|---|---|---|
| *Critical Reading* | *Mathematics* | *Writing Skills* | |
| 42–48 | 35–38 | 33–39 | Superior |
| 37–41 | 30–34 | 28–32 | Very good |
| 32–36 | 25–29 | 23–27 | Good |
| 26–31 | 21–24 | 17–22 | Above average |
| 20–25 | 17–20 | 12–16 | Average |
| 12–19 | 10–16 | 7–11 | Below average |
| less than 12 | less than 10 | less than 7 | Inadequate |

## ANSWER EXPLANATIONS

### Section 1  Critical Reading

1. **(D)** Fast-food restaurants are growing more popular in France. The traditional café is therefore growing less popular (falling "victim to the growing popularity" of McBurgers) and is slowly *becoming extinct* (vanishing, disappearing; dying out).

2. **(E)** *Although* signals a contrast. You would expect the coach to be *jubilant* (extremely joyful) about her team's victory. Instead, she was *disheartened* (discouraged).

3. **(A)** *Bantering* or joking remarks are clearly *inappropriate* in a serious speech.

4. **(D)** People uncomfortable with math would be likely to think the field should be *left to* those gifted in such an *esoteric* (hard to understand; known only to a chosen few) subject.

5. **(B)** A writer whose work was universally acclaimed or applauded and whose reputation was not yet *tarnished* or stained would be at the *zenith* or high point of her career.

6. **(B)** The Pilgrims have traditionally been held up or *cited* as defenders of democracy.

7. **(A)** In challenging the traditional image of the Mayflower Compact as a cornerstone of American democracy, the author reveals himself to be a *debunker*, one who exposes false claims or attacks established beliefs.

8. **(C)** Unlike the author of Passage 1, the author of Passage 2 speaks in the first person. "To *me*," he says, "the Mayflower Compact will always be a cornerstone of American democracy." Thus, he makes use of *personal voice*.

9. **(E)** The opening sentence of Passage 1 asserts that the Mayflower Compact had little impact on the growth of freedom in America. The author of Passage 2, however, maintains that the compact "laid a sound foundation" for American democracy. Clearly, he doubts that Passage 1's opening assertion is true. In other words, he would argue that the assertion was of *dubious validity*.

10. **(C)** The entire passage examines Bethune's beliefs in the ultimate victory of racial justice and in the possibility of winning whites to her cause. In addition, it clearly shows Bethune, in her work to get her people represented in all public problems, having an impact on her people's progress.

11. **(C)** You can arrive at the correct answer by the process of elimination.

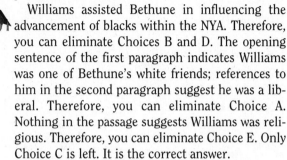

Williams assisted Bethune in influencing the advancement of blacks within the NYA. Therefore, you can eliminate Choices B and D. The opening sentence of the first paragraph indicates Williams was one of Bethune's white friends; references to him in the second paragraph suggest he was a liberal. Therefore, you can eliminate Choice A. Nothing in the passage suggests Williams was religious. Therefore, you can eliminate Choice E. Only Choice C is left. It is the correct answer.

12. **(A)** Bethune's success in getting Dickerson's appointment is a clear example of her impact.

Choice B is incorrect. The author is stressing how helpful Bethune was to Dickerson, not how different Bethune's career was from Dickerson's. Choice C is incorrect. Dickerson is not the subject of the paragraph that follows. Choice D is incorrect. The author brings up Bethune's belief in the "New Negro" well after he mentions her assistance to Dickerson. He draws no connection between Dickerson and the "New Negro." Choice E is incorrect. The author is making a point about Bethune, not about Dickerson.

13. **(E)** Bethune was the intermediary who helped arrange for Dickerson's new position. She was instrumental or *helpful* in gaining this end.

14. **(B)** By leading America to a "full realization of its democratic ideas," the New Negro would be *helping America accomplish its egalitarian goals*.

15. **(B)** The author compares and contrasts Bethune with her white liberal friends. The author directly quotes the wording of Bethune's 1944 appeals for black representation. The author gives concrete examples of the ways in which Bethune remained a black partisan champion of the New Deal. The author constantly reiterates the idea that Bethune

 **Note the following icons, used throughout this book:**

Time saver    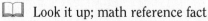Look it up; math reference fact    Helpful Hint

Educated guess    Prefixes, roots, and suffixes    Caution!

Did you notice?    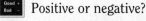Positive or negative?    A calculator might be useful.

had an ongoing influence on black progress during the Roosevelt years. However, the author uses figurative language only minimally and never develops an extended metaphor.

16. **(A)** Dickens implies that Gradgrind is so peremptory (absolute; dogmatic) about facts that he would insist upon the fact that his given name was, in fact, Thomas.

17. **(E)** Gradgrind carries scales and a rule in his pocket to "weigh and measure any parcel of human nature." Though Dickens plays upon several meanings of *rule* here, the word basically refers to a ruler or measuring stick.

18. **(B)** As he walks home, Gradgrind is in "a state of considerable satisfaction." He is pleased with himself and with the school he has created; his mood is clearly one of *complacency* or smugness.

19. **(D)** Dickens is poking fun at Gradgrind's teaching methods and is thus *broadly satirical* (full of ridicule).

20. **(C)** Gradgrind never introduces his pupils to nursery rhymes or to fantasy creatures such as ogres. This suggests that he rejects from his curriculum anything that is in the least *fanciful* or imaginative.

21. **(D)** Dickens has written the passage from the point of view of an omniscient narrator, *an observer who knows all about Gradgrind's thoughts and feelings*. The narrator knows all about Gradgrind's emotional state, his goals as headmaster, his manner of speech. In short, he knows Gradgrind through and through.

22. **(B)** The little Gradgrinds, having studied the Great Bear and Charles's Wain, had never "known wonder on the subject of stars." This suggests that the Great Bear and the Wain are constellations, or *groupings of stars*.

23. **(E)** Gradgrind's main idea is to fill his pupils full of *facts*, particularly facts about *science* (statistics, constellations, graminivorous quadrupeds, etc.).

24. **(E)** The famous cow with the crumpled horn ("The House That Jack Built") and the yet more famous cow who swallowed Tom Thumb in the folk tale are legendary *fictional characters* with whose celebrity the young Gradgrinds are unacquainted.

## Section 2  Mathematics

For many problems, the explanation provides a reference to one or more **KEY FACTS** from Chapter 7. These are the mathematical facts that you need to solve that problem. If a solution refers to **KEY FACT J2**, for example, the solution depends on the second **KEY FACT** discussed in Section J of Chapter 7.

For some problems, an alternative solution, indicated by two asterisks (**), follows the first solution. When this occurs, usually one of the solutions is the direct mathematical one and the other is based on one of the tactics discussed in Chapters 6 and 7.

See page 244 for an explanation of the symbol $\Rightarrow$, which is used in several answer explanations.

1. **(C)** $35 = (7-2)(7-m) = 5(7-m) = 35 - 5m$. So, $5m = 0$, and, therefore, $m = 0$.

2. **(C)** Since the sum of the measures of the three angles of a triangle is 180° (**KEY FACT J1**), then

$$40 + 2a + 3a = 180 \Rightarrow 40 + 5a = 180 \Rightarrow$$
$$5a = 140 \Rightarrow a = 28.$$

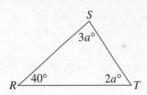

**Use TACTIC 6-6.** If you trust the diagram, there are many ways to go. If $a$ were 45, $2a$ would be 90, which is clearly wrong. Likewise, if $a$ were 10, $2a$ would be 20, which is also way off. In fact, $\angle S$ appears to be *about* a 90° angle. So, $3a \approx 90$, which means $a \approx 30$. Choose 28.

3. **(D)** To convert 225 minutes to hours, divide by 60: the quotient is 3 and the remainder is 45. Therefore, 225 minutes from 10:05 A.M. is 3 hours and 45 minutes from 10:05 A.M., which is 1:50 P.M.

**If you divide 225 by 60 on your calculator, you get 3.75, and then you have to convert 0.75, or $\frac{3}{4}$, of an hour to 45 minutes.

4. **(B)** The easiest solution is to quickly reduce, by repeatedly dividing each side by 9:

$$(\cancel{9})^{1}(\cancel{9})^{1}(\cancel{9})^{1}n = \frac{{}^{3}(27)^{1}(27)^{3}}{n}. \text{ So } n = \frac{1}{n} \Rightarrow n = 1.$$

**Of course, you can rewrite the equation as $n^2 = \frac{(27)(27)}{(9)(9)(9)}$ and use your calculator: $n^2 = 1$.

5. **(C)** Since the two angles, $x$ and $y$, form a straight angle, $x + y = 180$ (**KEY FACT I2**). Also, it is given that $x = y + 140$. Therefore,

$$(y + 140) + y = 180 \Rightarrow 2y + 140 = 180 \Rightarrow$$
$$2y = 40 \Rightarrow y = 20.$$

   **Use **TACTIC 6-1** and backsolve. Start with 20, Choice C. If $y = 20$, then

   $x = 140 + 20 = 160$, and $20 + 160 = 180$;

   so it works. The answer is Choice C.

6. **(D)** If $x^2 = 10$, then

$$x^6 = x^2 \cdot x^2 \cdot x^2 = 10 \times 10 \times 10 = 1000.$$

   **Use your calculator: $x = \sqrt{10}$, and $(\sqrt{10})^6 = 1000$.

7. **(B)** The average of four consecutive integers is the average of the middle two and so is always 0.5 more than an integer: the average of 1, 2, 3, and 4 is 2.5; the average of 10, 11, 12, and 13 is 11.5; and the average of 98, 99, 100, and 101 is 99.5. Only II is true.

8. **(A)** The formula for the area of a circle is: $A = \pi r^2$.

   Divide both sides by $\pi$: $r^2 = \dfrac{A}{\pi}$

   Take the square root of each side: $r = \sqrt{\dfrac{A}{\pi}}$.

   The diameter is twice the radius: $d = 2r = 2\sqrt{\dfrac{A}{\pi}}$.

   **Let the radius of the circle be 1. Then, the area is $\pi$, and the diameter is 2. Which of the five choices is equal to 2 when $A = \pi$? Only $2\sqrt{\dfrac{A}{\pi}}$.

9. **(A)** Calculate each 2012 salary by multiplying each 2010 salary by (1 + the percent change). Ann had the highest 2012 salary:

$$\$4200(1.06) = \$4452.$$

10. **(C)** For some number $x$, the measures of the angles are $x$, $x$, and $2x$; so

$$180 = x + x + 2x = 4x \Rightarrow x = 45.$$

   Therefore, the triangle is a 45-45-90 triangle, and, by **KEY FACT J5**, the ratio of the sides is $1:1:\sqrt{2}$.

11. **(D)** Draw diagrams. $A, B, C$ could be the vertices of a right triangle (I is true). If $A, B, C$ were the vertices of a square, then $AC = \sqrt{2}(AB)$ (II is false). $A, B, C$ could all lie on a circle. In fact, the only way that three points couldn't lie on a circle would be if they all were on the same line (III is true). Statements I and III only are true.

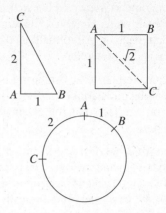

12. **(A)** On the first painting, Ross made a 20% profit; so if he bought it for $x$ dollars and sold it for $1200,

$$1200 = x + .20x = 1.2x \Rightarrow x = 1200 \div 1.2 = 1000.$$
His profit was $200.

   On the second painting, Ross lost 20%; so if he bought it for $y$ dollars and sold it for $1200,

$$1200 = y - .20y = .80y \Rightarrow y = 1200 \div .80 = 1500.$$
His loss was $300.

   In all, he lost exactly $100.

13. **(D)** Draw a picture.

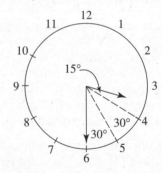

   The minute hand, of course, is pointing right at 6. The hour hand, however, is *not* pointing at 3. It was pointing at 3 at 3:00, half an hour ago. The hour hand is now one-half of the way between the 3 and 4. So there are 15° between the hour hand and 4 and another 60° between 4 and 6, a total of 75°.

   **If you can't figure the answer out exactly, guess. From the picture, you should see that the angle definitely measures more than 60° and less than 90°. Eliminate Choices A, B, and E.

14. **(B)** Check each statement. The only factors of 15 are $\pm 1$, $\pm 3$, $\pm 5$, and $\pm 15$. If $m$ is any of these, $\dfrac{15}{m}$ is an odd integer. (I is false.) Eliminate Choices A and D. Could $\dfrac{m}{15}$ be an even integer? Sure, it could be *any* even integer; for example, if $m = 30$, $\dfrac{m}{15} = 2$; if $m = 150$, $\dfrac{m}{15} = 10$. (II is true.) Eliminate Choice C. Could $15m$ be prime? No, $15m$ is divisible by 15. (III is false.) II is the only true statement.

15. **(B)** Since 1, 2, 3, and 6 are each divisors of 6, the remainder is 0 when they are divided into 6. The only nonzero remainders occur when 6 is divided by 4, in which case the remainder is 2, and when 6 is divided by 5, in which case the remainder is 1. The sum of the remainders is 3.

16. **(C)** Since $a < b$, when $a$ is divided by $b$, the quotient is 0 and the remainder is $a$; so $a*b = a$. When *any* number is divided by $a$, the remainder must be less than $a$, and so the maximum value of $b*a$ is $a - 1$. Therefore, the greatest possible value of $a*b + b*a$ is $a + (a - 1) = 2a - 1$.
    \*\*Use **TACTIC 6-2**: plug in numbers. Let $a = 2$ and $b = 3$. When 2 is divided by 3, the quotient is 0 and the remainder is 2:
    $$2 = 0(3) + 2. \text{ So } 2*3 = 2.$$
    When 3 is divided by 2, the quotient is 1 and the remainder is 1:
    $$3 = 1(2) + 1. \text{ So } 3*2 = 1.$$
    $2*3 + 3*2 = 2 + 1 = 3$. Which choice equals 3 when $a = 2$ and $b = 3$? Only $2a - 1$.

17. **(A)** Use **TACTIC G3**: When you have more than two equations, add them
    $$\begin{aligned} x + y &= 10 \\ y + z &= 15 \\ \underline{+\ x + z} &= \underline{17} \\ 2x + 2y + 2z &= 42 \end{aligned}$$
    Divide by 2:       $x + y + z = 21$
    To get the average,
    divide the sum by 3:    $\frac{x + y + z}{3} = \frac{21}{3} = 7$
    (*Note:* you *could* solve for $x, y, z$, but you shouldn't.)

18. **(D)** Check each choice. (A) If $x = 5$, $\sqrt{x - 1} = 2$. (B) This one is more difficult; the only possibility is $x = 1$, in which case $\sqrt{x^2 - 1} = 0$. If you don't see that immediately, keep Choice B under consideration, and test the rest. (C) If $x = 1$, $\frac{1}{x} = 1$. (D) For positive $x$, $\frac{x + 2}{x + 1}$ is always greater than 1 but less than 2; $\frac{x + 2}{x + 1}$ cannot be an integer—that's it. If you didn't reason that out, check Choice E. $\frac{7}{x + 1}$ is an integer if $x = 6$. You should have eliminated at least Choices A, C, and E.

19. **(E)** Any odd number is the sum of two consecutive integers: $6 + 7 = 13$ and $7 + 8 = 15$. Eliminate Choices B and D. Next try the sum of three consecutive integers: $3 + 4 + 5 = 12$. Eliminate Choice A. Now try four consecutive integers: $2 + 3 + 4 + 5 = 14$. Eliminate Choice C. The answer must be 16.

20. **(A)** If $p$ painters can complete a job in $d$ days, then 1 painter will take $p$ times as long: it would take 1

painter $pd$ days to complete the job and $\frac{1}{4}pd = \frac{pd}{4}$ days to complete 25%, or $\frac{1}{4}$, of the job. Finally, if the work is divided up among $q$ painters it would take $\frac{pd}{4} \div q = \frac{pd}{4q}$ days.

\*\*Use **TACTIC 6-2**: plug in easy-to-use numbers. If 2 painters can complete the job in 4 days, it would take them 1 day to complete 25% of the job. It would take 1 painter twice as long—2 days. Which choice is equal to 2, when $p = 2$, $d = 4$, and $q = 1$? Only $\frac{pd}{4q}$. Remember: Test each choice with your calculator and eliminate a choice as soon as it is clear that it is not equal to 2.

## Section 3 Critical Reading

25. **(A)** Because it can now be grown successfully in America, the once-rare fruit is now *accessible* or readily available to American consumers.

26. **(C)** Someone always searching for new ways to do things is by definition *an innovator* (someone who introduces changes into the existing ways of doing things).

27. **(C)** A trip to France, with all the chances for conversing in French it would provide, would be a practical or *pragmatic* test of how much you had learned of conversational French.

28. **(A)** Since Cherokee society already granted certain rights to women, it did not break with or *violate* Cherokee custom to allow women their rights.

29. **(E)** Though scientists might be upset by *erroneous* (faulty) or *derivative* (unoriginal) work, the scientific community would be most shocked by *fraudulent* or faked research that was intentionally *deceptive* or deceitful.

30. **(C)** The key phrase "of few words" indicates that Eastwood's characters are *laconic*, untalkative types.

31. **(E)** *Insipid* (flavorless; dull and uninteresting) is a term that applies equally well to food and to conversations.

32. **(D)** Someone *crabbed* (bad-humored; harsh; morose) seldom smiles; someone *parsimonious* (stingy; miserly) never gives away money. Note how parallel structure determines word order: the first missing adjective relates to the first verb ("seldom smiled"); the second missing adjective relates to the second verb ("never gave away").

33. **(C)** The passage contrasts the image of Nightingale, the night nurse carrying a lamp as she walked the wards, with the image of Nightingale, the hospital authority. What is more, it states that Nightingale "came into her own as the world's most renowned authority on hospital reform." To come into one's own is to achieve one's potential, to become fulfilled. According to the author, Nightingale did not reach her full potential until she became a recognized authority on hospital reform. To the author, therefore, *her greatest accomplishments were in improving hospital planning and administration.*

34. **(D)** When Nightingale addressed these aspects of hospital construction and management, she *dealt with* them thoroughly and in great detail.

35. **(E)** In this passage, the author celebrates the return into print of Green's novels and makes a case for her as the mother of detective fiction. Thus, the author's purpose is most likely to *reclaim* Green, *a forgotten literary pioneer*, from a century's worth of neglect, in process restoring her reputation.

36. **(C)** The publication of *The Leavenworth Case* marked or *denoted* (signaled) the first appearance of Inspector Gryce.

37. **(B)** In extending the pilot's control of the plane and making extreme actions (loops, sudden swerves, dives, etc.) comfortable, acrobatic flying *extends a pilot's range of capabilities.*

38. **(D)** The medium of the air is the *environment* in which flying creatures function.

39. **(B)** In the course of doing a loop, you lose sight of the horizon and must tilt your head backward to catch sight of the horizon line again. Thus, to pick up the horizon line is to *spot it visually.*

40. **(A)** Earlier in the passage, the author describes the experience of doing a loop as being "as far outside instinctive human behavior as you can go." In grabbing at the sides of the cockpit during the loop, the author is reverting to *instinctive*, involuntary behavior.

    Choice B is incorrect. The experience of doing a loop was terrifying; grabbing the sides of the cockpit was not. Choice C is incorrect. It was not essential for the author to grab the sides of the cockpit; his seat belt was strong enough to keep him from falling out of the plane. Choice D is incorrect. The author did not wind up making a habit of grabbing the sides of the cockpit; he did it only that once. Choice E is incorrect. The experience of doing a loop may have seemed life threatening; grabbing the sides of the cockpit was not.

41. **(E)** In saying the belt held, the author means that it did not slip or come unfastened; instead, it *maintained its grasp*, keeping him safe.

42. **(C)** The instructor tells the author to put his arms out of the cockpit so that he can learn to have confidence in his seat belt's ability to hold him in the plane. He does so, *relying totally on his seat belt to keep him safe.*

43. **(B)** By stressing the terror that went into learning how to fly a loop, the author makes you feel that *satisfying* is an extremely mild word to describe the exhilaration of overcoming such an extreme fear and mastering such an unnatural skill. It is clearly an *understatement.*

44. **(D)** The author was not a fan of stunt flying; she was reluctant to pay attention to the aerial display. Therefore, this particular aerial display must have been unusually *captivating* to capture her attention.

45. **(D)** The author describes the audience's longing for a particular effect in the stunt-flying demonstration ("a certain kind of roll or climb, or a return to a certain portion of the air"). This is akin to a reader's longing for a particular effect in a poem—for example, a certain kind of image or rhyme or the return of an earlier refrain. Poets, however, play with their readers' expectations, sometimes varying exact end-rhymes with an occasional assonance or consonance (*slant* rhymes), as when Emily Dickinson unexpectedly rhymes *came* with *home*. Thus, in saying that Rahm "fulfilled your hope slantingly, like a poet," the author means that he *refused to satisfy your expectations directly* but gave you something unexpected instead.

46. **(C)** By "moving back the boundaries of the humanly possible" the author is talking about becoming aware *of new potentials for humanity*. This new knowledge leaves her gladdened and *exhilarated.*

47. **(E)** Passage 1 is both descriptive and informative. In recounting the story of the flying lesson, it is anecdotal. However, in comparison with Passage 2, it is not particularly poetic or *lyrical.*

48. **(A)** The author of Passage 1 talks about how useful acrobatic flying is in improving the skills of pilots. The author of Passage 2, however, looks on acrobatic flying as *an aesthetic experience*: she responds to Rahm's aerial demonstration as a new form of beauty, a performance that engages her aesthetically. Therefore, she would most likely consider the assessment of aerial flying in Passage 1 *too utilitarian* (concerned with practical usefulness) to be appropriate for an aesthetic experience.

## Section 4 Mathematics

For many problems, the explanation provides a reference to one or more **KEY FACTS** from Chapter 7. These are the mathematical facts that you need to solve that problem. If a solution refers to **KEY FACT J2**, for example, the solution depends on the second **KEY FACT** discussed in Section J of Chapter 7.

For some problems, an alternative solution, indicated by two asterisks (**), follows the first solution. When this occurs, usually one of the solutions is the direct mathematical one and the other is based on one of the tactics discussed in Chapters 6 and 7.

See page 244 for an explanation of the symbol ⇒, which is used in several answer explanations.

21. **(D)** $2x - 1 = 9 \Rightarrow 2x = 10 \Rightarrow x = 5$. Then $20x = 100$ and $20x - 1 = 99$.

22. **(B)** Since $8 - (8 + w) = -w$, the equation becomes $-w = 8$. So, $w = -8$.

23. **(D)** Let the numbers be $x$ and $\frac{1}{5}x$. Then
$$20 = x\left(\frac{1}{5}x\right) = \frac{1}{5}x^2 \Rightarrow x^2 = 100 \Rightarrow$$
$$x = 10 \text{ or } x = -10.$$

Since the numbers are positive, $x = 10$, $\frac{1}{5}x = 2$, and their sum is 12.

**You can avoid using algebra by just testing pairs of small numbers, where one number is 5 times the other: 1 and 5? No. 2 and 10? Yes.

24. **(C)** Let $x$ be Mr. Riccardo's number.

Then $x + 3 = 3x \Rightarrow 3 = 2x \Rightarrow x = 1.5$.

**Use **TACTIC 6-1** and backsolve. Start with Choice C:

$1.5 + 3 = 4.5$ and $1.5 \times 3 = 4.5$. It works.

25. **(C)** If a team lost $l$ of the $g$ games it played, it won the rest: $g - l$. The fraction is $\frac{g-l}{g}$.

**Use **TACTIC 6-2** and choose easy-to-use numbers. If the team lost 1 of its 3 games, it lost $\frac{1}{3}$ of them and won $\frac{2}{3}$ of them. Only Choice C equals $\frac{2}{3}$ when $g = 3$ and $l = 1$.

26. **(B)** When 200 is divided by 7, the quotient is 28 and the remainder is 4. Therefore, 200 days is 4 days more than 28 weeks. Twenty-eight weeks after a Friday is again a Friday, and 4 days after that is Tuesday. (Note that it is irrelevant that the *date* was August 13, 2010; this problem concerned only the day of the week.)

27. **(B)** Since the area of the square is 20, each side is $\sqrt{20}$. The radius of each semicircle, therefore, is $\frac{\sqrt{20}}{2}$.

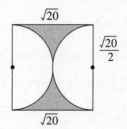

The area of the two semicircles is equal to the area of a circle of radius $\frac{\sqrt{20}}{2}$:

$$\pi\left(\frac{\sqrt{20}}{2}\right)^2 = \pi\left(\frac{20}{4}\right) = 5\pi.$$

So the area of the shaded region is
$$20 - 5\pi = 5(4 - \pi).$$

**Use **TACTIC 6-6**: trust the diagram and use your calculator, if necessary, to eliminate absurd answer choices. Clearly, the shaded area is less than half the area of the square, so it is surely less than 10. Approximating $\pi$ by 3 and the square root of 20 by 4 or 5, we see that choices A, B, C, D, and E are about 17, 5, 12, 22, and 40, respectively. Clearly, the answer is choice B.

28. **(C)** Adding the three equations, we get immediately that $a - d = 60$.

**Pick any number for $d$; say $d = 10$. Then $c = 40$, $b = 60$, and $a = 70$. Finally, $70 - 10 = 60$.

29. **(7.5 or 15/2)** $\triangle ABC$ is a right triangle; its area is given by $\frac{1}{2}(AB)(AC)$. Since $\overline{AB}$ is vertical, find its length by subtracting the $y$-coordinates: $AB = 4 - 1 = 3$. Similarly, since $\overline{AC}$ is horizontal, find its length by subtracting the $x$-coordinates: $BC = 6 - 1 = 5$. Then, area of $\triangle ABC = \frac{1}{2}(3)(5) = \frac{15}{2} = 7.5$.

30. **(52.5)** Since the sum of all the angles around a point is 360° (**KEY FACT I3**),
$$90 + a + a + 60 + a + a = 360 \Rightarrow$$
$$4a + 150 = 360 \Rightarrow 4a = 210 \Rightarrow a = 52.5.$$

31. **(360°)** By **TACTIC E1**, if the average of five numbers is 100, their sum is $5 \times 100 = 500$. Since $20 + 30 + 40 + 50 = 140$, the fifth number, $x$, is $500 - 140 = 360$.

32. **(50)** Since 40% of the members of the club are boys, then 60% are girls. Let $m$ be the number of members of the club.

Then $.60m = 30 \Rightarrow m = 30 \div .60 = 50$.

33. $\left(\frac{7}{12}\right)$ Use the slope formula (**KEY FACT N4**) to calculate the slope of line $l$: $\frac{7-3}{4-1} = \frac{4}{3}$. By **KEY FACT N6**, the slope of $m$ is also $\frac{4}{3}$ and the slope of $n$ is $-\frac{3}{4}$, the negative reciprocal of $\frac{4}{3}$. So the sum of

the two slopes is $\frac{4}{3} + \left(-\frac{3}{4}\right) = \frac{7}{12}$.

34. **(67)** Write out enough terms of the sequence until you see a pattern.

$$1, 2, 3, 5, 8, 13, 21, 34, 55, \ldots$$

There are several patterns you might notice, but one observation is that the terms are

<u>odd, even, odd, odd, even, odd,</u> . . .

with the sequence <u>odd, even, odd</u> repeating indefinitely. The first 99 terms consist of 33 groups, with 2 odd numbers in each group, for a total of 66 odd numbers. The 100th number is the first number in the next group, which is odd. So there are 67 odd terms.

35. **(25)** $5(\sqrt{x} - 3) = 3\sqrt{x} - 5 \Rightarrow$

$$5\sqrt{x} - 15 = 3\sqrt{x} - 5 \Rightarrow$$
$$2\sqrt{x} - 15 = -5 \Rightarrow$$
$$2\sqrt{x} = 10 \Rightarrow \sqrt{x} = 5 \Rightarrow x = 25.$$

36. $\left(\frac{15}{8} \text{ or } 1.87 \text{ or } 1.88\right)$ Use $b$, $c$, and $t$ for "bangs," "clangs," and "tangs," respectively. Then the given equations are: $3b = 2c$ and $4b = 5t$. Multiply the first equation by 4 and the second by 3:

$$12b = 8c \text{ and } 12b = 15t$$
So
$$8c = 15t \Rightarrow c = \frac{15}{8}t$$
So
$$1 \text{ clang} = \frac{15}{8} \text{ tangs.}$$

37. **(138)** Since 40% of 25 is 10, there are 10 girls and $25 - 10 = 15$ boys in the class. The total weight of the 10 girls is $10 \times 120 = 1200$ pounds and the total weight of the 15 boys is $15 \times 150 = 2250$. Therefore, the average weight of all 25 children is

$$\frac{1200 + 2250}{25} = \frac{3450}{25} = 138.$$

38. **(1)** By **KEY FACT K9**, the area of a square whose diagonal is $d$ is $\frac{d^2}{2}$. Since the area of the black region is the area of the large square minus the area of the middle square, the black area is:

$$\frac{1}{2}(5^2) - \frac{1}{2}(4^2) = \frac{1}{2}(25) - \frac{1}{2}(16) =$$
$$12.5 - 8 = 4.5.$$

The striped region is a square whose diagonal is 3, and so its area is $\frac{1}{2}(3^2) = \frac{1}{2}(9) = 4.5$. Therefore, the two areas are equal, and so the ratio of their areas is 1.

## Section 5  Writing Skills

1. **(A)** Sentence is correct.

2. **(C)** The two errors in diction (*imminent* for *eminent* and *stood* for *stayed*) are corrected in Choice C.

3. **(D)** This corrects the sentence fragment.

4. **(C)** Choice C corrects the sentence fragment.

5. **(C)** Comma splice. Choice C corrects the run-on sentence and expresses the author's meaning directly and concisely. All other choices are indirect, ungrammatical, or do not retain the meaning of the original sentence.

6. **(B)** Choice B corrects the run-on sentence.

7. **(A)** Sentence is correct.

8. **(B)** Error in coordination and subordination. Choice B corrects the conjunction *neither . . . nor* (not *neither . . . or*) and retains the meaning of the original sentence.

9. **(C)** Error in pronoun number agreement. Use *this kind of story* or *these kinds of stories*.

10. **(D)** The omission of the correct verb form is corrected in Choice D.

11. **(C)** Error in modification. The dangling participle construction is corrected in Choice C.

12. **(E)** Error in modification and word order. Choice E corrects the misplaced modifier and eliminates the unnecessary use of the passive voice.

13. **(A)** The use of the semicolon to separate the pair of clauses is correct.

14. **(B)** Choice B expresses the author's meaning directly and concisely. All other choices are indirect, ungrammatical, or do not retain the meaning of the original sentence.

15. **(E)** Double negative. Change *without scarcely a murmur* to *with scarcely a murmur*.

16. **(A)** Sentence is correct.

17. **(D)** Error in usage. Do not confuse *respectively* (singly in the order mentioned) and *respectfully* (politely and deferentially).

18. **(D)** Error in usage. The story is *incredible* or improbable; the jurors are *incredulous* (skeptical, disbelieving).

19. **(C)** Error in relative pronoun use. Relative pronouns are noun substitutes that serve to introduce subordinate clauses. Replace *which* with *a state of affairs that*.

20. **(E)** Dangling modifier. Ask yourself who is welding. Certainly not the goggles!

21. **(E)** Sentence is correct.

22. **(A)** Error in sequence of tenses. Change *has adopted* to *adopted*.

23. **(B)** Error in diction. Change *irregardless* to *regardless*.

24. **(C)** Error in subject-verb agreement. The subject *she and her staff* is plural; the verb should be plural—*are*.

25. **(B)** Error in diction. Change *or* to *nor*.

26. **(C)** Error in diction. Change *affect* to *effect*.

27. **(D)** Error in pronoun agreement. Change *his and her* to *their*.

28. **(B)** Error in pronoun case. Change *you* to *your*.

29. **(E)** Sentence is correct.

30. **(E)** Sentence is correct.

31. **(D)** Error in parallelism. Change *an increase in interest rates* to *interest rates increase*.

32. **(C)** Adjective and adverb confusion. Change *special prepared* to *specially prepared*.

33. **(C)** Error in tense. Change *been creating* to *created*.

34. **(E)** Sentence is correct.

35. **(C)** Choice A is a sentence fragment.
Choice B violates standard English idiom. The phrase *for example* should be followed by a noun, not by a prepositional phrase.

Choice C is a complete sentence and serves as an appropriate topic sentence for the second paragraph. It is the best answer.
Choice D serves neither as a good transition from the first to the second paragraph nor as an effective topic sentence for the second paragraph.
Choice E is a sentence fragment; also the phrases *for instance* and *for example* are redundant.

36. **(C)** Choice A contains an error in subject-verb agreement. The plural subject *rights* should have a plural verb, *were*.
Choice B shifts verb tenses from present perfect (*have seized*) to past perfect (*had repressed*). Confusion ensues.
Choice C succinctly and accurately revises the original sentence. It is the best answer.
Choice D is a confusion of verb tenses, which renders the sentence almost incomprehensible.
Choice E has a severe pronoun reference problem. It is unclear to whom the pronouns *they, their,* and *them* refer.

37. **(A)** Choice A clearly and succinctly explains the fate of the kulaks. It is the best answer.
Choice B is wordy and awkwardly expressed.
Choice C is wordy and contains a usage error. Because *forcing* is a gerund, *Stalin* should be possessive (*Stalin's*).
Choice D contains a dangling participle. It says that Stalin lost this right to own private property, an idea contrary to what the writer intended.
Choice E is not accurately expressed and contains an error in subject-verb agreement. The compound subject *loss* and *collectivization* requires a plural verb.

38. **(E)** Choices A, B, and C are trite and abrupt transitions. They should be avoided.
Choice D is not a good answer because the essay does not discuss international agreements on human rights.
Choice E accurately and smoothly provides a link between the content of the essay and the concluding paragraph. It is the best answer.

39. **(A)** Only Choice A accurately describes the function of the last paragraph. The conclusion—that people will eventually claim their rights—grows out of the discussion in paragraphs 1, 2, and 3. Therefore, Choice A is the best answer.

# After the PSAT/NMSQT

After the scores of the PSAT/NMSQT are received, you, your parents, and your guidance counselor can begin to make plans for college. Here are some Barron's reference books that will be very helpful to you.

***Barron's SAT*** by Sharon Weiner Green and Ira K. Wolf (2014, 27th Edition). This classic includes a diagnostic test and five additional practice tests that enable you to practice under exact SAT format and test conditions; all tests have answer keys and answer explanations. Extensive review and practice is provided for each type of test question. The Critical Reading review also includes the 3500 word list, with definitions and parts of speech. The Writing review includes common grammar and usage errors. The Mathematical Reasoning review covers basic arithmetic through high school algebra and geometry. Testing tactics and strategies are featured. Two additional practice tests are provided on an optional CD-ROM.

***Critical Reading Workbook for the SAT*** by Sharon Weiner Green (2012, 14th Edition), ***Math Workbook for the SAT*** by Lawrence Leff (2012, 5th Edition), ***Writing Workbook for the SAT*** by George Ehrenhaft (2012, 3rd Edition). These workbooks provide the detailed review you may need for specific sections of the test. Each book contains hundreds of practice questions with answers and extensive review specific to the topic.

***Grammar Workbook for the SAT, ACT...and More*** by George Ehrenhaft (2014, 3rd Edition). This workbook provides a review of the grammatical issues you are most likely to be asked about on the SAT, ACT, and other standardized tests. You'll learn terms you need to know and how to avoid the grammar pitfalls that give almost everyone a headache. And you will learn how to write a proper exam essay. The book includes plenty of practice questions with complete answer explanations.

***Hot Words for the SAT*** by Linda Carnevale (2010, 4th Edition). This book includes hundreds of words, grouped by concept, with definitions, sample sentences, and quizzes.

***SAT 2400*** by Linda Carnevale and Roselyn Teukolsky (2014, 5th Edition). Written for the student who is aiming for that perfect score, this book breaks down the toughest questions and analyzes why they are tough. Practice tests are provided for each of the three SAT sections: critical reading, writing, and math. An optional CD-ROM contains a complete practice SAT test and fifty additional practice questions.

***SAT Flash Cards*** by Sharon Weiner Green and Ira K. Wolf (2011, 2nd Edition). This handy boxed set includes 200 math cards with 75 important math facts, strategies, and sample multiple-choice and grid-in questions; 200 grammar cards covering parts of speech, sentence construction, and more; and 100 vocabulary cards with definitions and sample sentences.

***Essays That Will Get You Into College*** by Daniel Kaufman, Chris Dowhan, and Adrienne Dowhan (2014, 4th Edition). More than fifty model essays that have worked for applicants, with advice, discussion, and commentary, reveal the secrets of successful essay writing.

***Barron's Profiles of American Colleges*** (2014, 31st Edition). Profiles of more than 1,600 regionally accredited four-year American colleges and universities give the prospective student a preview of his or her relationship to a particular college—based on its facilities, outstanding features and programs, admission requirements, costs, available financial aid, extracurricular activities, programs and major offerings, degrees awarded, enrollment, religious affiliation, housing facilities, and social and honorary societies. CD-ROM included.

# Index

## How to Use the CD-ROM

The software is not installed on your computer; it runs directly from the CD-ROM. Barron's CD-ROM includes an "autorun" feature that automatically launches the application when the CD is inserted into the CD-ROM drive. In the unlikely event that the autorun feature is disabled, follow the manual launching instructions below.

### Windows®

1. Click on the Start button and choose "My Computer" or "Computer."
2. Double-click on the CD-ROM drive, which will be named **PSAT_NMSQT.exe**.
3. Double-click **PSAT_NMSQT.exe** to launch the program.

### MAC®

1. Double-click the CD-ROM icon.
2. Double-click the **PSAT_NMSQT** icon to start the program.

### SYSTEM REQUIREMENTS

(Flash Player 10.2 is recommended)

| Microsoft® Windows® | MAC® OS X | Linux®, and Solaris™ |
|---|---|---|
| Processor: Intel Pentium 4 2.33GHz, Athlon 64 2800+ or faster processor (or equivalent).<br>Memory: 128MB of RAM.<br>Graphics Memory: 128MB.<br>Platforms:<br>Windows 7, Windows Vista®, Windows XP, Windows Server® 2008, Windows Server 2003. | Processor: Intel Core™ Duo 1.33GHz or faster processor.<br>Memory: 256MB of RAM.<br>Graphics Memory: 128MB.<br>Platforms:<br>Mac OS X 10.6, Mac OS X 10.5, Mac OS X 10.4 (Intel) and higher. | Processor: Intel Pentium 4 2.33GHz, AMD Athlon 64 2800+ or faster processor (or equivalent).<br>Memory: 512MB of RAM.<br>Graphics Memory: 128MB.<br>Platforms:<br>Red Hat® Enterprise Linux (RHEL) 5 or later, openSUSE® 11 or later, Ubuntu 9.10 or later.<br>Solaris: Solaris™ 10. |